INTERNATIONAL ECONOMIC LAW SERIES

General Editor: John H. Jackson

THE DEFINITION OF SUBSIDY AND STATE AID

WTO and EC Law in Comparative Perspective

The Definition of Subsidy and State Aid

WTO and EC Law in Comparative Perspective

LUCA RUBINI

Lecturer in Law and Deputy-Director of the Institute of European Law
Birmingham Law School

OXFORD
UNIVERSITY PRESS

This book has been printed digitally and produced in a standard specification in order to ensure its continuing availability

OXFORD
UNIVERSITY PRESS

Great Clarendon Street, Oxford OX2 6DP

Oxford University Press is a department of the University of Oxford. It furthers the University's objective of excellence in research, scholarship, and education by publishing worldwide in

Oxford New York

Auckland Cape Town Dar es Salaam Hong Kong Karachi Kuala Lumpur Madrid Melbourne Mexico City Nairobi New Delhi Shanghai Taipei Toronto

With offices in

Argentina Austria Brazil Chile Czech Republic France Greece Guatemala Hungary Italy Japan South Korea Poland Portugal Singapore Switzerland Thailand Turkey Ukraine Vietnam

Published in the United States by Oxford University Press Inc., New York

Reprinted 2011

ISBN 978-0-19-953339-8

Ai miei genitori.
Senza i loro sacrifici, nemmeno una parola di questo libro avrebbe visto la luce.

General Editor's Preface

One of the most complex and difficult issues in the context of the world trading system rules is the subject of subsidies. Subsidies are inherently troublesome for policy makers and governments. In many situations, subsidies are an essential tool of governance, and can be a substantial benefit for societies in carrying out important and valid measures to benefit their citizens. On the other hand, some 'subsidies' can have important damaging effects, including 'distortions' of the market system, in the eyes of economic analysts. Often there is a constant and deep tug of war between these and other various viewpoints of benefits conferred by governments on citizens and constituents. Also often there are very fundamental but controversial policy goals, including distributional allocations among competing interest in society. Consequently it should not be surprising that the subject of 'subsidies' in the reality (as well as the theory) of international economic regulation and measures (including taxation and regulatory benefits) create (or reveal) major tensions and conflicts. Often these tensions and conflicts develop into major juridical cases, including such cases in the WTO dispute settlement system. In that context the 'subsidy' (or SCM agreement) cases represent a major portion of all the WTO dispute settlement cases which have been brought there so far.

This book, *The Definition of Subsidy and State Aid*, published by Oxford University Press in its series on International Economic Law, is not only timely, but is immensely important in probing in a strikingly fundamental way, many of the perplexing treaty textual and policy issues of the subject. The title 'Definition' only begins to chart a pathway of analysis in this book which constantly poses and seeks to answer core assumptions and premises which bedevil the subject. The author, Dr Luca Rubini, has clearly gone beyond the normal roadmaps which chart the rules and practices of an international law subject, and has probed deeply into the inevitable mix of treaty text in the context of difficult policy choices and 'balancing' processes often encountered in such subject.

The book begins with an important overview of the analytical structure it undertakes, which is to peer deep into the depths of the policy maze and then to build upon that undertaking to address questions that may seem simple and solvable, but when sliced open often have implications of enormous importance to society and international peace and security. For example, the author discusses the meaning of 'advantage' as indicated in the WTO subsidy rules, and immediately reveals that analysis must often go beyond 'mere economics'.

The author also pays attention to another body of international rules in the context of the European Union 'State aids', to enlighten with comparisons, the policy maze involved.

Likewise, the author perceptively notes that many of the international rules concerning subsidies require 'comparisons' to some 'benchmark' such as the market paradigm. So the comparisons often imply the need for balancing, which of course raises important questions in what manner should the balance be controlled, and by whom.

It is a delight once again, to see this OUP series providing a book of this profound importance, and stimulating and penetrating analysis.

John H. Jackson

Foreword

As we have noted on the occasion of the publication of the last broad comparative study of the subsidies disciplines of the WTO and the EU, such studies are rare. This statement, made three years ago, remains valid today. To our knowledge, this is only the second time that a similar enterprise has been undertaken. But it is distinct from its predecessor in at least two aspects: first, with respect to its subject matter and second, its approach.

A quick look at the table of contents shows that: Luca Rubini's book is essentially devoted to *one* major theme, ie, the definition of the *scope* of the rules on subsidies under the WTO and on State aids in the EU. Conversely, the author does not examine what might be called the other side of the coin, ie, the reasons which may *justify* the granting of a subsidy or a State aid. The distinction between scope and justification is a 'Leitmotif' of the book. The author emphasizes repeatedly that scope and justification must not be conflated but kept strictly separate.

Institutional issues are alluded to but they remain marginal compared with the main subject of the book.

The author's approach to the analysis of the notion of subsidy and State aid is highly *conceptual*. The author abundantly discusses existing WTO and EU case law, but this discussion is neither purely descriptive or apologetic nor critical in measuring the coherence of the jurisprudence in using only the parameters set by the Appellate Body of the WTO or the ECJ itself. The author develops and uses his own yardsticks. He is not only interested in the subsidy and State aid rules as they are, but also as they should be.

The author's approach is nicely encapsulated in the three 'essential', most fundamental questions, which should be posed in progressive and escalating order. 'What is the purpose of the subsidy/State aid definition? What is the purpose of the discipline of which it is part and defines its scope? And, ultimately, what are the more general, overall objectives of the political and legal system which accommodates the subsidy discipline.'

To be distinguished from these fundamental systemic issues is the question of the objective(s) pursued by the measure under examination itself. Normally, this question does not belong to the determination of whether the measure at issue is a subsidy, ie, a matter of scope, but whether the measure can be justified, ie, a matter of justification. That is particularly true where the government pursues an economic activity and where the 'market' is therefore the only appropriate benchmark for determining whether the measure confers an advantage.

However, the situation is different if the government pursues a non-economic activity, such as taxation. In this case, the only appropriate benchmark is the rationality of the government's own action. In examining this rationality, objectives count. The author distinguishes judiciously between inherent/internal and external objectives. Differences in taxation which are justified by the inherent/internal logic of the tax do not derogate from the norm and therefore do not constitute an advantage. Conversely, differences which result from external objectives do constitute a derogation and confer an advantage, and are therefore considered as subsidies.

Why do we mention this point specifically? Because we believe that it is a major contribution to the qualification of taxation under WTO subsidy and EU State aid rules. The qualification of differences resulting from taxation, while little explored in the WTO, is one of the most difficult and controversial areas of EU State aid law. The increasing use of taxes as incentives and disincentives, in particular in the fight against global warming, will further augment the importance of this question.

The finding that a measure is a countervailable or actionable subsidy under the WTO or that it fulfils the conditions of Article 87 (1) EC has, of course, major consequences. These consequences are more visible and serious under the EC Treaty. The finding that a measure is a State aid under Article 87 (1) EC entails, according to Article 87 (3), the obligation of EU Member States to notify the measure to the Commission before it is put into effect, to respect the standstill obligation, and to recover any aid put into effect in violation of the standstill obligation. The recognition that a measure constitutes a State aid thus entails a dramatic shift of responsibilities and, ultimately, power from the Member States to the Commission.

It is likely that institutional considerations are the hidden agenda of the jurisprudence of the ECJ, which limits the notion of State aid to measures that operate a transfer of *public* resources to certain undertakings. The ECJ has thus excluded from the scope of the State aid rules those advantages that flow from regulatory schemes which put the burden on *private* enterprises. This jurisprudence, which culminated in the famous *PreussenElektra* ruling, appears to be rather counter-intuitive, as it leads to a notion of State aid under the EC Treaty which is narrower than the corresponding notion of subsidy under the SM Agreement of the WTO, although the EU pursues more ambitious goals than the WTO. It is not surprising that Rubini criticizes this jurisprudence as formalistic and leading to results which do no make much sense from the point of view of their economic effect. Instead, he advocates use of the selectivity criterion to distinguish between advantages flowing from purely regulatory measures which are caught by Article 87 (1) of the EC Treaty as opposed to those which are not. This would, of course, require a more in depth examination of the selectivity requirement, which so far has been relatively little explored in EU law.

This consideration leads us back to the fundamental questions asked by the author and in particular to the issue of what purpose the subsidy/State aid rules serve in the two legal systems. The author believes that more emphasis should be put on the distortion of competition among competitors than on the obstacles to international trade, frustrating market access. He therefore advocates focusing more on the distortion of competition requirement expressly mentioned in Article 87(1) EC. It is well known that this requirement is scarcely given any real relevance in past and present EU decision making, as the distortion of competition is presumed to flow automatically from an advantage given to certain enterprises.

The author's views can easily be accommodated under the EC Treaty. They are more difficult to follow in the WTO context. For the time being, the main obstacles are the wording of the SCM Agreement and the methods of interpretation applied by the Appellate Body, which remain stricter than those of the ECJ, although the Appellate Body has become more flexible in recent years. A competition oriented interpretation of the injury or serious prejudice standard might be possible, but it would require the case law to make a step forward. Rubini suggests a way that this could be done. In any case, in line with the books approach, he provides good food for thought.

This observation leads us to our final remark. Comparative studies are of enormous value for both legal systems—the WTO and the EU. They enable a clearer perception of the strengths and weaknesses that each system presents.

The EU particularly will benefit from such studies. The basic EC Treaty rules are broader and therefore more flexible than the corresponding, detailed provisions of the SCM agreement. The EU's capacity to enact implementing legislation is surprisingly well functioning, in spite of the increase to 27 Member States and the absence of fundamental Treaty reform. Such legislative capacity is practically lacking in the WTO. Further, the EU has a policy-making institution, the Commission, at their disposal, which has no equivalent in the WTO. Finally, the ECJ is less constrained in its interpretative approach than the Appellate Body of the WTO.

We would even go a step further. We would suggest that the EU will not only benefit, but that it also needs the comparison with the WTO rules on subsidies. These rules constitute the only legal system from which the EC can learn to refine its own State aid discipline. Other States have laws on countervailing duties. But to our knowledge, no legal system other than the WTO has an all-embracing mechanism which controls and limits the granting of subsidies, although one might expect such control mechanisms in federal States, such as the USA or Canada. There is therefore no transatlantic dialogue on subsidies comparable to the vivid discussions on antitrust law which have contributed so much to the shaping and implementation of EC competition law in recent in recent years.

EU State aid law has of course influenced the existing WTO rules on subsidies. But these rules have to be—and are—interpreted by panels and the Appellate Body.

It is useful for the EU to observe the evolution of this WTO jurisprudence. Such attention might contribute to the further evolution and maturing of the EU's own system of State aid control, and ultimately avoid future conflicts.

Thus the encouragement, notably to the members of the steadily growing WTO subsidy and EU State aid 'constituency', to reflect on Rubini's impressive monograph, his findings, and his recommendations.

Claus-Dieter Ehlermann
Brussels
August 2009

Acknowledgments

In Michael Powell's and Emeric Pressburger's masterpiece movie *A Canterbury Tale*, one of the main themes is that of Chaucer's pilgrims going to Canterbury 'to receive a blessing or to do penance'. The process of writing a PhD thesis and then a book springing from it may well be compared to a pilgrimage – a long, intense journey with much effort (and adventures!) along the way and great expectations about its outcome. On many occasions, I have asked myself whether this 'pilgrimage' was more about receiving a blessing or doing penance. The answers have been varied, changing depending on the occasion. Now that the journey has ended, looking back, I can see that it has definitely been a bit of both. To be true, I hope that the final stage, with the book on the shelves, ready for review, will be like that of Thomas Colpeper, the magistrate of Chillingbourne, in Canterbury. He was expecting 'to do penance'. What he eventually found was 'a blessing'.

I have encountered many people during my journey, and there are many I need to thank.

My first expression of gratitude goes to Piet Eeckhout and Andrea Biondi. Their PhD supervision has been marked by attentive support and sincere friendship. One cherished thought goes also to my Alma Mater, King's College London, and particularly its Centre of European Law, a first-class intellectual hub that has shaped my way of thinking, nurtured my spirit of exploration, and taught me what being a scholar means. The debt to my PhD examiners, Claus-Dieter Elhermann, who also kindly accepted to write the foreword, and David O' Keeffe, is huge. Their questions, comments, and advice have all helped me to dramatically improve my reach. The attention they have shown towards my project has gone far beyond examination duties and has been remarkable. I also need to thank the many people who, in different ways, through discussions and interviews, suggestions and criticisms, have assisted me in testing findings and conclusions reached in my doctoral thesis and in my efforts to improve it. Particular mention is needed for John Baldwin, Jean-Francois Bellis, Americo Beviglia-Zampetti, Sadeq Bigdeli, Jane Bradley, Marco Bronckers, Marc Busch, Giuseppe Conte, Thomas Cottier, Richard Diamond, Vittorio Di Bucci, Giuseppe Fazio, James Flett, Todd Friedbacher, Jennifer Hillmann, Gary Horlick, Henrik Horn, Gary Hufbauer, John Jackson, Jesse Kreier, Gustavo Luengo Hernandez de Madrid, David Luff, Petros Mavroidis, Djakhongir Saidov, Ben Slocock, and Eric White. The people at OUP have been outstanding in their professional support and efficiency. I wish, in particular, to thank John Louth, Alex Flach, and Darcy Ahl. I also need to thank the British Academy for the award of a Small Research Grant for a visit to the Institute of International Economic law at Georgetown University in the 2007

Fall term, something that has proved pivotal in upgrading the book. Of course, I cannot fail to remember my wife Barbara who has always being there, providing support on all occasions, often enduring bigger or smaller renunciations (which – I promise – will all soon be redressed). My final and deepest thoughts go to Miranda and Adriano, my parents, to whom this book is dedicated. It has never been more true that, without their patient and silent sacrifices, not a single letter of this work would have seen the light of day.

Birmingham, 1 June 2009

Contents—Summary

V DISTORTION OF COMPETITION

Contents

IV BENEFICIARIES

Table of cases

EUROPEAN COURT OF JUSTICE AND COURT OF FIRST INSTANCE

A. Alphabetical

B. Numerical

GATT/WTO DISPUTE SETTLEMENT CASES (IN ALPHABETICAL ORDER OF SHORT TITLE)

NATIONAL COURTS

Table of legislation

EUROPEAN UNION

Tokyo Round Subsidies Code (Agreement on Interpretation and Application of Articles VI, XVI and XXIII of the General Agreement on Tariffs and Trade)

WTO Agreement

DISPUTE SETTLEMENT BODY DECISIONS

OTHER GATT DOCUMENTS (IN CHRONOLOGICAL ORDER)

Various GATT reports

GATT negotiations documents

URUGUAY ROUND NEGOTIATIONS DOCUMENTS

Documents of the Secretariat or the negotiating parties

List of abbreviations

AB	Appellate Body
AD	Antidumping
AG	Agreement on Agriculture
BISD	Basic Instruments and Selected Documents
BTA	Border Tax Adjustment
CFI	Court of First Instance
DG	Directorate General
DOC	Department of Commerce (US)
DSB	Dispute Settlement Body
DSM	Dispute Settlement Mechanism
DSU	Understanding on Rules and Procedures Governing the Settlement of Disputes
EEC	European Economic Community
EC	European Community
ECJ	European Court of Justice
ECR	European Court Reports
ECSC	European Coal and Steel Community
EU	European Union
GATT	General Agreement on Trade and Tariffs
GATS	General Agreement on Trade in Services
GBER	General Block Exemption Regulation
ILC	United Nations International Law Commission
ILO	International Labor Organization
NI	Nullification of impairment
NVNI	Non-violation nullification or impairment
nyr	not yet reported
OECD	Organization for Economic Cooperation and Development
OFT	Office of Fair Trading
OJ	Official Journal of the EC
PSO	Public Service Obligation
SAAP	State Aid Action Plan
SCM	Agreement of Subsidies and Countervailing Measures
SG	Agreement on Safeguards
SGEI	Service of General Economic Interest
SME	Small and Medium sized Enterprises
SPS	Sanitary and Phytosanitary Measures
TBT	Technical Barriers to Trade
TRIMs	Agreement on Trade-Related Investment Measures

UK	United Kingdom
UN	United Nations
US	United States
VAT	Value Added Tax
VCLT	Vienna Convention on the Law of Treaties
WTO	World Trade Organization

PART I

INTRODUCTION AND FOUNDATIONS

The Chairman concluded the roundtable noting that the discussion has raised more questions than it answered. The major problem identified is the issue of the definition—not just the definition of a subsidy but also the question of how to determine what is legitimate and what is not legitimate.[1]

Put simply, apart from clear instances of grasping monopoly, why should the international community be the keeper of national export morals? The answer is also simple: unbridled and competing national subsidies can undermine world prosperity. Whatever the analytic merits of a purist free trade, turn-the-other-cheek approach, the Great Depression taught the world that protective policies can quickly end distructively spread from nation to nation.[2]

A subsidy is treated in the GATT framework as a 'distortion' of international trade, that is, as creating a disparity between the actual costs incurred in producing a particular good and those which must be borne by the firm undertaking its production. In fact, however, much (perhaps all) government support can be defended as being a 'correction' rather than a 'distortion' of the market process.[3]

[1] OECD, *Competition Policy in Subsidies and State Aid*, Competition Policy Roundtable, DAFFE/CLP (2001) 24, OECD, Paris, 179.

[2] GC Hufbauer and J Shelton Erb, *Subsidies in International Trade* (Cambridge, Massachusetts: MIT Press, 1984) 8.

[3] WF Schwartz and EW Jr Harper, 'The Regulation of Subsidies Affecting International Trade' (1972) 7 Michigan Law Review 831, 833.

Overview

The first part of the book has a two-fold objective. First, to introduce the topic, its importance and immediately address the main questions arising out of it. Secondly, to lay down the more general foundations in the area that enable a proper understanding of the specific subject of the book.

The introduction (chapter 1) addresses three main issues. First, the desirability and feasibility of defining the notion of subsidy through a comparative approach of the two most developed disciplines of subsidies, the WTO and the EC. In so doing, a point of method ('in comparative analysis context matters') is made and exemplified through the case-study of the approaches to legal interpretation in the two systems. This case-study also provides a valuable insight into the principles of legal interpretation used in the construction of the definition of WTO subsidy and EC State aid. The introduction to the comparative discourse is closed with a brief section which addresses the issue of the possible inconsistencies between the definitions of EC State aid and WTO subsidy, an issue which is particularly topical because the two relevant disciplines may well apply cumulatively, with the result that normative conflicts may arise and need to be solved.

The second and third issues are more theoretical. One focuses on the 'definition of the definition' of subsidy. In other words, we identify the characteristical elements of an abstract definition of subsidy, while showing how we reached this result and reassuring the reader that abstract analysis is always connected to the practical examination of the actual definitions of subsidy in WTO and EC law. The second issue focuses on the important interaction between scope and justification, a true recurring theme of the whole book, with important conceptual and practical effects. It is suggested that the inherent attraction of justification considerations at the level of the definition centres around the philosophical concepts of distributive justice and substantive equality.

Chapter 2 addresses two foundational questions which, it is submitted, have an important impact on the more confined topic of the definition of subsidy. Why do we, and should we, control subsidies? If so, how do we devise an international system of control? We spend more time on the first question, identifying two justifications for subsidy control, one trade-related (linked to market access), the other competition-related (linked to distortions of competition). We also underline the important role that subsidy play in remedying market failures and pursuing other laudable public policy objectives. On the basis on these findings, we sketch the main features of the systems of subsidy control in the WTO and EC as they are, and as we suggest they should be.

1

Introduction

After introducing the reader to the subject of this book in the first section, section II focuses on the desirability and feasibility of the adoption of a comparative (WTO-EC law) approach in its analysis. The importance of a 'contextual' examination is underlined and discussed using a case-study on the attitudes to legal interpretation prevailing in the two systems at issue. The author then briefly addresses the possibility that inconsistent definitions in the two legal systems might lead to a normative conflict.

In section III the main elements of the analysis are singled out by clarifying what the author considers as 'definition' of subsidy in this book. After that, section IV introduces a crucial relationship—that between 'scope and justification'—and its impact on the boundaries of the 'definition' of subsidy. This interaction, which is a recurring theme of the book, is set into the broader theoretical discourse by linking the issue of subsidies with the concepts of distributive justice and equality. The analysis is closed with a roadmap of our trip, outlining the main parts of the book and its chapters.

I. The definition of WTO subsidy and EC State aid: the topic and its importance

Governments have always granted subsidies for various reasons, in various forms, and producing various effects.[1] In an era of increasing interdependence among countries and markets, and with government intervention on the rise in the current economic crisis, these effects are often felt in other constituencies. This triggers responses of various types which in turn produce other effects across the border. At the same time, the case for controlling subsidies and responses to them,

[1] Adam Smith devoted a whole chapter of his *An Inquiry into the Nature and Causes of the Wealth of Nations* of 1776 to 'bounties'. He concluded that 'the effect of bounties, like that of all the other expedients of the mercantile system, can only be to force the trade of a country into a channel much less advantageous than that in which it would naturally run of its own accord.' Alexander Hamilton's judgment was not much different. An interesting passage from his 1791 *Report on Manufacturers* can be found in JH Jackson, *The World Trading System – Law and Policy of International Economic Relations* (2nd edn, Cambridge Massachussetts: MIT Press, 1997) 417.

and for entering into international treaties defining governments obligations, is easily raised.[2]

These few lines sketch the background of the topic of this book. The word 'subsidy' is used many times and the reader might have the impression that this notion is not an issue. This is not the case. As the initial quote from the OECD's workshop indicates, in the already extremely controversial area of subsidies and their control, one of the most controversial topics has always been the definition of its main subject.

Although useful in addressing specific issues, economic science, for example, is not able to provide a definition of subsidy with sufficiently clear contours. According to Calamai and De Moor, 'any measure that keep prices for consumers below the market level or keep prices for producers above the market level, or that reduce costs for consumers and producers by giving direct or indirect support can be considered a subsidy'.[3] This definition certainly captures some features of the phenomenon but it is still too vague. Snape notes that, 'in considering which government actions may be regarded as providing subsidies, the term can be all-embracing. Virtually *every* government action can be regarded as a subsidy for someone, and virtually all such actions can affect international trade'.[4]

These words seem to dispel any hope of finding a definition with *operational* value. And this is an issue of paramount conceptual and practical significance because it ultimately determines whether a certain discipline applies or not, whether a governmental measure is allowed or not.

This book is about defining subsidies, in particular from the legal perspective. More precisely, the author attempts to define the concepts of 'subsidy' and

[2] International treaties have increasingly tackled the issue of subsidies, mainly referring to the use of countervailing duties, ie the imposition on foreign imports of a duty to compensate the subsidy. In 1923, 29 treaties containing rules on subsidies, of which seven were signed after 1900, were counted by J Viner, *Dumping: A Problem in International Trade* (New York: Kelley, 1966), 166–8.

One of them was the Brussels Sugar Convention of 1902 which introduced rules to curb export bounties on sugar. The significance of this treaty goes beyond the limited area of subsidies. In the words of HP Moura Filho, through it 'multilateralism had been established as a conceptual alternative and a practical possibility' ('Pioneering Multilateralism: The Sugar Agreements 1864–1914', paper presented at the XVI International Economic History Congress, Helsinki, Session 109, 2006, 1). This, just before the outbreak of World War I in 1914 and the subsequent period of protectionism which would have culminated with World War II. Only thereafter was the idea of multilateralism resurrected. The Brussels Sugar Convention of 1902, however, was never forgotten: 'the compromise treaty package that was agreed established for the first time a multilateral trading regime, albeit for one commodity, that contained many elements that would become standard in the General Agreement on Tariffs and Trade (GATT) and other later twentieth-century liberal trade regimes', observes GA Pigman, 'Hegemony and Trade Liberalization Policy: Britain and the Brussels Sugar Convention of 1902' (1997) Review of International Studies, 185, 199.

[3] P Calamai and A De Moor, *Subsidizing Unsustainable Development—Undermining the Earth with Public Funds* (Geneva: Earth Council, 1997) 1.

[4] R Snape, 'International Regulation of Subsidies' (1991) 14:2 The World Economy 139, 140 (emphasis in the original text).

'State aid' used in the WTO and EC respectively, the two most developed systems of control of this type of policy instrument in the world.[5]

The motivation for this effort is the desire for clarity and rationality in a land where both seem to be rare commodities, and to do so through a comparative analysis. The goal is to provide an analytical and conceptual framework of these two legal definitions. This, it is hoped, will aid both the interpreter and policy-maker in their effort to make sense of two disciplines which may apply (separately but even simultaneously) to this important instrument of industrial policy.[6]

II. Comparing WTO law and EC law

One of the peculiar aspects of this book is that the concept of subsidy is defined through a comparative analysis of WTO and EC law. This approach begs two questions. The first delves into the various reasons, often of general order, that justify comparisons. Its answer lays down a solid conceptual and practical foundation for the book's analysis. The second question touches on a delicate point that is sometimes raised which challenges the feasibility itself of a comparison between two legal systems which are arguably very different. The outcome of its analysis highlights the importance of 'contextual' considerations. A case-study on legal interpretation illustrates this point in action. Finally, the last part of the section briefly addresses the legal scenario of the possible cumulative application of, and conflict between, WTO subsidy and EC State aid laws, particularly when inconsistencies are found between the two definitions of subsidy and State aid.

A. Why compare?[7]

'The British don't know how to make a good cup of coffee. You don't know how to make a good cup of tea. It's an even swap.' This witty sentence can be found in the *Instructions for American Servicemen In Britain* of 1942. Although the meaning conveyed is just one of respect, based on equal dignity (and mutual ignorance), the other side of the coin of that dignity (and particularly that ignorance) is the existence of a 'knowledge opportunity'. And this opportunity is there to be exploited.

This is indeed the rationale of any form of comparative analysis. Although war efforts demanded that energy be channelled to tasks which were certainly

[5] It should be clarified immediately that, unless referring to one of the two specific legal systems, we use the terms 'subsidy' and 'State aid' indifferently. In fact, the former, which is arguably more common, even in economic and political circles, is used more frequently.

[6] The issue of the possible cumulative application of, and conflict between, WTO subsidy and EC State aid laws is analysed in section II.D below.

[7] More generally on the benefits and method of comparative analysis see the classic treatise of K Zweigert and H Kötz, *An Introduction to Comparative Law* (Oxford: Oxford University Press, 1999) chapters 1–3.

more important, the sentence above could have been rephrased, for the sake of our argument, in a more positive way. 'The British don't know how to make a good cup of coffee. You don't know how to make a good cup of tea. You can learn from each other.'

Experience has taught us that comparisons enhance knowledge. Law is no exception. The premise is: if the same problem has arisen in a different legal system, it may be interesting to enquire how that other legal system addressed and resolved the problem. The focus of comparative analysis is on searching for differences and similarities, to attempt to explain them, and eventually evaluate them, their strengths and weaknesses.[8] A similar point can be made for multi-disciplinary approaches. To view the same issue from different perspectives may contribute to a better understanding of that issue.

The enhancement of knowledge is, however, only the first fruit that comparative law can offer. The ultimate aim and benefit is *critical.*

Drawing inspiration from the solutions adopted in the other system, the lawyer is naturally led to verify the correctness of the solutions of his (or even of the two) system(s) and to propose new ones. This important critical phase prevents comparative law from being merely an exercise of 'piling up blocks that no one will build with'.[9] It shows the various practical dimensions of comparative law. The comparative exercise may prompt new interpretations of the existing law, or proposals for law reform.[10] It may even contribute to the development of legal systems.[11]

Finally, in the current context of a globalizing world in which relationships between different legal systems are of tremendous importance, the role to be played by comparative law is increasingly 'urgent'.[12] The most urgent of these responsibilities is *conflict-avoidance.* If different legal systems have to be applied to the same problem, a proper understanding of those different systems may minimize inconsistencies in interpretation. The increasing proliferation, and fragmentation, of various

[8] The reference to the 'other' and to the recognition that 'there is a world elsewhere' has a deep cultural, pedagogical, even moral, value. In other words, comparative law can raise the awareness that no system is perfect (a sort of benchmark) and that we can learn from foreign laws. See R Sacco, *Introduzione al Diritto Comparato* (Turin: UTET, 1992) chapter 1.

[9] K Zweigert and H Kötz, *An Introduction to Comparative Law* (Oxford: Oxford University Press, 1999) 47.

[10] The SCM Agreement is a good example in this regard, since many of its provisions draw inspiration from EC or US law.

[11] An excellent example is the role played by comparative law in the development of the general principles and the protection of fundamental rights in EC law. See FG Jacobs, 'The Uses of Comparative Law in the Law of the European Communities, Legal History and Comparative Law', in R Plender (ed), *Legal History and Comparative Law: Essays in Honour of A. Kiralfy* (London: Frank Cass, 1990); NL Brown and FG Jacobs, *The Court of Justice of the European Communities* (5th edn, London: Sweet and Maxwell, 2000) chapter 15.

[12] W Twining, *Globalization and Legal Theory* (London: Butterworths, 2000) chapter 7.

sources of international law gives an added value to interpretation as an instrument for legal coherency and certainty.[13]

B. Can WTO subsidy law and EC State aid law be compared?

The needs of critical understanding and reform, as well as that of conflict-avoidance, make the comparison between WTO subsidy law and EC State aid law not only desirable but even necessary. That said, this section attempts to answer a preliminary, more basic question which is sometimes put forward and directly undermines this conclusion. In a word, can WTO subsidy and EC State aid rules *really* be compared?

It is clear that the general (legal, political, historical, economic and other) context and objectives of the WTO and EC[14] are different and may therefore have an impact on the comparison of a specific set of rules.

The radical but natural query is whether, in consideration of these important differences, any meaningful comparison is *possible*. The problem would occur not only at a macro level (ie comparison between general traits of the systems) but also at the micro level of the rules that specifically regulate certain phenomena, eg tax discrimination, regulation, justifications, or subsidies.[15] With respect to the latter, it has been argued that the differences between WTO and EC discipline would be so many and 'fundamental' as to render 'the interest in a comparative analysis . . . limited to providing useful insights into both disciplines, but no more than that'.[16]

'Is the glass half empty or half full?' We think that the whole debate can be reduced to this question, which highlights how the issue is more one of perception

[13] See the 'Analytical study' *Fragmentation of International Law: Difficulties Arising from the Diversification and Expansion of International Law* of the Study Group of the UN ILC, Finalized by M Koskenniemi, A/CN.4/L.682, 13 April 2006, and also the 'Conclusions', A/CN/.4/L.702, 18 July 2006. For a commentary see J Pauwelyn, 'Fragmentation in International Law' in Max Planck Encyclopedia of Public International Law, 2008. The same author carried out an excellent analysis of the issue of 'conflict of norms'. See *Conflict of Norms in Public International Law How WTO Law Relates to Other Rules of International Law* (Cambridge: Cambridge University Press, 2003).

In the regulation of public subsidies, a convergence in the interpretation of WTO subsidy and EC State aid rules cannot but be beneficial. This point will be addressed in part D below.

[14] See chapter 2, section I.

[15] Although not spelled out expressly, this kind of objection was certainly in the mind of Eeckhout when, introducing his comparison between the law on free circulation of services in the EC and in the WTO law, and making it clear that he was not proposing that one system should have been the model for the other, he felt it necessary to acknowledge that: 'There are obvious differences, in wording, objective, context, and scheme of liberalization mechanisms in the respective systems. But that does not mean that comparison could not be enriching'. See P Eeckhout, 'Constitutional Concepts for Free Trade in Services', in G De Búrca and J Scott (eds), *The EU and the WTO Legal and Constitutional Issues* (Oxford: Hart Publishing, 2001) 212.

[16] J Flett, AC Jessep, and K Talaber-Ritz, 'The Relationship between WTO Subsidies Law and EC State Aid Law' in 'EC State aid law-Le Droit des Aides d'Etat dans la CE, Liber Amicorum Francisco Santaolalla Gadea (Kluwer Law International, 2008) 441, 442.

than of substance. The viability of carrying out a comparative exercise between rules that govern the *same phenomenon* and, from this perspective, pursue the *same function*,[17] is not precluded by the differences, even in objectives, in the general legal systems. Far from being an obstacle *to* the comparison between rules that regulate the same fact, these differences are an important factor that, along with others, has to be taken into account *in* the comparison to avoid incorrect conclusions.[18] In other words, rather than being an absolute barrier, diversity is an essential reminder that—to be meaningful—the analysis has always to be *contextual*.[19]

It could also be added that, at a more general level, when comparing the regulation of economic activities, differences often tend to wither. This is certainly due to the ongoing globalization process that produces an impact, even culturally, towards uniformity which goes well beyond the limited arena of commercial struggle.[20] Without diminishing the importance of the caveat just made ('context matters'), this trend confirms that the comparison between the rules that in various legal systems govern these phenomena is appropriate.[21]

[17] See K Zweigert and H Kötz, *An Introduction to Comparative Law* (Oxford: Oxford University Press, 1999). Comparisons are possible only between those rules that, irrespective of their possible domestic qualification, perform the same *function* since they regulate the same phenomenon. In other words, only comparables can be compared, and 'in law the only things which are comparable are those which fulfil the same function' (id, 34).

[18] This is indeed the approach taken by those that have carried out more recent comparisons between EC State aid and WTO subsidy law. See B Slocock, 'EC and WTO Subsidy Control Systems Some Reflections' (2007) European State Aid Law Quarterly 249; CD Ehlermann and M Goyette, 'The Interface between EU State Aid Control and WTO Disciplines on Subsidies' (2006) European State Aid Law Quarterly 695; G Luengo Hernández de Madrid, *Regulation of Subsidies and State Aids in WTO and EC Law—Conflicts in International Trade Law* (Alphen aan den Rijn: Kluwer Law International, 2006); id, 'Conflicts Between the Disciplines of EC State Aids and WTO Subsidies: Of Books, Ships and Aircraft' (2008) European Foreign Affairs Review 1.

The OECD too, in discussing subsidy control, compared the WTO and EC approaches (together with the experience of no less than seven different countries). See OECD, *Competition Policy in Subsidies and State Aid*, Competition Policy Roundtable, DAFFE/CLP (2001) 24, OECD, Paris.

[19] There are numerous interesting examples of parallels between EC and WTO law made from various perspectives. See, eg, F Ortino, *Basic Legal Instruments for the Liberalisation of Trade—A Comparative Analysis of EC and WTO Law* (Oxford: Hart Publishing, 2004); G De Búrca and J Scott, *The EU and the WTO—Legal and Constitutional Issues* (Oxford: Hart Publishing, 2001); JHH Weiler (ed), *The EU, the WTO and the NAFTA—Towards a Common Law of International Trade* (Oxford: Oxford University Press, 2000).

[20] The aim to reach a certain—albeit minimal—degree of liberalization of the economy seems to represent a *leit motif* in the regulation of economic activities and of the obstacles to it. See G Bognetti, *Introduzione al Diritto Costituzionale Comparato* (Turin: Giappichelli, 1994).

[21] The line of this argument could be taken even further. Not only is it common to find similarities in the rules concerning economic facts, but, more generally, there is an increasing propensity, even 'urgency', to give more *legal* relevance also to non-economic considerations, such as the environment, health and safety, labour conditions, and more generally fundamental rights. For an analysis of the increasing importance of non-economic values see chapter 2 section I.

C. 'Context matters': a case-study on legal interpretation

Legal interpretation is a fascinating topic, particularly in the context of international law. Lord McNair once said that there was no part in the law of the treaties which he approached with more trepidation than that of interpretation. Certainly, most of the passion that interpretation arouses is due to the elusive nature of a process that is more an art than a science.[22]

The interpreter has at his disposal various rules of interpretation. The fact is, however, that their actual scope is not settled, and, most importantly, the relative weight of these rules in the hermeneutic process may vary significantly. Further, as seen in the previous section, a crucial factor that may impact the approach to interpretation and its outcome is the broader legal context. This impact, and particularly that of WTO and EC law, is the subject of the next case-study.

Legal interpretation in the WTO

The second sentence of Article 3.2 of the Understanding on Rules and Procedures Governing the Settlement of Disputes (DSU) states that the dispute settlement system serves to clarify the existing provisions of the covered agreements 'in accordance with customary rules of interpretation of public international law'. In its first two cases, the newly constituted Appellate Body construed this phrase as referring to the Vienna Convention on the Law of Treaties (VCLT).[23] However, if we recognize that the rules of VCLT are 'materially principles of logic and order', it is clear the concept of 'customary rules of interpretation' should not be limited to the formal rules enshrined in the VCLT, but should in fact encompass other non-codified rules, or principles, of interpretation which are considered as such in international law.[24]

Whatever it may be, the two pillars of WTO law interpretation are constituted by Articles 31 and 32 of the VCLT. The former is particularly important since it embodies the 'general rule on interpretation':

> a treaty shall be interpreted in good faith in accordance with the ordinary meaning to be given to the terms of the treaty in their context and in the light of its object and purpose.[25]

[22] I Sinclair, *The Vienna Convention on the Law of Treaties* (2nd edn, Manchester: Manchester University Press, 1984) 118. See also NL Brown and FG Jacobs, *The Court of Justice of the European Communities* (5th edn, London: Sweet and Maxwell, 2000) 323.

[23] *US—Gasoline*, para 3 (for Article 31 of the VCLT); *Japan—Taxes II*, para 97 (Article 32). See also, for Article 33, *US—Softwood Lumber IV*, para 59.

[24] I Van Damme, 'Jurisdiction, Applicable Law, and Interpretation' in D Bethlemen, D McRae, R Neufeld, and I Van Damme (eds), *The Oxford Handbook of International Trade Law* (Oxford: Oxford University Press, 2009) 298, 323–4.

[25] Article 32 provides that 'recourse may be had to supplementary means of interpretation, including the preparatory work of the treaty and the circumstances of its conclusion, in order to confirm the meaning resulting from the application of Article 31, or to determine the meaning when the

In 2002, Professor Ehlermann, a former Appellate Body judge, synthesized the approach of the Appellate Body with respect to these criteria.[26] The greatest importance is attached to the 'ordinary meaning of the terms of the treaty'. The 'context' is given less weight than the first, but it is certainly been more relied upon than the third, the 'object and purpose'. By contrast, little importance is attributed to the 'preparatory work of the treaty' under Article 32.

Although this schematic outline offers a good picture of the inner balance struck by the VCLT and WTO's approach to legal interpretation, it needs to be developed a little further to produce a more comprehensive understanding.

Article 31 of the VCLT includes a 'general *rule* of interpretation'. The use of the emphasized singular clearly indicates that the process of interpretation is 'a single combined operation',[27] or, to use a more sophisticated term, 'holistic' exercise[28]. What VCLT rules, and in particular Article 31, however do is 'reflect an attempt to assess the *relative value* and *weight* of the elements to be taken into account in the process of interpretation rather than to *describe the process of interpretation itself*.'[29] Indeed, apart from implying that the process of interpretation should be a unitary operation, its actual operation is not described, and it is for the interpreter to carry it out in each individual case.

The text constitutes the natural starting point of any process of interpretation as well as its centre of gravity. As Pauwelyn notes, the text of the treaty is the necessary *reference for* and at the same time the *limitation of* the other tools of treaty interpretation.[30] Since interpretation is about giving meaning to existing rules and not about creating new rules, it cannot go either beyond or against the text of the rule in question.

interpretation according to Article 31: (a) leaves the meaning ambiguous or obscure; or (b) leads to a result which is manifestly absurd or unreasonable'.

[26] CD Ehlermann, 'Six Years on the Bench of the "World Trade Court"—Some Personal Experiences as Member of the Appellate Body of the World Trade Organization' in (2002) Journal of World Trade 605, 615 16. This finds confirmation in the personal accounts of other judges of the Appellate Body. See J Bacchus, 'Appellators: The Quest for the Meaning of And/Or' (2005) World Trade Review 499; G Abi-Saab, 'The WTO Dispute Settlement and General International Law' in R Yerxa and B Wilson (eds), *Key Issues in WTO Dispute Settlement—The First Ten Years* (Cambridge: Cambridge University Press, 2005) 7.

[27] See the UN International Law Commission, *Draft Articles on the Law of Treaties with Commentaries, Yearbook of International Law Commission*, 1966, Vol II, 219–20. See also I Brownlie, *Principles of Public International Law* (6th edn, Oxford: Oxford University Press, 2003) 633; MN Shaw, *International Law* (5th edn, Cambridge: Cambridge University Press, 2003) 656.

[28] See Appellate Body, *EC—Chicken Classification*, para 176: 'Interpretation pursuant to the customary rules codified in Article 31 of the Vienna Convention is ultimately a holistic exercise that should not be mechanically subdivided into rigid components.'

[29] I Sinclair, *The Vienna Convention on the Law of Treaties* (2nd edn, Manchester: Manchester University Press, 1984) 117 (emphasis added).

[30] J Pauwelyn, *Conflict of Norms in Public International Law—How WTO Law Relates to Other Rules of International Law* (Cambridge: Cambridge University Press, 2003) 245.

It is with these considerations in mind that it is noted[31] that the consistent reliance on the 'ordinary meanings of the terms of the treaty' by the Appellate Body and the Panels has contributed to 'providing security and predictability of the multilateral trading system'[32] and has had a legitimizing effect of the activity of the dispute settlement organs, by keeping at bay the criticisms that they were attempting to 'add or diminish the rights and obligations provided in the covered agreements'.[33]

But this reliance on the text is not the same as mere textualism.

First, the 'ordinary meaning' of legal rules does not result from a pure grammatical or linguistic analysis, or a dictionary meaning, but necessarily has to take their practical application into due account. Secondly, the analysis of the 'ordinary meaning' inevitably requires a significant degree of 'contextualization'.[34] Article 31(1) of the VCLT itself notes that the terms of the treaty should not be read in the abstract but should be put 'in their context' which is constituted by the text of the treaty, including its preamble and annexes, and other rules that satisfy certain requirements.[35] Most significantly, the inherent need for contextualization may lead well beyond the strictures of the requirements of the VCLT. Thirdly, the interpretation of the 'ordinary terms of the treaty in their context' shall be read 'in the light of' the 'object and purpose' of the treaty.[36]

The phrase 'in the light of' arguably indicates that, although significant, purposive or teleological interpretation is seen as a secondary and ancillary tool.[37]

[31] CD Ehlermann, 'Six Years on the Bench of the "World Trade Court"—Some Personal Experiences as Member of the Appellate Body of the World Trade Organization' in (2002) Journal of World Trade 605, 616–17. In a similar vein see J Bacchus, 'Appellators: The Quest for the Meaning of And/Or' (2005) World Trade Review 499.

[32] Article 3.2 of the DSU, first sentence.

[33] Article 3.2 of the DSU, third sentence.

[34] FG Jacobs, 'Varieties of Approach to Treaty Interpretation: With Special Reference to the Draft Convention on the Law of Treaties before the Vienna Diplomatic Conference' (1969) International and Comparative Law Quarterly 318, 334; M Lennard, 'Navigating by the Stars: Interpreting the WTO Agreements' (2002) Journal of International Economic Law, 17, 24.

[35] I Van Damme, 'Jurisdiction, Applicable Law, and Interpretation' in D Bethlemen, D McRae, R Neufeld, and I Van Damme (eds), *The Oxford Handbook of International Trade Law* (Oxford: Oxford University Press, 2009) 298, 326 et seq.

[36] M Lennard, 'Navigating by the Stars: Interpreting the WTO Agreements' (2002) Journal of International Economic Law, 17, 27, observed that also the object and purpose of the *provision* under examination may become relevant insofar as it is evidence of the object and purpose of the treaty.

[37] As confirmation of the centrality of the text of the treaty, the object and purpose of a treaty are primarily to be gathered from it, and particularly, if there is any, from its preamble. M Lennard ('Navigating by the Stars: Interpreting the WTO Agreements' (2002) Journal of International Economic Law, 17, 29) notes that the UN International Law Commission (*Draft Articles on the Law of Treaties with Commentaries, Yearbook of International Law Commission*, 1966, Vol II, 221) considered the 'object and purpose' of the treaty as referring to *expressed* objects and purposes, particularly, but not exclusively, as mentioned in the preamble. See also I Sinclair, *The Vienna Convention on the Law of Treaties* (2nd edn, Manchester: Manchester University Press, 1984) 118; FG Jacobs, 'Varieties of Approach to Treaty Interpretation: With Special Reference to the Draft Convention on the Law of Treaties before the Vienna Diplomatic Conference' (1969) International and Comparative Law Quarterly 318, 337.

The anchorage to the text of the treaty may thus circumscribe the risk that the interpreter imports his own object and purpose of the treaty. It is in any case a fact that, for various reasons, the identification of treaty object and purpose may be particularly difficult. Most treaties, and this is especially true for multilateral conventions, like the WTO, have more than one purpose, and quite often these may be in conflict with each other.[38]

It has been noted that non-codified rules of interpretation play an important role. One of the most important is the principle of effectiveness, or *effet utile*. This requires that 'when the treaty is open to two interpretations one of which does and the other does not enable the treaty to have appropriate effects, goods faith and the objects and purpose of the treaty demand that the former interpretation should be adopted'.[39] In the same vein, the Appellate Body noted that 'interpretation must give meaning and effect to all the terms of the treaty. An interpreter is not free to adopt a reading that would result in reducing whole clauses or paragraphs of a treaty to redundancy or inutility'.[40] As Pauwelyn observed, 'words cannot be *interpreted "out of"* WTO provisions'.[41]

As a final point, the quote from the ILC commentary above may lead one to wonder whether the principle of effectiveness really differs from the interpretation 'in the light of the object and purpose of the treaty', or whether they are rather two different ways—possibly with a different emphasis (one referring to the text, the other to the object and purpose)—of describing the same thing.[42] Most importantly, both principles raise the same concern with respect to the 'centre of gravity' of interpretation in international law. They can be close allies of the text, giving full meaning to it, but, if pushed too far, they may turn against it.[43]

[38] I Sinclair, *The Vienna Convention on the Law of Treaties* (2nd edn, Manchester: Manchester University Press, 1984) 130–1.

[39] UN International Law Commission, *Draft Articles on the Law of Treaties with Commentaries, Yearbook of International Law Commission*, 1966, Vol II, 219.

[40] *US Gasoline*, para 23; confirmed in, *inter alia, Japan—Taxes II*, para 12.

[41] J Pauwelyn, *Conflict of Norms in Public International Law How WTO Law Relates to Other Rules of International Law* (Cambridge: Cambridge University Press, 2003) 249. It has also been noted that the Appellate Body reinforced the textual approach to the treaty by responding to the previous alleged 'tendency of panels to overlook exact textual wording in order to give effect to what they see as the "object and purpose" of the treaty as a whole'. See MJ Trebilcock and R Howse, *The Regulation of International Trade* (3rd edn, London: Routledge, 2005) 133–4.

[42] I Sinclair, *The Vienna Convention on the Law of Treaties* (2nd edn, Manchester: Manchester University Press, 1984) 118.

[43] See J Pauwelyn, *Conflict of Norms in Public International Law How WTO Law Relates to Other Rules of International Law* (Cambridge: Cambridge University Press, 2003) 249.

The Appellate Body itself seems to have understood the risks of a too much liberal interpretation (that is too remote from the text and the object and purpose of the treaty) when it noted that the Vienna Convention 'principles of interpretation neither require nor condone the imputation into a treaty of words that are not there or the importation into a treaty of concepts that were not intended'. See Appellate Body, *India—Patent*, para 45. This finding shows two things. First, that, in the same way as it is not possible to read words 'out of' the treaty, words cannot be read 'into' the treaty. See J Pauwelyn, *Conflict of Norms in Public International Law – How WTO Law Relates to Other Rules of International Law* (Cambridge: Cambridge University Press, 2003) 249. Secondly, it shows the

Legal interpretation in the EC

Article 220 EC reads: 'The Court of Justice and the Court of First Instance, each within its jurisdiction, shall ensure that in the interpretation and application of this Treaty the law is observed.' Unlike WTO law, there is no express reference to any method of interpretation.[44] It has therefore been for the Court itself to define its own approach to legal interpretation.[45]

In fact, the principles of interpretation are not different from those analysed in the previous section. What differs (a memento that 'context matters' in comparative analysis) is their relative weight, and the process of interpretation itself.

In this regard, the words uttered in 1976 by Kutscher, former President of the Court, are still relevant: 'The literal and historical methods of interpretation recede into the background. Schematic and teleological interpretation . . . is of primary importance.'[46] Further, contextual and purposive interpretation 'are closely interlocked in the case-law of the Court'.[47]

The main, important implication that can be drawn is that the text does *not* generally represent a limit. This is partly because the Court soon realized the limitation of textualism.[48] Brown and Jacobs noted:

> [f]aced as it often is with texts which are vague, ambiguous or incomplete, the Court has recognised the limitations for itself of the literal methods of interpretation. Particularly, after 1958, when the Court was confronted with the more programmatic EC Treaty, its interpretation shifted perceptibly towards the contextual and teleological, with emphasis on the *ratio legis* and the objectives of the Treaty.[49]

connection between 'extensive' and 'purposive' interpretation. The first part of the finding refers to imputing into the treaty 'words that are not there', with a clear emphasis on the text, the second part, which mentions the importation into the treaty of 'concepts that were not intended', seems to use a different language which may well hint at a broader analysis of the object and purpose of the treaty.

[44] No reference can be found in the Statute of the Court or the relevant Rules of Procedures.

A corollary is that the ECJ does not follow the methods of interpretation prevailing in public international law when interpreting EC law. The case is of course different when it is necessary to interpret international agreements binding on the Community. See P Eeckhout, *External Relations of the European Union – Legal and Constitutional Foundations* (Oxford: Oxford University Press, 2004) 256 et seq.

[45] It is interesting to consider that, in the WTO context too, despite some guidance was provided by the DSU, it was the judiciary (the Appellate Body) to actually define the rules of the game and call in the VCLT.

[46] H Kutscher, 'Methods of Interpretation as Seen by a Judge of the Court of Justice', in *Reports of the 1976 Judicial and Academic Conference* (Luxembourg: Office for the Official Publications of the EC, 1976) 16.

[47] Ibid, 40.

[48] A Arnull, *The European Court of Justice* (2nd edn, Oxford: Oxford University Press, 2006) chapter 16 traces the cultural roots of this approach back to the civil law origins of the EC system and, in particular, to the 'move away from literalism that . . . followed codifications' in the 19th century.

[49] NL Brown and FG Jacobs, *The Court of Justice of the European Communities* (5th edn, London: Sweet and Maxwell, 2000) 326.

In another passage, the preference for the teleological approach is again explained as being 'peculiarly appropriate in Community law where . . . the Treaties provide mainly a broad programme or design rather than a detailed blue-print'.[50] This is convenient on the premise that the EC and EU Treaties are (already) substantially a Constitution and the Court of Justice a Constitutional Court.[51]

The Court's reasoning therefore puts a heavy reliance on context and, in particular, on teleology and *effet utile* with the result that EC law is usually interpreted quite liberally.

Indeed in EC law purposive interpretation has various applications. Referring to the crucial objective of integration underlying the internal market, the expression 'integrationist' interpretation has also been used.[52] One of the most notable examples is the famous *Van Gend en Loos* case[53] where the Court laid down the principle that the Community constitutes a 'new legal order of international law for the benefit of which the states have limited their sovereign rights . . . and the subjects of which comprise not only Member States but also their nationals'. Community law can thus have direct effect, that is, it can give rise to rights that individuals can invoke before national courts and that the latter have to protect. It is appropriate to take a moment to look at the reasoning of the Court to fully appreciate what is meant by the contextual, purposive and integrationist approach in the EC context.[54]

This approach has sometimes been negatively dubbed 'judicial activism' and subjected to strong criticism.[55] In any event, it cannot be concluded that the Court never feels constrained by the Treaty language. In the *UPA* case,[56] contrary to the

[50] NL Brown and FG Jacobs, *The Court of Justice of the European Communities* (5th edn, London: Sweet and Maxwell, 2000) 339.

[51] FG Jacobs, 'Is the Court of Justice of the European Communities a Constitutional Court?', in D Curtin and D O'Keeffe (eds), *Constitutional Adjudication in European Community and National Law* (Dublin: Butterworths, 1992) 25, 32; T, Tridimas, 'The Court of Justice and Judicial Activism' (1997) European Law Review 199; A Albors-Llorens, 'The European Court of Justice: More than a Teleological Court' (1999) Cambridge Yearbook of European Legal Studies 373.

It should not be taken for granted that a Constitution should always be construed flexibly or liberally. It is instructive in this regard to consider the contrasting positions of two current Justices of the US Supreme Court, Stephen Breyer and Antonin Scalia. See S Breyer, *Active Liberty: Interpreting a Democratic Constitution* (rev edn, Oxford: Oxford University Press, 2008) and A Scalia, *A Matter of Interpretation: Federal Courts and the Law* (Princeton: Princeton Universoty Press, 1998) which, together with the relevant essay of Justice Scalia, also includes commentaries from Professors Gordon Wood, Laurence Tribe, Mary Ann Glendon, and Ronald Dworkin.

[52] P Pescatore, *The Law of Integration: Emergence of a New Phenomenon* (Leiden: Sijhoof, 1974).

[53] Case 26/62.

[54] On this landmark case, see P Pescatore, 'The Doctrine of 'Direct Effect': An Infant Disease of Community Law' (1983) European Law Review 155.

[55] The strongest attack came from H Rasmussen, *On Law and Policy in the European Court of Justice* (Lancaster: Martinus Nijhoff, 1986). The author does not enter this debate except to note, together with A Arnull, *The European Court of Justice* (2nd edn, Oxford: Oxford University Press, 2006) chapter 16, that 'the view that the Court of Justice ignores the wording of Community provisions in order to pursue an agenda of its own is a parody of its approach'.

[56] Case 55/00P *UPA*.

powerful and convincing Opinion of Advocate General Jacobs, the Court found that it was not able to construe the notion of 'individual concern' in Article 230(4) EC more liberally, and hence was unable to ensure better access to justice for 'non-privileged' applicants seeking judicial review of EC acts, since this would have meant running *against* the *text* of the Treaty.

Brief parallel between WTO and EC law

Professor Ehlermann summed up the difference in approach to interpretation in the two legal systems:

> [w]hile the Appellate Body clearly privileges 'literal' interpretation, the ECJ is a protagonist of 'teleological' interpretation.[57]

The big difference between the two systems depends on the different weight given to textual and purposive interpretation respectively. And this has an impact on how the process of interpretation itself is conducted. Ultimately, this difference in approach to legal interpretation explains different judicial styles.

If one has to be—or at least has to be seen to be—particularly faithful to the wording of a treaty (like in the WTO) this will require a particularly elaborate style where every step of the reasoning is laid out, sometimes several times and with different formulations. Conversely, the style of the Court of Justice is definitely more concise, sometimes even cryptic.

From the interpreter's perspective, the two styles are extreme, in either direction. WTO dispute settlement organs, particularly Panels, would do better to attempt to simplify. On the other hand, the Court of Justice should sometimes be less hermetic in its reasoning. That said, we should not forget the political dimension. Like the different emphasis in the use of the methods of legal interpretation, it may well be argued that the two different judicial styles—extremely elaborate vs extremely concise—are ultimately a reflection of the different need for *legitimacy* required by the two tribunals. Further, hermetism or lack of clarity often tell a different story and may be explained by lack of consensus.

A word of conclusion, and reconciliation too. We see—at least beneath the surface—a common denominator which can reduce the apparently wide distance between the two approaches to legal interpretation in the WTO and EC. In both systems, there seems to be a recognition that mere textualism does not take us very far. The text is the natural starting point of any form of interpretation but we cannot stop there. Although the emphasis is clearly different, calls for more 'contextualization' or, if the system allows and requires this, 'teleology', constitute a step in this direction.

[57] CD Ehlermann, 'Six Years on the Bench of the "World Trade Court" – Some Personal Experiences as Member of the Appellate Body of the World Trade Organization' in (2002) Journal of World Trade 605, 616.

D. A matter of importance: 'inconsistencies' between WTO subsidy law and EC State aid law at the definition level

There is an important conceptual and practical dimension deriving from the comparative exercise between WTO subsidy and EC State aid rules. This issue has broad ramifications which go beyond the definitional issues and hence the specific subject of this book. What is therefore attempted here is merely to sketch the terms of the problem, from the perspective of the definition of subsidy/State aid. At the same time, however, while signalling the issue, the reader is provided with a 'problem-framework' to usefully approach the core of the analysis of the book and this potential conflict dimension.

The fact is that there are real possibilities of 'conflicts' between the two systems. Conflicts are situations where (for example, two) contrasting normative obligations do not offer any alternative to complying with one and breaching the other. To be more precise, in the present context, the scenario would be that of (i) inconsistency of EC State aid law *with* WTO subsidy law, (ii) generally resulting in a situation where what is legal in the EC is illegal in the WTO.[58] Although the final determination that there is a conflict would require a comprehensive analysis of both disciplines as a whole, since only such analysis can provide a definite conclusion on the obligations of the relevant State, *inconsistencies* pointing towards a conflict situation could already come out at the level of the definition of State aid and subsidy and of its various constituent elements.

Indeed even similar requirements may be construed differently in the two definitions. Admittedly, many differences could be ironed out through 'consistent interpretation'. This would mean interpreting the relevant requirement(s) of the definition of EC State aid in line with the corresponding one(s) in the WTO. Two comments may be made. First, in the light of the flexible approach to legal interpretation the EC shows, one would expect that it would be quite easy to construe, so far as necessary and possible, the relevant definition of State aid in line with that of WTO subsidy. Similar claims have been put forward, as defences, in a number of cases before the Community courts which have however consistently rejected the relevance of any reference to the WTO notion of subsidy (for the lack of 'direct effect' of WTO law in the EC law internal system).[59]

Secondly, the reasoning above is predicated on the stated objective to *avoid a possible conflict* and assumes that the whole responsibility would fall on the EC shoulders. A quite separate, and more general, issue is whether this one-way alignment is always desirable. It may well be that differences between the two legal systems at the definitional level can be explained with the fact that the EC 'solution' is more correct. If any adjustment should be made, it could be argued that this

[58] The opposite situation (EC—illegal but WTO—legal) is more difficult to visualize.

[59] See, eg, See C-351/98 *Spain v Commission*, para 44 and Case C-409/00 *Spain v Commission*, para 56.

should operate in the opposite direction, with WTO subsidy law following suit. The discovery and assessment of the several differences and divergences (together with the similarities and convergences) between the two definitions is the main subject of the critical and comparative analysis of this book. The reader is therefore referred to the relevant passages where the possible inconsistencies between the two laws are uncovered and explained.

That said, it is the author's impression that, on balance, the most common causes of real conflict between EC State aid and WTO subsidy laws would not come from the definition side but rather from other aspects of the substantive discipline (for example, the current stark difference in the regulation of 'subsidy justifications'). In very broad terms, the most frequent situation is that, due to its more developed and integrated approach, the EC is more lenient than the WTO towards public subsidies. In short, it is likely that many practices that would be permitted in the EC would be objectionable in the WTO. However, this is a very limited and approximate conclusion. As said, the issue of possible conflicts between EC State aid and WTO subsidy law is complex and requires a thorough analysis which goes beyond the scope of this book.[60]

III. Defining the definition

The subject of the book is the definition of subsidy in the WTO and State aid in the EC.

We should, however, first define what we intend for definition of subsidy or State aid. This is a difficult exercise. Those who seek definitions, particularly legal definitions, deal with elusive substance. The legal concept of subsidy does not exist *in rerum natura*: it is not a fact but an artificial construct of a given legal system with a given practical purpose.[61]

The starting point of the quest for a 'legal definition' of subsidy comes from the main point of the previous section on comparative analysis. The concept of 'subsidy' cannot be defined in general but depends substantially on its *context*, be it legal, political, economic, etc. The legal system, with its material provisions, procedural rules and remedies, and ultimately its objectives, does influence the actual definition of subsidy in *that* 'legal system'. The second remark is that, more than just a description, the definition of subsidy refers to the *characteristics*

[60] See, eg, G Luengo Hernández de Madrid, *Regulation of Subsidies and State Aids in WTO and EC Law—Conflicts in International Trade Law* (Alphen aan den Rijn: Kluwer Law International, 2006); id, 'Conflicts Between the Disciplines of EC State Aids and WTO Subsidies: Of Books, Ships and Aircraft' (2008) European Foreign Affairs Review 1. See also CD Ehlermann and M Goyette, 'The Interface between EU State Aid Control and WTO Disciplines on Subsidies' (2006) European State Aid Law Quarterly 695.

[61] On the complexity of legal definitions see the classic analysis of HLA Hart, 'Definition and Theory in Jurisprudence' (1954) Law Quarterly Review 70.

that are normally and positively present when that legal system concludes 'we have a subsidy', or 'this subsidy is objectionable' or rather 'this subsidy is permissible'.

These two considerations seem to jeopardize *any* effort of abstraction from a given legal system, and to make it possible to define a subsidy only in relation to WTO law or a State aid in relation to EC law. However, we still believe that an exercise of abstraction is possible, and indeed desirable. Looking at things from distance, with some measure of detachment, often produces a more comprehensive and objective understanding.

As we will see, the consideration of the characteristics of subsidies in those two legal systems (which constitute the most important regulations of subsidies at an international level) represents the starting point of the analysis. It is by deconstructing these elements, and examining them, that we can suggest a more abstract definition of subsidy. If this exercise does not claim to be exhaustive, it can however certainly claim to represent a useful conceptual framework within which to analyse issues and suggest solutions. The premise of this exercise will always be constituted by the problems legal systems, in our case the WTO and the EC, face in regulating those phenomena that are called 'subsidies'.

Reasoning in the GATT/WTO world, Professor Diamond, of Georgetown University, has recently outlined a 'conceptual map' constituted by 'a five step heuristic for identifying actionable subsidies'.[62]

The first step, which includes 'government actions that increase producer wealth', 'defines the broad universe of actions that might be considered actionable government subsidies. The remaining four steps serve as filters or tests that each action must pass to be considered an actionable subsidy.' These are: exclusion based on the nature of recipients (ie specificity) or governmental action (steps 2 and 3), exclusion based on market comparison (step 4), and requirement of damage to competing producers (step 5).

In this book, a similar theoretical exercise is attempted. Going beyond the actual definitions in the WTO and EC law, the attempt is to devise a conceptual framework that could provide a better understanding of *a notion of subsidy inserted in a subsidy regulation pursuing certain objectives*.[63]

How has this framework been shaped? From the initial stages of the research a few general elements, outlined below, have naturally emerged as essential characteristics, and hence useful tools of interpretation, of a more abstract concept of subsidy. Through the reflexive process of the critical and comparative analysis

[62] R Diamond, 'Privatization and the Definition of Subsidy: A Critical Study of Appellate Body Texturalism' (2008) Journal of International Economic Law 649, 664–669. In a discussion with the author, Professor Diamond acutely observed that it is easier to define what is *not* a subsidy than what is a subsidy.

[63] An analysis of the objectives of subsidy control in the WTO and EC can be found in chapter 2.

itself, issues and tests, concepts and categories have come out, and have been increasingly developed. The result is a 'subsidy language' that will accompany us.

The abstract level of analysis has been continuously connected to, and nurtured from, the normative one, and more particularly the complex 'legal formants' that characterize the relevant regulation in the WTO and in the EC.[64] This analysis inevitably draws on various sources. But two of them stand out particularly. The most important is certainly teleology, that is the discourse on the goals that the two legal systems in general, and the two subsidy disciplines in particular, do (or should) pursue. Secondly, an important role is played by the meta-juridical discourse, which involves other disciplines, such as economics, political science and political economy.

We should repeat that the goal of our conceptual framework is to introduce a flexible analytical toolbox, not a logical straitjacket.[65] Alternative classifications and terminology can certainly be contemplated. Completeness was not our aim, and is surely not our result. Intuition, however, seems to have married well with theory in respect of certain hard issues, principles and tests. Indeed, they seem to be characteristic of any subsidy definition, and, for this reason, deserve centre stage in our analysis.

Three elements emerge as essential to a minimal, even commonsensical, notion of subsidy: first, a form of public action; secondly, the grant of an economic advantage; thirdly, an impact on the competitive process. Perplexities might be raised with respect to the third element. It could indeed be argued that this means leaving the narrow concept of 'subsidy' to approach the broader concept of 'objectionable subsidy'.[66] However, this author thinks that the competitive impact of the subsidy deserves to be included in the elements defining the scope of the discipline because of its link with the justification of subsidy control.[67]

IV. The definition of subsidy and the interaction between scope and justification

Part I begins with a quotation from the conclusions of the OECD's roundtable on subsidies and State aids: 'The major problem identified is the issue of the definition'.

[64] The concept of 'legal formant' has been defined by R Sacco, 'Legal Formants: A Dynamic Approach to Comparative Law' (1991) American Journal of Comparative Law 343; id R Sacco, *Introduzione al Diritto Comparato* (Turin: UTET, 1992).

[65] In the same vein see the premise of O Black, *Conceptual Foundations of Antitrust* (Cambridge: Cambridge University Press, 2005) 4–5.

[66] Interestingly, Diamond's heuristic focuses on the broader notion of 'actionable subsidy'.

[67] See chapter 2. By contrast, despite the attraction between definition and justification, which warrants their inclusion in the 'issue of the definition' (see next section), the positive externalities produced by subsidies, and the relevant regulation, do not belong to the definition of subsidy and are not therefore dealt with in this book. The analysis of the justifications of subsidies and their possible international discipline will be the subject of a later project.

Crucially, the Chairman went on to specify that the 'issue' is 'not just the definition of a subsidy but also the question of how to determine what is legitimate and what is not legitimate.'[68]

The inclusion of both questions under the 'issue of the definition' shows the close relationship between the two. One of the crucial questions of interpretation of the definition of subsidy in both legal systems is the recurring risk of conflation of justification considerations into scope analysis. This is one of the main themes of this book.

The scope/justification attraction revolves around the role of the objectives in the analysis of subsidies. Subsidies are an important public policy tool and are often used to remedy a disadvantage. Depending on how this objective is considered in the subsidy context, three possible situations can arise.

First scenario. There is no subsidy because the measure, being a mere application of the general rule, does not confer an advantage at all, and hence cannot distort or alter the playing field in any way.

Second scenario. There is no subsidy because, even if formally a differential treatment is present, the measure does not really confer an advantage because it compensates a disadvantage and thus levels the playing field.

Third scenario. Under circumstances similar to the second situation, since there is a measure derogating from the norm and granting an advantage, we do indeed have a subsidy but this would ultimately be legitimate, or justified, because the measure achieves a recognized laudable objective.

To sum up, reasoning in terms of 'scope/justification' binomial, there are two alternatives. Either (i) because there is no differential treatment, at formal or substantive level, we do not have an advantage in the first place (no 'scope'), or (ii) since there is a differential treatment, we have an advantage (and possibly a distortion), but this is permitted ('justification').

Now, the issue is that there is often a tendency to conflate the two levels of scope and justification at the *preliminary* level of the definition (ie 'scope') concluding that the measure does *not* in fact constitute a subsidy. This depends on both practical/political and conceptual reasons. As regards the former, for any defending government the first line of defence is that there is no subsidy in the first place. Hence the relevant (subsidy) rules do not apply. If any, other disciplines might be triggered but there is no subsidy issue to handle—one less problem.

A. Scope and justification, equality and distributive justice

At a conceptual level, the scope/justification attraction depends on the elusiveness of the boundaries of the twinned concepts of *equality* and *distributive justice*.

[68] OECD, *Competition Policy in Subsidies and State Aid*, Competition Policy Roundtable, DAFFE/CLP (2001) 24, OECD, Paris, 179.

The analysis of the philosophical idea of 'justice as equality' may help in understanding the operation of the definition of subsidy.[69] Mere common sense suggests that the concept of subsidy involves a measure that does not accord equal treatment to similar situations but rather confers an advantage to some. As thoroughly analysed in Part III of the book, the determination of the existence of this advantage is not easy. In *The Concept of Law* Hart notes that the idea of justice:

> consists of two parts: a uniform or constant feature, summarised in the precept 'Treat like cases alike' and a shifting or varying criterion used in determining when, for any given purpose, cases are alike or different.[70]

These words convey the instability lying at the heart of any judgment of equality, which is inevitably reflected into the concept of subsidy (the reader is referred again to the analysis in Part III), and leads to the attraction between scope and justification highlighted in the previous paragraph, and, in particular, to the possible consideration of the justification *already* at the level of the definition.

The usual starting point of most discussions on justice is Aristotle's *Ethica Nicomachea* where we find the principle that things that are alike should be treated alike, while things that are unalike should be treated unalike, in proportion to their unalikeness.[71] This broad concept of justice, firmly embedded in that of equality, can be subdivided into two separate ideas. Whereas corrective or commutative justice merely requires that all equals are treated equally, distributive justice means giving each according to his merit or need. Compared to the former, whose ethos simply reflects a given balance, often reinstating the *status quo* (and hence remains at a somewhat formal level), the latter would inevitably require more discretion, inherent in how the 'proportion of inequality' is actually defined and applied to achieve a fixed target of just distribution (and progressively focuses on more prospective and substantive levels of equality).

Drawing inspiration from this discussion for our purposes, whereas this distinction seems to be satisfactory at a conceptual level, it may be less so when we attempt to test it using practical cases of alleged differential treatment and try to establish whether in the instant case we have a measure conferring an unfair advantage and consequently a subsidy.

Is the legislation at hand merely an application of formal equality based on a commutative and largely automatic relationship which, almost by definition, would not amount to a subsidy? (In this regard, a good question is whether market-based transactions can be explained simply in these terms.) Further: where does formal equal treatment end and substantive equal treatment begin?

More intriguingly, can we distinguish between acts of distributive justice? Can we differentiate measures based on a distributional logic, and introduced to reach

[69] And even the broader universe of its justification and the relevant discipline.

[70] HLA Hart, *The Concept of Law* (2nd edn, Oxford: Clarendon Press, 1994) 160.

[71] Book V.3, 1131a, 1131b.

equality at a more substantive level, which do not constitute unequal treatment and subsidization on the one hand, and measures of a similar nature that should in contrast be considered as conferring an undue advantage and hence a subsidy on the other? If the answer is yes, *where* and *how* should we draw the line? These questions lie at the very heart of the legal definition of subsidy.

These difficulties are particularly clear if we consider few examples in the area of taxation.

First example: environmental taxes. Inasmuch as they are based on the 'polluter-pays' principle, environmental taxation may be looked at as being there merely to correct an unjust situation and hence represent a classic example of commutative justice. Special treatment in favour of 'heavy-polluters' can by contrast be seen as based on a 'distributional' aim.

If we consider these two examples, the former represents an example of just treatment and cannot constitute a subsidy. The latter, by contrast, clearly deviates from the 'corrective' logic of the 'polluter-pays' principle and hence is a subsidy. In sum, in these two cases we have a complete overlap between 'commutative' justice and 'scope' on the one hand, and 'distributive' justice and 'justification' on the other.

Second example: income taxes. When governments tax, they usually design the measure on the basis of the general principle of the 'ability to pay' of the taxable person. This principle takes account of a distributive logic, operating proportionally on the basis of income (the same would apply for other taxes using other indicators such as consumption, wealth, etc). In general, differential treatment which is based on the 'ability to pay' principle is not held to constitute unequal treatment and a subsidy. This applies for example to a normal application of progressivity, which is undoubtedly an incarnation of the 'ability to pay' principle, and is not generally considered to confer an unjust advantage.

However, depending on its design, the redistributive effect of progressivity may be more or less accentuated. Although the borderline is not clear, it can be imagined that, at a certain stage, the redistributive logic becomes so marked that the tax measure would be considered a derogation from the normal rule, conferring an unfair advantage and eventually qualifying as a subsidy.

Contrary to the previous case of corrective taxes, this example shows that there may be cases when the neat overlap and distinction between (i) 'commutative' justice and scope and (ii) 'distributive' justice and 'justification' ceases to exist. In other words, some acts of distributive justice would *not* qualify as subsidy, not falling within the 'scope' of the rules, in the first place.

It is in the grey area between accepted and unaccepted distribution that the task of distinguishing between what is within and outside the scope becomes testing.

The elusive concept of distributive justice, and particularly its core of *substantive equality*, comes out often in the legal debate of the subsidy definition. More or less consciously, distributive or redistributive considerations play a prominent role in the debate at the core of the concept of subsidy, particularly in the analysis of advantage the measure allegedly confers.[72] As indicated by Hart, this is determined by the uncertain outcome of the equality assessment. The fact is that this analysis is charged with moral values and symbols. Leaving aside the technical side, the bottom line is that '[j]udgments about like and unlike—about equality and discrimination—seem to have an inexorable moral logic to them in ordinary human discourse'.[73]

Two conclusions present themselves. First, the boundaries of the definition of subsidy are often not clear because of the vagueness of the kind and/or degree of (re)distribution that the legal definition of subsidy is ready to accept. Secondly, the elusiveness, and invasiveness, of distributive considerations and equality argumentation tend to lead to the merger of scope and justification levels. But, as the next paragraph explains, this distinction is of great importance.

B. Scope or justification: does it really matter?

Separating definition—and scope—from justification on the one hand, or conflating justification arguments into definitional discouse on the other, is extremely important, and from many perspectives, of both legal and political order. In this short paragraph we merely sketch, with general remarks, the differences that can derive from the following two alternative conclusions. *First*: there is no breach. *Second*: there is a breach but this is justified.

From a practical perspective, the differences depend on the rules applicable in either case.[74] At a *material* and *procedural* level, these rules may provide different (more/less numerous, stringent, clear, etc) requirements and typically their burden of proof is allocated differently.[75] Further, the applicability of different rules has important *institutional* and *constitutional* implications. Thus, if a certain set of rules apply, (supra-national) bodies may be involved in the scrutiny of the measure. There may be, for example, duties of notification and prohibitions of implementation until and unless a formal authorization is granted. The breach of these rules may have consequences, in the context of the administrative appraisal of the measure, or, subsequently, in case of litigation.

[72] We should not forget that subsidies are a typical tool of public intervention to tackle market failures and pursue other public policy objectives.

[73] MJ Trebilcock and R Howse, *The Regulation of International Trade* (3rd edn, London: Routledge, 2005) 111.

[74] At this stage, we remain at a general level. These observations will materialize in the following chapters when their substantive, procedural and institutional considerations will apply to the two legal systems at issue.

[75] It is usually for the complainant to put forward evidence of the breach, whereas, once a breach of a given rule has been established, the possible justifications are the defendant's responsibility.

We should not overlook the distinct *symbolic* value that the two situations above ('we have not breached the rules'; 'we have breach the rules but we are justified') involve.[76] There are two dimensions to this.

On the one hand, the two alternatives may well refer to a different 'normative hierarchy' between values, with different 'default' and 'exception' norms. On the other hand, the *political* perception-reality of 'power' should be considered. If a certain legal discipline does apply, with all its normative, institutional, and procedural paraphernalia, governments, and their constitutencies, are 'constrained' and may thus feel 'vulnerable'. The existence of an 'external source of regulation' means that they do not ultimately control the decision of whether that measure (which, we should recall, has usually a definite public policy telos) can go ahead without further ado, or not.

In short, the scope/justification distinction is not only about *rules* and lawyers' technicalities, but, as always, the sharing and control of *power*, and *political symbolism*. And these do matter, a lot.

IV. Book outline

We provide here an outline of the parts of the book and the relevant chapters.[77]

Parts II, III and V deal with the three core elements of the definition of subsidy that we have identified above. They focus on the forms of governmental action covered in WTO and EC law (chapters 3 to 6); the analysis of the economic advantage that governments can grant through economic and non-economic conduct (chapters 7 to 10); and, finally, on the impact standards (that in the two legal systems capture the 'distortion of competition' subsidy) may cause (chapter 13).

Part IV analyses the various issues surrounding the identification of the beneficiaries (chapter 11) and the rationale and operation of the specificity test (chapter 12).

The final chapter, attempting few conclusions, closes our definitional journey.

[76] cf, for an analysis in the context of the role of 'regulatory purpose' between Articles III and XX of the GATT (discussed extensively in chapter 9), H Horn and JHH Weiler, 'EC – Asbestos', in H Horn and PC Mavroidis (eds), *The WTO Case Law of 2001* (Cambridge: Cambridge University Press, 2003) 14.

[77] A brief summary of each part and chapter can be found at the beginning of each of them.

2

Foundations: the purpose of subsidy control

Through a synthesis that gently draws on the findings of other (than law) disciplines, this chapter attempts to answer two fundamental questions. Why do we, and should we, control subsidies, particularly from an international perspective? The answer to the first question paves the way to the second which briefly focuses on the main features an international system of subsidy control may have.

It is argued that these questions on the goal(s) and operation of subsidy control (analysed in sections II and III) are of crucial importance in order to approach the various technical (but not only technical) issues of the legal definition of subsidy. In section I, we start our quest for meaning by considering the general objective(s) of the WTO and the EC since these may have important implications on the narrower issue of the purpose(s) of subsidy and State aid control.[1]

But before doing this, it may be useful to open with the difference, and relationship, between the three basic notions of 'market', 'trade' and 'competition'.

Prelude: market, trade and competition

The *market*, which may be domestic or international, is the place where trade and competition occur. Whereas *trade* is about the circulation of productive factors, and in particular goods and services, within the relevant market, *competition* is the process whereby those goods and services, and ultimately their suppliers, struggle with each other to strengthen and extend their position within that market. Firms, industries—and even countries—compete with each other through (international) trade. Without the possibility of trading, ie of putting products and services on the market (either domestically or by exporting to other countries), there would be no competition. In a sentence, *competition occurs through trade in a market.*

The generally accepted opinion is that, through trade and competition, market forces would naturally lead to the best, in the jargon of economics most efficient, allocation of resources, thus maximizing the benefit—technically the

[1] The reader may have noticed that, when referring to term such as 'goal', 'objective' or 'purpose' (all synomyms), this paragraph leaves open the possibility that there may be more than one. The fact is that we are dealing with complex phenomena. Not only can the plurality of explanation not be ruled out, it should almost invariably be presumed.

welfare—of society.[2] More tangibly, this should be represented by lower prices, better products and services, and broader choice. This optimal result would derive from the unconstrained functioning of, even conflicting, market forces. This belief is exemplarily summed up in the image of the 'invisible hand' forged by Adam Smith in the 18th century.

Leaving aside the philosophical controversies surrounding the concepts themselves of 'efficiency', 'welfare' and 'maximization',[3] the other side of the story is that the described optimal outcome may in any event occur only where certain conditions (such as an indefinite number of agents, perfect information and no governmental intervention) are present. In fact, such conditions are rarely present with the result that the market often fails to deliver its promised benefits. In short, it does not function efficiently. Further, and of possibly greater importance for our discussion, even when market forces reach an *efficient* allocation of resources, this may not be considered *equitable* by a given society. Policy choices are therefore made and policy measures (which may include public subsidies) are adopted to tackle these problems of efficiency and equity.

Despite market failings, the idea of competition remains an accredited paradigm. It is crucial to understand international trade, and the underlying rationale based on specialization and comparative advantages. It is useful to appreciate how firms behave in the market.[4] Finally, as the following analysis shows, it is pivotal to make sense of how firms may be advantaged or disadvantaged by subsidies—and hence of the rationale of subsidy control.

[2] The result of 'maximization' of efficiency or welfare is very elusive. The core issue is that society is complex and a given measure may constitute at the same time a loss to an individual/group and a gain to another individual/group. According to economics, the question of whether the welfare of 'society' is maximized or not is determined on the basis of two standards, one narrower and one broader. On the one hand, the stricter 'Pareto efficiency' standard refers to that equilibrium in which no feasible change can raise anybody's welfare *without lowering* that of somebody else. On the other hand, the looser 'Kaldor-Hicks efficiency' standard accepts that somebody's welfare is lowered, provided that this is *compensated by* the increase of that of somebody else. It is however important to underline that there is no actual payment from the winner to the loser, the compensation operating only in the abstract. Clearly, the second standard is more flexible and its use may be more amenable. However, the virtual and artificial nature of the underlying compensation requires a *political trade-off* that the society at issue should be ready to make.

[3] The uneasiness underlined in the previous note becomes here direct challenge, concentrating on the meaning itself of these terms and standards. The literature on these topics is huge and increasing. A good analysis is offered by O Black, *Conceptual Foundations of Antitrust* (Cambridge: Cambridge University Press, 2005) chapter 2. A very personal, and limited, selection of further reading on these themes includes the two classic essays of R Dworkin, 'Is Wealth a Value?' and 'Why Efficiency?' both in *A Matter of Principle* (Cambridge MA: Harvard University Press, 1985) 237 and 267 respectively; and also A Sen, *On Ethics and Economics* (Oxford: Blackwell, 1987), and JK Galbraith, *The Affluent Society* (5th edn, London: Penguin, 1998).

Inevitably, the conceptual uneasiness with traditional welfarism translates into the debate on the validity of statistical criteria to measure economic performance. It has been suggested for example that indicators, such as the Gross Domestic Product (GDP), should be replaced with more comprehensive standards to measure prosperity and progress of society.

[4] The premise of standard economics being that agents would be rational and always act self-interestedly. In chapter 8 the fundamental criticism of this premise is addressed.

I. The objectives of the WTO and the EC

The more general objectives of the WTO and EC may have important implications on the issue of the objectives of subsidy and State aid control. A brief overview of the former is therefore desirable.

A. An analysis of the WTO

As with European integration, the nature of the WTO is the subject of highly inspiring analysis.[5] Howse has recently summarized various approaches to the purpose(s) of the WTO. His clear exposition, with a final useful reference to agreements regulating subsidies, merits a full quotation:

> For economists like Bagwell and Staiger, the purpose of WTO rules is to facilitate internationally efficient outcomes through negotiated improvements in market access, consistent with states' domestically efficient outcomes (taking their policy objectives as given). Much different is the notion of the WTO as a global economic constitution, a charter of rights for free and fair competition in world markets (Ernst-Ulrich Petersmann). A further, alternative conception of the WTO rules is that they serve to entrench a view of what are good domestic public policies and tie the hands of governments in their choice of policies, helping them to pursue rational rather than irrational domestic policies, despite demands of concentrated domestic interest groups for the latter (what I shall call the good governance approach). Then there is the view that I have propounded with Kalypso Nicolaidis, [footnote in the original text omitted] a renewed 'embedded liberalism.' This view begins from the notion that the trading system is about assisting domestic political communities to achieve their chosen collective objectives in a manner that reinforces and does not undermine global community goals: peace and security as the Bretton Woods planners had in mind in thinking of the social and political effects in the interwar period of spiraling protectionism, but now also sustainable development as reflected in the preamble to the WTO Agreement and human rights, many of which have achieved the status of customary law, binding on all states to the extent that they have not contracted out (in the case of non preemptory norms). [. . .] Finally, there is a political bargain view of the WTO, that understands the rules as a set of political compromises with which the parties are able to live; governments may well have accepted rules in some areas that reduced domestic welfare (say TRIPs or subsidies or anti-dumping) in return for benefits flowing from other agreements (such as agriculture). On this approach, it makes little sense to ask whether particular rules are 'efficient' or welfare-improving for all WTO Members, at least without bearing in mind the underlying

[5] The starting point for the analysis of the GATT/WTO should be represented by the various writings of JH Jackson. The reader is referred to three of them in particular: *The World Trading System: Law and Policy of International Economic Relations* (2nd edn, Cambridge MA, MIT Press, 1997); *The World Trade Organization: Constitution and Jurisprudence* (London: Royal Institute of International Affairs, 1998); JH Jackson, *Sovereignty, WTO and Changing Fundamentals of International Law*, Cambridge: Cambridge University Press, 2006).

See, also, J Pauwelyn, 'The Transformation of World Trade' (2005/2006), Michigan Law Review 1, which follows JHH Weiler's famous analysis in the European context: 'The Transformation of Europe' (1990–1991) Yale Law Journal 2403.

political trade-offs, including across issue areas. From the political bargain perspective, the legal constraints on subsidies could, even if not otherwise efficient be a desirable cost of a bargain that curbs the unilateral use of countervailing duties against subsidies, if this is the necessary price for getting users of countervailing duties (historically the predominant user is the US) to accept such curbs.[6]

The reading of this passage gives a flavour of the complexity of the WTO, the organization and legal system in charge of administering world trade. More than that, it shows the diversity of the *views* on the WTO, and particularly its underlying 'bargain' as well as its 'ethos'.

The attempts to explain what the GATT/WTO, and more generally trade agreements, are for, are flourishing. The insights, and inspirations, offered by these analyses are numerous.[7] Although the author does have a preference (which will shortly be disclosed), a solid—not surprising—finding is that virtually each theory has something to offer to the debate and can help to explain, at least partly, a complex reality. In some cases, these explanations overlap considerably and what changes is the perspective (eg economic, political, philosophical). In other cases, they conflict with each other (eg by preferring a merely domestic vs global, or an economic vs non-merely-economic approach).

The question of why countries enter into commitments which, to varying extents, restrict their power to unilaterally set trade (but not only trade) policies, is a complex one which requires a complex answer. A one-size-fits-all explanation will not do. Trade agreements, and particularly those creating an organization to administer them, regulate different and often sensitive subjects which inevitably go beyond mere trade discourse and impinge on core societal value choices. Furthermore, they should be placed in the negotiation, political and historical context, with different stakeholders and trends leading to different directions. Priorities are set, choices made, compromises accepted. Finally, in some cases one important factor—proof that agreements and rules do not always belong to the realm of logic and rationality—should be accounted for. The impact of accidental circumstances, the use of not fully intended formulation and even the fortuitous contracting of commitments cannot be excluded.

The time has come to disclose the author's view. There is indeed a bottom-line, substantially based on standard economic thinking, which explains the basic rationale for entering into trade agreeements, and for the existence of

[6] R Howse, 'Do the World Organization disciplines on domestic subsidies make sense? The case for legalizing some subsidies' in KW Bagwell, GA Bermann, and PC Mavroidis (eds), *Law and Economics of Contingent Protection in International Trade* (Cambridge: Cambridge University Press, forthcoming 2009). The author's view, developed with Nicolaides, can be found in R Howse and K Nicolaides, 'Enhancing WTO Legitimacy: Constitutionalization or Global Subsidiarity?' (2003) Governance 73.

[7] Reference should be made to a very recent work which is providing a fresh understanding on the beginnings of the GATT: DA Irwin, PC Mavroidis, and AO Sykes, *The Genesis of the GATT* (Cambridge: Cambridge University Press, 2008).

the GATT/WTO.[8] Referring to the GATT, but with conclusions that can safely be extended to the whole WTO, Mavroidis has thus recently concluded that:

the more plausible rationale is that the GATT is probably there in order to constrain unilateralism. The various GATT instruments are there to guarantee that the multiple negative effects stemming from unilateral definition of trade policies will be addressed.[9]

In the same vein, Regan observed that 'trade agreements are mostly for restraining protectionism'.[10] This, however, is just the bottom-line.

If it explains why countries decide to enter into trade agreements (to prevent negative externalities), it may not fully explain how the 'terms and conditions' of these agreements are drafted and eventually interpreted. In other words, if there is a 'mischief' (unilateral negative externalities; protectionist measures) which radically justifies the need to sit around a table and negotiate and enter into mutual commitments, it is equally true that there is often (not always!) a 'public policy choice' that justifies, or is in any event involved in, the adoption of those same measures that cause undesired international spillovers.

The challenge for trade agreements in the 21st century is how they take all these policies into account and reach a balance in their regulation. This author thinks, therefore, that while economic theory may help to justify the first half of the story (the 'mischief'), we should trascend it and resort to other readings to understand the other half (the 'redemption'). This would offer a more comprehensive view and enable to capture the directions that the WTO could, and should, take even in the near future.[11]

[8] The literature on the economics of trade agreements is gaining prominence. See, among others, K Bagwell and RW Staiger, *The Economics of the World Trading System* (Cambridge MA: MIT Press, 2002), and DH Regan, 'What Are Trade Agreements For? Two Conflicting Stories Told by Economists, with a Lesson for Lawyers' (2006) Journal of International Economic Law 951.

[9] P Mavroidis, *Trade in Goods* (Oxford: Oxford University Press, 2008) 20. In another interesting paper, BM Hoekman and P Mavroidis ('Policy Externalities and High-Tech Rivalry: Competition and Multilateral Cooperation Beyond the WTO' (1996) Leiden Journal of International Law 273) add two other interesting dimensions to this need for economic cooperation. The two authours posit that the two concepts of 'market contestability' and 'conditions of competition' 'underline much of what is in the GATT and the WTO Agreements, and are useful in characterizing both past and current approaches to treaty-based multilateral cooperation in the economic policy sphere' (ibid, 276).

[10] DH Regan, 'What Are Trade Agreements For? Two Conflicting Stories Told by Economists, with a Lesson for Lawyers' (2006) Journal of International Economic Law 951.

[11] To be clear, it is not suggested that economic explanations should be trumped. The point is about adding a new level of analysis, not subtracting its basis. This is clearly recognized by Howse: 'The Howse and Nicolaidis approach, in its emphasis on empowerment of domestic polities as *the starting point* for the determination of optimal trade rules, is quite compatible with the framework of analysis of economists like Bagwell and Staiger in most respects: it simply adds a further evaluative criterion, asking whether or how the rules advance or undermine the goals of the emerging global juridical community as a whole'. See R Howse, 'To the World Organization disciplines on domestic subsidies make sense? The case for legalizing some subsidies' subsidies' in KW Bagwell, GA Bermann, and PC Mavroidis (eds), *Law and Economics of Contingent Protection in International Trade* (Cambridge: Cambridge University Press, forthcoming 2009).

In other words, the changing ethos of the WTO is about reconciling the 'mischief' of protectionism with the 'redemption' of legitimate domestic (and not only domestic) policy choices.[12] Trade interests do not sit in a vacuum. The 'linkages' with other values, policies and challenges (eg environment and climate change, human rights, safety, health, development) are becoming ever clearer and pressing. (World) trade law is connected to other areas of the law, at various levels, be they international, regional, national, sub-national.[13]

Quite often these statements are inserted in a 'constitutional' discourse which underlines the impending (some would say current) 'constitutionalization' of the WTO.[14] With variations, this would generally refer to a broadly coherent system, often based on a defined and balanced institutional structure, that would regulate both economic and non-economic values.

Without entering the debate, two main necessities nevertheless emerge. First, policies and organizations, and various governance layers, should interact with each other and strive for 'coherency'. Secondly, the above mentioned critical issues should be governed at the most appropriate and effective level in a logic of 'subsidiarity'. A key consideration is indeed that the process should not obscure but rather engage with the preferences and requests coming from national and even more local and non-governmental stakeholders.

In the same vein, borrowing from Ruggie's famous theory of 'embedded liberalism',[15] and applying it to the current trading scenario, which is dramatically different from that of GATT 1947, Pauwelyn recently outlined the traits of a newly emerging 'trade politics'. He suggested that:

> [t]hese 'new trade politics' are grounded in a new form of 'embedded liberalism', combining a world-wide, general support for free markets and globalization with calls for policy space to protect the environment, workers, consumers and citizen concerns at large, as well as to enact industrial and rural policies to boost economic development.[16]

[12] Which, in turn, may themselves constitute the 'mischief' to address with international action.

[13] See, among others, T Cottier, *The Challenges of WTO Law: Collected Essays* (London: Cameron May, 2007); C Joerges and EU Petersmann, *Constitutionalism, Multilevel Trade Governance and Social Regulation* (Oxford: Hart, 2006), R Howse and K Nicolaides, 'Enhancing WTO Legitimacy: Constitutionalization or Global Subsidiarity?' (2003) Governance 73; and JP Trachtman, 'The Constitutions of the WTO' (2006) European Journal of International Law 623.

[14] A good analysis of this issue, and the various 'constitutional theories' applied to the WTO, is DZ Cass, *The Constitutionalization of the World Trade Organization: Legitimacy, Democracy, and Community in the International Trading System* (Oxford: Oxford University Press, 2005). See also the references in the previous footnote. An illuminating account can be found in Pauwelyn's review to Professor Cass' book: (2006) American Journal of International Law 986. For a general analysis see also J Habermas, 'Does the Constitutionalization of International Law Still Have a Chance?' in J Habermas, *The Divided West* (Cambridge: Polity Press, 2006) 115.

[15] JG Ruggie, 'International Regimes, Transactions, and Change: Embedded Liberalism and the Post-War Economic Regimes' (1982) International Organization 195.

[16] J Pauwelyn, 'New Trade Politics After the Doha Round', *Center for Trade and Economic Integration, Working Paper 1/2008*, 16.

The key features in the 'new trade politics' are represented by the underlined importance of values and dimensions *other* than trade and economic ones, and in the need to offer more 'policy space' to domestic constituencies, in both developed and developing countries.[17] It is a small step further to link the idea of domestic policy space to that of subsidiarity.[18]

The catalyst for the WTO's new directions is the *urgency* of meeting certain *common challenges* like 'environmental degradation' (particularly, in its most acute and devasting form represented by climate change), the safeguard of 'basic human rights' (especially those recognized in the zeroth level of protection of *jus cogens*), the 'development' (intended in its broadest possible sense: see UN right to development)[19] of those that constitute the large majority of the world's countries and population, and, recently but emerging dramatically, the 'financial crisis' and the ensuing 'economic recession'. All these huge and pressing challenges, a testament to the multi-faceted interdependence of an increasingly globalizing world, are inextricably linked with international trade and its regulation. We will soon focus on the fundamental change, a true political *metanoia*, that may be required to gather consensus on their solution, which directly revolves around the pivotal concepts of *shared interests* and *community*.

This section has introduced to the complexity of the discourse concerning the WTO and its objectives. This analysis is of great importance for understanding the subject matter of this book since it constitutes the inevitable background for the definition of the goals of subsidy control and their actual regulation.

B. A parallel with the EC

European integration represents a unique phenomenon in international law.[20] Its nature and role have thus elicited endless discussions.[21]

[17] This argument, which is expressly referred to by Pauwelyn, has been developed by D Rodrik, 'How to Save Globalization from its Cheerleaders', John F Kennedy School of Government, Harvard University, Faculty Research Working Papers Series, September 2007, RWP07–038, 4, where he concludes that '[a] good argument can be made that it is a lack of policy space—and not lack of market access—which is (or likely to become soon) the real binding constraint on a prosperous global economy.' It is however clear that certain challenges—climate change is a good and topical example—can only be effectively met with an intervention at the international level.

[18] Which also means that certain values, and emergencies, should be effectively tackled, or at least coordinated, only at a global level.

[19] UN Declaration on the Right to Development, Res 41/129 (1986). See A Sengupta, 'The Human Right to Development' (2004) Oxford Development Studies 179. See also BA Andreassen and SP Marks (eds), *Development as a Human Right Legal, Political, and Economic Dimensions* (Cambridge MA: Harvard School of Public Health, 2006).

[20] Suffice reading the visionary words of the Court of Justice in the 1963 *Van Gend en Loos* case where it emphatically laid down that the EC constitute a 'new legal order in international law'. See Case 26/62 *Van Gend en Loos v Nederlandse Administratie der Blastingen* [1963] ECR 1.

[21] Four titles may be singled out to help the reader in this respect. The first two are highly regarded collections: JHH Weiler, *The Constitution of Europe* (Cambridge: Cambridge University Press, 1999); JHH Weiler and M Wind, *European Constitutionalism Beyond the State* (Cambridge: Cambridge

Although they were both born from the ashes of World War II, the degree of development and integration of the European Communities (and, since 1993, their higher structure, the European Union) soon surpassed the GATT. The same holds true for its successor, the WTO.

The differences between the GATT/WTO and EC systems are clear. They pursue different levels of integration with only a partial similarity in objectives. Unlike the WTO, which is still an 'economic', better a 'trade' organization, the catalogue of the objectives and policies of the EC is almost universal. A simple glance through the contents of the EC Treaty is enough to give the reader an appreciation of the comprehensiveness of the competencies of the EC. The EC does not merely pursue quite extensive economic policies (eg trade liberalization, competition, industrial policy, economic and monetary policy, infrastructure, transport, energy, agriculture) but is increasingly involved in other important policy areas (eg human rights, regional cohesion, health, consumer protection, culture, environment, immigration).

The different vocation of the two systems is also reflected in their membership. Despite a recent substantive enlargement which brought its membership to 27, the EC is a 'regional organization' constituted of a (still relatively) small and (still relatively) cohesive group of nations with a substantial degree of commonality of values and objectives. The WTO's universal vocation—it currently counts 153 members (and 30 governments with observer status)—necessarily shows a different picture.

These general differences in aims and membership have implications at the institutional level. The institutional structure of the EC is both complex and mature. Generally the three functions (judicial, legislative and executive) are clearly defined and equally strong with an overall satisfactory system of checks and balances of powers. The 'assignment of powers', 'subsidiarity', and 'proportionality' in Community action are cornerstone political and legal principles.[22] An element of further solidity is given by the integration between the EC legal system and the national systems of the Member States guaranteed by the direct effect of EC law and the consequent idea that national courts and administrations are EC 'organs'.[23] In the WTO, the institutional structure is less complex and less effective. There is virtually no legislative power and rule making is a problem. As an inevitable counterbalance, however, the judicial branch, the Dispute

University Press, 2003). To these is added a masterful biography of one of the fathers of the European Integration which provides the reader with an invaluable insight into the functionalist and pragmatic approach which is linked to the genetic origin of this process: F Duchêne, *Jean Monnet: The First Statesman of Interdependence* (New York: Norton, 1994). Finally, a concise but thoughtful intellectual history of European integration (which however lacks the constitutional process of the recent years) can be found in S Douglas-Scott, *Constitutional Law of the European Union* (Harlow: Pearson Longman, 2002) chapter 1.

[22] Article 5 EC.

[23] See *Van Gend en Loos*, n 19 above.

Settlement Mechanism (DSM), is highly developed and authoritative and has significantly contributed to the development of an important feature of the WTO system—its 'rule-orientation'.[24]

Having underlined the important differences between the GATT/WTO and the EC, it is nonetheless clear that the world trading system and the European system *share* some basic objectives of trade liberalization, and, increasingly, even important non-economic concerns (the best examples concern the environment, safety and health, development and human rights). Much of the analysis explaining what the GATT/WTO is about can be substantially transposed to the European context too. In particular, considerations of fostering economic cooperation and curbing adverse unilateral conduct and, more positively, opening market access, play a crucial role in the EC context, finding shape in the 'internal market' and 'competition' policies. At the same time, social and non-economic considerations find a natural habitat in the complex European model.[25]

That said, it should be remembered that the differences between the GATT/WTO and the EC are significant, and warrant specification and distinctions. Crucially, these differences may well have a bearing on the actual issues of subsidy control and consequently on the definition of subsidy (the essence of the caveat 'context matters' outlined in the previous chapter). Focusing on the EC for example, it is clear that its constitutional and institutional structure and its broad and diverse goals have an important impact on shaping its peculiar system of State aid control at the substantive, institutional and procedural levels.

C. Conclusions: constitution, community and shared interests

Addressing in 2000 the American Society of International Law, Cottier noted:

> This is my thesis: We currently lack the framework and tools to answer these fundamental questions of the trading system. The functionalist paradigm no longer allows a proper basis of analysis. Why is this so? I would argue that trade liberalization, at some point, inherently starts to require, rely upon and develop positive integration, ie, it depends on common and shared standards and perceptions, or at least, upon mutual recognition of national or regional standards. Moreover, trade liberalization, at some point, inherently leads to the adoption of flanking policies which are in a position to balance detrimental effects of trade liberalization. Of course, we have not reached this point on the global level. We are far from working under constitutional structures. [. . .] Yet, we may be reaching the point where a future framework of analysis needs to shift to constitutionalism, thus a framework which is capable of taking into account and reasonably balancing a broader range of issues and legitimate interests in its operation and dispute resolutions. Such interests are on the one hand horizontal and related to subject matter. They are, on the other hand, also vertical interests, affecting the balance of power between different levels of government, national or regional,

[24] See W Davey, 'The Dispute Settlement Mechanism', Illinois Public Law and Legal Theory Research Paper Series, Research Paper No 03-08, 25 June 2003.

[25] As noted in chapter 1, comparative exercises between the two systems are flourishing.

and international or global. In the present context, I refer to constitutionalism in a modest sense: it is understood to depict an attitude and a framework capable of reasonably balancing and weighing different, equally legitimate and democratically defined basic values and policy goals of a polity dedicated to promote liberty and welfare in a broad sense. It would seem to me that this is the essence of a constitution providing practical coherence, on whatever level it is placed: local, regional, national, supranational, or perhaps even international.[26]

While offering a balanced example of 'constitutional talk', these words nicely sum up the main terms of the issue examined here—the goals of the WTO/EC *and* their impact on subsidy regulation (and via this on the definition of subsidy). The core of the debate lies in the second point of Cottier's thesis, it is about 'taking into account' and 'reasonably balancing a broader range of issues and legitimate interests' with the traditional requirements of trade liberalization. This is crucial in the WTO, and its current challenge lies mostly in the first step (ie the recognition of broader issues and legitimate interests). The fifty-year path to European integration is marked by this sort of questions. Considering its almost universal coverage, the current challenge is centred more around the second step, ie the balancing exercise between trade and non-trade values.[27]

Putting these remarks into the context of our analysis, it is clear that the consideration of various interests, which should be weighed against the goals of trade liberalization, goes to the heart of the discipline and also of the definition of WTO subsidy and EC State aid. Subsidies are ambivalent inasmuch they may simultaneously produce different—indeed opposite—effects which go to the benefit/detriment of different constituencies. These effects impinge not only on economic efficiency but, more radically, on socio-economic or even distributional objectives. All this requires that the system at hand first recognizes these objectives and then weighs them. This is naturally a balancing exercise between winners and losers, a political trade-off between conflicting interests.

These considerations lead us to another issue tangentially raised by Cottier when referring to a shift towards 'positive integration' but that directs to a more general point. At a certain stage, trade liberalization requires a 'commonality of standards or perceptions'.[28] This echoes a crucial concept, which is strictly intertwined with the

[26] T Cottier, 'Limits to International Trade: The Constitutional Challenge' (2000) American Society of International Law Proceedings 220, 221.

[27] See, eg, Case C-112/00 *Eugen Schmidberger, Internationale Transporte und Planzüge v Republik Österreich* [2003] ECR I-5659, with a good comment from A Biondi, in 'Free trade, a mountain road and the right to protest: European economic freedoms and fundamental individual rights' (2004) European Human Rights Law Review, 51. See also Case C-36/02 *Omega* [2004] ECR I-9609; C-438/05 *International Transport Workers' Federation and Others v Viking Line ABP and Others* [2007] ECR I-10779; C-341/05 *Laval un Partneri Ltd v Svenska Byggnadsarbetareförbundet and Others* [2007] ECR I-11767.

[28] Or, at least, their mutual recognition.

previous remarks on the recognition and balancing of interests (and admittedly that of constitution), the sociological concept of *community*.[29]

Cho and Gerber have recently addressed this issue in the context of the WTO, the former in a general and comprehensive way,[30] the latter applying it to the 'relationship' between competition law and the WTO.[31] In this respect, the integration of competition law into the world trading system is significantly used as a case-study to test the sense of community in the WTO. Gerber's findings, *mutatis mutandis*, are therefore useful to understand the problems the WTO is currently encountering (consider the difficulties in the Doha Development Round) and, more specifically, the issue raised in this section, ie the interplay between the overall system's goals and the control of subsidies.[32]

The concept of community rests on various factors that Gerber identifies in the respect of the interests of all members, the alignment of interests and incentives, the presence (and perception) of shared interests, the clarity of the goals of the organization and its appreciation as a shared resource, and the confidence in the institutional, procedural and decisional structure of the organization. In the European context, Jacobs notes that 'part of what makes up a community' are 'shared values', and 'in these respects, the European Community can be seen to share, at a fundamental level, some common values'.[33] Although the unique context of European integration fully justifies the conceptual upgrade (from 'interests' to 'values'), it is argued that the bottom-line is pretty much the same. It is real, or—to some extent—perceived, *commonality* that ensures *cooperation*.

The engagement of the *interests* of all members, particularly by making them *shared*, is crucial. To be clear, a community does not necessarily mean that the organization, and its policies, should be able to always benefit all members and their interests. What is required is a sense that 'members must perceive their interests to be associated and interwowen with goals, projects or processes that they share with the other members' and, more practically, the creation of 'justified expectations that the net benefits to members' (ie the benefit ultimately flowing to them after discounting the relevant costs) 'will be widely and relatively evenly distributed'. A sense of fairness in the distribution of benefits and costs is therefore required which is at odds with the perception that only certain members or groups

[29] F Tönnies, in J Harris (ed), *Community and Civil Society* (Cambridge: Cambridge University Press, 2001). In our analysis, the term 'community' is used in a rather loose way and does not closely follow Tönnies' distinction between *Gemeinschaft* ('community') and *Gesellschaft* ('society' or 'association'). Apart from the fact that these types often tend to partly overlap in theory and in practice, we believe that this usage is more than sufficient to introduce the main traits of the issue.

[30] S Cho, 'The WTO's *Gemeinschaft*' (2004) Alabama Law Review 483.

[31] DJ Gerber, 'Competition Law and the WTO: Rethinking the Relationship' (2007) Journal of International Economic Law 707.

[32] This may be particularly true if we accept that subsidies and their control substantially raise competition issues. See below section II, B and C.

[33] FG Jacobs, *The Sovereignty of Law The European Way*, The Hamlyn Lectures 2006 (Cambridge: Cambridge University Press, 2007) 51 (emphasis added).

are systematically advantaged or damaged. In specific instances, there will definitely be winners and losers but, overall, a community requires an even distribution of benefits and costs.

The temporal perspective of the goals would be crucial too.[34] Short-term assessment is often inappropriate with the result that, in some cases, the effects should be considered only in the longer term. Further, 'gradualism in steps' may also be a key component in fostering a sense of community. This idea is two-fold. On the one hand, it cannot be expected that highly ambitious programmes be created from one day to the other. On the other hand, the consideration of the interests of all Members (which we have seen to constitute an important factor in the idea of community) may require a different treatment with an integration into the system that should be progressive.[35]

It is clear that the concept of community outlined above—like those of global welfare or efficiency—may have some aspirational features. It is equally clear, however, that this concept is pivotal to make an organization, and keep it going. This is particularly correct the more complex (in terms of number of members and interests) the organization is. Only an entrenched sense of community can engender widespread confidence in the WTO's norms and procedures[36] and create the conditions to make the current Doha Round Negotiations reach a successful outcome, and one which would be regarded as beneficial by all WTO Members.[37]

[34] Gerber makes the particularly appropriate example of development which is certainly a complex goal that cannot be achieved in a relatively short period of time. We could add to this the emergency of climate change and, more generally, the challenges posed by environmental degradation. Recent times have also seen the dramatic return of recession. Many forecasts point to a long period of recovery.

[35] It is however also clear that the idea of gradualism (and its inherent relativity) may be seen as directly clashing with that of community (and its seemingly natural absoluteness). The risk may be that, under empty rethoric about further cooperation, Members may be content to reach a suboptimal compromise which they see as final. Technical ingeniousness in crafting the actual regulation, and political willingness to reach the ultimate more ambitious goal may help in striking a fair and acceptable balance where gradual regulation would really embody the idea of *progressivity towards integration* and thus, eventually, reinforce the sense of community.

To conclude with an example, gradualism is the core of the critical concept of special and differential treatment for developing countries. For a new approach to this concept see T Cottier, 'From Progressive Liberalization to Progressive Regulation in WTO Law' (2006) Journal of International Economic Law 1.

[36] The reader should not have the impression that this discussion on the concepts of constitution, community and on the presence of shared interests should be confined to the WTO context only. The current constitutional debate (or crisis?), prompted by the successive popular rejection of the 2003 'Constitution for Europe' and 2007 'Treaty of Lisbon', show that the European 'Community' is always in search of a meaning to its name. W Hallstein noted in the 1960s ('The European Economic Community' (1963) Political Science Quarterly 161, 162), that the European Community is a polity 'in the process of continuous creation'. A handy account on the present constitutional debate is that of N McCormick, *Who's Afraid of a European Constitution?* (Exeter: Imprint Academic, 2005). See also the witty comments of JHH Weiler, in his editorial 'Marking the Anniversary of the Universal declaration; The Irish No and the Lisbon Treaty' (2008) European journal of International Law 647.

[37] It is interesting in this regard to consider the wording of the final clauses of the Ministerial Declaration adopted on 14 November 2001 at Doha, WT/MIN(01)/DEC/11. Paragraph 49 reads

The concept of community: implications for subsidy control

This concept of community would play a crucial role in ensuring that a complex subject such as subsidy control, with all its ambivalences, finds an appropriate discipline in the world trading system. The concept of community is the determining factor in deciding how ambitious such a system could be and in making it acceptable.

In the first place, it would be necessary to ensure clarity about what the system of subsidy control is about and what its goals are—which turns on how the negative and positive effects of subsidies are tackled. This requires the recognition that subsidies are not a narrow technical issue but raise public policy considerations. Strong political support is needed, and this can be found only if the system itself is considered as a 'shared resource'. In turn, this can only happen if the right balance from both the substantive and institutional/procedural perspectives is struck. On the one hand, the regulation should consider and precisely identify all interests at stake (be they political, economic and social, eg protection of competition; remedy of market failures and other legitimate objectives) and reach that even balance necessary to make them 'shared'. On the other hand, norms must be drafted, procedures devised, and institutions involved, in a way that allows all Members to have confidence in them.

II. The goals of subsidy and State aid control in the WTO and EC

The analysis of the goals of subsidy control is inextricably linked to their effects. It is therefore necessary to analyse these in some depth. It is proposed to do this from two perspectives, the *trade* and *competition (and welfare)* ones.[38]

inter alia: '[The negotiations] shall be conducted with a view to ensuring benefits to all participants and to achieving an overall balance in the outcome of the negotiations'.

[38] In doing this I have drawn (often liberally) from several sources. For the GATT/WTO context see, eg, KW Bagwell and PC Mavroidis, 'Too Much, Too Little . . . Too Late?' and R Howse, 'To the World Trade Organization Disciplines on Domestic Subsidies Make Sense? The Case for Legalizing some Subsidies' in KW Bagwell, GA Bermann, and PC Mavroidis (eds), *Law and Economics of Contingent Protection in International Trade* (Cambridge: Cambridge University Press, forthcoming 2009); D Neven and V Verouden, 'Towards a More Refined Economic Approach in State Aid Control' in W Mederer, N Pesaresi, and M Van Hoof (eds), *EU Competition Law—Volume IV: State Aid* (Leuven: Claeys and casteels, 2008) Book 1, Part 1, chapter 4; AO Sykes, 'The Economics of WTO Rules on Subsidies and Countervailing Measures', Chicago M John. Olin Law and Economics Working Paper No. 186 (2nd Series), May 2003; DK Tarullo, 'Norms and Institutions in Global Competition Policy' (2000) American Journal of International Law 478; OECD, *Consistencies and Inconsistencies between Trade and Competition Policies*, Joint Group on Trade and Competition, COM/TD/DAFFE/CLP(98)25/FINAL, 1999, OECD, Paris; BM Hoekman and P Mavroidis, 'Policy Externalities and High-Tech Rivalry: Competition and Multilateral Cooperation Beyond the WTO' (1996) Leiden Journal of International Law 273; E Fox, 'Competition Law and the Agenda for the WTO: Forging the Links of Competition and Trade' (1995) Pacific Rim Law and Policy Association 1.

For a similar analysis with respect to the EC, see, eg, HW Friederiszick, LH Röller, and V Verouden, 'European State Aid Control: An Economic Framework' in Bucirossi (ed), *Handbook of Antitrust*

We focus first on the connection between subsidies and the concept of market access. In particular, we will concentrate on the political balance of trade liberalization deals, considering the links between subsidies and market access on the one hand and between the relevant commitments (on subsidies and market access) on the other. Secondly, the examination shifts to the level of the competitive process and its failures. This requires the analysis of the complex welfare (in terms of efficiency and equity) implications of subsidies.

Taking stock of the findings of this two-level investigation, the final step of our analysis will concern the objectives of subsidy control in the WTO and EC, as they currently are, and as it is suggested they should be.

A. First perspective: subsidies and market access

Subsidies can first be looked at from a *trade* perspective, particularly in terms of their impact on market access of (competing and foreign) non-subsidized products. With this in mind, the following analysis considers the interplay between subsidies, and their discipline, and other commitments or policies of the broader system where they should be set.

The heart of the GATT bargain: the protection of market access

The first level of analysis of the goals of subsidy control revolves around the concept of *market access*. This centres on the extent to which markets—the place where trade and competition take place—are open to products and services coming from abroad. From another viewpoint, it refers to whether those products and services encounter more or less direct governmental barriers to entry, operating at the border or after it.[39] The following analysis invites the reader to consider subsidies as barriers to access to the market.

The main concern of the GATT is to eliminate or reduce through negotiation the most 'explicit and obvious governmentally imposed trade obstacles',[40] that is

Economics (Cambridge MA: MIT Press, 2008) 625; A Biondi and P Eeckhout, 'State Aid and Obstacles to Trade' in A Biondi, P Eeckhout and J Flynn (eds), *The Law of State Aid in the European Union* (Oxford: Oxford University Press, 2004) 103; K Mortelmans, 'Towards Convergence in the Application of the Rules on Free Movement and on Competition?' (2001) Common Market Law Review 613; D O'Keeffe and A Bavasso, 'Four Freedoms, One Market and National Competence: In Search of a Dividing Line' in M Andenas and D Fairgrieve (eds), *Judicial Review in International Perspective: Liber Amicorum in Honour of Lord Slynn of Hadley* (London: Aspen, 2000) 541; CD Ehlermann, 'The Contribution of EC Competition Policy to the Single Market' (1992) Common Market Law Review 257.

[39] Using a different language, we could refer to the 'contestability' and the 'conditions of competition' of the markets. See BM Hoekman and P Mavroidis, 'Policy Externalities and High-Tech Rivalry: Competition and Multilateral Cooperation Beyond the WTO' (1996) Leiden Journal of International Law 273, 275 et seq.

[40] M Matsushita, TJ Schoenbaum, and PC Mavroidis, *The World Trade Organization—Law, Practice, and Policy* (2nd edn, Oxford: Oxford University Press, 2006) 259.

tariffs, quotas and other border obstacles to market access. With respect to tariffs, better market access is achieved through negotiated reciprocal concessions. However, since the effects of reduced, or dismantled tariffs, can be easily replaced with other policy tools with an equal impact,[41] the credibility, and viability, of the whole system requires a guarantee that concessions made do not become meaningless and that the degree of market access legitimately expected is not undermined, or 'nullified'. Failing this, the 'balance of rights and obligations' underlying the political and economic bargain of trade liberalization of the GATT would be compromized. Confidence in the value of offering concessions which can be easily *circumvented* by other policies producing similar effects would mean that, prospectively, fewer would be entered and eventually the whole process of liberalization of trade would risk being jeopardized.

Although domestic policies may have an impact on market access, they are difficult to 'contract' since they are strictly linked to regulatory diversity and societal choices. The GATT guards against the protectionistic (ie *anti*-market access) tendencies of internal tax and regulation through a simple prohibition of discrimination.[42]

Domestic subsidies may directly offset the effect of a reduced or eliminated tariff producing the same protective effect. Domestic subidies, however, constitute an important policy instrument often used to target market failures or pursue other policy objectives. Unlike internal taxation and regulation, the discipline of subsidies is not limited to a prohibition of discrimination. Their treatment is more complex and has faced an evolution over time which has eventually led to a strict discipline which does not consider the legitimate policy objectives they may pursue.[43]

So far, we have been reasoning in a simplified two-countries world. Subsidies may erode concessions and frustrate market access expectations even in another type of setting. Suppose that countries A and B export to country C. Imagine also that country A decides to grant exports subsidies, ie subsidies contigent on exportation. Among the various effects that these subsidies may produce will be the potential to impinge on the market access into country C that country B could expect in a scenario *without* export subsidies aiding country A's competing industry. Even in this case, the grant of a subsidy has the effect of impairing market access expectations and eroding the value of concessions made with the ultimate result of

[41] The potential of this policy substitution is shown by Lerner's equivalence theorem.

[42] Article III of the GATT. The SPS and TBT agreements add additional proxies to indicate the absence of protectionist intent. A different route to liberalization is followed in the sensitive area of services (GATS). On all these issues see M Matsushita, TJ Schoenbaum, and PC Mavroidis, *The World Trade Organization—Law, Practice, and Policy* (2nd edn, Oxford: Oxford University Press, 2006) chapters 7, 13 and 16.

[43] The 'tariff > subsidy policy substitution' scenario which affects market access expectations is directly addressed by one type of objectionable 'adverse effects' which specifically refers to the nullification and impairment of 'benefits of concessions bound under Article II of GATT 1994'. See chapter 14.

undermining the political credibility of the system. This scenario is regulated quite harshly in the WTO since (all) export subsidies are prohibited.

State aids and the EC internal market

The considerations made for the GATT/WTO can easily be translated into the EC context too.

With the completion of the more integrated internal market, which goes further than the corresponding global regulation of trade in many respects,[44] the attention of the EC has increasingly shifted towards those other measures that could impair the functioning of the internal market, particularly State aid. The concern is similar to the one outlined in the GATT.[45] Member States would not have accepted a prohibition on customs duties, quotas and other equivalent measures if their effect had substantially been replaced by State subsidies. It is exactly in this regard that it has been noted that '[t]here are basic political and economic reasons to justify [the] EC competence'.[46] The idea that State aid should be controlled to guarantee that the internal market objective and bargain is safeguarded is therefore solidly based in EC law.

More generally, we will see how close the link between the 'internal market' (law) and State aid (law) is, and how strongly it affects the debate on the purpose and definition of State aid. That said, the 'policy space' offered by the use of State aid is properly considered. This translates into the political and legal recognition that, even when distorting competition and affecting the internal market, State aid may also pursue legitimate policy objectives. This positive impact, moreover, is not only looked at as a domestic issue but is fully inserted into a 'Community' perspective. In other words, the EC State aid system of control is not only concerned with trade or competition distortions in the internal market but also recognizes that public intervention in the economy may be warranted for various reasons, and these may be in the 'Community interest'.

Back to the GATT: striking the bargain's right balance

In a recent research, Bagwell and Staiger have made a finding which seems to contradict previous analysis.[47]

[44] By requiring the abolition of customs duties, quantitative restrictions and measures of an equivalent effect, and by introducing significant harmonization measures.

[45] B Bishop, 'From Trade to Tutelage: State Aid and Public Choice in the European Union', Presentation to Conference to ACE, Copenhagen, 2 December 2005, 1.

[46] J Pelkmans, *European Integration—Methods and Economic Analysis* (2nd edn, London: FT-Prentice Hall, 2001) 241. The 'equivalent' effect of subsidies-tariffs/quotas represents the 'political' reason justifying EC State aid control. The 'economic' rationale is linked to efficiency considerations deriving from 'undistorted competition' and is analysed below, in the context of our second level of competition analysis.

[47] K Bagwell and RW Staiger, 'Will International Rules on Subsidies Disrupt the World Trading System?' (2006) 96:3 The American Economic Review, 877.

Rather than protecting tariff concessions, subsidy disciplines would *deter* them. In fact, their conclusion incorporates a more sophisticated result. While too few constraints on subsidies would deter tariff concessions (for the reasons outlined above), too many constraints would also lead to the same result. The reduction of 'policy space' following stricter subsidy disciplines would make countries more redundant to relinquish their capacity to use tariffs as a policy tool. Bagwell and Staiger draw the consequence that the more lenient GATT (ie pre-WTO) discipline on domestic subsidies, which, apart from unilateral remedies,[48] substantially permitted them was more efficient. Crucially, any market access-unfriendly impact of domestic subsidies could have been addressed by the route of 'non-violation nullification or impairment' (NVNI) complaint under Article XXIII of the GATT.[49]

Howse notes that the cure suggested might not be as appropriate as the diagnosis of the disease.[50] Rather than relying on the uncertainties of the NVNI remedy,[51] he suggests an alternative route which would offer members their desired 'policy space' for domestic subsidies. The possibility of (re)introducing a category of subsidies that are non-actionable should be considered, and—addressing Bagwell's and Staiger's concerns—this could be shaped so that it does not interfere with Members' incentives to offer tariff concessions.

B. Second perspective: subsidies, competition and market failures

Subsidies not only interact with trade, ie the flows of goods and services, more profoundly they interfere with the conduct of economic operators—their recipients and, through them, the latter's competitors. Under certain circumstances, they may distort the competitive process (which is a better expression than 'level playing field'). At the same time, however, governments do not generally grant subsidies inadvertently or unjustifiably. Subsidies are one of the preferred (although not always the best) tools to remedy all sorts of malfunctionings of that delicate machine that is the market and improve society's welfare.

This section consider subsidies from a *competition* and *welfare* perspective.

[48] In the form of countervailing duties imposed by the importing country on the subsidized exports causing material injury to its domestic industry.

[49] For an analysis of this remedy in the WTO context see M Matsushita, TJ Schoenbaum, and PC Mavroidis, *The World Trade Organization—Law, Practice, and Policy* (2nd edn, Oxford: Oxford University Press, 2006) 121 2, or Van den P Bossche, *The Law and Policy of the World Trade Organization—Text, Cases and Materials* (2nd edn, Cambridge: Cambridge University Press, 2008) 182 6. For an analysis of NVNI complaints see chapter 14.

[50] R Howse, 'To the World Organization disciplines on domestic subsidies make sense? The case for legalizing some subsidies' in KW Bagwell, GA Bermann, and PC Mavroidis (eds), *Law and Economics of Contingent Protection in International Trade* (Cambridge: Cambridge University Press, forthcoming 2009), 5–7.

[51] Which has also to be set in the new WTO setting, particularly in its new 'adverse effects' context.

Introducing complexity: competition assessment, welfare analysis and political judgement

We have seen the connection between subsidies, their discipline and market access. The finding was intriguing. By impairing trade opportunities, subsidies may endanger trade liberalization and make markets less open. At the same time, however, their discipline may encroach on the (often legitimate) policy decisions of domestic constituencies, and, if too strict, may equally impinge on trade liberalization.

This section proceeds to a second, and deeper, level of analysis of subsidies and their effects, focusing on the *welfare* discourse, notably their ability to directly and actually impact the 'competitive process' and to address the equally important 'failures of the market'.

The deeper level of welfare analysis shows that the implications of subsidies and their regulation are far from clear and unequivocal.[52] This depends on subsidies' complex net of negative and positive effects, or externalities, which may involve various subjects in different circles and constituencies.

On the one hand, subsidies are said to distort market functioning and introduce inefficiencies at various levels.[53] The ideas of distortion and inefficiency are strictly linked with each other, and the close connection between subsidization and distortion-inefficiency crucially relies on the *competitive* impact that subsidies have on firms' behaviour.[54] On the other side of the ledger, subsidies may produce positive effects. Intuitively, subsidization often means cheaper inputs or end-products/ services. More deeply, this kind of public intervention may target market imperfections or pursue other important non-economic, social or distributive objectives. This is nicely conveyed by Schwartz and Harper when they note that subsidies can 'correct' the market process at least as much as they 'distort' it.'[55]

The judgement on the desirability of subsidies is a political exercise which depends on which interests (of rivals, consumers, taxpayers) are considered and

[52] The necessary assumption is that market conditions are imperfect. Otherwise, subsidies would not produce any noticeable effect.

[53] Subsidies may lead to *allocative* inefficiency (if resources are not used in the best possible way), *productive* inefficiency (if goods and services are not produced at least cost), *dynamic* inefficiency (if firms are encouraged to undertake the wrong amount/type of innovation, for example research and development), and *X*-inefficiency (when public support induces opportunism in the firm's management and workforce and hence leads to reduced productivity). The inefficiency of public support means waste of public money to the loss of the taxpayer. Further, from a more general perspective, subsidies easily create emulation and races at an international level, producing a further waste of resources which should be added to the previous ones.

[54] Black's *Oxford Dictionary of Economics* defines distortions as 'economic situations in which the incentives facing firms and individuals fail to reflect true social opportunity costs' (125). A social opportunity cost is 'the amount of goods which has to be forgone because resources are used to make some particular good. When any goods or services are produced, the resources used to make them are not available for other purposes' (ibid, 434). In simpler words, distortions create a misallocation of resources because they induce firms to act in a certain, undesired, way, in a word, inefficiently.

[55] See full quotation and reference in the cover of Part I.

which perspective (domestic, global) is taken.[56] In short, on which *welfare standard* (effect on competitors, consumer, total; more/less domestic/global) is adopted.

The final verdict depends on a balancing act that is not only about evaluating data reflecting economic efficiency but almost invariably involves equity considerations, and hence policy choices which are in turn entrenched on societal values and preferences, often of constitutional rank. Further, if there are winners there will be losers, which makes the judgement more difficult, especially if the underlying trade-off has to be made in a broader, transnational context.

With subsidies, what is ultimately involved is the confrontation between different philosophical, political and societal conceptions of the role of state intervention in the economy. In their seminal work, Hufbauer and Shelton-Erb identified two different stances on state subsidization.[57]

The 'injury-only school' considers that subsidies play an important role in correcting market failures and in achieving important goals. While underplaying the negative effects of subsidies, and suggesting that any discipline on subsidies should come mainly from 'domestical processes, not international rules', it accepts that 'micro-problems' should be addressed by trade remedies on the basis of a proof of injury. By contrast, the 'anti-distortion school' views the use of subsidies more negatively, considering the distortions produced as detrimental to the functioning of market forces, reducing world economic efficiency, affecting comparative advantages, enabling countries to first-mover-advantages in new industries and avoiding adjustment in old industries, and provoking dangerous emulations. While, even in this quarter, it is in principle accepted that subsidies may be used to tackle market imperfections, this argument is considered to be 'vastly exaggerated'. A more interventionist attitude against subsidies is therefore advocated, with substantially lower thresholds to trigger action.

Bourgeois observed that 'both schools of thought admit that subsidies can create or correct market distortions. They disagree, in practice, on what should be the basic attitude towards subsidies. Should they be allowed, unless their trade distortive effects are proved, or should there be a gereral, but rebuttable, presumption of the existence of such effects?'[58]

The complex *welfare analysis* and *political judgement* of subsidies, which is the subject of this part of the chapter, should be set against this background. The negative and positive effects of subsidies are disentangled and fleshed out.

[56] We should not assume that these interests and perspectives are always fully alternative to each other and completely impermeable. The discussion on consumer welfare below is instructive in this regard.

[57] GC Hufbauer and J Shelton Erb, *Subsidies in International Trade* (Cambridge, Massachusetts: MIT Press, 1984) 19 21.

[58] JHJ Bourgeois, 'The GATT Rules for Industrial Subsidies and Countervailing Duties and the New GATT Round: The Weather and the Seeds', in EU Petersmann and M Hilf (eds), *The New GATT Round of Multilateral Trade Negotiations: Legal and Economic Problems*, Vol. V (Deventer: Kluwer, 1991) 231, 232.

However, before doing this, two case-studies that show welfare standards in operation are analysed.

Two case-studies on welfare standards

Case-study 1: export and domestic subsidies

There seems to be a general consensus that export subsidies reduce overall global welfare.[59] The results are however more contradictory if we consider the various perspectives separately.

While subsidies would reduce the welfare of the subsidizing country and of third countries' exporters, they would be mainly beneficial for the importing country. Apart from limited (and rarely successful) cases of predatory behaviour, cheap subsidized imports benefit consumers. The rival domestic industry might suffer but this is not inevitable. On the one hand, it could make the most of the competitive pressure and economize its loss and/or divert towards more profitable activities. On the other, any significant damage could be addressed by the imposition of defensive measures (ie 'countervailing' duties) on the imports. Now, assuming the benefit to consumers is sufficient to outweigh any loss to the domestic industry, from the importing country's perspective, the final assessment of the various subsidy externalities would be positive. This substantially positive situation for both consumers and domestic industry—we now complicate the model with a further actor—would be enough to compensate (in the Kaldor-Hicks efficiency sense)[60] the damage suffered by displaced third countries' exporters.

This has recently led Janow and Staiger to conclude that export subsidies are substantially beneficial and their *prohibition* is an economic puzzle.[61] Provided that the importing country retains the option to resort to measures of defence of its aggrieved industry, nobody should complain. To put it bluntly, export subsidies (though this argument could be predicated more generally for any subsidy) would increase trade flows and would thus be in line with the purpose of the world trading system. The provocative—but consequential—conclusion is that we should *incentivize* the use of export subsidies rather than restrict it.

This reading, based on formal economic analysis, and formulated on the basis of the said assumptions, is thought-provoking. Two remarks can be made immediately. First, there is certainly no inevitability in concluding that export subsidies should always be prohibited. Rather than relying on a strict prohibition

[59] AO Sykes, 'The Economics of WTO Rules on Subsidies and Countervailing Measures', Chicago M John. Olin Law and Economics Working Paper No. 186 (2nd Series), May 2003.

[60] See n 2 above.

[61] ME Janow and RW Staiger, 'United States Measures Treating Export Restraints as Subsidies' in H Horn and P Mavroidis *The WTO Case Law of 2001* (Cambridge: Cambridge University Press, 2003) 200; ME Janow and RW Staiger, 'Canada—Measures Affecting the Importation of Dairy Products and the Exportation of Milk' in H Horn and P Mavroidis *The WTO Case Law of 2001* (Cambridge: Cambridge University Press, 2003) 236.

rule, a hypothetical regulation may well ask that the alleged negative externalities produced be proved.[62] Secondly, it has indeed been put forward that export subsidies may produce *positive* externalities in some cases, particularly for developing countries.[63]

That said, there are however important counter-arguments that prevents endorsement of the view that, while dropping the prohibition of export subsidies, incentives should be created to grant them.

First, the model outlined above relies on one important condition, that the importing country retains the ability to respond, that is the right to resort to unilateral reaction. Under the current state of the law, this is the case. But it must be noted that countervailing action is subject to various sorts of criticisms.[64] It is, for example, particularly vulnerable to capture and protectionist use and creates international tensions. Moreover, by adding further distortion(s) rather than eliminating an undesired one, it often produces inefficient outcomes.

Secondly, if the (global) problem of imperfectly competitive markets is underproduction, export subsidies, by increasing production levels and trade flows, may represent a solution to the problem, but this may easily turn out to be a short-term one and—considering possible trade reactions and the ensuing waste of resources—one that is ultimately ephemeral. Apart from those exceptions outlined above where export subsidies would lead to an efficient outcome (often in terms of more products available), the more general solution to underproduction is represented by a discipline which strenghtens international competition 'on the merits', protecting *efficient* actors, and not one which generally and unqualifiedly endorses a 'doped' version of it (and which might trigger the adoption of further distorting measures).

In other words, there may well be cases where subsidies are justified because they pursue an efficient or legitimate objective. Although for export subsidies this seems to be more the exception than the rule, this may provide a case for revisiting an overly strict approach in favour of a more nuanced one capable of differentiating the good from the bad. This is however different from a blanket authorization subject only to the possibility of controversial unilateral defences.[65]

[62] The standards to be met may differ but the idea that the negative impact be established would remain the underlying approach.

[63] For the analysis of this case, and other limited cases where export subsidies might be justified (experience goods and oligopolies), see A Green and M Trebilcock, 'The Enduring Problem of WTO Export Subsidies Rules' (2007) in CA Bermann, PC Mavroidis, and KM Bagwell (eds) *Law and Economics of Contigent Protection in International Trade* (Cambridge: Cambridge University Press, forthcoming 2009), where references to further literature can be found.

[64] See MJ Trebilcock and R Howse, *The Regulation of International Trade* (3rd edn, London: Routledge, 2005) 286–92.

[65] And addressing the damage to third country's exporters through a virtual 'Kaldor-Hicks' compensation. See n 2 above.

Two further arguments may be made, which can indeed be asserted with respect to any subsidy, and which are the result of a 'political economy' perspective. They represent the gist of Hufbauer and Shelton-Erb's position, quoted at the very beginning of this part: 'unbridled and competing national subsidies can undermine world prosperity'. Far from representing an unconditional negative attitude towards subsidies, this is a warning against a lack of any international control of them.

On the one hand, the emulative effect of subsidies, and the risk of rent-seeking and subsidy wars, with the collateral effects of resource inefficiency and international tensions, should not pass unnoticed. In other words, it cannot be excluded (and this is probably an understatement) that, rather than merely resorting to defensive measures, the import country might decide to follow the protectionist path to the end, subsidizing its industry and thus triggering a subsidy race. This would admittedly lead to a global waste of resources and to international rows (possibly leading to other inefficiencies).

On the other hand, the tensions and inefficiencies of 'strategic' subsidization are known, and are considered on their own a good justification for disciplining subsidies internationally.[66] In 'prisoners' dilemma' type situations, cooperation, in the form of a discipline restraining subsidies, would be superior to unilateral *and* concurrent subsidization, leading to a 'positive-sum game'.

The case of domestic subsidies is more controversial. Like export subsidies, domestic subsidies may damage competing importers. At the same time, however, and more than export subsidies, they may be granted to pursue important positive economic and social objectives, which, depending on the case, may produce positive spill-overs across the border as well. They may tackle a market failure, such as a negative externality (eg pollution) or a positive externality (eg insufficient R&D investment), or pursue a redistributive objective (eg regional development). The issue of the grounds that may justify a public intervention in the economy is not considered in detail here, nor is the question of whether a subsidy is the best tool to solve the problem in a particular set of circumstances. These questions will be analysed below.

Two remarks can be made by way of conclusion. First, to say that there is a justification to discipline subsidies at the international level is not the same as endorsing a blanket prohibition of them. Because of their often across-the-border negative externalities, there may be a *need* to control them. The *type* of control (straight prohibition, differentiated impact standard approach, balancing of various effects and objectives) is a different question entirely.

[66] PC Mavroidis, *Trade in Goods* (Oxford: Oxford University Press, 2008) 180. For the seminal analysis of the case when 'strategic' subsidization may be efficient from the perspective of the subsidizing country see K Brander and B Spencer, 'Export Subsidies and International Market Share Rivalry' (1985) Journal of International Economics 82. For a commentary on 'strategic trade theory' see PR Krugman and M Obsfeld, *International Economics—Theory and Policy* (5th edn, London: Addison Wesley, 2000) chapter 11.

Secondly, the assessment of whether a subsidy is good or bad depends in the end on the welfare standard adopted. If this is a purely 'effect on rivals' welfare standard, the result will be that the subsidy is bad because it adversely affects the competing industry. If we adopt a broader perspective, based on 'total welfare', which in turn may be more 'domestic' or 'global' oriented, the conclusion may be different. In the example of environmental subsidies, the gain for the environment may be considered more than sufficient to compensate for the loss to injured competitors. Again, the application of this economic principle of 'compensation' requires a political 'trade-off'. This balancing is inherently a political exercise which relies on a policy choice. The bottomline is that this policy choice ultimately depends on the broader objectives of the political/economic organization/agreement.

Case-study 2: subsidies and consumer welfare

An intriguing argument that is sometimes advanced is that, inasmuch as they result in the availability of cheaper products or services, subsidies are beneficial to consumers.

In the context of countervailing duty actions, it is thus argued that from the perspective of the importing country the import of subsidized goods would be beneficial.[67] It is true that these may create some difficulty for the competing domestic industry but a comprehensive welfare analysis (ie an analysis considering gains and losses of all involved stakeholders) would often lead one to conclude that the overall net effect for the importing country is positive, particularly if the gains to consumers—who can buy cheaper products—are considered. Accordingly, apart from the extreme (and difficult to succeed) scenario of predation, levying a countervailing duty on subsidized imports would not be justified and would simply mean imposing a higher price on consumers. Indeed, it is often suggested that the importing country should simply send a 'thank you note' to the embassy of the government of the exporting country for the windfall received.

The radicalism of this argument can be explained partly by its context, in particular by the (correct) criticism of unilateral trade reactions. In other words, a strong argumentation is deployed to reject the soundness of countervailing duties (which, far from eradicating the problem of subsidies, would introduce new distortions in the market and tensions in the political sphere). These circumstances lead the argument to be slightly overreaching.

There is indeed some agreement from those quarters too that, from a more general perspective, subsidies may be distorting and should be regulated. Even from a more narrow focus, as will be shown, subsidies may damage competition. Simple economics itself highlights a paradox of the 'cheap-subsidized-goods' argument

[67] See, eg, AO Sykes, 'International Trade: Trade Remedies' in AT Guzman and AO Sykes (eds), *Research Handbook in International Economic Law* (Cheltenham: Edward Elgar (2007) 62; id, 'Countervailing Duty Law: An Economic Perspective' (1989) Columbia Law Review 199, 210 et seq; JJ Barceló III, 'Subsidies and Countervailing Duties—Analysis and a Proposal' (1977) Law and Policy in International Business 799.

whereby the short-term benefit to the consumer would be greater in those very cases (when markets are concentrated and goods are not very differentiated) where the negative effects on competitors are stronger.[68]

A more sophisticated approach should be adopted when dealing with the complex net of externalities of subsidies.

First, short-term, static and one-perspective-only analysis does not do full justice to the mechanism of externalities caused by subsidies nor to the dynamics of the competitive process. Apart from the immediate (and provocative) appeal of the 'cheap is good' mantra, the complex action of subsidy effects warrants a deeper analysis. The dynamics, and gains, of a *healthy competitive process* are just as important (if not more so) than the immediate dividends of a distorted process. The benefit to consumers should not be exclusively assessed on a static and short-term basis. Even without reaching the self-evident, extreme and rare case of predation, the development of competition in the medium, and indeed longer term, is also significant.[69] We cannot forget that, in most cases, the availability of cheaper but subsidized products or services is just a perverse concomitant of the distortion of the competitive process, and, as seen above, this often occurs in those cases where the said distortion is more severe.

Secondly, the focus on the damage caused to efficient rivals seems to be a good proxy to consider *also* consumers' interest.[70] But we could go further than merely showing an 'alignment' of the interests of efficient rivals/consumers from this viewpoint. It has already been observed that welfare analysis is complex, and so are the interests/perspectives which are considered in this analysis. In the context of antitrust law, in rejecting the use of a 'consumer welfare objective' (in favour of a 'total welfare' approach),[71] Motta makes a general observation which is of great

[68] R Nitsche and P Heidhues, *Study on Methods to Analyse the Impact of State Aid on Competition*, Report prepared for the European Commission, Directorate General for Economics and Financial Affairs (Final Report ECFIN/R/2004/004): Bruxelles (2005) 5.

[69] See, eg, M Motta, *Competition Policy: Theory and Practice* (Cambridge: Cambridge University Press, 2004) chapter 1; R Whish, *Competition Law* (6th edn, Oxford: Oxford University Press, 2008) chapter 1. It is interesting to note that similar considerations also apply in the context of competition laws when the imposition on a dominant firm of a duty to supply, license or grant access to a facility is at issue, and what emerges is the dilemma of what choice better protects innovation, property and competition. In this regard, in the EU context, the reader's attention is drawn to the landmark Opinion of Advocate General Jacobs in the *Oscar Bronner* case, where (at para 56) he warned about focusing too much on the benefits that a short-term solution may seem to yield.

[70] HW Friederiszick, LH Röller and V Verouden, 'European State Aid Control: An Economic Framework' in Bucirossi (ed), *Handbook of Antitrust Economics* (Cambridge MA: MIT Press, 2008) 625.

[71] To a large extent economists seem to agree that 'total welfare' is, more or less directly, the standard against which subsidies should ultimately be judged. See, eg, AO Sykes, 'The Economics of WTO Rules on Subsidies and Countervailing Measures', Chicago M John. Olin Law and Economics Working Paper No. 186 (2nd Series), May 2003; HW Friederiszick, LH Röller, and V Verouden, 'European State Aid Control: An Economic Framework' in Bucirossi (ed), *Handbook of Antitrust Economics* (Cambridge MA: MIT Press, 2008) 625.

It should further be noted that although 'total welfare', however it is interpreted, might be the ultimate objective of subsidy control, when it comes the operation of the system it may be necessary

value to this analysis. In today's economies, where most companies draw their capital (directly or indirectly) from the public, there is a considerable 'overlap' (and not mere alignment) between 'consumers' and 'producers' which often makes it difficult to oppose their interests fully.[72]

A disclosure of a close interest could be made by another subject, ie the 'taxpayer'. Taxpayers are crucial actors in the play of subsidization and its revenge: they ultimately pay for the subsidy, they may eventually gain from the duties collected (in terms of consequent lower fiscal pressure). They also play an important part in the case where the more efficient competitor is injured. The difficulty or failure of a firm, or even an industry, may well have a broader impact on the economy, calling on the government to intervene with various rescue measures or adjustments (such as the restructuring of a damaged competitor, social assistance to a workforce that has been laid off). This will ultimately be financed through taxation. It does not take much to prove this point in these recession-hit times with a high tide of bail-outs. It should not be forgotten that the 'consumer' and the 'taxpayer' are one and the same subject.

Finally, note the presence of another actor in this play, the 'employees' of the injured company. That 'consumers' may have some empathy with their position (as an expression of sympathy, national pride, concern for possible economic and social ripercussions) cannot be excluded.[73]

The approach presented so far enables the reader to fully appreciate the most direct negative externality a subsidy may cause in the context of market functioning and hence the justification of its control. That said, taking stock of the complex dynamics of subsidy effects, and of the policy objectives they often pursue, a mature subsidy discipline should go beyond proxies of harm and carefully consider the positive externalities for all interested stakeholders (including consumers, taxpayers and employees). For the sake of conceptual and even operational clarity, it is however argued that this should occur separately, at a second stage when the positive effects of subsidies are considered and when the intrinsically political balancing exercise of all effects—negative and positive—is made.

Giving substance to subsidies' distortion: a competition-oriented approach

Leaving aside for a moment more general political economy considerations (eg avoidance of rent-seeking, protectionist reactions, subsidy wars and global

to distinguish. In this regard, it is submitted that a preliminary, or in any event separate, reliance on the narrower negative effects on rivals should be considered.

[72] M Motta, *Competition Policy: Theory and Practice* (Cambridge: Cambridge University Press, 2004) 21. The clarity of his argument deserves full quotation: 'in today's advanced economies consumers often own firms (partly or fully), directly or through pension and investment funds. Accordingly, dividends are distributed to a vast number of citizens who would be hurt if profits were reduced. If the adoption of a consumer welfare standard were intended to favour "citizens" as opposed to "firms", it would not be clear that such a goal would be achieved.'

[73] Again, a testing recession climate provides some support in this regard.

inefficiency) which may well justify the control of subsidies (and particularly certain kinds of subsidies), it is now time to focus more precisely on the negative effects subsidies may have on market functioning. In doing so, an attempt will also be made to identify a workable test capable of capturing these negative externalities.

We begin our examination with the concept of *distortion*, one of the true paradigms in the field, which is crucial when it comes to considering the effects of subsidies and State aids, their control and the remedies against them.

The concept of distortion is however very ambiguous. As Professor Jackson reminds us, 'in some sense, every governmental action that impinges on the economy creates a "distortion"'.[74] What has to be asked is whether a more workable concept of distortion, in line with the economic rationale for controlling subsidies, can be identified as the main *catalyst* of many, if not all, of the forms of economic inefficiency outlined above.[75]

A big debate on basic conceptual issues, including that of distortion, arising from subsidy rules under the GATT commenced within the North-American academic world in the 1970s and is ongoing to this day.[76] The debate has been mainly

[74] JH Jackson, *The World Trading System—Law and Policy of International Economic Relations* (2nd edn, Cambridge Massachussetts: MIT Press, 1997) 298.

[75] See n 53.

[76] The paper that started off the discussion was WF Schwartz and EW Harper Jr, 'The Regulation of Subsidies Affecting International Trade' (1972) Michigan Law Review 831.

Many followed suit (the various contributions devoted to the 'specificity' requirement are referred to in chapter 13): see, eg, JJ Barceló III, 'Subsidies and Countervailing Duties—Analysis and a Proposal' (1977) Law and Policy in International Business 799; CJ Goetz, L Granet, and WF Schwartz, 'The Meaning of "Subsidy" and "Injury" in the Countervailing Duty Law' (1986) International Review of Law and Economics 17; R Diamond, 'Economic Foundations of Countervailing Duty Law' (1989) Virginia Law Journal of International Law, 767; AO Sykes, 'Countervailing Duty Law: An Economic Perspective' (1989) Columbia Law Review 199.

The 1980s closed with a Symposium of the Countervailing Duty Law at Georgetown University Law Centre in 1989. The relevant contributions touched the main concepts and rationale of subsidies and countervailing duty response and were published in a special issue of Law and Policy in International Business of the same year. In particular, beginning at p 503, the reader can find: WF Schwartz, 'Countervailing Duty Law for the 1990's—A New Look at the Law and Economics of Subsidies'; R Diamond, 'A Search for Economic and Financial Principles in the Administration of United States Countervailing Duty Law'; RA Cass, 'Trade Subsidy Law: Can a Foolish Inconsistency be Good Enough for Government Work?'; WN Eksridge Jr, 'Dynamic Interpretation of Economic Regulatory Legislation (Countervailing Duty Law)'; AO Sykes, 'Second-Best Countervailing Duty Policy: A Critique of the Entitlement Approach'; MJ Trebilcock, 'Is the Game Worth the Candle? Comments on *A Search for Economic and Financial Principles in the Administration of US Countervailing Duty Law*'; and JH Jackson, 'Perspectives on Countervailing Duties'.

More recent contributions, already in the WTO context, are: AO Sykes, 'The economics of "injury" in antidumping and countervailing duty cases', RA Cass, and MS Knoll, 'The economics of "injury" in antidumping and countervailing duty cases: A reply to Professor Sykes', RD Boltuck, 'Innovations in support of the unitary injury test in US unfair trade cases', all in JS Bhandari and JS Sykes (eds), *Economic Dimensions in International Law* (Cambridge: Cambridge University Press, 1997) at 83, 126 and 166 respectively; AO Sykes, 'The Economics of WTO Rules on Subsidies and Countervailing Measures', Chicago M John. Olin Law and Economics Working Paper No. 186 (2nd series) May 2003; G Grossman and PC Mavroidis, 'Here Today? Gone Tomorrow?' in H Horn

conducted in the context of the analysis of trade remedies, that is, the unilateral imposition of duties to countervail subsidized imports.[77] In the EC, despite the existence of a comprehensive system of State aid control since the 1950s, a serious analysis of the effects of State aid and particularly of the welfare standards and techniques to measure them did not really start till the late 1990s.[78] The debate has recently gathered momentum with the suggestion of adopting a 'more refined economic approach' put forward in the State Aid Action Plan (SAAP) launched by DG Comp in mid-2005.[79] The work done in the OECD on public subsidies should also be mentioned.[80]

It should be noted at the outset that most of the results of these significant strands of analysis are of general validity since they are based on economic findings which often abstract from the specific normative framework at issue and provide a useful insight into why subsidies 'distort' and should thus be controlled.

Benitah has identified two ideas of distortion in the GATT/WTO law.[81] This distinction, which may be extented to the EC too, may be of help in developing the

and PC Mavroidis (eds), The WTO Case Law of 2001 (Cambridge: Cambridge University Press, 2003) 170; G Grossman and PC Mavroidis 'Recurring Misunderstandings of Non Recurring Subsidies' and H Horn and PC Mavroidis, 'United States—Preliminary Determination with Respect to Certain Softwood Lumber from Canada: What is a subsidy?', both in H Horn and PC Mavroidis (eds), *The WTO Case Law of 2002* (Cambridge: Cambridge University Press, 2005) at 78 and 220; AO Sykes, 'International Trade: Trade Remedies' in AT Guzman and AO Sykes (eds), *Research Handbook in International Economic Law* (Cheltenham: Edward Elgar 2007) 62.

The latest word in the debate goes back to one of its initiators: R Diamond, 'Privatization and the Definition of Subsidy: A Critical Study of Appellate Body Texturalism' (2008) Journal of International Economic Law 649.

[77] This occurred for two main reasons. First, till the advent of the WTO, the strongest 'track' to tackle subsidies was the unilateral one (see below for an exposition of the rules and their evolution). Secondly, the debate took place in the US, a country which, historically, has been the strongest user of countervailing duties.

[78] Probably the best example is the European Competition Law Annual Conference organized by Professor Ehlermann at the Robert Schuman Centre of the European University Institute, in Florence, in June 1999. The conference proceedings are available in: CD Ehlermann and M Everson (eds), *European Competition Law Annual 1999: Selected Issues in the Field of State Aids* (Oxford: Hart Publishing, 2001).

[79] Various studies and publications are coming out. Some references (particularly contributions by economists) can be found in chapter 14 when various economic issues of the distortion of competition are analysed. In the author's opinion, three works stand out for their comprehensiveness and accessibility: D Neven and V Verouden, 'Towards a More Refined Economic Approach in State Aid Control', in W Mederer, N Pesaresi, and M Van Hoof (eds), *EU Competition Law—Volume IV: State Aid* (Leuven: Claeys and Casteels, 2008) Book 1, Part I, chapter 4; HW Friederiszick, LH Röller, and V Verouden, 'European State Aid Control: An Economic Framework' in Bucirossi (ed), *Handbook of Antitrust Economics* (Cambridge MA: MIT Press, 2008) 625; and J Derenne and M Merola (eds), *Economic Analysis of State Aid Rules Contributions and Limits* (Berlin: Lexxion, 2007).

[80] See, eg, the study produced by the Committee on Competition Law and Policy in 2001: OECD, *Competition Policy in Subsidies and State Aid*, Competition Policy Roundtable, DAFFE/CLP (2001) 24, OECD, Paris.

[81] M Benitah, *The Law of Subsidies under the GATT/WTO System* (The Hague : Kluwer Law International, 2001) 251–80; id, 'Les divers sens du concept de distortion et leur rôle dans la définition juridique actuelle d'une subvention compensable: Les normes internationales et le cas des États-Unis' (1996) Canadian Yearbook of International Law, 137.

type of distortion that subsidy control should tackle and in providing an interesting framework for various elements of the definition of subsidy. On the one hand, the *simple* view of distortion would rest on the subsidy's interference with the 'natural' market mechanism governing the allocation of resources in the subsidizing country and subsequently with a disturbance of international economic relations. Clearly, the standard of proof of this simple view is not very demanding and many subsidies would arguably be found to match it.

On the other hand, there would be a more *sophisticated* idea of distortion. Compared with the simple approach, the sophisticated view of distortion, in principle, requires a thorough economic analysis of the impact of the subsidy and may thus be more demanding from the evidential perspective.[82] This concept would be the direct and immediate focus of any regulation of public subsidies.

Under the relevant entry, the *WTO glossary* reads that we have a distortion '(w)hen prices and production are higher or lower than levels that would usually exist in a competitive market'. The hint to an impact on prices and output and the reference to a 'competition' baseline are quite promising. One of the most accredited versions of the sophisticated idea of distortion crucially relies on the *impact* of the subsidy on the *competitive process* which could be divided into two consequential steps: (i) the impact of the subsidy on the conduct of the recipient and (ii) the ensuing adverse effect on the position of its competitors.[83]

In general, it cannot be concluded that one view is better than the other. Everything depends on context and function. Whereas the simple idea of distortion is particularly suitable to explain certain elements of the definition of subsidy, which are there to capture the 'potential' to lead to a misallocation of resources (such as the 'advantage' examined in Part III, or 'specificity' in chapter 13), the sophisticated idea, and particularly the one that focuses on the impact of subsidies on the competitive process, is more appropriate when it comes to ultimately determine the possible negative economic impact of the subsidy.

Addressing market failures: subsidies and political judgements

It has been seen that subsidies may create negative externalities, and in particular may distort the competitive process. We have identified this as the main rationale for controlling subsidies. Subsidies are however ambivalent because they can also produce positive effects.[84] It is widely and increasingly recognized that the market does not always deliver desirable or acceptable outcomes. This may be explained in terms of inefficiency or more simply of inequity.

[82] Even in this context, however, more simple rules like presumptions might be used if, for example, no significant distortion is expected or, on the contrary, the conduct is highly likely to distort.

[83] This concept of distortion of competition and its operation are discussed fully in chapter 13.

[84] See, eg, WF Schwartz and EW Harper Jr, 'The Regulation of Subsidies Affecting International Trade' (1972) Michigan Law Review 831.

Although there is a great degree of overlap, we divide our analysis into two levels, one technical and one normative.

Technical issues

The concept of market failure is not a clear one. There are different taxonomies, and views, among economists. Stiglitz lists six basic market failures, namely, imperfect competition, public goods (such as *some* infrastructures and services), externalities (which can be divided into negative ones—such as pollution, and positive ones—such as research and development investment), incomplete markets (like capital markets), imperfect information, unemployment and other macroeconomic disturbances (such as inflation and disequilibrium).[85] Sometimes, all these forms of imperfection are summarized into what are seen as the two main categories: public goods and externalities. Stiglitz also refers to two other categories that, strictly speaking, cannot be explained in terms of inefficiency of the market but rather lack of equity, that is redistribution and merit goods (such as culture).[86]

In these cases, governments intervene to tackle the imperfection of the market. Various instruments may be used to reach this goal, and public subsidies are amongst them. The choice of the instrument, and its design, are important, and at this level economics plays an important role.[87] However, this area is complex, and for various reasons. On the one hand, it is inherently *normative*, ie it is the place where political and policy decisions are made (this is particularly evident with respect to equity problems).

On the other, even leaving aside the level of value choices and decisions (which are fundamental in this area and to which we return later), there are difficulties of a more technical nature. Economic science may indeed play a role in detecting a market failure and in indicating the most efficient instrument to tackle it. However, although this may be easy and straightforward in principle, it may become very woolly at the practical level where 'identification' and 'quantification' issues come out. Also, accurate information is crucial in this area, but, unfortunately, the whole subject of market failures and actions to address them is marked by information deficiencies.

Let us analyse with more precision these technical issues. In the first place, it is sometimes testing to *identify* the problem (indeed there may be more than one imperfection in the market). Secondly, the market failure may be difficult to *quantify*. Thirdly, and most importantly from the perspective of the justification of subsidies, it may be questionable whether a subsidy is the *best* tool to achieve the

[85] JE Stiglitz, *Economics of the Public Sector* (3rd edn, New York: Norton, 2000) chapter 4.

[86] Market failures are not mutually exclusive. We may have situations where the market does not function for more than one reason. Further, in some cases, we have a mix of efficiency/equity problems.

[87] D Rodrik, 'Industrial Policy for the Twenty-First Century', November 2004, CEPR Discussion Paper No. 4767 offers an extremely useful insight into a new approach to 'industrial policy' to target market failures.

desired objectives. In other words, subsidies often represent a *second-best* option which does not directly tackle the issue and may add further distortion(s).[88] Fourthly, if it is concluded that a subsidy in the best available option, it may be difficult to *quantify* the amount of aid which is necessary to correct market failures and the conditions that should be attached to it. These problems also depend on the more general context, ie on the effects of other policies, and more generally other circumstances. Along this line, the 'net' impact of the intervention may be uncertain as the positive and negative effects are difficult to disentangle and to balance with each other to eventually make a decision on whether it should be efficient and legitimate.[89] Finally, the risk of regulatory capture by rent-seeking lobbies should not be underestimated. Nor more generally, should the possibility that, just as the market may fail, so too may the government fail in its intervention.

Normative issues

We can now return to the *normative* discourse, where value choices are made and where the system fundamentally decides whether and when public intervention, in the instant case in the form of subsidy, is warranted. In other words, the discussion shifts from the level of *technical viability* to that of *political legitimacy*.

A fundamental proposition should be made. Any system of subsidy control that pretends to be balanced should take into account of (at least some of) the public policy objectives pursued and positive externalities produced by subsidies. A simple but illuminating confirmation can be found in other areas of the law, like trade rules, where more or less broad provisions or exceptions are made available to

[88] In an ideal world, a 'first-best' policy, directly addressing the problem, should be adopted. On the 'first-' and 'second-best' theories see n 89 below.

[89] In some cases, it may even be argued that the measure is not a *distortion* but rather a *correction* of a previously existing distortion. This issue evokes the important interplay between scope and justification analysed in the introduction. In a nutshell, to determine whether there is or not a distortion has important conceptual and practical implications since it may eventually determine whether the measure at issue does qualify (or not) as a subsidy in the first place.

J Pelkmans, *European Integration—Methods and Economic Analysis* (2nd edn, London: FT-Prentice Hall, 2001) 242, has for example argued that 'if the aid is paid to overcome a market failure, it is not distortive—indeed, it is to restore efficiency'. Similarly, after explaining the second-best theory, A Evans, *European Community Law of State Aid* (Oxford: Clarendon Press, 1997) 80, suggests that 'since competition requires efficient allocation of resources, aid which merely corrects inefficient allocation associated with market failure may not be regarded as distorting competition.' In economic language, unlike the 'first-best' theory which presupposes the possibility of the removal of the *only* existing distortion in the market to achieve full-efficiency, the 'second-best' theory says that, if this is not possible, because there are more than one distortions, the solution is to introduce a new *distortion* to offset the *distortions* that already exist (see D Begg, S Fisher, and R Dornbusch, *Economics* (5th edn, London: MacGraw-Hill, 1997) 247).

A final, unsettling, word is uttered by R Nitsche and P Heidhues, *Study on Methods to Analyse the Impact of State Aid on Competition*, Report prepared for the European Commission, Directorate General for Economics and Financial Affairs (Final Report ECFIN/R/2004/004): Bruxelles (2005) 109, who underline that the issue—is it distortion or correction?—ultimately depends on the (narrow or broad) concepts of welfare and market failure that are adopted (sic!).

address economic or non-economic justifications of measures which otherwise breach other rules.[90]

As a matter of principle, the author does not see any reason why a similar approach should not be followed in the area of public subsidies as well.

On this assumption, two general guidelines can be advanced. First, by contrast with negative externalities, the system should endorse a welfare standard which, *ideally*, should consider the interests of all the various stakeholders (ie 'total welfare'). Secondly, *so far as possible*, the perspective should tend to be more global rather than domestic. The two emphasized provisos inserted in the previous statements already give an idea of the difficulty of regulating the positive externalities of subsidies.

Crucially, how far to go in recognizing them ultimately depends on the specific political, economic, social, historical, etc context of which the system of subsidy control is part. The variables are so many and diverse that it is very difficult to draw firm conclusions in this regard. As has been suggested above, the inclusion/exclusion of certain justifications may ultimately depend on the how entrenched the sense of *community* is. This point is developed below with some examples.

The agreement that certain objectives are important may be particularly strong. We may be talking of 'global commons' where the positive effects of the subsidy would clearly be felt across the board, or in any case of other 'failures' that are high in the political agenda.

One topical case is climate change.[91] Although subsidies are by no means the only, nor always the best, tool to address this alarming emergency, it is highly desirable that any discipline of subsidies should recognize interventions with this target.[92] Other emergencies have recently hit the headlines showing the dramatic interdependence of a world that cannot afford to act in a schizophrenic way. Energy security and affordability, and the stability and regulation of the financial system undoubtedly constitute 'shared interests'. Another important category relates to effective public action to assist development (broadly intended) which affects every corner of an increasingly globalized world in various ways (think of migration).[93]

Indeed, climate change and environmental degradation, poverty and development, and energy, financial and economic crises are increasingly proving that the world is truly interdependent, and is facing challenges that are crucially interconnected

[90] See, eg, Article 30 of the EC or the 'mandatory requirements' under Article 28 of the EC in the European internal market context, and Article XX of the GATT and its 'general exceptions'.

[91] A forward-looking analysis of the status of measures to fight climate change under WTO law is GC Hufbauer, S Charnovitz, and J Kim, *Global Warming and the World Trading System* (Washington DC: Peterson Institute for International Economics, 2009).

[92] More generally, but also more controversially considering its breadth, we could also think of the goal of environmental protection.

[93] The ILO's reminder that '[p]overty anywhere constitutes a danger to prosperity everywhere' is deeply appropriate. Constitution of the International Labor Organization, Annex (Declaration concerning the aims and purposes of the International Labor Organization), para I (c).

with each other. Common and coherent action is required. A balanced international subsidy compact should take all this into account.

Other market failures or socio-economic goals (such as research and development; regional development; adjustment for sectors in difficulty; employment or training) may be considered too. From an economic standpoint, a subsidy may in principle represent a suitable tool to handle any of those failures. Their accreditation under subsidy rules again substantially depends on the political consensus that can be gathered on their acceptability.

The crux of the issue is always the same, and it is terribly simple. Whereas the measure may certainly produce significant negative externalities across the border, the benefit may not necessarily (and immediately) be felt beyond the boundaries of the subsidizing country. The scenarios may be different, and may give rise to different welfare situations, depending for example on the time span considered. The fact remains that, at least from a direct and short-term perspective (which is often the one that prevails, at least politically), the beneficial effect may well be produced only at a local level and the distortions at an international level. Now, the crucial issue for an international discipline of subsidy control is how to address these asymmetries and ultimately how to take all welfare interests into account. As stated above, the degree of acceptance of subsidies producing this kind of mixed externalities rests on political considerations in the end.

The above analysis can only generate a good rule of thumb on the acceptability of a positive objective pursued by subsidies:

> the higher the rank of the interest is, and the broader the impact of the (net) benefit is, the easier the acceptance of the 'trade-off' may be.[94]

From a political and sociological perspective, developed above, this turns ultimately on whether the system is based on a sufficiently rooted sense of *community*.

C. Conclusions: goals of subsidy control in the WTO and EC

So far, the discussion has mainly been about what goals subsidy control could, or should, have. We have reasoned about an ideal benchmark. We now turn to analyse the disciplines in the WTO and EC and outline the goals actually emerging from these rules. Inevitably, the status quo is tested, or at least our interpretation of it, against the said ideal.

The goals of subsidy control in the GATT/WTO

The goal, or indeed the goals, of the Agreement on Subsidies and Countervailing Measures (SCM) Agreement are not fully clear. The SCM Agreement's lack of a preamble, which usually provides some indication on the relevant instrument's

[94] The 'net' benefit is the one that discounts the negative externalities caused by the subsidy.

purposes, is highly significant in this regard. The area is so controversial that Members could not agree on, and did not even wish to expressly spell out, even in a general fashion, the goals of the agreement.[95] For its part, the Dispute Settlement Body (DSB) remains in vague terms which however provide a starting point, indicating as its main aim that of regulating 'distorting subsidies' and unilateral remedies for them.[96]

The interpreter's labours in attempting to find meaning are strenuous. It should be underlined immediately that the analysis proceeds on the basis of the original version of the SCM Agreement. It is argued that this allows a more comprehensive view of the current status quo, and a preview of how the regulation should be.

In our quest for goals, we incrementally add layers of meaning. The premise is that, in line with the general consideration that unilateral conduct creating negative effects should be controlled (the justification of the trade agreement), the SCM Agreement is a multilateral discipline regulating the grant of subsidies and responses to them that may cause negative effects. More specifically, one of the main objectives is to discourage subsidies that may harm competing foreign producers in two ways, either by breaching their market access expectations or by affecting their competitive position. The other important objective of the SCM Agreement is to control the unilateral reaction to those subsidies that injure domestic industries, ensuring that it is justified and proportionate and hence its possible damage is limited.

Hence, the SCM Agreement is about discouraging subsidies that may harm producers' interest (thus reflecting an 'effect on rivals' welfare standard). However, this is only part of the story. If there are no doubts that the SCM Agreement is currently not about 'advancing global economic efficiency',[97] the initial situation (the one provisionally in force till the end of 1999)[98] crucially recognized the legitimacy of certain subsidies targeting market failures and other policy objectives and permitted them.

It is understood therefore that—at least initially—the deal leading to the SCM Agreement embraced a complex, and (albeit not perfect) overall balanced, welfare analysis which went beyond producers' interests. More particularly, the original setting seemed to rely substantially on a mix of welfare standards embodied in separate provisions.[99]

[95] It may be useful to recall the two confronting schools of thought ('injury-only' and 'anti-distortion') examined above.

[96] See, eg, Panel, *Canada—Aircraft*, para 9.119; Panel, *Brazil—Aircraft*, para 10.11; Appellate Body, *US—DRAMS*, para 115.

[97] See G Grossman, and PC Mavroidis, 'Here Today? Gone Tomorrow?' in H Horn and PC Mavroidis (eds), *The WTO Case Law of 2001* (Cambridge: Cambridge University Press, 2003) 170, 180–6; R Diamond, 'Privatization and the Definition of Subsidy: A Critical Study of Appellate Body Texturalism' (2008) Journal of International Economic Law 649, 654.

[98] See section III below for an analysis.

[99] Although the mechanism of operation is different, broadly similar conclusions can be drawn with respect to the regulation of agricultural subsidies in the AG.

On the one hand, while outlawing certain subsidies (mainly export subsidies), it acknowledged that other subsidies, which respect legitimate policy choices, should be accepted. In both cases, the system seemed to be modelled on a broad welfare perspective, going beyond domestic boundaries. While the prohibition of certain subsidies could largely be explained in both economic and political economy terms (avoidance of subsidy wars, protection of global efficiency and competing producers), the authorization of certain categories of subsidies was a recognition of other (economic but not only economic) interests pursued by subsidies and, at the same time, of a significant 'policy space' for domestic constituencies.

On the other hand, other subsidies were objectionable only if they produced an adverse impact on those undertakings competing with the subsidized entity. In so doing, the various impact tests seem to rely either on an 'effect of rival' welfare standard which, according to the author's reading, is not only about protecting competitors but the competitive process itself, or on the 'protection of market access' expectations.[100]

Despite inconsistencies and weaknesses, it is submitted that the initial setting of the SCM Agreement clearly reflected the core idea that subsidies are ambivalent in their rationales and effects, a recognition which dates back to the GATT era.[101] In this regard, although there has been an evolution of the system from the GATT to the WTO, the bargain embodied in the original compact of the SCM Agreement does not depart from its GATT origins but rather represents an organic growth of them.[102]

Since the year 2000, with the expiry of the non-actionable subsidies, and proposals about enlarging the prohibited subsidies category,[103] the system seems to be

[100] See chapter 14 for an analysis.

[101] See Articles 8 and 11 of the Tokyo Sudsidy Code in this regard. See section III below.

[102] Others seem to suggest a different reading, notably that the stricter approach towards subsidies in the WTO would represent a change of approach. See, eg, M Matsushita, TJ Schoenbaum, and PC Mavroidis, *The World Trade Organization—Law, Practice, and Policy* (2nd edn, Oxford: Oxford University Press, 2006) chapter 10. In the author's view, what seems to have happened is certainly a shift from a *softer (flexible and even indeterminate) approach* (with a looser stance towards export subsidies and an unclear, better inconclusive, treatment of domestic subsidies) towards a *harder (more determined and precise)* one (straight prohibition on the one hand, clear distinction between objectionable and non-objectionable domestic subsidies on the other).

This may well be just an expression of a general change from the GATT (*bargaining-centre* perspective) to the WTO (*rule-based* perspective). See JH Jackson, *The World Trading System—Law and Policy of International Economic Relations* (2nd edn, Cambridge Massachussetts: MIT Press, 1997) 115–16; for a critical analysis of the relationship between these two perspectives, see HE Hudec, 'GATT or GABB? The Future Design of the General Agreement on Tariffs and Trade' (1971) Yale Law review, 1299; see also JHH Weiler, 'The Rule of Lawyers and the Ethos of Diplomats: Reflections on the Internal and External Legitimacy of WTO Dispute Settlement', Harvard Jean Monnet Working Paper, 9/00).

Whatever the correct explanation for this evolution may be, it is a fact that the barycenter of the SCM Agreement that was provisionally in force for the first five years of the WTO was still very much aligned to the GATT's one. Things have dramatically changed with the expiration of the category of permited subsidies, shifting the centre of gravity towards an unambiguously stricter approach.

[103] See Proposal from the US, TN/RL/GEN/146.

unbalanced, and to have slipped at least one step back from the organic development indicated above. The balance is now tipped too far towards *subsidy aversion.* An increasing number of calls about the importance of a newly defined public intervention in the economy is being heard from various quarters.[104] So is the need to recognize more 'policy space' to domestic constituencies.[105] The case for reforming subsidy regulation, particularly by reintroducing a category of non-actionable subsidies, possibly after few necessary amendments, is increasingly advanced[106] and is, in the author's view, particularly strong.[107]

The goals of State aid control in the EC

EC State aid control has been in a situation of relative quiescence for many years, almost decades. It was there, modestly performing its duty. It was not in the spotlight, quite the contrary, often being referred to as the 'ugly duckling' in EC competition law. With the completion of the internal market,[108] the increasing liberalization/privatization trends and coordination in economic policies, and the devolution of monetary policies (for the Euro-zone Members), the provisions of the EC Treaty on State aid control have inevitably come into preminence. State aid has become one of the latest, most visible tools of industrial policy in the hands of Member States.

The adoption by the Commission (more precisely, DG Competition) of the 2005 'State Aid Action Plan' (SAAP), a consultation paper which under the motto of 'less and better targeted State aid' advocates a 'more-refined use of economic analysis', more transparency and consolidation of legislation, has seemingly triggered a process of rejuvenation of State aid governance. Brussels has become a powerhouse and various legislative acts (in the form of both soft and hard law)

[104] See, eg, D Rodrik, 'Industrial Policy for the Twenty-First Century', November 2004, CEPR Discussion Paper No. 4767.

[105] See, eg, J Pauwelyn, 'New Trade Politics After the Doha Round', *Center for Trade and Economic Integration, Working Paper 1/2008*; and D Rodrik, 'How to Save Globalization from its Cheerleaders', JF Kennedy School of Government, Harvard University, Faculty Research Working Papers Series, September 2007, RWP07–038.

[106] R Howse, 'To the World Organization disciplines on domestic subsidies make sense? The case for legalizing some subsidies' in KW Bagwell, GA Bermann, and PC Mavroidis (eds), *Law and Economics of Contingent Protection in International Trade* (Cambridge: Cambridge University Press, forthcoming 2009).

[107] By redressing the balance, this suggestion would somewhat meet the concerns of those that have strongly warned that the SCM Agreement is currently 'one of the least economics-informed agreements in the WTO': M Matsushita, TJ Schoenbaum, and PC Mavroidis, *The World Trade Organization—Law, Practice, and Policy* (2nd edn, Oxford University Press, 2006) 394. See also the various references in that chapter (chapter 11) to the arguments put forward in this direction by various scholars, mostly economists: Bagwell, Grossmann, Horn, Janow and Staiger.

[108] Following the abolition of customs duties, quantitative restrictions and measures having an equivalent effect to the latter, and harmonization of various national measures impinging on the free movement of economic factors.

are being adopted. The cases before Community and national courts are increasing. The topic is occupying larger spaces in the scholarly debate.

Most interestingly for our purposes, the SAAP has ignited a lively debate on the objectives of EC State aid control. What we have is the confrontation between a 'competition' quarter that, following the example of the current process centred on an 'economic-oriented' approach to the antitrust rules of the EC Treaty (Articles 81 and 82 of the EC), proposes an injection of more economic analysis into the interpretation of State aid law, both at the level of the definition, for example with respect to the requirements of the distortion of competition or the effect on intra-Community trade, and at that of the justifications.[109] Various economic studies have recently been carried out to fill a perceived gap in the literature on State aids.[110] In analysing externalities and distortions produced by the latter, at a more general level, the debate crucially revolves also around the welfare standards ('rival', 'consumer', 'total') that the system should embrace overall and the level of the various steps of application of the rules.[111]

The confronting quarter, which could be dubbed 'internal market school', believes on the contrary that State aid rules are not completely competition rules and hence can be construed only partly by referring to traditional antitrust provisions. With historical and systemic arguments (to some extent supported in earlier statements of the case-law: cf *Philip Morris*),[112] it is underlined that they should more correctly be assimilated to the internal market provisions which aim to remove obstacles to trade. State aid then is seen as more of a barrier to intra-Community trade rather than a distortion of competition (which reminds us of the first level of analysis of the negative effects produced by subsidies, and particularly the impact on market access). It is underlined that the main difference between 'competition rules' and 'State aid rules' is that whereas the former focus on competition between undertakings, the latter would *also*—'and perhaps to a greater extent'—concentrate on macro-economic rivalry between Member States.[113]

As with internal market law where there is no need for a 'more refined economic analysis', no such need should be felt with respect to State aid law. Thus, the 'distortion of competition' should automatically follow and be ultimately presumed, 'as a necessary consequence of a measure that fulfils the other requirements' of the State

[109] Underlining that if State aid is a policy tool to tackle market failures, it should be important to properly diagnose the disease, identify the most appropriate cure while limiting any side effect.

[110] Some predating, maybe even anticipating, the SAAP. For various references see chapter 14.

[111] Apart from the references in the previous note, see J Derenne and M Merola (eds), *Economic Analysis of State Aid Rules—Contributions and Limits* (Berlin: Lexxion, 2007).

[112] See chapter 14.

[113] JL Buendia-Sierra, 'Not like this: Some Skeptical Remarks on the "Refined Economic Approach" in State aid', in Proceedings of 4th Experts' Forum on New Developments in European State Aid Law, 18 and 19 May 2006, European State Aid Law Institute (Berlin: Lexxion, 2006) 59, 61–2. In other words, State aid control would have been introduced to safeguard the internal market by tackling a specific risk, that of unfair financial competition between 'have' and 'have-nots'.

aid definition.[114] Along the same lines, as in the EC internal market, there should not be any *de minimis* rule.[115] Further, it is highlighted that, unlike traditional antitrust law, it would be erroneous to put exclusive reliance on efficiency arguments.[116] State aid law is by definition a tool of public policy and non-efficiency (ie social-redistributional) rationales naturally play a crucial role in it. Another strand of this school pushes the alleged relationship with internal market logic even further. Following the *Cassis de Dijon* line, it endorses a 'rule of reason' approach under Article 87(1) of the EC, eventually allowing justification considerations to find space, and be balanced, at the level of the definition.[117]

Leaving aside this debate (with this author tending to side with the first quarter, although there is some merit in the second school of thought),[118] it is nonetheless clear that, if compared with GATT/WTO, Europe goes *much further*.

Two examples on the substantive discipline (analysis of the institutional/procedural mechanism is left to section III below) can be provided. First, EC State aid law, as a regulation to ensure competition within the internal market, is capable of tackling situations where competitors are only domestic (in the context of an increasingly integrated internal market, the 'effect on trade' requirement is generally easy to prove). Secondly, there are far more justifications, some clearly based on a Community interest or on non-efficiency rationales.

[114] V Di Bucci, 'Comments on the Paper "Selectivity, Economic Advantage, Distortion of Competition and Effect on Trade"', in J Derenne and M Merola (eds), *Economic Analysis of State Aid Rules—Contributions and Limits* (Berlin: Lexxion, 2007) 156, 159.

[115] Which is still the mainstream position in the case-law. See JL Buendia-Sierra, 'Not like this: Some Skeptical Remarks on the "Refined Economic Approach" in State aid', in Proceedings of 4th Experts' Forum on New Developments in European State Aid Law, 18 and 19 May 2006, European State Aid Law Institute (Berlin: Lexxion, 2006) 59, 62; V Di Bucci, 'Comments on the Paper "Selectivity, Economic Advantage, Distortion of Competition and Effect on Trade"', in J Derenne and M Merola (eds), *Economic Analysis of State Aid Rules—Contributions and Limits* (Berlin: Lexxion, 2007) 156, 159.

[116] JL Buendia-Sierra and B Smulders, 'The Limited Role of the "Refined Economic Approach" in Achieving the Objectives of State Aid Control : Time for Some Realism', in 'EC State aid law-Le Droit des Aides d'Etat dans la CE, Liber Amicorum Francisco Santaolalla Gadea (Kluwer Law International, 2008) 18, 21–2.

[117] A Biondi, 'Some Reflections on the Notion of "State Resources" in European Community State Aid Law' (2007) Fordham International Law Journal 1426, 1441. Just a gloss may be appropriate here, to show the paradoxical—even schizophrenic—consequences that a full adoption of an 'internal market' approach might envisage. Whereas the main concern raised by the 'more refined economic approach' is the possible flexibility that this may entail with the result that troublesome measures might escape control (ie a *risk* of *under-inclusion* of the regulation), the adoption of a balancing exercise, such as that inherent in the 'rule of reason', at the level of the definition, might lead right towards that direction. It would indeed provide arguments that *some* measures, which might in fact be objectionable because of their effects, do not actually confer an advantage and hence cannot be regarded as State aid. The feared under-inclusion would thus become a reality.

[118] Including the need to contain too much enthusiasm for a not fully internalized economic approach.

Coda: State aid and subsidy rules as competition regulation

After answering the first fundamental question on the goals of subsidy control in the WTO and in the EC, this closing section enquires whether WTO subsidy rules and EC State aid rules should be considered as 'trade' or 'competition' rules. This is an important conceptual and practical point.

Right at the beginning of this chapter, it was underlined that *competition occurs through trade in a market.* In this context, while trade rules aim to remove barriers to trade and ensure market access, competition rules directly focus on the protection of the competitive process in the market. Crucially, we have seen that subsidies may act as obstacles to trade (and hence raise a market access issue), and, at the same time, affect competition. Depending on the approach taken, therefore, rules governing subsidies might in principle be considered as trade or competition rules.

What is posited here is that both EC State aid and WTO subsidy rules should be looked at mainly as *competition* rules.

Trade and competition: united in diversity

It is certainly the case that the boundaries between trade and competition regulation are blurring, and there are various signs of this in the evolution of the law in both legal systems. It is observed that the *policies* of trade liberalization and competition (generally intended, including antitrust) are inextricably linked with each other.[119] More interestingly, it is noted that in both legal systems there is increasing convergence, even in language, between the relevant *rules*.[120] It has been observed, for example, that the 'rule of non-discrimination in WTO law (effectively a free-trade rule) contains a clear undistorted-competition element'.[121] Reference is made to Article III of the GATT, and particularly to its consistent interpretation as a legal

[119] CD Ehlermann, 'The Contribution of EC Competition Policy to the Single Market' (1992) Common Market Law Review 257, has clearly underlined the interplay between EC competition policy and internal market policy. For a more global analysis, which often draws on the European experience, characterized by a close alignment of trade, competition and industrial policies, see E Fox, 'Competition Law and the Agenda for the WTO: Forging the Links of Competition and Trade' (1995) Pacific Rim Law and Policy Association 1; id, 'Toward World Antitrust and Market Access' (1997) American Journal of International Law 1 (where she underlined how '[t]he leaders of the European Union have long understood the symbiosis between trade and competition law', p 4).

See also the study of the OECD, *Consistencies and Inconsistencies between Trade and Competition Policies*, Joint Group on Trade and Competition, COM/TD/DAFFE/CLP(98)25/FINAL, 1999, OECD, Paris.

[120] See, eg, A Biondi and P Eeckhout, 'State Aid and Obstacles to Trade' in A Biondi, P Eeckhout and J Flynn (eds), *The Law of State Aid in the European Union* (Oxford: Oxford University Press, 2004) 103; K Mortelmans, 'Towards Convergence in the Application of the Rules on Free Movement and on Competition?' (2001) Common Market Law Review 613; D O'Keeffe and A Bavasso, 'Four Freedoms, One Market and National Competence: In Search of a Dividing Line' in M Andenas and D Fairgrieve (eds), *Judicial Review in International Perspective: Liber Amicorum in Honour of Lord Slynn of Hadley* (London: Aspen, 2000) 541.

[121] A Biondi and P Eeckhout, 'State Aid and Obstacles to Trade' in A Biondi, P Eeckhout and J Flynn (eds), *The Law of State Aid in the European Union* (Oxford: Oxford University Press, 2004) 103, 105.

tool aiming at 'equality of competitive conditions'.[122] It should however be underlined that, according to the consistent case-law, the obligation of national treatment is breached even if the trade effects are 'insignificant or even non-existent' since 'Article III protects *expectations* not of any particular trade volume but rather of the *equal competitive relationship* between imported and domestic products'.[123] In other words, Article III of the GATT is mainly about safeguarding *competitive opportunities*.[124]

The interpretation which has been made of certain elements of Article III seems to indicate that the impact of the measure is not overlooked.[125] The *Korea—Beef* dispute is instructive in this respect. The issue was whether, under Article III:4, imported beef was treated less favourably than domestic beef by an internal regulation which required a separate retail distribution system for the former. After saying that the measure 'constitute[d] in itself differential treatment' to the detriment of imported products, the Panel carried out an attentive analysis of the impact of the dual-distribution system on the 'competitive opportunities' of imports.[126] For its part, the Appellate Body started by repeating that the controlling standard requires an examination of 'whether [the] measure modifies the conditions of competition in the relevant market to the detriment of imported products'.[127] Then, while rejecting the argument that the simple 'formal separation' of the distribution system could amount to prohibited less favourable treatment, it eventually reached the (same) conclusion that the new system meant a 'drastic reduction of commercial opportunity' for imported beef.[128] Now, the attentive analysis into the factual circumstances of both Panel and Appellate Body may be misleading. If one reads these findings carefully, what emerges is that the analysis of the impact of the measure is still centred around the preliminary level of the *competitive conditions or opportunities*[129] and does not really question the *actual negative* effect on the trade flows of those imports.[130]

In sum, despite the GATT findings indicating an assessment of some effects under the national treatment provision, this stops at the level of *market access*,

[122] Appellate Body, *Japan—Taxes II*, page 16; id, *EC—Asbestos*, para 97. This statement has its origin in GATT jurisprudence: see *US—Superfund*, para 5.1.9; *Japan—Taxes I*, para 5.5(b).

[123] Appellate Body, *Japan—Taxes II*, p 16 (emphasis added).

[124] PC Mavroidis, 'Come Together? Producer Welfare, Consumer Welfare, and WTO Rules' in EU Petersmann and J Harrison (eds), *Reforming the World Trading System—Legitimacy, Efficiency and Democratic Governance* (Oxford: Oxford University Press, 2003) 277 , 280.

[125] See, eg, Appellate Body, *Chile—Taxes*, paras 56–76, with respect to the interpretation of the expression 'applied so as to afford protection' under the second sentence of Article III:2.

[126] Panel, *Korea—Beef*, paras 629–36.

[127] Appellate Body, *Korea—Beef*, para 137.

[128] ibid, paras 143–8.

[129] ie the plain restriction produced by the dual retail system with respect to imported beef.

[130] Which was probably none, since the WTO-consistent quota for beef had been virtually fully utilized.

A reading similar to that of *Korea—Beef* can be made of other disputes on Article III of the GATT. See, eg, the *Dominican Republic—Cigarettes* dispute.

which is clearly one of the conditions necessary to compete. The analysis does not go beneath the surface to engage with the *competitive process* itself. Hence the consistency with the customary statements that the provision is only about expectations and the impact of the measure on the actual trade flows and volumes is irrelevant. In short, although there is clearly a convergence in direction, the focus of each examination remains different. The emphasis is on the protection of the competitive opportunities and not of the actual competitive process. Crucially, from a *practical* viewpoint, the outcome of both analyses may, but does not necessarily need to, be the same.[131]

With these remarks in mind, a similar exercise can be carried out with EC law. If we consider Article 28 of the EC, which prohibits quantitative restrictions and measures having an equivalent effect, it is easy to find comments emphasizing a convergence with competition law. Biondi and Eeckhout have advanced that the increasing 'emphasis on market access may lead to references to undistorted competition' and what is a required is 'but a small step'.[132] At this stage, mention is usually made of Advocate General Jacobs' analysis in *Leclerc-Siplec* where he endorsed the guiding principle '[t]hat all undertakings which engage in a legitimate economic activity in a Member State should have unfettered access to the whole of the Community market, unless there is a valid reason for denying them full access to a part of that market'.[133] In EC circles this test has been read as moving internal market rules closer to a 'competition-based' approach. In the same case, Jacobs also proposed that this 'market access' test be tempered with a *de minimis* test,[134] a sieve typical in EC competition law, and so far consistently rejected in EC internal market law.

The convergence between the trade parlance (based on barriers to trade and market access) and competition parlance (based on the effects on competition) is fascinating.[135] Despite similarities, however, a conclusion similar to that drawn

[131] These considerations may enable us to distinguish the similar terminology one sometimes finds in competition cases. A paradigmatic example in EC antitrust law is *Delimitis v Henninger Bräu* (Case C-234/89) where the ECJ clearly held that, to determine whether an exclusive purchasing agreement has the effect to distort competition, it is necessary to analyse its effects (together with those of similar agreements) on competitors' opportunities to gain access to the beer market. Despite the correspondence in language with that in the previous Article III of the GATT cases, a close reading of the EC decision shows that both the centre of interest and the degree of analysis are different. The competition case is solidly geared to comprehensively and positively evaluate the actual effect of the conduct at issue on competitor's entry into the market. If, like in GATT Article III cases, the term 'opportunity' appears, this is arguably used in a stronger sense.

[132] A Biondi and P Eeckhout, 'State Aid and Obstacles to Trade' in A Biondi, P Eeckhout, and J Flynn (eds), *The Law of State Aid in the European Union* (Oxford: Oxford University Press, 2004) 103, 106.

[133] Case C-412/93 *Lederc-Siplec*, para 41 of the Opinion.

[134] ibid, paras 42–8.

[135] Two notable examples of convergence between the two areas in EC law can be noted. One is the *Tobacco Advertizing Directive* case (Case C-376/98 *Germany v European Parliament and Council*) where the Court, in interpreting Article 95 of the EC, which empowers the Council to adopt harmonization measures for the establishment or functioning of the internal market, found that such

in the WTO context can also be made here. Internal market rules and competition rules operate differently. The Court clearly held this, noting that, despite their objective possibly being the 'same',[136] 'the application of those provisions presupposes distinct conditions peculiar to the two kinds of State measure which they are intended to govern and they differ, furthermore, as to their legal consequences', particularly with respect to the implementation and the leading role played by the European Commission in the State aid field.[137] In other words: 'in the internal market area there is no need to prove the actual effects of the trade measure for the prohibition to apply. It is enough to show that the measures are potentially restrictive of the exchanges.'[138]

But, leaving aside for a moment the difference in focus and operation between trade and competition rules, what is the element underlying the convergence between the trade and competition laws and policies?

In the EC context, Biondi and Eeckhout (relying on the consistent case-law) formulate a sweeping conclusion:

> [t]he assumption upon which the entire reasoning is based is the recognition that both sets of rules are pursuing an *identical* aim, namely that of ensuring the free movement of goods under normal conditions of competition.[139]

O'Keeffe and Bavasso noted that 'the aim of creating an internal market constitutes a unifying thread or, at least, an interface between EC internal trade law and EC competition law'.[140] Both sets of rules are therefore clearly going in the same

measures must genuinely contribute to such an objective. In particular, with a significant equation, the Court noted that these measures must either contribute to eliminating obstacles to free movement or they must purport to eliminate an appreciable distortion of competition.

The other example is the *Wouters* decision (in Case C-309/99) which has clearly shown a convergence between Articles 81 and 82 EC on the one side and free movement rules on the other, particularly at the level of the operation of the justification.

[136] And using a language strikingly similar to that of the GATT/WTO by referring to the 'distortion of the *conditions* of competition' within the internal market (emphasis added).

[137] See, eg, Case C-234/99 *Nygård*, para 55.

[138] JL Buendia-Sierra, 'Not like this: Some Skeptical Remarks on the "Refined Economic Approach" in State aid', in Proceedings of 4th Experts' Forum on New Developments in European State Aid Law, 18th and 19th May 2006, European State Aid Law Institute (Berlin: Lexxion, 2006) 59, 62.

It should be noted that Buendia-Sierra utters these words to confirm his view, outlined in the previous paragraph, that EC State aid law should *not* belong to competition logic but should be construed similarly with EC internal market rules (and in line with that case-law which does not require a State aid to produce actual effects on trade and competition). The comment of Buendia-Sierra is all the more true when discrimination is involved. A paradigmatic example is Case 249/81 *Buy Irish*, paras 25 and 26.

[139] A Biondi and P Eeckhout, 'State Aid and Obstacles to Trade' in A Biondi, P Eeckhout, and J Flynn (eds), *The Law of State Aid in the European Union* (Oxford: Oxford University Press, 2004) 103, 108 (emphasis added).

[140] D O'Keeffe and A Bavasso, 'Four Freedoms, One Market and National Competence: In Search of a Dividing Line' in M Andenas and D Fairgrieve (eds), *Judicial Review in International Perspective: Liber Amicorum in Honour of Lord Slynn of Hadley* (London: Aspen, 2000) 541, 543.

direction, that of the liberation of the economic forces of the market. The 'unifying thread' or 'interface' between the two disciplines—and this applies to both the EC and the WTO—is the goal of creating a place, the market, where competition and trade occur.

Now, assuming that the target is the same, or in any event similar, the duties are complementary but different. In particular, the difference between trade and competition rules is not only *conceptual* but, as has been underlined in the analysis of both legal systems, mostly *practical*. It concerns the operation of the rules.

In the application of competition law, the attention shifts from the level of mere 'conditions and opportunities' to that of 'effects'. This analysis usually enquires about the impact of competitive relationships, the behaviour of the economic players, and significantly rests on economic analysis.[141] The OECD highlights this difference:

> at a risk of some over-simplification . . . competition policy emphasises a fact specific, case by case approach. . . . Similarly, competition policy often emphasises issues of actual competition in particular markets, while trade policy often focuses on issues of potential competition in the sense of safeguarding competitive opportunities. . . . These differences may have implications for the means and mechanisms employed by both policies . . .[142]

Therefore, it is the emphasis and operation that differ. The effects of a measure (and their assessment) do indeed involve various consequential stages or steps, and these may be set in a progressive sequence. Terms such as 'competitive' 'opportunities' and 'conditions', 'potential' or 'actual' 'impact' or 'effects', and even 'market access', may mean many things, depending on the step of the causal chain in which they are set, and on the aim and context of their assessment. They may demand a more or less exacting empirical or economic analysis.[143] Although, as the OECD warns, we should not be tempted into easy generalizations and reach the absolute conclusion of a neat divide between trade and competitions rules, a discriminant does exist and is constituted by the *focus* of the rules, and policies, which alternatively may be more on the safeguard of trade flows (read: market access), on the working of competition, or in between, in the land where trade openings intersect

[141] On the premise that trade policy and competition law have 'different aims and premises', Tarullo notes that, from the trade policy perspective, '[w]hether foreign markets are workably competitive in an economic sense is essentially irrelevant'. See DK Tarullo, 'Norms and Institutions in Global Competition Policy' (2000) American Journal of International Law 478, 483.

[142] OECD, *Consistencies and Inconsistencies between Trade and Competition Policies*, Joint Group on Trade and Competition, COM/TD/DAFFE/CLP(98)25/FINAL, 1999, OECD, Paris, para 18.

[143] Thus, for example, the operation of trade rules is usually triggered as soon as the measure (eg unlawful tariff or quota) has been found to exist. Alternatively, if some sort of enquiry of the impact of the measure (eg differential tax or regulation) on the 'equality of the conditions of competition' is to be done, this would hardly go as far as demanding proof of an actual distortion of the competitive process and, to do so, base itself on economic analysis.

with competition opportunities. Importantly, this difference in focus may (not necessarily must) have an influence on *how* rules *actually work*.[144]

Returning to the image evoked by Biondi and Eeckhout, a small step, but still *a* step, between 'market access' and 'competition' is required.

Conclusion: a matter of practical importance

The analysis lends itself quite readily to conclusions.

As indicated by its language and position in the EC treaty (in Chapter 1 of Title VI on the 'rules on competition'), State aid law is clearly a competition regulation and should be interpreted and applied as such. While there is a close relation to the internal market objective and to its rules,[145] the determination of whether the measure 'distorts competition' remains a requirement.

This should generally involve an assessment of the impact of the measure on the behaviour of economic agents, and, in particular, the effect of the measure on the cost/revenue structure of the subsidy recipient and on the consequent harm to (at least) equally efficient competitors. This may rely on the use of economic analysis.[146]

The same conclusion applies to WTO law. If it is true that subsidies can be viewed as barriers to trade, and that some provisions in the GATT/WTO (like the standard of NVNI) have been introduced with this concern in mind, the analysis in this chapter has shown that the deepest concern raised by subsidies is their possible negative impact on the competitive process, and accordingly found that this is one of the most important justifications for regulating subsidies. It is natural therefore that rules and tests should take this crucial factor (the 'mischief' of the discipline) into account. Now, if the focus and operation of the relevant rules is based on the effects of the measure on the competitive process, subsidy regulation cannot but be regarded—ie drafted and, so far as possible, interpreted—as competition law. In the end, more than a terminological or conceptual nicety, it is a practical difference that matters.[147]

[144] If it is true that trade rules do not employ a comprehensive effects analysis, it is known that, in significant cases, competition law too resorts to *per se* rules and presumptions, or is satisfied with evidence of a mere 'threat' of damage. In all these cases, an empirical or economic analysis is postponed, taken for granted, or, more simply, not done at all. This rigorous approach makes competition rules similar to trade rules.

[145] See chapter 6, section III for an analysis of the interplay between State aid and other rules, particularly internal market rules.

[146] These issues, and in particular the required impact standards, are analysed in detail in chapter 14.

[147] The crucial point is repeated that considering a set of rules as trade or competition may be important in practical terms. The tests may differ, and, as a consequence, we may end up with situations of 'over-inclusion' (ie rules covering measures that should not be convered) or 'under-inclusion' (ie rules covering measures that should be covered). Typically, the former case may occur if we adopt a stricter 'trade' approach, the latter a more flexible 'competition' one. These issues are analysed at length in chapter 14.

III. The operation of subsidy control in the WTO and EC: overview and critique

After examining the goals that a system of subsidy control could have, and those that are actually pursued by the WTO and the EC, the operation of the two legal systems at issue is briefly examined. This serves to provide the reader with a background understanding of the substantive and procedural framework built up on the actual definition of subsidy. An important finding is that, as with the goals of the system of subsidy control and the more general goals of the whole legal system, the 'operative rules' too (ie those on remedies, procedures, institutions) are closely connected to the actual definition of subsidy and may actually have an impact on it. The final section makes some critical remarks on how subsidy rules, control and remedies could be devised.

A. Summary of WTO and EC rules

The WTO subsidy regime

From GATT to WTO

Only two provisions in the GATT explictly regulate subsidies. On the one hand, Article VI essentially provides that the importing country may impose countervailing duties on subsidized imports that cause or threaten material injury to an established domestic industry. On the other hand, Article XVI:1 introduces a duty to notify all subsidies increasing exports of, or reducing imports to, the subsidizing country and a consultation procedure for limiting subsidization that causes serious prejudice to other countries. Three paragraphs of Article XVI deal with export subsidies[148] and, although fairly inaccurate, and largely ineffective,[149] already show a more stringent treatment of this type of subsidy.[150]

It cannot pass unnoticed that, from the normative perspective, the difference between trade and competition regulation follows the distinction between 'rules' and 'standards'. This will be taken up again in the critical discussion of how subsidy control regulation may be shaped. See section III below.

[148] In particular, 'contracting parties' should 'seek to avoid' the grant of subsidies on the exports of primary products, or, in any event, to guarantee that their application does not result 'in that contracting party having more than an equitable share of world export trade in that product' (Article XVI:3). Export subsidies to 'any product other than a primary product resulting in the sale of that product at a price lower than the comparable price charged for the like product in the domestic market' are prohibited (Article XVI:4).

[149] As disputes have shown, the most troublesome parts of these two provisions concerned the 'equitable share' language in para 3 and the 'bilevel pricing' test in para 4. See HC Hufbauer and J Shelton Erb, *Subsidies in International Trade* (Cambridge, Massachusetts: MIT Press, 1984) chapter 3. See also RE Hudec, *Enforcing International Trade Law—The Evolution of the Modern GATT Legal System* (Salem, New Hampshire: Buttherworth Legal Publishers 1993).

[150] It is worth remembering that, in 1960, a Working Party drafted a list of measaures considered as forms of export subsidies: GATT Working Party Report of 19 November 1960 on the Provisions of Article XVI:4, BISD 95/185 (1961) 186–7.

In 1979 the first general comprehensive plurilateral discipline on subsidies and countervailing measures was adopted.[151] The 'Tokyo Round Subsidies Code' represents an important advancement in the regulation of subsidies at global level.[152] The code expanded the GATT's obligations. Track I explained in more detail the procedure leading to the imposition of countervailing duties and the concept of injury. Track II dealt with the discipline on the grant of subsidies affecting international trade. It reinforced the prohibition on export subsidies, introduced a regulation of domestic subsidies, and partly developed enforcement and remedies.[153]

The Tokyo Code showed an ambivalent attitude towards domestic subsidies, recognizing that they may be used to promote important objectives of social and economic policy, and that, at the same time, they may cause adverse effects to the interests of other signatories.[154] This ambivalence was particularly evident in Article 11 which combined the recognition of the important goals pursued by governments with the use of domestic subsidies, providing a rich list of examples in this regard,[155] with the subsequent invitation on the contracting parties to avoid such practices that 'adversely affect the conditions of normal competition'. How and where the balance was to be struck was not however clear.

The WTO Agreement includes a new discipline on subsidies, the Agreement on Subsidies and Countervailing Measures (SCM Agreement). The SCM Agreement upgrades the discipline of the Tokyo Code in various respects.[156] For the first time a comprehensive definition of subsidy is introduced along with the concept of specificity. The actual discipline of subsidies, that is the determination of whether, and to what extent, they are legitimate, is far more clear than in the 'limbo' of Article 11 of the Tokyo Round Subsidies Code. Subsidies are clearly regulated under different 'categories' (the three original ones will be analysed below) with different procedural arrangements and remedies.[157]

[151] Agreement on Interpretation and Application of Articles VI, XVI and XXIII of the General Agreeement on Tariffs and Trade, GATT, BISD 26 Supp. 56 (1980) (Tokyo Round Subsidies Code).

[152] Although its impact was somewhat diminished because it was only binding on its signatories.

[153] One the one hand, it clarified the notification obligation under GATT Article XVI and the ensuing countries' peer-control (Article 7). On the other hand, it explictly disciplined consultations and dispute settlement which could lead, in the case of non-compliance with the Committee's recommendations, to the authorization of 'such countermeasures as may be appropriate' (Articles 12 and 13).

[154] Article 8:1.

[155] These were: 'a) To eliminate industrial, economic, and social disadvantages of specific regions; b) to facilitate the restructuring, under socially acceptable conditions, of certain sectors, especially where this has become necessary by reason of changes in trade and economic policies, including international agreements resulting in lower barriers to trade; c) generally to sustain employment and to encourage retraining and change in employment; d) to encourage research and development programmes, especially in the field of high-technology industries; e) to implement economic programmes and policies to promote the economic and social development of developing countries; f) to redeploy industry in order to avoid congestion and environmental problems.'

[156] First of all, being part of the WTO's single package', it is binding on all WTO Members.

[157] Further, building on the Tokyo Code, the SCM Agreement provides for more favourable treatment such as grace periods and exemptions for developing countries and economies in transition.

With respect to enforcement, through the Committee on Subsidies, notification and surveillance procedures are enhanced. Notification duties are developed, both in terms of content and regularity. The right of Members to seek information and clarification on a given programme is slightly increased. The Committee should thus operate as a 'clearing house' of 'peer-control'. Overall, however, the system does not seem to be particularly efficient. Members do not notify, and institutionalized peer control seems to have been replaced with a more confrontational approach.

As regards remedies, the two tracks of dispute settlement or unilateral countervailing duty action are confirmed and developed.[158] The big WTO development to which reference should be made is the newly established mechanism of dispute settlement (DSM).[159] In particular, Panels and the Appellate Body can review complaints regarding subsidy programmes adopted by Members. Depending on the category of subsidy, they may recommend the removal of the effects of the subsidy or even its withdrawal. They may also review national countervailing duty laws and their application by domestic agencies.

While there is no comprehensive regulation of subsidies in the Agreeement on Trade in Services (GATS),[160] more substantive obligations can be found in the Agreement on Agriculture (AG) which, in a nutshell, permits both export and domestic subsidies on certain agricultural products but subjects them to negotiated reduction commitments.[161]

One subsidy, three categories

One of the most significant characteristics of the regulation of industrial (ie non-agricultural and non-service) subsidies in the WTO is its 'taxonomic approach'. Subsidies are divided into categories according to the different impact they allegedly produce on international trade and competition.[162] The SCM Agreement initially provided three categories, those of 'prohibited', 'actionable' and 'non-actionable'

[158] Both avenues are possible although only one remedy can eventually be applied. See note 35 to Article 10 of the SCM.

[159] '. . . dispute settlement has become a matter of compulsory jurisdiction for all WTO Members. It is this compulsory character that distinguishes it from all other existing international dispute settlement systems': CD Ehlermann, 'Six Years on the Bench of the "World Trade Court": Some Personal Experiences as Member of the Appellate Body of the World Trade Organization' (2002) Journal of World Trade, 605, 607. See chapter 1, section II.C for the important topic of the rules on legal interpretation adopted by the DSM.

[160] Article XV principally calls upon Members to enter into negotiations with a view to developing the necessary multilateral disciplines to avoid trade-distorting effects. At the time of writing, no significant results seem to have resulted from these negotiations, mostly carried out in the context of the Doha Round. Further, in case of subsidies causing adverse consequences, consultations can be requested and 'shall be accorded sympathetic consideration'.

[161] In the context of the analysis of this book, some provisions of the AG that are particularly useful for definitional purposes will be referred to.

[162] These categories find their origin in the distinction between export and domestic subsidies, and their alleged or real impact, underlined above.

subsidies. Although the last one lapsed in 2000, it will be analysed briefly to assess its significance.

'Prohibited subsidies' include first export subsidies, ie those that are 'contingent' on export performance. To these are equated 'local-content' (or 'import-substitution') subsidies, ie those that are 'contigent' on the use of domestic over imported goods. These subsidies, particularly export ones, have always been perceived to pose a special threat to international trade and competition, they are difficult to justify in terms of legitimate domestic policy objectives and raise serious concerns over the prospect of mutually destructive subsidy wars.[163] Consequently, their discipline has always been particularly rigorous, with the ultimate result that in the WTO they are simply prohibited: 'a Member shall neither grant nor maintain' them, reads Article 3.2 of the SCM. In other words, the SCM Agreement does not require the establishment of any specificity or distortion. The occurrence of negative externalities, and serious ones, is presumed. Being prohibited, if granted, these subsidies must simply be 'withdrawn'.[164]

One of the most interesting issues that has arisen concerns the exact reach of this remedy. The controversial Panel report in *Australia—Leather (Article 21.5)* clarified this point, holding that, in the case of paid non-recurring subsidies, the term 'withdraw', in order to have some meaning, should encompass a retroactive repayment.[165] This report was so controversial that it came close to not being adopted because of a real chance of negative consensus within the DSB.[166] Aware of the issue, Panels and the Appellate Body in subsequent disputes have carefully

[163] Although supporting the prohibition of export subsidies, Sykes criticizes the similar treatment imposed on 'local content' subsidies. See AO Sykes, 'The Economics of WTO Rules on Subsidies and Countervailing Measures', Chicago John M Olin Law and Economics Working Paper No. 186 (2nd Series) May 2003,

[164] If the recommendation to withdraw the prohibited subsidy is not followed, the DSB can authorize the adoption of 'appropriate countermeasures'. See Article 4.10 of the SCM.

[165] According to the Panel, 'where any repayment of any amount of a past subsidy is required or made, this by its very nature is **not** a purely prospective remedy. No theoretical construct allocating the subsidy over time can alter this fact. In our view, if the term "withdraw the subsidy" can properly be understood to encompass repayment of **any** portion of a prohibited subsidy, "retroactive effect" exists' (para 6.22, the bold style is used in the original text). After considering the principles of Article 31 of the Vienna Convention of the Law of Treaties (VCLT) and the principle of effectivenesss, the Panel concluded that 'based on the ordinary meaning of the term "withdraw the subsidy", read in context, and in light of its object and purpose, and in order to give it effective meaning, [. . .] the recommendation to "withdraw the subsidy" provided for in Article 4.7 of the SCM Agreement is **not** limited to prospective action only but may encompass repayment of the prohibited subsidy' (para 6.39, the bold style is used in the original text).

The repayment, however, does not imply that interest should be paid as, according to the Panel, the remedy at issue is not 'intended to fully restore the *status quo ante* by depriving the recipient of the prohibited subsidy of the benefits it may have enjoyed in the past. Nor do we consider it to be a remedy intended to provide reparation or compensation in any sense' (para 6.49). This has led some to distinguish and conclude that the *Australia—Leather (Article 21.5)* Panel introduced some 'retrospectivity' but not real 'retroactivity'.

[166] See DSB, Minutes of Meeting, WT/DSB/M/75, of 7 March 2000.

avoided applying that drastic remedy.[167] The issue of prospective (only) or (partly) retrospective remedies is highly sensitive. It goes straight to the core of one of the most important issues in any legal system. The issue, and extent of remedies, is about making rules effective, and their breach ineffective. These sorts of questions are even more crucial and sensitive in the context of WTO law, and more generally in international law, where the general rule is that remedies are only for the future.[168]

Domestic subsidies are regulated under the second and third categories. Subsidies are 'actionable' if they cause 'adverse effects' to the interests of other Members. These effects, which follow the GATT terminology already present in the Tokyo Round Subsidies Code, are defined in Article 5 of the SCM as:

(a) injury to the domestic industry of another Member;
(b) nullification or impairment of benefits accruing directly or indirectly to other Members under GATT 1994, in particular the benefits of concessions bound under Article II of GATT 1994;
(c) serious prejudice to the interest of another Member.

Before turning to their discipline, it may be useful to spend a few minutes on the meaning of these tests which are analysed in chapter 14 in full.

The concept of 'injury' to the domestic industry is used in the same sense as in the context of countervailing duty and anti-dumping duty procedures. Article 15 of the SCM specifies this concept in great detail. The term 'nullification or impairment' (NI) has the same meaning as in the relevant provisions of GATT 1994, notably Article XXIII:1 and, 'in particular', to item (b) 'non-violation' situations where we have a 'breach' of the 'GATT bargain' described in section II.A above. In particular, it concerns those cases of 'non-violation nullification or impairment' (NVNI) where a Member that has given a tariff concession acts in a way that—despite not contravening any specific GATT obligations—nonetheless denies the competitive opportunity that other Members could reasonably expect. With regard to the 'serious prejudice' standard, Article 6 of the SCM provides a thorough elaboration. The resulting discipline is quite complex. The first paragraph,

[167] See, eg, Appellate Body, *US—FSC*, para 178. A retrospective remedy was not asked for in the case. Considering its factual background (a widespread export tax exemption granted for years), if it had been asked for, and granted, one can imagine the devasting economic consequences for the losing party (and its economy).

[168] Against this background, it is noteworthy that the *Australia—Leather (Article 21.5)* Panel confirmed that 'withdraw the subsidy' is *different* from 'bring the measure into conformity' in Article 19.1 of the DSU (paras 6.30–6.31 and 6.41–6.42). Accordingly, 'that a "retrospective" remedy might not be permissible under Article 19.1 of the DSU (a question which we do not here decide) does not preclude us from concluding, on the basis of the text of Article 4.7 of the SCM Agreement, that "withdraw the subsidy" is **not** limited to purely prospective action, but may encompass repayment of prohibited subsidies' (para 6.42, the bold style is used in the original text).

For an analysis of the issue of remedies in the WTO see the critical notes below.

which lapsed in the year 2000, originally laid down some presumptions,[169] which could be rebutted demonstrating that the subsidy had not produced any of the effects described in the crucial paragraph 3. This provision concludes that a 'serious prejudice may arise' if one or more of the 'effects of the subsidy' enlisted therein are present.[170]

We come now to the treatment of 'actionable' subsidies. Whereas 'prohibited' subsidies cannot be granted or maintained, in this case, Members should simply not cause 'adverse effects', in any of the form of NVNI, serious prejudice or injury outlined above. Admittedly, if these effects are removed the Member may continue to grant the subsidy. The DSB may determine that the subsidy 'should be withdrawn' or that 'appropriate steps' should be taken 'to remove the adverse effects'.[171] What is not clear is whether, as in the case of prohibited subsidies, the withdrawal of actionable subsidies has some retrospective effect, requiring their repayment. For the same argument used above, aimed at guaranteeing the *effet utile* of the provision, this is probably the case at least for 'non-recurring' subsidies.

The second category of domestic subsidies (now expired) was one of the new features of the WTO regulation.[172] These subsidies were neither actionable nor countervailable because they were considered non-distorting or because they served economic and social objectives of overriding importance. These measures, whose requirements were spelled out in detail in Article 8 of the SCM Agreement, included subsidies for research activities, for tackling regional disadvantages, and for promoting the adoption of environmental standards.[173] Procedurally, any of

[169] A serious prejudice was deemed to exist when (i) subsidization exceeded a certain percentage of the product value (normally 5%); (ii) in case of subsidies to cover operating losses to an industry or enterprise (unless, in the latter case, they were a non-recurrent measure and were given merely to provide time for the development of long-term solutions and to avoid acute social problems); and (iii) when debt was directly forgiven, or when grants to cover that debt were given.

[170] These effects are (a) displacement or impediment of imports of a like product of another Member into the subsidizing Member's market; (b) displacement or impediment of exports of a like product of another Member from a third country market; (c) significant price undercutting of the subsidized product as compared with the price of a like produce of another Member, significant price suppression, depression, or lost sales in the same market; (d) increase in the world market share of the subsidizing Member in a particular subsidized primary product.

It should be highlighted that, from an evidential perspective, these 'effects' have a double relevance for the determination of serious prejudice. On the one hand, if one of them is established, serious prejudice *may* arise (Article 6.3). On the other, if it is proved that none of them is present then *no* serious prejudice may be established (Article 6.2).

[171] According to Article 7.9 of the SCM, in the event that 'appropriate steps' to remove those effects or to withdraw the subsidy have not been taken, and that the parties have not agreed on some form of compensation, the DSB may authorize countermeasures 'commensurate with the degree and nature of the adverse effects'.

[172] As said, this category lapsed in the year 2000 as it was not possible to reach a consensus to extend their application, along with that of Article 6.1 of the SCM, 'either as presently drafted or in a modified form' (Article 31 of the SCM).

[173] In particular, Article 8.2 of the SCM refers to the following three categories of non-actionable subsidies:

(a) subsidies for research activities conducted by firms or by higher education or research establishments on a contract basis with firms if, in particular, the assistance does not exceed a certain

these subsidies should have been notified 'in advance of its implementation' to the Committee on Subsidies and there was a review system.[174] Crucially, the satisfaction of all legal requirements did not make the subsidy in question completely safe. If it were proved that a subsidy otherwise complying with these, and hence in principle 'non-actionable', was in fact causing '*serious* adverse effects' to the domestic industry of a Member (such as to cause damage that would have been difficult to repair), consultations could be requested.[175] If no mutually acceptable solution could be reached, the matter was referred to the Committee which could have recommended the modification of the programme to remove the effects, but, significantly, not the 'withdrawal' of the subsidy.

The EC State aid regime

The main features of the EC State aid system of control were already present since its inception in 1957.

From the substantive point of view, the main provision is Article 87 of the EC which reads in its first paragraph that:

> save as otherwise provided in this Treaty, any aid granted by a Member State or through State resources in any form whatsoever which distorts or threatens to distort competition by favouring certain undertakings or the production of certain goods shall, in so far as in affects trade between Member States, be incompatible with the common market.

This provision, which outlines the 'definition' of State aid, and will therefore be subject to extensive dissection and analysis in the following chapters, already outlines, in its opening and closing words, two interesting features.

First, a measure with those requirements, which expressly include the 'distortion competition', is 'incompatible with the common market'. The link between State aid and internal market functioning is already present at the definitional level.[176] Secondly, the incipit makes it clear that there are other provisions in the Treaty of

cost level, depending on whether the activity is of 'industrial research' (75%) or 'pre-competitive development' (50%), and if it is limited to certain classes of costs;

(b) subsidies in favour of disadvantaged regions given pursuant to a general framework of regional development and non-specific within eligible regions provided that the region is clearly definable, it is considered as disadvantaged on the basis of neutral and objective criteria such as income or GDP per capita or the unemployment rate;

(c) subsidies to promote adaptation of existing facilities to new environmental requirements imposed by law and/or regulations which result in greater constraints and financial burden on firms, provided that the assistance is *inter alia* a one-time non-recurring measure, limited to 20% of the cost of adaptation, directly linked to and proportionate to the plan of reduction of nuisances and pollution, and is available to all firms that can adopt the new equipment or production processes.

[174] A system of yearly updates of the notification, including, in particular, information on modification of the subsidy programmes, was also envisaged. Further, on request by a Member, the Secretariat and the Committee should have reviewed the notifications to determine whether the conditions and criteria laid down above had been met. See Article 9 of the SCM.

[175] As underlined by the emphasis, the impact standard under this category was stricter than 'adverse effects' of 'actionable' subsidies'.

[176] On the interplay between State aid and internal market rules see chapter 6, section III.

Rome which can rebut the preliminary conclusion of 'incompatibility'. The main references are Articles 87(2) and (3) of the EC on the one hand and Article 86(2) (which provides a general justification for the safe performance of public services) on the other.[177] Article 87(2) of the EC provides three forms of State aid (which, overall, are of limited importance) that 'shall' be automatically compatible with the common market.[178] Article 87(3) of the EC is certainly a provision with a bigger impact which deserves full analysis. It reads:

> The following may be considered to be compatible with the common market:
>
> (a) aid to promote the economic development of areas where the standard of living is abnormally low or where there is serious underemployment;
>
> (b) aid to promote the execution of an important project of common European interest or to remedy a serious disturbance in the economy of a Member State;
>
> (c) aid to facilitate the development of certain economic activities or of certain economic areas, where such aid does not adversely affect trading conditions to an extent contrary to the common interest;
>
> (d) aid to promote culture and heritage conservation where such aid does not affect trading conditions and competition in the Community to an extent that is contrary to the common interest;
>
> (e) such other categories of aid as may be specified by decision of the Council acting by a qualified majority on a proposal from the Commission.

The justifications of State aid in the EC Treaty thus find their recognition in rather general clauses. The monopoly for their application has been for the European Commission which is held to enjoy a wide discretion in the complex economic and political assessment. If the welfare analysis of subsidies means that its assessment of market failures and distortions of competition naturally involves the often difficult balancing of values and effects, this is particularly true in the European legal order, where EC State aid policy does not stand in a vacuum but is influenced by other EC objectives and policies, primarily by the internal market.[179]

The broad language of Article 87(3) of the EC has allowed the Commission to consider various objectives and to slowly develop its State aid policy. In terms of normative development, the trend can be described as follows. We passed from the interpretation of general clauses to policy definition and consolidation, often

[177] This provision, and its role in the State aid debate, particularly with respect to the issue of the financing of public services, will be analysed in the case-study closing chapter 11.

[178] These are: 'a) aid having social character, granted to individual consumers, provided that such aid is granted without discrimination related to the origin of the products concerned; b) aid to make good the damage caused for natural disasters or exceptional occurrences; c) aid granted to the economy of certain areas of the Federal Republic of Germany affected by the division of Germany, in so far as such aid is required in order to compensate for the economic disadvantages caused by that division.'

[179] The discretional element inherent in this policy-creation exercise is clear not only if we consider the broad language of the individual categories but, more simply, one little word in the *chapeau* of para 3: 'The following *may* be considered to be compatible with the common market' (emphasis added).

tested before the Community Courts. Individual decisions have built up a practice which, for the sake of good administration, transparency and legal certainy, has been increasingly codified in the form of various 'soft law' instruments (letters, communications, notices, guidelines, frameworks) to eventually reach, in some cases, the stage of 'hard law'. The final step of the process, which leads to a significant change in the governance of EC State aid law, is the adoption of 'block exemptions' regulations. The underlying concept, already successfully trialed in antitrust law, is to render automatically permissible (ie without any prior authorization) State aid measures that pursue horizontal objectives and that satisfy the prescribed conditions. The most dramatic development in this regard is the recent entry into force of a single 'General Block Exemption Regulation' (GBER).[180] The main principles inspiring the GBER, and the most recent action of DG Competition, are those of the already mentioned 'State Aid Action Plan' adopted in the summer of 2005.[181] The buzz-words are 'more-refined economic analysis', more transparency and legislative consolidation, cooperation between Commission and Member States in State aid governance.

The GBER covers different types of State aid, notably aid for regional development, SMEs, research, development and innovation, environment, employment, training, social aid (for disabled or otherwise disadvantaged workers) and aid for promoting female enterpreneurship.[182] Apart from the GBER, and leaving aside sectoral aid,[183] there is a comprehensive and complex legislation on justifications which is (still) often embodied in 'soft law' instruments.[184] Just to give a flavour of this, a few documents, based on Article 87(3)(a) and (c) of the EC, may be noted such as the guidelines on environmental aid,[185] on rescue and restructuring aid[186] and regional aid,[187] the frameworks on aid for research, development and

[180] Commission Regulation (EC) No. 800/2008 of 6 August 2008 declaring certain categories of aid compatible with the common market in application of Articles 87 and 88 of the Treaty ('General block exemption regulation') OJ L214, 9.8.2008, 3. The impact of this instrument, which entered into force in late August 2008, has still to be tested. It is a crucial step in the procedural administration of EC State aid that should mean decentralization and simplification, and ultimately lead to freeing resources to be better used in the control of more troublesome cases of State aid.

[181] Commission, State Aid Action Plan—Less and better targeted aid: a roadmap for state aid reform 2005–2009 ('SAAP'), consultation document, 7 June 2005. See section II.C above.

[182] The block exemption applies only if certain conditions, mainly referring to aid intensities and cost-eligibility, transparency and incentive effect, are present.

[183] Covering sectors such as coal, steel, shipbuilding, public service broadcasting, postal services, cinematographic and other audiovisual works.

[184] In this fast developing area, an excellent and handy overview is offered by the *Vademecum on State Aid Rules* which is regularly updated by the Commission (the latest edition states the law as of 30.9.2008).

[185] Community Guidelines on State aid for environmental protection, OJ C 82 of 01.04.2008, 1.

[186] Community Guidelines on State aid for rescuing and restructuring firms in difficulty, OJ C 244, 1.10.2004, 2.

[187] Guidelines on national regional aid for 2007–2013, OJ C 54, 4.3.2006, 13–45.

innovation,[188] and the communications in response to the current economic and financial crisis.[189]

Strong enforcement and (procedural and substantive) remedies constitute the two characteristic features of the EC system of State aid control, making it unique, particularly if contrasted with the WTO.

From the enforcement perspective, the cornerstone of the EC system of State aid control is that Member States are under two closely connected obligations which can be derived from Article 88(3) of the EC. First, they have to notify any proposed new aid, or alteration of existing aid, to the European Commission.[190] Secondly, they cannot implement their plans until the Commission has given the green light.[191] The Commission's role of exclusive arbiter to determine whether a State aid, otherwise prohibited under Article 87(1) of the EC, is nonetheless 'compatible with the common market', is protected by national courts that act as guardians of the compliance with the procedural obligations of notification and non-implementation ('standstill').[192] The most dramatic consequence of this role is the power to order the recovery of State aid granted 'unlawfully', ie without having being notified to and/or authorized by the Commission. In other words, aid that is procedurally unlawful.

Through the years the Court has laid down important principles in this regard, to guarantee the full effectiveness of the preventive control of the Commission, and creating a very strong 'procedural remedy'. It has accordingly held that the 'standstill' obligation gives rise to subjective rights in favour of individuals that

[188] Community Framework for State aid for Research and Development and Innovation, OJ C 323 of 30.12.2006, 1.

[189] The Commission has adopted four communications so far: (1) Communication from the Commission—The application of State aid rules to measures taken in relation to financial institutions in the context of the current global financial crisis (2008/C 270/02) adopted on 13.13.2008, OJ C270, 25.10.2008, 8 ('banking communication'); (2) Communication from the Commission—The recapitalisation of financial institutions in the current financial crisis: limitation of aid to the minimum necessary and safeguards against undue distortions of competition adopted on 8.12.2008, OJ C10, 15.1.2009, 2 ('recapitalization communication'); (3) Communication from the Commission—Temporary framework for State aid measures to support access to finance in the current financial and economic crisis—adopted on 17.12.2008 and amended on 25.2.2009, consolidated version published in OJ C83, 7.4.2009, 1 ('temporary framework'); (4) Communication from the Commission on the Treatment of Impaired Assets in the Community Banking Sector, adopted on 25.2.2009 ('impaired assets communication').

[190] 'Existing' aids are subject to the constant review of the Commission pursuant to Article 88(1) of the EC and Regulation (EC) No. 659/1999 of 22 March 1999 laying down detailed rules for the application of Article 93 of the EC Treaty, OJ L83, 27 March 1999, 1.

[191] The role of the Council, which directly represents the interests of the Member States, is limited to 'exceptional circumstances'. See Article 88(2), second and third sentences, EC. See also Case C-110/02 *Commission v Council*.

[192] Which depends on one of the main constitutional feature of EC law, ie direct effect. On their part, Community courts may be involved in two ways. On the one hand, the Court of First Instance (CFI) may review the decisions adopted by the Commission. On the other hand, the European Court of Justice (ECJ) may clarify, via preliminary rulings, any doubt national courts might have on the definition of State aid in their watchdog role of Member States duties.

national courts are bound to safeguard. In particular, national courts must offer the certain prospect that all the necessary inferences will be drawn, in accordance with their national law, as regards the validity of measures giving effect to the aid, the recovery of financial support granted in disregard of that provision, and possible interim measures.[193] As national courts and the Commission fulfil complementary and separate roles, the fact that the Commission is investigating a given aid measure does not release the national courts from their duty to safeguard the rights of individuals in the event of a breach of the prohibition of implementation.[194]

Further, it has been consistently held that, even when the Commission eventually approves the aid as being compatible with the common market, that decision does not have the effect of regularizing *ex post facto* a measure that is still procedurally invalid, since otherwise the direct effect of that prohibition would be impaired and the interests of individuals would be disregarded.[195] This is the ultimate consequence of the force of the procedural remedies, particularly with respect to the repayment of unlawful aid, national courts could award. The Court of Justice repeatedly underlined that any other interpretation would have the effect of according a favourable outcome to the non-observance by the Member Sate concerned of the last sentence of Article 88(3) of the EC, and would deprive that provision of its effectiveness.[196]

A recent decision of the the Court in the *CELF II* case has apparently mitigated this consolidated stance.[197] If the unlawful aid is eventually declared compatible by the Commission, 'Community law does not impose an obligation of full recovery of the unlawful aid'.[198] To avoid any undue advantage deriving from the precocious implementation of the aid, as a matter of EC law, national courts must only order the 'aid recipient to pay interest in respect of the period of unlawfulness'.[199] Crucially, it is for domestic law to determine whether further remedies, such as the recovery of the unlawful aid or the compensation for damage caused by the unlawful implementation, are appropriate.[200]

The old solution was not fully practical. Following the recovery, the Member State could re-implement the aid declared 'compatible', even immediately. What was guaranteed by the strict consequences of this remedy, however, was the full effectiveness of the system of control. Against the previous consolidated case-law,

[193] Case C-354/90 *FNCE*, para 12.

[194] Case C-29/94 *SFEI v La Poste*, paras 41 and 44.

[195] Case C-354/90 *FNCE*, para 16. It is also interesting to note that, under Article 14.1 of Regulation No. 659/1999, which codifies the previous practice, the Commission too shall order the recovery of any unlawful aid but only when it adopts a negative decision.

[196] Case C-354/90 *FNCE*, para 16; Case C-39/94 *SFEI v La Poste*, paras 45 and 69.

[197] C-199/06 *Centre d'exportation du livre français (CELF) and Ministre de la Culture et de la Communication v Société internationale de diffusion et d'édition (SIDE)*. Advocate General Mazak delivered a contrary Opinion.

[198] *CELF II*, para 46.

[199] ibid, para 52.

[200] ibid, para 53.

the first impression given by the *CELF II* decision is that of a drastic retreat. One is left with the question of whether, by delegating the power to impose more far reaching remedies on national courts and national law, the effectiveness of EC State aid control ends up diminished.[201] Will domestic adjudicators always manage the difficult question of whether repayment of simple interest is enough to make up for the procedural breach and to safeguard competitors? Would it not have been more appropriate to give national courts a clearer mandate in this regard? More radically, does *CELF II* represent the death of 'private enforcement' in the State aid field?[202]

It is important to underline that, contrary to what happens in the WTO, when we talk of 'repayment' and 'recovery' of State aid that is 'incompatible' (and hence not simply 'unlawful' from a procedural standpoint but not permissible under any of the justifications), the rule is 'retroactivity'.[203] The aid has to be repaid with interest and Member States cannot make excuses for not abiding by this obligation. The only possible defence is absolute impossibility which is very hard to prove. For its part, the Commission shall order the recovery of any aid which has been granted 'unlawfully' *and* is also eventually 'incompatible with the common market', that is, which cannot find any justification under EC law.

The final comment concerns another element of stark difference between the EC and WTO systems. Unilateral remedies are not available to Member States. Under no circumstances may Member States apply unilaterally countervailing duties to defend themseleves against subsidies granted by other Member States. In other words, if an objectionable State aid has been granted, this has to be repaid in full and with interest. This may occur following a national court's decision and/or a Commission's decision.

The previous analysis has shown the clear differences that exist between the EC and the WTO both in terms of enforcement and remedies. These are the strong scrutinizing role carried out by the Commission, based on a generalized obligation of prior notification and a prohibition of implementation, the role played by national courts as guardians to the respect of the enforcement mechanism, and the retroactive nature of the repayment of State aid that is not compliant with EC law.

[201] The exact impact of the case will not be apparent for some time to come. In the meantime, the Court has handed down the first confirmation of *CELF II* in Case C-384/07 *Wienstrom*. For a thorough analysis of the *CELF II* case see T Jaeger, 'The CELF-Judgment: A Precarious Conception of the Standstill Obligation' (2008) European State Aid Law Quarterly 279; PJ Slot, 'Case note on Case C-199/06, *Centre d'exportation du livre Francais (CELF)* v. *Société internationale de diffusion et d'édition (SIDE)*' (2009) Common Market Law Review 623.

[202] C Arhold, 'The 2007/2008 Case Law of the European Court of Justice and the Court of First Instance on State Aid' (2008) European State Aid Law Quarterly 441, 480.

[203] Although, according to the recent *CELF II* jurisprudence, this does not apply to merely 'unlawful' aid.

B. Critical analysis

This final section makes some critical remarks on how subsidy rules, control and remedies could be drafted. In doing so, the overview of the two systems just carried out is drawn upon, as are the findings of the previous analysis.

Drafting tests and provisions

This paragraph focuses on the substantive law and in particular on how to draft provisions and tests.

There are three starting considerations. First, in the light of their more general context, tests and provisions should be sound but they should also be easily administrable. Secondly, as the analysis in this chapter has shown, the role of the objectives of the subsidy system should be taken into account in drafting substantive law.

Finally, when drafting requirements defining the crucial elements of the definition of subsidy, or indeed its justifications, we should bear in mind the important distinction between 'rules' and 'standards'[204] in the context of antitrust and subsidy regulation. Although a strict divide is difficult, rules tend to be more precise in defining their requirements and also their consequences. They are thus more easily administrable. The classic example is that of clear *per se* rules, in the form of either prohibition or permission.[205] For their part, standards are less detailed, and more open-ended. They are characterized by more flexibility and often leave substantial issues to be determined at the adjudication level on a case-by-case basis. Of course, these are the two extremes of the spectrum, and middle-positions are possible.

Thus, with respect to 'impact standards', a mixed approach can be considered. Building on experience, the use of standards can be nicely combined with the use of rules and presumptions. If an individual assessment of complex economic situations is needed, a 'standard' approach should be preferred. If, by contrast, the impact of that type of subsidy, in those type of circumstances, is already clear, a more definite 'rule' can be the answer.

In principle, the same mixed approach can be suggested with respect to the provisions on justifications. However, contextual considerations, and in particular those on the type of control, play a fundamental role in this respect. The EC experience is one of general exception clauses (definitely extremely broad 'standards'!) whose application has been fully left to the discretion of the Commission. Over the years, policy has consolidated into a more detailed discipline which, in certain areas, is constituted of extremely detailed conditions and requirements.

[204] See L Kaplow, 'Rules Versus Standards: An Economic Analysis' (1992) Duke Law Journal 557.

[205] Depending on the case, the risks of 'rules' are however those of under-inclusion (also known as 'negative' positive or Type II error) or over-inclusion ('false' positive or Type I error).

If we move to the WTO, the EC's original broad approach to justification with full delegation for its application to a supranational body is not conceivable. The most sensitive topic of permissible subsidies should be dealt with great precision. If the idea itself of having embedded justifications in a subsidy compact has any chance to resurrect, a detailed rule approach (similar to that prevailing in most of current EC legislation) is preferable. The drafting technique of the now expired non-actionable category was a good example in this respect.

Type of control and remedies

Supranational and/or unilateral

The type of control is strictly linked to the issue of remedies, and in various respects. There is first a temporal dimension. Whereas, normally, remedies operate only after the subsidy has produced its harm, control can, in principle, take place before or after the grant of the subsidy.

The second factor is one of identity. In other words, a remedy to a harm can also act as a tool to control the conduct causing the harm, or at the very least, the harm itself. This is the typical function of unilateral remedies like countervailing duties. They do not aim to have the subsidy removed. The target is just to neutralize the negative impact of the subsidy by imposing a duty which should not surpass the margin of subsidization. More precisely, the ambit of action is confined to the domestic constituency and to the harmful effects produced by the subsidy therein. The impact produced elsewhere, in other countries and market, is simply outside the focus of the remedy.

The type of control offered by this type of unilateral mechanism is obviously limited, and not only in its intended aims. Although under the binding umbrella of international rules (the SCM Agreement), it is administered locally, often on impulse of the aggrieved domestic industry. The risk for more or less deliberate capture is not negligible. The purely domestic perspective is thus particularly apt to attract more or less genuine criticisms, and in any case to create international tensions.

Further, the narrowness of the objectives of unilateral action does not intuitively concur with more global apprehensions about subsidies' negative externalities. If there is a deterrent effect in imposing countervailing duties, this may well be felt only where the reaction occurs (for example by exporting the relevant products at a higher price in the future). It may concurrently discourage the practice of subsidization itself[206] but this is only speculative.

[206] JH Jackson, *The World Trading System—Law and Policy of International Economic Relations* (2nd edn, Cambridge Massachussetts: MIT Press, 1997) chapter 11.

Despite the criticisms of countervailing duty laws just sketched,[207] it seems clear that unilateral remedies are here to stay.

That said, if they are limited and do not capture the complexity of the negative externalities a subsidy may produce internationally, they should be complemented by an effective supranational system of control. This may take various forms, being truly multilateral (like the GATT/WTO) or plurilateral/regional (like the EC). Its core is generally constituted of a more or less independent body that receives (prior or successive) notifications of subsidy practices. The actual mode of control may then vary dramatically. At one end of the spectrum (say the GATT/WTO), we may have a system where the relevant body represents a forum for clarification and discussion between the parties concerned. At the other end (say the EC), the system may fully entrust a function of surveillance and decision, with the power to authorize or not notified subsidies, to a truly autonomous body.

The existence of such different types of control is evidence itself of the extremely different 'contexts' of the two political and legal systems, the WTO and EC, at large.[208] While the EC system is largely effective, there is widespread agreement that, from an enforcement perspective, the WTO system should be improved. It is interesting in this regard that, when discussing how to improve the WTO mechanism, reference is sometimes made to the EC.[209] However, although the EC system of control can provide inspiration for solutions in certain respects, it cannot completely represent a model for the WTO.

It should be noted finally that there is an alternative system of controlling subsidies, adopted in the regulation of support in the agricultural sector, which relies on negotiated and progressive reductions of certain categories of subsidies. Once ceilings and modalities have been defined, this method offers the advantage of a relatively easy administration. As the current Doha Round shows, however, the whole political burden is shifted at the level of the negotiations of the reductions.

Trasparency and control

In the light of the previous paragraph, it is clear that our main focus here should be on the WTO system of control. There is widespread agreement that the enforcement mechanisms should be improved.[210]

[207] And most of them could apply to the 'upgraded version' of unilateral remedy, that is, countervailing subsidies. See chapter 3, section V.A.

[208] This was the important caveat underlying comparative analysis made in section II.A of chapter 1.

[209] See, eg, MJ Trebilcock and R Howse, *The Regulation of International Trade* (3rd edn, London: Routledge, 2005) 290–1. In the GATT era, see JJ Barceló III, 'Subsidies and Countervailing Duties—Analysis and Proposal' (1977) Law and Policy in International Business 779.

[210] It is useful to refer to the current negotiations on fisheries subsidies. Despite the existence of different views, interesting proposals have been put forward. See, eg, the New Draft Consolidated Chair Texts of the AD and SCM Agreements, TN/RL/W/236, circulated on 19 December 2008, by the Chair of the Negotiating Group on Rules which include a 'roadmap for discussions' on fisheries

The starting consideration is that the simple introduction of legal *obligations* is pointless if these are ineffective. More transparency and control should be the aims. But before rushing to identify the cure, the desease should be properly identified.

In terms of legal tools to make enforment more effective, if obligations do not bite, they are not sufficient. The clearest example is that of the notification under Article XVI:1 of the GATT which should represent the centrepiece of the enforcement system envisaged in the GATT/WTO. It is certainly an obligation, which has been there since 1947. Not respecting it is, in principle, a breach of a WTO obligation. Despite all this, the compliance record has been particularly poor, and the WTO advent has not improved the situation.[211]

In the absence of a very strong mechanism like the EC one, which involves various actors in ensuring the effectiveness of the centralized control and the respect of the procedural obligations of Member States, it may be necessary to introduce rules to create the correct *incentives* for countries to notify their measures, to do so in a comprehensive way, and to promptly respond to request for information of other Members. The environment should be conducive to real 'peer-control'. In short, the Committee on Subsidies should be used as a true 'clearing-house' of subsidy measures. If this works then the surveillance function of the same committee can be consolidated, and maybe even expanded.

As previously noted with general remarks that well apply to this specific context too,[212] what is necessary is the consciousness that this system is in the common interest, that it is a 'shared resource'. What is ultimately needed is an underlying stronger sense of 'community'.

The dynamics of enforcement are however diabolical. They can operate as a vicious, or rather as a virtuous, circle. If one element of the system does not work (and, in our case, the cornerstone is the notification duty) it will inevitably impact other subsequent steps. No one will put any effort into something which does not work. No country will cooperate *within* an enforcement framework if the others simply do not. To express it in economic jargon, there are many externalities, opportunities for moral hazard, and network effects, in the realm of enforcement. The proper incentives need to be put in place to make it work, and to do so efficiently.

Horlick has expressed the inefficiency of the enforcement in the WTO system with a wonderful image. The most important problem with respect to WTO subsidy

subsidies. See also the first draft text on a discipline, included in the Draft Consolidated Chair Texts of the AD and SCM Agreements,TN/RL/W/213, circulated on 30 November 2007, and the following Working Document From the Chairman, TN/RL/W/232, circulated on 28 May 2008, which in Annex C includes delegations' reactions to the first draft and new proposals since.

[211] Writing in 2001, but with a conclusion applicable even now, see GN Horlick, 'Subsidies Discipline Under WTO and US Rules' in CD Ehlermann and M Everson (eds), *European Competition Law Annual 1999: Selected Issues in the Filed of State Aids* (Oxford: Hart, 2001) 593, 601.

[212] Section I.C.

discipline would be that governments are trapped in a 'glass-house'.[213] In other words, 'members may not wish to challenge each other's domestic subsidies, on the traditional principle that governments which live in glass houses do not throw stones'. The truth of Horlick's statement is not confined to domestic subsidies but is of general application. It explains how a 'glass-house' problem may, from the very beginning, prevent the success of any system of control where everybody has to reveal, at least to some extent, his fault.

For the system to work, it is crucial to break these deadlock situations. There are several ways of doing this and although lack of space does not permit us to examine the operative proposals that could create 'the right incentives' noted above, some food for thought is offered.

There are three areas of intervention which should not be considered as mutually exclusive.

First, the use of procedural devices can represent a very powerful way to reach important targets in an easy way. Two examples can be given. The first comes from an EC proposal, which was clearly modelled on the stronger internal system of EC State aid control, and which was abandoned at the very last stage of the Uruguay Round Negotiations. What was being suggested was that 'actionable' subsidies be prohibited, or at the very least suspended, prior to notification.[214] This is just a procedural device—it does not look at objectives or effects of the measure at issue. It does, however, create a huge incentive to notify, and a great benefit to transparency.

The second example of how to use procedural elements to improve the efficiency of the system is the allocation of the burden of proof. Compared to the previous example, this may be more intrusive since the issue of 'who needs to prove, or rebut, what' clearly impacts the substance of the case too. But it may be a very powerful way of improving the effectiveness of a legal/political mechanism.

Secondly, remedies. It has been noted how sensitive this area is and it will be discussed further below. It cannot, however, be excluded that the procedural level of enforcement be connected to that of remedies, as, for example, with leniency in antitrust.

[213] GN Horlick, 'Subsidies Discipline Under WTO and US Rules' in CD Ehlermann and M Everson (eds), *European Competition Law Annual 1999: Selected Issues in the Field of State Aids* (Oxford: Hart, 2001) 593, 602–3. See also PA Clarke, J Bourgeois, and GN Horlick, 'WTO Dispute Settlement Practice Relating to Subsidies and Countervailing Measures', in F Ortino and EU Petersmann (eds), *The WTO Dispute Settlement System, 1995–2003* (Kluwer Law International, 2004) 353, 378: 'To date, there has been virtually no discipline on non-prohibited subsidies—perhaps because all Members live in "glass houses" and do not wish to throw stones at each'.

[214] This is reported by GN Horlick, 'Subsidies Discipline Under WTO and US Rules' in CD Ehlermann and M Everson (eds), *European Competition Law Annual 1999: Selected Issues in the Field of State Aids* (Oxford: Hart, 2001) 593, 603. Along the same lines, the EC also suggested that, before benefitting from protection, 'non-actionable' subsidies not only had to be notified but also authorized. Clearly, this is not a simple procedural device but involves the 'delegation' of a substantive control to the SCM. And this is sensitive, irrespective of the degree of control and the discretion involved.

Thirdly, institutional adjustments. As just one example of an intervention which would build upon the existing institutional structure, the relatively underutilized Group of Experts could be rejuvenated and given new purpose in a broader enforcement context.[215] The current rules already provide that it should offer confidential advice to members on whether certain measures amount to subsidies, and may be requested to assist a Panel on the issue of whether the measure in question is a prohibited subsidy. Interestingly, according to Article 4.5 of the SCM, this advice is binding on the Panel.

One suggestion might be to enable a country not only to seek a confidential advice on the nature of a measure but also to obtain an official assessment from the Group. Should the answer be that the measure is not a subsidy, this could trigger a presumption in this respect and exclude the duty of notification.

Remedies

As regards remedies, a brief outline of the alternatives will be noted, followed by an analysis of the controversial issue of the temporal effect of the removal of the subsidy.

Countervailing duties (and subsidies) by their nature focus on the effects of subsidies and counteract them.[216] If the remedy concentrates on the subsidy itself, two possibilities can be envisaged. The action could go to the root of the problem by seeking the removal of the subsidy. Alternatively, it could merely focus on the latter's effects.

Although conventional wisdom suggests that it is always better to cure the cause rather than the effect, this may not always be possible or indeed desirable. The fact is that, as has been noted in this chapter, subsidies are ambivalent. They often represent a society's legitimate choice to address an important objective. As such, it would not seem wise, or indeed possible, to simply remove them if, together with a positive impact, they concomitantly produce negative effects. The lessening, or even the elimination of the negative effects, may be possible. This route should in principle always be sought. If that is not feasible, it is for the legal system, and its subsidy discipline, to operate that inherently political balancing act underlined above.

Finally, one remedy which should be considered, particularly because it directly empowers the victims of the harm, is the possibility of compensation for the damage caused by subsidization. As antitrust laws teaches us, this 'private enforcement' route, which has been mentioned in the EC context, raises various questions. There are however specific obstacles that it could face in the world trade context, mainly

[215] The following remarks build up on conversation with a former member of the Group of Experts.

[216] This type of remedy has already been discussed extensively.

depending on the effect of WTO law in domestic legal systems and on its consistency with subsidy laws.[217]

As regards the most effective remedy, subsidy removal, a highly controversial issue focuses on whether this remedy should only be prospective or, at least to some extent, retrospective. Although in different terms, we have seen that a similar debate takes place in both the WTO and EC. It has been noted already how this issue goes to the heart of any legal system, and it is particularly difficult in a legal order such as international law.

In general, it seems that a merely prospective remedy, particularly in the context of a weak enforcement system (where, for example, there is no requirement for prior notification and/or authorization), is not satisfactory.[218] The main reason is that it significantly diminishes the effectiveness of a rule-based system of subsidy control. This is self-evident in the extreme case of non-recurring subsidies. The *Australia—Leather (Article 21.5)* Panel was clearly right in its reasoning and conclusion. When the subsidy is constituted of 'one-shot' only, and has already been paid, if repayment is excluded on principle, what could be the recommendation of the DSB? In such cases, the remedy must, by necessity, be retrospective.[219]

The same kind of reasoning applies, in the author's view, in the context of remedies for breaches of procedural rules. This refers to the question of the 'recovery' of 'unlawful' but 'compatible' State aid in the EC.

Although the former state of the law was probably leading to excessive, and paradoxical, situations,[220] the current stance of *CELF II* (which, as a matter of EC

[217] See Article 32.1 of the SCM in particular, extensively analysed in chapter 3, section V.A. The legal issue is: would a domestic rule entitling aggrieved parties to compensation for injury caused by subsidies be considered as a 'specific action against a subsidy of another Member' which is prohibited under the said provision? Extending the scope of the analysis to the identical provision in the AD Agreement (Article 18.1), can we really conclude that domestic antitrust laws, which punish discriminatory or predatory pricing, and provides for compensation of private parties, be illegal under the WTO inasmuch as it would constitute 'specific action against dumping of exports from another Member'? As the next chapter shows, everything turns on the interpretatiton of the terms 'specific' and 'against'. The issue is however intriguing, and with possible far-reaching consequences.

[218] See P Eeckhout, 'Remedies and Compliance' in D Bethlemen, D McRae, R Neufeld, and I Van Damme (eds), *The Oxford Handbook of International Trade Law* (Oxford: Oxford University Press, 2009) 438, 448–51.

[219] In fact *ex tunc* remedies were granted by some GATT panels in the fields of anti-dumping and countervailing duies. cf PC Mavroidis, 'Remedies in the WTO Legal System: Between a Rock and a Hard Place' (2000) European Journal of International Law 763, 775 et seq.

For the issues raised by the *Australia—Leather (Article 21.5)* Panel, and broader questions on remedies in the WTO, see also G Goh and A Ziegler, 'Retrospective Remedies in the WTO after *Automotive Leather*' (2003) Journal of International Economic Law 545; P Grane, 'Remedies under WTO Law' (2001) Journal of International Economic Law 755; A Green and M Trebilcock, 'Enforcing WTO Obligations: Whan Can We Learn From Export Subsidies?' (2007) Journal of International Economic Law 653; PC Mavroidis, cit.

[220] 'You have to recover the State aid because you granted it in breach of the procedure. But, you can give it back immediately because it is compatible.'

law, simply requires the payment of the interest, leaving the availability of further remedies to national laws) dramatically dimishes the force of the previous remedy which provided for a full retroactive repayment (of capital plus interest) and ultimately its justification, that is the need, beyond legal requirements, to give governments an incentive for notifying their plans and wait for their implementation. A rethink of the remedy is required, which realigns legal obligations with political and financial incentives.

PART II

FORMS OF GOVERNMENTAL ACTION

The core concept of 'subsidy' is extremely pliable. The term normally means the transfer by the government of something of value to a producer which increases the producer's profitability. The most common kinds of subsidies involve transfers of money, goods or services, either for free or at below market prices. But from an economic viewpoint anything the government does which alters the producer's costs or revenues in a favorable direction could just as easily be called a subsidy. The political perception is primarily a matter of visibility. Once the helping hand of government becomes conspicuous, it tends to elicit 'subsidy' objections no matter what form the help takes.[1]

[1] RE Hudec, Difference in National Environmental Standards: The Level-Playing-Field Dimension, (1996) 5 Minnesota Journal of Global Trade 1, 15.

Overview

The initial step of the analysis is to concentrate on the first requirement of the definition of subsidy or State aid which is the action of the government. Having in mind the words of Hudec, the objective of this Part of the book is to assess the *forms* of governmental action that may constitute a subsidy in WTO and EC law.

The key premise underlying this book, and consequently this chapter too, is worth being repeated. Legally, a State aid or a subsidy is an operational concept that is artificially defined within a given legal and political system. Not every action of the government which is likely to produce, in one way or another, a certain economic result by interfering with the functioning of international trade and competition will amount to a subsidy under a specific legal definition. Boundaries must be drawn. While certain forms of governmental action will be included in that definition, others will not. What is important is to determine which ones are covered, and further to answer how and why they are covered.

This Part of the book attempts to answer three questions. The conceptual analysis of Chapter 3 focuses on what measures *may* be considered as subsidies. Building on its findings, the remaining chapters (4, 5 and 6) seek to answer two other questions. What forms of action *do* in fact constitute a subsidy or a State aid in the two legal systems? And, finally, what forms *should* the two regimes consider as such? In the final chapter, after summarizing the findings of the analysis made so far, the discussion is enriched with the examination of other (than subsidy) rules whose application may affect the definition of subsidy in the two legal systems.

3

Introduction: governmental intervention in the economy and subsidies

This introductory chapter focuses on the *forms* of public intervention in the economy that may in general give an economic advantage and may thus in principle be covered by subsidy or State aid rules. In doing so, and in particular in distinguishing those cases that are commonly held to be subsidies (those of 'financial assistance') from those that are more controversial (those of 'regulation'), an attempt is made to provide a conceptual explanation of this different treatment. This is followed by the examination of the legal techniques that can be used to determine the legal relevance of governmental action in the context of a definition of subsidy. A final section concentrates on the significance of the objectives of the measures, and maps their position within the issue of the definition of subsidy.

This conceptual exercise should enable a better understanding of the economic, political and ultimately legal perspectives surrounding the definition of subsidy and pave the way to the analysis of the law in the two systems and to its critique.

I. Distinguishing financial assistance and regulation

As various branches of economics and political science explain, governments intervene in the economy for various reasons, and do so in different ways and with different results.[1] They tax and spend (fiscal policy), control interest rates and the supply of money (monetary policy), regulate trade with other nations (trade policy), and, more generally, involve themselves in various aspects and sectors of the economy (regulation).

If we immediately attempt to determine whether a(ny) measure(s) of fiscal, monetary, trade and regulatory policy may constitute a subsidy, and pose this question to an economist or a political scientist, their answer would probably

[1] It should at once be underlined that to intervene in the economy does not necessarily mean that the government operates 'in the market' as its conduct may affect the economy, and hence undertakings, also when it acts *qua* government, for example by levying taxes or introducing rules. Part III shows that the distinction between market and non-market conduct has an important impact on the analysis of the advantage, and in particular of the benchmarks that are used therein.

discourage our definitional effort from the beginning. '[F]rom an economic viewpoint, anything the government does which alters the producer's costs or revenues in a favorable direction could just as easily be called a subsidy', Hudec reminded. In the same vein, in his remarks reported at the beginning of chapter 1, Snape noted that 'the term subsidy can be all-embracing' and 'virtually *every* government action can be regarded as a subsidy for someone' and, finally, and crucially for an international discipline, 'virtually all such actions can affect international trade'.[2] Clearly, this approach is not practicable in the context of a discipline which should regulate and provide directions.

What this chapter attempts to do is to focus on the forms of governmental action that *may* be regarded, at least in principle, as subsidies or State aids. Before embarking on the technical analysis of legal definitions (and the specific definitions within two given legal systems, the WTO and the EC), an initial analysis of what is generally more likely and what is generally less likely to be considered a subsidy is useful. Even more useful is the analysis of the conceptual elements underlying this different classification since this may have an impact on the techniques that legal systems use to define the (legal) relevance of certain forms of public intervention.

Hudec's quotation provides us with some guidance on this first preliminary act of differentiation. By putting the 'all-embracing' political economy concept of subsidy into some perspective, it highlights two things. First, the classification of certain measures as subsidies is widely accepted. These substantially belong to the typical tools of fiscal policy, such as financial transfers, and, the author would add, tax measures. The second indication is that, as soon as we leave this familiar territory, the frontier of the concept becomes increasingly elusive and its delineation is subject to political contention and legal disputes.

On this basis, a brief overview of various forms of governmental action giving economic advantages is given. In the light of their degree of acceptance as subsidies, 'financial assistance' and 'regulation' will be distinguished.

A. Forms of financial assistance

The government may provide financial advantages to undertakings by transferring economic resources to them in various ways, for example, with grants, capital injections, loans, guarantees, provision or purchase of goods or services. Apart from spending, government can equally use its taxation powers to confer economic benefits, by granting special or differential tax treatment. Despite a sometimes gradual process of acceptance, these measures of fiscal policy are now commonly recognized as subsidies.

Governments may also provide goods or services (such as infrastructures, education, public order) that, despite being in principle open to all members of society

[2] R Snape, 'International Regulation of Subsidies' (1991) The World Economy 139, 140.

(hence generally called 'public goods'),[3] may in certain circumstances have a favourable impact on certain undertakings only. Mainly because of their general character and availability, the classification of this category of fiscal policy has been a continual source of difficulties.

All these measures of fiscal policy can be grouped together under the general expression 'financial assistance'. In conclusion, despite the uncertain case of public goods, financial transfers and tax measures are commonly considered as forms of governmental action that may constitute subsidies.

B. Forms of regulation

It is clear that it is possible to confer economic advantages on undertakings by regulating their business environment, by introducing or removing rules and restrictions on economic activities. The frontier of the definition of subsidy, which regularly attracts claims of subsidization and where contention is high (particularly, as Hudec teaches, if 'the helping hand of government becomes conspicuous'), is constituted of 'regulatory measures' or 'regulation', elusive terms that can be intended broadly.

Through regulation the government may control the functioning of markets, for example the quantity and price of goods or services. Governments may affect prices and quantities in quite an *immediate* way by fixing (minimum or maximum) prices and/or imposing obligations to sell or buy the relevant products or services. In some cases, with a course of action called 'deregulation', governments may relax, or remove altogether, rules and restrictions[4] that are applicable to undertakings and thus benefit them.[5]

Governments may also adopt a *less direct* course of conduct, for example by introducing border (trade) measures, such as import or export barriers (think of quotas and tariffs) which, by respectively reducing or increasing the quantity of goods or services in the market, may result in an advantage for those undertakings that sell or buy them in terms of respectively higher or lower prices. Leaving aside any legal consideration, the classification of quotas and tariffs as subsidies is immediately puzzling for one reason. In economics, subsidies are themselves considered to be trade barriers which may be used as an alternative to tariffs and quotas. Assuming this is correct, logic would seem to preclude that alternatives could also be considered one and the same measure. It is however the 'pliability' of subsidy definition that explain the possibility of such an expansion from a political and legal perspective.[6]

[3] For an analysis and application of the proper meaning of the economic concept of public good see chapter 7.

[4] The list of examples can be endless: eg labour, environmental or product safety standards, corporate, insolvency or antitrust rules.

[5] We leave aside for a moment the different case when there is *no* regulation at all on the subject and analyse it below.

[6] As will be seen in chapter 6, a systemic insight may help in solving the conundrum.

Within a broad understanding of those measures that may regulate the economy, we could also consider the case of monetary policies. For both their general character (cf public goods) and their clear distance from the traditional forms of financial transfers and taxation, these measures have not easily been linked to subsidization. As a paradigmatic example of the extremely 'pliable' nature of the concept of subsidy, allegations have recently been suggested that the substantial devaluation of a currency would constitute a subsidy.[7]

II. Conceptualizing the distinction between financial assistance and regulation

It is now apt to compare the two categories of governmental action ('financial assistance' and 'regulation') identified above.[8] The goal is to *conceptualize the grounds* underlying the distinction between those types of intervention (ie financial transfers and tax measures) that are commonly accepted as subsidies and those (ie border trade measures and regulatory measures) that are more controversial. In particular, the examination of the *characteristics* of these forms of public intervention may shed some light on their varying degree of acceptance (under subsidy rules), and, ultimately, enable a more correct interpretation of the law and, if necessary, an informed discussion of its reform.

In this regard it is argued that (i) the *degree of complexity* of the *action* and of the *transfer of economic resources* and (ii) the *nature* of the *prerogatives* exercised by the government in the instant case are all useful in understanding the political and legal status of the forms of financial assistance and regulation under subsidy disciplines.

A. The complexity of the action

In general, financial assistance and regulation often differ with respect to the degree of complexity of the action of the government and of the relevant transfer of economic resources. In short, the mechanism whereby the economic advantage is conferred is usually more complex in regulatory rather than in financial cases.

[7] Reference is made to the US challenge of the Chinese devaluation of the renmenbi. On the various issues raised, including the possible categorization of this practice as subsidy, see RW Staiger and AO Sykes, 'Currency Manipulation and World Trade', December 2008, NBER Working Paper No. W14600; GC Hufbauer and C Brunel, 'The US Congress and the Chinese Renminbi' in M Goldstein and NR Lardy, *Debating China's Exchange Rate Policy* (Washington: Peterson Institute for International Economics, 2008); A Mattoo and A Subramanian, 'Currency Undervaluation and Sovereign Wealth Funds: A New Role for the World Trade Organization', World Bank Policy Research Working Paper 4668 (July 2008).

[8] For a similar distinction, referring to tax, expenditure and regulatory policies, see AO Sykes, 'The Economics of WTO Rules on Subsidies and Countervailing Measures', Chicago John M Olin Law and Economics Working Paper No. 186 (2nd Series), May 2003.

This element of complexity may have a crucial impact on the application of the relevant rules, which may be specific in their requirements, making it more difficult to subject the conduct to a given definition of subsidy.

The first element of complexity of regulatory conduct may depend on its *indirect* course. When the government provides financial assistance, it often (although not necessarily) does so directly. This is not the case for regulatory measures which often involve an intermediary in the transfer of economic resources.

The main issue of an indirect action is whether the conduct of the third party—which, in principle, may act autonomously—may be *attributed* or *imputed* to the government. The direction exercised by the government in this regard does not always feature the same degree of clarity, immediacy and intensity, ranging from a straight order to do something to merely creating the conditions where a similar conduct with a similar effect will be performed. If compared with measures of indirect financial assistance, indirect regulatory measures are often connoted by less clear, immediate and intense degrees of direction. That is to say, the 'mechanism of transmission' of the benefit is more elaborate.

A good example is when the government attempts to influence the quantity and the price of a product in the domestic market by introducing *border measures* such as export or import restrictions or tariffs. Although economics can help us in predicting their impact on the conduct of economic operators, it cannot be denied that the causal chain of the measure is more complex (ie it involves more steps) as compared to a straight order or prohibition on them.[9] The possibility of deviation from the anticipated is not entirely negligible.

Another difficulty of the indirect action, that is particularly common in regulatory contexts, is to determine whom the government is actually directing. This may have great practical importance since it eventually turns on whether the conditions of the legal definition concerning indirect courses of action are satisfied or not.

Think of *price regulation*. With respect to a mandated minimum price, shall we say that it is the buyer who is ordered to pay it or, from another perspective, the supplier is ordered to charge it? The converse is obviously true for maximum prices. Is it the producer who is prohibited from charging more, or is it rather the buyer who is entitled to pay that price? Arguably, the most reasonable reading is that it is the party that is most immediately subject to the direction of the government—and the one that has an opposite interest to the measure—who is the intermediary through which the financial support is effected.

[9] cf the illuminating words of R Diamond, 'Privatization and the Definition of Subsidy: A Critical Study of Appellate Body Texturalism' (2008) Journal of International Economic Law 649, 664: '. . . subsidy law covers a particular mode of government action. The government does not directly order exporting producers to change their behavior. Rather, the government presumes that companies are rational actors that respond to market signals. The foreign government changes the market signals that its producers see. These changes cause profit maximixing producers to alter their behavior in a manner that causes injury to domestic producers'.

A different conclusion can be drawn in some cases of *deregulation* where the governmental measure seems to be immediately directed to the beneficiary undertaking, for example by exempting it from certain rules or restrictions (such as labour or environmental standards). This measure almost inevitably affects a third party.[10] It seems however that this third party, which, at least inasmuch as its financial dimension is concerned, may still be considered as the vehicle of governmental conduct, is subject to a lesser degree of direction as compared with, say, an order or a prohibition immediately directed to it.

In other cases, where there is a dedicated authority to enforce the rules (eg antitrust laws), it may be argued that we have a normal situation of delegation where the economic advantage clearly passes through the action of the delegated authority (which, in the example, would be required to apply more benign antitrust rules). If the enforcement is less institutionalized (for example because there is no specific authority to enforce antitrust rules) we would return to the scenario described immediately before.

B. The complexity of the financial dimension

The complexity of the mechanism of conferral of the economic advantage may have an impact on the clarity of its financial dimension. Although any public intervention is liable to produce an economic impact on undertakings, and more specifically an allocation of economic resources (whereby the benefit for one party quite often corresponds to the burden for another), it is not always possible to identify a clear *transfer* of economic resources from one party to another. And this may have implications from a definitional perspective.

In the case of indirect financial assistance, the existence of a transfer of economic resources is normally particularly clear. The measures do not involve a great degree of complexity since we are usually dealing with commonly accepted forms of subsidy linked to the traditional taxation/expenditure functions of governments.

By contrast, a transfer of economic resources is more difficult to identify in some forms of regulatory action. We may think of the cases of deregulation discussed above (labour and environmental standards) where the direct addressee of the action of the government seems to be the beneficiary of the measure and a third party is only affected derivatively. In this scenario, can we so easily conclude that the employees affected by lower labour conditions, the public damaged by higher pollution, or even the companies operating in a no more profitable market for environmental services, are 'transferring' economic resources to the beneficiary undertakings? While economics would probably answer positively, things may be more difficult if the issue has to considered 'within' a specific normative framework.

[10] Following the examples above, we can think of the employees; the public damaged by pollution or the undertakings supplying environmental devices or services.

What seems to emerge from these cases is that the clarity of the transfer is proportionately linked to the role played by the intermediary. In other words, the *less active* the latter is the *less clear* the former seems to be.

An ancillary point concerning the financial dimension of the action focuses on the origin of the resources that are used to finance the transfer. Generally, whereas the large majority of cases of financial assistance involve a transfer of 'public' resources, regulatory measures normally call for a use of 'private' resources. In the former the government usually acts directly, in the latter it almost invariably relies on the role of third parties. The most commonly accepted forms of subsidy, which certainly belong to the category of financial assistance, are strictly linked to the government's prerogative to tax and spend the collected revenue (which is quite separate from the prerogative to regulate).

C. The significance of prerogatives

The final comments of the previous section suggested a useful perspective to appreciate the difference between forms of financial assistance and regulatory measures, focusing on the type of prerogatives that are exercised by the government in the instant case.

Measures of financial assistance are characterized by both a particularly clear and a rather immediate transfer of economic resources. This palpable financial component follows the exercise of the *governmental prerogative to tax and spend the collected revenue*. By contrast, the financial dimension of regulatory measures is not always represented by clear and immediate transfers of economic resources. It is the introduction or removal of rules (and restrictions) that plays a crucial role in the, often less direct and more complex, mechanism of conferral of the economic advantage with the consequence that they are characterized by a regulatory component, connected to the different *governmental prerogative to regulate the economy*.

Questions similar to those which arose in the analysis of the degree of complexity of the action and of the transfer of economic resources arise again here. In particular, from a *legal standpoint* (in the context of the requirements of an already drafted or contemplated definition of subsidy), to what extent does this difference in governmental prerogatives mark the dividing line between what is and what is not a subsidy? Most crucially, from a *policy* perspective (where the goals of a subsidy discipline are considered), where should we draw a justifiable line?

III. Techniques to define the legal relevance of the governmental action

After exploring the conceptual traits of the distinction between various forms of public intervention, we examine the legal techniques that may be used to to define the legal relevance of the public intervention. In other words, to determine what forms of governmental action are actually covered by the definition. These techniques, which significantly reflect most of the terms of the previous analysis, will be used in the examination of the actual coverage of WTO subsidy and EC State aid rules and in its critique.

Four techniques can be usefully adopted to set the boundaries of a definition of subsidy or State aid. Importantly, they are not mutually exclusive and their operation often overlaps.

The more general and intuitive technique is the *formulation of the definition*. Definitions may be drafted in different ways. They may be general or specific, and more or less comprehensive. They may be sufficiently explicit so as to cover only certain forms of action, say those that involve clear and direct transfers of economic resources. By contrast, they may be more generally worded with a potentially wider coverage, comprising more indirect and complex measures granting economic advantages. Further, and most importantly, they may, more or less clearly, distinguish measures according to the (financial or regulatory) *nature* of the action of the government.

The second technique refers to those cases of indirect action when the government acts through a third party, or, in any event, the transfer of economic resources involves a third party. The main legal issue is whether, and, if so, under what conditions, the government may be held responsible for the conduct of the third party.[11]

We have seen that the direction of the government may be characterized by various aspects of complexity. Definitions reflect this complexity in the relevant *rules of imputability*. These may be crafted in different ways, which are more or less sophisticated and comprehensive. For example (and in order of a progressive strictness), they may simply demand a classification of the financing body as public, or, if the focus is on the actual conduct, they may require proof of a definite causal nexus or rather expect a more intense and clear act of direction, like an order.[12]

The third method to determine the relevance of the measure at issue focuses on the *origin of the resources* used to finance the action of subsidization. A long-standing issue in the two systems is whether the definitions of subsidy and State aid necessarily require a cost to government or may also be financed with private resources.[13]

Finally, the fourth technique of definition concerns the *objectives* of the public intervention. The government usually acts in the pursuit of various public policy

[11] For the international law perspective, see International Law Commission, *Draft Articles on Responsibility of States for International Wrongful Acts, with Commentaries, Yearbook of International Law Commission*, 2001, Vol II, Part II. See also J Crawford, *The International Law Commission's Articles on State Responsibility—Introduction, Text and Commentaries* (Cambridge: Cambridge University Press, 2002).

[12] It is important to underline that, even if the involvement of the government in the conferral of the economic advantage is generally clear, for example in the cases of deregulation discussed above (where there may be a clear mandate), the determination of its actual legal responsibility under the provision at issue may still be an issue since it fully depends on the formulation of the relevant rule of imputability.

[13] The next two chapters will devote much space to the analysis of this issue.

objectives. A recurring theme of our analysis is what role is played by the objectives of the measure in subsidy definitions. This chapter closes with a section which first enquires whether the objectives of the measures may be significant in the definition of what forms of governmental action are subsidies, and then more generally maps their position within the issue of the definition of subsidy.

In conclusion, an awareness of these techniques of definition is particularly useful not only for the legislator but also for the interpreter. A full knowledge of their relevance enables more coherent and sound legal interpretations to be achieved.

IV. Legal treatment of regulatory measures

One of the most challenging definitional issues is the treatment of 'regulatory measures' under WTO subsidy and EC State aid rules. The previous analysis has provided both background and framework to this topic.

What can already be anticipated is that this question cannot be given an easy or general answer. Regulatory measures may take various forms and legal provisions may be drafted in different ways. Most importantly, the broader context (which includes the goals of the legal system and the 'other' provisions) should be duly considered before advancing a conclusion.

What we can do, however, is to immediately dispose of one argument put forward to negate the possibility that some regulatory measures should be considered as subsidies.

Consider the case of two States with two different levels of regulation (one higher, one lower) with respect to, for example, labour or environmental standards. It is sometimes observed that it would be implausible to consider a country's *omission* to enact regulation as a subsidy.[14] In the absence of measures of harmonization at the international level, it is within the sovereignty of each State to decide the standard of environmental or labour protection most appropriate to its society. Accordingly, if differences in standards (and, more generally, in how regulatory regimes are drafted) between various States may affect competition,[15] they cannot be relevant *as such* for subsidy rules. In short, they are the expression of a *general* policy choice. And subsidy is antonym to norm.[16]

Consequently, if the imposition of lower standards is not simply an omission but does in fact constitute *derogation* from the general policy in the country in

[14] M Benitah, *The Law of Subsidies under the GATT/WTO System* (The Hague: Kluwer Law International, 2001) 70. See also P Didier, *WTO Trade Instruments in EU Law—Commercial Policy Instruments: Dumping, Subsidies, Safeguards, Public Procurement* (London: Cameron May, 1999) nn 76–231.

[15] OECD, *Competition Policy in Subsidies and State Aid*, Competition Policy Roundtable, DAFFE/CLP (2001) 24, Paris, OECD, 27–8, analyse the issues of differences in regulatory regimes, in terms of higher/lower standards and in the choice of the 'initial entitlements'.

[16] As will be discussed fully Part III, the core idea of subsidy is that of a derogation from the relevant norm.

favour of certain undertakings, there are no reasons why this form of deregulation may not be capable of being regarded, at least in principle, as a form of subsidy. The answer will depend on whether that form of action is covered by the relevant discipline and, crucially, whether it is liable to confer a competitive advantage.

V. Forms of governmental action and objectives

One of the techniques to define the legal relevance of a certain action of the government is to refer to the *public policy objectives* pursued by the latter. In this section we will consider briefly the role played by the public objectives in the regulation of subsidies. Considering their general applicability both EC and WTO law will be analysed together.

There is a specific reason why this technique is dealt with at the beginning, before examining the other methods of delimitation, ie the formulation of the definition, the rules of imputability and the origin of the resources. The question of the role played by the objectives of the measure is a recurring theme in the various stages of the analysis of the 'issue of the definition' of WTO subsidy and EC State aid.

A. Self-defence and permitted remedies in rule-oriented systems: the case of retaliatory subsidies

It should at once be underlined that some objectives do *not* justify distorting subsidies. The most notable example is that of 'retaliatory' or 'countervailing subsidies', granted to counter the effects of similar practices of other Member States.

This is a difficult topic which demands a precise analysis. First, apart from the relevance of any efficiency argument on whether a subsidy may be the best remedy to the distortions caused by other subsidies (particularly as compared to countervailing duties),[17] there are more general considerations concerning subsidy-races and potential political and diplomatic tensions which cause this practice to be looked at with scepticism, if not concern. Countervailing-subsidies are liable to undermine any rule-oriented system founded on cooperation and on an agreed regime of control of subsidies. This order of considerations seems to have been translated to the legal level in both the GATT/WTO and EC. The general thrust is that subsidies that are liable to distort international trade and competition cannot be permitted only because they compensate the negative effects of other Members' subsidies.

[17] R Meicklejohn, 'The Economics of State Aid' in European Commission (Directorate General for Economic and Financial Affairs) 'State Aid and the Single Market', (1999) European Economy—Report and Studies 25, 31.

The main principle was clearly laid down in the seminal GATT *US—DISC* case where the Panel noted that '[i]t could not accept that one *distortion* could be justified by the existence of another'.[18] A few years afterwards, the Court of Justice formulated a similar principle in the context of EC law observing that '[t]he effects of more than one *distortion* of competition on trade between Member States do not cancel one another out but accumulate and the damaging consequences to the common market are increased'.[19]

There is another viewpoint—that countervailing subsidies or aids are a form of *self-defence*. This is in principle an *extrema ratio*, being accepted only in exceptional and residual circumstances.[20] In solidly rule-based or rule-oriented systems such as the EC and the WTO they are not permitted at all.[21] In the context of GATT/WTO (but not in the EC), what is exceptionally permitted (constituting an express derogation—but always a derogation—from Article II of the GATT) is only, in certain circumstances and according to certain procedures, the application of countervailing *duties*.[22] An important gloss should be noted here. It has been said that countervailing subsidies or aids are not permitted at all in the EC/WTO. This statement requires more precision. What is not allowed are countervailing subsidies or aids that 'distort to the requisite standard'. If this is not reached, the two systems of subsidy control simply do not bother. From their perspective, any remedying effect produced is not noticeable and hence irrelevant.[23]

An important affirmation of the importance of the observation of the 'rule of law' in the WTO comes from Article 32.1 of the SCM which provides that 'no specific action against a subsidy of another Member can be taken except in accordance with the provisions of GATT 1994, as interpreted by this Agreement'. The dispute settlement organs had the opportunity to interpret this provision with

[18] Paragraph 79 (emphasis added).

[19] Case 78/76 *Steinicke v Germany*, para 24 (emphasis added).

[20] See, more generally, MN Shaw, *International Law* (5th edn, Cambridge: Cambridge University Press, 2003) 1024 et seq.; I Brownlie, *Principles of Public International Law* (6th edn, Oxford: Oxford University Press, 2003) 697 et seq.

[21] In the EC, this principle has been affirmed also with respect to the grant of aid by third countries which cannot justify the non-application of the EC Treaty rules in the EC. The issue is better addressed in the context of EC's external policy (see the 1994 Commission's Guidelines on the application of Articles 92 and 93 of the EC Treaty and Article 61 of the EEA Agreement to State aids in the eviction sector, OJ C350 of 10.12.1995, 5, para 11). cf the different view of Advocate General VerLoren Van Themaat in Case 169/84, *COFAZ*, p 407, who argues for the admissibility of countervailing aid.

[22] And, even with respect to this more limited act of self-defence, many criticisms have been made. For a general analysis see JH Jackson, *The World Trading System—Law and Policy of International Economic Relations* (2nd edn, Cambridge Massachussetts: MIT Press, 1997), 279 et seq. A more comprehensive account can be found in MJ Trebilcock and R Howse, *The Regulation of International Trade* (3rd edn, London: Routledge, 2005), 282 et seq.

[23] It is in this light that the analysis of CD Ehlermann and M Goyette, 'The Interface between EU State Aid Control and WTO Disciplines on Subsidies' (2006) European State Aid Law Quarterly 695, should be considered.

respect to the US Byrd Amendment.[24] The Appellate Body considered this measure a 'specific action against a subsidy' and thus found it contrary to Article 32.1 of the SCM. [25] This provision was again subject to analysis by the DSM in the *EC—Commercial Vessels* case. This dispute concerned the grant of EC State aid to the shipbuilding industry in response to a similar Korean initiative. The Panel construed the phrases 'action' and 'against' in a very restrictive fashion with the result that the EC scheme escaped prohibition. Clearly, however this should *not* be interpreted as a green light to countervaling subsidies. It simply tells us that the interpretation of prohibition of Article 32.1 of the SCM is demanding, not that subsidies that fall foul of the impact standards of the SCM Agreement should simply be allowed. Subsidies may still be objectionable, but following the ordinary route of control.

Finally, as we will see in the following analysis, subsidies to compensate for disadvantages of a given domestic industry as compared with foreign competing industries are not generally accepted because of their direct interference with comparative advantages and hence with international competition and trade.[26] The case might be different when these specific forms of intervention are justified by other independent circumstances,[27] or certainly when general measures, that is measures applicable to the whole of the economy, are concerned.

B. The place of objectives in subsidy legal analysis

In chapter 2 it has been posited that any balanced regulation of subsidies should take into account, at least to a certain extent, the objectives pursued by governments when they intervene in the economy.

That said, the analysis of the objectives of government action may be one of the techniques to define the latter's legal relevance. This seems, for example, to have occurred in a strand of the EC case-law where the Court's decision that the measure at issue did not constitute a State aid seems to have partly been influenced by the need to compensate for some disadvantages faced, for various reasons,

[24] Which provided that the proceeds of antidumping and countervailing duties should have been distributed to affected domestic producers. Quite interestingly, AF Lowenfeld, *International Economic Law* (2nd edn, Oxford: Oxford University Press, 2008) 216, n 1, observes that the intellectual origin of the Byrd Amendment might probably be traced back as far as 1791 and the famous Report on Manufactures of Alexander Hamilton.

[25] US-Offset Act (Byrol Amendment), paras 263–74.

[26] The main authority in the field in the EC is Case 173/73 *Italy v Commission*, para 13. See also Joined Cases 6 and 11/69 *Commission v France*, para 21; Case C-6/97 *Italy v Commission*, para 21. As for WTO law, see the Panel, *US—FSC*, para 7.122. For a useful comment on the latter see RE Hudec, 'Industrial Subsidies: Tax Treatment of "Foreign Sales Corporations" in EU Petersmann and MA Pollack (eds), *Transatlantic Economic Disputes–The EU, the US, and the WTO* (Oxford: Oxford University Press, 2003) 175, 189.

[27] Such as a regional handicap or an industrial restructuring, but this crucially depends on how far positive law goes in recognizing these aims.

by the beneficiary undertakings.[28] Another more plausible argument is that these measures have not been considered to be a State aid because of their *regulatory nature*.

On a proper construction of the rules, and in accordance with the consistent case-law, State aids should be defined objectively, on the basis of their effects,[29] and public policy goals should not be relevant, at least at the level of the definition of which forms of public action should fall within the scope of the rules. A similar conclusion can certainly be drawn with respect to WTO law where, although it is often recognized that governments may act for various policy reasons,[30] the assessment of the action of the government is always maintained at an objective level.

More generally, policy objectives may play a role in the legal analysis of subsidies, but at subsequent and different levels. The issue is about the relevance of the aims or objectives pursued by the measure in the analysis of the advantage (see Part III), of the generality or specificity of the measure (chapter 12), of its distorting effect (chapter 14) and, beyond the boundaries of the definition, of the consideration of the exceptions (chapter 2). As was noted at the end of our analysis in chapter 1, within the context of the definition, the main issue is how scope and justification considerations, inevitably permeated by the social aims pursued by governments, interact. And how, within the framework of the definition, they should be distinguished.

[28] See, for example, the *Sloman Neptun*, *Kirsammer-Hack*, *Viscido*, *Cigliola* decisions thoroughly examined in chapter 5.

[29] Case 173/73 *Italy v Commission*, para 13. See, generally, chapters 5 and 8.

[30] See, for example, Panel, *US—Export Restraints*, para 8.31; Panel, *US—Softwood Lumber III*, para 7.16. cf, in the context of the GATT/Tokyo Round Subsidies Code (and its Art 11; see chapter 2), Panel, *US—Atlantic Salmon I*, paras 235–41, and Panel, *US—Lead and Bismuth I* (unadopted), paras 441–51. See, generally, chapter 8.

4

The forms of governmental action covered by WTO subsidy rules

After analysing in the previous chapter the forms of public intervention in the economy that *may* in principle qualify as a subsidy, and the techniques to establish their legal relevance within the definition at hand, we may now proceed to answering the second and third questions formulated at the beginning of Part II—what forms of action *actually* constitute a subsidy or a State aid in the WTO and EC, and what forms of action *should* be considered as such.

We begin with the examination of the state of the law in the WTO. The analysis focuses on the legal treatment of subsidies in both the GATT and the WTO.

In so doing we concentrate on the first three techniques described above. The first two (the formulation of the definition and rules of imputability) are analysed together, mainly depending on the tight link between the two aspects in the most important provision under examination (Article 1.1(a)(1) of the SCM). Finally we move to the third method of delimitation, the origin of the resources.

I. Formulations of the definition of subsidy and rules of imputability

A. GATT era

The GATT did not include any express definition of subsidy, and hence of its main constituent elements such as the forms of governmental action covered. It is known from an early Panel report that this was not considered as 'necessary [or] feasible' and that it 'would probably be impossible to arrive at a definition that would at the same time include all measures that fall within the intended meaning of the term in Article XVI without including others not so intended'.[1] Certainly the lack of a definition was due to differences of views, as comes out clearly from a report of a group of experts adopted one year earlier.[2]

With respect to the meaning of the word 'subsidies', a large majority of the experts considered that it covered only subsidies granted by governments or by semi-governmental bodies.

[1] Report on 'Operation of the Provisions of Article XVI' adopted on 21 November 1961, BISD 10th Supp/201 (1962) para 23.

[2] Second report on 'Anti-dumping and Countervailing Duties' adopted on 27 May 1960, BISD 9th Supp/194 (1961) para 34.

Three experts considered that the word should be interpreted in a wider sense and felt that it covered all subsidies, whatever their character and whatever their origin, including also subsidies granted by private bodies.

Despite this divergence, however,

[i]t was agreed that the word 'subsidies' covered not only actual payments, but also measures having an equivalent effect.

The resemblance between this conclusion and the language used by the European Court of Justice a few months later is striking. The Court quite ingeniously distinguished the terms 'aid' and 'subsidy' saying that the former does not cover only positive benefits (ie subsidies) but also those forms of financial support that 'are similar in character and have the same effect' as positive benefits.[3]

Returning to the GATT, some linguistic hints against a limited coverage could be found in various provisions which alternatively referred to 'any subsidy' (Articles VI:3 and Article XVI:1 of the GATT) or to 'any form of subsidy' (Articles XVI:3 and 4), or which noted that subsidies could be granted directly or indirectly (Articles VI.3, XVI:3 and XVI:4 of the GATT) or, with a particular emphasis on the effects of the measure, that they could affect imports or exports in a direct or indirect way (Article XVI:1 of the GATT).

From the beginning, the consistent reading of the term subsidy has thus been quite extensive. The Tokyo Round Subsidies Code, for instance, mentioned some 'examples of possible forms of subsidies', encompassing 'government financing of commercial enterprises, including grants, loans or guarantees; government provision or government financed provision of utility, supply distribution and other operational or support services or facilities; government financing of research and development programmes; fiscal incentives; and government subscription to, or provision of, equity capital'.[4] An examination of the GATT disputes confirms that various measures of assistance have been regarded as subsidies (such as payments, loans, guarantees, tax deferrals and exemptions).[5]

Although it was debated whether more complex regulatory mechanisms such as lax environmental or labour standards could also be included in the notion of subsidy,[6]

[3] Case 30/59 *Steenkolenmijnen*, p 19. See chapter 4 for an analysis.

[4] Article 11.3. We can also mention a 1960 Working Party that, during the negotiations to put the provision of Article XVI:4 fully into effect, reported a proposal of a quite detailed list of measures considered as export subsidies. Quite interestingly, it was thought it necessary to underline that 'this list should not be considered exhaustive or to limit in any way the generality of the provisions of paragraph 4 of Article XVI'. See Report 'Provisions of Article XVI:4', BISD 9th Supp/185 (1961), para 5.

[5] See, eg, *Australia—Ammonium Sulphate* (1950); *US—DISC* (1981); *France—Income Tax* (1981); *Netherlands—Income Tax* (1981); *Belgium—Income Tax* (1981); *EEC—Oilseeds I* (1990); *US—Softwood Lumber II* (1993); *US—Atlantic Salmon* (1994). Although expressly recognized in the Tokyo Round Subsidies Code, the status of certain measures, particularly capital injections, raised much controversy in the *US—Lead and Bismuth I* (1994) with the result that the Panel report was not adopted.

[6] *Pro* M Bronckers and R Quick, 'What is a Countervailable Subsidy under EEC Trade Law?' (1989) 6 Journal of World Trade 5, 22; A O'Brien, 'Countervailing Low Wage Subsidies: A Counter

it seems that, despite its comprehensive nature, the GATT concept of subsidy was limited to measures involving a clear transfer of economic resources and, in the case of action through intermediaries, requiring a rather close involvement of the government.[7] This is the interpretation made by an early Panel[8] and confirmed prior to the Uruguay Round by the Group of Experts on the Calculation of the Amount of a Subsidy (a body operating under the Tokyo Round Committee on Subsidies and Countervailing Measures), which noted that:

> there can be no subsidy in the absence of a financial contribution by government . . . there is a necessary link between a subsidy and the taxation function of government, exercised either directly or delegated to other, private bodies.[9]

In particular, the concept of 'financial contribution', construed with reference to the link with the 'taxation function of the government', clearly hints at the forms of intervention involving a *quite defined transfer of economic resources connected with the 'sovereign right of governments to collect revenue and spend it'*.[10] These correspond to the most commonly accepted forms of subsidy. On the other hand, the rule of imputability of the forms of indirect action shows a particularly tight degree of government involvement by using the term 'delegation'.

What emerges therefore is that in the GATT there was a certain agreement that only clear and established forms of financial assistance would be covered in the definition of subsidy with the exclusion of more complex forms of regulatory measures.

B. WTO era

The regulation of subsidies in the WTO is included in two main instruments, the SCM Agreement and the Agreement on Agriculture (AG). The analysis of the forms of governmental action covered concentrates on two provisions which are particularly significant, the 'financial contribution' in the general definition

to the Leveling of Labor Conditions' (1994) 4 Transnational Law and Contemporary Problems 825; *contra* M Benitah, *The Law of Subsidies under the GATT/WTO System* (The Hague: Kluwer Law International, 2001), 68.

[7] It was accordingly concluded that price support systems which are maintained by indirect methods such as quantitative restrictions, flexible tariffs or similar charges, would not constitute a subsidy. See Panel Report 'Review pursuant to Article XVI:5', BISD 9th Supp/188 (1961) para 11.

[8] ibid, para 12.

[9] This view was incorporated in a Note by the GATT Secretariat on 'Subsidies and Countervailing Measures' presented during those negotiations (MTN.GNG/NG10/W/4, Section 4.1.A). It may be noted that these findings of both the Panel (ibid) and the Group of Experts anticipate, almost verbatim, the future wording of the financial contribution requirement of Article 1.1 of the SCM, and will play a significant role in its interpretation by the Panel, *US—Export Restraint* (see para 8.71).

[10] Emphasis added. This expression was used by the said Group of Experts on the Calculation of the Amount of a Subsidy and was referred to in the GATT Secretariat note mentioned in the previous note.

of subsidy of Article 1.1(a)(1) of the SCM and the form of export subsidy in Article 9.1(c) of the AG.

SCM Agreement

The SCM Agreement, which constitutes the most general regulation of subsidies in the WTO, has introduced for the first time a fairly sophisticated definition of subsidy in Article 1.

In particular, under Article 1.1(a), the action by the government may be constituted by two alternative elements, a 'financial contribution' or 'any income or price support', which should confer a 'benefit'.

Article 1.1(a)(1) of the SCM: the financial contribution requirement

Article 1.1(a)(1) of the SCM requires that for a subsidy to exist there must be a 'financial contribution' by a government or any public body. The provision also includes an elaborate list of various forms of financial contribution which occur where:

- (i) a government practice involves a direct transfer of funds (eg grants, loans, and equity infusion), potential direct transfers of funds or liabilities (eg loan guarantees);
- (ii) government revenue that is otherwise due is foregone or not collected (eg fiscal incentives such as tax credits);
- (iii) a government provides goods or services other than general infrastructure, or purchases goods;
- (iv) a government makes payment to a funding mechanism, or entrusts or directs a private body to carry out one or more of the type of functions illustrated in (i) to (iii) above which would normally be vested in the government and the practice, in no real sense, differs from practices normally followed by governments.

For the purposes of the present analysis, the important questions to answer are the following: How should this requirement be interpreted, and what is its role? What is the meaning and role of its fourth subparagraph? Does the financial contribution require a cost to government?

Leaving the issue of financing to the next section, the first questions will be answered.

Interpretation and function of the financial contribution

The Appellate Body has promptly underlined that the 'financial contribution' is *separate from* the 'benefit' and that these two elements *together* determine whether a subsidy exists.[11] These are the important background findings to keep in mind in order to fully appreciate the following analysis.

[11] Appellate Body, *Brazil—Aircraft*, para 157. See also *Canada—Aircraft*, para 156.

The report of the *US—Export Restraints* Panel will be examined.[12] This is a landmark document for the definition of subsidy, casting light on both the interpretation and function of the requirement of financial contribution.[13]

The core of the debate is 'nature versus effect' of governmental action.

The main issue in *Export Restraints* was whether an 'export restraint' could constitute a financial contribution in the form of the government-entrusted or government-directed provision of goods in the sense of Article 1.1(a)(1)(iii) and (iv) of the SCM.[14]

The central argument of the United States, the defendant, which mirrored its position on the notion of subsidy in the Uruguay Round negotiations, was based on an exclusive emphasis on the (beneficial) effects produced by the governmental intervention in the economy.

An export restraint can be caught by the fourth subparagraph when its *effect* is to induce domestic producers to sell their products, in greater quantities or exclusively, to domestic users. In other words, when the producer of the restrained goods has no other practical or commercial option than to sell in the domestic market, an export restraint would be functionally or conceptually equivalent to an 'entrustment' or 'direction' to that producer to 'provide' those 'goods' in the domestic market under Article 1.1(a)(1)(iv) of the SCM, the difference being merely semantic. In such circumstances, it would be *as if* the government had explicitly and affirmatively ordered those producers to do so.

In response to the 'effects approach' advocated by the US, the Panel underlined that the determination of whether a financial contribution exists must concentrate on the examination of the *nature* of the action by the government and not on its effects.

The interpretation whereby, irrespective of its nature, any governmental action producing a certain result would effectively amount to a financial contribution,

[12] See, in particular, paras 8.15–8.76.

[13] The president of the Panel was Michael Cartland, the Hong Kong Permanent Representative to the GATT who played a pivotal role in the Uruguay Round, particularly in the negotiations on subsidies, by chairing the Negotiating Group on Subsidies and Countervailing Duties. Thanks to his presence, the Panel undoubtedly enjoyed a comprehensive insight into the delicate negotiations of the notion of subsidy and of the spirit of the delicate balance reached in the final agreement. This biographical element does give a special aura of authority to the Panel's findings. It probably also helps to explain why, despite the findings touching a legal issues intensely debated during the negotiations as well as a crucial allegation in the controversial and long-standing *US—Canada* dispute on lumber, the report was not appealed. For a report of the history of the export restriction complaint in the GATT era (and under the US-Canada Free Trade Agreement) and an assessment at the beginning of the WTO, see Hudec, 'Differences in National Environmental Standards: The Level-Playing-Field Dimension' (1995) 5 Minnesota Journal of Global Trade 16–19.

[14] The Panel considered as an export restraint 'a border measure that takes the form of a government law or regulation which expressly limits the quantity of exports or places explicit conditions on the circumstances under which exports are permitted, or that takes the form of a government-imposed fee or tax on exports of the product calculated to limit the quantity of exports'. In so doing, the Panel followed the definition proposed by the claimant, Canada. It is worth noting that the US proposed a broader definition, ie 'an action or an act that holds back or prevents exports' (ibid, para 8.16).

would eventually mean reading the financial contribution requirement out of the SCM Agreement. The Panel concluded that the focus of the financial contribution assessment must therefore be on the government's *action* rather than its possible effects on, or the reactions to it by, those specifically affected, even if those effects or reactions can be expected. From another perspective, it was noted that the reaction of private entities to given governmental measures cannot constitute the basis of establishing a Member's compliance with WTO law.

The Panel then crucially found that the SCM Agreement regulated *only certain forms* of governmental action that distort or may distort international trade.[15] It is with this express purpose in mind that the definition of subsidy (with its three 'gateways': financial contribution, benefit and specificity)[16] was drafted. In other words, the *function* of the financial contribution requirement is to ensure that not all government measures that confer benefits can be deemed to be subsidies. As a corollary of this function of limitation, according to the Panel, those forms (listed in items (i) to (iii)) should be considered exhaustive.[17]

The following jurisprudence substantially confirmed the limiting role of the financial contribution element. After underlining that 'Article 1.1(a)(1) *makes clear* that a "financial contribution" by a government or public body is an *essential component* of a "subsidy" ',[18] the Appellate Body has recognized that 'paragraphs (i) through (iv) of Article 1.1(a)(1) set forth the situations *where there is* a financial contribution by a government or public body'.[19] Consequently, 'not all government measures capable of conferring benefits would necessarily fall within Article 1.1(a)' as, otherwise, there would be no need for the financial contribution 'because all government measures conferring benefits, *per se*, would be subsidies'.[20]

[15] This would be in line with the object and purpose of the SCM Agreement. See, eg, Panel, *Canada—Aircraft*, para 9.119; Panel, *Brazil—Aircraft*, para 7.26.

[16] Strictly speaking, according to the SCM Agreement (see Articles 1.2 and 2.1 SCM), the specificity test is not part of the definition of subsidy.

[17] Whereas, on the one hand, the four modes of subsidy under point (a)(1) are introduced by the phrase 'ie where' (thus suggesting the exclusiveness of the list), on the other hand, point (a)(1)(iv) refers to the 'functions illustrated in (i) to (iii) above' (thus indicating the contrary). The function of limitation of the financial contribution requirement is particularly clear from the introducing phrase 'ie where'. The discordant term 'illustrated' is just a remnant of the very first draft of the provision where the list was introduced by 'such as where' (MTN.GNG/NG10/W/38, so called 'Cartland I' text). Whereas the latter was subsequently replaced by 'ie' (MTN/GNG/NG10/W/38/Rev. 1, 'Cartland II') and eventually by the final form 'ie where' (MTN/GNG/NG10/W/38/Rev. 2, 'Cartland III', MTN/GNG/NG10/W/38/Rev. 3, 'Cartland IV', MTN.TNC/W/FA, 'Dunkel' text), the former term remained untouched due to a clear oversight.

Further, a restrictive, albeit not necessarily an 'exclusive', approach seems to be confirmed by the coda to subparagraph (iv) which makes it clear that the conduct of the intermediary 'would normally be vested in the government and the practice, in no real sense, differs from practices normally followed by governments'. For the interpretation of these crucial expressions see below.

[18] Appellate Body, *US—DRAMS*, para 107 (emphasis added).

[19] ibid, para 108 (emphasis added).

[20] ibid, para 114 building on its finding in *US—Softwood Lumber IV*, para 52, n 35. See also Panel, *EC—DRAMS*, para 7.58.

In the light of the previous construction of the financial contribution element, the *US—Export Restraints* Panel notes that the *function* of the fourth subparagraph is not to encompass forms of action other than those provided in subparagraphs (i) to (iii), and consequently to enlarge the coverage of the definition of subsidy, but rather to avoid circumvention of those subparagraphs by a government simply acting through a private body (or, indeed, through a funding mechanism).[21] Using a particularly illuminating expression at paragraph 8.53, the Panel noted that that provision has to do with the identity of the *actor* and not with the *nature* of the actions covered by the financial contribution requirement.

It should finally be noted that, according to the Panel, all forms of financial contribution involve a clear transfer of economic resources in the form of a transfer of something of value, either money, goods or services, from the government or an intermediary to a private entity. Crucially, as a consequence of the function of limitation of the financial contribution, the converse is not necessarily true, that is, not *all* transfers of economic resources constitute a financial contribution under the SCM Agreement.

The fourth subparagraph of Article 1.1(a)(1) of the SCM: rules of imputability and 'guarding' mechanisms

Subparagraph (iv) between restrictiveness and expansiveness The inherent and intriguing tension between two findings should be evident by now. On the one hand, the *restrictiveness* of the conclusion that subparagraph (iv) cannot extend the coverage of the financial contribution—which is just a corollary of the general finding that the function of the financial contribution requirement is to limit the forms of governmental action regulated under it. On the other hand, the natural *expansiveness* of any mechanism to counter circumvention—which has been recognized as the true function of subparagraph (iv). To ease this tension, what is crucial then is to find an appropriate *balance* between these two objectives, a point of equilibrium between two conflicting forces.

Any legal norm is comparable to a valve. As the exposition of the various interpretations made by dispute settlement organs show, this is particularly true for the rules of imputability under the fourth subparagraph. Depending on which of the two objectives indicated above ('limited coverage' or 'anti-circumvention' of the financial contribution) prevails, more or less courses of conduct will pass through the valve, enlarging or restricting the scope of the financial contribution requirement and, consequently, of the definition of subsidy.

As underlined in chapter 1, the canons of interpretation of the Vienna Convention on the Law of Treaties (VCLT) demand that the balance between the two tendencies should *mainly* emerge from, and be consistent with, the text of the financial contribution requirement itself.

[21] This anti-circumvention function has been confirmed by the Appellate Body. See *US—DRAMS*, para 113; *US—Softwood Lumber IV*, para 52.

The quest for a balance: the development of the law What we see with respect to the financial contribution through a private party can be viewed as a quest for a balance between two opposing objectives. We begin with an examination of the development of the law on the relevant rules of imputability, and then provide a critique.

In *US—Export Restraints*, the US were substantially claiming that the key factor in the interpretation of the terms 'entrust' and 'direct' was the *proximity of the causal relationship* between the action by the government and the conduct of the private body. An export restraint would thus fulfil the required 'direction' when the producer of the restrained goods has no other choice but to sell in the domestic market.

The Panel disagreed and gave a restrictive interpretation of those two terms. The ordinary meanings of the concepts of 'entrust' and 'direct' necessarily conveyed an idea of 'explicit and affirmative action [of] delegation or command'.[22]

A first step towards a more liberal interpretation was taken in the *US—DRAMS*, *Korea—Commercial Vessels* and *EC—DRAMS* Panels (hereinafter referred to as 'the Panels'). While they agreed that the terms 'entrust' and 'direct' must respectively contain an 'element of delegation or command', and that they should invariably take the form of an 'affirmative' act, they disagreed as to whether they necessarily needed to be explicit insofar as they could be 'explicit or implicit, informal or formal'.[23]

It is in the *US—DRAMS* dispute, however, that the Appellate Body took a significant step further by rejecting the view that the concepts of entrustment and direction be limited to the notions of delegation or command.

On the one hand, the concept of entrustment would generally be connoted by an *action of giving responsibility* to someone for a task or an object. This interpretation is not limited to acts of delegation, either formal or informal, as there may be other means, be they formal or informal, that governments could employ to give responsibility to carry out one of the functions listed in paragraphs (i) to (iii) of Article 1.1(a)(1) of the SCM.[24] On the other hand, the Appellate Body found that the notion of direction is connected with the *exercise of governmental authority* over a private body. 'A "command" . . . is certainly one way in which a government can exercise authority over a private body in the sense foreseen by Article 1.1(a)(1)(iv), but governments are likely to have other means at their disposal to exercise authority over a private body', some of which are *more subtle* or *may not involve the same degree of compulsion*.[25] As regards the complexity of the act of entrustment or direction, it should also be noted that, unlike all previous dispute settlement

[22] Panel, *US—Export Restraints*, paras 8.29 8.30.

[23] Panel, *US—DRAMS*, para 7.33; Panel, *Korea—Commercial Vessels*, para 7.370; Panel, *EC—DRAMS*, para 7.57.

[24] Appellate Body, *US—DRAMS*, para 110.

[25] ibid, para 111.

organs, the Appellate Body did *not* request that the action of the government be 'affirmative'.

The quest for a balance: analysis of the law An attempt will now be made to explain these interpretations in the light of the observations that have been made with respect to the two conflicting objectives within the financial contribution element, and the need to strike an appropriate balance between them.

The main concern, and hence the focus, of the *US—Export Restraints* Panel was to show that the financial contribution requirement *only covers* certain forms of public intervention. It is against this background that the admittedly strict interpretation of the tests of imputability under subparagraph four (which would require the explicitness of the action) can be properly understood.

In the following cases, a shift in emphasis can be noted. The role of delimitation of the financial contribution was not an issue.[26] What we have is an attempt to give an *effective* interpretation to the anti-circumvention device of the fourth subparagraph. Thus the Panels underlined that to require that the action of delegation and command be always explicit would undermine the utility of Article 1.1(a)(1)(iv) as it would enable governments to circumvent their commitments.[27] In *US—DRAMS*, the Appellate Body searched for the essence of the terms 'entrustment' and 'direction' which it found in the broad concepts of conferral of responsibility to or exercise of authority over somebody. In so doing, it eventually rejected the assimilation with the notions of delegation and command.

This final outcome (entrustment and direction are respectively different from delegation and command), however, raises some concerns.[28]

This may be illustrated by the analysis of the Appellate Body's construction of the term 'direct'.[29] Using the orthodox approach, and applying the 'customary rules of interpretation in public international law', we begin with the ordinary meaning of the word set in its immediate context. In particular, the choice of the appropriate meaning of 'direct' would be significantly influenced by the *syntax* of the phrase 'direct a private body to carry out'. To direct somebody to do something cannot but mean to *order* him or her to do something.[30] The examination of the meanings of the corresponding verbs in the French and Spanish versions (respectively 'ordonner' and 'ordenar'), when inserted in similar syntactical structures ('ordonner à quelq'un de faire quelque chose'; 'ordenar a alguien a hecer algo'),[31]

[26] cf Appellate Body, *US—DRAMS*, para 114; *US—Lumber IV*, para 52, n 35; Panel *EC—DRAMS*, para 7.58.

[27] Panel, *US—DRAMS*, para 7.33, n 50, Panel, *Korea Commercial Vessels*, para 7.370, n 209; Panel, *EC—DRAMS*, para 7.57, n 65.

[28] See M Matsushita, TJ Schoenbaum, and PC Mavroidis, *The World Trade Organization—Law, Practice, and Policy* (2nd edn, Oxford: Oxford University Press, 2006) 345.

[29] A similar exercise could be entertained with the interpretation of 'entrust'.

[30] For a similar reading cf Panel, *US—Export Restraints*, para 8.28.

[31] Together with English, French and Spanish are official languages in the WTO. According to Article 33(3) of the Vienna Convention, '[t]he terms of the treaty are presumed to have the same meaning in each authentic text'.

would confirm the conclusion that the phrase at issue refers to an '*order to* somebody *to* do something'.[32]

The textual interpretation of 'direct' thus refers to a course of conduct, which might well be 'explicit or implicit, informal or formal' as it was found by the Panels, but which is necessarily characterized by a *well defined, and rather marked, degree of direction* and *compulsion* in the governmental action. Crucially, this interpretation sits uneasily with the conclusion of the Appellate Body that a 'command is not necessary' and that even forms of action that are 'more subtle' or that do 'not involve the same degree of compulsion' are covered.[33]

Legal interpretation does not depend exclusively on grammatical analysis. The already underlined importance of the textual approach in the WTO however requires that the letter of the law should not be disregarded. An excessively broad interpretation of subparagraph (iv) inevitably risks expanding too much the scope of the financial contribution requirement and endangers the difficult balance between its two consolidated functions of limitation and anti-circumvention. It has already been suggested that if a balance between the two conflicting objectives has to be struck, this has to be consistent with the letter of the law. In this regard, it is interesting to compare for a moment the Appellate Body's construction with the reading made by the Panels which is *textually* and *contextually* more correct and hence more successful in achieving an appropriate balance.

Interestingly, the Appellate Body concludes its reasoning by underlining that its interpretation is in line with the object and purpose of the SCM Agreement, which, using its words, 'reflects a delicate balance' between those Members that sought more discipline on the use of subsidies and those that sought more discipline on the application of countervailing measures.[34] This general statement is correct, and will be used in our analysis, in particular when we attempt to make some conclusive remarks on the coherency of the definition of subsidy in the WTO.[35] It is however beside the point. It does not address the more specific concern about the different—and inner—balance between the two conflicting objectives of limitation and anti-circumvention that have emerged from the analysis of the financial

[32] The Appellate Body analyses the meaning of the verbs 'ordenar' and 'ordonner' but does not consider the specific meaning they have when a certain syntax, that of subpara (iv), is considered.

[33] It is worth noting that the Appellate Body too started its analysis from similar dictionary meanings of to 'direct' ('give authoritative instructions to' and 'order (a person) to do'). The Appellate Body itself seems to have recognized that the degree of compulsion required by the term 'direct' is the same of the term 'mandate' (which undoubtedly means 'command' or 'order'). This finding was made in the context of the interpretation of the phrase 'governmental action' in Article 9.1(c) AG. See *Canada—Dairy (Article 21.5)*, para 128: 'Article 9.1(c) does not require that payments be financed by virtue of government "mandate", or other "direction". Although the word "action" certainly covers situations where government mandates or directs that payments be made, it also covers other situations where no such compulsion is involved' (emphasis in the original).

[34] Appellate Body, *US—DRAMS*, para 115.

[35] See section III of chapter 6.

contribution itself, concern that is also motivated by the need to fully respect the text and hence the object and purpose of the SCM Agreement.

Even assuming, for the sake of the reasoning, that the Appellate Body's novel interpretation of the term 'direct' is correct, there is no clear guidance on the applicable standard. The Appellate Body itself recognizes the difficulty of the assessment when it hastens to add that the relevant determination 'will hinge on the particular facts of the case'.[36] What is still difficult to grasp is the impact of the general finding that the concept of direction refers to situations where the government exercises its authority over a private body on the more specific finding that this may be more subtle than a command and does not necessarily involve the same degree of compulsion. Further, how can the latter, loose interpretation be reconciled with the sweeping statement that the two standards of imputability under item (iv) are not met with 'mere policy pronouncements' or 'imply a more active role than mere acts of encouragement'?[37]

With an express reference to the *nature* of the form of intervention, the Appellate Body has emphatically ruled out that the interpretation of paragraph (iv) can be so broad as to cover measures whereby governments merely exercise their 'general regulatory powers'.[38] Not only is this a vague statement, but it leaves open, in the author's view, the question of whether, by relying on the more liberal interpretation of the term 'direct' the Appellate Body suggested,[39] complex regulatory mechanisms, such as those involving lax labour or environmental standards or import and export restraints, could now fall—at least under certain circumstances—within the scope of the provision.

Finally, it cannot pass unnoticed that, despite the Appellate Body's stated intention, the proposed liberal interpretation has the potential to weaken the finding that the financial contribution focuses on the *nature* and not on the *effects* of the action of the government. The more we leave clear notions such as command, moving towards more subtle and less intense courses of action, the greater the risk that the financial contribution be defined on the basis of the *circumstances of the case* and the *behaviour of third parties*.[40]

Interlude on the other form of indirect action (payments to funding mechanism) We may pause for a moment in our analysis of the action involving an entrustment or direction of private bodies to draw a brief parallel with the other form of action

[36] Appellate Body, *US—DRAMS*, para 116.

[37] ibid, para 114.

[38] ibid, para 115.

[39] And the same could equally be said for the term 'entrust'.

[40] Citing the *US—Export Restraints* Panel, the Appellate Body confirmed that entrustment and direction cannot cover 'the situation in which the government intervenes in the market in some way, which may or may not have a particular result simply based on the given factual circumstances and the exercise of free choice by the actors of the market'. Government entrustment or direction 'cannot be inadvertent or mere by-product of governmental regulation' (*US—DRAMS*, para 114).

under the fourth subparagraph of Article 1.1(a)(1) of the SCM where 'a government makes payments to a funding mechanism'.

The meaning of the two terms 'funding' and 'mechanism' does not need much clarification. The provision refers to those cases where the government makes payments to a system that is established to transfer financial resources to entitled categories.[41]

It has been said that the two forms of indirect action under the fourth subparagraph 'are aimed at capturing equivalent government actions'.[42] How correct this assimilation is, however, is put into doubt by the recent interpretation of the term 'entrust' in the other form of indirect action which, according to the Appellate Body, would not necessarily refer to an act of delegation. If this is correct, the financial contribution through a funding mechanism would arguably be characterized by a more direct and intense course of action than the entrustment of a private body to carry out a financial contribution. The government makes a payment to a funding mechanism which—unlike other private bodies—is there exclusively to finance somebody, and hence any payment received from the government should almost automatically be used for such mission.

Two provisos consolidating the function of the financial contribution The concepts of 'entrustment' and 'direction' are crucial within the context of subparagraph (iv), and, more generally, of the whole financial contribution requirement. The interpreter would however be mistaken if his or her reading ended with those two concepts. Indeed the provision includes two important statements that could easily pass unnoticed but which should not do so.[43] We quote again the provision *in extenso*, emphasizing the two expressions.

> a government makes payment to a funding mechanism, or entrusts or directs a private body to carry out one or more of the type of functions illustrated in (i) to (iii) above which *would normally be vested in the government* and *the practice, in no real sense, differs from practices normally followed by governments.*

These two admittedly repetitive statements could be seen as examples of bad drafting, appearing too obvious, almost tautological, or too obscure. In both cases they would seem unable to add any real meaning to the previous 'hard' concepts of entrustment and direction. In a word, they would be substantially *inutile.* This approach would however run counter to the principle of effective treaty interpretation.[44] A more convincing alternative recognizes the firm intention of the drafters to convey a distinct meaning, and possibly an important one, with the provisos playing a role in this respect. The proper construction of the two statements

[41] It is interesting to note the very similar wording used by the GATT Panel Report 'Review pursuant to Article XVI:5', in BISD, 9th Supp/188 (1961) para 12.

[42] Panel, *US—Export Restraints*, para 8.32.

[43] Most, if not all, the works in the area are surprisingly silent on these two requirements.

[44] See chapter 1, section II.C.

requires that they are put within the broader context of letter (iv), and, more generally, of the financial contribution requirement.

The starting point of our analysis is worth repeating. The presence of these two requirements makes it immediately clear that to establish that a private body has been 'entrusted' or 'directed' to carry out one of the functions under items (i) to (iii) is *not* sufficient under subparagraph (iv). Howse noted that '[t]he relevant provision *also* requires that the function entrusted or delegated to the private body be one that is *normally* performed by government'.[45]

If it is clear that the two sentences specify the indirect action of subparagraph (iv), what is not clear is how they do this. They could be interpreted in different, opposite, ways which substantially follow the two approaches (nature vs effect) underlying the conflicting interpretations of the concepts of 'entrustment' and 'direction', and more generally of the financial contribution requirement itself, which we have analysed above.

Two important findings emerging from the case-law should inform our analysis. First, as with the notions of 'entrustment' and 'direction', it is clear that these two sentences cannot reduce or enlarge the defined scope of the financial contribution which is exhaustively defined by (i) to (iii).[46] The immediate impression is that the objective of the two provisos seems in particular that to *avoid the scope of the financial contribution via a third party being unduly broadened.* In other words, the two sentences are there to ensure that there is no distortion of the financial contribution requirement by arguing that complex triangular transfers of economic resources would be caught in through an unbridled construction of the key concepts of 'entrustment' or 'direction'. Secondly, and consequently, they play a crucial role in reinforcing the idea that the 'difference between subparagraphs (i)-(iii) on the one hand and subparagraph (iv) on the other has to do with the identity of the actor, and not the nature of the action'.[47]

[45] R Howse, 'Post-Hearing Submission to the International Trade Commission: World Trade Law and Renewable Energy: The Case of Non-Tariff Measures', 5 May 2005, Renewable Energy and Intenrnational Law Project, 22. See also A Reich, 'Privately Subsidized Recycling Schemes and their Potential Harm to the Environment of Developing Countries: Does International Trade Law Have a Solution?', Bar Ilan University Public Law Working Paper No 2–5, 4 March 2004, 11 et seq.

Note also RE Hudec, ('Differences in National Environmental Standards: The Level-Playing-Field Dimension' (1996) 5 Minnesota Journal of Global Trade 1, n 35) that applies subpara (iv), including the two final provisos, to the 'export restraints' that have long been subject to the *US—Canada Lumber* confrontation. The background is the known Congressional intention to cover within the newly ratified Uruguay Round subsidy disciplines also a broad concept of 'regulatory' subsidy. Hudec notes that, whereas 'governments have often given subsidies by selling raw material inputs below fair market value', the issue of '[w]hether the resulting reduced-price sale "in no real sense differs from practices normally followed by governments" is debatable'. He concludes by noting: 'Interestingly, the US implementing legislation struck "in no real sense differs" and substituted "does not differ in substance"'.

[46] Panel, *US—Export Restraints*, paras 8.56–8.59.

[47] Panel, *Korea Commercial Vessels*, para 7.32, referring in n 26 to Panel, *US—Export Restraints*, para 8.53.

With these findings in mind, an interpretation of each sentence can be advanced.

The first sentence focuses on the governmental course of the 'functions under (i) to (iii)' highlighting that they should 'normally' (which can safely be replaced with adverbs such as 'usually' or indeed 'indifferently') be carried out by the government.

The actual benchmark of 'normality', the term which is also found in the second proviso,[48] can be particularly testing, and proves important for the proper definition of the scope of subparagraph (iv). Various alternatives can be thought of. We can dispose of Canada's reference to the concept of 'habitual' in *US—Export Restraints* for which the Panel expressed 'serious doubts' because of its inappropriate limiting effect on the scope of subparagraph (iv).[49] Quite similarly, it seems that the possibility of using more generally the Member at hand as a benchmark should be excluded since it may too lead to circular, and auto-justificatory, reasoning. Reich has observed that two alternatives could be 'what most governments do' or a 'defined, commonly accepted standard'.[50] He shows that, despite the diversity in governmental policies and traditions, the former 'factual' approach, with its flexibility,[51] may be more appealing and acceptable to dispute settlement. Whatever it may be, we think that in practice the distinction among these benchmarks may be more apparent than real.[52]

The second sentence, the 'added-value' closing clause of subparagraph (iv), fundamentally precludes that complex regulatory mechanisms be included in the provision. The 'practice' of the government should 'differ', 'in no real sense', 'from practices normally followed by governments'. It should be noted immediately that, whereas the focus of the first proviso was the 'function' carried out by the government, this sentence concerns the 'practice', ie the action of carrying out that 'function' through a private party.

The words 'practices normally carried out by governments' are the true (hermeneutic) core of this proviso—and more generally of the whole subparagraph (iv). It seems that *normal governmental practice* should be given a specific meaning, referring in particular to the forms of action that involve the *exercise of the prerogatives of taxation and expenditure*. This is the view that has passed across time from the GATT to the WTO. The view expressed by the Group of Experts in 1987 during the Uruguay Round Negotiations, which was interpreting a 1960 Panel,

[48] For its meaning in that context see below.

[49] Panel, *US—Export Restraints*, para 8.59.

[50] A Reich, 'Privately Subsidized Recycling Schemes and their Potential Harm to the Environment of Developing Countries: Does International Trade Law Have a Solution?', Bar Ilan University Public Law Working Paper No 2–5, 4 March 2004, 12–13.

[51] The presence of a 'significant number of governments' performing a certain function should be enough to satisfy the evidential burden.

[52] Factual and theoretical questions may easily blend into what would emerge as the relevant, and possibly rather abstract, standard of normality.

and which was relied on by the *US—Export Restraints* Panel in 2001 with the following words:

we . . . find very significant the Group of Experts' interpretation that the 1960 Panel's reference to 'practice . . . in no real sense different from those normally followed by governments' was a general reference to the *delegation* to private parties of the particular government functions of taxation and expenditure of revenue, and *not* a reference to government market interventions in the general sense, or the effects thereof.[53]

Having defined what 'normal governmental practice' means, we should consider how the conduct at issue relates to it. This depends on the terms 'differ' and 'in no real sense'. Whereas the latter hints at the need for a clear and close correspondence, for its part, '[not to] differ' could be read as requiring an *equivalence in effects* between the practice at issue and those usually performed by governments. An uncontrolled reading of this type would however result in a potential enlargement of the scope of subparagraph (iv) and of the financial contribution requirement and thus run counter to the function of subparagraph (iv)—which does not alter the forms of actions already indicated in items (i) to (iii)—and would also be inconsistent with the immediate contextual indications of the phrase 'in no real sense'. At the other side of the spectrum '[not to] differ' could be construed as requiring *an equivalence in nature* between the practice actually under examination and those that governments normally execute. This interpretation, by substantially requiring that the two practices are virtually the same, would exclude any expansionist outcome, and would be fully in line with the role attributed to letter (iv) as well as with a stringent reading of 'in no real sense'. In short, while '[not to] differ', put in context, seems to evoke a strong connection, what is not fully clear is how strong this should actually be. While a simple reference to a correspondence in effects seems too loose, to require a full uniformity in nature may be too strict.

In conclusion, these two statements seem to share the role to specify the standards of imputability of 'entrustment' and 'direction' and, through this, to consolidate (the function and interpretation of) the financial contribution. This is done by linking the financial contribution to the government powers of taxation and expenditure.[54] This reading has been confirmed by the *Korea—Commercial Vessels Panel.*

We note Korea's argument that Article 1.1(a)(1)(iv) of the *SCM Agreement* refers to functions 'normally (. . .) vested in the government' and 'practice [that] in no real sense, differs from practices normally followed by governments'. We note that this language was addressed by the panel in *US—Export Restraints.* That panel referred to the report of the Group of Experts on the Calculation of the Amount of a Subsidy, which in turn referred to a

[53] Panel, *US—Export Restraints*, para 8.72.

[54] Following this reasoning, there are two interesting questions to ask: whether the guarding function of these two provisos may have an impact (i) on the interpretation of the concepts of 'entrust' and 'direct' and (ii) on whether a 'cost to government' would be needed under the financial contribution requirement (this issue is analysed at length below).

1960 panel report. Like that panel, we too 'find very significant the Group of Experts' interpretation othat the 1960 Panel's reference to "practice . . . in no real sense different from those normally followed by governments" was a general reference to the *delegation* to private parties of the particular government functions of taxation and expenditure of revenue, . . .'. The Panel notes that the reference to functions 'normally vested in the government' textually mirrors the reference to 'practices normally followed by governments'. Accordingly, the Panel considers that the reference to functions 'normally vested in the government' should also be understood to mean functions of taxation and revenue expenditure. Thus, a function may be said to be 'normally vested in the government' if that function involves the levy of taxation or the expenditure of revenue.[55]

The Panel is saying two interesting things. First, by establishing a clear link between two sentences 'which textually mirror' each other, it underlines that they substantially pursue the same aim. Secondly, it confirms the strong connection between the notion of financial contribution on the one hand and the governmental functions of taxation and expenditure of revenue on the other hand. This would exclude more complex exercises of regulatory power from subparagraph (iv).[56] Howse has clearly expressed this delimitation:

The requirement that a private body be performing a normally governmental function guards against the possibility that *all* 'command-and-control' regulation, which directs private bodies and which always has *some* distributive effect as between different private economic actors, could be deemed a subsidy.[57]

[55] *Korea—Commercial Vessels*, para 7.30.

[56] It is necessary to mention that, in the continuation of the passage quoted, the Panel is admittedly creating a bit of confusion with respect to the coverage of regulatory measures within the financial contribution requirement.

Korea's main argument was that 'government practice' under subpara (i) would only refer to the exercise of 'governmental authority, eg regulatory powers and taxation regulation', and this would have been confirmed by the context represented by the two final sentences in subpara (iv).

In rebutting this argument, whereby 'governmental practice' is (wrongly) equated to 'governmental authority', the Panel makes disorienting findings, by indiscriminately and unjustifiably using the two examples made by Korea. According to the Panel 'government practice' would cover 'all acts of government or public bodies, irrespective of whether or not they involve the exercise of regulatory powers or taxation authority' (para 7.29). Following this reasoning, in the coda of para 7.30, after holding that functions 'normally vested in the government' should involve 'the levy of taxation or the expenditure of revenue', the Panel concludes: '[a]ccordingly, since loans and loan guarantees involve revenue expenditure, they may be treated as functions "normally vested in the government", *whether or not they are provided pursuant to the exercise of regulatory powers or taxation authority*' (emphasis added).

In the author's view, these findings do not mean much. They can be dismissed as unhappy slips of the pen. First, the two measures at issue in the case (loans and loan guarantees) are clear examples of 'taxation and expenditure of revenue'. Secondly, a landmark conclusion that the financial contribution could involve the exercise of regulatory powers would have warranted more reasoning in its support, particularly if it could be read as patently contradicting the previous reasoning.

[57] R Howse, 'Post-Hearing Submission to the International Trade Commission: World Trade Law and Renewable Energy: The Case of Non-Tariff Measures', 5 May 2005, Renewable Energy and International Law Project, 22.

Taking a step back, we should however ask whether the 'hard-and-fast' connection between 'financial contribution' and 'taxation/expenditure of revenue' advanced in the case-law is fully justified.

This is the most immediate and easiest, but equally the most restrictive interpretation. While, as seems to emerge from the case-law itself (which ostracizes any 'reference to government interventions in the general sense, or the effects thereof'), and from the literature,[58] the goal is to exclude *more complex* forms of regulatory intervention in the market, the risk of a too restrictive stance, focusing only on 'financial assistance' measures, is to leave out—irrespective of their qualification—*equally immediate* forms of support.

This would create an easy incentive to circumvent the law, or, to use more dignified parlance, an opportunity for 'policy substitution'. It would further be in stark contrast to the other line of jurisprudence which concludes that there is no need for a 'cost to government' under subparagraph (iv).[59] Coherency being at stake, one of the two findings is thus clearly not fully sound. While, admittedly, it may be difficult to think of a different benchmark than 'taxation-expenditure', what may be asked instead is whether it is *really* necessary to draw a fast line. There are good reasons for the definition of subsidy to be able to capture measures that appear to be *just* across the border. A different interpretation of the proviso whereby the practice should, in no real sense, differ from those normally followed by governments could be adopted, one which would still require a strong, but not inconsiderate, correlation.

This long excursus can be concluded with one topical example.

'Feed-in tariff' systems, which combine a minimum price with a purchase obligation, are commonly used to support the production of energy from renewable sources. This mechanism was tested under EC State aid rules in the *Preussen Elektra case*.[60] The German *Stromeinpeisungsgesetz* imposed on local electricity distributors to buy all the electricity produced with renewable energy sources in their area at a price higher than market one. The European Court of Justice concluded that this measure was not a State aid because of the lack of use of State resources.

What would be the status of such a measure under WTO law? Whilst the imputability standards of 'entrust' or 'direct' would be satisfied,[61] the testing point is the application of the two provisos of subparagraph (iv), particularly the final one.[62] Depending on the approach and interpretation followed, the result will be different. An unqualified acceptance of the 'hard-and-fast' connection noted above would mean exclusion of the practice from the wrath of subsidy laws. A more

[58] cf Howse.

[59] As we see below, the two issues are closely linked to and mutually dependent on each other.

[60] The case is examined at length in chapter 5, section III.

[61] The purchase obligation is mandated by statute.

[62] R Howse, 'Post-Hearing Submission to the International Trade Commission: World Trade Law and Renewable Energy: The Case of Non-Tariff Measures', 5 May 2005, Renewable Energy and International Law Project, 21–2.

flexible, although not necessarily lenient, approach would mean this kind of measures could be caught.[63]

Conclusions

The concept of financial contribution substantially follows the GATT notion of subsidy. It generally refers to well-defined and commonly agreed forms of governmental action involving a clear transfer of economic resources, which, directly or indirectly, call for the exercise of the powers of taxation and expenditure, forms of 'financial assistance' in the conceptual jargon of the introductory section of chapter 3.[64]

Despite the uncertainty raised by recent Appellate Body's findings on the standards of imputability in the case of indirect action, a proper construction of the concepts of 'enstrument' and 'direction', and of the two last sentences in subparagraph (iv), would preclude that more complex course of regulatory action, which have so far been excluded, could now be covered. The borderline, however, is not fully defined.

[63] Howse (ibid) disagrees. In any case, even if not constituting a 'financial contribution' under Article 1.1 (a)(1) of the SCM, the same measure may well qualify as a form of 'price support' under the other requirement of governmental action (Article 1.1(a)(2)). See SZ Bigdeli, 'Incentive Schemes to Promote Renewables and the WTO Law of Subsidies', in SZ Bigdeli, T Cottier, and O Nartova (eds), *International Trade Regulation and the Mitigation of Climate Change* (Cambridge: Cambridge University Press, 2009).

It is interesting to note that, in the *US—Export Restraints* litigation, the EC supported an interpretation of the final provisos of subpara (iv) which is in line with our suggestion. In particular, these provisos would be satisfied if the private body is acting under conditions 'pre-determined' by the government (see the Replies to the Third Party Questions of the Panel, paras 17 and 18). Even more interestingly, the EC used an example that closely resembles 'fixed-tariff mechanisms'. Although it concerns a 'sale obligation', and not a 'purchase obligation', the substance is the same: 'a private electricity company will provide an "indirect financial contribution" to the domestic aluminium producers if it is specifically directed by the government to provide electricity to these producers at a fixed price' (Executive Summary of the Written Submissions, para 20).

For the sake of the analysis, we can also imagine courses of conduct at the 'pre-marketing' stage and ask whether they could amount to a 'financial contribution'. We are thinking in particular of two examples discussed with Professor Diamond and which involve what we could call 'production requirements'. First example: a law orders a company, or industry, to produce steel. Second example: a law requires that all cars be made of steel. Without entering into a detailed analysis, the first, but firm impression is that, although the economic effect of these measures may be clear, they do not feature the *same* degree of directness of requirements to *buy* or *sell*. They should rather be assimilated to 'border measures'. Following the image proposed in the body of the analysis, they are therefore a little bit further than '*just* across the border'.

[64] See, eg, R Howse, 'Post-Hearing Submission to the International Trade Commission: World Trade Law and Renewable Energy: The Case of Non-Tariff Measures', 5 May 2005, Renewable Energy and International Law Project, 21–2; M Benitah, *The Law of Subsidies under the GATT/WTO System* (The Hague: Kluwer Law International, 2001), 68–74; JH Jackson, *The World Trading System—Law and Policy of International Economic Relations* (2nd edn, Cambridge Massachussetts: MIT Press, 1997), 296; A Beviglia Zampetti, 'The Uruguay Round Agreement on Subsidies—A Forward-Looking Assessment' (1996) Journal of World Trade 5, 28. Dissenting views, under GATT rules, can be found in A O'Brien. 'Countervailing Low Wage Subsidies: A Counter to the Leveling of Labor Conditions' (1994) 4 Transnational Law and Contemporary Problems 825) and M Bronckers and R Quick, 'What is a Countervailable Subsidy under EEC Trade Law?' (1989) Journal of World Trade 5, 22.

Article 1.1(a)(2) of the SCM: any income or price support—an additional concept in search of an expansive reading

According to Article 1.1(a)(2), a subsidy shall be deemed to exist when there is 'any form of income or price support in the sense of Article XVI of GATT 1994'.

Income and price supports are forms of government intervention aimed at sustaining the income of a certain category or at maintaining the price of a certain commodity at a given, usually minimum, desired level.[65] The phrase 'in the sense of Article XVI of GATT 1994' means that the measure must operate to increase exports of the product benefiting from the subsidy or decrease the imports of competing products. This refers to the *effect* of the subsidy, that is to the strengthening of the beneficiary of the subsidy and, ultimately, to the consequent increase of its exports or decrease of its competitors' imports.

Before analysing the scope of Article 1.1(a)(2), it should be noted at the outset that, to do justice to its separate mention in the definition and hence to its utility, this provision should naturally regulate measures *different* from those considered as 'financial contribution' under Article 1.1(a)(1). The Appellate Body has expressly confirmed this when, after setting forth the 'financial contribution' and the various forms of government action disciplined in the four subparagraphs of Article 1.1(a)(1), it noted that '[t]his range of government measures capable of providing subsidies is *broadened still further* by the concept of "income or price support" in paragraph (2) of Article 1.1(a)'.[66]

We can now move to the *scope* of the expression 'any income or price support'. In so doing, it may be useful to draw a parallel with the previous findings on the financial contribution.

One reading would indicate a fairly restrictive coverage. An early (1961) GATT Panel focused on price-support schemes and 'discussed the circumstances under which a system which fixes domestic prices to producers at above the world price level might be considered a subsidy in the meaning of Article XVI'.[67] The Panel emphasized that there could be cases in which a government maintained a fixed price without resort to a subsidy, ie without a 'loss to the government'. One example would be the case of a minimum price fixed by law 'which is maintained by quantitative restrictions or flexible tariff or similar charges'.

One of those cases where 'a government maintained a fixed price above the world price without resort to a subsidy' was considered by *US—Export Restraints* Panel. It was noted that the support of the price of a commodity by imposing high tariffs on imports would not constitute a subsidy within the meaning of Article 1. In particular, it was doubted whether the 'concept of financial contribution

[65] This formulation largely corresponds to the entries 'income support' and 'price support' that can be found in Black's *Oxford Dictionary of Economics*, 225 and 336.

[66] Appellate Body, *US—Softwood Lumber IV*, para 52 (emphasis added).

[67] Panel Report 'Review pursuant to Article XVI:5', BISD 9th Supp (1961), 188, at para 11.

contained in Article 1.1(a)[1] of the SCM Agreement seeks to bring such government action within the ambit of the SCM Agreement'.[68] The comparison between the findings of the GATT Panel and the *US—Export Restraints* Panel highlights a high degree of similarity with respect to the degree of government involvement required by the criteria of financial contribution and of income or price support. In other words, it seems that, although producing a transfer of economic resources, complex regulatory mechanisms involving border measures, such as tariffs and export restraints, cannot be caught within the scope of either provision.[69]

There are however various indications in support of a *more expansive reading* of Article 1.1(2)(a) of the SCM. They are partly based on a textual interpretation of the provision, which would attempt to give it full and independent meaning from the financial contribution, and partly based on the trend made evident by the recent jurisprudence on the definition of the public intervention.

On the one hand, unlike the financial contribution requirement, the phrase 'any income or price support' is not limited to specific forms of governmental action. Its general wording is capable of encompassing various forms of public intervention that may be deployed to execute *any* income or price support. Further, and most importantly, there is no express indication and qualification of the standard of government involvement required. It is not therefore difficult to imagine that that phrase could also catch more complex regulatory measures, like purchase or sale obligations or even border measures, that would not constitute a financial contribution.

On the other hand, inspiration can be drawn from some recent findings on the more elaborate language of the financial contribution requirement. Leaving aside for the moment the issue of the 'loss to government', which the GATT Panel required for price support schemes, and which, as we will see, is probably not good law anymore,[70] it is interesting to focus on the recent relaxation of the rules of imputability of the financial contribution by the Appellate Body in *US—DRAMS*. This interpretation has already been extensively examined and criticized because it does not completely fit with the complex text of subparagraph (iv) of Article 1.1(a)(1) of the SCM. Irrespective of its correctness, what can however be appreciated in the context of our analysis is the more liberal approach towards the degree of government involvement requested emerging from the more generous interpretation of the standards of 'entrustment' and 'direction' in

[68] Panel Report, *US—Export Restraints*, para 8.38. It may be useful to recall that, in that dispute, the Panel was actually analysing whether, an export restraint, a regulatory practice similar to a tariff but with complementary effects (by limiting exports, export restraints increase the quantity of goods produced domestically and decrease its price; by limiting imports, tariffs decrease competitive pressure from outside the domestic market and hence contribute to maintain a certain price level), was covered by subpara (iii) read in conjunction with subpara (iv).

[69] In this regard, it has been suggested that the restrictive *US—Export Restraints* Panel would condition the interpretation of Article 1.1(a)(2). See RW Staiger and AO Sykes, 'Currency Manipulation and World Trade' (paper, 13 July 2008), 31, n 57.

[70] See section II.C below.

subparagraph (iv) of the financial contribution. This approach is particularly appealing inasmuch as it is more liberal than that of the *US—Export Restraints* Panel which, in turn, we have found to be rather similar to the early GATT interpretation of price support schemes.

The conclusion is that the tide might be changing. With its potentially broad language, the phrase 'any income or price support' may well include complex regulatory measures, such as those involving border measures, which were originally considered not to be covered, and which still remain outside the scope of the financial contribution requirement.

Agreement on Agriculture (AG)

After analysing the formulation of the definition and the rules of imputability of the notion of subsidy under the SCM Agreement, it is useful to move to the AG.

Introduction: AG and SCM Agreement, definitions and relationships

The most striking difference between the AG and the SCM Agreement—at least from the perspective of this book's subject—is that the former does not include any definition of subsidy.

The answer to the question of the definition depends on the relationship between the two agreements. Recent disputes, particularly *EC—Sugar* and *US—Cotton*, have made it evident that this can be particularly complex.[71] To a large extent this relationship can be described as one between *lex specialis* and *lex generalis*.[72] The SCM, which applies to any sector of the economy (except for services), represents the general discipline of subsidies. Its generality is arguably reflected in the primary provisions, first of all those on definitions. Whereas there may well be differences between the SCM Agreement and other instruments regulating subsidies, these seem to mainly concern the *discipline* rather than the most fundamental concepts.

[71] It should be noted that the issue was completely different in the two cases. In *US—Cotton* there was no real overlap of regulation between the two instruments since the AG did not provide *any* discipline for local-content subsidies. Thus the relevant SCM provision (Article 3.1(b)) could apply without any particular problem. As recognized by the Appellate Body itself, the issue in *EC—Sugar* was somewhat more complex revolving around the *cumulative* application of 'similar' subsidy rules, that is rules regulating a similar type of measure, ie export subsidies. What had to be determined was whether Article 3 SCM (that *inter alia* prohibits export subsidies) could apply to export subsidies listed in Article 9.1 AG and granted in excess of the relevant scheduled commitments. In other words, the issue was whether the SCM subsidy provisions could apply *in addition to* those of the AG. For some notes on the systemic issues emerging from the *US—Cotton* and *EC—Sugar* cases see L Rubini, 'Comments on the US—Cotton dispute' in Ortino and Ripinsky (eds) *WTO Law and Process* (London: British Institute of International and Comparative Law, 2006) 133, 134–6. See also PC Mavroidis, *Trade in Goods* (Oxford: Oxford University Press, 2008) 208–10.

[72] Article 21.1 of the AG reads: 'The provisions of GATT 1994 and of the other Multilateral Trade Agreements in Annex 1A to the WTO Agreeement shall apply subject to the provisions of this Agreement'. See PC Mavroidis, *Trade in Goods* (Oxford: Oxford University Press, 2008) 208.

The relationship between the SCM Agreement and the AG is still not fully clear though, in particular because of the various references, or cross-references, between the two instruments. Article 21.1 of the AG generally affirms the speciality of its agreement over other covered instruments, including the SCM Agreement.[73] Likewise, Article 3 of the SCM gives precedence to the AG. More intriguingly, however, other provisions, such as Articles 5, 6 and 7 of the SCM, expressly refer to the application of Article 13 of the AG, the so-called 'peace-clause', which partly sheltered subsidies complying with the requirements of the AG from the application of the SCM Agreement discipline. However, this protection no longer exsists, having expired on 31 December 2003.

In conclusion, while Article 21.1 AG would still be there to guard, in some way, the 'speciality' of the AG's discipline, the main elements of subsidy regulation would more and more find their 'natural' place in the SCM Agreement. The broader policy context should also be considered. Beyond rules and their relationship, the trend seems to be one of an increasing confluence of the agricultural sector into the general regulation of subsidies.[74] One example of this trend would be the expiration of the peace-clause itself which was good evidence of the 'ancillarity' of the AG towards the SCM Agreement.

For these reasons, when reading the AG, and in particular when defining the notion of subsidy, it seems appropriate to look at the SCM Agreement for contextual guidance. Since these two instruments are 'integral parts of the same treaty [the WTO Agreement]', they should be read harmoniously.[75] The Appellate Body thus interpreted the term 'subsidy' by drawing on the definition of subsidy in Article 1.1 of the SCM, and in particular both elements of financial contribution and benefit. It observed accordingly that a subsidy involves a transfer of economic resources from the grantor to the recipient for less than full consideration.[76]

It should be noted finally that the absence of a definition of subsidy in the AG, and the reliance on the SCM Agreement for these purposes, does not mean that the former does not have anything to offer for definitional purposes. In fact various provisions give valuable indications with respect to the 'forms of public intervention' covered under that agreement and hence to their characteristic elements. This is the subject of analysis of the following paragraphs.

The forms of governmental action under the AG

As the first step of our analysis, it is useful to give a brief overview of the rules in the AG that regulate subsidies. This exercise may offer useful definitional indications

[73] The text of the provision is in n 72.

[74] Which would admittedly be in line with the 'long-term objective' of the AG 'to establish a fair and market-oriented agricultural trading system' as reported in the preamble to the agreement.

[75] Appellate Body, *US—Cotton*, para 549.

[76] Appellate Body, *Canada—Dairy*, para 87; *US—FSC*, para 136.

and may give some immediate guidance on what forms of public intervention are at issue.

Article 9 of the AG encloses a list of export subsidies concerning scheduled products which are subject to reduction commitments. In these provisions, many features of the forms of governmental action covered have been usefully described. Either because of their formulation or because of their anchorage to the definition of financial contribution of Article 1.1 of the SCM, *all* those provisions (apart from Article 9(c), fully analysed below) seem to encompass measures of financial assistance featuring a clear transfer of economic resources. Depending on the formulation of the provision, they may involve only a direct or also an indirect course of action. Most interestingly, with respect to the cases of indirect conduct, the relevant rules of imputability seem to involve different degrees of intensity, from the more demanding one embodied in the term 'mandate' in subparagraph (e)[77] to the potentially more comprehensive one expressed by the word 'provide' in subparagraph (d).[78] Subparagraph (f) stands out for its indeterminacy by merely regulating 'subsidies'.

Analogously, the examination of the measures of 'domestic support'[79] indicates the characteristics of the forms of action that are regulated as domestic subsidies.

For example, most of the measures of domestic support involve a transfer of economic resources.[80] Moreover, it is clear that, at least in some cases, domestic support may also be granted indirectly. An important issue concerning indirect action is whether *more complex* actions of support, such as those carried out through border measures (consider the case of export restraints) can also be covered. In this regard, it is significant that the AG distinguishes between import quotas and other non-tariff border measures on the one hand and forms of domestic support, including income and price support measures, on the other.[81] While the former are

[77] Subparagraph (e) regulates internal transport and freight charges on export shipments, provided or mandated by governments, on terms more favourable than for domestic shipments. It may be noted that the verb 'to mandate' is particularly clear (it means 'to command' or 'to order'; see *Shorter Oxford English Dictionary on Historical Principles* (5th edn, Oxford: oxford University Press,2002) Vol I, 1688) and, consequently, cannot raise the sort of interpretative doubts that we have seen with respect to the verb 'direct' in Article 1.1(a)(iv) of the SCM.

[78] Subparagraph (d) refers to the provision of subsidies to reduce the costs of marketing exports of agricultural products and the costs of international transport and freight. The verb 'provide' features 'to make available' among its various meanings (*Shorter Oxford English Dictionary on Historical Principles* (5th edn, Oxford: Oxford University Press, 2002) Vol II, 2382).

[79] We may safely assume that the term 'support' is very similar in meaning to 'subsidy'. Even a quick scan through the various meanings of the verbs 'to support' and 'to subsidize' shows a great deal of similarity: see *Shorter Oxford English Dictionary on Historical Principles* (5th edn, Oxford: Oxford University Press, 2002) Vol II, 3090 and 3119. The equation support-subsidy is especially evident from Annex 3 to the AG, on the methodology used to calculate aggregate measurement of support, and in particular at paras 1 and 2 thereof. Finally, after a comprehensive analysis of the AG, the *US—Cotton* Panel (see paras 7.420–7.423) has explained that 'all relevant types of support for the purposes of the *Agreement on Agriculture* are subsidies'.

[80] See, eg, Article 6 and Annexes 2, 3 and 4.

[81] Export subsidies are regulated in a separate part (V) of the AG.

treated under the 'market access' chapter and assimilated to tariffs, the latter are subject to a different regulation.[82] Article 4 on 'Market Access' provides that Members shall not maintain, resort to, or revert to any measures of the kind which have been required to be converted into ordinary customs duties. These measures include various examples of border measures or regulatory measures.[83] The Appellate Body has made it clear that these measures should have been converted into ordinary customs duties before the entry into force of the WTO Agreement and are thus subject to the same mechanism of liberalization constituted by bindings and reductions.[84] If they have not been converted, they should not be maintained, and they are prohibited under Article 4.[85] The important question for our purposes is whether these measures should *also* be considered as 'domestic support' and be subject to the relevant subsidy discipline.

We can now concentrate on the form of subsidy under subparagraph (c) of Article 9.1 of the AG, and in particular on its rule of imputability.

The rule of imputability in Article 9.1(c) of the AG

Article 9.1(c) of the AG subjects to reduction commitments 'payments on the export of an agricultural product that are financed by virtue of governmental action, whether or not a charge on the public account is involved . . .'.

From a definitional perspective, this provision is particularly important for its rule of imputability, embodied in the phrase 'financed by virtue of governmental action'. This standard has been thoroughly analysed by the Appellate Body in the three stages of the *Canada—Dairy* dispute.

In the original proceedings, governmental agencies played a crucial role at every step of the supply of cheaper milk with the result that there was no difficulty in concluding that the payment took place 'by virtue of governmental action'. After a substantial deregulation of the market for export milk, the regulatory framework under examination in the two implementation proceedings was more elusive. The Appellate Body was thus forced to concentrate more attentively on the various elements of the standard of imputability.

The phrase 'governmental action' is 'somewhat open-ended, perhaps even abstract', with the result that the provision 'extends, in principle, to *any* governmental action'[86] whereby the government 'regulates', 'controls' or 'supervises' individuals.[87] For its part, the word 'finance' refers 'generally to the mechanism

[82] The AG provides for reduction commitments of domestic support measures.

[83] A footnote mentions 'quantitative import restrictions, variable import levies, minimum import prices, discretionary import licensing, non-tariff measures maintained through State-trading enterprises, voluntary export restraints and other similar border measures other than ordinary customs duties'.

[84] cf Appellate Body, *Chile—Price Band System*, paras 206 and 207.

[85] cf ibid, para 207.

[86] Appellate Body, *Canada—Dairy (Article 21.5)*, paras 129 and 131 (emphasis in the original).

[87] Appellate Body, *Canada—Dairy (Article 21.5)*, para 112; id, *Canada—Dairy*, para 97.

or process by which financial resources are provided to enable "payments" to be made'.[88]

What is crucial in the definition of the standard of imputability is the determination of the nexus between the governmental action and financing which is determined by the phrase 'by virtue of'. This would require that:

there must be a demonstrable link between the *governmental action* at issue and the *financing* of the payments, whereby the payments are, in some way, financed as a result of, or as a consequence of, the governmental action.[89]

The Appellate Body underlined that 'it is extremely difficult . . . to define in the abstract the precise character of the required link between the governmental action and the financing of the payments'.[90] It then noted:

[g]overnments are constantly engaged in regulation of different kinds in pursuit of a variety of objectives. For instance, we can envisage that governmental action might establish a regulatory framework merely enabling a third person freely to make and finance 'payments'. In this situation, the link between the governmental action and the financing of the payments is too tenuous for the 'payments' to be regarded as '*financed* by virtue of governmental action' (emphasis added) within the meaning of Article 9.1(c). Rather, there must be a tighter nexus between the mechanism or process by which the payments are *financed*, even if by a third person, and governmental action. In our opinion, the existence of such a demonstrable link must be identified on a case-by-case basis, taking account of the particular governmental action at issue and its effects on payments made by a third person.[91]

Importantly, according to the Appellate Body, the existence of a 'demonstrable link' does not necessarily require the exercise of compulsion. Article 9.1(c) 'does not require that payments be financed by virtue of government "*mandate*", or other "*direction*". Although the word "action" certainly covers situations where government mandates or directs that payments be made, it also covers other situations where no such compulsion is involved'.[92] In this regard, the first Article 21.5 Panel noted that 'by virtue of' does not refer only to those cases where obedience is 'enforced' but also those where action is simply 'influenced' as 'in both instances the result would not occur *but for* the power to enforce or influence'. In other words, 'whether the government "forces" or merely "encourages" producers to sell into the commercial export market are *qualifications* of the causal relationship required under Article 9.1(c)'.[93]

These findings recall immediately the case-law under Article III:4 and XI of the GATT where the attribution of a private practice to the government was at issue

[88] Appellate Body, *Canada—Dairy, (Article 21.5—II)*, para 132.
[89] Appellate Body, *Canada—Dairy (Article 21.5—I)*, para 113.
[90] ibid, para 115.
[91] ibid; see also Appellate Body, *Canada—Dairy (Article 21.5—II)*, para 134.
[92] Appellate Body, *Canada—Dairy (Article 21.5—II)*, para 128 (emphasis in the original).
[93] Panel, Appellate Body, *Canada—Dairy Products (Article 21.5—I)*, paras 6.35 and 6.44 (emphasis in the original).

and where Panels have consistently concluded that the mere *inducement* of private parties, or creation of *incentives* on them, to act in a certain way was enough to attribute the conduct to the government and thus have a 'measure' under the relevant rules.[94] It is however a comparison with the rule of imputability under Article 1.1(a)(iv) of the SCM that can bear more fruit for our analysis of the definition of subsidies. This exercise will feature at the end of this section.

Abstract rules of imputability: the definitions of 'government agency' and 'public body'

The definitions of 'government agency' under Article 9.1(a) of the AG and of 'public body' under Article 1.1(a)(1) of the SCM are two good illustrations of a particular technique to determine whether the conduct of a public entity is imputable to the government.

Article 9.1(a) of the AG subjects to reduction commitments export subsidies that consist of 'the provision by governments and their agencies of direct subsidies, including payments-in-kind'.

The Appellate Body noted that:

> [t]he essence of 'government' is . . . that it enjoys the effective power to 'regulate', 'control' or 'supervise' individuals, or otherwise 'restrain' their conduct, through the exercise of lawful authority. This meaning is derived, in part, from the *functions* performed by a government and, in part, from the government having the *powers* to perform those functions.[95]

The Geneva-based body turned then to the notion of 'government agency' and found that it referred to 'an entity which exercises powers vested in it by a "government" for the purpose of performing functions of a "governmental" character'.[96] The key elements were therefore the delegation by the government of powers and the performance of functions of governmental character. By contrast, and quite interestingly, the fact that the agency enjoyed a certain degree of discretion in the exercise of its duties and that it was composed, completely or partially, of individuals representing production sectors was not relevant.

The most important indication of *Canada—Dairy* is that the operation of the rule of imputability underlying the action through governmental agencies seems to be inherent in the classification of the body as 'government agency'. In this process, the degree of government influence is certainly considered but at a general and abstract level with the result that the standard of imputability is rather strict. In short, once a given body is found to be a 'governmental agency', virtually every instance of its conduct is caught by the discipline.

[94] See, eg, *Japan—Semi-conductors* (for Article XI) and *Japan—FIRA* (for Article III:4). For a commentary (and a critique) see PC Mavroidis, *Trade in Goods* (Oxford: Oxford University Press, 2007) 45–50.

[95] Appellate Body, *Canada—Dairy*, para 97.

[96] ibid.

Significantly, the phrase 'financial contribution by a government or any public body' in the *chapeau* of Article 1.1(a)(1) of the SCM can be read in a similar fashion.

The SCM Agreement provides for a clear distinction between 'public' and 'private' bodies. This distinction is particularly relevant in the context of Article 1.1(a)(1) of the SCM as different parts of the provision, and different rules of imputability, may apply. The *US—Export Restraints* Panel has indicated that any entity that is neither a government nor a public body would be a private body.[97] As the notion of private body is residual, and it can be assumed that the meaning of government is the same as that provided in the AG, we may focus on the concept of 'public body'. The *Korea—Commercial Vessels* Panel has made it clear that:

> an entity will constitute a 'public body' if it is controlled by the government (or other public bodies). If an entity is controlled by the government (or other public bodies), then any action by that entity is attributable to the government and should therefore fall within the scope of Article 1.1(a)(1) of the *SCM Agreement*.[98]

It is clear that this definition, with its general reference to the control exercised by the government, leaves many interpretative issues open. There may be cases where the boundaries between the concepts of 'public body' and 'private body' are not easy to draw. We can think, for example, of the case of public undertakings that can be generally defined as those undertakings that are 'under the control of' the government. Should they simply and always be regarded as public bodies? Some fine-tuning may be required with respect to the notion of control.[99] This leads to a second comment. We should ask whether the assimilation between 'public bodies' and 'government', which is explicitly made by Article 1 SCM, indicates that further elements should be considered in order to define an entity as a 'public body' and, in particular, whether these should be represented—as in the definition of governmental agency in Article 9.1(a) of the AG—by the conferral of public powers for the performance of governmental functions.

The most significant point, however, is that the improbability test emerging from the phrase 'financial contribution by a government or any public body' is remarkably similar to that of the phrase 'provision by government and their agencies of direct subsidies' in Article 9.1(a). What seems to suffice is a *general* and *abstract* assessment of the control of the government, and not an analysis of *actual* control in the instant case.

97 Panel, *US—Export Restraints*, para 8.49.

98 Panel, *Korea—Commercial Vessels*, para 7.50.

99 It is true that in the *Korea—Commercial Vessels* case, the Panel carried out a very comprehensive and detailed analysis that established the existence of governmental control over *KEXIM* referring to various circumstances (see paras 7.50–7.55). It seems however indicative that the first and 'primary' justification for this conclusion was considered the 100% governmental ownership of the latter (see para 7.50). In other words, the general definition of 'public body' laid down by the Panel, with its mere reliance on the open-ended notion of 'control', begs the question of whether—in other cases—adjudication bodies will be content with more limited evidence, such as a simple proprietary control.

Two concluding parallels

This long section on the forms of governmental action covered in WTO subsidy law, which focused on the two techniques of delimitation of the formulation of the definition and of the standards of imputability, can be concluded with two comparisons which, by highlighting the different coverage of different legal provisions, sharpen our awareness of the relativity of subsidy definitions—and its underlying creativity.

Comparing Article 9.1(c) of the AG and Article 1.1(a)(iv) of the SCM

We may attempt to draw a parallel between Article 9.1(c) of the AG and Article 1.1(a)(iv) of the SCM.

It may be noted immediately that the two provisions have a different approach with respect to the forms of governmental action that are covered. In both systems a transfer of economic resources is necessary.[100] Whereas, however, the financial contribution element under Article 1.1(a)(1) of the SCM encompasses only certain forms of governmental action, Article 9.1(c) of the AG in principle extends to a broader class of governmental actions, the only notable qualification being that we are dealing with export subsidies. In particular, the latter provision generally refers to 'payments', a term which is broadly contrued to cover various types of transfer of economic resources, including transfers of goods and services ('payments in kind'),[101] and even financial transfers within the same economic entity ('cross-subsidization').[102]

The analysis becomes particularly inspiring if we concentrate on the rules of imputability under those provisions.[103] The jurisprudence of the Appellate Body seems to offer contradictory indications.

On the one side, it is said that neither provision requires a high degree of compulsion, in the form of, respectively, a 'mandate' or 'direction',[104] or 'delegation' or 'command'.[105] The same reports, however, provide in the small print of the footnotes conflicting indications when expressly comparing the rule of imputability under Article 1.1(a)(1)(iv) of the SCM and that under Article 9.1(c) of the AG. Whereas in the second implementation report in *Canada—Dairy*, Article 9.1(c) of the AG has been 'contrasted' to Article 1.1(a)(1)(iv) of the SCM to explain that the former does *not* require a standard of attributability *as high as* that of the latter,[106]

[100] See Panel, *US—Export Restraints*, para 8.73; Appellate Body, *Canada—Dairy*, para 107.

[101] Appellate Body, *Canada—Dairy*, paras 103–14.

[102] Appellate Body, *EC—Sugar*, paras 257–71. This finding may raise some perplexities but, from an economic perspective, and bearing in mind the broad and non-formalistic reading of the term 'payment', it is by all means defensible. See B Slocock, 'EC and WTO Subsidy Control Systems—Some Reflections' (2007) European State Aid Law Quarterly 249, 253–4.

[103] The two final provisos of subparagraph (iv) are left to one side for now.

[104] Appellate Body, *Canada—Dairy (Article 21.5—II)*, para 128.

[105] Appellate Body, *US—DRAMS*, paras 110 and 111.

[106] Paragraph 128, n 113.

in *US—DRAMS* the Appellate Body interpreted Article 1.1(a)(1)(iv) by making an express reference to Article 9.1(c) thus suggesting that, in its view, the two standards of imputability *are substantially comparable*.[107] An explanation of the last statement may depend on the sensitive loosening of the rule of imputability under subparagraph (iv) as interpreted by the *US—DRAMS* Appellate Body.

In fact, on closer scrutiny it is clear that the two standards of imputability do *not* have the same scope. The relaxed interpretation of the Appellate Body of the term 'direct' still leaves a great deal of uncertainty. It has been suggested that, to avoid the letter of the law being disregarded, a *well-defined, significant* degree of direction and compulsion is still desirable. That is not necessarily the case with respect to the phrase 'financed by virtue of governmental action'. Although it is not easy to define with certainty the required 'demonstrable link', it seems clear that it is broader than that of the SCM provision both in terms of (i) *complexity* of the causal nexus (encompassing even less direct actions) and of (ii) *intensity* of the action (including also actions of encouragement).[108]

Comparing the two standards of imputability, there has been a clear progression from a *more formalistic* approach, whereby only certain, well-defined, forms of action are relevant, to a *more sophisticated* one, where what matters is not the classification of the form of intervention but rather a more comprehensive analysis of its impact in the context of the circumstances of the case (including the behaviour—or reaction—of the affected parties). Using the language adopted in the previous analysis, these two approaches could be described as *nature*-based and *effect*-based respectively.

The conclusion that Article 9.1(c) of the AG and subparagraph (iv) of Article 1.1(a)(1) of the SCM do differ in terms of the forms of indirect governmental action that they cover does not only rely on the difference between the relevant standards of imputability, but also on their 'context'. Thus, contrary to what happens to the AG provision, subparagraph (iv) features two further gates, which by correlating the 'financial contribution' to the exercise of the governmental prerogatives of taxation and revenue expenditure, firmly guard against the possibility that regulatory measures providing benefits be covered.

These comparative remarks on the respective coverage of Article 9.1(c) of the AG and Article 1.1(a)(iv) of the SCM can be concluded with the words of the Appellate Body.

> Article 9.1(c) of the [AG] describes an *unusual form of subsidy* in that 'payments' can be made by private parties, and need not be made by governments. Moreover, 'payments' need not be funded from government resources, provided that they are 'financed by virtue of governmental action'. Article 9.1(c), therefore, contemplates that 'payments' may be made

[107] Paragraph 114, n 184.

[108] In the context of Article 1.1(a)(1)(iv) of the SCM, the Appellate Body made it clear that mere policy pronouncements and acts of encouragement cannot be enough (*US—DRAMS*, para 114).

and funded by private parties, *without that type of governmental involvement ordinarily associated with a subsidy.*[109]

What is intriguing is that the Appellate Body is expressly contrasting the *unusual* form of subsidy regulated by Article 9.1(c) of the AG with the *other* forms of subsidies governed by *other rules*. In this regard, there can be no mistake if our thoughts go immediately to Article 1.1 of the SCM. This would confirm the general nature of the definition of subsidy included in the SCM Agreement. Further, and leaving aside for now the reference to the issue of financing, the striking conclusion is that the 'type of governmental involvement' of the AG provision is different, that is lower, from that which is *ordinarily* requested under subsidy law, notably Article 1.1 of the SCM.

Comparing abstract and concrete rules of imputability

The examination of the first two techniques of delimitation can be concluded with a parallel between the *abstract* rules of imputability emerging from the expressions 'government or any public body' and 'governments and their agencies' and those resulting from the fourth subparagraph of Article 1.1(a)(1) of the SCM and Article 9.1(c) of the AG. When compared with the former the latter can certainly be defined as *concrete.*

Whereas the two cases regulated under the fourth subparagraph of Article 1.1(a)(1) of the SCM and Article 9.1(c) of the AG *describe the action* of the government, the phrases 'financial contribution by a government and any public body' and 'provision by governments and their agencies of direct subsidies' put a considerable stress on the *definition of the agent*, be it the government, a public body or a government agency. The existence of a directing public hand is implied in this definition.

This structural characteristic plays an important role in the definition of the rules of imputability.

Under the *chapeau* of Article 1.1(a)(1) of the SCM and Article 9.1(a) of the AG, the crucial interpretive step is the classification of the body under scrutiny as a 'public body' or a 'government agency'. In this regard, general considerations, such as those concerning the statute or the nature of the body, or the general control or influence by the government, certainly play a more important role than the assessment of the government influence actually exercised in the case at issue which is, by contrast, required—albeit in different ways—under Article 1.1(a)(1)(iv) of the SCM and Article 9.1(c) of the AG.

The crucial consequence is that, since they feature rules of imputability which are 'more or less stringent', the relevant provisions are accordingly 'more or less comprehensive' with respect to the forms of public intervention that they cover. For example, a less demanding rule of imputability (eg an abstract one) will make

109 Appellate Body, *Canada—Dairy (Article 21.5—II)*, para 87 (emphasis added). See also Appellate Body, *EC—Sugar*, para 259.

it more likely that the conduct at issue is covered. Conversely, a more demanding rule of imputability (eg a concrete one) can raise the standard of proof and thus make it less likely that the conduct is eventually caught. Further, each type of rule, particularly when focusing on the conduct of the government, can rely on various standards (again more or less demanding). A comparison between the two different standards of Article 1.1(a)(1)(iv) of the SCM and Article 9.1(c) of the AG is again illuminating in this respect.

II. Origin of the resources

There now follows an examination of the regulation of subsidies in the GATT/WTO focusing on the third technique to define the legal relevance of the public intervention, that is the origin of the resources used to finance the subsidy.

It is worth starting with an examination of the terminology used.

A. Premise on definitions: costs between economics and accounting

When discussing the financing of a subsidy, various concepts have been used in the GATT/WTO such as 'financial contribution', 'charge on the public account', 'budgetary expenditure', 'loss of public revenue', 'loss or cost to government', 'governmental resources'. It is therefore particularly important to clarify these concepts and the possible relationship between them.

The notion of 'financial contribution' is rather ambivalent. It may equally refer to the *action* of the government that transfers economic resources, as we have seen in the first part of this chapter, and to the governmental *origin* of the resource. 'Budgetary expenditure' and 'charge on the public account'[110] seem to refer to the use of public revenue which, according to accounting practice, is recorded in the public accounts. These accounts usually take note of actual expenditure (such as a payment), potential expenditure (such as guarantees), and capital loss (such as when revenue, like a credit, is waived). By contrast, the expressions 'loss of public revenue' and 'loss or cost to government',[111] which can be compared to that of use of 'governmental resources', are more general, and include any form of financing involving government resources irrespective of whether any trace is left in the public accounts. In particular, they can be construed to include opportunity costs, in the form of, for example, foregone interests.

[110] The latter is commonly used in the legislation. cf Article 9.1(c) of the Agreement on Agriculture and item (l) of the Illustrative List of Export Subsidies enclosed, as Annex I, to the SCM Agreement. cf also the GATT Panel Report 'Operation of the Provisions of Article XVI' adopted on 21 November 1961, GATT, 10th Supp BISD 201 (1962), para 5.

[111] The expression 'loss to government' can be found in the GATT Working Party Report 'Provisions of Article XVI:4' adopted on 19 November 1960, GATT, 9th Supp BISD 185 (1961), para 11.

The concept of opportunity cost, which can be distinguished from that of accounting cost, and is the one that is particularly significant in economic terms,[112] refers to the amount lost by not using the resource at hand, such as capital, in its best alternative use. In other words, whereas this economic concept is concerned with the best allocation of available resources, the accounting notion of cost is focused on the actual payment made by a firm which should leave a trace in its accounts.[113]

In fact, all the notions above are used indiscriminately and the meaning that prevails is the actual or potential use of governmental resources, whether noted or not in the public accounts. In the remainder of the analysis the expression 'cost to government' is generally used. It may be useful to note too that the concept used in the EC ('grant through State resources') also focuses on the actual use of government resources, or, to put it another way, on a financial burden, rather than on budget recording.[114]

Once it is accepted that a cost to government is necessary, which, as the following exposition shows, has been subject to a long legal controversy, the main legal issue is to determine whether this has been incurred in the case at hand, which, as the EC case illustrates, can also raise disagreement.

B. GATT era

One of the most controversial issues in the debate on the definition of subsidy has always been whether a cost to government is required. Different views have been adopted and defended along the years by the various Contracting Parties, in particular the US (traditionally arguing that a cost to government is not necessary) and the EC (claiming the contrary). The conflict sparked during the US/EC 'Steel War' in the early 1980s,[115] the clash perpetuated itself through the Uruguay Round negotiations and was eventually settled in the WTO era (courtesy of judicial interpretation).

The official position on the issue in the GATT is difficult to ascertain. Whereas the disputes did not offer any significant indication, various reports in the early

[112] D Begg, S Fisher, and R Dornbusch, Economics (5th edn, London: MacGraw-Hill, 1997), 6 and 94.

[113] In our context, the issue of opportunity costs usually arises when it has to be determined whether 'soft loans' amount to a subsidy. This occurs when, for example, the government lends money to an undertaking at an interest rate (say 9%) that is above the rate at which the government borrows (say 8%) but below the relevant rate in the private market (say 10%). The government can be said to have incurred an opportunity cost by 'giving up a portion of the interest it could obtain': JH Jackson, *The World Trading System—Law and Policy of International Economic Relations* (2nd edn, Cambridge Massachussetts: MIT Press, 1997) 295.

[114] See chapter 5, section III.

[115] M Bronckers and R Quick, 'What is a Countervailable Subsidy under EEC Trade Law?' (1989) 6 Journal of World Trade 5, 17 refer to the 1981–1982 'steel war' between US and EC as the first point in time when the latter argued for the necessity of a cost to government.

1960s substantially lend support to the view that a cost to government was necessary.[116] Not featuring a definition of subsidy, the Tokyo Round Subsidies Code does not give any definitive answer on the issue either. It has sometimes been argued that the requirement of a cost to government emerged from its annexed Illustrative List of Export Subsidies.[117] The language used in most of the examples of export subsidy (such as 'allowance', 'exemption', 'remission', 'deferral', 'drawback') seems to suggest the use of public resources.[118] A particular confirmation of this reading seems to derive from the closing item (l) which, by referring to 'any other charge on the public account constituting an export subsidy', was read as indicating a common denominator of all previous examples.

This has also been the view taken by the European Court of Justice in the two *Fediol* cases decided in the late 1980s. The Court noted that the various items of the Illustrative List on Export Subsidies, and in particular item (l), justified the fact that 'in the mind of the Community legislature the concept of export subsidy necessarily implied a financial burden borne directly or indirectly by public bodies'.[119]

In fact the Tokyo Round Subsidies Code did not resolve the issue. The reliance on the Illustrative List is not decisive because it merely refers to some examples of export subsidies and not to the definition of subsidy itself.

A close reading of the *Fediol* decisions shows that the Court of Justice itself was aware of this. It rejected the more affirmative arguments of the Commission and Advocate General Mancini. The former distinguished the concept of GATT subsidy from that of State aid—which according to the reading prevailing at the time did not involve a financial burden for the State. The latter went even further arguing that, 'although unsupported by rules of Community or international law', it is 'semantically and logically indisputable' that the requirement of cost to government is inherent in the notion of subsidy. The Court more cautiously found that '[t]he concept of subsidy thus understood is not incompatible with the

[116] See the Panel Report 'Review pursuant to Article XVI:5' adopted on 24 May 1960, GATT, 9th Supp. BISD (1961), p 188, paras 11 (on price support schemes) which refers to 'loss to the government' and 12 (on the action through intermediaries) which underlines the importance of the 'source of the funds'. See also the incidental recognition that subsidies would involve a 'charge on the public account' in Panel Report 'Operation of the Provisions of Article XVI' adopted on 21 November 1961, GATT, 10th Supp. BISD (1962), p 201, para 5.

[117] See JF Beseler and AN Williams, *Anti-Dumping and Anti-Subsidy Law—The European Communities* (London: Sweet and Maxwell, 1986) 123–4. Contra M Bronckers and R Quick, 'What is a Countervailable Subsidy under EEC Trade Law?' (1989) 6 Journal of World Trade 5, 14. The illustrative list is a revision of a list included in a 1960 Working Party Report (Report on the 'Provisions of Article XVI:4' adopted on 19 November 1960, GATT, 9th Supp. BISD (1961), p 185, para 5), and is substantially reproduced in Annex I of the WTO SCM Agreement.

[118] Admittedly, some support to the opposite argument could be found in item (c) which, by simply referring to measures 'mandated' by government, is broad enough to cover also transfers financed with private resources.

[119] See para 11 of Case 187/85; para 12 of Case 188/85. The piece of legislation the Court is referring to is Regulation No 2176/84 which implented the Tokyo Round Subsidies Code.

Community's obligations under international law, in particular under GATT and agreements concluded in the framework thereof'.[120] It pointed out that, in GATT law, there has never been an express definition of the term 'subsidy'. Accordingly, the Commission 'was not wrong or arbitrary in concluding that the concept of subsidy in Article 3 of Regulation No 2176/84 presupposes the grant of an economic advantage through a charge on the public account'.[121]

The conclusion that the Community was entitled, but not required, to take the view that a charge on the public account was necessary in its countervailing duty law (see, to this effect, the use of the negative syntax in the two statements) cannot be justified simply by the usual deferential approach in the judicial review of Community's acts. It is the Court's acknowledgement that the choice of EC countervailing duty law was just an option, permitted by the GATT. The latter did not provide for an express definition of subsidy and hence a final word on the cost to government.

C. WTO era

In the analysis of the cost to government issue in WTO law, we concentrate mainly on the definition of subsidy in Article 1 SCM, and in particular on the financial contribution. The SCM is the most general regulation of subsidies in the WTO and it is with respect to the definition of subsidies therein that there was a fierce confrontation during the Uruguay Round.

The situation is different with respect to agriculture. Indeed it seems that the issue of the financing of subsidies has not been as controversial in the context of the AG. In some cases, it is the actual provision that seems to indicate that there is no need that government resources are used. Article 9.1(c) of the AG, for example, regulates payments financed by virtue of governmental action, 'whether or not a charge on the public account is involved'.[122] In other cases, this may be easily inferred, for instance with respect to the forms of domestic support that do not fulfil the condition of Article 1(a) Annex 2 (that is that 'the support in question shall be provided through a publicly-funded programme (including government revenue foregone) not involving transfers from consumers').[123] In other cases, for example Article 9.1(a) ('provision by governments or their agencies of direct subsidies, including payments-in-kind'), the dispute settlement has made it clear

[120] Paragraph 12 of Case 187/85; para 13 of Case 188/85.

[121] Paragraph 13 of Case 187/85; para 14 of Case 188/85.

[122] See Appellate Body, *Canada—Dairy (Article 21.5—I)*, para 114; id, *Canada—Dairy (Article 21.5—I)*, paras 132 and 133.

[123] That might be the case of a parafiscal charge imposed on consumers or even on producers at large.

that there is no need for a transfer of government resources[124] and, quite probably, the relevant findings can be transposed also to other items of Article 9.1.[125]

SCM Agreement

The financial contribution: uncertain compromise or creeping victory?

The two opposite views on the cost to government issue, and, more generally, on the definition of subsidy, were confronted with each other during the Uruguay Round negotiations and were mainly heralded by the United States on the one side and the European Communities on the other.[126] The former's more extensive approach contrasted with the stricter approach of the latter.[127]

The United States position was very much 'effect-oriented'. It proposed that a subsidy be defined as 'any measure or combination of governmental measures which confers a benefit on the recipient enterprises'.[128] According to this view, which corresponds to the broad approach to the definition of subsidies in US countervailing duty law history,[129] what matters is the distorting effect of the measure and not its form or how it is financed.

Together with other negotiating countries, the European Communities counter-argued that 'actions by public authorities which do not imply expenditure of public funds, or, anyway, a charge on the public account, are not subsidies and thus *a fortiori* cannot be actionable or be otherwise subject to subsidies discipline'.[130] The concern was that the omission of such a requirement would cause an indefinite number of measures to be caught (and subject to US countervailing duty action).

The *chapeau* of Article 1.1(a)(1) of the SCM provides that, for a subsidy to be deemed to exist, it is necessary to have 'a financial contribution by a government'. Then we have a list of three forms of financial assistance and a provision, item (iv), which envisages that the government may make the financial contribution through intermediaries, such as a private body.

Starting with the expression 'financial contribution', although the negotiating history shows that it has often been regarded as a synonymous to cost to

[124] See Panel, *Canada—Dairy*, para 7.56.

[125] Consider, eg, paras (d), (e) and (f).

[126] PJ McDonough, 'Subsidies and Countervailing Measures' in TP Stewart (ed), *The GATT Uruguay Round—A Negotiating History* (1986–1992), Vol I (Deventer: Kluwer, 1993) 809, 898–9; see also P Didier, *WTO Trade Instruments in EU Law—Commercial Policy Instruments: Dumping, Subsidies, Safeguards, Public Procurement* (London: Cameron May, 1999) 230–3.

[127] The *US—Export Restraints* dispute, thoroughly discussed above, offers a good insight in this regard.

[128] GATT Document MTN.GNG/NG10/W/29.

[129] See PJ McDonough, 'Subsidies and Countervailing Measures' in TP Stewart (ed), *The GATT Uruguay Round—A Negotiating History (*1986–1992), Vol I (Deventer: Kluwer, 1993) 899.

[130] cf GATT Document MTN.GNG/NG10/W/31.

government,[131] taken in itself, its meaning remains uncertain. Moreover, the wording of item (iv) of Article 1.1(a)(1) of the SCM, which also covers the case where 'a government entrusts or directs a private body to carry out' a financial contribution, is capable of encompassing also those cases where the transfer of economic resources is not actually financed by the government but rather by the intermediary.

The scope of Article 1.1(a)(1) of the SCM is thus ambiguous. And this ambiguity was the price for reaching an agreement between two very different positions. However, the content of the *compromise* remains *uncertain*. Is it the positive expression of an 'agreement to disagree'? Or, rather, should the use of a sufficiently flexible language be interpreted as a veritable victory, one which could ironically be claimed by each side to the dispute? Certainly, the ambiguity of the provision, and in particular its capability to include the more extensive position, provides significant ammunition to a creeping victory of the latter. These are only suppositions, however. The fact remains that both the expression 'financial contribution' and the wording of item (iv) are vague enough to accommodate both positions. The only certainty we are left with is that the legislative stage seems to have kept the issue open.

Scholars disagree on which position ultimately succeeded.[132] Thus, for example, while McDonough and Didier suggest that a cost to government would not be necessary,[133] Low maintains that the 'financial contribution' in Article 1.1(a)(1) of the SCM implies a 'financial outlay' by the government.[134] Along the same lines, others argue that an important implication of the new definition may be to prevent the use of the SCM Agreement to attack 'regulatory subsidies' (ie the failure of governments to provide certain levels of regulation, such as environmental protection

[131] This is well illustrated in the Secretariat's note MTN.GNG/NG10/13, p 4. If we wanted to carry out this exercise through the various documents, we would find that this equivalence is expressly made by Japan (MTN.GNG/NG/W27, p 2) and can almost certainly be inferred from the words of Canada (MTN.GNG/NG/W25, p 4). Some doubts might be entertained with respect to India's position (MTN.GNG/NG/W16, p 1; MTN.GNG/NG/W 33, p 3).

[132] JHJ Bourgeois, 'EU Rules on State Aids and WTO Provisions on Subsidies Compared: The Case of State-Owned Banks', in CD Ehlermann and M Everson, *European Competition Law Annual 1999: Selected Issues in the Field of State Aids* (Oxford: Hart Publishing, 2001) 209, 220–1.

[133] PJ McDonough, 'Subsidies and Countervailing Measures' in TP Stewart (ed), *The GATT Uruguay Round—A Negotiating History* (1986–1992), Vol I (Deventer: Kluwer, 1993) 899, points out that the language of Article 1.1(a)(1)(iv) of the SCM 'apparently encompasses' the forms of 'private subsidies' 'wherein benefits are conferred on recipients from private sources but at the direction or mandate of government'. cf also P Didier, *WTO Trade Instruments in EU Law—Commercial Policy Instruments: Dumping, Subsidies, Safeguards, Public Procurement* (London: Cameron May, 1999) 232–3 who underlines that 'the dispute on the financial contribution concept was settled by a compromise which reflects, in the main, the US position'. As regards the term 'financial contribution', 'while excluding non financial contributions' he argues that it seems 'sufficiently wide to encompass many forms of State intervention which have financial consequences, whether or not they imply a call on the public purse'.

[134] P Low, 'The Treatment of Subsidies in the WTO Framework' in CD Ehlermann and M Everson, *European Competition Law Annual 1999: Selected Issues in the Field of State Aids* (Oxford: Hart Publishing, 2001) 103, 111.

or labour standards) which, as seen in the previous chapter, often do not involve any cost to the government.[135]

The Appellate Body has arguably solved this ambiguity. Before outlining its findings, it may be worth saying a few words on the other limb of Article 1 of the SCM which concerns the public intervention and which, like the financial contribution, raises an issue of the origin of financing.

Article 1.1(a)(2) of the SCM: forms of income or price support

A 1960 GATT Panel report concluded that, under Article XVI of the GATT, only 'price support' measures requiring a 'loss' to the government could be regarded as subsidies.[136] This interpretation is consistent with the general position as to the definition of subsidy and the cost to government issue in the GATT.

Article 1(a)(2) of the SCM now regulates 'any form of income or price support in the sense of Article XVI of GATT 1994'. The issue of whether measures of income support can be fully assimilated to those of price support may be left aside. The interesting question is whether the new provision should be interpreted as the GATT Panel did with Article XVI of the GATT, or whether a new reading is possible instead, particularly if the general position with respect to the issue were changed with respect to other forms of public intervention, notably those provided in the financial contribution.

It does not seem that this point has been discussed during the Uruguay Round negotiations. Some support for the more extensive interpretation can be found in the literature. Low thus argues that, whereas 'income and price supports will often imply a financial outlay of some kind by the government', it is indeed possible to devise a minimum price regime which does not involve a financial outlay and which would certainly distort trade in a GATT 1994 Article XVI sense.[137]

As anticipated, a more liberal position would definitely be strengthened by a broader finding that the more general concept of the definition of subsidy defining the action of the government—the 'financial contribution'—does not require a cost to government. This point is analysed in the next paragraph.

Clarifying the ambiguity of the financial contribution: *Canada—Aircraft*

The wording of Article 1.1(a)(1) of the SCM does not expressly indicate whether a subsidy requires a cost to government but is ambiguous on this point. Whatever reading is given to the resulting ambiguity—as we have suggested, either 'agreement

[135] JH Jackson, *The World Trading System—Law and Policy of International Economic Relations* (2nd edn, Cambridge Massachussetts: MIT Press, 1997) 296; M Benitah, *The Law of Subsidies under the GATT/WTO System* (The Hague: Kluwer Law International, 2001) 71 and 73–4.

[136] GATT Panel Report adopted on 24 May 1960 (Review pursuant to Article XVI:5 GATT), BISD 9th Suppl 1961 188, at p 191.

[137] P Low, 'The Treatment of Subsidies in the WTO Framework' in CD Ehlermann and M Everson, *European Competition Law Annual 1999: Selected Issues in the Field of State Aids* (Oxford: Hart Publishing, 2001) 103, 111.

to disagree' or uncertain but creeping victory of either side (with the odds more in favour of the extensive approach)—it was predictable that, sooner or later, the issue would be subject to the scrutiny of the newly-established dispute settlement organs for a decision. However, what was not fully predictable is the direction that would be taken.

The issue of whether a 'cost to government' is relevant in the context of Article 1.1(a) of the SCM arose in the *Canada—Aircraft* dispute. The context of the debate, however, was not the interpretation of the 'financial contribution' element in Article 1.1(a)(1) but rather the definition of the 'benefit' under Article 1.1(a)(2). In particular Canada was arguing that the notion of 'cost to government' is relevant in the interpretation of the term 'benefit' within the meaning of the latter. By rejecting the argument, the Panel noted that:

> if 'benefit' were to include the notion of net cost to government, it could exclude from the definition of 'subsidy' situations explicitly identified in Article 1.1(a)(1) itself as constituting government financial contributions even though no cost to the government might be involved. Specifically, Article 1.1(a)(1)(iv) identifies as a 'financial contribution' the situation where a government directs a private body to make 'financial contributions' within the meaning of Article 1.1(a)(1)(i)–(iii). In such a situation, the net cost could be incurred entirely by the private body rather than the government. Canada's interpretation of 'benefit' (ie, to include net cost to government) would render Article 1.1(a)(1)(iv) meaningless, since a form of 'financial contribution' explicitly included in Article 1.1(a) would automatically (ie, because it would never meet the net cost to government test) be excluded by Article 1.1(b).[138]

Although the argument of effectiveness is excessively marked,[139] the position of the Panel does not leave much room for doubt.

Albeit using more laconic language, the Appellate Body confirmed that a 'cost to government' is not implied in the context of the 'financial contribution'. Crucially, it observed that Canada's argument, whereby the concept of 'cost to government' would be relevant in the interpretation of the 'benefit',

> would exclude from the scope of that term those situations where a 'benefit' is conferred by a private body under the direction of government. These situations cannot be *excluded* from the definition of 'benefit' in Article 1.1(b), given that they are specifically *included* in the definition of 'financial contribution' in Article 1.1(a)(iv).[140]

The importance of the conclusion (confirmed in the report of the momentous *US—Export Restraints* dispute)[141] cannot be underestimated. Both the Panel and the Appellate Body were fully aware of the long-standing debate on the cost to

[138] Panel, *Canada—Aircraft*, para 9.115.

[139] The consideration that the alternative reading 'would render Article 1.1(a)(1)(iv) meaningless' seems to want to prove too much. We may certainly have cases of indirect action financially supported by the public fisc.

[140] Appellate Body, *Canada—Aircraft*, para 161.

[141] Paragraph 8.73, n 167.

government issue and of the significance of *any*, even *incidental*, finding on the issue. Moreover, this finding is highly significant not only in the context of the financial contribution requirement. This interpretation may have a spill-over effect with respect to a more extensive reading of the other form of government intervention concerning 'any income or price support'.

The only regret is that this controversial issue was not raised in its natural context—the financial contribution—which would have required the dispute settlement organs to provide a full reasoning.

The objective of next paragraph is to 'supplement the analysis' of the Panel and the Appellate Body by addressing the issue in the context of the financial contribution and by using the 'customary rules of interpretation' of the VCLT.

Exercise of interpretation: the financial contribution and the 'cost to government' It may be recalled that the 'general rule of interpretation' of Article 31.1 of the VCLT reads that 'a treaty shall be interpreted in good faith in accordance with the ordinary meaning to be given to the terms of the treaty in their context and in the light of its object and purpose'. According to Article 32 of the VCLT, this may be complemented by the use of supplementary means of interpretation, such as the preparatory works, in order to confirm the discovered meaning or to determine it when the general rule has left it ambiguous or obscure.

In few words, as found in chapter 1, under the 'customary rules of interpretation of public international law', duly embodied in the VCLT, the text of the treaty represents the 'centre of gravity' of legal interpretation. This does not however mean that it is self-sufficient, since it necessarily needs to be contextualized in various ways.[142]

Textual and contextual interpretation A quick check of the dictionary meanings of the constituent elements of 'financial contribution' indicates that this expression substantially refers to a payment, ie to a transfer of financial or economic resources. Whereas 'financial' means 'of or pertaining to revenue or money matters',[143] the examination of the most relevant dictionary meanings of 'contribution' ('something paid or given (voluntarily) to a common fund or stock; an action etc. which helps to bring about a result; the action of contributing')[144] seems to indicate that the meaning conveyed by the phrase 'financial contribution' essentially refers to *a payment* which is most probably executed to reach a particular aim. This is in line with the findings of the previous analysis of financial contribution which concluded that it refers to forms of action that involve a financial transfer.

[142] The reader is directed to section II.C of chapter 1 for a more comprehensive analysis of the approach to legal interpretation in the WTO.

[143] *Shorter Oxford English Dictionary on Historical Principles* (5th edn, Oxford: Oxford University Press, 2003) Vol I, 959.

[144] ibid, 506.

What is not so clear, however, is that this definition would necessarily refer to the *origin* of the resources involved. Although the phrase 'financial contribution' has often been used as a synonym of cost to government or charge on the public account, this does not seem to be its main focus and its wording is actually general enough to encompass cases with no use of governmental resources as well. This conclusion can be confirmed if we concentrate on the form of financial contribution in the fourth paragraph of Article 1.1(a)(1) of the SCM which, as we know, regulates the case where the government entrusts or directs a private party to carry out one of the previous forms of action. As the dispute settlement organs in *Canada—Aircraft* noted, this form of financial contribution is certainly *capable* of encompassing transfers of economic resources which are actually provided by the intermediary, and not by the government.

One significant contextual factor could restrain this capability. A consolidated view, expressed in the interpretation of the two final provisos of subparagraph (iv), is that the latter would imply 'a general reference to the *delegation* to private parties of the particular government functions of taxation and expenditure of revenue, and *not* a reference to government market interventions in the general sense, or the effects thereof.'[145] Now, if one relied on the first part of this statement, and required that *every* form of financial contribution, be it direct or indirect, involve the exercise of the government prerogatives of taxation and revenue expenditure, it would be quite easy to conclude that *every* subsidy should by necessity require a 'cost to government'. If, however, this finding is put into perspective, by noting that it was made in order to exclude *complex* regulatory mechanisms from the scope of the financial contribution requirement, it is still possible to conclude that a transfer of economic resources could be carried out through a private party without a burden for the fisc.[146] This would be confirmed by the second part of the statement above. The delegation to private parties would always be possible *unless* the 'government practice' were 'a reference to government market interventions in the general sense, or the effects thereof'.

The difficulty with the apparent *hard-and-fast connection* 'financial contribution'-'functions of taxation/revenue expenditure' is that, if we exclude *all* 'regulatory measures' from the scope of subparagraph (iv) altogether, an indirect subsidy without the use of public resources may become *impracticable*. In other words, cases of delegation without use of government money are very likely to be considered 'regulation' (not covered) rather than 'financial assistance' (covered). In the author's view, irrespective of the possible classification of the measure, a balanced answer

[145] Panel, *US—Export Restraints*, para 8.72; Panel, *Korea—Commercial Vessels*, para 7.30.

[146] Interestingly, those scholars who support a strict interpretation of the two final provisos of subpara (iv) also recognize that a financial contribution may be granted *via* a 'private body' without any cost to government. See R Howse, 'Post-Hearing Submission to the International Trade Commission: World Trade Law and Renewable Energy: The Case of Non-Tariff Measures', 5 May 2005, Renewable Energy and Intenrnational Law Project, 22.

should lie in a more flexible interpretation allowing to catch (at least) the *more immediate and linear* forms of indirect support.[147]

The results of our textual and contextual analysis are therefore that:

A The expression 'financial contribution' seems mainly to refer to the *action of transfer of financial resources*, and not to the *source* of the latter,

B This definition does *not* necessarily refer to the origin of the resources, particularly the fourth item of article 1.1(a)(1) of the SCM.

That said, an uncompromising (but undesirable) interpretation of the fourth item of Article 1.1(a)(1) of the SCM by reference to the exercise of the functions of *taxation* and *revenue expenditure* might lead to the practical result that every form of financial contribution *does* require the use of public resources.

This author does not find any other contextual guidance in support of or against these conclusions either in other provisions of the SCM or in other WTO instruments.

On the one hand, provisions such as Article 14 of the SCM or Article 1 of Annex IV to the SCM Agreement, which are relied on by Didier,[148] are not relevant because they do not provide the appropriate context for the interpretation of the financial contribution requirement. The former refers to the concept of *benefit* (more particularly, to the calculation of the amount of the subsidy for countervailing duty actions), the latter to the (now expired) presumption of *serious injury* under Article 6.1(a) of the SCM.

On the other hand, the interpreter might be tempted to look at similar definitional provisions of other WTO instruments, such as the AG. Irrespective of the fact that these do not provide unequivocal indications, the most fundamental obstacle is of a systemic nature. The reference to a *specific* discipline (on agriculture), may be of limited help when we should interpret the *general* discipline of subsidies (such as the SCM Agreement), and in particular its most general norm, that which (expressly) lays down the definition of its subject and determines its scope of application.

Interpretation 'in the light of the object and purpose' of the treaty Some support for the interpretation of Article 1.1(a)(1) as generally referring to a transfer of economic resources provided by the government but not to its method of financing can be found in the analysis of the object and purpose of the SCM Agreement.

The object and purpose of the treaty should mainly be derived from its text, and in particular its preamble which usually spells out the background and the objectives of the relevant discipline.

[147] For an analysis of the issue in the context of the two final provisos of subpara (iv) see above.

[148] P Didier, *WTO Trade Instruments in EU Law—Commercial Policy Instruments: Dumping, Subsidies, Safeguards, Public Procurement* (London: Cameron May, 1999) 232.

The absence of a preamble in the SCM Agreement evidences the considerable disagreement on the 'subsidy issue'. The dispute settlement organs have thus been cautious in defining the object and purpose of the SCM Agreement and formulating arguments based on it.[149] Generally speaking, only general statements can be found, which summarize it as the establishment of a multilateral discipline on the premise that some forms of government intervention distort international trade, or have the potential to distort international trade, or, with an alternative and more laconic formulation, as a multilateral discipline on subsidies which distort international trade.[150]

Admittedly, along with the *US—Export Restraints* Panel, it could be underlined that the SCM Agreement does not regulate 'every government intervention that might in economic theory be deemed a subsidy with the potential to distort trade'.[151] This general statement could be made more specific by the reading outlined above that a financial contribution could be established only when the government is taxing or spending. If this is true, it should be concluded that Members wanted to regulate only those forms of governmental action that *involve* a cost to government.

Another plausible reading is possible however. Despite the caution noted above, some agreement on the purpose of the subsidy discipline can be reached. By relying on the consideration that subsidies are regulated because they cause, or may cause, *distortions*,[152] it could indeed be suggested that no relevance should be given to a factor, the financing of the measure, which, in general, does not seem to be relevant in assessing its distorting capacity.[153]

Effectiveness, preparatory works, restrictive interpretation Arguments on the basis of the principle of effectiveness, which would flow directly from 'good faith' and 'the object and purpose of the treaty' under Article 31(1) of the VCLT, do not seem to shift the balance substantially as they would not add any more weight to the arguments already based on purposive interpretation.

[149] It has been noted that 'the SCM Agreement does not contain any express statement of its object and purpose. We therefore consider it unwise to attach undue importance to arguments concerning the object and purpose of the SCM Agreement'. cf Panel, *Canada—Aircraft*, para 9.119.

[150] The two definitions can be found in Panel, *Canada—Aircraft*, para 9.119, and Panel, *Brazil—Aircraft*, para 10.11 respectively.

[151] Panel, *US—Export Restraints*, para 8.62.

[152] Although in the different context of the construction of the 'benefit', the importance of the 'trade-distorting' potential of the 'financial contribution has been duly considered by the Appellate Body (*Canada—Aircraft*, para 157).

[153] Admittedly, certain conduct, such as predation, ie under-cost selling, are more likely to succeed if they draw from the resources of the clearly deep pockets of public coffers. However, this does not lend any support to considering the cost to government *as a requirement* of the definition of subsidy. It merely indicates that, in some cases, the fact that a practice is publicly subsidized should be taken into account when the impact of the measure is analysed because of the increased likelihood of its endangering the competitive process.

Similarly, the author does not consider recourse to the preparatory works useful in confirming our interpretation. The general reservations with respect to the utility and reliability of this method have already been noted.[154] This is particularly true in the case at issue. The negotiating history can only tell us that there was a heated debate but it is silent on whether one of those positions in the end prevailed and, if so, which one.

Similarly, despite the Appellate Body expressly endorsing the principle of restrictive interpretation (also known as *in dubio mitius*) in *EC—Hormones*,[155] the author does not consider this to be reliable, concurring instead with critics of this principle.[156]

[154] The recourse to the preparatory works is not very common. This is partly due to the fact that these are accorded a secondary role in the process of interpretation. However, the caution in referring to them seems more radically to depend on two other arguments clearly summarized by Sinclair. The relevant passage deserves a full quotation: 'the obscurity of a particular text will often find its origin in the *travaux préparatoires* themselves. The natural desire of negotiators to bring negotiations to a successful conclusion will often result in the adoption of vague or ambiguous formulations. Sometimes the parties will have deliberately wished to avoid too much precision in order to allow themselves in future to argue that the provision as formulated does not commit them to an inconvenient or too onerous obligation. Finally, the *travaux préparatoires* are unlikely to reveal accurately and in detail what happened during the negotiations, since, more often than not, they will not disclose what may have been agreed between the heads of delegations during private corridor discussions'. See I Sinclair, *The Vienna Convention on the Law of Treaties* (2nd edn, Manchester: Manchester University Press, 1984) 142. cf also I Brownlie, *Principles of Public International Law* (6th edn, Oxford: Oxford University Press, 2003) 636.

Whereas Sinclair's first argument highlights the substantial *inconclusiveness* of the recourse to the preparatory works, the second argument warns against the *unreliability* of the records of negotiations. Crucially, both these arguments suggest that the insight into negotiations, far from providing the clarification sought, might in fact divert from the results that, despite some uncertainty, have emerged from the primarily textual interpretation under Article 31 VCLT.

[155] The Appellate Body noted that 'if the meaning of the term is ambiguous, that meaning is to be preferred which is less onerous to the party assuming an obligation, . . . or involves less general restrictions upon the parties' (para 165). It seems however that this principle was not actually relevant in solving the *Hormones* dispute, a textual interpretation of the provision at issue (Articles 3.1 and 3.2 of the SPS Agreement) being sufficient.

[156] This principle is increasingly less used and is generally subject to criticism. See, eg, I Brownlie, *Principles of Public International Law* (6th edn, Oxford: Oxford University Press, 2003) 636; J Pauwelyn, *Conflict of Norms in Public International Law—How WTO Law Relates to Other Rules of International Law* (Cambridge: Cambridge University Press, 2003) 186.

As early as in 1961, Lord McNair expressed the view that the principle was of declining importance and dated 'from an age in which treaties were interpreted not by legal tribunals, and not even much by lawyers but by statesmen and diplomats'. Underlying the *in dubio mitius* principle is the idea of deference towards the sovereignty of the states, wittily dubbed by Professor Jackson as one of the 'mantras' of WTO. See JH Jackson, *Sovereignty, WTO and Changing Fundamentals of International Law* (Cambridge: Cambridge University Press, 2006). The fact is that, in a treaty, very much like in any contract between private parties, one party's obligation usually corresponds to another party's right. As Pauwelyn noted, 'to interpret obligations for one State restrictively could, indeed, amount to not giving the intended effect to the rights of another State'. See *Conflict of Norms in Public International Law—How WTO Law Relates to Other Rules of International Law* (Cambridge: Cambridge University Press, 2003) 186, n 57. A treaty is the result of a sophisticated exercise of balance of obligations and rights as has been recognized by the Appellate Body itself in the *Japan—Taxes II* case. The particularly illuminating passage deserves full quotation: '[t]he *WTO Agreement* is a treaty—the international equivalent of a contract. It is self-evident that in an exercise of their sovereignty, and in pursuit of their

Conclusion The result of the exercise of interpretation is that, on balance, the conclusion of the dispute settlement organs that the financial contribution, and *more specifically* the fourth subparagraph of Article 1.1(a)(1) of the SCM, does not necessarily involve a cost to government, is substantially supported by the interpretation of the 'financial contribution' requirement 'in accordance with the customary rules of international law'. This conclusion seems essentially to rest on a textual and contextual interpretation, with some support from the teleological perspective.

own respective national interests, the Members of the WTO have made a *bargain*. In exchange for the benefits they expect to derive as Members of the WTO, they have agreed to exercise their sovereignty according to the commitments they have made in the *WTO Agreement*' (para 15, emphasis in the original).

It is posited that the admittedly balanced approach of the mainly textual analysis of the Vienna Convention is already capable of capturing, in each given case, the bargain underlying the words of the WTO Agreement.

5

The forms of governmental action covered by EC State aid rules

This chapter deals with questions similar to those that were analysed in the previous chapter on WTO law. Following the first three techniques to define the legal relevance of the conduct of the government (formulation of the definition, standards of imputability, origin of the resources), we analyse the forms of governmental action that are covered by Article 87(1) EC, and, where necessary, provide a critique.

I. Formulation of the definition of State aid

Unlike in WTO law, there is only one provision featuring a definition of State aid in the EC.[1] Article 87(1) EC regulates 'any aid granted by the State or through State resources in any form whatsoever'.

A. Broad language between potentially wide coverage and prevailing interpretation

Even a first reading seems to indicate that this provision should not be interpreted formally or narrowly. The wording refers to '*any* aid' 'in *any* form *whatsoever*' which is 'granted by the State *or* through State resources'.[2] Many linguistic elements thus hint towards a particularly comprehensive reading, broad enough to cover various forms of governmental action that provide assistance to undertakings.

Crucially, what is underlined here is merely the *capacity* to interpret the definition broadly. This does not necessarily, or always, correspond to its *prevailing interpretation*. Different, more extensive or restrictive, interpretations may depend on policy choices. These policy choices are, however, contrained by various considerations. They should be in line with the constitutional values, with the overall structure of the legal system (taking into account of the possibility of unwanted policy substitution), and with the coherency of internal choices with

[1] Other provisions (like Articles 36 and 73 EC, or the now expired Article 4(c) of the ECSC) refer to 'aids' or 'subsidies' without defining them. It is therefore customary to rely on the concept outlined in Article 87(1) EC.

[2] Emphasis added.

international commitments. Most importantly, they should be sound and balanced in terms of the legal interpretation of the definition itself. In other words, given a certain policy objective (for example, that of excluding certain measures from the scope of the rules), this should be done in the most clear and appropriate way. This is not only for the sake of conceptual neatness, but also for transparency and legal certainty.

A broad interpretation of Article 87(1) EC was arguably in the minds of the Fathers of the Treaty of Rome as clearly expressed at various points of the *Spaak* Report which underlines the irrelevance of the form of the public intervention:

> [l]es aides accordées par les Etats doivent donc être examinees de très près, *indépendamment de la forme extérieure qu'elles revêtent*... La règle générale est que sont incompatibles avec le marché commun les aides, *sous quelque forme qu'elles soient accordées*...[3]

Crucially, what is unclear is how broad the Fathers imagined the notion of aid could be. A safe assumption is that they were thinking of most common cases where the *governmental prerogatives to tax and spend the levied revenue* were exercised.[4] Equally, it can be assumed that the contemplation of the possible applicability of other, more appropriate, rules was certainly an important factor in the back of their minds.[5] Whatever it may be, it is clear that the interpretation of provisions drafted more than fifty years ago should not be set in stone. If necessary, it may well be, and should be, subject to an evolutive and teleological interpretation.

The potential of State aid control was immediately captured by the European Court of Justice. In 1961, in the first State aid case, it had to interpret the expression 'aid or subsidy' in Article 4(c) ECSC. In a finding, which has also become a standard in the context of Article 87(1) EC, and which is clearly in line with the vision of the Fathers,[6] it held that the concept of aid is wider than that of a subsidy

> because it embraces not only positive benefits, such as subsidies themselves, but also interventions which, in various forms, mitigate the charges which are normally included in the budget of an undertaking and which, without, therefore, being subsidies in the strict meaning of the word, are similar in character and have the same effect.[7]

[3] Rapport des Chefs de Délegation Aux Ministres des Affaires Etrangères, Comité Intergouvernemental créé par la Conférence de Messine, Brussels, 21 April 1956 (Spaak Report) 57.

[4] This is confirmed by the two examples set out by the *Spaak Report* itself: 'l'exemption accordée à une catégorie d'entreprises ou à une branche d'industrie au regard des charges de droit commun comporte les mêmes effets et relève des mêmes critère d'examen qu'une subvention sur fonds publics' (ibid).

[5] As will be examined, this 'external dimension' is particularly important, not only for its implications with respect to the different substantive requirements of the law but also with respect to the institutional and constitutional implications. See chapter 6, section III.

[6] Reproducing the two examples mentioned in the *Spaak Report*. See n 4.

[7] Case 30/59 *Steenkolenmijnen*, p 19. cf also ibid, at 27.

The subsequent case-law of the Court of Justice has consistently confirmed the rather open-ended coverage of Article 87(1). The Court has thus found various forms of governmental assistance to constitute State aids. These range from the most obvious, such as grants, loans, capital injections, guarantees, fiscal exceptions, debt renegotiation, to more unconventional ones, like exemption from the normal application of insolvency rules, purchases at market conditions but without the presence of a real need, allocation of pollution permits and licences of UMTS frequencies.[8]

This broad scope seems to be favoured by an interpretation which puts emphasis on the *effects* of the conduct at issue. This has already been seen in the *Steenkolenmijnen* decision. In another *locus classicus* the Court of Justice laid it out even more clearly: '[Article 87] does not distinguish between the measures of State intervention by reference to their causes or aims but defines them in relation to their effects'.[9] In the same tone, it has been said that the concept of State aid is an *objective* one.[10]

The Court of Justice has also repeatedly stated that Article 87(1) EC covers not only measures granted by the State, which does not include only central national authorities but also regional and local ones,[11] but also by other bodies which, in one way or another, are under its control. The Court made it clear that State aid law regulates all subsidies threatening the play of competition coming from the public sector,[12] a notion that generally refers to 'that part of the economy or an industry that is controlled by the government'.[13] This notion of public sector clearly reminds us of the definition of 'public undertaking' adopted in the Transparency Directive whereby a public undertaking is 'any undertaking over which the public authorities may exercise directly or indirectly a dominant influence by virtue of their ownership of it, their financial participation therein, or the rules which govern it'.[14] Using broader language, the Court has also held that Article 87(1), which merely refers to any aid 'granted by the State or through State resources', should be construed so as to cover subsidies granted directly by the State as well as those 'granted indirectly by public or private bodies established or appointed by the State to administer the aid'.[15]

[8] For an examination of these forms and particularly of the analysis of the advantage granted see chapters 8 and 10.

[9] Case 173/73 *Italy v Commission*, para 13.

[10] Case T-67/94 *Ladbroke Racing v Commission*, para 52.

[11] cf, eg, Case 248/84 *Germany v Commission*, para 17.

[12] cf Case C-305/89 *Italy v Commission*, para. 13; Joined Cases C-27-73/91 *Sloman Neptun*, para 19; Case T-358/94 *Air France v Commission*, para 56.

[13] BA Garner (ed), *Black's Law Dictionary* (7th edn, St Paul, Minnesota: West Group, 1999) 1246; an almost identical meaning can be found in the *Shorter Oxford English Dictionary on Historical Principles* (5th edn, Oxford: Oxford University Press, 2002) Vol II, 2394.

[14] See Article 2(1)(b) of the Commission Directive 80/723/EEC.

[15] Case 78/76 *Steinicke v Germany*, para 21; Case 290/83 *Commission v France*, para 14. See also Case C-279/98 *PreussenElektra*, para 58, and the other cases referred to.

B. Boundaries

Despite this openness, Article 87(1) EC does have limits and attempts to extend its application will not necessarily be warranted.

On the one hand, the Court has set down some clear limits to the inherent expansiveness of a purely effect-based analysis. Accordingly, there is no such concept as that of a 'measure having an effect equivalent to State aid', modelled on a measure having an effect equivalent to a quantitative restriction under Article 28 EC and triggered by the general duty of cooperation imposed on Member States by Article 10 EC.[16] Although this finding does not preclude the possibility of interpreting Article 87(1) EC extensively, it certainly draws a line. On the basis of Article 10 EC, the scope of other rules of competition law, which are addressed to undertakings, can exceptionally be extended to cover the anti-competitive conduct of Member States. This is not the case for State aid rules which already specifically address a certain type of anti-competitive conduct of Member States.

It is interesting to compare the similarity of the conclusion of the Court—there is no such concept as a measure having an effect equivalent to State aid—with the findings in the *US—Export Restraints* dispute where the Panel rejected the attempt to extend the scope of the financial contribution requirement of Article 1.1(a)(1)(iv) of the SCM to other forms of action that produce a similar effect.[17]

On the other hand, the case-law of the Court of Justice has indicated that certain forms of public assistance featuring a regulatory element (price fixing; lax labour/social, insolvency laws) are not generally caught by State aid rules.[18] The reasoning underlying these decisions is not fully clear. On the one side, there is a heavy emphasis on the lack of *use of State resources,* which, under the current State of EC law, is required of any State aid. On the other side, it may well be that in certain cases the *regulatory nature* and/or *the objectives* of the measure at issue have played a role in the decision. By contrast, as the next section shows, it does not seem that the imputability to the State of the measure under scrutiny was an issue under the applicable standard.

II. Rules of imputability under Article 87(1) EC

The coverage of Article 87(1) EC is thus in principle particularly broad, encompassing various forms of financial assistance by governments. One element which contributes to such wide coverage is the possibility that public intervention conferring

[16] Article 10(2) EC reads: '[Member States] shall abstain from any measure which could jeopardise the attaiment of the objectives of the Treaty'.

[17] See chapter 4, section I.B.

[18] See, eg, Case 82/77 *Van Tiggele*, Joined Cases C-72/91 and C-73/91 *Sloman Neptun*, Case C-189/91 *Kirsammer-Hack*, Joined Cases C-52/97, C-53/97 and C-54/97 *Viscido*, Case C-200/97 *Ecotrade*, Case C-295/97 *Piaggio*, Case C-379/98 *PreussenElektra*, Case C-59/03 *Cigliola*.

an economic advantage be carried out through an intermediary. As in the WTO, in such cases the main legal issue is one of imputability.

A. No precise rule of imputability

The question of imputability occurs when the State uses a public or a private body as a vehicle to grant aid. What has to be determined then is whether the action of that body, which may well act independently, should in fact be attributed to the State.

It may be immediately underlined that, unlike Article 1.1(a)(1)(iv) of the SCM, Article 87(1) EC does *not* provide for a defined rule of imputability. The provision at issue here simply requires that the aid be 'granted by the State or through State resources'. Leaving aside the thorny issue of financing, this wording has been construed in a liberal fashion, to encompass many cases where the government provides financial support indirectly.[19] In particular, there does not seem to be a precise rule of imputability, instead a flexible approach seems to prevail.

In some cases the direction of the State, and hence the imputability of the measure, is particularly clear. The State may for example introduce legislative or administrative measures requiring the provision of assistance.[20] It may also specifically establish or appoint a public or private body to administer the aid or, in any event, give an order or an instruction to grant it.

There is also another case where the imputability seems to be rather clear-cut. We have seen that in some cases of deregulation the governmental direction immediately empowers the beneficiary, for example by exempting it from certain standards, and a third party, which effectively provides the financing, is affected only rather indirectly. Some examples of these measures of deregulation have not been considered as forms of State aid. The possible reasons for such a conclusion have been hinted at. What is important to repeat here is that this does not seem to depend on difficulties with respect to their imputability to the State—this is clear, especially in the light of the general language of Article 87(1) EC.

The most significant findings of the case-law concerning the issue of governmental direction will now be examined, followed by an assessment of these findings.

[19] Case 78/76 *Steinicke v Germany*, para 21; Case 290/83 *Commission v France*, para 14. For a similar conclusion, although linking the point to the 'State resources' debate, see Case C-279/98 *PreussenElektra*, para 58.

[20] Although the State aid point was not discussed by the Court, this was clearly the situation in Case 21/88 *Du Pont de Nemours Italiana* where the provision in Italian legislation that required public bodies and companies to purchase 30% of their supplies from companies established in the Mezzogiorno was by definition imputable to the State.

B. A brief review of the case-law

In the *Stardust Marine* case, Advocate General Jacobs has analysed the case-law on the issue of imputability and noted the variety of standards under this concept. The clear exposition, and the classification, of the Advocate General should be followed closely.[21]

There have been some cases where the 'Court established in concreto that the particular measure at issue had been the result of action of the State'. In *Commission v France* ('Poor farmers')[22] the Court thus held that a solidarity grant to farmers was covered by Article 87(1) because it was 'decided and financed by a public body' (the *Caisse Nationale du Crédit Agricole*), its implementation was 'subject to the approval of the public authorities', the detailed rules for its grant corresponded to 'those for ordinary aid' and it was 'put forward by the Government as forming part of a body of measures in favour of farmers which were all notified to the Commission' under Article 88(3) EC.

In other cases, the concrete involvement of the government 'has been inferred from the circumstances taken as a whole'. The *Van der Kooy*[23] case concerned a preferential tariff for natural gas applied by Gasunie with respect to glasshouse growers. The Court found, first, that the State directly or indirectly held 50% of the shares of Gasunie and appointed half of its supervisory board (whose powers included that of determining tariffs). Secondly, the 'Netherlands Government was empowered to approve the tariffs applied by Gasunie and could thus block any tariff which did not suit it and, third, the Netherlands Government had on two occasions successfully exercised its influence over Gasunie in order to seek an amendments of its tariffs'. In conclusion, according to the Court, 'considered as a whole, these factors demonstrate that Gasunie in no way enjoys full autonomy in the fixing of gas tariffs but acts under the control and on the instructions of the public authorities. It is thus clear that Gasunie could not fix the tariff without taking account of the requirements of the public authorities'.[24]

In other cases, it seems that the Court has been content to find that the body at issue 'operated in general under the control of the government'. In *ENI-Lanerossi* and *Alfa Romeo*, the Court found that the members of the boards of directors and the management boards of the two Italian holdings ENI and IRI were appointed by decree and did not have full freedom of action since they had to take the directives of the CIPE, the ministerial committee for economic planning, into account.

[21] Case C-482/99 *Stardust Marine*, paras 58–62 of the Opinion.

[22] Case 290/83 *Commission v France*, para 15.

[23] Joined Cases 67, 68 and 70/85 *Van der Kooy v Commission*. cf also Case C-56/93 *Belgium v Commission*, para 10.

[24] *Van der Kooy*, paras 36 8.

Thus the conclusion was that, 'taken as a whole' those factors showed that ENI and IRI operated, 'in essence', 'under the control' of the Italian State.[25]

Finally, in other cases, the Court seems to have focused mainly on the public or private nature of the body at issue without examining 'whether it took its decisions—in the actual case or even in general—under the decisive influence of the public authorities'. In the *Air France* case the Court of First Instance found that the measure, although formally granted by a limited company governed by private law, was in reality carried out at the decisive instigation of the majority shareholder of the company, a public body, the *Caisse des Dépôts et Consignations*. 'The Caisse was established by law, it was placed under the supervision and guarantee of the legislature, its tasks was the administration of public and private funds composed of compulsory deposits, it was governed by statutory and regulatory rules and its Director-General and directors were appointed by the President of the Republic and the French Government. Those factors were sufficient for it to be held that the Caisse belonged "to the public sector" and the Commission was accordingly entitled to treat the Caisse as "a public-sector body whose conduct is attributable to the French State". The public nature of the Caisse was not called into question by the existence of rules which ensured that the Caisse enjoyed legal autonomy.' According to the Court, those rules did 'not call into question the principle itself of the public nature of that body'.[26]

The exposition of these cases shows that the assessment of the government involvement may operate, under one and the same provision (Article 87(1) EC) at a *progressively more concrete* or *abstract* level, and may be *more* or *less sophisticated* (conclusion which clearly echoes our analysis of the various rules of imputability under the WTO provisions). Advocate General Jacobs put forward a convincing explanation of the variety of these rules, and of the seeming tension between these cases. The intensity of the standard, and hence of the Court's review, would 'depend on how far the public authorities are likely to be involved'.[27]

C. The *Stardust Marine* test

In *Stardust Marine* the Court attempted for the first time to elaborate the rule of imputability under Article 87(1) EC.[28]

In so doing, it relied heavily on the suggestions in the Opinion of Advocate General Jacobs.[29] Significantly, he had begun his analysis by noting that 'it is not easy to establish a general test to determine whether a given measure of a public undertaking is attributable or imputable to the State'. The same consideration

[25] See Case C-303/88 *Italy v Commission* ('ENI-Lanerossi'), para 12; Case C-305/89 *Italy v Commission* ('Alfa Romeo'), para 14.

[26] Case T-358/94 *Air France v Commission*, paras 57–62.

[27] Case C-482/99 *Stardust Marine*, paras 62 and 63 of the Opinion.

[28] Case C-482/99 *Stardust Marine*, para 50 et seq.

[29] ibid, paras 64–8 of the Opinion.

would certainly be true for the conduct of private undertakings as well. He underlined that mere control over a body should not be sufficient inasmuch as 'the fact that the public authorities may exercise directly or indirectly a dominant influence does not prove that they actually exercised that influence in a given case'. At the same time, to avoid the risk of circumvention, it should not be required that the involvement of the State be represented by an explicit instruction. In his view, it should 'be sufficient to establish on the basis of an analysis of the facts and circumstances of the case that the undertaking in question could not take the decision in question "without taking account of the requirements of the public authorities"'.[30]

On the one hand, the Court upheld that a measure should not be imputed to the State merely because it is taken by a public undertaking. Being in the position to control a public undertaking does not mean actually exercising it in a particular case because 'a public undertaking may act with more or less independence, according to the degree of autonomy left to it by the State' (hence, general control is not enough). On the other hand, the Court denied that it is necessary to demonstrate that the public authorities have specifically incited the public undertaking to take the aid measure in question (hence, more or less explicit/express instruction is not necessary). Having regard to the close and privileged relations between the State and public undertakings, that would provide an incentive to grant aid in a non-transparent way. It would also make it difficult for a third party to demonstrate in a particular case that aid measures were in fact adopted on the instructions of the public authorities.

Having taken out the two most extreme benchmarks (mere control and explicit instruction), the Court seems to have subscribed a quite broad *standard of assessment*. What has to be examined is

> whether the public authorities must be regarded as having been *involved, in one way or another, in the adoption of those measures*.[31]

Moving to the *standard of proof*, the Court followed the pretty flexible approach suggested by Advocate General Jacobs, concluding that:

> the imputability to the State of an aid measure taken by a public undertaking may be inferred from a *set of indicators* arising from the *circumstances of the case* and the *context* in which that measure was taken.[32]

[30] As examples of the facts and circumstances which could be taken into account he listed the evidence that the measure was taken at the instigation of the State; the scale and nature of the measure; the degree of control which the State enjoys over the public undertaking in question; and a general practice of using the undertaking in question for ends other than commercial ones or of influencing its decisions. Again to cope with any danger of circumvention, he indicated that, in his view, a generous approach should be taken with regard to proof, which should include circumstantial evidence.

[31] Para 52 (emphasis added).

[32] Para 55 (emphasis added).

In line with the previous case-law and the Opinion of Advocate General Jacobs, a significant consideration was the fact that the decision to grant aid could not be made without taking the requirements or directives of public authorities into account. It underlined that, 'in certain circumstances', 'other indicators *might* be relevant in concluding that an aid measure taken by a public undertaking is imputable to the State, such as, in particular, its integration into the structures of the public administration, the nature of its activities and the exercise of the latter on the market in normal conditions of competition with private operators, the legal status of the undertaking (in the sense of its being subject to public law or ordinary company law), the intensity of the supervision exercised by the public authorities over the management of the undertaking, or any other indicator showing, in the particular case, an involvement by the public authorities in the adoption of a measure or the unlikelihood of their not being involved, having regard also to the compass of the measure, its content or the conditions which it contains'.[33]

D. The *Pearle* case: the double role of the concept of control in a boundary-case

We may now digress a bit by focusing on a boundary-case,[34] which, as such, does not depart from the previous case-law, and in particular from the doctrine elaborated in *Stardust*.[35]

A public body (a trade association) imposed on its members a compulsory earmarked levy to finance a collective advertising campaign for opticians' businesses. This levy was introduced on the initiative of a group of opticians belonging to the trade association, and was in the interest of all its members.

Contrary to the usual situation, what emerges even from such a brief review of the facts is that it is the public body here that is used as vehicle of private action. Although the reasoning of the Court is brief and not fully clear in distinguishing between the determination of imputability and the definition of the origin of financing,[36] it seems that the fact that the measure was taken at the initiative of a private group of opticians (and in the interest of all members of the public body) was considered to be sufficient to exclude its imputability to the public body.[37]

[33] Paragraph 56 (emphasis added). It may be interesting to note that, applying the test above to the instant case, the Court concluded for the incorrectness of the adoption of the sole *organic* criterion, whereby the various measures of financing would have been imputable to the French State because *Crédit Lyonnais* and its two subsidiaries, as public undertakings, were under the control of the State.

[34] Case C-345/02.

[35] L Hancher, 'A Pearle of Wisdom' (2004) European State Aid Law Quarterly 363.

[36] B Vesterdorf, 'A Further Comment on the New State Aid Concept as this Concept Continues to be Reshaped—Pearle—A Further Piece of the State Aid Puzzle?' (2005) European State Aid Law Quarterly 393, 399 suggests that the Court conflated the separate questions of control of resources and imputability. For a similar merger see Case T-136/05 *EARL Salvat*, paras 129–65 (it is interesting to contrast paras 136 and 140 in this regard), and Case C-206/06 *Essent*, paras 65–75.

[37] E Gambaro, A Nucara, and L Prete, 'Pearle: so much Unsaid!' (2005) European State Aid Law Quarterly 3,5.

What is important in *Pearle* is the revelation of the close link between the two separate questions of imputability and financing, which has come out also in the more recent *Essent* case.[38] The connecting element is given by the concept of 'control' which, as shown in *Stardust*, plays a crucial role in both issues.[39] On the one side, to determine imputability we consider the public control over the acting third party. On the other side, as we will see, the qualification of resources as 'State resources' requires the establishment of public control over them.

E. Analysis of the rule of imputability under Article 87(1) EC

This section analyses the findings of the Court in various cases and in particular the test developed in the *Stardust* case which represents the first attempt to elaborate the rule of imputability under Article 87(1) EC.

The Stardust*'s rationalization: towards a flexible and case-by-case rule*

We have seen, and concurred with, Advocate General Jacobs' explanation of the variety of standards applied by the Court in the case-law preceding *Stardust*, which was based on the likelihood or intensity of the involvement of public authorities in the conduct of the third party.

What we see in *Stardust* is a rationalization of the previous case-law which takes the shape of a defined rule of imputability. Nevertheless, and inevitably, if both the variety of real situations and the looseness of the wording of Article 87(1) EC are considered, the test developed by the Court is characterized by *flexibility* rather than by precision.[40] After taking out the two extremes—a mere situation of control is not enough; an express instruction is not necessary—what the Court requires is a *case-by-case analysis* (both with respect to the rule of imputability and the relevant standard of evidence). The imputability, depending on the involvement 'in one way or another' in the adoption of the measure, may be inferred from a set of indicators arising from the circumstances of the case, and changing on the basis of the context surrounding the measure.

The Court's clear stand on the relationship 'public control'–'imputability' should be noted. There is indeed a shift from a *formalistic* to a *functional* test.[41] The Court excluded that a mere situation of control on the public undertaking is enough to attribute all its activity to the State. What is required is an assessment of the *actual* exercise of such control in the case at hand.

[38] Case C-206/06 *Essent*, paras 65–75.

[39] L Hancher, 'Case note on Case C-482/99 French Republic v Commission ("Stardust Marine")' (2003) Common Market Law Review 739, 748 and 749.

[40] A Alexis, 'Notion d'Aide d'Etat Remarques sur l'arrêt Stardust Marine du 16 mai 2002' (2002) European State Aid Law Quarterly 149, 152.

[41] L Hancher, 'Case note on Case C-482/99 French Republic v Commission ("Stardust Marine")' (2003) Common Market Law Review 739, 749.

This might seem to be partly contradicted by the reference, 'in certain circumstances', to other indicators that 'might' be relevant and that often seem to involve a rather *abstract* link with the public power[42] and thus to simply correspond to the fact that the undertaking in question is under public control.[43] In fact, there is no contradiction in the findings of the Court if it is accepted that they constitute a rationalization of the indications of the previous case-law. The key words are flexibility and case-by-case analysis. Whereas what is usually required is an assessment of the actual exercise of direction, in other cases, considering that the government involvement is likely, more abstract, even organic, elements are sufficient to establish imputability.

Beyond Stardust*: imputability and regulatory measures*

It should now be asked whether regulatory measures, which always involve the role of a third party, should be considered as 'granted by the State' and thus satisfy the requisite standard of imputability under Article 87(1) EC.

We may start with the measures of 'deregulation'. The peculiarity of this course of conduct is that the State's direction is clearly addressed to the beneficiary undertakings, which are immediately exempted from rules or restrictions, with the third party, which effectively finances the operation, playing a passive role. Clearly, the test developed in *Stardust*, which focuses on acts of direction addressed to the intermediary, does not apply here. To say that the measures at issue are not 'granted by' the State would however be absurd. Since the State's conduct directly affects the beneficiary undertakings by exempting them from rules and restrictions, the former's involvement is self-evident.

The next question is whether more complex cases where the government may be viewed as guiding a third party to carry out a measure of support but certainly does *not* do so in an *immediate* way, such as where the benefit is conferred through 'border measures',[44] could equally be regarded as 'granted by the State'. There is no case-law on the point. And, like in the case of regulatory measures, the Court does not seem to have had these cases in mind when it laid down the *Stardust*'s rule of imputability. Despite its inherent flexibility, this test seems to refer to more classic cases, where, if present, the involvement of the government is to provide financial support, particularly direct support.

That said, generally speaking, although less immediate, the involvement of the government can certainly be established in some cases. Especially in certain circumstances, when the *causal nexus* between the border measure and the third

[42] See, for instance, the integration of the public undertaking into the public administration, or its legal status.

[43] T Lübbig and M Von Merveldt, 'Stardust Marine: Introducing Imputability into State Aid Rules Plain Sailing into Calm Seas or Rowing Back into Shallow Waters?' (2003) European Competition Law Review 629, 633.

[44] Whose legal status under GATT/WTO law has been extensively analysed in chapter 4.

party's conduct is particularly *proximate*, the imputability to the State may be particularly clear (cf the US argument in *US—Export Restraints*). For its part, as *Stardust* shows in any case, Article 87(1) EC does not face the strictures of a well-defined test (such as that of Article 1.1(a)(1)(iv) of the SCM) or, more generally, of a rigid textual approach (such as in the WTO). In chapter 1 it has already been noted that, because of the heavy influence of teleological considerations, the approach to interpretation in EC law is quite liberal. If policy will is there, legal provisions are certainly more receptive.

Arguments against the coverage of these 'border measures' under Article 87(1) EC would thus be similar to those deployed with respect to cases of deregulation, revolving around the *source of financing*, the *nature or objectives of the measures*, or indeed *systemic considerations* depending on the applicability of other rules of EC law.

III. Origin of resources

In the EC, a controversy similar to the GATT/WTO one on the 'cost to the government' has come from the interpretation of the hermetic expression 'granted by the State or through State resources' in Article 87(1) EC.

The current official position, as stated in the *PreussenElektra* decision, is that the definition of State aid necessarily implies the use of State resources. It is argued however that the stability of this jurisprudence is somewhat weakened by other, often concomitant, hesitant and contradictory statements. The fact is that, if the policy choice is that regulatory measures have to be excluded by the scope of EC State aid law, the reliance on the public or private origin of the resources used is not the best way to do this.

Before the State resources requirement is analysed, it may be useful to examine the jurisprudence of the Court on the issue.

A. The case-law on the 'State resources'

It may be convenient to divide the exposition of the case-law in three parts, the first concerning the initial period, where the case-law was not yet settled, the second relating to the period where the Court consolidated its jurisprudence whereby financing through State resources is necessary, and the third referring to the period where the jurisprudence is arguably characterized by contradictions, uncertainties and paradoxes.

It may also be useful to recall that in the reasoning of the Court the argument on the financing is often blended with other considerations which seem to be based on the *regulatory nature* or on the *objective* of the measure. Although this ambivalence emerges from the following exposition, the reader is invited to concentrate his attention on the point concerning the *origin of the resources* which will then be subject to analysis. A final note on style. For clarity's sake, extensive quotations of the significant findings of the Court are provided.

The first period: fluctuations

In the first period the Court was still fluctuating. We therefore find decisions with contradictory statements.

The *Van Tiggele* case concerned a measure fixing a minimum price for gin.[45] One of the issues was whether, apart from constituting a measure having an effect equivalent to a quantitative restriction on imports under Article 28 EC, 'price-control rules' could amount to a State aid under Article 87(1) EC. The Court followed the Opinion of Advocate General Capotorti[46] and concluded that:

> [w]hatever definition must be placed on the concept of an 'aid' within the meaning of [Article 87] it is clear from the wording thereof that a measure characterized by the fixing of minimum retail prices with the objective of favouring distributors of a product at the exclusive expense of consumers cannot constitute an aid within the meaning of Article [87].[47]

In the next paragraph the Court added:

> [t]he advantages which such an intervention in the formation of prices entails for the distributors of the product are not granted, directly or indirectly, through State resources within the meaning of Article [87].[48]

The issue was subsequently raised in the *Norddeutsches Vieh- und Fleischkontor* case which concerned the allocation of special tariff quotas for the importation of frozen beef and veal from non-member countries.[49] Three traders challenged German legislation that determined the allocation of national quota shares between domestic traders also on the ground that it constituted State aid in favour of certain other traders. Advocate General VerLoren van Themaat opined that it was possible to argue, on the basis of the distinction made in Article 87(1) between 'aid granted by a State' and 'aid granted through State resources', that the independent grant of pecuniary advantages which were not paid for by a Member State were caught by Article 87 EC. He mentioned, as an example, the case of reduced rates which Member States might require private electricity companies or haulage contractors to grant to certain undertakings or in respect of certain products.[50] The Court disagreed and found that:

> the financial advantage which traders derive from receiving a share in the quota is not granted through State resources but through Community resources because the levy which

[45] Case 82/77.

[46] See para 8 of the Opinion.

[47] Paragraph 24.

[48] Paragraph 25.

[49] Joined Cases 213 and 215/81.

[50] ibid, page 3617.

is waived is part of Community resources. Although the term 'aid granted through State resources' is wider than the term 'State aid', the first term still presupposes that the resources from which the aid is granted come from the Member State.[51]

In *Commission v France ('Poor Farmers')* what was at issue was a solidarity grant to poor farmers which was financed by the operating surplus of the French *Caisse nationale de crédit agricole*.[52] As we have seen, there was no doubt that the decision to grant the aid could be imputed to the State. The Commission considered that the resources used to finance the measure were generated from the management of private funds and not State resources. It nonetheless claimed that, although the measure under scrutiny was not, strictly speaking, a State aid, it should have been prohibited by Article 10 EC, being a measure having an effect equivalent to a State aid. On a different construction of the facts, Advocate General Mancini concluded that the use of State resources was indeed involved.[53] The Court did not examine whether the grant was financed by State resources. It noted, however, that:

> [b]y the generality of the terms employed in that provision any State measure, in so far as it has the effect of according aid in any form whatsoever, may be assessed on the basis of Article [87] for its compatibility with the common market.
>
> As is clear from the actual wording of Article [87(1)], aid need not necessarily be financed from State resources to be classified as State aid.[54]

The persisting fluctuations of the Court can be appreciated in two cases decided shortly afterwards, *Van der Kooy* (where the point is not clearly decided)[55] and *Greece v Commission* (which fully upholds *Commission v France*).[56]

The second period: towards stability?

The *Sloman Neptun* decision represents a robust *revirement* towards a restrictive approach with respect to the 'State resource' issue which, after more than fifteen years, is now firmly consolidated.[57]

[51] Paragraph 22.

[52] Case 290/83.

[53] It is useful to recall the firm stance of the same Advocate General in the *Fediol* cases (Cases 187/85 and 188/85) where he underlined that, 'although unsupported by rules of Community or international law', it is 'semantically and logically indisputable' that the requirement of cost to government is inherent in both the notions of GATT subsidy and EC State aid (see pp 4177 and 4178).

[54] Paragraphs 13 and 14.

[55] Joined Cases 67/85, 68/85 and 70/85. Although the emphasis of the analysis of the Court seems to be on the issue of imputability, there is indeed a brief reference to the lower profit that the State would have received from the application of a lower tariff (see para 28). What is not clear, however, is whether this reference should be viewed as a recognition that a financial burden is a necessary requirement of the notion of State aid or, more simply, of a conferral of an out-of-the-market advantage.

[56] Case 57/86, para 12.

[57] See Joined Cases C-72/91 and C-73/91.

The national legislation under examination enabled certain shipping undertakings flying the German flag to subject seafarers who were nationals of non-member countries to working conditions and rates of pay less favourable than those applicable to German workers. Albeit not fully clear, the reasoning of the Court relies heavily on the fact that the legislation at issue would not allegedly involve a transfer of State resources.

Neither the Commission nor Advocate General Darmon thought that a transfer of State resources was necessary under Article 87(1) EC. Contrary to its position with respect to the notion of subsidy under GATT law,[58] the Commission argued that a measure of whatever nature which entails a relief for a particular sector that is not part of a comprehensive system, and hence implies a derogation or exemption from it, is State aid even if it is not financed from public funds. This conclusion derived from both the wording of Article 87(1), and in particular the distinction between aid granted by a State and aid granted through State resources, and from the purpose of State aid rules to protect competition. In any event, the loss of tax revenue resulting from the level at which rates of pay were fixed supported the view that the measure at issue was financed from State resources. Advocate General Darmon argued that the origin of the financing of an aid measure was not relevant. In his view, Article 87(1) required only that the aid measure was the result of conduct for which a Member State was responsible and conferred an advantage on certain undertakings by derogating from the relevant system.

The Court rejected these arguments and, referring to its decision in *Van Tiggele*, held that:

> only advantages granted directly or indirectly through State resources are to be regarded as State aid within the meaning of Article [87(1) EC]. The wording of this provision itself and the procedural rules laid down in Article [88 EC] show that advantages granted from resources other than those of the State do not fall within the scope of the provisions in question.[59]

Revisiting one *dictum* in *Steinicke und Weinlig* in the light of the finding on the origin of the resources,[60] the Court then underlined the anti-circumvention purpose of the distinction set forth in Article 87(1) EC aimed at catching both direct and indirect action of subsidization:

> [t]he distinction between aid granted by the State and aid granted through State resources serves to bring within the definition of aid not only aid granted directly by the State, but also aid granted by public or private bodies designated or established by the State.[61]

[58] See Cases 187/85 and 188/85 *Fediol*. See chapter 4, section II.B.

[59] Paragraph 19.

[60] Case 78/76 *Steinicke und Weinlig*, para 21.

[61] Paragraph 19.

Turning to the crucial question of whether the advantages deriving from the measure at issue were to be viewed as being granted through State resources, the Court crucially held:

[t]he system at issue does not seek, through its object and general structure, to create an advantage which would constitute an additional burden for the State or the abovementioned bodies, but only to alter in favour of shipping undertakings the framework within which contractual relations are formed between those undertakings and their employees. The consequences arising from this, in so far as they relate to the difference in the basis for the calculation of social security contributions, mentioned by the national court, and to the potential loss of tax revenue because of the low rates of pay, referred to by the Commission, are inherent in the system and are not a means of granting a particular advantage to the undertakings concerned.[62]

The principle of *Sloman Neptun* was upheld in *Kirsammer-Hack* and *Viscido*. In the first case the Court concluded that the exclusion of small businesses from a legal regime requiring payment of compensation in the event of unfair dismissals of employees, and at the same time exempting the latter from bearing the legal costs incurred in the relevant legal proceedings, did not constitute a grant of aid.[63] Following the line of *Sloman Neptun*, the Court found that:

the exclusion of a category of businesses from the protection system in question does not entail any direct or indirect transfer of State resources to those businesses but derives solely from the legislature's intention to provide a specific legislative framework for working relationships between employers and employees in small businesses and to avoid imposing on those businesses financial constraints which might hinder their development. It follows that a measure such as the one in question in the main proceedings does not constitute a means of granting directly or indirectly an advantage through State resources.[64]

A similar conclusion was reached in *Viscido* where the measure at issue allowed only one undertaking, Ente Poste Italiane, to derogate from the general rule under Italian law that employment contracts should be of indeterminate duration, and permitted the recruitment of staff under fixed-term contracts.[65] Contrary to the two previous cases, the Court did not refer to the *regulatory nature* or the *objective of the legislation* but merely concluded that the measure at issue 'does not involve any direct or indirect transfer of State resources' to the benefited undertaking.[66]

The principle that the notion of State aid under Article 87(1) necessarily requires a transfer of State resources has also been followed in the *Ecotrade* and *Piaggio* decisions.[67] Two brief comments can be made on those decisions. On the one hand, we cannot avoid noting the language used by the Court in its reasoning

[62] Paragraph 21.
[63] Case C-189/91 *Kirsammer-Hack*.
[64] Paragraphs 17 and 18.
[65] Joined Cases C-52/97, C-53/97 and C-54/97 *Viscido*.
[66] Paragraph 15.
[67] Respectively, Case C-200/97, para 35; Case C-295/97, para 35.

which alternatively refers to the concept of 'State resources' and, with a reminiscence of *Sloman Neptun*,[68] to the notion of 'additional charge for the State'. Frankly, no explanation for this linguistic variation, nor any argument affecting the substance of the debate, can be found. On the other hand, it is more intriguing to highlight the inconsistency between the reasoning, which unequivocally requires a burden for the State, and the conclusions of that reasoning[69] and the corresponding operative parts of both decisions where the use of State resource is merely formulated as an *alternative* requirement. What is interesting to ask is whether this can quite simply be explained by poor drafting or is more tellingly ascribable to a sort of Freudian slip . . .

The last vigorous attack to the 'State resources' doctrine concerned a 'feed-in tariff' in the electricity sector[70] which fascinatingly echoes the example[71] used by Advocate General VerLoren van Themaat almost twenty years before in the *Norddeutsches Vieh- und Fleischkontor* case to conclude that a 'cost to government' is not always necessary to have a State aid. In the *PreussenElektra* case, the Court followed the well-reasoned Opinion of Advocate General Jacobs and reaffirmed its position.[72] The Court concluded that national legislation requiring private electricity supply undertakings to purchase electricity produced in their area of supply from renewable energy sources at minimum prices higher than the real economic value of that type of electricity[73] did not constitute State aid within the meaning of Article 87(1) because there was no direct or indirect use of State resources.

Indeed the financial burden resulting from that purchase obligation was distributed by the legislation between those electricity supply undertakings and upstream private electricity network operators.[74]

With this highly debated case the controversy was apparently put to rest and the jurisprudence seemed to have eventually achieved *stability*. The necessity of a transfer of State resources to have a State aid was finally confirmed.

The third period: perplexities

The cases that follow show that *PreussenElektra* had not resolved all the uncertainties. Four cases which, in the author's view, are exemplary have been selected. These decisions raise perplexities about the solidity of the jurisprudence of the second period, particularly with respect to the persuasiveness of the reliance on the financial

[68] See para 21 therein.

[69] See *Ecotrade*, para 45, and *Piaggio*, para 43.

[70] For a definition of these systems see Directive 2001/77, recital 14.

[71] Imposition on private electricity companies of reduced rates for certain undertakings.

[72] Case C-379/98.

[73] Hence, comparing it to the example of *VerLoren van Themaat*, what was at issue was a procurement, and not a supply, of electricity.

[74] Paragraphs 58–60.

origin of the measure as technique of definition of State aid. To enable a full appreciation of their significance, the dry style of exposition adopted so far has been departed from, and some words of commentary added.

In *Cigliola*[75] the Court was asked by the Tribunale di Genova whether Italian legislation which 'allows an undertaking, Ferrovie dello Stato, to dismiss its older employees—thereby creating a situation in which the undertaking can save on labour costs (salaries and insurance obligations), with an immediate resulting burden to the State in the form of reduced contribution revenue and the payment of pensions to dismissed workers—fall within the concept of aid that is incompatible with the common market within the meaning of Article 87 of the Treaty'.[76]

Considering that the answer to the question referred by the national Court could be clearly deduced from the existing case-law, the Court disposed of the case by way of order.[77] However, even from a brief reading of the question referred, it emerges that the factual and legal background was not really the same as that in the previous case-law and that the issue as to whether, in this case, State resources had been used or not would have requested a more thorough analysis, probably with an Opinion of the Advocate General, a hearing, and, ultimately, a judgment duly published.[78]

The reasoning of the order refers to the previous case-law, particularly to *Sloman Neptun*.[79] It seems nonetheless that at least two circumstances distinguished this case from *Sloman Neptun*. First, the national measure allowed the *dismissal* of employees, thus clearly impacting on ongoing relationships, and, most importantly, on labour costs *currently* borne by the undertaking at issue. This is why in its reference the national court probably highlighted the *immediacy* of the burden for the State finances. Secondly, the financial impact of the measure could indeed be increased by another distinguishing element, that is the fact that, as a consequence of the said dismissal, the State was obliged to pay the dismissed workers' pensions immediately. Oddly, this factor is not considered at all by the Court.

Admittedly, doubts could be entertained about whether the *overall* impact of the measure was really to involve a use of State resources. The measure at issue was intended to give flexibility to the beneficiary undertaking, and thus the actual assessment of any *net burden* for the State, which would depend on the future circumstances of that undertaking, might be difficult to ascertain. In this regard it is

[75] Case C-59/03 *Cigliola v Ferrovie dello Stato*.

[76] See OJ 2003 C83/12, 5 April 2003.

[77] The relevant legal basis is Article 104(3) of the Rules of Procedure which allows the Court to decide a case with reasoned order (and without Advocate General's Opinion) 'where a question referred to the Court for a preliminary ruling is identical to a question on which the Court has already ruled, where the answer to such a question may be clearly deduced from existing case-law or where the answer to the question admits of no reasonable doubt'.

[78] Only a notice with a provisional translation of the operative part of the order has been published in OJ 2004 C106/17.

[79] A copy of the order in the language of the case (Italian) has been obtained from the Registry of the Court on 7 November 2005.

interesting to refer to the penetrating observation of Advocate General Jacobs in *Viscido* that underlines the uncertainty and non-quantifiability of the cost to the government in such circumstances.[80] The Court has accordingly underlined that the focus of the State resources condition is whether there is an immediate shortfall of public money, and not whether the measure ultimately results in a net increase in revenues for the Member State concerned.[81]

In *Cigliola*, however, the Court was quite sure about which position to take, and this is apparent from the language of its conclusion which follows almost word for word the (controversial) question referred. Considering its significance, a full quotation, with emphasis of the appropriate passages, is needed:

> [a] national law which allows an undertaking to terminate the contracts of employment of its oldest workers, setting aside ordinary law that permits continuation of the employment relationship and which thereby creates a situation in which the undertaking can save on labour costs, with *an immediate resulting burden on the State in the form of reduced contribution revenue and the payment of pensions to dismissed workers*, does not constitute State aid within the meaning of Article 87(1) EC.[82]

The *contradiction* with the previous case-law is clear. The Court expressly recognizes that the measure produces 'an immediate resulting burden on the State in the form of reduced contribution revenue and the payment of pensions to dismissed workers'. This, however, does not amount in its view to a use of State resources.

In *Enirisorse II*[83] the 'State resources' issue arises again in the Opinion of the Advocate General which represents an authoritative analysis and critique of the requirement. What was under examination was Italian legislation that, in derogation from the general law, enabled an undertaking to withdraw from a company controlled by the State but on condition that it relinquished all claims over that company's assets.

Although the Court could have disposed of the case easily following the consolidated case-law on the financing of the measure,[84] interestingly it did not focus on this aspect, but only on whether the system at issue, and the two interrelated exceptions (right to withdraw from the company/ right to deny any financial claim on the latter's assets), conferred an advantage. Advocate General Maduro concentrated also on the 'State resources' requirement and provided an extremely insightful analysis which is worth being reported in full detail.

After acknowledging that the application of the traditional approach would have meant that the measure at issue could not have been considered a State aid because of the lack of use of State resources, he moved on to criticize this test.

[80] C-54/97 *Viscido*, para 15 of the Opinion.

[81] Cases C-182 and 217/03 *Belgium and Forum 187 v Commission*. See also the Opinion of Advocate General Léger, at paras 307–9.

[82] See para 25 and the operative part (emphasis added).

[83] Case C-237/04.

[84] The alleged advantage was financed exclusively from private funds.

In doing so he provided an explanation of the success of the 'transfer of State resources' requirement but suggested a shift towards the *selectivity* test.

He commenced his analysis by underlining the need to draw *boundaries* in State aid law. Not every measure capable of conferring an 'economic advantage' or affecting the 'competitive environment in the single market', and deriving 'from mere differences in legislation between Member States', can constitute a State aid.[85] Consequently, 'the circumstances in which the granting of an advantage can properly be subject to the Community State aid rules need to be carefully circumscribed'.[86] He detected a crucial distinction:

> [i]n its case-law, the Court seems to wish to draw a distinction between distortions resulting from the adoption of *measures to regulate economic activities* and *those caused by a transfer of public resources to certain undertakings*. Only the latter are such as to affect the competitive environment. The former must be accepted in as much as their only purpose is to establish the parameters within which business is carried on and goods and services produced.[87]

This consideration led him to the core of the matter:

> [t]he reason for the distinction is clear to see. The Court is seeking to *guard against the scope of Community rules being broadened* to cover distortions of competition that are simply the result of differences in legislative policy between Member States. That caution stems from a concern not to encroach on powers reserved to the Member States. There is a danger that the extension of the State aid rules might result in all economic policy decisions of Member States being brought under the scrutiny of the Community authorities, without any distinction being made between *direct interventions in the market* and *general measures to regulate economic activities*. It would also result in a substantial increase in the workload of the Community's supervisory authorities, the Commission and the Court.[88]

In a word, the purpose of State aid rules is to control 'only those distortions of competition brought about by a Member State seeking to give a *particular* advantage to certain undertakings' with 'measures that depart from its overall policy approach'.[89] Now, if the 'restrictions set by the Court are . . . entirely legitimate'—Advocate General Maduro crucially notes—the use of 'transfer of State resources test' is not fully appropriate.[90] Referring to the seminal findings of Advocate General Darmon in *Sloman Neptun*, he moved his attention towards the *selectivity* criterion. This is the correct test to discriminate between forms of governmental action under State aid law for three reasons. First, a regulatory measure may well

[85] Paragraph 43 of the Opinion.

[86] ibid.

[87] Paragraph 44 of the Opinion (emphasis added).

[88] Paragraph 45 of the Opinion. The 'institutional factor' underlined by Maduro, which revolves around the share of competence and powers between Member States (either directly or through the Council) on the one hand and the Community (mainly the Commission) on the other plays a crucial role in the definition of what a State aid is in the EC. We will look at this aspect in more detail in chapter 6, section II.B.

[89] Paragraph 46 of the Opinion (emphasis added).

[90] Paragraph 47 of the Opinion.

entail an indirect charge on the State budget and this may be far more significant than that arising from a transfer of State resources.[91] Secondly, the selectivity test is better able to catpure the distortions created by relative economic advantages on undertakings.[92] Thirdly, 'with the growing interpenetration of the public and private sectors of the economy', there is a danger that Member States 'may be tempted to use their *regulatory* powers to *encourage* or *compel* private entities to alleviate costs of certain undertakings'.[93] Relying on the 'State resources' requirement would mean excluding from the net many State measures that have 'all the *effects* of State aid'.[94] According to the Advocate General, '[s]uch an outcome would be *manifestly at variance with the objectives* pursued by the Treaty and the principles laid down by the Court in its case-law'.[95]

The third case to consider is *Essent*,[96] a case which concerned Dutch legislation providing a surcharge on the price for electricity to pay certain 'stranded costs', ie investment costs incurred before the opening of the market to competition and not recoverable after liberalization.[97] The proceeds of the surcharge levied by net operators from customers were paid to a private company that was delegated by law to transfer them to four private regional generating companies, which jointly owned the delegated company.

In its reasoning the Court seems to merge in one single step the analysis of the imputability of the measure and that of its financing, although the focus of the analysis clearly concerns the issue of whether the measure is financed through State resources (since its attributability to the State seems difficult to deny).[98] The Court goes on to find that the relevant amounts have their 'origin in a State resource' (the surcharge), always remain under public control and cannot be used for 'other purpose that that provided for by the Law'. We thus have 'State resources'.

It emerges that the issue of whether the measure at issue was financed through 'State resources' was subject to great debate both before the referring national court (Groningen District Court) and the European Court of Justice. The main authorities which were put forward to challenge this nature, and where the Court famously found that no public resources were at issue, were *PreussenElektra* and *Pearle*.

What is striking in the case is the scrupulous effort made by both the Advocate General and the Court to establish that the proceeds of the charge were 'State resources', and remained as such even when they were in the hands of the collecting

[91] Paragraph 48 of the Opinion.

[92] Paragraph 49 of the Opinion.

[93] Paragraph 50 of the Opinion (emphasis added).

[94] ibid (emphasis in the original).

[95] ibid (emphasis added).

[96] Case C-206/06 *Essent*.

[97] For this reason, also known as 'non-market compatible costs'.

[98] The Opinion of Advocate General Mengozzi confirms this almost exclusive focus. See paras 92–118.

net operators and the statutorily-designated company. Indeed it seems difficult to doubt the continuing public nature of the *revenue of a tax destined to a specific purpose*, particularly in the light of the broad approach to the concept of 'State resources' usually endorsed by the Court.

The lack of confidence in dealing with the 'State resource' definition, and the need to receive, even from external sources, validation in this regard, comes out strikingly in the very recent *Iride* case. This decision involves a legal scenario similar to, but probably even clearer than, that in *Essent* (with a public, and not a private, body involved in the administration of the sums).[99] But, this decision is the latest confirmation that uncertainties, and even signs of lack of self-confidence, could be expected. Indeed everything flows from the previous case-law of the Court itself, particularly *PreussenElektra*.

It is time for some important final questions. Is the Court's position, as epitomized by the *PreussenElektra* decision, correct? Assuming that there is a need to draw the line and fix boundaries (which is, incidentally, the role of definitions), are these to be found in the existence of a 'transfer of State resources'? From another viewpoint, are these cases really decided on the basis of the technical argument of the 'State resources' requirement? Or, rather, has this increasingly become a burdensome tool and must the real rationale of the decisions be found elsewhere?

B. Analysis of the 'State resources' requirement

The determination of whether the notion of State aid necessarily requires a use of State resources has always been the subject of a heated debate. The phrase 'granted by the State or through State resources' in Article 87(1) EC has usually been open to two contrasting interpretations.

Extensive interpretation

According to the first, more extensive approach,[100] only the second part of that phrase would refer to a financial burden for the State. The first part, quite generally

[99] Case T-25/07. The case is analysed at length below.

[100] See eg, M Slotboom, 'State Aid in Community Law: A Broad or Narrow Definition?' (1995) European Law Review 289; M Ross, 'State Aids: Maturing into a Constitutional Problem' (1995) Yearbook of European Law 79; K Bacon, 'State Aids and General Measures' (1997) Yearbook of European Law 269; GM Roberti, *Gli aiuti di Stato nel diritto comunitario* (Padova, CEDAM, 1997); G Conte, 'Aiuti di Stato e procedure concorsuali nazionali nella recente giurisprudenza comunitaria: il caso della "Legge Prodi"' (1999) Il Diritto dell'Unione Europea 539; M Ross, 'State Aids and National Courts: Definitions and Other Problems—a Case of Premature Emancipation?' (2000) Common Market Law Review 401. On the widespread criticism of the recent *PreussenElektra* decision see, among others, M Bronckers and R Van der Vlies, 'The European Court's PreussenElektra Judgment: tensions between EU Principles and National Renewable Energy Initiatives' (2001) European Competition Law Review 458; J Basquero Cruz and F Castillo de la Torre, 'A Note on

referring to 'any aid granted by the State', would include all remaining measures which, although attributable to the State, are not financed by it. This interpretation is consistent with the broad wording of Article 87(1) EC, which prohibits 'any aid in any form whatsoever', and, in particular, with the focus on the *effects* of the measures which is usually derived from it.[101]

The most important argument in support of this position is the teleological one. If, according to Article 3(g) EC, the main purpose of State aid rules is to safeguard the functioning of competition from distortions created by public intervention in favour of certain undertakings and production, the source of the financing of that measure is not material, at least insofar as it is considered as a requirement of the definition. The too formalistic interpretation of Article 87(1) EC, whereby only advantages financed through State resources would be considered as State aid, would eventually create an incentive on Member States to circumvent State aid regulation. The clearest example would occur when the State, rather than granting aid through a fund financed by private contributions, decided to mandate private individuals or undertakings to make payments directly (ie without the intermediary of any fund) to given undertakings. The State would achieve its aim without suffering any cost. The potential distorting effect of the two measures would not be different, but their legal classification would. This point has been clarified by Advocate General Darmon in *Sloman Neptun*:

> [l]et us take, for the sake of argument, a public measure which requires individuals—consumers, workers, trading companies or any other category of private persons—to pay certain sums to a given undertaking or a given sector of the industry. In my view, it follows from the *ratio legis* of Article [87], namely maintaining *equal conditions of competition* between rival traders, that such a measure ought to be classified as aid. The 'public' nature of the aid which is implicit in Article [87(1)] relates more to the authority which adopted the measure—the State and its agencies—thereby disrupting normal market conditions, than to the body or person financing the aid.[102]

PreussenElektra' (2001) European Law Review 489; A Goossens and S Emmerrechts, 'Case Note on Case C-379/98 PreussenElektra AG v Schleswag AG' (2001) Common Market Law Review 991; Rubini, 'Brevi note a margine del caso PreussenElektra, ovvero come "prendere seriamente" le norme sugli aiuti di Stato e la tutela dell'ambiente nel diritto comunitario' (2001) Diritto Comunitario e degli Scambi Internazionali 473.

[101] See Case 173/73 *Italy v Commission*, para 13; Case 78/76 *Steinicke und Weinlig*, para 21.

[102] Paragraph 40 of the Opinion. An additional argument is that the restrictive interpretation is likely to prejudice the power of control of the Commission under Article 88 EC. In the *PreussenElektra* case, the Commission itself underlined the importance for State aid control of such procedure, particularly in the light of the recent developments in the EU (the completion of the internal market and the introduction of the EMU). Indeed, 'selectively applied aid measures are the last remaining instrument which the Member States can use to confer competitive advantages on domestic undertakings' (cf para 146 of the Opinion of Advocate General Jacobs).

Restrictive interpretation

The other approach, which, as we have seen, is supported by the consistent case-law of the Court, construes the notion of State aid in a more restrictive fashion.[103] The principle is that only advantages granted directly or indirectly through State resources can be considered as State aid. The reference in Article 87(1) to aid 'granted through State resources' would only mean that that provision covers not only State aid granted directly by the State but also that granted through other public or private entities.

In his Opinion in the *PreussenElektra* case Advocate General Jacobs put forward various arguments in support of this more restrictive position whereby the use of State resources is a constituent element of the notion of State aid. In particular, he observed that this is so because it 'provides more legal certainty'. In his view:

> the more extensive interpretation would oblige the Member States, affected undertakings, the Commission, national courts and ultimately the Community Courts to decide in respect of all legislation regulating the relationship between enterprises whether it does confer selective advantages on certain undertakings within the meaning of Article [87(1)]. Since such an assessment is a difficult exercise with an uncertain outcome, it seems preferable that *legislation regulating the relationship between private actors* is *as a matter of principle excluded from the scope of the State aid rules.*[104]

This argument, which leads to exclude, 'as a matter of principle', all regulatory measures, from the definition of State aid, is similar to the pragmatic argument advanced in the Opinion in *Viscido*. After observing that the measures at issue did not involve a use of State resources, Jacobs rejected the notion that State aid rules could cover 'all labour and other social measures' that are selective and might distort competition because 'to investigate all such regimes would entail an inquiry on the basis of the Treaty alone into the entire social and economic life of a Member State'.[105] In *PreussenElektra* he observed further that the 'risk of circumvention', that is the danger that Member States resorted to large scale support for certain domestic undertakings which is financed through private resources, producing the same anticompetitive effects as State aid but escaping the Commission's control, should not be exaggerated. He concluded by noting that other provisions of the domestic and Community order are indeed likely to apply to those measures.[106]

[103] See, eg, R Plender, 'Definition of Aid' in A Biondi, P Eeckhout, and J Flynn (eds), *The Law of State Aid in the European Union* (Oxford: Oxford University Press, 2004) 3; A Biondi and P Eeckhout, 'State Aid and Obstacles to Trade' in A Biondi, P Eeckhout, and J Flynn (eds), *The Law of State Aid in the European Union* (Oxford: Oxford University Press, 2004) 103.

[104] Opinion in *PreussenElektra*, para 157 (emphasis added).

[105] Opinion in *Viscido*, para 16.

[106] Opinion in *PreussenElektra*, para 158.

Method of financing and legal certainty

Leaving aside for the moment the important issue of the possible applicability of other rules (which can be summed up in the question of 'regulation of policy substitution' and has fundamental *substantive*, *institutional* and *constitutional* implications),[107] some time will be spent on the important argument concerning legal certainty. In particular, what we want to test is whether the 'State resources' requirement really provides for the legal certainty that we would lack in its absence.

Before focusing on this important point, some general remarks will be made on the role of the *method of financing* a measure of support.

First, a subsidy to a given industry or undertaking will in general alter the level playing field *irrespective of* whether it is financed with public or private money (it is sometimes wittily underlined that State resources are financed with taxes and hence, in the last analysis, with resources coming from the private sphere).

This does not however detract from the fact that the method of financing of the measure *may* indeed produce a different impact. Aid systems financed through various fiscal measures have provided the opportunity for interesting findings. In the old *France v Commission* decision, the Court suggested that the method of financing the aid could not be isolated from the 'aid as such' so that the former, in conjunction with the 'aid in its narrow sense', could render the 'whole' incompatible with the common market.[108] It is thus a factor that the Commission has to take into account when examining a plan to grant State aid under Article 88 EC.[109] The most recent case-law has gone even further indicating that 'taxes do not fall within the scope of the provisions of the EC Treaty concerning State aid unless they constitute the method of financing an aid measure, so that they form an integral part of the measure'. For this to happen the tax must be 'hypothecated' to the aid measure, that is its revenue must be allocated for the financing of the aid and must have a direct impact on its amount.[110]

The allocation of the financial burden of the State aid measure may indeed *aggravate* the distorting effect of the advantage conferred by it. That would occur, for example, if an aid to certain undertakings were financed by its competitors.[111]

[107] See the last section of chapter 6 on the 'external perspective' of subsidy/State aid regulation.

[108] Case 47/69 *France v Commission*, para 4.

[109] ibid, para 14.

[110] Case C-206/06 *Essent*, paras 89 and 90; Case C-174/02 *Streekgewest*, paras 25 and 26; Case C-175/02 *Pape*, paras 14 and 15; Case C-325/02 *Distribution Casino France*, para 34. As a direct consequence of the 'integration' of the hypothecated tax into the aid measure, the duty to notify the former is now firmly established (*Essent*, para 93; Joined Cases C-261/01 and C-262/02 *Van Calster and Others*, para 51; *Streekgewest*, para 26).

[111] This is exactly what happened in *PreussenElektra*. See also Advocate General Jacobs in Joined Cases C-261/01 and C-262/01 *Van Calster*, para 40 of the Opinion, where he suggested that the recovery of charges financing an illegal aid scheme is particularly important 'if they themselves create distortions of competition and trade which would add to and reinforce the distortion produced by the aid itself. That may occur if they are imposed on competitors of the beneficiaries of the aid or if the charges are such as to produce a protective effect and give some form of advantage to the domestic market'.

With more specific regard to the 'State resources' issue, the mere fact that the State grants aid, and, most importantly, provides the resources to finance it, may raise particular concerns because of the virtually unlimited government resources, or, in any event, in times of budgetary constraints, potentially greater if compared with private ones. Thus predatory conduct backed by the hugely 'deep pocket' of public actors has definitely more chance to succeed as, by definition, there is no need to 'recoup' when competitors have been driven out of the market.[112]

That said, to require in general terms the use of State resources as a necessary element of the notion of State aid is not justifiable from the point of view of the stated objective of State aid rules, the protection of competition. For this reason, the reading that seems to be more in line with the *purpose* of State aid rules is the more extensive one, ie Article 87(1) EC does not require that a State aid be necessarily financed through State resources. Although in some cases, public financing may have a bigger potential to disrupt competition and trade, it can in general be said that the nature of the resources used to finance a State aid is not crucial for definitional purposes. In other words, the method of financing the measure should be significant in assessing the *effects* of the State aid, but not to define the *boundaries* of its definition.[113]

We can now concentrate on the important argument, put forward by Advocate General Jacobs various times, concerning legal certainty. To briefly repeat the point: the 'State resources' requirement would constitute a useful tool of selection of measures since, in its absence, the State aid regime might be confronted with 'all legislation regulating the relationship between enterprises' and ultimately with 'the entire social and economic life of a Member State'.

The starting point should be the case-law defining 'State resources'.

In *Ladbroke* the Court confirmed that this concept 'covers all the financial assistance by which the public sector may actually support undertakings, irrespective of whether or not those means are permanent assets of the public sector'. What would matter is that these resources 'constantly remain under the control' of the State.[114] In explaining the previous case-law, Advocate General Jacobs noted:

> [t]he common denominator of the relevant cases is that the State exercised *direct* or *indirect control* over the resources in question despite the fact that the funds did not come from the State budget. In the case of parafiscal charges the funds were first brought under the State's

[112] Predation is a common—and controversial—topic in competition and antitrust laws. For an analysis of EC and also US law, and for further references, see R Whish, *Competition Law* (6th edn, Oxford: Oxford University Press, 2008) 729–41. Predation is also an important topic in subsidy law (and anti-dumping law). See JH Jackson, *The World Trading System—Law and Policy of International Economic Relations* (2nd edn, Cambridge Massachussetts: MIT Press, 1997), 283; MJ Trebilcock and R Howse, *The Regulation of International Trade* (3rd edn, London: Routledge, 2005) 283.

[113] Otherwise, the risk could be run of paradoxically narrowing the scope of application of the discipline and hence excluding the possibility of considering *any* distorting potential altogether.

[114] Case C-83/98P *France v Ladbroke Racing and Commission*, para 50. The same finding was previously made by the CFI in Case T-358/94 *Air France*, paras 66 and 67. See also Case C-482/99 *Stardust*, paras 37–8.

control before they were redistributed to the undertakings concerned. In the case of a waiver of revenue the State renounced funds which it was legally entitled to claim. State resources are therefore those resources which are *directly* or *indirectly under the control* or in other words at the disposal of the State.[115]

The position of the Advocate General was upheld by the Court which thus adopted an *extensive notion* of 'use of State resources'. Two comments can be made straight away. First, this broad approach to the notion of State resources is not formalistic, and, to some extent, may be regarded as a counter-balance to the previous, more rigorous, finding in *PreussenElektra* where the unclear wording of the phrase 'granted by the State or through State resources' of Article 87(1) EC was read as requiring a 'cost to government'. Secondly, it is interesting to note that the concept of 'public control' used to impute the conduct of the public undertaking to the State, which often complexly intersects with the separate question of the public origin of the financing (the 'double meaning' of control highlighted above), is *overall stricter* than that used to define State resources. While the Court almost inevitably finds that the resources of public undertakings are under the control and at the disposal of the State and hence constitute State resources, what it requires to attribute the conduct of the public undertaking to the State is the actual exercise of its influence on the former.

It is fundamentally argued that this broad notion of State resources does *not* provide a useful key of interpretation, and a contribution to legal certainty. The point is that the exact boundaries of the scope of 'public control' are difficult to define. In other words, the issue is: how far can this crucial concept be stretched? It could in fact be pointed out that it has the potential to include if not all, at least most of the cases where the State is somewhat involved in the financing (Jacobs talks of *direct* or *indirect* control).

The comparison between measures that are commonly held to be State aid and measures that are not makes this difficulty evident.

Whereas it is clear that a measure funded through a *tax* borne by consumers would clearly be regarded as a State aid (cf *Essent*), it is not clear why support through a government-mandated minimum *price* scheme, which is financed by consumers, would not constitute a State aid (*Van Tiggele*). Quite similarly, while it is accepted that there is a use of State resources when the State empowers a private body to levy *parafiscal charges* on undertakings or consumers to support other undertakings (*Essent* again), that is not the case when, through a *purchase* obligation, the State mandates private undertakings to make payments in favour of other undertakings (*PreussenElektra*) or *imposes an obligation* for television operators to *earmark* a percentage of their operating revenue for the pre-funding of films in certain languages (*UTECA*).[116]

Further, it can be asked how it is possible to distinguish between the non-application of employment legislation with the result that labour costs of certain

[115] Paragraph 41 of the Opinion in Case C-482/99 *Stardust* (emphasis added).

[116] Case C-222/07.

undertakings (including social contributions) are reduced, which does not amount to State aid (*Sloman Neptun*), and the introduction of special legislation, notably training and experience contracts, providing for a reduction of social security contributions, which has been found to constitute State aid (*Italy v Commission*).[117] In particular, the Court's argument in the first line of cases about the 'inherency in the system' of the loss of social contribution (which can also be viewed as referring to the *remoteness* of the loss) is not very convincing. A similar conclusion can probably also be drawn with respect to the potential loss of tax revenue deriving from lower employees' wages.[118]

The fact is that, there are *no* overwhelming *technical* and *policy* reasons to distinguish between the cases set out above.[119] In all of them, it can reasonably be held that the resources used to finance the aid measure are, 'directly or indirectly', 'under the control' or 'at the disposal' of the State. On the basis of the current case-law, maybe through a progressive (or, more simply, clear) interpretation, they could all be regarded as involving a use of State resources.

The differential approach of the Court is too much *formalistic* and not in line with the purpose of State aid rules underlined in the case-law itself. With its Byzantinism, it provides the Member States with an easy way, if not an incentive, to circumvent the rules. At the same time, and most importantly, it is not fully satisfactory because, with all its unreasoned distinctions, it does not provide clear and consistent directives, or, to put it simply, legal certainty.

The instability of the concept of 'State resources' shows two different and diverging trends which add to its *uncertainty*.

On the one hand, this concept is construed *broadly* with the result that it is easier to show that there is a State aid. Two examples can be given, the first focusing on the already noted wide notion of 'control' supported in the case-law, the second relying on the fact that 'State resources' may be present even if their use is only 'potential'.

Despite its inherent impalpability, the revenue that is foregone in the case of opportunity costs should be considered 'at the disposal of' the lender. 'Soft loans' are thus usually regarded as State aids. Further, in a recent and controversial decision the Commission has introduced a novel concept of aid, suggestively defined 'virtual' or 'psychological'. A mere announcement by the government of a loan to a public untertaking was sufficient to constitute a potential burden on State resources, even though the loan agreement was never signed.[120] The consideration

[117] Case C-310/99

[118] See also C-200/97 *Ecotrade*, para 36; C-379/98 *PreussenElektra*, para 62.

[119] An attempt to rationalize the possibility of distinguishing the cases has been made by Advocate General Mengozzi in Case C-206/06 *Essent*, paras 107–9.

[120] Decision 2006/621/EC of 2 August 2004, *France Télécom* [2006] OJ L257/11, under appeal in Cases T-425 and 444/04 *France and France Télécom* v *Commission*. For a comment see P Kirch, O d'Ormesson, JW Rodriguez Curiel, 'Transfer of State Resources' in J Derenne and M Merola (eds), *Economic Analysis of State Aid Rules—Contributions and Limits* (Berlin: Lexxion, 2007) 105, 113 et seq.

that the offeree could sign it at any time, and that, in any case, the government had publicly committed its reputation were enough to establish that State resources could potentially be involved.

On the other hand, sometimes the proof that resources are public may be *unduly demanding* thus engendering the risk that it may be more difficult or burdensome to establish that there is a State aid.

In *Essent* the issue was whether a government-mandated surcharge on the electricity price to compensate certain 'stranded costs' incurred by generating undertakings involved 'State resources'. The 'double role' of control emerges clearly in the reasoning of the Court which combines the analysis of 'imputability' with that of 'State resources'. Indeed, as shown by *Pearle*, although conceptually distinct, the issue of financing is not only intertwined with that of imputability but is in fact *dependent* on it.[121] After finding that the proceeds at issue 'have their origin in a State resource', the Court carried out a painstaking analysis of whether that classification remained as such, through the constant 'control' of the State, at every level of the mechanism. The fact that the measure (a parafiscal charge destined for a specified purpose) was *clearly* imputable to the government should have meant that it was equally patent, particularly in the light of the broad concept of 'State resources' laid down in the case-law, that the resources involved always maintained a public nature.[122] This was not the case, and arguably, if there is a lesson to be learned, it is that the 'State resources' requirement may not only be superfluous but may even lead to an unnecessarily pedantic evidential exercise.

More fundamentally, this decision uncovers an interesting psychological story made of a lack of self-confidence in the utility of the intruments at disposal to resolve the issue. The very recent *Iride* case, dealing with similar facts, proves this point.[123] The need to seek confirmation that the resources deriving from the supplemented electricity tariff are public reaches a new high.[124] The CFI not only refers to the usual language of 'control' over the resources but relies on the new concept of 'property'. And, in doing so, it intriguingly seeks *external* validation in the case-law of the Italian Supreme Court of Cassation for the classification of these sums as 'State property'.[125]

[121] Accordingly, in *Pearle* the resources were held *not* to be public because the measure was *not imputable* to the public body concerned. This dependency does make complete sense if it is premised on the finding already made that the concept of control is more difficult to establish in the context of the proof of imputability. Hence, once this obstacle is overtaken, almost by necessity, the conclusion that the resources at issue are under control will be drawn.

[122] In this regard, *Essent* is the opposite of *Pearle*.

[123] Case T-25/07 *Iride*. One significant factual difference from *Essent* was that the body administering the fixed component of the electricity tariff paid by consumers for compensating the stranded cost was public, which should have made the reasoning more straightforward.

[124] ibid, see paras 22–38.

[125] The ultimate finding is self-explanatory: '[t]he Court [of First Instance] does not have jurisdiction to put into question the interpretation of Italian law carried out by the Supreme Court of Cassation.' See para 38.

Is there any specific *cause* for this psychological fragility and hermeneutic overgrowth, and more generally for all the uncertainties underlined so far? The author believes the answer is yes, and the original sin should be sought in the case-law of the Court itself, when it was required that the use of 'State resources' should always be necessary.

The two main cases which were invoked in *Essent* to suggest that the surcharge at issue, and its use, did *not* involve 'State resources' were *PreussenElektra* and *Pearle*.[126] While it can be conceded that the difference from the *Pearle* case was self-evident (in no way, a *voluntary contribution* can be equated to a *compulsory charge*), doubts may be expressed with respect to *PreussenElektra*. Leaving aside name/form (*price*, *surcharge*) the reality is that both monetary transfers were *mandated by law* and the relevant resources were subject to *public control*. To repeat a point already made above, how can we meaningfully distinguish between the two? Is the complexity (?) of the mechanism through which they reach the beneficiary sufficient to justify a different classification?

The root of all uncertainties is exactly this need to differentiate between measures that, paraphrasing Advocate General Maduro, have 'all the *effects* of State aid'.[127] Such distinctions are difficult, and their results often raise perplexities. As the previous paragraphs have shown, the argument that the 'State resources' requirement would provide *legal certainty* seems to be contradicted from the analysis of the guiding concept of 'control' (which it crucially shares with the condition of 'imputability') and of various cases which have been considered (or not) as State aid.

C. Conclusions

The previous analysis has shown that the use of 'State resources' is not the most appropriate tool to define the *boundaries* of the notion of State aid.

The four cases (*Cigliola*, *Enirisorse II*, *Essent*, and *Iride*) taken as examples from the third jurisprudential period, and the case-law on the concept of 'State resources' itself, show the doubts, contradictions and paradoxes of a not fully internalized solution, and the substantial *inutility* of this requirement. The transfer of State resources is the imprecise *technical* argument which the Court relies on to follow up an unjustified *policy* choice, and to eventually reach uncertain and

[126] As may be recalled, the former case concerned a 'feed-in tariff' mechanism, whereby regional electricity supplier were mandated to *buy* all electricity produced in their area from renewable sources at a certain (above-market) *price*. The latter case was about an advertising campaign decided and funded through a *self-imposed levy* by the members of a trade association (a public body). The public body—the Court found—was not responsible for the campaign since it was merely used as a *vehicle* by the members. Hence, the revenue of the levy was not under the control of the body and accordingly could not possibly be considered as a 'public resource'.

[127] Advocate General Maduro in Case C-237/04 *Enirirorse II*, para 50 of the Opinion (emphasis in the original).

arbitrary decisions. Through this element, which deceitfully promises to represent a safe shelter, but in fact hides insidious pitfalls, the Court disposes of cases that it does not consider as State aid for *other reasons*. These mainly, and, as we will see in chapter 6, unjustifiably, relate to the *regulatory nature* and/or the *objective* of the measure at issue.[128] This was expressed masterfully by Advocate General Jacobs in *PreussenElektra*: 'legislation regulating the relationship between private actors is *as a matter of principle* excluded from the scope of the State aid rules.[129]

Now, and we come to the second conclusion, if this is the policy choice the EC wishes to take—and assuming, for the sake of reasoning, that it is the correct one—why not *simply* use clear statements and avoid using an unreliable requirement? The Court should clarify, with a *neat formulation*, i) *what forms* of governmental action should be caught ('financial assistance'?) and which one should be excluded ('regulation'?), and ii) *why* this is so.

Some passages of the case-law already contain some hints to this end.[130] Duly stripped of any 'State resources' argument, they may represent a starting point. But, transparency, and hence legal certainty and political legitimacy, demand that the decision to exclude from the scope of State aid law (all or some of the) measures which are the expression of the exercise of regulatory powers should be based on solid ground, on fully developed arguments such as the ones we find in the learned Opinions of the Advocates General (Capotorti,[131] Jacobs,[132] Darmon,[133] Maduro)[134] that have tackled this delicate issue. This point is analysed further in the critical and comparative section in the next chapter.

If, by contrast, the Court decided to make an historic *revirement*, a fourth period, characterized by rethinking and synthesis, may be open. A ray of hope has come from the Opinion of Advocate General Maduro in *Enirisorse II*, analysed in detail above. However, no momentous change is predicted.

[128] This true rationale was indeed caught by P Davies, 'Market Integration and Social Policy in the Court of Justice' (1995) Industrial Law Journal 49, an article which was also significantly cited by Advocate General Jacobs in his Opinion in *Viscido*.

[129] Opinion in *PreussenElektra*, para 157 (emphasis added).

[130] See, eg, Joined Cases C-72/91 and C-73/91 *Sloman Netptun* and Case C-189/91 *Kirsammer Hack*.

[131] Case 82/77 *Van Tiggele*.

[132] Joined Cases C-52/97, C-53/97 and C-54/97 *Viscido*; *Case C-379/98 PreussenElektra.*

[133] Joined Cases C-72/91 and C-73/91 *Sloman Netptun* and Case C-189/91 *Kirsammer Hack*.

[134] C-237/04.

6

Forms of governmental action: internal and external perspectives

I. Critical and comparative analysis, internal and external perspectives

This final chapter of Part II features three different characteristics.

First, we attempt to provide a conclusive *critical assessment* of the state of the law with respect to the forms of governmental action that constitute a subsidy or a State aid in the WTO and EC, and provide suggestions about whether the law, or its interpretation, should be changed. In other words, we mainly focus on the third question that we set ourselves at the beginning of our analysis (what action *should* be considered a subsidy or State aid under the two legal systems).[1]

Secondly, this final critical assessment will be carried out from a marked *comparative* standpoint. The analysis of the similarities and differences between the two disciplines, and the two legal systems as a whole, will help us to better evaluate the correctness of the solutions adopted in each legal system.

Thirdly, the analysis is twofold, adopting two different viewpoints. On the one hand, we assess the regulation of subsidies and State aids 'in itself' (which we may call 'internal perspective'), focusing in particular on the concerns about the *expansiveness* of the definition in terms of forms of governmental actions covered. On the other hand, taking an 'external perspective', we briefly look at the 'other rules' that in the two legal systems might apply to the same or similar forms of governmental action and address possible worries about *system coherency*.

II. The regulation of subsidies and of State aids: the 'internal perspective'

A. Recapitulation of the state of the law in the two legal systems

We begin with a brief summary of the state of the law with respect to the forms of public action covered in the two systems.

[1] See Part II, Overview.

WTO law

In the WTO, the definition of subsidy in the SCM Agreement (Article 1) is distinguished by a heavy reliance on the *forms* or *nature* of the action of the government. The 'financial contribution' requirement seems to cover mainly forms of financial assistance, as we have defined it at the beginning of chapter 3, ie those involving the exercise of the government prerogatives to tax and spend revenue. With respect to the action through third parties, the scope of Article 1.1(a)(1)(iv) is not fully settled. Despite an increasing relaxation of the standards of imputability, and in particular the interpretation of the crucial notions of 'entrustment' and 'direction', the wording of the provision, and in particular the indications coming from the judicial interpretation of the final sentences of subparagraph (iv), seem to direct us towards a rather rigorous reading, with the result that *more complex* forms of regulatory action would be excluded. What is not fully clear, however, is whether that same reading might exclude even *more linear* forms of regulatory intervention.[2] Finally, although the exact remit of Article 1.1(a)(2), covering 'any income or price support', has not been subject to official interpretation recently, it cannot be doubted that it has the potential for significantly expanding the forms of action covered by the definition.

The examination of the AG has provided interesting results with respect to the forms of intervention covered, in particular from the angle of the rules of imputability for indirect action. The test under Article 9.1(c), which covers payments 'financed by virtue of governmental action', expressly relies on a rule of imputability which is *less formalistic* than the ones examined under the SCM Agreement, particularly Article 1.1(a)(1)(iv). What is paramount here is the *degree of causality*, which the Appellate Body calls 'demonstrable link', between the government's conduct and the financial support through an intermediary.

With respect to the 'cost to government', the Appellate Body has momentously found that it is not necessary under the definition of subsidy under Article 1 of the SCM, at least with respect to the cases of indirect action under Article 1.1(a)(1)(iv). While it can be predicted that a similar reading will soon be adopted for the forms of 'income and price support' of Article 1.1(a)(2), it has been highlighted that this conclusion, sound but not fully reasoned, might reveal a *contradiction* with the other case-law which expressly noted the connection between the indirect action under Article 1.1(a)(1)(iv) and the prerogative to tax and particularly expend revenue. If this second strand is applied strictly, this might mean that there is not much room for regulatory action, which is usually supported with private and not public resources, in the provision.

Finally, the analysis of the public objectives does not play any role at the level of the identification of the actions caught by the definition of subsidy.

[2] This issue is linked to the legal status of the financing of the measure. See below.

EC law

The analysis of EC law has focused on the definition of State aid in the first paragraph of Article 87 EC.

Despite a broader language as compared with that of Article 1 of the SCM, we have noticed a remarkably similar interpretation with respect to the forms of governmental action covered. In other words, only forms of financial assistance (as intended above) seem to be covered by the provision with the exclusion of *virtually all* forms of regulation. The arguments, of both textual and judicial origin, which are relied on to reach this conclusion partly refer to the *nature* or *form* of the measure (as occurs in WTO law), to the use of 'State resources' (differently from the WTO) and, to some extent, on the *objectives* of the measure (differently from the WTO).

With respect to the financing of the measure, a 'transfer of State resources' is required of any form of support. It has also been seen that the test used to define 'State resources'—ie whether they are 'under the control' of the State or not—is relatively broad and consequently not easy to apply. The boundaries of the resulting concept are difficult to draw with precision and often seem to lead to perplexing, if not arbitrary, results, to the detriment of legal certainly. A similar test of 'public control', which is generally interpreted more strictly, is used as rule of imputability to determine whether the conduct of third parties can in fact be attributed to the State.

B. Critical and comparative assessment

The time has come for a final critical and comparative assessment.

The 'internal perspective' is about *expansiveness*, that is about whether the scope of the relevant regulation is too comprehensive or, put it in another way, it is excessive. The issue is therefore where *boundaries* should be more appropriately set.

We start with WTO law, directing our observations to the main discipline, that is the SCM Agreement, and in particular to the 'financial contribution' requirement, which the author believes to be the most significant provision.

The balance struck by Article 1.1(a)(1) is essentially sound. The difficult outcome of the negotiators' efforts, the wording of the financial contribution requirement, has generally been construed correctly by the jurisprudence of the dispute settlement organs.

The financial contribution element thus represents the middle way between the two extremes vigorously put forward during the Uruguay Round negotiations. On one side, the US wanted to push through a definition of subsidy which singled out the benefits and effects produced by governmental intervention in the economy without paying any attention whatsoever to the form or nature of that conduct. On the other side, the EC wanted the focus to be only on those forms of governmental action that produce a charge on the public account. The solution of

Article 1.1(a)(1) of the SCM is a reasonable balance between these two positions: (i) the form or nature of the financial contribution *does* matter and (ii) the origin of the resources *does not* matter.

Despite some uncertanties arising from the juxtaposition of these two lines of the case-law,[3] while rejecting the significance of the origin of the financial resources, the SCM mainly includes in the definition of subsidy those forms of financial assistance that are generally considered as subsidies, and, conversely, leaves out the most controversial forms of regulatory action. That the exact line of the boundary is not fully clear, however, was probably inevitable. The balance might be tipped slightly in favour of a more expansive definition of subsidy when Article 1.1(a)(2), concerning 'any income or price support' scheme, is considered.

This middle position is certainly consistent with the current limited degree of economic integration of the WTO (cf the different EC context). In other words, this solution is in tune with a certain degree of deference towards the regulatory and domestic policies of Member States.[4] Further, it is in line with customary rules of interpretation of the Vienna Convention, and their emphasis on textual approach.

This leads us to consider the double relevance played by the definition of subsidy in the WTO regulation of subsidies where, beside the multilateral track, ie international obligations on the use of subsidies, there also exists a unilateral track, ie imposition of countervailing duty on subsidized imports. Defining subsidy too widely would risk expanding too much the resort to the broadly criticized countervailing duty path.[5] With an extreme but forceful argument Professor Jackson underlines how an unduly broad definition of subsidy would expose too many government measures to countervailing actions (which already constitute an exception to Article II of the GATT) with the ultimate risk of undermining the whole system of post-World War II liberal trade. The foregone conclusion is that 'the international system should be trying to define a subset of a certain type of "subsidy" with which it will be concerned'.[6] Having a single definition of subsidy for both 'tracks', one controlling *subsidies*, one controlling *reactions to subsidies*, it was particularly important to reach a balanced interpretation of the financial contribution element. This would in turn have resulted in a balanced approach to the remedy-issue. The importance of this equilibrium has been underlined by the Appellate Body:

> . . . the object and purpose of the *SCM Agreement* . . . reflects a delicate balance between the Members that sought to impose more disciplines on the use of subsidies and those that

[3] See section II.A above.

[4] From another perspective, the method of liberalization of the GATT is mainly *negative*, removing obstacles to international trade, and not *positive*, introducing measures of harmonization of domestic laws and policies. Indeed, the role of harmonization in the WTO is limited, in particular as compared with the EC.

[5] Particularly, if the US, the major user so far of countervailing duty actions, traditionally favours an extensive notion of subsidy.

[6] JH Jackson, *The World Trading System—Law and Policy of International Economic Relations* (2nd edn, Cambridge Massachussetts: MIT Press, 1997) 293–4.

sought to impose more discipline on the application of countervailing measures. Indeed, the Appellate Body has said that the object and purpose of the *SCM Agreement* is 'to strengthen and improve GATT disciplines relating to the use of both subsidies and countervailing measures, while, recognizing at the same time, the right of Members to impose such measures under certain conditions' [*US—Softwood Lumber IV*, paragraph 64].[7]

After analysing WTO law, we now turn our attention to EC law. For the sake of fairness, the result of the appraisal should be anticipated in this case too. The current State of the law is substantially *unsatisfactory* with respect to the forms of governmental action covered by Article 87(1) EC.

The starting point is that the scope of EC State aid rules, at least with respect to the forms of governmental action covered, is *substantially equal* to, if not even *narrower*, than that of WTO subsidy rules.

This is indeed paradoxical as we would have expected a different coverage but, arguably, the other way round, with WTO proceeding at a slower pace. Unlike the financial contribution requirement in Article 1 of the SCM, Article 87(1) provides for a broad and potentially comprehensive language: 'any aid granted by the State or through State resources in any form whatsoever'. This has been accompanied by a consolidated 'effect-based' approach with an eye more on the distorting impact of the measure of support rather than on its form. Further, considering the procedural and remedy side, in the EC, Members have granted the EC Commission a monopoly over subsidy control and consequently do not have the possibility to resorting to unilateral defensive measures such as countervailing duties. In this regard, the argument put forward in the WTO in support of a balanced and cautious interpretation would thus not be applicable with respect to the definition of State aid of Article 87(1). This provision, and its wording, should also be set in the broader EC context where we certainly have a higher degree of economic, and not only economic, integration, and where the approach to interpretation is quite flexible, being characterized by a heavy reliance on teleology.

These elements taken together—broader language, centralized control (and exclusion of unilateral reactions), higher integration, more reliance on teleological arguments—would all lead to a particularly comprehensive reading of Article 87(1) EC from various perspectives. It could be argued that Article 87(1) should not cover only the more commonly accepted and traditional forms of financial assistance, expression of the prerogatives to tax and expend revenue, but also some forms of regulation. This is certainly and ultimately a *policy choice* (very much like the currently prevailing more conservative one) but, as has been shown, there are strong arguments for at least a partial enlargement of the coverage of the State aid rules to encompass *some* cases of regulatory action[8] which are liable to distort competition very much in the same way as more traditional

[7] Appellate Body, *US—DRAMS*, para 115.

[8] To be clear, we are thinking more of *PreussenElektra*-type measures rather than *US—Export Restraints*-type ones. See chapters 4 and 5 for an exposition of these cases.

forms of financial assistance. This extension would also tackle the most obvious cases of circumvention.

To explain the restrictive approach of the EC towards certain regulatory measures and towards the issue of financing, a comparison is appropriate. It is interesting to consider the interpretation of State aid in EC 'internal' law together with that of subsidy in EC 'external' relations (the one defended during the Uruguay Round negotiations). With respect to the latter, the motive that has led the EC to introduce the 'cost to government' requirement was to limit the concept of subsidy and through this keep at bay the aggressive use of countervailing duty actions made by the US. Interestingly, while this additional element was required of the definition of GATT subsidy, at the same time, in EC law, the concept of State aid was generally held (surely by the Commission) not to demand a use of 'State resources'.[9] It has thus been rightly observed that 'the Community seems to have elevated a tactical move to the level of policy'.[10]

A similar attempt of limitation can be found in the restrictive interpretation of the definition of EC State aid. This move, which is heavily based on the use of the technical requirement of 'State resources', is aimed at excluding *regulatory measures* from the coverage of State aid rules and hence a *certain type of EC control.*

The most immediate explanation lies in reasons of constitutional deference towards Member States' policies since the *institutional* balance of EC State aid control is sensibly shifted towards the Community, with a system of preventive notification to, and authorization of, the Commission.

However, three remarks may partly diminish the power of this argument. First, the non-application of State aid rules does not necessarily preclude the application of other EC rules, and, most importantly, although *postponed*, control at Community level is always possible and in the end may be significantly intrusive. Secondly, significant procedural developments in the context of the State Aid Action Plan (SAAP), especially the recent adoption of the General Block Exemption Regulation (GBER), which lead to a noticeable decrease in the direct and individual scrutiny by the Commission, and at the same time offer a higher predictability of the criteria which make a State aid compatible with EC law, may somewhat ease the pressure felt by Member States when a State aid claim is aired. Finally, the crude reality may well be that Member States may not be that reluctant to play the 'State aid game'. Bishop has put forward an interesting 'public choice' justification

[9] The jurisprudence was more ambiguous. See the 'first period' of the case-law on the 'State resources' requirement in chapter 5, section III.A. For the position of the Commission, reference is once again made to the latter's arguments in the *Fediol* cases (Case 187/85 and Case 188/85): see paras 32 and 34 of the two Report of the Hearing respectively.

[10] M Bronckers and R Quick, 'What is a Countervailable Subsidy under EEC Trade Law?' (1989) 6 Journal of World Trade 5, 18. See also M Slotboom, 'Subsidies in WTO Law and in EC Law: Broad and Narrow Definitions', (2002) Journal of World Trade 517, 532.

of State aid control in Europe.[11] Member States would have agreed to a 'tutelage' exercised by the Commission on their spending powers for the possibility to 'shift' to the latter 'the responsibility and blame' for decisions their constituency might find unpopular, and also for the relative ineffectiveness of repayment of State aid.[12] State aid control would thus be substantially reduced to a 'pantomime'.

Whatever the merits of the previous arguments, the attempt to exclude certain regulatory measures from the coverage of State aid law can be put in its historical context. Cases such as *Sloman Neptun* and *Kirsammer-Hack*, which indicated that the tide was turning, belong to the same generation as *Keck*.[13] Both produced the limitation of the scope of, respectively, Article 87 and Article 28 EC by sheltering, in different senses, 'certain' *regulatory measures*. It is important to make two remarks in this regard. First, although partly overlapping, the concept of 'regulation' is used in different senses in the two contexts. In the State aid context it is opposed to 'financial assistance', in the internal market context to 'restrictions to trade' which may well include regulatory requirements concerning, for example, products characteristics and packaging. Secondly, *Keck* does not exclude 'certain selling arrangements' from the scope of Article 28 EC altogether, but merely prohibits discrimination in favour of domestic products.

The imbalance of the *status quo* in EC State aid law is not only due to the too narrow coverage of the definition (which is a *policy* issue) but concerns also the reasoning used in its support (which is *technical* matter). In other words, the problem is not only the result but also the means to achieve it.

Apart from the consideration of the *public objectives* of the measure at the level of the definition of the kinds of governmental action covered, which is not in line with the consolidated emphasis on the *effects* of the measure, the main shortcoming—as has been highlighted recently by Advocate General Maduro—concerns the repeated reference to the necessity of a use of 'State resources'. This requirement should be put aside inasmuch as it does not make sense from an economic and competition perspective. What matters is that an undertaking or an industry receives an unfair economic advantage, and not who is burdened as a consequence. This concern is made particularly acute in the context of an increasingly completed internal market and mixed public-private participation in

[11] B Bishop, 'From Trade to Tutelage: State Aid and Public Choice in the European Union', Presentation to Conference to ACE, Copenhagen, 2 December 2005.

[12] The latter point being partly reinforced by the latest decision of the Court of Justice in Case C-199/06 *CELF II* which has substantially watered down the recovery obligation of unlawful aid, subsequently declared compatible by the Commission, by simply requiring the payment of interest. See chapter 2, section III for an analysis.

[13] Joined Case C-267 and 268/91 *Keck* was decided on 24 November 1993. While *Kirsammer-Hack* was decided only six days afterwards, its precursor, *Sloman Neptun*, was judged a few months earlier (17 March). On the link between *Keck* and the other State aid cases see P Davies, 'Market Integration and Social Policy in the Court of Justice' 24 (1995) Industrial Law Journal 49, 59; M Ross, 'State Aids: Maturing into a Constitutional Problem' (1995) Yearbook of European Law 79, 82 and 83.

the economy. Moreover, far from guaranteeing the expected legal certainty, the criterion is loosely and broadly defined by referring to the elusive notion of public control. The result is that the definition of what constitutes 'State resources' is uncertain—if not contradictory—when it comes to its actual application. Perplexing decisions have been taken in this regard which differentiate particularly between measures which, because of the similar effects, should be treated in the same way. As a consequence, the room and incentive for Member States to circumvent the rules may be significant. Finally, in some cases, it may even result in unduly burdensome and artificial proof requirement, not adding any value to the assessment of a measure which should already clearly qualify as State aid.

The fact is that the 'State resources' argument was a *technical surrogate* for disposing of certain forms of action on the basis of their *regulatory nature*. If this is the policy decision, however, a sounder approach should be chosen. This should take the WTO 'financial contribution' approach as a model and should rely on a judicial formulation of what forms of governmental actions are included in the definition of State aid and what are excluded. This could be done with general statements and examples. Rather than concentrating on the origin of financing, express reference should be made to the *form* or *nature* of the action of the government.

III. The other rules: the 'external perspective'

In our quest for boundaries, although the findings of the 'internal perspective', ie EC State aid and WTO subsidy laws, are crucial, we cannot ignore the 'external perspective' since this may well have an impact on the former. This external scrutiny concerns the *other rules*, those that might in principle apply to measures which may be classified as, or are similar to, a subsidy or a State aid. The direct focus of this analysis is *system coherency* which, in many respects, represents the counterpart of the concerns about the *expansiveness* of subsidy and State aid rules typical of the 'internal' view.

Before commencing, two remarks should be made. First, the following observations are not confined to the limited issue of the forms of governmental intervention caught by the definition but concern more generally all aspects of subsidy and State aid regulation. Further, since the topic is huge and goes beyond our research focus, the following paragraphs are more about raising issues than providing answers.

A. Sketching the terms of the problem: rules and system

The importance of placing each set of rules in its wider context can be underlined from the outset. Lawyers tend to look at legal systems as *coherent* complexes where the scope of the various sets of rules, and the relationships between them, are well-defined.

Applied to the current context, the goal of *system coherency* means asking whether measures that are alleged to be caught by subsidy or State aid rules should more appropriately be covered by other rules. A related and delicate issue is that of *circumvention of the law* or, with a less censuring wording, *policy substitution*. The legal system may present a lacuna or a gap in the regulation, which, to be as such, should be non-deliberate and unjustifiable, enabling certain courses of conduct that *should* be regulated by a certain set of rules to fall outside its scope, or, even, of any rule altogether.

The application of different rules bears crucial consequences, at various levels. The substantive regulation, for example with respect to scope, prohibitions, justifications, may well be different. Different procedural rules may apply, and different institutions may be called to participate in the process. Ultimately, all this may have important implications for the constitutional share of competence and powers.

B. Rules interplay and system coherency

It may be argued that too expansive a scope of subsidy and State aid rules would entail a danger for the coherency of the system. The first and fundamental question, however, is whether there is really any such thing as *system coherency*. In this regard, it may be particularly useful to commence with Professor Ehlermann that, by drawing from his considerable double experience as EC and WTO lawyer, noted:

> [f]rom the beginning, I have been impressed by what seems to me to be a rather important difference between the two legal orders. Substantive WTO law appears to me to be less structured than EC law. The same contested measure is often examined under a series of provisions, possibly contained in different covered agreements. All of these provisions and agreements seem to apply simultaneously and cumulatively. There seems to be no—or at least little—structure, and overall architecture, which would allow distinguishing between *lex generalis* and *lex specialis*.[14]

Ehlermann gave some examples. Quite interestingly, one of them was the 'relationship between the GATT, the GATS and the Subsidies Agreement'. Crucially, he concluded by wondering 'whether it would not be necessary (or appropriate) to determine a dividing line between these three agreements, in order to avoid a systematic overlap of the three texts'.[15]

We can draw some conclusions.

[14] CD Ehlermann, 'Six Years on the Bench of the "World Trade Court"—Some Personal Experiences as Member of the Appellate Body of the World Trade Organization' (2002) Journal of World Trade 605, 630.

[15] The author wonders whether this remark is partly linked to Ehlermann's experience. The cumulative application of the GATT, SCM and GATS came out in the *Canada—Autos* case which was presided over, at the appellate level, by Ehlermann himself.

In general, it seems that any legal system, in order to be *such* (ie a *system*), should inevitably aspire to *coherency*.[16] In other words, it should reflect a 'structure', substantially made of 'relationships' between different sets of 'rules', and ultimately informed by its constitutional and policy choices.[17]

Three kinds of relationships between rules may be thought of. First, two (or more) given rules may apply alternatively. Secondly, two (or more) given rules may apply cumulatively (to the entirety of the measure at issue or only to certain aspects of it). Thirdly and finally, as specification of the previous relation, one (or more) rule(s) may, or shall, be taken into account in the application of another rule.

Since theoretical thinking should now make room for practical application, we will apply this framework to both EC and WTO law with respect to subsidies and State aids.

C. An application: subsidies in EC and WTO law

In this section we consider four types of public measures (ie quotas, tariffs, internal taxes, and regulation) and analyse their subjection to subsidy rules and/or other provisions in both EC and WTO law. We do this through the conceptual scheme on norm relationships just indicated. After that, we focus on the various legal and political implications that the applicability of different norms may have.

Alternative application, exclusion of subsidy rules

It is clear that certain measures, considered on their own, and not as part of more complex mechanisms, do *not* constitute subsidies in either system. We are referring in particular to tariffs, quotas and bans (which essentially correspond to a 'zero quota'). Although the often indirect advantage conferred by these border measures could be perceived as an indirect subsidy, there are specific rules that apply to them in WTO (Articles II and XI of the GATT)[18] and in EC law too (Articles 23 and

[16] All this does not exclude the fact that conflicts between different norms may arise, but, because of the said inherent aspiration towards coherency they should be solved, either through interpretative means or law reform.

[17] The need for coherency of the legal system has been recognized both in the WTO and the EC. It is known that the WTO is legally based on a 'single package', since all 'agreements and associated instruments are integral parts' of the Marrakesh Agreement Establing the World Trade Organization (see Article II:2 thereof). By referring to the principle of effectiveness, the Appellate Body in *Argentina—Footware Safeguards*, para 81, noted: 'a treaty interpreter must read all applicable provisions of a treaty in a way that gives meaning to *all* of them, harmoniously' (emphasis in the original). In the 'new legal order' of the EC (see Case 26/62 *Van Gend en Loos*), the Court held: 'Every provision of Community law must be placed in its context and interpreted in the light of the provisions of Community law as a whole, regard being had to the objectives thereof and to its state of evolution at the date on which the provision in question is to be applied.' See Case 283/81 *CILFIT*, at p 3430. The said aspiration to coherency is particularly marked in more mature legal systems, such as the EC.

[18] See *US—Export Restraints*, para 8.37 (using the example of tariffs). R Diamond, 'Privatization and the Definition of Subsidy: A Critical Study of Appellate Body Texturalism' (2008) Journal of International Economic Law 649, 665 (referring to tariffs, quotas, export bans).

28 EC). Since these measures constitute the most obvious restrictions to trade, they are generally prohibited.

Quite similarly, the elusive and broad category of regulatory measures is generally considered to be beyond the reach of subsidy laws and is subject *only* to other provisions. We have seen that both EC State aid and WTO subsidy rules have generally been construed in a restrictive fashion, thus covering measures linked to the functions of taxation and revenue expenditure (that we tagged 'financial assistance') and excluding regulation. This conclusion depends mainly on interpretation (like in the EC and in the GATT) or also on normative formulation (like, at least partly, in the WTO). Regulatory measures remain the true, and unclear, frontier of subsidy laws.

As a consequence, regulatory intervention has been the traditional object of other provisions. The breadth of the concept of regulation entails that its legal treatment is particularly complex in both EC and WTO law, and often involves difficult distinctions between measure and measure.

In the EC, if the measure regulates product characteristics (and production methods), it is equated to a measure having an equivalent effect to a quota, and is accordingly subject to the prohibition of Article 28 EC (or 29 in the case of export restrictions).[19] If, by contrast, the measure affects the marketing of the product, what is prohibited is only discrimination between domestic and imported products (caught, via judicial interpretation, under the same Article 28 EC).[20] The WTO discipline is different, and overall less stringent. Article III:4 of the GATT subjects internal regulation concerning *product chacteristics* to a *mere* non-discrimination obligation towards imported products (so-called 'National Treatment'). What is still unclear, though, is the role of Article XI of the GATT, which prohibits quantitative restrictions and 'other measures'. In particular, there is the question of whether a regulation which essentially *prevents access* to the market should really be considered as an example of internal regulation or whether it should squarely fall foul of this provision and hence be prohibited. Further, when the regulation concerns process or production methods (PPMs), Article III is held not to be applicable and the more stringent Article XI may come into play.[21]

[19] For three interesting examples where restrictions based on the 'manner of production' were banned under the applicable provision (Article 29 EC) see, eg, Case C-5/94 *Hedley Lomas*; Case 1/96 *Compassion in World Farming*; Case C-169/89 *Gourmetterie*.

[20] See C-267–268/91 *Keck* which introduced the famous category of 'selling arrangements'.

[21] On the status of PPMs under the GATT see MJ Trebilcock and R Howse, *The Regulation of International Trade* (3rd edn, London: Routledge, 2005) chapter 3; R Howse and D Regan, 'The Product/Process Distinction—An Illusory Basis for Disciplining "Unilateralism" in Trade Policy' (2000) European Journal of International Law 249.

To conclude, it is interesting to note that it is exactly with regard to those measures (border measures; regulation) for which there are serious perplexities about the classification as subsidies, that the applicability of other rules is fairly clear.[22]

Cumulative application, subsidy and other rules

Other measures may be subject to both subsidy and other rules.

Thus, for example, internal taxation which discriminates against imported products is prohibited in the EC (Article 90 EC) and WTO (Article III of the GATT).[23]

But a discriminatory internal tax may also constitute a subsidy. Indeed, the GATT—at its core—clearly establishes a link between the concepts of discrimination and subsidy (see chapter 9 for a detailed analysis). Two remarks should be made immediately. First, the different approach to internal regulation (no subsidy) and taxation (subsidy) should not surprise, and can easily be explained by the already repeated historical correlation between subsidization and taxation government prerogatives. Secondly, Article III of the GATT raises an interesting, and largely still open, interpretative issue on the possibility of applying the provision on national treatment *when* the same conduct is also a subsidy. Paragraph 8(b) of Article III reads: 'The provisions of this Article shall not prevent the payment of subsidies exclusively to domestic producers . . .'. Everything depends on the scope attributable to this exception. As such, and also to avoid an important principle like national treatment being rendered ineffective, it should be given a restrictive interpretation.[24] What this provision certainly does not preclude is that certain aspects of a measure amounting to a subsidy may be subject to Article III.

More generally, in EC law too, the possibility of assessing a measure under State aid law *and* also under free movement rules (namely Article 25, 28, 31, and 90 EC) has been consistently repeated.[25]

If a measure qualifies as a State aid under Article 87(1) EC, it will be subject to State aid rules, and hence to the centralized and discretionary scrutiny of the Commission. At the same time, however, according to the famous test of

[22] This conclusion can be tested with two controversial cases we have extensively analysed above: *US—Export Restraints* and *PreussenElektra*.

[23] For EC law see, eg, Case 73/79 *Commission v Italy*, para 9; Case 17/81 *Pabst and Richarz*, para 22; Case C-234/99 *Nygård*, para 55. In the WTO, see, eg, *Japan—Taxes II*, *Chile—Taxes*.

[24] See P Van den Bossche, *The Law and Policy of the World Trade Organization Text, Cases and Materials* (2nd edn, Cambridge: Cambridge University Press, 2008) 344.

[25] The latest interesting statements of the law can be found in Case C-222/07 *UTECA*, Judgment of 5 March 2009, and in Case C-333/07 *Société Régie Networks*, Judgment of 22 December 2008. In the former case, the possibility of a cumulative application (although *in casu* there was no State aid for lack of 'State resources') seems to involve virtually all fundamental freedoms (services, establishment, workers, and even capital). The interesting systemic issue on justifications will be analysed below.

'severability' laid down in *Iannelli v Meroni*,[26] those aspects of the measure breaching free movement provisions that can be 'separated' from the aid, since they are not 'indissolubly linked' to its object, will also be independently subject to those rules (and to the control of national courts).[27]

Interestingly, as Biondi and Eeckhout have observed, the Court has always found that in the measure there were aspects separable from the aid itself, or that, in any event, should not have been excluded from a *further scrutiny* to ensure the effective application of EC law to national measures which could constitute an obstacle to trade.[28] In short, the fact that the measure could be classified as State aid did not mean that it could escape the prohibition laid down in other provisions.[29] This certainly confirms the crucial role played by 'internal market' provisions, which permeates other areas of EC law, including State aid law, in various respects. It is noteworthy that, in all cases where claims based on internal market rules and State aid rules were made, the Court has invariably concluded that the former applies, *even if* the latter does not. This seems to support the conclusion that 'internal market' law and policy do indeed constitute the basis of EC law and policy.

From the inverse perspective, however, the Court has also confirmed that the application of fiscal measures does not mean that State aid rules cannot apply.[30] As seen in chapter 2, internal market and State aid rules share a common objective but attain it in different ways.

In general, it seems that a situation similar to that prevailing in the EC (with a cumulative application of State aid and internal market rules to different aspects of the measure and in the pursuit of different objectives) also occurs in WTO law. There are indeed no special reasons why, as a general approach, a measure falling within the scope of subsidy rules should not, at least with respect to *certain aspects*, be covered also by other provisions such as Articles II, III or XI GATT.[31]

[26] Case 74/76 *Iannelli v Meroni*, para 14.

[27] We have already mentioned (see chapter 5, section III.B) the case-law for which 'taxes do not fall within the scope of the provisions of the EC Treaty concerning State aid unless they constitute the method of financing of the measure, so that they form an integral part of the measure.' In the context of the present discussion, it should be noted that the issue in those cases is exclusively whether the method of financing is part of the State aid and should hence be subject to the same notification obligations. In other words, the possibility of assessing it under other rules is not in question.

[28] A Biondi and P Eeckhout, 'State Aid and Obstacles to Trade' in A Biondi, P Eeckhout, and J Flynn (eds), *The Law of State Aid in the European Union* (Oxford: Oxford University Press, 2004) 103, 100. This prerogative has been forcefully endorsed by the Court in Case C-234/99 *Nygård*, paras 56–64.

[29] See, eg, Case 249/81 *Commission v Ireland*, para 18; Case 18/84 *Commission v France*, para 13. See also Case 91/78 *Hansen*, para 9.

[30] See, eg, Joined Cases C-78/90 to C-83/90 *Compagnie Commerciale de L'Ouest*, para 32; Joined Cases C-149/91 and C-150/91 *Sanders*, para 24; Case C-17/91 *Lornoy*, para 28; Case C-114/91 *Claeys*, para 21; Joined Cases C-144/91 and C-145/91 *Demoor Gilbert*, para 24; Case C-266/91 *CELBI*, para 21; Case C-72/92 *Scharbakte*, para 18; Case C-234/99 *Nygård*, para 53.

[31] In the passage quoted above, Ehlermann explained the alleged 'lack of structure' of WTO substantive law when he noted that '[t]he same contested measure is often examined under a series of

State aid compatibility and other rules

In the context of the assessment of the compatibility of EC State aid with the 'common market', the Commission should also take into account the compliance of the measure at issue with other *specific* provisions of the EC Treaty.

It has thus been consistently stated that, although State aid rules leave a wide discretion to the Commission to come to a decision on the compatibility of a system of State aid with the requirements of the common market, it is clear from the general scheme of the Treaty that that procedure must never produce a result which is contrary to the specific provisions of the Treaty.[32]

This important finding confirms once again that EC State aid law, and in particular the justification of an otherwise distorting subsidy, does not sit in a regulatory and policy vacuum but has to be in line with the prevailing directions coming from the overall system, and particularly 'internal market' ones.

Applicability of different rules: implications

The application of one rule rather than another has several implications.

First of all, it is clear that different rules often have different *substantive requirements and tests*. In other words, rules may vary from an operational perspective. A good example is given by the distinction between 'trade' and 'competition' rules thoroughly analysed in chapter 2.[33] In the EC context the Court of Justice noted that the application of internal market rules and State aid rules presupposes 'distinct conditions peculiar to the two kinds of State measure' and 'they differ furthermore as to their legal consequences'.[34]

Among the most important substantive issues is that of *justifications*. The case of WTO law is particularly instructive in this respect. To classify a measure as a trade barrier covered by Article XI GATT or as a discriminatory regulation under Article III:4 GATT opens up, at least in principle, the possibility of applying the general exceptions under Article XX GATT. If, by contrast, the same measure is examined under subsidy rules only, the possibility of justification is much more

provisions, possibly contained in different covered agreements.' This finds indeed confirmation in WTO practice and case-law. It is interesting to refer to a revealing finding of the old Panel in *Indonesia – Automobile Industry*. The Indonesian government was arguing that only the SCM Agremeent should have applied to the dispute to the exclusion of the GATT, notably its Article III, and the Agreement on Trade-Related Investment Measures (TRIMs). At para 14.56, the Panel held: 'we reject Indonesia's general defense that the only applicable law to this dispute is the SCM Agreement. We consider rather that the obligations contained in the WTO Agreement are generally cumulative, can be complied with simultaneously and that different aspects and sometimes the same aspects of a legislative act can be subject to various provisions of the WTO Agreement.'

[32] See, eg, Case 73/79 *Commission v Italy*, para 11; Case C-234/99 *Nygård*, para 54.

[33] See the coda to section II.C.

[34] See, eg, Case 91/78 *Hansen*, para 9.

limited in scope, since we could only resort to the category of 'non-actionable subsidies' under the SCM.[35]

The issue becomes particularly intriguing if *both* sets of provisions, ie GATT and SCM provisions, are held to apply cumulatively. Does a justification under one agreement, for instance the GATT, suffice to shelter the practice from the wrath of the other agreement, say the SCM? Further, considering that the category of 'non-actionable' subsidies is for now dead letter, can the general justifications under Article XX become relevant again also with respect to the subsidy issue? The author would answer this question positively.[36] This is an interesting legal and policy issue, since Article XX of the GATT would, for example, provide a broad justification for the environment (particularly as compared to the strict requirements of the corresponding category of non-actionable subsidies).[37]

[35] As the law currently stands, this possibility is however only moot. The category of 'non-actionable' subsidies expired in 2000.

[36] Certainly, the SCM Agreement is a development of the GATT provisions on subsidies, being *lex specialis* with respect to them. On its part, Article XX of the GATT regulates 'general exceptions' to any breach of GATT provisions. GATT provisions and the other covered agreements do not live in isolation. The WTO Agreement is a 'single undertaking' and its provisions are part of an 'integrated' legal system. See in this regard the interesting findings of the Appellate Body in *Brazil—Desiccated Coconut*, paras 11–14, on the different normative framework between GATT and WTO, and on the relationship between GATT and SCM provisions on subsidies.

The General Interpretative Note to Annex 1A on Multilateral Agreements of Trade in Goods provides that in case of *conflict* between the GATT and another provision of any agreement on trade in goods (including the SCM Agreement), the latter will 'prevail to the extent of the conflict'. Now, it could be argued that a conflict situation could exist between Art XX of the GATT (on general exceptions) and Art 8 of the SCM (on non-actionable subsidies), the necessary assumption being that both those rules regulated the same subject matter. In this regard, it should be asked whether it should also be assumed that the notion underlying non-actionability is one of 'exception' (thus making it comparable to Art XX). If we consider the ambivalent nature of subsidies (see Arts 8.1 and 11.1 of the Tokyo Round Subsidies Code in this respect; more generally, see the discussion in chapter 2 above), this qualification could be disputed.

Assuming, for the sake of the reasoning, an overlap between the two sets of rules, and a relationship of speciality, it could be argued that, in presence of the category of non-actionability, the role of Art XX of the GATT was quite limited. But now that the non-actionable category is expired the author does not see any source for conflict between the GATT and the SCM Agreement in this respect. There are no reasons why, irrespective of the previous 'general-exception' nature of the rules in Art 8 of the SCM, the flexible discipline on general exceptions in trade in goods should not play its role in the subsidy field as well. Truly, from another perspective, other covered agreements, such as the TRIMs, do make express reference to the applicability of Art XX of the GATT. Further, from a policy viewpoint, the broadly phrased language of Art XX, coupled with the demonstrated willingness of the AB to construe it liberally, could raise concerns.

The issue of the availability of the general exceptions under Art XX of the GATT with respect to subsidies covered by the SCM is still open. The dispute settlement has not tackled it expressly. See, eg, the recent *US—Shrimp from Thailand Customs Bond Directive* dispute where the Appellate Body did not address India's general claim that Art XX of the GATT would not be applicable in the context of an anti-dumping case.

[37] The possibility of using Article XX of the GATT to justify measures—including subsidies—to fight climate change breaching other provisions of the GATT (or indeed other covered agreements) is currently one of the most discussed possibilities of application of this provision. See, eg, the testimony of J Pauwelyn before the US 'Subcommittee on Trade of the House Committee on Ways and Means' on 24 March 2009, 9.

The recent European *UTECA* case has raised interesting systemic issues, particularly on the relationship between different justifications.[38] The facts are straightforward. Spain ordered television broadcasters to commit a specific part of their revenue to pre-fund the production of European films in one of the original languages of the country. From the legal perspective, the measure was found to breach various internal market freedoms, notably free movement of services, establishment, workers and capital. It was however held to be justified by overriding reasons of public interest, ie culture. At the same time, the measure was considered under State aid rules and, only because of the lack of 'State resources' (the funding came from private sources), the assessment was negative in this respect.

The interesting question which arises is the impact that a positive assessment under one set of rules (in the instant case, internal market) may have on that under another set of rules (State aid). More specifically, can the former have an impact on the definition of State aid or on the judgement as to its compatibility by the Commission?[39]

Another important implication of the application of one rule rather than another focuses on the *remedies* side. One of the most significant peculiarities of the GATT/WTO system is that to consider a measure as a subsidy may open the way to the imposition of a unilateral countervailing duty on the relevant imports, which would not occur if the same measure is covered *only* under Article XI or III GATT (or indeed Article II GATT to which Article VI, permitting countervailing duties, is just an exception).

EC law provides another important example. For obvious reasons of legal certainty, legal systems do not look with favour at retroactive remedies. Thus, under EC law, the prohibition of retroactivity still seems to be the general rule, albeit with limited exceptions, most notably when there is an important Community interest and legitimate expectations are not breached.[40]

The situation is markedly different with respect to State aids where the rule is that aid 'incompatible' with the common market should be repaid in full. As has been underlined in chapter 2, the stance with respect to 'unlawful' aid, that is aid Member States grant in breach of their procedural obligations of priori notification and non-implementation, is currently under reconsideration.

[38] Case C-222/07 *UTECA*.

[39] Advocate General Kokott (at para 115 of the Opinion) has incidentally answered a different, indeed opposite question, noting that an authorization by the 'Commission in the context of State aid does not . . . prejudice the interpretation of other provisions of the EC Treaty, particularly fundamental freedoms.' This conclusion seems essentially in line with the prevailing case-law.

It may be asked whether this inference would work the other way round (a justification under fundamental freedoms 'does not prejudice' the interpretation of the Commission). The line of the case-law which, while recognizing the wide discretion of the Commission, warns that the State aid 'procedure must never produce a result which is contrary to the specific provisions of the Treaty' comes immediately to mind and increases the sense of discomfort of the interpreter.

[40] See P Craig and G De Búrca, *EU Law—Text, Cases and Materials* (4th edn, Oxford: Oxford University Press, 2007) 551–58.

For a long time, the retroactive repayment of 'unlawful aids' has been strongly affirmed and subject to virtually no limitations. Aggrieved parties could ask the competent national court to order the full repayment and to draw any necessary legal consequence. Quite remarkably, the availability of this remedy was untouched by the fact that the Commission had started to investigate the matter, and even where it had eventually declared the aid 'compatible'. The stain of the breach of the procedural cornerstone of the system could not be removed.[41] The recent *CELF II* case seems to have signalled a change in emphasis.[42] If an unlawful aid is eventually declared compatible, *as a matter of EC law*, national courts are only required to order the payment of interest for the relevant period. While the possibility of seeking the full recovery (and compensation) is still available, it is left to a decision of national law and domestic courts.[43]

From the procedural and institutional, and hence constitutional standpoint, subsidies seem to be considered as different from other State measures, like taxation, regulation, tariffs or quotas. Member States are free to design and implement tax and regulatory measures and, only if their assessment is not correct, are they subject to scrutiny by judicial or administrative authorities. As for tariffs, they are either prohibited from introducing them or they can do so only within the agreed limits. Quotas are simply prohibited. Again, no control by an independent authority is required.

The case is different for subsidies. Both the GATT/WTO and the EC require that they be notified to a supra-national body.[44] The intrusiveness of the control is markedly different in the two systems. In the WTO it is 'light-touch' (mainly based on peer review) and largely ineffective. The sovereign prerogatives of Member States are thus marginally constrained, and no real differences can be found with respect to the regulation of other State measures.

By contrast, the institutional and procedural framework of EC State aid law, with a fully independent institution exclusively in charge to decide whether planned aid is justified, is in stark contrast to the discipline of other forms of public action (like taxation and regulation). Sovereign choices are significantly restricted.

[41] The momentous *Lucchini* decision (Case C-119/05) has shown that, in the case of aid granted in flagrant breach of both procedural and substantive law, even the principle of *res judicata* would be overcome.

[42] Case C-199/06.

[43] For an analysis of remedies under EC State aid law, and the questions left open by the CELF II decision, see chapter 2, section III.

[44] Albeit in different ways, the need for a special monitoring of subsidies is indeed present in both systems. For the EC, see JL Buendia-Sierra, 'Not like this: Some Skeptical Remarks on the "Refined Economic Approach" in State aid', in Proceedings of 4th Experts' Forum on New Developments in European State Aid Law, 18 and 19 May 2006, European State Aid Law Institute (Berlin: Lexxion, 2006) 59, 62, who refers to the early statement of the ECJ in Case 74/76 *Iannelli v Meroni*, para 12. As regards the GATT, an interesting insight can be found in the preparatory works. See, eg, the 'Anglo-American Discussions Under Article VII: Commercial Policy', Public Records Office BT 11/2215, at part VII.1, reported by DA Irwin, PC Mavroidis, and AO Sykes, The Genesis of the GATT (Cambridge: Cambridge University Press, 2008) 238.

A parallel with the 'internal market' field may be useful. If we are within the latter, the direct decisional power is mainly (although not exclusively) in the hands of Member States (either at a decentralized level or at the EC level—the Council—for harmonization measures). If, by contrast, we have a State aid issue, the Commission is heavily involved in the decisional phase. The restraint on Member States' room for manoeuvre is coupled with the limited, indeed exceptional, role played by the Council.

A good example of these differences is given by the *PreussenElektra* case. The 'feed-in tariff' mechanism was analysed under both State aid rules and internal market rules. The conclusion that the measure was not a State aid in the first place meant *removing it from* the control of the Commission and *leaving it within* that of Member States. Significantly, from the substantive perspective, the final outcome might not be different (there is a breach of competition and trade but this should be justified for environmental considerations). What, however, changes dramatically is the balance of power that may lead to that decision.

Conclusions

The previous analysis of the 'external' perspective has shown how systemic considerations are important, and how the broader context may, from a political and legal standpoint, have an impact, and often a considerable one, on the 'internal' analysis of a given set of rules. The main reason is that the application of different rules entails the application of different political and legal 'regimes' bringing with them distinct technical, institutional, constitutional and even symbolic features.

PART III

THE ADVANTAGE ANALYSIS

Things that are alike should be treated alike, while things that are unalike should be treated unalike, in proportion of their unalikeness.[1]

The idea of justice consists of two parts: a uniform or constant feature, summarised in the precept 'Treat like cases alike' and a shifting or varying criterion used in determining when, for any given purpose, cases are alike or different.[2]

Judgments about like and unlike—about equality and discrimination—seem to have an inexorable moral logic to them in ordinary human discourse.[3]

[1] Axiom attributable to Aristotle, Ethica Nichomachea (Oxford: Clarendon Press, 1925) bk V.3, 1131a, 1131b (Ross trans. 1925).

[2] HLA Hart, *The Concept of Law* (2nd edn, Oxford: Clarendon Press,1994) 160.

[3] MJ Trebilcock and R Howse, *The Regulation of International Trade* (3rd edn, London: Routledge, 2005) 111.

Overview

The analysis of Part II has shown that various public measures may be considered to be subsidies. This does not mean however that *any* measure that happens to take any of those forms is a subsidy. The matter warrants further analysis, and the next fundamental step is to establish whether the measure at issue grants an economic advantage.

Borrowing again from Hudec's words quoted at the beginning of Part II, this corresponds to 'something of value' that eventually 'increases the producer's profitability'.[4] Diamond has nicely summarized this effect: 'It is the ability to produce at lower cost that constitutes the competitive advantage subsidy recipients enjoy.'[5]

Indeed, the crucial importance of the subject of this Part—the legal definition of the concept of *advantage*—can be fully appreciated only if this element is placed in its context. It is the advantage produced by the public intervention in the economy that eventually makes the subsidy liable to produce negative externalities, in the form of a distortion of international competition and trade.[6] Those negative externalities mostly depend on the positive 'impact on profitability' of the recipient, and consequently on the negative impact on its competitors. Ultimately, the analysis of chapter 2 has led us to conclude that the most convincing of the justifications of subsidy control is the conferral of this *competitive advantage*.

Although often consequential, the concepts of *advantage* and *competitive advantage* are separate. They have a different focus and require a different type of analysis. More bluntly, the proof of an advantage does not invariably lead to that of a competitive edge. They therefore constitute two separate definitional steps which warrant a distinct examination.

The following chapters explore the *advantage analysis*, ie the process to determine the existence of an advantage in the two systems, and the main difficulties emerging from it. Like in the previous Part we commence with a conceptual tone. Chapter 7 introduces the basic notions of 'comparison' and 'benchmark', the underlying core idea of 'derogation from the norm', and the political and economic context of the advantage analysis. The exposition then follows a twofold pattern, depending on whether the public intervention occurs in the market

[4] RE Hudec, Difference in National Environmental Standards: The Level-Playing-Field Dimension, (1996) 5 Minnesota Journal of Global Trade 1, 15 (emphasis added).

[5] R Diamond, 'Privatization and the Definition of Subsidy: A Critical Study of Appellate Body Texturalism' (2008) Jounal of International Economic Law 649, 654.

[6] And also, which goes beyond the actual definition of subsidy, positive externalities, in the form of remedy to an undesired socio-economic situation.

or outside it. The economic activity of governments is examined in chapter 8, their non-economic activity in chapters 9 (WTO law) and 10 (EC law).

The role played by the public policy objectives pursued by governments through subsidies is thoroughly examined. Chapter 11 summarizes the point on this *leitmotiv* and goes on to explore it through the topical case-study of the financing of public services. The advantage analysis is the main place of the 'objectives talk'. It is the step in the definition of subsidy where we directly witness the vivid attraction between scope and justification outlined in chapter 1, and where *equality* and *justice* considerations come more directly into play. This is why the opening quotes immediately direct the reader's attention to these two concepts.

7

The advantage analysis: an introduction

In *Canada—Aircraft* the Appellate body laid down findings whose generality makes them a suitable starting point for explaining the operation of the advantage analysis in both legal systems. As expressed by its ordinary meaning, the concept of 'benefit' under Article 1.1(b) of the SCM 'clearly encompasses some form of advantage'.[1] This intuitive, almost tautological and still skeletal idea is immediately given some flesh:

> the word 'benefit', as used in Article 1.1(b), implies some kind of *comparison*. This must be so, for there can be no 'benefit' to the recipient unless the 'financial contribution' makes the recipient '*better off*' than it *would otherwise have been*, *absent* that contribution. In our view, the marketplace provides an *appropriate basis for comparison* in determining whether a 'benefit' has been 'conferred' . . . whether the recipient has received a 'financial contribution' on terms more favourable than those available to the recipient in the market.[2]

The emphasized words highlight the general steps of the advantage analysis. The determination of the conferral of 'some form of advantage' is based on (i) 'some kind of comparison' which in turn requires (ii) an 'appropriate basis' for it, that is an appropriate benchmark.[3] Crucially, this comparative process should lead to a determination of (iii) whether the recipient is 'better off' than 'would otherwise have been, absent' the government measure. These findings are now examined in turn.

I. Comparison and benchmarks

Common sense leads us to understand that the question of whether someone has received an advantage immediately begs another question: 'advantage in relation to what and in relation to whom?' This means that it is necessary to make a *comparison* and, to do so, to find a suitable benchmark. Only this exercise can disclose whether any advantage has been received. In other words, to be a subsidy a measure has to be tested against a *baseline* and it is only after this comparison is made that we will

[1] Appellate Body, para 153; cf also Panel, para 9.112.

[2] Appellate Body, para 157 (emphasis added); cf also Panel, para 9.112.

[3] The reference to the marketplace depended on the circumstances of the case—the government was acting on the market—and this should not necessarily be considered as a rule in all cases.

be able to tell whether the government intervention is subsidizing that consumer or producer by increasing his returns.[4]

This is exactly what the Appellate Body noted in *Canada—Aircraft* and this conclusion is plainly transposable to the EC. Referring to the definition of State aid, Ross underlines that '[n]o advantage can be identified without a comparator first being found as a benchmark for treatment'.[5] And confirmation can be found in the case-law too. Advocate General Cosmas, for example, underlined that the concept of advantage under Article 87(1) EC is based on the ideas of 'comparison' and 'point of reference'.[6]

A. Benchmarks: an insight from economics

Sykes has recently explained what an economist would consider as a 'natural benchmark': a 'hypothetical market equilibrium without any governmental presence'.[7] Since this State of nature is impossible to find, intellectual rigour would require to take *any* tax, expenditure and regulatory policy into account. If, as a consequence of the measure, net returns are increased, the relevant activity can be said to be subsidized, if they are reduced, it will be taxed. The problem with this extremely analytical approach is its sheer difficulty of application. It is just impossible to take into consideration every instance of public intervention in the economy that may affect the costs and revenues of enterprises.

Three alternatives are thus suggested which will be referred to in the analysis of the legal requirements used to define a subsidy.[8] The simplest one, which is at the core of the logic of the advantage analysis outlined in this chapter, is 'to look at each government measure in isolation and to ignore the question of whether any benefit it confers may be offset by costs elsewhere'. The second alternative is to consider generally applicable policies as not conferring any subsidy. This is the essence of the requirement that only specific measures can be objectionable under subsidy rules (we analyse this alternative in chapter 13). Finally, the third alternative, which, although theoretically appealing if one wishes to capture any *international*

[4] The reader should note that, whereas in the context of the analysis of the *advantage*, the issue is whether the measure increases the wealth of the recipient, the focus of the the analysis of the *competitive advantage* is different, being whether the measure—through the advantage—makes the recipient more competitive. For a clear explanation of the distinction (and its importance in the context of subsidy laws) see R Diamond, 'Privatization and the Definition of Subsidy: A Critical Study of Appellate Body Texturalism' (2008) Journal of International Economic Law 649.

[5] M Ross, 'State Aids and National Courts: Definitions and Other Problems—A Case of Premature Emancipation?' (2000b) Common Market Law Review 401, 407.

[6] Case C-353/95P *Ladbroke v Commission*, para 30 of the Opinion. cf also Case T-308/00 *Salzgitter v Commission*, para 81.

[7] AO Sykes, 'The Economics of WTO Rules on Subsidies and Countervailing Measures', Chicago M John. Olin Law and Economics Working Paper No. 186 (2nd Series), May 2003, 3. See also BM Hoekman and MM Kostecki, *The Political Economy of the World Trading System* (Oxford: Oxford University Press, 2001) 170.

[8] AO Sykes, 'The Economics of WTO Rules on Subsidies and Countervailing Measures', Chicago John M Olin Law and Economics Working Paper No. 186 (2nd Series), May 2003, 3–5.

alteration of the playing field, is also extremely difficult to apply in practice, would require a comparison of the impact of the government measure with that of other governments' measures on similarly situated entities elsewhere.

The first two alternatives (which we could respectively dub 'gross benefit' and 'selective benefit') are relatively easier to administer than the 'universal benchmark' stylized at the very beginning on the one hand, and the 'cross-governmental benchmark' of the last alternative on the other. Despite deficiencies and difficulties, they therefore represent two consolidated criteria to identify and select public measures that should be regulated as subsidies from others that should not.

B. Economic and non-economic activity, market and normative benchmarks

The 'appropriate' benchmarks may be disparate. The government may intervene in the economy, and produce an impact on it, in two ways. This distinction is important to identify the correct benchmark. If the public body performs an *economic* activity in the market, its conduct is tested against the *market* benchmark applicable in the circumstances. If, by contrast, the public body carries out a conduct which is *not economic* but governmental, the suitable benchmark will be *normative* since it has to be found in the relevant regulation or legal system.

It is worth underlining that the two-fold distinction between economic and non-economic activity, and market and normative benchmarks, is not based on the *objectives* pursued by the government, which in both cases are presumed to be for the common good, but rather on the *nature* of the action and the context in which grantor and recipient operate. This important point is clarified further in section III below.

II. How the analysis works

So far, we are still at a superficial level. To say that the advantage analysis implies 'some kind' of comparison and that an 'appropriate' benchmark needs to be found (be it a market or normative one) is still descriptive. It does not explain how this analysis actually works and, eventually, how the determination that an advantage has, or has not, been conferred can be made. To do so the comparative process mentioned above has to be embodied into an *operative test* with more defined steps to follow and precise concepts to rely on.

A. Norm and exception: the derogation test

Again *Canada—Aircraft* provides a useful pointer. The Appellate Body noted that the comparison refers to what 'would otherwise have been' in absence of the measure at issue. In the case of economic activity, this means focusing on whether the measure has taken place on 'terms more favourable than those [otherwise] available in the market'.

The term 'otherwise' (be it express or naturally implied) is central in the language above. The advantage analysis centres around the construction of this key term. Three concepts are clearly hinted at. First, the benchmark in the analysis is linked to an idea of *norm* or *normality*. Secondly, the advantage would be the result of an *exception* to this norm. Thirdly, this deviation operates to the economic benefit of someone.

This analysis finds confirmation in EC law. In the early *Steenkijomenen* case, the Court of Justice famously found that the concept of aid 'embraces not only positive benefits, such as subsidies themselves, but also interventions which, in various forms, mitigate the charges that are *normally* included in the budget of undertakings . . . .'[9] The idea that the concept of aid would involve a departure from normality is clear, and is in line with the previous analysis made in the WTO context. Two illustrious Advocates General underlined that it is necessary to establish whether there is an economic advantage which would not have been granted in the *normal course of events*.[10] Referring to a market transaction, the Court itself found that 'in order to determine whether a State measure constitutes aid, it is necessary to establish whether the recipient receives an economic advantage which it would not have obtained *under normal market conditions*'.[11] The EC language thus expressly refers to the idea of normality. Now, the logical implication is that the existence of an advantage would result from a derogation from this norm.[12]

This analysis leads us to conclude that the 'derogation from the norm', which could be dubbed 'derogation test', is the core of the advantage analysis, the operative test we were looking for.

We should immediately underline that, far from representing a mechanical deductive exercise, applied in a doctrinaire fashion and producing almost automatic solutions, this test involves a *complex process* made of *delicate steps*. As this chapter shows, irrespective of whether we are dealing with a market or normative context, the two crucial steps of the analysis—the definition of *norm* and *exception*—are by no means straigthforward.[13]

[9] Case 30/59 *Steenkijomenen*, p 19 (emphasis added).

[10] cf Advocate General Slynn in Case 84/82 *Germany v Commission*, p 1501; Advocate General Jacobs in Cases 278-280/92 *Hytasa*, para 28.

[11] Case C-39/94 *SFEI*, para 60 (emphasis added).

[12] An express reference to a 'derogation from the norm' can be found in the Commission's practice with respect to taxation and State aid. See chapter 10.

[13] The final step, focusing on the actual existence of an economic advantage, is usually relatively simple, even evident sometimes.

B. Defining the norm, determining the exception: variations on the theme

Sometimes a different formulation of the process to establish the advantage can be found. This immediataly echoes the principle of *equality* and focuses on whether the *situation at issue is treated like comparable situations.*

Thus in interpreting the phrase 'otherwise due' under Article 1.1(a)(1)(ii) of the SCM, the Appellate Body found that, in determining whether a tax measure favours someone, 'like will be compared with like' and, in particular, the 'fiscal treatment of legitimately comparable income' will be compared.[14] In a similar vein in the EC, in *Adria-Wien* the Court noted that to conclude that we have a State aid, we have to establish whether a State measure favours certain undertakings 'in comparison with other undertakings which are in a legal and factual situation that is comparable in the light of the objective pursued by the measure in question'.[15] Sometimes the link with the general principle of equality is expressly made.[16]

All these formulations lay down what can be called 'comparative test'. The interesting question is whether there is a link between this language of equal treatment (or non-discrimination) of comparable situations on the one hand, and that of derogation from the norm on the other. Do they refer to two different tests? Or, more simply, is what we have two different formulations of essentially the same test? Although we address these questions when we deal with the *US—FSC* dispute in chapter 9, it is useful to anticipate the main finding.

The derogation test focuses directly on the *logical process* to determine whether the measure grants an advantage, by expressly using the suggestive language of 'derogation' or 'exception'. The other formulation seems to be more low-profile in this regard, usually emphasizing the quite neutral concept of 'comparison' rather than the expressive idea of 'discrimination'. In the author's view, all this means that the comparative test is particularly helpful when it comes to define the *benchmark* used in determining the existence of an exception. It will be seen that the reference to 'comparable or like situations' represents the key concept around which the difficult notion of 'general rule' or 'norm' should be construed.

The substantial identity of the two tests is confirmed by the fact that the language used to express them is often overlapping, even in this book. There may be a reference to the existence of a 'derogation' from or 'exception' to the rule,[17] or to a 'differential treatment' or 'discrimination' between undertakings. In all cases the meaning ultimately conveyed is the same, being whether this apparent anomaly is in fact an anomaly and an undue advantage conferred. Whatever language is used,

[14] Appellate Body, *US—FSC* (Article 21(5)), paras 90 and 91. See chapter 9 for a further analysis.

[15] Case C-143/99 *Adria-Wien*, para 41.

[16] Case C-353/95P *Ladbroke v Commission*, at para 30 of the Opinion. See also M Ross, 'State Aids and National Courts: Definitions and Other Problems—A Case of Premature Emancipation?' (2000) Common Market Law Review 401, 407.

[17] Or, indeed, to a 'deviation' from or 'exemption' to it.

the underlying process is the same and requires a complex analysis which focuses on similarities and differences between various situations, objectives and justifications, and eventually on the delicate interplay of rules and exceptions.

In other words, whilst the intrinsic mechanics is the same, the 'comparative' and 'derogation' tests clarify different working parts of it, and different steps of the advantage analysis, respectively what is the *norm* and what is the *exception*. A music afficionado would say that the two formulations are variations of the same theme rather than two distinct themes. Like variations in melody, rhythm, harmony or embellishment show different facets of the theme to the benefit of beauty, conceptual variations in law, and indeed in other scientific areas, may clarify different issues and perspectives to the benefit of better understanding.

III. The context of the advantage analysis: market and public role redefinition

A. Two characters in search of identity: the market and the government

The advantage analysis, and more generally the debate on public subsidies, can be understood only if the more general economic and political context is properly considered.

Recent times have seen the emergence of phenomena which involve strong cultural and ideological, financial and political forces. First, there is a trend, well known at least in western economies, towards liberalization of the economy and privatization of public undertakings.[18] Sectors that till recently were public reserves (such as health, education, transport and public utilities—post, communications, water, electricity, gas) have increasingly been opened to the private sector. The justifications are various but can be fairly summed up in the belief that competitive markets are more beneficial to consumers with private actors being able to operate more efficiently. Ultimately, the greater budgetary constraints faced by governments also played a role in their retreat from direct intervention in the economy, at least in its more traditional forms, to less interventionist forms of regulation.

What has not changed but is instead facing a renewed recognition is the belief that the public interest should still be pursued and that the 'government' has a crucial role to play in this regard. The social dimension of public action faces a renewed recognition.[19] One of the most notable examples, which we analyse at the

[18] See, in general, JE Stiglitz, *Economics of the Public Sector* (3rd edn, New York: Norton, 2000) chapter 1.

[19] For two recent and interesting collections of essays focusing on the EC debate see G De Búrca (ed), *EU and the Welfare State—In Search of Solidarity* (Oxford: Oxford University Press, 2006) and M Dougan and E Spaventa (eds), *Social Welfare and EU Law* (Oxford: Hart Publishing: 2005). More generally, see also D Rodrik, 'Industrial Policy for the Twenty-First Century', November 2004, CEPR Discussion Paper No 4767.

end of chapter 11, focuses on the public services debate, occuring in the EC and the WTO alike. In general, the cases for social (and often global) action are endless, ranging from sustainable development and climate change to the access to natural resources and the food emergency, and, more generally, poverty and the need to have a fairer society where wealth is redistributed in a more just way.[20] All this has to be set against the 'globalization' debate, with its 'discontents', and their real or putative representatives, voicing their concerns.[21] A globalized economy, largely based on the 'Washington consensus', has produced great economic benefits. The simple fact is, however, that many parts or regions of global society have not noticed them.

The previous factors are therefore pushing governments, at home and in multinational fora, to rethink their main purpose, the safeguard of the general welfare, and in particular the means to achieve this.

The current financial and economic crisis, which has led us to recession (and in the near future possibly to depression) represents an additional, key factor in making this process of redefinition of the public role in the economy particularly painful and urgent. In recent months we have witnessed a wave of rescues and nationalizations of banks, financial institutions and other key national industries, that are showing how the trend is very different from that of previous decades. An exclusive reliance on 'supply side' economic policies, based on the idea that long-term considerations would have sustained a continuous growth, has shown its weakness. The swing of the pendulum may now considerably shift to 'demand side' policies. Waiting for an ideal mix of the two perspectives, a greater assertion of government intervention ('depression economics', using Krugman's expression) in the coming years is an easy prediction.[22] Government spending will be increased. More subsidies will be granted and infrastructure investment financed. The inevitable twist of this story is the real risk that, in times of deep crisis and widespread panic, there is a return to protectionism.[23] The antidote is always the same: the recognition that global challenges need common and concerted action.

Since the origin of the current financial and economic downturn has to be found in both regulatory and market failures, the market itself is in a delicate process of redefinition. More radically, however, it may be society that will eventually undergo a process of self-reflection, and possibly change.[24]

What is certain is that, at the time of writing, governments and market very much resemble two characters in search of identity.

[20] See, eg, Oxfam, *Rigged Rules and Double Standards: Trade, Globalization, and the Fight Against Poverty*, 2002, 17.

[21] See, eg, JE Stiglitz, *Globalization and its Discontents* (London: Penguin, 2002); J Bhagwati, *In Defence of Globalization* (Oxford: Oxford University Press, 2004).

[22] PR Krugman, *The Return of Depression Economics and the Crisis of 2008* (2nd edn, London: Penguin, 2008) chapter 10.

[23] See, 'The Return of Economic Nationalism', *The Economist*, 7–13 February 2009.

[24] See JK Galbraith, *The Affluent Society* (5th edn, London: Penguin, 1998).

Returning to the topic of our book, this volatile economic, political and social background, offers the opportunity for a *conceptual clarification* which is fundamental for the advantage analysis.

B. Economic and non-economic activities: a conceptual clarification

Liberalization and privatization have led to a crucial redefinition of the public presence in the economy. It is often said that governments have changed their role from providers to regulators.[25] Many activities, such as the provision of infrastructure or public services, which were typically supplied by the government, and traditionally considered public, have at various stages increasingly involved private actors.

The evolution of the public intervention in the economy offers an opportunity for a conceptual clarification between (i) those activities that are truly non-economic because they *would not* be carried out, even in principle, by private agents, and (ii) those that, although involving a public interest and thus the responsibility of the State, are economic because they *can* take place in a market scenario.

This difference is crucial for the operation of the advantage analysis because it tells us what activity is subject to the market, its logic and rules, and what activity is not. A brief exposition of some basics of welfare economics, and in particular the distinction between public and private goods, may be useful to better understand this important conceptual, and operational, divide.[26]

Public and private goods

Economics teaches us two key concepts, those of *public* and *private* goods. Public goods are those goods or services which, if provided, are open to use by all members of society. Conversely, private goods are any goods or services which, if used by one individual or firm, are not available to others. More specifically, public goods are characterized by the fact that it is not possible to exclude any individual from their benefits without incurring high costs (this is the property of *excludability*). Another characteristic, less significant for the purposes of this analysis, is that of non-rival consumption.[27]

The importance of the distinction between public and private goods is that, assuming that private agents normally act rationally and not altruistically, public

[25] See, eg, G Majone, 'The Rise of the Regulatory State in Europe' (1994) West European Politics 77; A La Spina and G Majone, *Lo Stato Regolatore* (Bologna: Il Mulino, 2000).

[26] The following exposition draws from JE Stiglitz, Economics of the Public Sector (3rd edn, New York: Norton, 2000) chapters 6 and 8. For a quick reference to the basic concepts used in the text, the reader is directed to J Black, *Oxford Dictionary of Economics* (2nd edn, Oxford: Oxford University Press, 2002).

[27] This means that public goods can be used simultaneously by more persons without this causing any particular additional cost.

goods are *not* normally supplied by the private sector, mainly because individuals cannot be excluded from, and hence charged for, their use. For this reason, they are considered a paradigmatic example of market failure justifying public intervention.

Crucially, *pure* public goods, ie those goods or services that fully satisfy both properties above, ie non-excludability and non-rival consumption, are rare, the classic examples being defence, lighthouses, and street-lighting. The large majority of goods and services should be regarded as private since there are usually means to exclude access to, and charge for, their use. In other words, most of these goods and services can be provided by the private sector.

It is true, however, that the concept of 'public good' is often used in a more general fashion. In this usage, it refers to those situations where, for various reasons, there is a lack of private initiative and the result is that the relevant goods or services are not offered in the market.[28]

Publicly provided private goods

Certain cases, mainly involving *public services* (and often significant *infrastructures* to supply them), are more controversial.

Goods or services that, strictly speaking, may be considered private goods—because exclusion is possible—have often been directly supplied by the public. These are so-called 'publicly provided private goods'. Leaving aside the political, cultural or ideological reasons, which may have an impact on this choice, according to standard economic reasoning the provision of *private goods* by the government may be justified for either *efficiency* or *equity* reasons.

Some examples illustrate this point. The private sector may run hospitals and schools or universities. However, there is usually a large marginal cost associated with supplying additional individuals. This may result in *high prices* being charged to patients and students. The government may thus think that the general interest requires that it should provide these services directly, and for a lower fee or indeed free of charge. This is an *equity* justification.

The existence of increasing returns of scale[29] may make markets not competitive because economic efficiency requires that there is only a limited number of players. In some industries, called natural monopolies,[30] the increasing returns of scale are *so* important that the market can support only one firm. The creation of a substantial infrastructure, usually a network, to provide the service may involve

[28] In the following analysis, we refer mainly to the more precise notion discussed above. When we refer to the broader usage, we will duly note this.

[29] Where productivity increases with output; put simply, the cost declines when production increases.

[30] Notable examples are some public utilities and often transportation.

considerable sunk costs.[31] Although the marginal additional cost for supplying the actual service may be relatively insignificant, the sunk costs associated with the network creation may represent a substantial investment as well as a crucial barrier to entry for would-be competitors.[32] The incumbent may thus be in the position to abuse its monopolistic power and exploit consumers with high prices. This failure of competition is an *efficiency* justification for the public provision of what are, in general, private goods.

It is worth repeating the crucial point. In all these cases, either for equity or efficiency reasons, the government may decide to provide goods and services that the private sector may well provide. Alternative (private) ways of providing them may indeed be possible. As the liberalization/privatization trend clearly shows, the private sector has been increasingly involved in their supply. However, to ensure more efficient or equitable outcomes, governments may still intervene, complementing private production with regulation and/or subsidization (and taxation).

A good example is that of 'universal service obligations'. The government may wish to ensure that certain essential services should be offered at affordable prices and be accessible to everybody. If the private supplier is not in a position to guarantee these conditions (for example, in the case of postal services, because mail delivery in remote areas is particularly costly and hence too expensive to provide), some form of public intervention may be needed. Otherwise, neither the necessary infrastructure nor service will be provided.

We can concentrate on the provision of the service because it is its economic viability which is crucial (and which directly influences the decision to create or extend the network). The government may decide that a uniform price be offered to all consumers throughout the country. In this case, the financial viability of the supplier will in principle be ensured by internal cross-subsidization, between those users that pay more and those that pay less than the cost for the service. So far, no public intervention is necessarily present. The government *may* however need to intervene if there is a risk that other operators decide to enter the market and 'cream off' the most profitable part of the business (in the example of postal services, urban areas) by charging often considerably lower prices than the incumbent. The public tool to ensure the financial feasibility of the uniform price may thus be to grant an exclusive right to the supplier, ie a statutory monopoly in the relevant business. An alternative may be direct subsidization, more commonly to the supplier of the service than to the user.

[31] That is costs that cannot be recovered by the undertaking if it ceases operation even in the long run.

[32] Arguably, in some cases, the costs of a network or infrastructure may be so high to simply make its creation financially and economically impossible for the private sector.

The example of 'universal service obligations' is particularly instructive because it shows that, whereas *in general* the private sector may well deliver the relevant services, there may still be a need for further public intervention if, mainly for equity reasons, the private sector is required to supply them *at certain conditions*.

It is the importance given to these regulatory conditions that explains the divergence between those who consider these services to be private goods and those who regard them public goods.

The author's preference is for the first reading, and its more abstract approach. Like in the case of education and health, these services *may in principle* be performed by the private sector which, can exclude from, and charge for, their use. It is the resulting price which may be not acceptable in the end, by the government and/or the users, and may justify public intervention. In other words, it is an *equity* reason which justifies either their direct provision by the government, or the imposition of certain standards and obligations and hence some form of public intervention to assist the private sector to supply them accordingly.[33]

Two lessons for the advantage analysis

The previous examination offers two valuable lessons for the advantage analysis of public intervention in the economy.

The first is that the distinction between *economic* and *non-economic* activities, and market and normative benchmarks, should follow the distinction between private and public goods.

Admittedly, this distinction is not always entirely clear. On the one hand, we may have cases where, out of altruism or ostentation, private agents do provide public goods. But this seems to represent more the exception than the rule. On the other hand, and most importantly, the boundary may depend on the circumstances of the case at hand, and on the more general context which may change, and rapidly. It has thus been consistently noted that, far from being absolute, the distinction between private and public goods is a matter of 'degree'.[34] The concepts of public and universal service (which are often crucial to the distinction) are 'dynamic and flexible' and should be 'redefined periodically in order to be adapted to the social, economic and technological environment'.[35] Despite these uncertainties, and inevitable blur, the author believes that the distinction provides a sound and sufficiently reliable standard to distinguish between non-economic and economic activities for the purposes of the advantage analysis.

[33] It should be underlined that, so far, we have talked about pricing but there is also another important variable in the equation, which is the *quality* of the goods and services supplied.

[34] JE Stiglitz, *Economics of the Public Sector* (3rd edn, New York: Norton, 2000) 134–5; J Black, *Oxford Dictionary of Economics* (2nd edn, Oxford: Oxford University Press, 2002) 369.

[35] Commission White Paper on Services of General Interest, COM(2004) 374, 12 May 2004, para 3.3.

The second important lesson is that the concept of *responsibility of the government* cannot be equated to that of *(inherent) governmental activity.* The example of infrastructures is clear in this regard. These are crucial to the socio-economic development of a country and are often necessary for the supply of public services. Being in the public interest, the proper planning, creation and maintenance of infrastructures (and the relevant public services) is undoubtedly part of the *responsibility* of governments. This does not however necessarily mean that they have to be provided by the government since they can in principle often be provided by private agents as well.

C. Public interest between scope and justification

The previous examination of the ways through which the public interest may be pursued gives the opportunity to recall one of the main recurring themes of the book, which is the analysis of the interplay between *scope* and *justification.*[36]

This issue, which has a huge political and legal impact, looks at the role played by the public interest at the various stages of the legal analysis of the regulation of subsidies and State aids.

Phrased differently, the question is about *what is covered* by the rules and *what is permitted.* Two scenarios are possible. In the first, the conduct is not caught at all by the rules. The pursuit of a public interest, which is considered at the very preliminary stage of the definition, leads to the conclusion that there is no advantage. In the second scenario, the presence of a public interest does not preclude the conduct from granting an advantage. If the other requirements of the definition are fulfilled, the measure falls within the scope of application of the rules and, in some cases, is prohibited. The pursuit of a public interest may be recognized at a further stage of the analysis, when other provisions recognizing that the subsidy is justified come into play, and the conduct may eventually be permitted.

The 'legal and political' difference between the two scenarios becomes vivid when it is applied to the two legal systems under examination.

In the WTO it makes a great difference to hold that a measure does not constitute a subsidy in the first place or to consider it a subsidy which is (was) non-actionable. Whilst in the former case the measure falls outside the scope of application of the SCM Agreement altogether (and, if any, may be governed by other provisions), in the latter it is still subject to the SCM Agreement and to obligations, controls, and actions thereunder (notification, surveillance, and, quite crucially until—and provided that—the category of non-actionability is resurrected, to unilateral and multilateral actions). Not only the substantive but also the procedural, institutional and constitutional implications of this distinction cannot pass unnoticed.

The situation in the EC is similar. The case where the measure does not confer an advantage and hence cannot be a State aid is very different from that where there

[36] This has been extensively discussed in section IV of chapter 1.

is a State aid which is in principle prohibited but which is eventually 'compatible with the common market' As above, this difference does not only concern the substantive rules that are applicable (in the first scenario State aid rules do not apply, in the second case they do). Most significantly, it has an impact on the procedural, institutional and eventually constitutional setting of the EC system of State aid control. It should be recalled that, in the EC system of State aid control, it is only for the European Commission to authorize planned State aid measures. This is done through a complex balancing between distortions of competition and other positive effects in the public interest. In this context, Member States' power to influence the Commission's decision is very limited.

Returning to the distinction between economic and non-economic activity, this determination does not have a direct impact on whether or not the measure falls within the scope of application of the law.[37] In the context of the advantage analysis, the goal of the classification is the identification of the appropriate benchmark—market or normative—to test the conduct at issue and eventually determine whether or not it derogates from the appropriate norm.

The issue of whether or not the conduct is economic is not however completely neutral.

One distinction arises immediately. Whereas in the case of non-economic conduct the benchmark is the general rule in the area which the government itself defined, the standard to test a public economic activity, ie the market, is by definition external to any form of interference. Further, it cannot be denied that to define a conduct as economic, and to subject it to market logic, might actually result in a stricter standard to be adhered to, at least in some circumstances. This may for example depend on how abstract/concrete the benchmark actually applied is.

With more specific regard to the scope/justification issue, the economic classification makes the identification, and separation, of public policy considerations, easier. This is more difficult when we are fully in the realm of non-economic conduct where public motives are inherently more pervasive. A public interest objective is more likely to be invoked at the level of the advantage analysis, arguing that there is no discrimination or derogation and, consequently, that the measure falls outside the scope of the rules.

The following chapters analyse the role played by the public interest, in the context of the advantage analysis with respect to both economic and non-economic governmental activities.

[37] Unlike in other contexts. See, for examples, the definition of 'service' and 'undertaking' under various provisions of EC law. A good analysis can be found in the Opinion of Advocate General Maduro in C-205/03P *FENIN*. cf also the definition of 'service' in the GATS. See chapter 11, section II.C.

8

Economic activity and the advantage analysis

Whilst chapters 9 and 10 concentrate on the advantage analysis of the forms of conduct that are non-economic and hence inherently public, such as taxation and regulation, this chapter focuses on the economic activity of governments.

The first part deals with the general principle of the market. The focus is on the complexities and difficulties involved in the application of the actual benchmarks derived from this paradigm. In the second part, two case-studies explain the relationship between public intervention in the economy and market benchmarks. The attempt is to show, in the current context of redefinition of the roles of public and private actors in the economy, the interplay of two contrasting forces and their critical impact on the advantage analysis. A shift from complexity discourse to outspoken criticism is the subject of the final part. The fundamental critiques about the possibility, consistency and, ultimately, the legitimacy of using market benchmarks to test the economic conduct of public bodies are examined, and we conclude with an attempt to provide a balanced rehabilitation of the market paradigm.

I. The market: a complex paradigm

A. The adoption of the principle

The market is one of the most important principles of the advantage analysis. Although based on an arguably solid rationale, it will however become immediately apparent that its application is not free from complexities and difficulties.

From reticence to consolidation

Article 1.1 of the SCM provides that a subsidy shall be deemed to exist if a 'financial contribution' or a 'form of income or price support' confers a 'benefit'. However, the concept of 'benefit' is not developed at all in the SCM agreement, seemingly as a result of disagreement between the negotiating parties, some seeking to refer to commercial benchmarks, others to the cost to the subsidizing government, others to the recipients of the subsidy.[1] This can be contrasted with the 'financial contribution'

[1] P Low, 'The Treatment of Subsidies in the WTO Framework' in CD Ehlermann and M Everson, *European Competition Law Annual 1999: Selected Issues in the Field of State Aids* (Oxford: Hart Publishing, 2001) 103, 114–15.

requirement which, albeit not entirely unambiguous, is highly elaborated. Although important issues, such as the cost to government and the treatment of certain regulatory measures, could not be resolved during the negotiations, it was not difficult to codify with a certain degree of precision at least the forms of financial contribution that were commonly regarded as subsidy in the GATT.[2] Article 87(1) of the EC generally prohibits 'any aid' which 'favours' certain undertakings or the production of certain goods. Like the SCM, the EC Treaty does define an 'aid' and, in particular, the advantage inherent in it. Such a definition cannot be found in the previous, and now expired, ECSC Treaty.

A simple, and at the same time general, explanation has already been suggested in the previous chapters. These two treaties of the 1950s share the same reticence, and immaturity, with respect to the definition of public subsidies that can be found in the context of the GATT, signed only a few years earlier. This silence not only concerned the forms of action that should be regarded as a subsidy or an aid but inevitably affected another central—and *equally elusive*—element of the definition, the advantage.

When the legislator is silent, it is for administrative and judicial bodies, which are called to apply the rules, to provide some clarification. The *market* has consistently been referred to as the standard to test the public activity in the market, thus becoming, despite the difficulties and criticisms which we are about to examine, a true *paradigm* in the advantage analysis.

Some examples of this recognition may be provided. We may commence with the GATT. As our first example, in the early 1980s, the US and the EC were confronted by the 'steel war', which was the second time the issue of the definition of subsidy had arisen in the global context.[3] Although GATT dispute settlement was never involved, there was great controversy over the application of 'commercial considerations' to establish whether various forms of financial assistance into State-owned enterprises constituted a countervailable subsidy.[4] Our second example took place just a few months before the advent of the WTO when a Panel report was issued in the *US—Lead and Bismuth I* dispute. This report was never adopted but it contains significant findings which support the use of commercial criteria to test various forms of public economic activity.[5]

[2] cf, eg, the examples of domestic subsidies in Article 11(3) of the Tokyo Round Subsidies Code.

[3] The first time being the GATT *DISC* litigation at the beginning of the 1970s. See chapter 9.

[4] See C Barshefsky, AL Mattice, and WL Martin II, 'Government Equity Participation in State-Owned Enterprises: An Analysis of the Carbon Steel Countervailing Duty Cases' (1983) Law and Policy in International Business 1101; MF Dominick, 'Countervailing State Aids to Steel: A Case for International Consensus' (1984) Common Market Law Review 355; F Benyon and J Bourgeois, 'The European Community—United States Steel Arrangement' (1984) Common Market Law Review 305; GC Hufbauer and J Shelton Erb, *Subsidies in International Trade* (Cambridge, Massachusetts: MIT Press, 1984) 100–2; JHJ Bourgeois (ed), *Subsidies and International trade—A European Lawyers' Perspective* (Deventer – Boston: Kluwer, 1991) passim.

[5] See section III.B below.

It was not until the advent of the WTO that the first sweeping formulation of the market as general standard was made.

In *Canada—Aircraft*, the market was referred to as the 'only logical basis' (Panel) and 'an appropriate basis for comparison' (Appellate Body) to establish the benefit. The Appellate Body noted that 'the marketplace provides an appropriate basis for comparison in determining whether a "benefit" has been "conferred", because the trade-distorting potential of a "financial contribution" can be identified by determining whether the recipient has received a "financial contribution" on terms more favourable than those available to the recipient in the market.'[6] Numerous findings of the European Court of Justice echo this definition. In one of the most quoted we read: 'in order to determine whether a State measure constitutes aid, it is necessary to establish whether the recipient receives an economic advantage which it would not have obtained under normal market conditions.'[7] The attentive reader will have noticed the striking similarity of the language of the two courts. A true tribute to the market paradigm.

First comments

Conceptually, the reference to the market is no more than an application of the general and core paradigm of the advantage analysis, ie that the advantage should result from a *derogation from the norm*. In the case of economic activity, the *norm* is represented by the market. Obviously, findings whereby the market is the 'only logical basis' or 'an appropriate basis for comparison' can be correct only with respect to the economic activity of governments. Borrowing from the second Opinion of Advocate General Léger in the famous *Altmark* case, 'it appears . . . that in the field of State aid the Court distinguishes between two categories of situation: those where the intervention of the State is of economic nature and those where it forms part of the exercise of public power'.[8] Different criteria—*economic* or *normative*—apply to the two different types of conduct and the derogation test accordingly takes different shapes in both legal systems.

More interestingly, if the market should be the norm in the field of economic activities, the Appellate Body's express reliance on the 'trade-distorting potential' of the financial contribution as *the* justification for the use of market benchmarks seems to reveal that the assessment should be based only on those economic considerations that may indicate distortions in the market, more particularly to the competitive process.

The further implication is that, inasmuch as the distorting impact (or, to put it more clearly, the 'potential' as the Appellate Body simply states) of the subsidy remains, the role to be played at this stage by any *public policy objectives* pursued by

[6] Paragraph 157.
[7] Case C-39/94 *SFEI v La Poste*, para 60.
[8] Paragraph 20.

the measure can be quite limited. This interim finding, which is of crucial importance for the advantage analysis and more generally the definition of subsidy, will be thoroughly addressed below.

Finally, the notion of the market still remains a general principle. In order to be fully operative, it needs to be developed into precise benchmarks, applicable to the various forms of economic activity carried out in the market. This is the focus of the next paragraph, and it is at this level that the paradigm begins to show its complexity.

B. Market benchmarks: complex decisions, difficult reviews

The complexity of business decisions

As the conduct in the market can be varied (eg equity and debt financing, guarantees, purchase or sale transactions) so are the benchmarks which define whether that conduct is commercially sound. Within this diversity, two variables stand out as crucial in any business decisions, the *risk* of the investment and the expected *remuneration* for that risk.

The complexity of commercial decisions, and of their subsequent scrutiny, can be understood at two different levels, one objective and one subjective. On the one hand, the key variables of risk and remuneration are significantly affected by many other factors and by the various circumstances of the transaction at hand. Information may be scarce, time limited and the context may change, and quickly. As a result, those involved in commerce have to make difficult economic, financial and managerial assessments in a complex and dynamic, competitive environment.

On the other hand, although sophisticated technical tools are increasingly being developed to make sense of this objective complexity, ultimately the decision-making process cannot be solely described as *objective* and *rational*. The *subjective*, one should say human, factor plays a significant role. Ultimately, it all depends on the personal judgement of the entrepreneur or manager which is based on his/her intuition and experience.

Without necessarily adhering to the radical criticism examined below (market forces and its operators are *not* predictable; hence there are *no* rules that could be followed), clearly business is far from being an exact science (or a science at all). Its decisions naturally require a good element of not fully ponderable discretion, and vagaries may unexpectedly impact the calculated and much aspired goal.

Normative latitude: 'standards' vs 'rules'

The complexity of business decisions cannot be fully captured by the legal provisions setting forth the relevant benchmarks.

This is not just a matter of inadequate drafting. The problem is more radical than that and depends on the fact that the process underlying commercial decisions itself is so multifaceted and variable that virtually any criterion—irrespective of its precision—can become really meaningful *only* when it is applied in practice. In other words, if the starting point is certainly given by good, precise and clear criteria, shaped around sound indicators, it is only a case-by-case analysis that eventually allows to determine whether the actual decision is commercially sound.[9]

The European Commission shows awareness of this flexibility when it underlines that various financial and economic factors have to be analysed and balanced to determine whether the contribution is commercially sound. Another good example of the recognition of this latitude inherent in commercial decisions can be found in Article 14 of the SCM which provides guidelines to calculate the amount of the subsidy in the context of countervailing duty procedures and which, by underlining the circumstances under which a given form of governmental action 'shall not be considered as *conferring* a benefit' (emphasis added), can clearly be used as relevant context for the interpretation of the term 'benefit' under Article 1.1(b) of the SCM as well.[10] These guidelines refer to concepts such as 'usual investment practice', the difference between amounts actually paid and payable on the market, and 'adequate remuneration'. In their generality, they do not constrain the complexity of business decisions. They require a specific enquiry. To take another illustration, to say that the expected remuneration for a capital injection into a company is defined by the rate of return on equity[11] is certainly more precise but, again, it cannot hide the fact that what is required in the instant case is the determination of the actual rate which is a complex exercise involving complex economic, financial and managerial assessments and, as noted above, involving an ineluctable element of discretion.

To sum up, the complexity of business activity can only be tested by benchmarks that, from a normative perspective, should be translated into 'standards', rather than 'rules', ie on rather general provisions that should be applied on a case-by-case basis.[12]

[9] See Commission Communication, Application of Articles 92 and 93 of the EEC Treaty and of Article 5 of Commission Directive 80/723/EEC to public undertakings in the manufacturing sector, OJ C307, 13.11.1993, 3, para 37.

[10] See, eg, Panel, *Canada—Aircraft*, para 9.113, Appellate Body, id, paras 155–8. cf also P Didier, *WTO Trade Instruments in EU Law—Commercial Policy Instruments: Dumping, Subsidies, Safeguards, Public Procurement* (London: Cameron May, 1999) 220, n 33.

[11] Panel, *Canada—Aircraft*, para 9.165. In the EC see, eg, The Commission's Position, Application of Articles 92 and 93 [now 87 and 88] of the EEC Treaty to public authorities' holdings, Bulletin EC 9-1984, para 3.3, and the Commission Communication, Application of Articles 92 and 93 of the EEC Treaty and of Article 5 of Commission Directive 80/723/EEC to public undertakings in the manufacturing sector, OJ C307, 13.11.1993, 3, paras 35, 43 and 44. For two cases that offer a revealing example of the complexity of the determination of the rate of return of a public investment see Case T-296/97 *Alitalia I*; Case T-301/01 *Alitalia II*.

[12] cf L Kaplow, 'Rules Versus Standards: An Economic Analysis' (1992) Duke Law Journal 557.

The review of business decisions

The reader has probably gleaned from these brief remarks that the author's purpose is not to provide a detailed analysis of the application of the various market benchmarks, and of the quite often highly technical tools that are used in market analysis, but rather (i) to highlight the degree of *complexity* of commercial *decisions* and, as a direct consequence, (ii) the *difficulty* of their *review* by administrative and judicial bodies.

In this regard, it should not be forgotten that what is at issue in most of the cases is the review by an administrative or judicial body of an investment decision that a public body has taken, or wishes to take. The complexity of business decisions is inevitably reflected in their review making it a particularly difficult task. The role of the examining body is certainly to check whether the decision at issue is commercially sound. However, the (objective/subjective) complexity outlined above should be duly taken into consideration.

It is thus commonly accepted that any review should be based only on the information that was, or could have been, available to the investor at the moment of the business decision (*ex ante* assessment). The premise is that the commercial environment is dynamic and that the success or failure of the venture may well depend on changes of circumstances which could not have been predicted when the decision was made.

Most importantly, business decisions—it should be repeated—are not calculations but *judgements*. They naturally imply discretion. This factor should be taken into account by the examining body which should resist the temptation to substitute the public body's business judgements with its own. In other words, if administrative or judicial bodies should certainly be controllers, they cannot pretend to be entrepreneurs.

Market benchmarks: examples of complexity

Before focusing on two case-studies which attempt to explain the interaction between public intervention in the economy and identification of the appropriate market benchmark, the following paragraphs aim to provide the reader with a flavour of the difficulty of application of market benchmarks. The approach is intentionally more descriptive than critical. Not much commentary is needed to highlight the point: complexity. In the exposition, we draw particularly on the abundant indications offered by the EC case-law whose validity may safely be extended to WTO law.

(a) Diversity of investment objectives

There are different types of investors, and the circumstances of the investment may change. In short, investment objectives may be disparate and varied. As a result, the two key variables of risk and remuneration indicated above may be perceived differently in the various cases.

One of the most apparent distinctions is that between ordinary investors, who aim to realize a profit in the relatively short term, and holding companies or groups of undertakings, which pursue a 'structural policy' and are generally 'guided by prospects of profitability in the longer term'.[13] Equity investment should also be distinguished from debt financing because only the former involves direct participation in the business. The application of market benchmarks to capital injections may thus be particularly complex since the 'value of the investment' is much more 'dependent on the personal goals of the investor'.[14]

The existence of a vested interest in the undertaking is another notable factor which has an impact on the evaluation of risk and remuneration. The fact that the investor is already a shareholder, a lender or a guarantor of the undertaking makes their situation completely different from that of one who does not have any interest in the relevant company and is considering whether to invest in it. This becomes particularly clear when the company is in difficulties. The 'owner' of the company may accept a lower return when this is necessary to preserve his investment. He may even consider covering the losses of his subsidiary for a limited period in order to enable it either to reorganize and become profitable again or to close down under the best possible conditions,[15] or to minimize the costs which he might incur as guarantor and sole shareholder.[16] To prevent a higher liability an investor may even decide to make a fresh investment.[17]

How investment objectives can change according to the circumstances is nicely illustrated by the example of loans. There is a fundamental difference between the case where the loan is negotiated and granted and the case where, after the loan relationship has been entered into, the debtor is in default. In the former, the investor is motivated by profit. Things *may* change however when the contractual relationship is already in place. The borrower may not pay or, more significantly, might become unable to pay. The default of the borrower usually triggers the application of penalties or interests higher than those normally due. The creditor's goal is *still* to make a profit out of the transaction. However, if the debtor is in difficulty and is not able to cope with the payments originally agreed, the investment objective changes. It is no longer to make a profit but to avoid a loss or at least to recover part of the credit.[18] The debt may need to be rescheduled and the interest charged may be different (usually lower) than that agreed when the loan was initially granted. Similarly, agreement to reduce the debts of a company in difficulty may be eco-

[13] C-305/89, *Alfa Romeo*, paras 19 and 20.

[14] C Koenig and A Bartosch, 'EC State Aid Law reviewing Equity Capital Injections and Loan Grants by the Public Sector: A Comparative Analysis' (2000) European Competition Law Review, 377, 383.

[15] Case C-303/88 *ENI-Lanerossi*, para 21.

[16] Case T-323/99 *INMA*, para 100.

[17] For an interesting example see Case T-98/00 *Linde*.

[18] Case C-342/96 *Tubacex*, paras 48 and 49; Case C-246/97 *DMT*, paras 24 and 25. See the discussion on the 'regulation of debt' in the EC context in chapter 10, section III.B.

nomically justified, in particular when, in the event of insolvency of the debtor, the creditor's loss would be considerably higher.[19]

Two remarks can conclude this paragraph. From the perspective of the review of the investment decisions, on the assumption that economic actors usually behave similarly in comparable situations, the consideration of what other investors do in the transaction at hand may be relevant. Thus, even making allowances for the discretion underlying any business judgement, the participation of other (especially private) investors in the operation may indicate its commercial soundness, in particular if their contribution is on equal terms and of real economic significance.[20]

The second, more intriguing, comment focuses on a crucial point but is limited to flagging an issue which is dealt with exhaustively below.[21] The issue is whether private investors may be motivated also by considerations that are not strictly economic, such as employment or regional development, and, if so, to what extent. This issue is of particular importance because public investors should by definition pursue public interest objectives. The tension here is clear. It is thus important to understand what role, if any, is played by these considerations at the level of the advantage analysis.

(b) Restructuring of companies in difficulties and investment of large sums

Two cases pose particular problems when it comes to making a business decision to provide financing and to subsequently assess it.[22] In these cases the evaluation of the risk of the investment and of its remuneration may be especially difficult.

The first concerns the financing of loss-making companies. We have already seen the impact that a situation of difficulty may have on investment objectives when the investor has a vested interest in the company. This paragraph builds on those considerations, but focuses on the more specific problem of investments aimed at the *restructuring* of a company in difficulty. The issue is whether the support is really aimed at reorganizing the undertaking, or whether it merely represents a means to keep an ailing and unprofitable undertaking alive. The answer depends on the assessment of the numerous conditions of the restructuring.[23] This is a very difficult assessment. There are several different elements to evaluate and balance in order to reach a decision and these elements may be judged differently by investors.

[19] Case T-123/97 *Salomon v Commission*, para 68.

[20] P Didier, *WTO Trade Instruments in EU Law—Commercial Policy Instruments: Dumping, Subsidies, Safeguards, Public Procurement* (London: Cameron May, 1999) 225. By contrast investment decisions of employees may not be significant as they may be motivated more by the desire to ensure the survival of their jobs than by prospects of profitability of the company: see Case T-296/97 *Alitalia I*, para 83.

[21] Section III.B.

[22] M Parish, 'On the Private Investor Principle' (2003) European Law Review 70, 71.

[23] Such as the economic, financial and managerial situation of the company and the market, the soundness of the restructuring plan, etc.

The second case where it is particularly difficult to determine whether a private investor would have stepped in is when large sums of money are involved. Again, this may occur when the restructuring of big groups is implicated. The fact that the financial resources necessary for the restructuring may be considerable is a further element that adds to the difficulty of an already difficult assessment. A case where the 'money' factor comes into special relevance is when it is necessary to build big infrastructures, such as extensive networks.[24]

(c) Ambivalence of market indicators

Market indicators, such as price and quantity, are not always reliable, particularly if considered separately. The assessment of whether we have a normal commercial transaction requires the consideration of all the relevant factors.

Normally, the procedure followed for the sale is important to establish whether the transaction is commercially sound.

The price resulting from the sale through an open and transparent tender procedure to the highest bidder will generally be held to be the market price. Although in a different factual setting, the celebrated *Almark* case, which focused on the procurement of local bus services, has provided a powerful confirmation of the importance of the procedure to exclude the existence of an advantage.[25] Crucially, the government here was not selling but buying, and the test was thus not about *profit* but *efficiency*.[26] This does not detract from the fact that the rationale—the transaction process has a fundamental impact in determining that the price is commercially sound—is the same. The case is similar with respect to shares or other securities traded on the stock exchange. The market price is the price at which the relevant shares or securities are traded.[27] An alternative procedure may be the evaluation by an independent expert.[28]

This is not the end of the story however. The payment of the market price, even though following a certain procedure which should in principle guarantee the correct operation of market forces, may not be enough to exclude that the transaction is not commercial. An analysis of the EC case-law is particular useful in this regard. The first warning was given in the *Bremer Vulkan* case where the Court underlined that sometimes considering the stock market price, without adequate explanation, as the sole determining factor of the value of shares may be

[24] The subsidy issues raised by infrastructures are numerous. See section II.B in this chapter. See also chapters 9 and 10 when 'public goods' are analysed.

[25] See Case C-280/00, para 95. See also the Opinion of Advocate General Jacobs in Case C-126/01 *GEMO*, para 119.

[26] M Hansen, A Van Ysendyck, and S Zühlke, 'The Coming of Age of EC State Aid Law: A Review of the Principal Developments in 2002 and 2003' (2004) European Competition Law Review 202, 204, n 16.

[27] ie sold at the price determined by the cumulative demand of buyers.

[28] cf Commission Communication on State aid elements in sales of land and buildings by public authorities, OJ C 209 of 10.07.1997, 3.

'too formal, rigid and restrictive'.[29] In other words, to rely only on one market indicator, and an important one such as the price, may not be enough, if the context demands a more complex analysis. The advantage may be conferred by other circumstances of the case.

A good illustration of this was given in two decisions of the Court of Justice. In the *BAI* and *P & O European Ferries* cases the issue was whether the conclusion by a public authority of an agreement to purchase travel vouchers for ferry travels between Spain and the UK at the market price could be regarded as State aid. Contrary to the Commission's finding, the Court of First Instance found that this was the case. In particular, the Court made it clear that 'the mere fact that a Member State purchases goods and services on market conditions is not sufficient for that transaction to constitute a commercial transaction concluded under conditions which a private investor would have accepted, or in other words a normal commercial transaction, if it turns out that the State did not have an actual need for those goods and services.'[30]

In other words, it seems that variables such as price (and even quantity) may not be fully significant if the actual decision to purchase goods or services from the market does not correspond to a real and actual need of the buyer.[31] In these cases, the result would be the grant of a clear *out-of-the market* advantage to the supplier that would be able to dispose of goods or services which—under normal market conditions—would not have been placed. Although it is not clear whether the fact that the purchase was concluded without a competitive procedure might have had an impact on the outcome, and despite some initial perplexities, this case-law seems to be substantially correct, particularly because it reminds us of the complexity of market transactions.

In conclusion, the advantage analysis of economic activity must be a comprehensive one which takes into account all relevant factors, among which the market price is an important but not an exclusive one. The ambivalence of certain market indicators, and in particular price, becomes apparent in the next section when an additional element of complexity—the public intervention in the economy—is inserted into the equation.

II. The interaction between public intervention in the economy and market

The previous section has shown the complexity inherent in business decisions and, of greatest importance from the perspective of subsidy control, in their assessment.

[29] For another interesting example, see Joined Cases C-329/93, C-62/95 and C-63/95 *Bremer Vulkan*, para 36.

[30] Joined Cases T-116/01 and T-118/01 *P&O*, para 117; see also Case T-14/96 *BAI*, para 74 et seq.

[31] Although the quantity itself may be a good yardstick of the absence of need.

This section analyses a further possible element of complexity in the advantage analysis of economic activity which is given by the *public intervention in the economy*, expression which generally refers to any public conduct—be it economic or not—that may have an impact on the market. Two case-studies, which emphasize different perspectives, and provide different teachings, are examined.

A. Case-study 1: influence of the public intervention in the economy on market analysis

Four WTO disputes are particularly significant in analysing the effect that various forms of public intervention in the economy may have on the identification of the appropriate market benchmark. The analysis touches both the SCM Agreement and the Agreement on Agriculture (AG). The brief exposition of the main arguments and findings in the various disputes is followed by some comments.

Regulation: Canada—Dairy *(Article 21(5) I)*

The first case is *Canada—Dairy* (Article 21(5) I). What was under examination was the definition of 'payments' in Article 9.1(c) of the AG. Drawing on the subsidy definition in the SCM Agreement, and in particular the 'benefit' under Article 1.1(b) of the SCM, the Appellate Body confirmed that the notion of 'payment' is meaningful only through a comparison with a market benchmark.[32]

That said, two findings are particularly significant for our analysis. First, the Appellate Body noted that it was not correct to consider the domestic price, fixed by the government in the context of a heavily regulated market, as a proper benchmark for determining whether the lower price of milk to processors for export represented an advantage. Secondly, in a clear exposition of micro-economics fundamentals, the Appellate Body indicated that the price is not the only useful market indicator. In its words,

> [a]lthough the proceeds from sales at domestic or world market prices represent two possible measures of the value of milk to the producers, we do not see these as the only possible measures of this value. For any economic operator, the production of goods or services involves an investment of economic resources. In the case of a milk producer, production requires an investment in fixed assets, such as land, cattle and milking facilities, and an outlay to meet variable costs, such as labour, animal feed and health-care, power and administration. These fixed and variable costs are the total amount which the producer must spend in order to produce the milk and the total amount it must recoup, in the long-term, to avoid making losses. To the extent that the producer charges prices that do not recoup the total cost of production, over time, it sustains a loss which must be financed from some other source, possibly 'by virtue of governmental action'.[33]

[32] Appellate Body, *Canada—Dairy* (Article 21(5) I), para 87. See also *US—FSC*, para 136.

[33] Appellate Body, *Canada—Dairy* (Article 21(5) I), para 87.

In a nutshell, the impact of the public intervention in the domestic market, in the form of heavy regulation, made the reference to the prices prevailing therein not reliable for the analysis in the export market. The use of another market benchmark, that is the costs of production, was therefore necessary.[34]

Economic and other policies: US—Lead and Bismuth II *and* US—Countervailing Measures on Certain EC Products

The issue of the impact of public intervention in the market, and of the significance of prices derived from it, came out again in the *US—Lead and Bismuth II* and *US—Countervailing Measures on Certain EC Products* disputes with respect to privatizations.

In *US—Countervailing Measures on Certain EC Products* the US had imposed countervailing duties on imports from privatized companies alleging that the benefit of the subsidies granted prior to privatization had 'passed through'. One of the legal issues was whether the payment of a fair market value for the company, in the context of an arm's length transaction and in compliance with commercial considerations, exhausted the benefit of subsidies previously received.[35] The same question arose in a previous dispute, *US—Lead and Bismuth II*, where the Appellate Body upheld the Panel's conclusion that this was the case but significantly restricted its ruling to 'the particular circumstances of the case' and to 'the facts of the case'.[36]

It is only in the *US—Countervailing Measures on Certain EC Products* dispute, however, that the Appellate Body more vigorously *qualified* the Panel's finding that privatizations at arm's length and for fair market value *always exclude* that the benefit is passed through. The crucial factor was the ability of governments to direct the conditions of the process of privatization, and in particular to influence the sale price, with the result that the latter cannot be considered the outcome of a genuine market process. The Appellate Body held that privatizations at arm's length *may* result in extinguishing a previously conferred benefit but this is *not necessarily* so. In the words of the Geneva-based body:

> the Panel's absolute rule of 'no benefit' may be defensible in the context of transactions between two private parties taking place in reasonably competitive markets; however, it overlooks the ability of governments to obtain certain results from markets by shaping the circumstances and conditions in which markets operate. Privatizations involve complex and long-term investments in which the seller—namely the government—is not necessarily always a passive price taker and, consequently, the 'fair market price' of a state-owned enterprise is not necessarily always unrelated to government action. In privatizations,

[34] See also, within the peculiar situation of a financial transfer within the same economic entity, Appellate Body, *EC—Sugar*, para 267.

[35] This issue is also analysed from the perspective of the identification of the beneficiaries of the subsidy in chapter 12.

[36] Paragraph 74.

governments have the ability, by designing economic and other policies, to influence the circumstances and conditions of the sale so as to obtain a certain market valuation of the enterprise.[37]

The conclusion was that an irrebuttable presumption that privatizations at arm's length and for fair market value always exhausts the benefit is not consistent with WTO law. The benefit may expire, and indeed there is a rebuttable presumption that a benefit ceases to exist after privatizations under those conditions, but inevitably the conclusion depends 'on the facts of each case'.[38]

We leave aside the important debate on whether the price paid is really relevant in the determination of whether a benefit continues to exist, discussion which turns on the distinction between the concept of 'advantage' and 'competitive advantage'.[39] For the present purposes, the crucial finding coming out of these two disputes, which is in line with *Canada—Dairy* (Article 21(5) I), is that prices produced by markets are not always indicative of a genuine market process, particularly when there is a significant public intervention in the economy, be it in the form of 'significant regulation' or, as in the cases at hand in this paragraph, of the 'design of economic and other policies'.

Commercial presence: US—Softwood Lumber IV

What was at issue in the *US—Softwood Lumber IV* dispute was the definition of the appropriate market benchmark following a significant commercial presence of the government in the market. The case is also interesting because—at a more general level—it gave the opportunity to clarify the important concepts of 'market' and

[37] Appellate Body, *US—Countervailing Measures on Certain EC Products*, para 124.

[38] ibid, para 127.

[39] The correlation market price > benefit exhaustion has been criticized with strong and convincing arguments by G Grossman and PC Mavrodis, 'Recurring Misunderstandings of Non Recurring Subsidies' in H Horn and PC Mavroidis (eds), *The WTO Case Law of 2002* (Cambridge: Cambridge University Press, 2005) 78; 'Here Today? Gone Tomorrow?' in H Horn and PC Mavroidis (eds), *The WTO Case Law of 2001* (Cambridge: Cambridge University Press, 2003) 170) and R Diamond, 'Privatization and the Definition of Subsidy: A Critical Study of Appellate Body Texturalism' (2008) Journal of International Economic Law 649. The main argument is that subsidy regulation should not focus on the financial wealth of the owners of a company but rather it should care about whether the competitive position of that firm is (still) advantaged. This remark echoes the already noted concepts of 'advantage' and 'competitive advantage'. The important interpretative question is whether the notion of 'benefit' under Article 1.1. of the SCM should be construed in line with the second concept, possibly through a contextual approach, or whether any 'competitive' assessment should be left at a second stage of the analysis. This is not just an academic point. It may have important practical consequences, particularly in the light of a 'divided' definition of subsidy ('benefit'-'distortion of competition'), and in the context of a 'bifurcated' administration of countervailing duty actions (like the US one). See Diamond (ibid, 674). For further analysis on this issue see chapter 12, section II.B. A final gloss. It should be reminded that the definition of subsidy endorsed in this book does include, although separately, both elements of 'advantage' and 'distortion on competition'. See chapter 1, section III above.

'prevailing market conditions'.[40] Considering these two special traits—effect of significant commercial presence and definition of the notion of market—the findings of this dispute deserve a detailed examination.

In one of the various stages of a never-ending trade contention, the United States had imposed countervailing duties on imports of certain softwood lumber products from Canada. The conferral by Canada of the right to harvest timber in Crown Land was considered a financial contribution in the form of provision of goods (under Article 1.1(a)(1)(iii) of the SCM) to lumber producers.[41]

The issue of interest for our analysis was whether these goods were also provided at less than adequate remuneration thereby conferring a benefit pursuant to Article 14(d) of the SCM.[42]

In its determination the United States Department of Commerce (US DOC) found that the prices of private timber sales in Canada did not represent a commercial market baseline because they were distorted by government intervention. The supply of lumber originating in Crown Land was so dominant in the market that the prices of the few private suppliers were not determined independently and were necessarily depressed and aligned to the lower level of governmental prices. The US DOC therefore used as a benchmark prices of stumpage in certain bordering states in the northern United States, making adjustments to account for differences in conditions between those states and Canadian provinces.

The WTO Dispute Settlement Mechanism was called to determine whether the United States' practice was consistent with Article 14(d) of the SCM which requires that the adequacy of the remuneration in the provision of goods should be determined 'in relation to prevailing market conditions for the good or service in question in the country of provision or purchase (including price, quality, availability, marketability, transportation and other conditions of purchase or sale)'. The main point of disagreement between the United States and Canada was whether it was permissible under that provision for an investigating authority to use a benchmark other than private prices in the country of provision. To address this issue, which technically revolved around the interpretation of the phrase 'in relation to',[43] both Panel and Appellate Body made interesting findings also with

[40] MJ Trebilcock and R Howse, *The Regulation of International Trade* (3rd edn, London: Routledge, 2005) 268.

[41] Panel, *US—Softwood Lumber IV*, paras 7.9–7.30; Appellate Body, *US—Softwood Lumber IV*, paras 46–76.

[42] The problem of the proper pricing of natural resources is not new. GC Hufbauer and J Shelton Erb, *Subsidies in International Trade* (Cambridge, Massachusetts: MIT Press, 1984) 95–9, cite, eg, three US countervailing duty cases of the beginning of the 1980s concerning crude petroleum, natural gas and (again) lumber. The authors ingeniously distinguished between non-transportable and transportable natural resources, concluding that the provision of non-transportable natural resources should not be subject to international scrutiny for the lack of a 'ready standard' (such as a worldwide or national price) to use as a benchmark. Whatever merits this distinction and conclusion may have, lumber is clearly transportable. A benchmark, and a market one, should be found.

[43] Contrary to the Panel, the Appellate Body construed this as not necessarily meaning 'in comparison with' but rather 'as regards' and 'with respect to'.

respect to the concepts of market and market conditions under Article 14(d) of the SCM.

The Panel found that 'prevailing market conditions' refer to the market conditions 'as they exist' or 'which are predominant' in the country of provision.[44] Thus, the United States' argument that the term 'market' means 'fair market value' or market 'undistorted by government intervention' was rejected.[45] In particular, the Panel underlined that 'as long as there are prices determined by independent operators following the principle of supply and demand, even if supply or demand are affected by the government's presence in the market, there is a "market" in the sense of Article 14(d) [of the] SCM Agreement'.[46] This conclusion was not predicated in absolute terms. The Panel appreciated the 'economic logic' of the US' argument, but, against the clear text of Article 14(d), it felt impossible to 'substitute its economic judgment for that of the drafters' of the SCM Agreement.[47]

At the appeal stage, although conceding that the United States' approach, whereby the term 'market conditions' would necessarily imply a market undistorted by the government's financial contribution, was going too far, the Appellate Body underlined that the Panel's interpretation was 'overtly restrictive', and that, in some cases, the prices of the country of provision may not be informative. The Panel itself had provided two examples of situations where it may not be possible to use in-country prices: where the government is the only supplier of the goods, and where the government administratively controls prices. The Appellate Body considered a third possibility noting that:

> [i]n terms of market distortion and effect on prices, there may be little difference between situations where the government is the sole provider of certain goods and situations where the government has a predominant role in the market as a provider of those goods. Whenever the government is the *predominant provider* of certain goods, even if not the sole provider, *it is likely that it can affect through its own pricing strategy the prices of private providers for those goods*, inducing the latter to align their prices to the point where there may be little difference, if any, between the government price and the private price.[48]

This interpretation required to consider benchmarks alternative to private prices in the country of provision, if the 'provision's purposes are not [to be] frustrated'.[49] In other words, although prices of similar goods sold by private suppliers in the country of provision should represent the starting point and the primary benchmark, they cannot be the exclusive benchmark if certain conditions make them unreliable. In these cases, alternative benchmarks should be considered. These should always 'relate or refer to or be connected with' the prevailing market

[44] Panel, ibid, para 7.50. See, along the same lines, the previous Panel in *US—Sofwood Lumber III*, para 50.

[45] Panel, *US—Softwood Lumber IV*, paras 7.50–7.51.

[46] ibid, para 7.60.

[47] ibid, para 7.59.

[48] Appellate Body, *US—Softwood Lumber IV*, para 100 (emphasis added).

[49] ibid, para 101.

conditions in the country of provision and could include 'proxies that take into account prices for similar goods quoted on world markets' or 'proxies constructed on the basis of production costs'.[50]

Comments on the case-study

The case-study has shown the variety of the public intervention in the economy. Governments may regulate markets, they may 'design economic and other policies', a formulation which is capable of including both economic activity and the exercise of public powers, and finally they can provide goods in the market in competition with private suppliers. The government is an important agent in the market and its conduct may affect, sometimes substantially, its functioning. This may be particularly clear when it exercises public powers, such as when it tightly regulates a market. This can be equally true when it acts commercially and enjoys a dominant position in the relevant market thus enabling it to dictate a certain price level.

The prominence of the public intervention in the market can even put into question the concept of market itself. The *US—Lumber IV* dispute provides an interesting debate in this regard. Irrespective of the technical correctness of the Appellate Body's conclusion in the context of Article 14(d) of the SCM, important elements emerged. The existence of 'a market', and hence the possibility of deriving benchmarks from it, does not necessarily require a theoretical—indeed utopian—place free from any form of external intervention by the public hand. However, since the public intervention in the economy may be significant and affect the working of market forces and outcomes, the advantage analysis may become difficult.

Most importantly, the identification and application of the appropriate benchmarks may be demanding, adjustments may be needed, 'proxies' may be resorted to. In some cases, the most common market benchmarks, such as prices, may lose their significance altogether and the reference to other commercial indicators, such as costs, may be required. The use of costs as appropriate commercial references is sound and is not novel. It is sound because, alongside prices and revenue, costs are among the basic factors taken into account by firms in their production decisions.[51]

[50] ibid, para 106. The reasoning of the Appellate Body has been criticized as being too liberal and far from textual indications. See M Matsushita, TJ Schoenbaum, and PC Mavroidis, *The World Trade Organization—Law, Practice, and Policy* (2nd edn, Oxford: Oxford University Press, 2006) 359. The result of the Appellate Body's findings is not only that the clear express reference to the 'country of provision or purchase' in Article 14(d) (but the same could be true for Article 14(a)) is put aside in certain conditions, but is more generally superfluous. It is indeed natural that the starting point of all benefit determinations under Article 1.1(b) and/or Article 14 of the SCM is necessarily the market where the government and the recipient operate.

[51] For this reason the author does not see any potential conflict with the use of the 'private investor test' as suggested by M Matsushita, TJ Schoenbaum, and PC Mavroidis, *The World Trade Organization—Law, Practice, and Policy* (2nd edn, Oxford: Oxford University Press, 2006) 352.

Its use is consequently not new in the field of anti-dumping, antitrust law,[52] and, as the case-study on the compensation of public services at the end of this Part shows, also in the area of State aid/subsidy law.

B. Case-study 2: market logic expansion and redefinition of the public intervention in the economy

Drawing on WTO law, the previous case-study has demonstrated the difficulties in determining the appropriate benchmarks when the market is significantly influenced by the public hand in the economy.

Using the examples of infrastructures, this case-study, based on the EC experience, has two aims: first, to confirm the special difficulties caused by the public intervention in the economy emerging from the WTO context, and, secondly, and most importantly, to highlight the (so far rigorous), trend of market liberalization, ie the extension of market logic to areas which were previously sheltered from it, and the consequent redefinition of the public role in the economy.[53]

[52] The much debated area of pricing abuses, particularly predation, constantly refers to costs as relevant benchmarks. For EC and UK law see R Whish, *Competition Law* (6th edn, Oxford: Oxford University Press, 2008); for US law see KN Hylton, *Antitrust Law—Economic Theory and Common Law Evolution* (Cambridge: Cambridge University Press, 2003).

[53] The phenomenon of expansion of market logic, which can be witnessed with infrastructures, has been recently confirmed in the EC context also with respect to other 'commons', such as the environment and radio frequencies. 'Common goods' or 'commons' are similar to 'public goods'. They are non-excludable and their use is non-rivalrous, with the result that, if we are referring to finite resources, for example clear air, we can expect a 'tragedy of the commons' situation, where a free and unrestricted use of the same resources eventually leads to over-exploitation and social harm. Although the expression 'tragedy of the commons' is attributable to a work of G Hardin published with the same title in 1968 in Science (1243), this condition had already been described by Thucydites (*The Peloponnesian War*, Book I, Sec. 141) and Aristotle (*Politics*, Book II, Chapter III, 1261b). To avoid a 'tragedy of the commons' situation the use of these resources can be subject to various forms of control such as permits.

Two examples that involve the regulation of 'finite resources', ie the environment (and its degradation: pollution) and radio frequencies for (UMTS) mobile communication, have raised interesting State aid issues. The legal question is whether the allocation of permits to pollute, or conversely 'green' certificates (confirming that the energy at issue had been produced with environmentally friendly methods), and of UMTS licences, may grant an advantage and thus amount to a State aid or a subsidy. The most important element in these cases, some actually scrutinized before competent authorities, others only discussed in academic circles, is that both the discourse and the conclusions show the apparently inexorable trend of expansion of market logic.

In Case T-475/04, *Bouygues*, the CFI found that, although radiofrequencies are a finite and public resource, they should be managed under economic conditions. Although it was concluded in the end that there was no aid, with an interesting reasoning which blends the State aid argumentation on the advantage and distortion to competition with that under the principle of non-discrimination, the important finding is that UMTS licences are held to have 'economic' value. On appeal (Case C-431/07P) Advocate General Trstenjak confirmed the CFI's decision (but interestingly distinguished the analysis of the advantage from that of the distortion; see para 150 of the Opinion). And so did the Court of Justice on 2 April 2009.

Another good example of market logic creeping into State aid discourse is Case T-233/04 *Dutch ETS* that concerned the establishment of an emission trading scheme for nitrogen oxides. Although, again, the relevant allocation of tradable pollution permits was eventually found not to be aid (because

The La Poste *saga: natural monopoly, network infrastructure and public services*

The long *La Poste* saga constitutes an excellent case-study for our analysis. It therefore deserves space, and (often extensive) quotations from the relevant rulings.

Let us first consider the background to the case. *La Poste* operates as a legal monopoly the ordinary mail service in France. It is further authorized by law to perform certain activities open to competition, and in particular express delivery services which are carried out by its subsidiaries, *Société Française de Messagerie International (SFMI)* and *Chronopost* (hereinafter *SFMI-Chronopost*). The crucial legal and economic issue in the saga was whether the logistical and commercial assistance provided by *La Poste* to *SFMI/Chronopost* was in line with market conditions. Called to give a preliminary ruling by the Tribunal de Commerce de Paris, the Court of Justice noted that:

> [i]n order to determine whether a State measure constitutes aid, it is necessary to establish whether the recipient undertaking receives an economic advantage which it would not have obtained *under normal market conditions.*
>
> In examining that question, it is for the national court to determine what normal remuneration for the services in question is. Such a determination presupposes an economic analysis taking into account *all the factors which an undertaking acting under normal market conditions should have taken into consideration when fixing the remuneration for the services provided.*
>
> In the light of the foregoing considerations, the answer to the first question must be that the provision of logistical and commercial assistance by a public undertaking to its subsidiaries, which are governed by private law and carry on an activity open to free competition, is capable of constituting State aid within the meaning of Article [87 EC] if the remuneration received in return is less than that which would have been demanded under normal market conditions.[54]

A few months after the preliminary ruling was delivered in 1996, the Commission adopted a decision and concluded that the logistical and commercial assistance provided by *La Poste* to its subsidiary did not constitute State aid because

of the lack of sufficient selectivity or because in any case the differentiation between the affected undertakings arose from the general nature of the scheme), the CFI clearly stated that these permits have economic value. A free, or in any event 'non-commercial', allocation may raise State aid concerns.

There are no reasons why similar legal issues could not be raised in the WTO framework too and treated accordingly.

[54] Case C-39/94 *SFEI v La Poste*, paras 59–61 (emphasis added). Building on the market economy investor principle, Advocate General Jacobs was more precise in the indication of the various factors to consider, most notably 'the cost of providing the assistance, the size of its investment in the undertaking and its return from it, the importance of the activity of the undertaking to the investing group as a whole, conditions on the market in question and the period for which the assistance is granted' (see para 61 of the Opinion). Immediately afterwards, Jacobs concurred with the French Government that 'deciding whether there is aid in the present case will entail extremely complex findings of an economic and financial nature'.

it corresponded to normal business conditions since it covered 'full-cost prices' (total costs plus a mark-up to remunerate equity capital investment).[55]

Reviewing the Commission decision, the Court of First Instance found that its economic analysis was not consistent with the guidelines laid down by the Court in *SFEI*.[56] The mere verification of the reimbursement of costs was not sufficient. Considering that *La Poste,* by virtue of its position of monopolist in the reserved sector, could have provided the services at a lower cost than a private undertaking not enjoying those rights, the possibility that aid had in fact been granted could not be excluded. The correct benchmark was the remuneration that would have been demanded by a private investor *not operating in a reserved sector*.[57]

The CFI's decision was appealed. The significance of the Court of Justice's reasoning deserves an extensive quotation.[58] For the reader's convenience, the main passages have been emphasized. The Court begins by repeating the main legal point laid down by the CFI:

> . . . the appellants allege that the Court of First Instance infringed Article [87(1) of the EC], by giving an incorrect interpretation of the concept of normal market conditions used in the *SFEI* judgment.
>
> In that regard, the Court of First Instance stated . . . that the Commission should at least have checked that the *payment* received by La Poste was comparable to that demanded by a *private* holding company or a *private* group of undertakings *not operating in a reserved sector.*

The remainder of the reasoning is devoted to the criticism of this conclusion, and its underlying suggestion of 'comparability'.

> That assessment, which fails to take account of the fact that an undertaking such as La Poste is in a *situation* which is *very different from that of a private undertaking acting under normal market conditions*, is flawed in law.
>
> La Poste is *entrusted with a service of general economic interest* within the meaning of [Article 86(2) of the EC] . . . Such a service essentially consists in the obligation to collect, carry and deliver mail for the benefit of all users throughout the territory of the Member State concerned, at uniform tariffs and on similar conditions as to quality.
>
> *To that end, La Poste had to acquire, or was afforded, substantial infrastructures and resources (the postal network), enabling it to provide the basic postal service to all users, even in sparsely populated areas where the tariffs did not cover the cost of providing the service in question.*
>
> *Because of the characteristics of the service* which the La Poste network must be able to ensure, *the creation and maintenance of that network are not in line with a purely commercial approach.*

[55] In reaching this conclusion the Commission also considered two facts. First, that the internal rate of return on investment exceeded the cost of capital. Secondly, the fact that the transaction had taken place between companies of the same group, with the result that the relevant strategic considerations and synergies could not be disregarded.

[56] Case T-613/97 *Ufex I*, para 64 et seq.

[57] ibid, para 75.

[58] Joined Cases C-83/01P, C-93/01P and C-94/01P, *Chronopost I*, paras 31–40.

> . . . Ufex and Others [ie the appellants] have indeed accepted that a network such as that available to SFMI-Chronopost is *clearly not a market network. Therefore that network would never have been created by a private undertaking.*
>
> Moreover, the *provision of logistical and commercial assistance is inseparably linked to the La Poste network*, since it consists precisely in making available that *network which has no equivalent on the market.*

The conclusion of the Court offers the proper interpretation of 'normal market conditions' in the instant case.

> Accordingly, in the absence of any possibility of comparing the situation of La Poste with that of a private group of undertakings not operating in a reserved sector, normal market conditions, which are necessarily hypothetical, must be assessed by reference to the *objective and verifiable elements* which are available.
>
> In the present case, the *costs* borne by La Poste in respect of the provision to its subsidiary of logistical and commercial assistance can constitute such objective and verifiable elements.
>
> On that basis, there is no question of State aid to SFMI-Chronopost if, first, it is established that the price charged properly covers all the additional, variable costs incurred in providing the logistical and commercial assistance, an appropriate contribution to the fixed costs arising from use of the postal network and an adequate return on the capital investment in so far as it is used for SFMI-Chronopost's competitive activity and if, second, there is nothing to suggest that those elements have been underestimated or fixed in an arbitrary fashion.[59]

Comments on La Poste

The *La Poste* saga is representative of the sort of 'uncharted' competition, notably State aid, questions emerging in sectors liberalized or under liberalization, often involving network industries and public service commitments.[60]

Three main orders of issues emerge from the case.

(a) The incomparable and the ineffable: the singularity of natural monopolies and the protean nature of public services

Following Advocate General Tizzano,[61] in *Chronopost I*, the Court correctly questions the premise of the reasoning of the Court of First Instance, ie the possibility

[59] The case was thus remanded to the Court of First Instance for a new decision based on the directions of the Court. In Case T-613/97 *Ufex II* the CFI annulled again the Commission's decision for insufficient reasoning on the costs of the logistical and commercial assistance. On appeal (C-341/06P *Chronopost II*), the Court of Justice eventually closed the saga. After reforming the CFI's finding that the reasoning of the Commission was insufficient, it ruled on the merits. The final words in a saga which lasted 17 years, and confronted the two Community Courts twice, were: 'no State aid'.

[60] I Atanasiu, 'Chronopost II: The Application of the Market Economy Investor Principle in Reserved Sectors' (2008) European State Aid Law Quarterly 571, 571.

[61] See paras 38–63 of the Opinion.

of comparing the situation of *La Poste* with that of a private group of undertakings, and in particular one not operating in a reserved sector.

The presence of the network, with its 'substantial infrastructures and resources', represents a unique factor as well as a fundamental obstacle to the possibility of finding any 'equivalent on the market'. This is correct if the industry of ordinary mail is considered as a typical example of 'natural monopoly', that is an industry where only one firm can operate in the market profitably because the latter can support only one network.[62] The Court also notes, however, that the 'creation and maintenance of that network are not in line with a purely commercial approach' with the result that it is 'clearly not a market network' since 'it would have never been created by a private undertaking'. Although this can be true on the facts of the case, it cannot be generalized.[63]

Being private goods, *postal services* can also be carried out by private undertakings. Further, at least hypothetically, a *postal network* could be created and run profitably by private entrepreneurs. The investment to create a vast national network may be considerable but it is not necessarily impossible to finance. What can make a difference, from a business perspective, is the provision of the service, particularly if there are standards and obligations that have to be complied with. A 'universal service obligation' can thus render the performance of the service particularly costly. Its viability may therefore depend on some form of public intervention. We have also noted, however, that this concept of 'universal service' (and, more radically, that of public service) is dynamic and liable to change rapidly (and there is no better example than ordinary mail). But, to repeat the point, there are no reasons why the private sector could not *in principle* provide these services. For these reasons, it was suggested in the previous chapter that the provision of *any* public service could be considered as an economic activity.[64]

[62] In this regard, it may be useful to refer to the previous discussion on public and private goods, and on natural monopolies and their problem. See chapter 7, section III.B.

[63] ibid

[64] For a broad finding that the supply of a public service (in the instant case unrelated to any infrastructure) not consistent with market conditions is liable to constitute an aid, see Case C-126/01, *GEMO*, paras 28–34. See also the Opinion of Advocate General Jacobs, paras 64–78.

More generally, note the intricate case-law interpreting the concept of 'economic activity' via that of 'undertaking' in EC competition law (including State aid law). In a nutshell, the substance is that certain activities, which are admittedly public services, are not considered 'economic' in the first place (and hence fall out of the scope of the rules) if they are predominantly organized on the basis of the variable principle of 'solidarity'. Intriguingly, a different outcome can be reached under the different rules on free movement of internal market law (ie those activities would be 'economic' and caught by the net). In this regard, it might be useful to read the Opinion of AG Maduro in Case C-205/03P *Fevin*.

Is there a contradiction between our conclusion and this case-law? Not necessarily. On the one hand, this legal fluidity confirms the volatile nature of these issues. On the other hand, the issue of whether a public service amounts to an 'economic activity' has a completely different aim and result in the present context. What we are doing here is simply determining what is the appropriate benchmark to test conduct which is *already caught by the rules*, and not to determine whether that conduct falls within the scope of the rules in the first place. It is however clear that the assessment of the activity

In conclusion, it does not seem justified to transcend the finding of the Court 'on the circumstances of the case' into a general formulation of absolute impossibility of the private sector to create and maintain the network and provide the relevant (universal) services. Although often some form of public support may be required, it cannot be completely excluded that the market can do this.

(b) 'Normal market conditions' and 'objective and verifiable elements'

After underlining the uniqueness of a natural monopoly, what is still to be answered is how to correctly interpret the 'concept of normal market conditions' of the *SFEI v La Poste* judgment. The Court notes that 'in the absence of any possibility of comparison the situation of *La Poste* with that of a private group of undertakings not operating in a reserved sector, normal market conditions, which are necessarily hypothetical, must be assessed by reference to the objective and verifiable elements which are available'.[65]

The author agrees. The fact that a comparable market situation cannot be found does not lead the Court to simply reject the reference to 'normal market conditions'. These are simply defined as 'hypothetical'. Admittedly, this term may be misleading, since it may raise the impression that we are not *really* talking of a 'market' and its 'rules', which is clearly not the case (albeit monopolistic, there is a market). This doubt is immediately dissipated by the reasoning of the Court. The monopolistic structure of the market makes usual market benchmarks, ie prices, difficult to rely on. As Advocate General Tizzano indicated, the only price that could have been used would have been the one that could have been obtained if the logistical and commercial services had been put on the market and that private investors would have been prepared to offer (but this eventuality did not occur).[66] Absent the possibility of referring to prices, the only 'objective and verifiable elements which are available' to assess the compliance with market conditions, are *costs*. This reasoning, which immediately calls into mind that of the Appellate Body outlined in the previous case-study, is highly persuasive. As Advocate General Tizzano underlines:

> in the absence of adequate information on the market value of the services offered and with no estimates associated with a general group strategy to go on, *an undertaking operating under normal market conditions would be obliged to fix the price of such services on the basis of their costs*'.[67]

The author does not share the criticism that this conclusion would be somewhat unorthodox and does not fit well with the consolidated use of the market economy

may become an issue of scope in the State aid context too, when it has to be determined whether the recipient—which might be entrusted with a public service obligation—is in fact carrying out an 'economic activity'. In this case, the author's approach may not be fully in line with the current case-law.

[65] Paragraph 38.

[66] Paras 54–5 of the Opinion.

[67] Paragraph 57 of the Opinion (emphasis added).

investor principle.[68] In a monopolistic market, the reference to costs as an appropriate baseline to assess the monopolist's conduct should not surprise. Although this exercise may be difficult (a recurring theme in the whole *La Poste* saga),[69] it is in line with the basic tenets of standard micro-economics[70] and indeed the mainstream competition law analysis of 'cross-subsidization'.[71]

Further, the parallel with the case-law on the compensation of public service obligations (which is analysed in chapter 11) is clearly inappropriate.[72] Although in both cases the issue is whether there is a State aid, and, to answer this question, the transaction is assessed by using a cost baseline, the context in the two cases is completely different. The public conduct element in each cases, and hence the way through which an (anticompetitive) advantage could be granted, are poles apart. In one case (*La Poste*) a public body is *transferring* something, in the other (compensation of public services) it is *receiving* something. Accordingly, in the former case the concern is about the '*under*-compensation' of the public body (and hence what is under scrutiny is its cost-structure), in the latter the '*over*-compensation' of the service provider (and its costs are accordingly examined). The first case is about whether the public body has renounced profit, the second case about whether it has wasted resources. Although in both cases costs are considered reliable economic indicators, their role is completely different.

(c) Access to infrastructures and market benchmarks

The most important lesson from *La Poste* is that, despite the difficulties raised by the presence of a natural monopoly and a significant network infrastructure (both necessary to perform a public service), the Court confirms that infrastructures, and in particular the services provided through them, should be managed

[68] A similar criticism has been raised in the WTO context. See n 51 above.

[69] See also E Morgan De Rivery, NL Le Berre-Doder, and S Thibault-Liger, (in M Dony and C Smits (eds), *Aides d'Etat* (Brussels : Editions de l'Université de Bruxelles, 2005), 157, 163 et seq) who underline the dangers posed by the use of costs. First, transparency needs to be ensured. This is achieved through accurate separate accounts for each activity carried out by the undertaking. (See in this regard Directive 80/723/EEC—the 'Transparency' Directive—last amended by Directive 2005/81/EC.) Secondly, in the specific context of the costs of a public undertaking, there is a risk that 'les coûts de l'opérateur public peuvent être minimisés par l'existence même de ce financement public'. In the instant case, however, the CFI in *Ufex II* did not take into account of the possible impact of lower taxation on costs (see paras 189–90).

[70] The reference to other benchmarks, such as the prices in other regulated network industries or even in other countries would pose clear difficulties. See I Atanasiu, 'Chronopost II: The Application of the Market Economy Investor Principle in Reserved Sectors' (2008) European State Aid Law Quarterly 571.

[71] See, in the general context of EC competition law (and also with a commentary of the 1996 Commission decision in the *La Poste* case) L Hancher and JL Buendia-Sierra, 'Cross Subsidization and EC Law' (1998) Common Market Law Review, 901; G Abbamonte, 'Cross-subsidization and Community Competition rules: Efficient Pricing versus Equity?' (1998) European Law Review 414.

[72] In a similar tone, see A Bartosch, 'Clarification or Confusion? How to Reconcile the ECJ's Rulings in Altmark and Chronopost' (2003) European State Aid Law Quarterly 375, 384–5.

under market conditions. The market is the paradigm to determine whether an advantage is conferred.

Underlying the Court's reasoning is the crucial consideration that, once an infrastructure has been created (regardless of whether the market would not have provided it, or whether it is needed for providing a public service), it should in principle be *run according to market logic*. There may doubts about the actual benchmarks to use but there is no doubt that the access to it—by operators wishing to manage it, service suppliers, and final users—should always be assessed on economic terms, in the Court's jargon 'under normal market conditions'. In a word, the hiatus between the creation of the infrastructure and its operation is so imperceptible that the whole emphasis is exclusively shifted towards the latter. The discussion about whether the creation of the infrastructure is economic or not becomes essentially otiose. When the dust of the works is removed what remains is *a facility* which *should be run economically*. The otherwise inevitable conclusion is that an advantage is granted.

Building on the lessons of the *La Poste* saga, the next paragraph attempts to analyse in more depth the relation between infrastructure and market, particularly with respect to the EC law debate but with some suggestions also for the WTO. We will discuss further how these findings on the economic/non-economic nature of infrastructures translate into the question that is ultimately important for our analysis. When does the provision of infrastructure grant an advantage?

Infrastructure and market under State aid rules

(a) The traditional approach

The language of the traditional approach stresses two elements. First, infrastructures are *non-economic*, mostly because the private sector would not provide them (example of 'public goods'). They belong, therefore, to the inherent public prerogatives. The implication is that they should be sheltered from the application of State aid law. The second argument is that infrastructures are normally *general*, ie available across the board, with the result that they cannot confer any special advantage. The only problem under State aid rules would occur if there was a discriminatory access. It is worth noting that this argument confuses the various meanings of the term general which is intended more with reference to the *tendentially universal subjective application* of the measure rather than with its *normal character*. The debate is thus usually (but incorrectly) put in the context of the specificity analysis rather than that of the advantage.[73] Although there is clearly an overlap between advantage and specificity analysis (with similar questions often asked in both contexts), the two levels can be separated conceptually.

[73] This confusion, which continuously recurs in the area, and the need to distinguish between the two levels of the analysis, is discussed in more detail below. See chapter 10, section I.B.

In short, the result of the traditional approach is that, unless specific access is proved, infrastructures are not a problem for State aid law.

(b) Market logic expansion and multi-layered analysis

Santamato and Westerhof[74] have questioned the force of the two main arguments of the traditional approach to infrastructure under State aid rules, that is the 'market failure' argument[75] and the 'non-selectivity' argument.[76]

More profoundly, it seems that what calls for a review of the old approach is the process of market liberalization. Although this may change with the current global economic climate, recent decades have witnessed the emergence of a dramatic trend. For various reasons (public budgetary contraints; the belief that the private sector can do better and operate more efficiently), markets have been liberalized, and companies privatized. This tide has particularly involved public utilities. The private sector has been involved in the provision and operation of network infrastructures and in the supply of the relevant services.[77] Governments have not left the field altogether though. Apart from their continuing regulatory role, as a real sign of a new type of 'mixed-economy', complex and long-term forms of cooperation with the private sector, often falling under the broad expression of 'Public-Private Partnerships' (PPP), have been created.

Finally, technology is another key-word in the debate. Technical developments have an impact on the provision of services, and in particular the infrastructure facilities necessary to supply them. New tools can be devised to achieve the same objective, often in a better and more efficient way. As a consequence, the political and legal definition of what constitutes a public or universal service may vary. Quite often these innovations come from, and are largely implemented by, the private sector. The field of 'communications' is paradigmatic in this regard with, for example, electronic communication increasingly rivalling traditional mail services.[78]

[74] S Santamato and JG Westerhof, 'Is Funding of Infrastructure State Aid?' (2003) Europaische Zeitschrift für Wirtschaftsrecht 645, 646.

[75] 'Non-excludable [public] goods are not very frequent: for most infrastructure there are technical means of charging a price for the use of the facility.'

[76] 'The presence of mechanisms to avoid discrimination between competitors is certainly capable of significantly reducing the distortion of competition. However, non-selectivity within a sector does not imply a total absence of potential distortion: the issue of selectivity between sectors or between territories remains open.'

[77] See, eg, S Santamato and JG Westerhof, 'Is Funding of Infrastructure State Aid?' (2003) Europaische Zeitschrift für Wirtschaftsrecht 645; C Koenig and A Haratsch, 'The Logic of Infrastructure Funding under EC State Aid Control' (2004) European State Aid Law Quarterly 393; C Koenig and S Kiefer, 'Public Funding of Infrastructure Projects under EC-State Aid Law' (2005) European State Aid Law Quarterly 415; D O'Keeffe and J Branton, 'State Aid and Urban Regeneration: A UK Perspective' (2007) European State Aid Law Quarterly 484.

[78] Broadband infrastructures are crucial to bridge the 'digital divide'. Their financing may however trigger the application of State aid law. The Commission is very active in this area. See, eg, the Draft 'Community Guidelines for the application of State aid rules in relation to rapid deployment of

All this has produced two phenomena with respect to infrastructure: an *expansion of market logic* and an *increase of the levels of public/private interaction*. In other words, there is an increasing recognition that infrastructures may involve economic activities and may thus be subject to market criteria. Further, there may be several of these activities—and relevant markets—with the result that the advantage analysis should be carried out at various levels.

Thus, if the government decides to fund the *construction* and/or the *management* of an infrastructure, in order to exclude any advantage, it has to comply with market benchmarks. In other words, it has to pursue in any transaction the (minimum) market price/cost resulting from an open, transparent and non-discriminatory procedure.[79] State aid concerns may also arise at the level of the *shareholders* of the owner/operator of the infrastructure.[80] Apart from a possible privileged access, shareholders may benefit from the distribution of dividends (which should therefore be in line with commercial practice) and from the sale of assets/shares (which may justify the imposition of a temporary ban). Finally, the level of the *users* of the infrastructure/service is also relevant. The two main criteria that should be followed to exclude any advantage are those of an open (ie non-discriminatory) access and, in any case, market pricing.[81]

broadband networks' ('broadband guidelines'), published on 19 May 2009, with which a consultation process has been opened.

For a commentary on the of the various State aid issues raised in this area see M Hencsey, O Reymond, A Riedl, S Santamato, and JG Westerhof, 'State aid rules and public funding of broadband' (2005) Competition Policy Newsletter 8; L Papadias, A Riedl, and JG Westerhof, 'Public Funding for Broadband Networks: Recent Developments' (2006) Competition Policy Newsletter 13; P Nicolaides, 'Where Is the Advantage? The Case of Public Funding of Infrastructure and Broadband Networks' (2007) European State Aid Law Quarterly 615.

[79] Further, if the service purchased can be defined as one of 'general economic interest' (essentially a synonym of 'public service'), the conditions laid down by the Court in *Altmark* should be fulfilled. The conditions are as follows. First, the provider must have actual public service obligations to discharge and those obligations must be clearly defined. Secondly, the parameters on the basis of which the compensation is calculated must be established in advance in an objective and transparent manner. Thirdly, the compensation cannot exceed that which is necessary to cover all or part of the costs incurred in the discharge of the public service obligations, taking into account the relevant revenue and a reasonable profit. Fourthly, and finally, when the company is not chosen through a public procurement procedure, the level of compensation must be determined in relation to an analysis of the costs that a typical company in the sector would incur (taking into account its revenues and a reasonable profit for the discharging of the obligations).

[80] C Koenig and A Haratsch, 'The Logic of Infrastructure Funding under EC State Aid Control' (2004) European State Aid Law Quarterly 393, 396–7.

[81] An interesting case where market logic expansion and multi-layered analysis can be seen is that of airport financing. The 2005 Commission Guidelines on Financing of Airports and Start-Up Aid to Airlines Departing From Regional Airports (2005/C 312/01), OJ C 312 of 09.12.2005, 1, confirm the two trends indicated above. On the one hand, there is the complexity of infrastructure under State aid rules since different markets have to be considered in order to determine whether there is aid (eg not only that of users, particularly airlines, but also that of airport operators). On the other hand, except for the public functions (such as safety and air traffic control), the Guidelines (see para 59) apply to all airports activities. Thus it seems that all activities concerning the construction, operation and other airport services are considered economic.

The analysis of the *creation* of the infrastructure raises an interesting issue.

The question is whether the fact that the government provides an infrastructure that the private sector 'would not have provided' may have an impact on the advantage analysis. To be clear, we are not referring to the *procedure* that is followed in building the infractructure, which clearly involves contracting activities and should be subject to the market place (and, if relevant, public procurement rules). We are thinking rather of the government's *bringing into existence* an infrastructure itself, and asking whether its creation would have occurred but for public action.

But, what does 'the market would not have provided' actually mean? It is extremely difficult to distinguish between those situations that are *within* the market and those that are *beyond* it. Although costly, it is not in principle impossible to create an infrastructure. On the premise that the lack of private initiative does not depend on a market failure (such as a public good scenario, or a situation of absolute financial and economic impossibility), are we still entitled to test the conduct of the government against a market benchmark? Or, rather, having identified a market failure, should we use a non-market baseline to establish whether the government has *derogated from* its *general infrastructure policy*?[82]

If the answer to either question is that the government has granted an advantage by *creating* the infrastructure in the first place, the issue is whether this may have an impact on the following analysis of the various activities involving the infrastructure. To put it differently, should the fact that these are run according to market logic (for example, that the market price is paid for the access to it) lead us to forget that—but for governmental intervention—the infrastructure itself would not have seen the light at all?

The regulation of infrastructure under WTO subsidy rules

Drawing inspiration from the previous analysis under EC law, and the expansion of market logic that has emerged, it is interesting to assess whether the conclusions reached above are applicable in the WTO context.

What is not fully clear, though, is to the extent to which the old statement of the previous guidelines (Community guidelines on the application of Articles 92 and 93 of the EC Treaty and Article 61 of the EEA Agreement to State aids in the aviation sector, OJ C 350 of 10.12.1994, 5) whereby 'the construction of (airport) infrastructure projects . . . represents a general measure of economic policy which cannot be controlled by the Commission under the Treaty rules on State aid' is still valid (see para 19 of the 2005 Guidelines). In the following analysis, the status of the 'creation' of the infrastructure is discussed.

For a commentary of the 2005 Guidelines see A Bartosch, 'Distortions of Competition on the Markets for the Operation of Airport Infrastructures: the Commission's New Guidelines' (2005) European State Aid Law Quarterly 621; U Soltész, 'The New Commission Guidelines on State Aid for Airports: a Step too Far' (2006) European State Aid Law Quarterly 719.

[82] An operative framework and some criteria to address the advantage question in this context can be found in chapter 9, section III.

(a) The exclusion of 'general infrastructure'

The starting point is one of the forms of financial contribution under Article 1.1(a)(1)(iii) of the SCM. This provision refers to those cases where 'a government provides goods or services *other than general infrastructure* . . .'.[83] Whatever reading is given to this phrase, the intention seems to be that general infrastructure should not be covered by subsidy rules.

That said, the argument whereby general infrastructures belong to the responsibilities of Member States and should thus be sheltered from the application of subsidy law should be immediately dismissed. Even sovereign prerogatives, such as the power to tax, find limitations in WTO law, for example in subsidy rules.

Two other explanations deserve more attention, and focus on the already noted ambivalence of the term 'general'. The most accredited reading is that 'general' should be viewed as referring to the fact that the infrastructure at issue should not be *specific*, ie that it should not apply to the exclusive advantage of a 'specific enterprise or industry or group of enterprises or industries'. McGovern observes that the mention 'seems unnecessary in view of the general requirement in Article 2 . . . that subsidies must be specific'.[84] It could be argued that, since the determination of whether the use of infrastructures is specific or generally available is notoriously difficult, the legislator might in some way have tried to emphasize immediately that those measures should fall outside the reach of the SCM.

Another possible explanation of the exclusion of general infrastructures from Article 1.1(a)(1)(iii) of the SCM is that, being general, infrastructures would not be liable to confer any advantage. 'General' is thus intended in an alternative meaning, as opposed to exception. In other words, only infrastructures that do not derogate from the *general (infrastructure) policy* of the government, and are hence 'general' in this sense, should fall outside the scope of the law. It is worth repeating that this is the case not because they are not specific but because they do not confer an advantage in the first place.

This reading may be less intuitive but can be nicely reconciled with the wording and context of Article 1.1(a)(1)(iii) of the SCM. Unlike the prevailing interpretation, which reads the phrase 'other than general infrastructure' as a pleonastic (ie useless) anticipation of the specificity test, it attempts to give the phrase, and within it, the term 'general', its own meaning. In particular, this interpretation recognizes that, before being a specificity issue, the question of infrastructure is in the first place a matter of advantage.[85]

[83] Emphasis added.

[84] E McGovern, *International Trade Regulation* (Exeter: Globefield Press, 1995) 11.31–11.34.

[85] In this regard, we would see an anticipation of the advantage analysis at the level of the assessment of the financial contribution, which is not rare (the same occurs for tax measures under Article 1.1(a)(1)(ii) of the SCM: see chapter 9, section I.A).

(b) Towards a new approach

The interpretation of 'general' that has just been suggested, although innovative, is premised on the fact that the infrastructure is provided by the government because of a market failure. This is in line with one of the tenets of the traditional approach to infrastructure (which sees them as naturally non-economic) but is increasingly put into question by the significant role that, for various reasons, the private sector plays in the provision of infrastructures. More fundamentally, it has been seen that the main indication of market logic expansion is that, once you have an infrastructure, irrespective of whether it is economic or not, this should be run economically, ie for profit. From the standpoint of the advantage analysis, this means that the operation of the infrastructure, including the provision of services through it, should be tested against market criteria. More radically, we have concluded our analysis of EC law by taking a step backwards and asking whether the *creation* of the infrastructure could represent an advantage in the first place. It has been indicated that this could be the case, and that the answer, and the criteria to use, depend on the relevant market or non-market scenario.

The crucial legal question now is whether these remarks can be taken into account in the interpretation of Article 1.1(a)(1)(iii) of the SCM which still seems essentially to reflect the old approach. 'General', that is non-economic and non-specific, infrastructures are safe.

It is clear first of all that the phrase 'provision of infrastructure' also refers to the *services* supplied through it. This is clear from the immediate context of subparagraph (iii): 'a government provides goods or *services* other than general infrastructure' which does not seem to exclusively confine the 'infrastructure' to its physical or static dimension but may well extend to cover its main telos, ie the provision of services.

Most importantly, in the context of the determination of the advantage, there is the question of whether the term 'general' can be construed not only as referring to the 'general infrastructure policy or plan', but also to include those cases where the provision of the infrastructure is in line with the *general market* norm. Although this might require a little more in the way of interpretative inventiveness, an approach in this direction cannot be completely excluded.

C. Concluding remarks on the case-studies: the interplay between two forces

After the examination of the complexities and difficulties inherent in commercial decisions and in their reviews, this section has analysed a particular element of complexity: the *public intervention in the economy.*

The two case-studies have shown that the interplay between the public intervention in the economy and the market operates at various levels.

At a superficial level both case-studies highlight the fact that the government's intervention in the economy can make the market advantage analysis more demanding. It is only at a deeper level, however, that the most intriguing and critical findings can be made. The background is the actual context of redefinition of the roles of public and private actors in the economy caused by processes of liberalization and privatization. The key finding is the existence of two forces currently at work and partly moving in opposite directions. What the two case-studies do is to explain the interplay between the two forces from each perspective.

The first case-study focused on various forms of public intervention in the economy and highlighted the impact of this 'public' force on the identification of market benchmarks. We have seen how the concept of market itself has, to some extent, been called into question.

What emerged from the second case-study is not only the confirmation of the significant impact of public intervention in the economy but, more radically (and, one could argue, as a kind of revenge), the expansion of market logic. This 'private' force is somewhat in opposition to the 'public' force underlined above. In the previous case it was the public intervention in the economy that produced an impact on the advantage analysis. Now, it is the 'market tide' which profoundly influences the legal position of public intervention in the economy in the first place, and consequently also the advantage analysis thereof. Crucially, as shown by the example of infrastructure, public conduct, whose status was previously substantially sheltered from the market and its rationale, is being redefined and is now more likely to be classed as economic, and finally subject to the market logic and its benchmarks.

As in any good story, there has been a final twist. We have highlighted (discussing the issue of the 'creation' of infrastructures) how, despite the pervasiness of market principles, the public presence in the economy cannot be simply ignored, and may in turn have an impact on market logic.

III. The step forward: from difficulty to criticism

Drawing from the difficulties which have emerged so far, this closing section concentrates on two sets of arguments that make a step forward. The legitimacy—in terms of possibility and consistency—of using the market and its criteria to test the public intervention is directly challenged. The two criticisms are strictly intertwined insofar as they both underline the risk of discriminating against public actors in favour of private ones.

A. First criticism: the fallacy of the market paradigm

The criticism and its refutation

The criticism analysed here does not concern the difficulty but, more radically, the *possibility* of using the market as principle and benchmark. The argument is that the conduct of public bodies in the market may not be assessed against *any* benchmark since it would not be possible to identify with precision the rules that guide private entrepreneurs in the first place. Market benchmarks are purely abstract. It is difficult to say how a private investor would behave in a given situation as entrepreneurs do not necessarily behave in the same manner. Repeating a recurring observation, Parish argues that:

> [f]inance is not a science; it is not even an imprecise one, as it is based on predicting events whose occurrence depends upon people, whose conduct can never be formalised in a set of rules no matter how much data one has. . . . Risk aversion is a quality that varies wildly from one investor to another. Even discounting different perceptions of risk, different investors may allow themselves to be motivated by a variety of different factors which are not strictly financial.[86]

Even disregarding personal differences, Malinconico observes provocatively that if a rule in the market should be found this would be represented by uncertainty and lack of transparency.[87] Predictions would not always be confirmed according to a regular causal nexus since it is a real possibility that 'it is exactly the improbable that results in the success or failure of an investment'. Somewhat caustically, Tarullo advances that the reference to a market standard would be just an exercise in 'mimicry'.[88] Ultimately, the imposition of an abstract standard of behaviour would result in a sort of *dirigisme* 'liable to mortify the public enterprise as compared to the private one'.[89]

Therefore, the core of this criticism is that the market paradigm is *inherently fallacious* and, since it cannot apply to private investors, its imposition on public investors is all the more liable to discriminate against them.

The fundamental nihilism of these critical arguments is too extreme. It seems clear to this author that (i) it is possible to talk of the market as a principle and of its underlying rules, and that (ii) the reference to them is the most natural way to assess the public intervention in the market. Although it is sometimes difficult to find or apply a precise benchmark, the conduct of private actors certainly follows certain principles generally resting on the fundamental premise of economics, focusing on the rational, self-interested and profit-maximizing *homo oeconomicus*.

This premise is often questioned. It is noted that entrepreneurs do not always behave rationally or with an individualistic goal (with arguments which intriguingly trespass into the second fundamental critique analysed below). Parish argues that a 'strong case can be made that private investors have regard to

[86] M Parish, 'On the Private Investor Principle' (2003) European Law Review 70, 71.

[87] C Malinconico, 'Aiuti di Stato' in MP Chiti and G Greco (eds), *Trattato di diritto amministrativo europeo* (Milan: Giuffré, 1999) 55, 92.

[88] DK Tarullo, 'Beyond Normalcy in the Regulation of International Trade' (1986/1987) Harvard Law Review 546, 570–9.

[89] C Malinconico, 'Aiuti di Stato' in MP Chiti and G Greco (eds), Trattato di diritto amministrativo europeo (Milan: Giuffré, 1999) 55, 92; see also G Karyfis, 'Le principe de l'opérateur économique privé, critère de qualification des mesure étatiques, en tant qu'aides d'Etat, au sens de l'article 87, par. 1 du Traité CE' (2003) Revue Trimestrielle de Droit Européen 389, 413.

"social, regional-policy and sector considerations" . . . as much as public investors' and that increasing wealth is not necessarily the motive of investors.[90] This may well be true in some, if not many cases. Readers should be aware of the fundamental debate concerning the very basic assumptions of economics, those that can be found in the first pages of any university textbooks, that agents in the market are 'self-interested', 'utility-maximising' and 'rational players'.[91] Behavioural decision theories, for example, tend to criticize these assumptions and suggest that individuals may be motivated by a broader range of reasons.[92]

There is nonetheless considerable empirical (and common sense) evidence supporting the presumption that normally *rationality* is adhered to as well as that *profit* is the main motivator of economic agents. Although sometimes difficult to uncover, criteria and benchmarks, which refer to the behaviour of a typical, and certainly to some extent idealized, economic operator situated in that particular set of circumstances, can be found and developed. Certainly, as with any idealization, adjustments may be needed but even factors such as uncertainty and lack of information can be duly taken into account in the application of these criteria.

Since the market has its principles and rules, the conduct of economic actors operating within the market should be judged according to those rules.

If an undertaking does not behave in a commercially sound way it is punished. The company may lose shares to competitors and, in the most extreme cases, be driven out of the market. The management may be put into question by shareholders and replaced. It seems natural and logical that if a public body decides to enter the market it should follow its rules and its conduct should be reviewed on the basis of these rules (which, considering the complexity of business reality and decision-making, may well be based on flexible 'standards'). Ultimately, this is not only natural and logical but also justified by the need *not* to *discriminate against private actors*.

The scrutiny according to these rules is particularly important for two reasons that specifically relate to public agents. On the one side, public bodies may well draw from considerable financial resources which may enable them to better withstand the misfortune of a commercial venture. On the other side, the kind of accountability in case of bad or simply unlucky public investments is less clear. Some stakeholders (consider the constituency of the region where an ailing, heavily subsidized industry is located) may well support the investment despite its inconsistency with market logic.

These two concerns about a particularly deep pocket and the lack of business accountability may be partly addressed by the trends towards increasing budgetary constraints and more efficient use of public money which, for political and cultural

[90] M Parish, 'On the Private Investor Principle' (2003) European Law Review 70, 71 and 75.

[91] For a thoughtful discussion see A Sen, *On Ethics and Economics* (Oxford: Blackwell, 1987).

[92] With respect to finance, see A Shleifer, *Inefficient Markets: An Introduction to Behavioural Finance* (Oxford: Oxford University Press, 2000).

reasons, have gained approval in recent years. The fact remains that, from a commercial perspective, the liaison between the government and the market may be dangerous. Thus, if the scrutiny of public intervention in the market will always raise controversies, there seems to be at least an increasing recognition of the need for better transparency with respect to the financial relations of governmental bodies.[93]

In conclusion, despite its shortcomings, a market benchmark can be found and used. The author also tends to a have a more positive attitude than those, such as Smits, who accept the notion of a market benchmark but consider it as 'la moins mauvaise des solutions'.[94] The author is certainly more in line with Smits' subsequent remark that '[p]lutôt que de le supprimer, il conviendrait de le clarifier'.[95] In this regard, a general suggestion, in the name of 'flexibility', is put forward in the next paragraph.

A flexible solution

Rather than radically negating the existence of rules in the market, the concerns about a too abstract and rigid approach, which constitute the substance of the criticisms deployed against the market principle, can be addressed by using the necessary degree of *flexibility* in the identification and application of the appropriate benchmarks. From the normative (be it legislative or judicial) side, this translates in the idea of relying more on 'standards' than 'rules',[96] and in adopting a reasonably deferential approach. With words equally applicable to EC law and WTO law, the Commission noted that:

> [the] analysis of risk [which is demanded by any investment] requires public undertakings, like private undertakings, to exercise entrepreneurial skills, which by the very nature of the problem implies a wide margin of judgment on the part of the investor. Within that wide margin the exercise of judgment by the investor cannot be regarded as involving State aid. . . .
>
> [i]t is not the Commission's intention to apply the principles in this communication (in what is necessarily a complex field) in a dogmatic or doctrinaire fashion. It understands that a wide margin must come into entrepreneurial investment decisions. The principles have

93 A good model is represented by the EC 'Transparency Directive' (Commission Directive 80/723/EEC on the transparency of financial relations between Member States and public undertakings as well as on the financial transparency within certain undertakings, OJ L195, 29.7.1980, 35, subsequently amended various times).

The need for increased transparency in the government-public sector's financial relations is increasingly felt at a global level too. See, eg, in the context of Doha subsidy negotiations the Proposal from the US, TN/RL/GEN/146, 5 June 2007. See, also, with respect to a compact regulating 'international investment subsidies', GC Hufbauer, T Moll, and L Rubini, 'Investment Subsidies for Cross-Border MandA: Trends and Policy Implications', Occasional Paper Series No 2, United States Council for International Business Foundation, New York, 2008.

94 C Smits, 'La notion d'avantage et le critère de "l'opérateur en économie en marché"', in M Dony and C Smits (eds), *Aides d'Etat* (Brussels: Editions de l'Université de Bruxelles, 2005) 53, 78.

95 That is, rather than get rid of it, it would be better to clarify it.

96 See section I.A above.

however to be applied when it is *beyond reasonable doubt that there is no other plausible explanation* for the provision of public funds other than considering them as State aid.[97]

Although consistently repeated, this principle has not always been followed. In the already cited *Bremer Vulkan* decision, the Court defended the need for a flexible approach and criticized the Commission for having considered, without adequate explanation, the stock market price as the sole determining factor in valuing shares, and noted that 'that view is too formal, rigid and restrictive. To apply that criterion absolutely and unconditionally, to the exclusion of all other elements, constitutes a purely mechanical exercise which can scarcely be reconciled with the system of the market economy and the economic choices made in the present case by undertakings of substantial size guided by prospects of profitability in the longer term'.[98]

The use of 'average benchmarks' provides an interesting illustration of the possible ambiguity of the notion of flexibility. At first glance, the use of 'average' indicators seems to represent a straightforward application of the principle. A closer look, however, reveals that 'average' criteria are by definition inelastic. Average benchmarks have thus been criticized as too restrictive since they inevitably become *minimum* standards and thus *outlaw* any *conduct* which, albeit below average, would be *acceptable* to *some* private actors.[99] Hufbauer and Shelton Erb underline the irony that '[t]his is a fairly rigorous test since, at any given time, approximately half the industrial firms in the country will be earning less than the average return on equity'.[100]

If used correctly, a flexible application of market criteria allows the taking into account of all the circumstances of the case and making the necessary accommodation. A couple of examples concerning public actors may be useful. One common criticism of the possibility of using market benchmarks with public entrepreneurs is that, even if a rule guiding private operators is found, there would be inherent *economic* differences between public and private undertakings, mainly dependent on the (allegedly) unlimited financial resources of governments.[101]

[97] Commission Communication, Application of Articles 92 and 93 of the EEC Treaty and of Article 5 of Commission Directive 80/723/EEC to public undertakings in the manufacturing sector, OJ C307, 13.11.1993, 3, paras 27 and 29 (emphasis added).

[98] Cases C-329/93, C-62/95 and C-63/95, para 36.

[99] The issue has recently come into prominence in the EC with the judicial review of a Commission decision which applied an 'average rate of return' test. The decision of the CFI in joined Cases T-228/99 and T-233/99 *WestLB* is not fully clear in dealing with the issue (see, eg, para 258 of the judgment). See M Hansen, A Van Ysendyck, and S Zühlke, 'The Coming of Age of EC State Aid Law: A Review of the Principal Developments in 2002 and 2003' (2004) European Competition Law Review 202, 207; C Smits, 'La notion d'avantage et le critère de "l'opérateur en économie en marché"', in M Dony and C Smits (eds), *Aides d'Etat* (Brussels : Editions de l'Université de Bruxelles, 2005) 53, 63–5.

[100] GC Hufbauer and J Shelton Erb, *Subsidies in International Trade* (Cambridge, Massachusetts: MIT Press, 1984) 101.

[101] M Hansen, A Van Ysendyck, and S Zühlke, 'The Coming of Age of EC State Aid Law: A Review of the Principal Developments in 2002 and 2003' (2004) European Competition Law Review 202, 203.

A flexible application of market criteria should arguably allow for these peculiar economic features to be taken into consideration and the necessary adjustments to be made.

There is another interesting scenario. Suppose that the government manages to practice better conditions than those prevailing in the market, or to provide products or services that are not available in it. The doubt may be that this does not depend on superior efficiency, that is ability, of the agent but rather on its public status. However, the possibility that a public agent not only matches its market competitors (which is usually tested in the 'market' advantage analysis) but is in fact doing better than them cannot be ruled out completely. Although the numerous critics of public entrepreneurial and managerial potential might almost instinctively dismiss this possibility, as a matter of principle, it cannot be excluded. A non-abstract and non-dogmatic application of the market principle should represent a useful tool to analyse these situations.

This issue could have been tackled in the *Canada—Aircraft II* dispute with respect to a particular type of equity guarantees. A slight digression into the facts may be useful. Brazil argued that first loss deficiency guarantees (that is government guarantees to protect an equity investor from the risks inherent in the equity market), which had been provided by the Government of Québec to favour Canadian regional aircraft industry, 'quintessentially' conferred a benefit because they were not available in the market. Quite regrettably, the Panel did not address the interesting issue of whether or not, *as a matter of law*, the provision by a government of support not available in the market necessarily confers a benefit, because it eventually found that market equivalents did in fact exist.[102]

Final gloss: advantage analysis and distortion

This paragraph can be dovetailed with the analysis of another line of 'criticism' of market criteria since this provides an interesting opportunity for considering the role of the advantage analysis in the definition of subsidy.

Benitah suggests that to say that an advantage is conferred because the conduct at issue is at odds with what market logic would require would rest on a simple, or simplified, idea of *distortion* of the market functioning.[103] This may well be true but it is perfectly in line with the role of the element of advantage in the broader context of the definition of subsidy and State aid. Although there is a clear link between the determination of an advantage and a possible negative effect on the market (we may recall the Appellate Body's finding about the 'trade-distorting potential' of conduct deviating from market logic), the assessment of whether a

[102] Paragraph 7.341.

[103] M Benitah, *The Law of Subsidies under the GATT/WTO System* (The Hague: Kluwer Law International, 2001) 263.

distortion has actually taken place should be carried out at a subsequent stage of the analysis (see chapter 14).

What the determination of an advantage, in the form of a derogation from normal commercial practice, does is just to provide an indication, certainly significant but not final, that a 'potential' distortion of competition and trade may occur/has occurred.

B. Second criticism: the inconsistency of the market paradigm with the public interest

The second criticism[104] highlights another aspect of alleged discrimination of public investors since the use of the market paradigm—whose soundness, in principle, is not challenged—would not take into account the crucial determinant of public intervention in the market, ie the pursuit of the *public interest.* The presence of public policy objectives would impede a parallel with private investors who, by definition, pursue purely individualistic goals. The 'private investor' criterion should therefore be substituted for a more comprehensive 'public investor' criterion, modelled on the public role of governments.[105]

Generally speaking, two issues need to be addressed. The first is a question of *policy.* Should the regulation of subsidies at hand take public policy objectives into account? If this is the case (and in chapter 2, the author has argued this point vigorously), the second question is more, albeit not exclusively, *technical.* At what stage of the analysis should these objectives be considered? In particular, should their examination already occur at the level of the assessment of whether the conduct is commercially sound, ie of the advantage analysis? Assuming that the answer to the policy question is positive, it is useful to concentrate on the second issue which touches on one of the *leit motifs* of this work, ie the interplay between scope and justification in the regulation of subsidies and State aids.

The reader will recall the Appellate Body's finding in *Canada—Aircraft* that the market should be the appropriate basis for comparison in the advantage analysis of the economic conduct of the government because of its ability to identify the 'trade-distorting potential' of the financial contribution. This finding led the author to formulate a broad hypothesis, ie that the advantage analysis of economic activity (in both WTO and EC law) should be based on those *economic* considerations that may signal a distortion to the competitive process and that *any* other consideration that might not be indicative from this perspective should be excluded. A measure deviating from market practice would clearly suggest a potential of

104 Which arguably does not seem to have much following any more.

105 For this line of argument with respect to the GATT and the EC see, respectively, M Coccia, 'Comment' in JHJ Bourgeois (ed), *Subsidies and International Trade—A European Lawyers' Perspective* (Deventer-Boston: Kluwer, 1991) 139, 148 et seq, and H Lesguillons, 'Comment' in JHJ Bourgeois (ed), *Subsidies and International Trade—A European Lawyers' Perspective* (Deventer-Boston: Kluwer, 1991) 151, 153 et seq.

distortion of the market. The further, important, implication was that public policy objectives could find with difficulty a place at this stage of the analysis. The time has now come to test that potentially far-reaching hypothesis in both WTO and EC law.

WTO law

Public intervention in the economy is normally justified by public policy considerations. Legally, it is important to determine the role played by the public interest, particularly in the context of the definition of subsidy. The issue is not new.

As early as 1961, a Panel attempted to consider the 'reasons for subsidies' under Article XVI of the GATT but, as emerges from the report, this attempt was abandoned. Consequently, Jackson seemed to conclude that the study of the purpose of subsides is 'not relevant to the question of whether it falls within the terms of Article XVI'.[106] The 'reasons for subsidies' were discussed during the Tokyo Round and the ensuing Subsidies Code deals with them, although ambivalently. Articles 8.1 and 11 simply recognize the possible opposite effects of subsidies (which may distort competition and trade and at the same time pursue important and legitimate socio/economic objectives). However, none of the provisions provide any indication of how to assess these effects, and, most importantly, how to balance them and solve any conflict. These provisions are thus more descriptive (of the ambivalent reality of subsidization) than prescriptive (of how this ambivalence should be regulated).

The issue of subsidy objectives came out prominently in one of the last GATT disputes, *US—Lead and Bismuth I* where the Tokyo Round Subsidies Code was the relevant law. Although the report was not adopted because the issues were negotiated in the context of the SCM Agreement, it had an impact on those negotiations.[107] For these reasons, and for the interesting statements contained therein, a full examination of the Panel report is justified.

The definition of subsidy in the Tokyo Round Subsidies Code and public policy objectives: *US—Lead and Bismuth I*[108]

The case concerned the imposition of countervailing duties by the US on certain steel imports from the EC.

The EC argued that the standard of 'reasonable private investor' used by the US Department of Commerce (DOC) to assess the provision of equity capital was contrary to the term 'subsidy' referred to in Article 4.2 of Part I of the Tokyo Round

[106] JH Jackson, *World Trade and the Law of GATT* (Indianapolis: Bobbs Merrill, 1969) 387.

[107] M Matsushita, TJ Schoenbaum, and PC Mavroidis, *The World Trade Organization—Law, Practice, and Policy* (1st edn, Oxford: Oxford University Press, 2003) 267. See also PJ McDonough, 'Subsidies and Countervailing Measures' in TP Stewart (ed), *The Gatt Uruguay Round—A Negotiating History (1986–1992)*, Volume I (Deventer: Kluwer, 1993) 809.

[108] The relevant paragraphs of the report are 434–51.

Subsidies Code because it failed to consider that governments often invest in pursuance of public policy objectives. In sum, 'government motives for investment, and therefore benchmarks for governments, [are] different from investment by private individuals' with the consequence that the appropriate standard should thus be that of a 'reasonable *public* investor'. This standard allows for the balancing of commercial factors and public policy objectives, considering that, unlike private investors, governments do not necessarily aim to achieve a maximum return on their investment. The test would *not* be met when the equity infusion is made 'for *social reasons only* and *without any serious chance of breaking even in the long run*' (emphasis added).

The US responded that 'public policy objectives [are] irrelevant to a determination of whether or not the provision of equity capital by a government [is] a subsidy'. The EC's reasoning was 'circular' since it 'could be used to rationalize any provision of equity capital by a government'. Moreover, the US claimed 'that the "reasonable public investor" criterion proposed by the EC was without logic in that from the standpoint of a government all subsidies could be said to be "reasonable"'. The quite blunt conclusion was that the 'EC was simply proposing an alternative test without explaining why the Agreement [ie the Tokyo Round Subsidies Code] required such a test'.

The importance of the interpretative issue was immediately recognized by the Panel: 'the rationale of the EC's argument was potentially applicable to a wide range of forms of government intervention'. Thus, 'the argument of the EC raised the *more general question* of whether or not, for the purpose of the determination of the *existence* of a countervailable *subsidy*, public policy objectives pursued by governments are to be taken into account by investigating authorities' (emphasis added).

The Panel analysed the overall Tokyo Round Subsidies Code for guidance.[109] It found nothing in the provisions of Part I on countervailing action (which was under examination in the case) to indicate that public policy objectives should be taken into account in order to determine whether a given measure constitute a countervailable subsidy. Although noting that a reference to the objectives of the subsidies was expressly made in Part II subsidy discipline (particularly, in Articles 8.1 and 11), the Panel crucially found that, *even in that context*, while recognizing the right of signatories to use subsidies in pursuance of various public policy objectives, Article 11 did

> not provide that such policy objectives are relevant to a determination of whether a particular practice constitutes a subsidy. Under Article 11, the *existence of a subsidy* and the *public policy objectives pursued* with that subsidy are *separate matters*.[110]

[109] The reader may recall that a significant interpretative issue raised by the Tokyo Round Subsidies Code was whether Part I (countervailing duties) and Part II (subsidy discipline) featured the same notion of subsidy. This point is now positively solved by the SCM Agreement: see Articles 1.2 and 10.

[110] Paragraph 448 (emphasis added).

The important conclusion was that, under both Parts of the Tokyo Subsidies Code, the determination of whether or not a particular practice constitutes a (countervailable) subsidy *does not require* the consideration of the public policy objectives eventually pursued by the government. Only market considerations are relevant when determining whether a subsidy exists. Policy objectives are a 'separate matter'.

The benefit requirement in the SCM and public policy objectives
The conclusion reached with respect to the Tokyo Round Subsidies Code may be easily transposed into the context of the SCM Agreement.[111] Not only is it now clear that only one definition of subsidy is applicable, but, most importantly, the fairly descriptive and inconclusive language of Articles 8.1 and 11 of the Code was fully developed in the SCM Agreement into a more prescriptive discipline.

The SCM Agreement did provide for 'separate provisions' for the definition of what constitutes a *subsidy*—and within it a *benefit*—on the one hand, and what subsidies are *non-actionable* because they pursue *public policy objectives* (notably: regional, research and development and enviroment) on the other. It does not seem, however, that the fact that the category of non-actionable subsidy expired in the year 2000, may affect the conclusion as to the role of public policy objectives and alter the structure of the SCM Agreement as it was designed. The only consequence of this lapse is that, at least for now, one important limb is missing and the current discipline does not provide for any justification of important policy objectives.[112]

EC law

The restrictive approach towards the role of public policy objectives in the context of the definition of aid was laid down in the mid-eighties in the *Meura* case. The Court found that the comparator of the public investor must be a private one which, in similar circumstances, takes a decision to invest 'having regard to the foreseeability of obtaining a return and *leaving aside all social, regional-policy and sectoral consideration*'.[113] In *Hytasa*, Advocate General Jacobs observed that aid is granted whenever a State makes available to an undertaking funds which in the normal course of events would not be provided by a private investor applying ordinary commercial criteria and *disregarding considerations of a social, political or philanthropic nature*.[114] The Court concluded that it is necessary to distinguish the

[111] See, eg, Panel, *US—Softwood Lumber III*, para 7.16.

[112] For an analysis of the possibility of relying on the general provision for general exceptions in Article XX of the GATT, see chapter 6, section III.C.

[113] Case 234/84 *Meura*, para 14 (emphasis added).

[114] See Joined Cases 278 to 280/92 *Hytasa*, para 28 of the Opinion (emphasis added).

obligations which the State must assume as owner of the share capital of a company and its obligations as a public authority.[115]

This is the current State of the law. It is, however, useful to analyse two cases where the issue of whether a different test should apply to public investors was thoroughly discussed. This analysis will also provide the opportunity for a parallel with the GATT.

In *Alfa Romeo* the Court drew an important distinction between ordinary investors and holdings or groups of companies, by highlighting that these may pursue different objectives in their investment decisions. In *ENI-Lanerossi* the Court accepted that a parent company may decide to cover the losses of one subsidiary for a limited period in order to enable it either to reorganize it or to close down under the best possible conditions, and in doing so it 'may be motivated not solely by the likelihood of an indirect material profit but also by other considerations, such as a desire to protect the group's image or to redirect its activities'. Nevertheless, in both cases the Court underlined that an injection of capital that disregards any prospect of profitability, even in the long term, should be regarded as aid.[116] It is interesting to note that the Court's reasoning makes reference only to factors, such as profitability, restructuring plan, overcapacity, image, etc, that are inherently economic.

Advocate General Van Gerven took a more open approach in his two Opinions.

In *ENI* he underlined that, although both private and public undertakings should always be guided by 'the laws of the market place', even a private investor, particularly if it is a large holding company, *would not be wholly uninfluenced by considerations of a social nature or of regional or sectoral policy*. Quite clearly, this would *a fortiori* apply to public holding companies.[117]

In *Alfa Romeo* he developed this line of thinking and introduced the concept of *reasonable* investor.[118]

This would include ordinary and stable private investors. However, while the ordinary investors would not be interested in a shareholding significant enough to influence the management of the company, stable investors, such as holding companies, would possess, or in any event would wish to possess, shareholdings large enough to influence the governance of the undertaking. Both would be guided by considerations of profitability. Stable investors would, however, consider a longer period of time, and—quite interestingly—would also have regard to *considerations of employment and economic development in a given region or sector*. A passage of the Opinion deserves a full quotation because it attempts to explain where the balance between profitability and other objectives is set.

> In shifting the emphasis from the 'private' to the 'reasonable' investor, I am not suggesting that the requirement of profitability may be left out of account. The reasonable investor or

[115] ibid, para 22 of the decision.

[116] C-305/89, *Alfa Romeo*, para 20; C-303/88, *ENI*, para 22.

[117] Paragraph 14 (emphasis added).

[118] See paras 11 and 12 of the Opinion.

holding company (whether from the private or public sector) must, in order to act responsibly, secure a normal return on its investments, even if in so doing it may have regard to a wider social and economic context and over a longer time span. It is above all in the case of public holdings that the profitability requirement must be underlined, since they are under less pressure than private holding companies to make profit for shareholders who (directly or indirectly) are 'ordinary' private investors, given that the risk capital of public holding companies is directly or indirectly financed by public funds.[119]

It is now interesting to take a step backward and compare the criterion of the 'reasonable investor' suggested by Van Gerven (which was not supported by the Commission and was rejected by the Court of Justice) and the position that the EC (ie the Commission) took in the GATT in the *US—Lead and Bismuth I* dispute where they sponsored a 'reasonable public investor' test.

Leaving linguistic differences aside, the substance is remarkably similar, if not identical. Reading the the test advanced in the GATT dispute is useful in this regard. The 'reasonable public investor' standard would allow for the balancing of commercial factors and public policy objectives, on the premise that, unlike private investors, governments do not necessarily aim to achieve a maximum return on their investment. The test would not be met when the equity infusion is made 'for social reasons only and without any serious chance of breaking even in the long run'.

The balance between the profit imperative and public policy objectives is just the same. One could then ask whether the adoption of an apparently more lenient approach towards public investment in the GATT as compared to that embraced in its internal system is justified. In the author's view, the answer is yes, and this is the case for various reasons.

The political and litigation context comes to prominence immediately. In *US—Lead and Bismuth I* the EC is 'defending' the conduct of its Member States. In *Alfa Romeo* and *ENI* it is closely scrutinizing it. The difference between the two situations can however be found at another, properly legal, level. It can be noted that Advocate General Van Gerven's 'reasonable investor' test is universal inasmuch as it applies to both public and private investors. The 'reasonable *public* investor' test put forward by the EC is contrasted to the 'reasonable *private*' test defended by the US. It draws a clear distinction between private investors and public investors and aims to apply *only* to the latter's conduct in the market.

Here is the core of the issue. The more lenient approach towards public investors adopted by the Commission in the GATT context can be understood by properly considering the fundamental structural difference between the two legal frameworks—the Tokyo Round Subsidies Code on the one side and EC Treaty on the other.

The former represented a regulation of subsidies at an embryonic stage. Although the importance of public policy objectives was expressly recognized,

[119] Paragraph 12.

their regulation and relative weight in the balance with the distortions produced by subsidies was totally unclear. The inherent ambivalence of subsidies (distortive but legitimate) could not find a sufficiently prescriptive regulation which could provide equilibrium as well as clarity. By contrast, the EC Treaty had already displayed a more mature legal framework since the beginning (1957), with specific provisions addressing the public interest justifications (Article 87(2) and (3) and Article 86(2) of the EC), clearly *separate* from the general definition/prohibition of distorting State aid (and administered through a centralized and supranational system of control). Crucially, a similar framework was present in the SCM Agreement before the expiry of the non-actionable category (which, by clearly modelling itself on EC law, had given flesh to the ambiguous recognition of the Tokyo Round Subsidies Code).

Consequently, in EC law the distinction between economic and public policy considerations is clearly embedded in the idea that the concept of State aid is *objective* and its assessment is *effect-based* and that *causes and aims* of the measure are *not relevant* at this stage.[120] The fact that the notion of aid is objective does not leave much room for discretion in its analysis. By contrast, the status of public policy objectives in WTO subsidy discipline is still unclear.[121]

Certainly, in the analysis of the advantage in both market and, as we will see, also in non-market situations, what prevails is *judgement* rather than *deduction*. But this judgement does not directly, and freely, engage with *any* policy motive underlying State intervention. It is simply a recognition that, albeit within certain defined boundaries, the yardstick to assess certain conducts, should by necessity be flexible since those conducts are themselves based on complex decisions. And, in the case of non-economic conduct, it may require a limited assessment of the 'internal objectives' of the measure in the analysis of the 'logic or structure' of the measure.[122]

In this regard, it is interesting that all the cases where the 'objective approach' to the concept of State aid has been laid down involved tax measures, that is a form of conduct that is inherently public (and hence non-economic). The definition of the role of public policy objectives in the advantage analysis is particularly complex in this area. The government is by definition acting in the public sphere and the various public motives are difficult to disentangle. Those resolute statements about 'objectivity' and 'effect' which are formulated in general terms, are *all the more* significant when it comes to assessing the *economic* activity of governments where the distinction between commercial and public interest considerations should be more apparent.

In conclusion, if the action of the government confers an advantage and also pursues policy objectives, it seems that these should not be considered at the stage

[120] The *loci classici* are Case 173/73 *Italy v Commission*, para 13; Case 78/76 *Steinike*, para 21; Case T-67/94 *Ladbroke*, para 52.

[121] See chapter 2, section III.A and chapter 6, section III.C.

[122] See chapters 9 and particularly 10, section I.C.

of the definition of State aid, and in particular at the level of the advantage analysis. The crucial factor is that the EC State aid system already provides specific provisions where the public interest should be taken into account.

Conclusions: distinction between market and public interest

One of the recurring themes of this book is the analysis of the role played by the public interest in the various stages of the analysis of the legal definition of subsidy. This is rephrased, from another perspective, as 'scope-justification' interaction.

The previous examination indicates that the advantage analysis of market activity requires in both WTO and EC law a *distinction* between *market logic* and *public policy objectives.*

It is natural that the advantage analysis of the economic conduct of the public investor is tested against the market and its benchmarks. Although this assessment should be flexible, this cannot go so far as to forget commercial logic in favour of public policy objectives. In short, both systems seem to endorse, at least with respect to the assessment of the economic activity of governments, a *distinction between scope (which is defined by the market paradigm) and justification (which is defined by the public interest).*

Despite everything, the author believes that those who fear too harsh a treatment of public investors and the public interest may be reassured. The story so far is by no means about irrelevance but distinction.

IV. A word of conclusion: the redemption of the market paradigm

The market is a paradigm. But, despite (or because of) this, it involves difficulties, complexities and criticisms. In particular, not only has it been advanced that the identification and application of market benchmarks may be complex and their review a difficult exercise; it has been argued more fundamentally that the use of the market as a comparator is neither possible nor legitimate.

Business is complex but it has some rules. To quote Professor Marcus (Sir Alec Guinness) in the comedy *Ladykillers* of 1955:

> It was a good plan you know . . . Except for the human element . . . But no really good plan could account for Mrs Wilberforce.[123]

The moral for our analysis? The 'human element' is crucial. Further, there might be a 'Mrs Wilberforce element' in every business situation which can make even the most 'perfect' plan unsuccessful. But this is part of the market game. *Risk* and *probability*, not *chaos*, are the keywords. And risk and probability can largely be

[123] The reader may recall Mrs Wilberforce, the little old lady capable of unexpectedly stymying the perfect robbery plan of a gang of five men, headed by Professor Marcus.

calculated and managed. Rules and benchmarks, albeit flexible ones, can be found and used after the necessary fine-tuning and adjustments.

Mainly in analysing the criticisms against the market principle, the author has thus attempted to offer a solution which, by taking stock of difficulties and concerns, could reach a balanced view of the utility of the market logic and its benchmarks in the advantage analysis of the economic activity of governments.

The two key conclusions have been (i) that a *flexible approach* is needed in the application of complex market criteria, especially at the level of the review of business decisions, and (ii) that legitimate and almost ubiquitous *public interest* considerations should be *distinguished* from the *market* analysis and should not be considered at the level of the advantage analysis.

9

Non-economic activity and the advantage analysis in the WTO

This chapter concerns the advantage analysis of those forms of action that are inherently public inasmuch as they are non-economic. These include taxation, regulation and (pure) public goods.

The analysis focuses mainly on tax measures, ie those measures whereby governments exercise their authority to impose and levy monetary payments, like direct and indirect tax and social contributions. This focus is for two reasons—on the one hand, unlike regulation, fiscal policy constitutes one of the most consolidated and increasingly common means to grant assistance, thus providing a great wealth of cases and issues to concentrate on in both systems. On the other hand, the observations made in the tax context are of more general validity and can be extended to regulation and public goods, should these be caught by the rules.

I. Tax measures

A. A methodological premise: the advantage analysis between 'financial contribution' and 'benefit'

The starting point of the advantage analysis for tax measures in WTO law should be the interpretation of the phrase 'government revenue that is otherwise due is foregone or not collected' in Article 1.1(a)(1)(ii) of the SCM.

Since it seems more natural to concentrate on the concept of benefit under Article 1.1(b) of the SCM, rather than on one of the forms of financial contribution, it is important to justify this choice immediately and make it clear that we are not attempting to drop one of the two criteria (notably the benefit) or to conflate them.

In general, although financial contribution and benefit are different requirements and should, in principle, be interpreted according to their own criteria,[1] they can certainly represent part of the relevant context of each other. This is particularly so in this case where the form of financial contribution under Article 1.1(a)(1)(ii) is clearly linked to the benefit analysis in various respects.

[1] See, eg, Appellate Body, *Brazil—Aircraft*, para 157. See also *Canada—Aircraft*, para 156.

To understand this point, it is useful to compare the assessment required by the phrase 'otherwise due' in subparagraph (ii) with the analysis of governmental activities in the *market* under the 'benefit' requirement. In *Canada—Aircraft* the Appellate Body held:

[w]e also believe that the word "benefit", as used in Article 1.1(b), implies some kind of comparison. This must be so, for there can be no "benefit" to the recipient unless the "financial contribution" makes the recipient "better off" than it would otherwise have been, absent that contribution.[2]

In the *US—FSC* dispute the Appellate Body construed the phrase 'government revenue that is otherwise due is foregone' in Article 1.1(a)(1)(ii) of the SCM as follows:

[i]n our view, the '*foregoing*' of revenue '*otherwise* due' implies that less revenue has been raised by the government than would have been raised in a different situation, or, that is, 'otherwise'.... We ... agree with the Panel that the term 'otherwise due' implies some kind of comparison between the revenue due under the contested measure and revenues that would be due in some other situation.[3]

The language of the two passages is strikingly similar and the analogy is particularly interesting. First, both terms, 'benefit' and 'otherwise due' would 'imply some kind of comparison'. This comparison is between the actual case and another benchmark situation that would have occurred 'otherwise' (respectively, the 'marketplace' and the appropriate 'tax rules').[4] Secondly, the language of both cases, in a more or less direct way, hints at the fact that this derogation from the relevant benchmark may confer an advantage. In fact there is a difference in the two passages because there is more emphasis on the favouring effect of the measure in the first case (the financial contribution is expressly said to make the recipient 'better off') than in the second (where the foregoing of revenue otherwise due logically implies that 'less revenue' is raised). It could not have been otherwise considering that the former case concerned the interpretation of the 'benefit' requirement. Nevertheless, this difference is arguably more a matter of *formulation* rather than of *substance* as the collection of 'less revenue' than would have occurred otherwise not only alludes to but almost invariably gives rise to a benefit for the exempted subject.

The analogies (and the difference) outlined above can be explained by considering both the *fabric* and *position* of the advantage analysis.

The fabric and the position of the advantage analysis

Conceptually, it is possible to divide the advantage analysis into two steps. The first is whether the measure at issue provides a *derogation from a given benchmark*.

[2] Appellate Body, *Canada—Aircraft*, para 157.
[3] Appellate Body, *US—FSC*, para 90.
[4] See Appellate Body, *Canada—Aircraft*, para 157; Appellate Body, *US—FSC*, para 90.

The second is whether this deviation operates *to the advantage of* the undertakings at issue.

The position of these two steps in the definition of subsidy in the SCM Agreement is different in the advantage analysis of economic conduct and taxation respectively. Whereas in the case of market conduct they are *both* located in the context of the benefit requirement under Article 1.1(b) of the SCM, in the case of tax measures they are indeed already and mainly to be found at the level of the financial contribution.

Subparagraphs (i) and (iii) of Article 1.1(a)(1), which regulate governmental economic activities, merely identify the form of the conduct of the government (transfers of funds, provision of goods and services, procurement of goods) but are quite neutral with respect to both (i) its derogating character and (ii) its advantage, thus leaving this determination entirely to the following and separate analysis of the benefit requirement under Article 1(b) of the SCM.

On the other hand, the identification of the form of financial contribution under subparagraph (ii), which refers to the case of 'foregoing' or 'non-collection' of government revenue 'otherwise due', is not neutral but *already includes* a test which inquires as to (i) whether the conduct of the government derogates from a benchmark situation (as it is hinted by the 'otherwise due' language) and—to a large extent—also (ii) whether it favours the tax payer (as it is suggested, as a matter of logic, by the 'foregoing'/'non-collection' language).[5] Indeed in these cases the subsequent analysis of the benefit under Article 1.1(b) is usually straightforward. Once it has been established that government revenue, otherwise due, has been foregone or not collected, the existence of a benefit can be safely assumed.[6]

In sum, substantially what we see in the case of tax measures is *the anticipated insertion* (under paragraph (ii) of Article 1.1(a)(1) of the SCM) of the (two steps of the) *advantage analysis* which is usually carried out under the benefit of Article 1.1(b) of the SCM. It is this anticipation that in the author's view justifies the examination of the first provision in this context.

B. Case study: the *US—FSC* dispute

The construction of the 'otherwise due' requirement under Article 1.1(a)(1)(ii) of the SCM was one of the crucial issues in the celebrated *US—FSC* dispute. The significant findings of the Panels and the Appellate Body makes this dispute an excellent case-study to analyse the various tests and benchmarks used to determine whether the measure at issue is liable to confer an advantage and constitute a tax

[5] It is interesting to ask whether it is possible to formulate the conduct of (preferential) fiscal treatment in a more neutral way similar to that of market conduct. If precision is the aim, it is not possible to phrase subpara (ii) differently. As soon as mention is made to the foregoing or non-collection of revenue, the inevitable implication—which does not need to be expressly worded—is that revenue that was 'otherwise due' has been waived to the 'advantage' of the tax payer.

[6] cf Panel, *US—FSC*, para 7.103; Panel, *US—FSC* (21.5 EC), para 8.46.

subsidy under WTO law. In our examination we draw substantially on the insightful analysis of Professor Hudec.[7]

Introduction

Traditionally under US tax law, income earned outside the country is taxed if there is an effective connection with a trade or business in the United States (under the principle of worldwide taxation). The *FSC* legislation introduced an exemption from taxation on a portion of the 'foreign trade income' of certain companies established outside the United States (*Foreign Sales Corporations*, or *FSC*).[8] The *FSC* tax exemption was adopted by the US to replace its predecessor *DISC* to comply with a '1981 Understanding' which ended the impasse over the adoption of the *DISC* litigation reports.[9] With this Understanding the parties accepted that 'economic processes located outside the territorial limits of the exporting country *need not be subject to taxation by the exporting country and should not be regarded as export activities*' (emphasis added). Two conditions had to be fulfilled however, namely that the exemption be limited only to *foreign economic processes* (ie sales activities taking place outside the government's territory) and to *foreign-source income* (which would have been ensured by calculating the exempt income on the basis of arm's length pricing).

Leaving aside the debated issue of the legal effect of the 1981 Understanding, according to most observers, the *FSC* tax exemption did not in any event meet the conditions set out above. The *FSC* legislation required very little genuine foreign

[7] RE Hudec, 'Industrial Subsidies: Tax Treatment of "Foreign Sales Corporations"' in EU Petersmann and MA Pollack (eds), *Transatlantic Economic Disputes—The EU, the US, and the WTO* (Oxford: Oxford University Press, 2003) 175.

[8] Various requirements had to be met for the definition of both 'foreign trade income' and *FSC*. The law is thoroughly exposed by the Panel *US—FSC* at paras 2.1–2.8.

[9] The expression DISC litigation refers to the four disputes (*US—DISC*, *Belgium—Income Tax*, *France—Income Tax* and *Netherlands—Income Tax*) decided in 1977 with four panel reports. These reports concluded that the US DISC tax exemptions on the one side and the application of the territorial systems of taxation of France, Belgium and the Netherlands on the other constituted export subsidies. The required unanimity to adopt the reports could not be found until a settlement was finally agreed with the '1981 Understanding' which was adopted by the Council. There is an extensive literature on the DISC cases and the *FSC* legislation/litigation. See, eg, JH Jackson, 'The Jurisprudence of International Trade: The DISC Case in GATT' (1978) American Journal of International Law 747; GC Hufbauer and J Shelton Erb, *Subsidies in International Trade* (Cambridge, Massachusetts: MIT Press, 1984) 57–63), JM Gray, 'Taxation: Foreign Sales Corporations Replace Domestic International Sales Corporations' (1985) Harvard International Law Review 293; J Klabbers and A Vregdenhil, 'Dispute Settlement in GATT: DISC and its Successor' (1986/1987) Legal Issues of European Integration 115; L Weizmann, 'The Making of an Export Subsidy: DISCs and FSCs in Compliance with the GATT' (1987) World Competition 57; AH Qureshi and R Grynberg, 'United States Tax Subsidies Under Domestic International Sales Corporation, Foreign Sales Corporation and Extraterritorial Income Exclusion Act Legislation within the Framework of the World Trade Organization' (2002) Journal of World Trade 979; RE Hudec, *Enforcing International Trade Law—The Evolution of the Modern GATT Legal System* (Salem, New Hampshire: Buttherworth Legal Publishers 1993) 53–100, and id, 'Industrial Subsidies: Tax Treatment of "Foreign Sales Corporations"' in EU Petersmann and MA Pollack (eds), *Transatlantic Economic Disputes—The EU, the US, and the WTO* (Oxford: Oxford University Press, 2003) 175.

economic activity and the pricing rules' percentages did not comply with the arm's length principle.[10] Eventually, the EC alleged a violation of *inter alia* the SCM Agreement and in 1997 filed a complaint with the WTO.

One of the debated points in the *FSC* dispute, which directly concerns the advantage analysis in taxation, focused on the interpretation of the 'otherwise due' requirement under Article 1.1(a)(1)(ii) of the SCM.

The 'but for' test between simplicity and inadequacy

The Panel: the choice of simplicity

After underlining that the reference benchmark in the interpretation of the 'otherwise due' requirement must be found in the tax regime of the defending Member State,[11] the Panel put forward a test which should be used in determining whether revenue otherwise due has been foregone. In a repetitive passage it noted:

> [i]n accordance with its ordinary meaning, we took the term '*otherwise* due' to refer to the situation that would prevail but for the measures in question. It is thus a matter of determining whether, absent such measures, there would be a higher tax liability. In our view, this means that a panel, in considering whether revenue foregone is 'otherwise due', must examine the situation that would exist but for the measure in question. Under this approach, the question presented in this dispute is whether, if the *FSC* scheme did not exist, revenue would be due which is foregone by reason of that scheme.[12]

The Panel interpreted the 'otherwise due' phrase as referring to the situation that would prevail *but for* or *in the absence of* the measure in question. The inherent 'instability' of this 'but for' test (and, more generally, of the 'otherwise due' language)[13] is evident. In particular, the problem in the 'but for' approach is that it does not offer any solid indication about the *benchmark* against which the measure has to be tested.[14] This lacuna was acknowledged by the Appellate Body when it underlined the need to refer to 'some defined, normative benchmark'.[15]

[10] cf RE Hudec, *Enforcing International Trade Law—The Evolution of the Modern GATT Legal System* (Salem, New Hampshire: Buttherworth Legal Publishers 1993) 95–8, and id, 'Industrial Subsidies: Tax Treatment of "Foreign Sales Corporations"' in EU Petersmann and MA Pollack (eds), *Transatlantic Economic Disputes—The EU, the US, and the WTO* (Oxford: Oxford University Press, 2003) 175, 180.

[11] Panel, *US—FSC*, para 7.43.

[12] ibid, para 7.45.

[13] M Benitah, *The Law of Subsidies under the GATT/WTO System* (The Hague: Kluwer Law International, 2001) 188.

[14] Using mathematical language, 'saying that an exemption amounts to "foregone revenue that is otherwise due" has no meaning if we do not have a universal reference set in which this exemption appears as a departure from the general regime': M Benitah, *The Law of Subsidies under the GATT/WTO System* (The Hague: Kluwer Law International, 2001) 188. The problem is that it is possible to identify different universal reference sets in any given case with the consequence that the assessment of the 'otherwise due' requirement may well lead to different results (ibid, 188 and 189).

[15] Appellate Body, *US—FSC*, para 90. Using the mathematical language of the previous note, we could describe the defined normative benchmark as the appropriate universal reference set.

The risk of this uncertainty is that the test be interpreted in a *mechanical* fashion by limiting the assessment to the *form* of the tax system without going beneath its surface. This danger was highlighted by the EC that was arguing that the 'but for' test was too much 'formalistic' and that a different test giving more consideration to 'substance' rather than to 'form' would be preferable.[16] It was necessary to identify 'a deviation from or exemption to the *generally* applied rate or basis for collection' of taxes[17] (proposition which corresponds to our 'derogation test'). This would occur when the exemption or exclusion from taxation is 'not based on neutral and objective criteria, ie the exemption or exclusion is special or programmatic'.[18] Despite heavily criticizing this test (and, in particular, the complexity of identifying general rules and exceptions, and the risk of confusion with the specificity test), the US did not propose any clear alternative test but generally shared the view as to the 'desirability of avoiding results that exalt form over substance' and 'the need to have clear rules'.[19]

The Panel acknowledged that there was a certain degree of convergence between the 'but for' test and the 'derogation test' as, in all probability, in many cases the same result would have been generated.[20] It nonetheless underlined that the 'but for' approach seemed more 'grounded in the actual text of the SCM Agreement' than the 'derogation' test.[21]

The conclusion that the 'but for' test is more in line with the wording of Article 1.1(a)(1)(ii) of the SCM than the 'derogation' test is however arguable.

The main reason for the adoption of the 'but for' approach is prosaic. It has never been really controversial that the *FSC* exemption constituted a tax subsidy. The application of the 'but for' test was therefore sufficient to show *in the case at hand* that in the absence of the measure in question there would have been a higher tax liability. In this context, the risks of excessive formalism that could derive from the counterfactual analysis of a 'but for' test (which had been hinted at by the EC) were not as concrete as the complexities of the more sophisticated search for general rules and exceptions of the derogation test (which had been exhaustively warned against by the US).

In short, the Panel opted for the route that, under the circumstances of the case, was the more straightforward and economical. It was thus mainly a *choice of simplicity*. The judicial philosophy underlying this choice is that simple cases require simple solutions.

[16] Panel, *US—FSC*, para 4.1063.
[17] ibid, para 4.591 (emphasis added).
[18] ibid, *US—FSC*, para 4.1057.
[19] ibid, paras 4.1095–4.1113.
[20] ibid, para 7.46.
[21] ibid.

The Appellate Body: the recognition of inadequacy

The doubts about the *inadequacy* of the 'but for' test and, in particular, about its risks of excessive formalism emerged more prominently in the appeal.

It is significant that the Appellate Body made it immediately clear that the 'otherwise due' phrase requires the identification of 'some defined, normative benchmark against which a comparison can be made between the revenue actually raised and the revenue that would have been raised "otherwise"'.[22] In a passage which nicely combined the principle of sovereignty of Member States in tax matters with the principle that WTO obligations must be respected, it generally stated that this benchmark must be found in the domestic tax rules of the Member State in question.[23] Then the time came to assess the 'but for' test:

> the Panel found that the term 'otherwise due' establishes a 'but for' test, in terms of which the appropriate basis of comparison for determining whether revenues 'otherwise due' is 'the situation that would prevail but for the measures in question'. In the present case, this legal standard provides a sound basis for comparison because it is not difficult to establish in what way the foreign source income of an FSC would be taxed 'but for' the contested measure.

In line with the previous remarks about the simplicity of the characterization of the *FSC* exemption, the Appellate Body thus approved of the use of the 'but for' test 'in the present case' because of its lack of difficulty. It could have stopped there but it did not. The world trade court decided to go on to comment on the general applicability of the 'but for' test in other situations.

After underlining that it had 'certain abiding reservations' about applying *any* legal standard such as the 'but for' test 'in the place of the actual treaty language' (and thus rejecting the possible suggestion that the 'but for' test was no more than a nice rephrasing of 'otherwise due'), it noted:

> we would have particular misgivings about using a 'but for' test if its application were limited to situations where there actually existed an alternative measure, under which the revenues in question would be taxed, absent the contested measure. It would, we believe, not be difficult to circumvent such a test by designing a tax regime under which there would be no general rule that applied formally to the revenues in question, absent the contested measures.[24]

The (un)expected conclusion therefore was that 'although the Panel's "but for" test works in this case, it may not work in other cases'.[25] The risks of excessive

[22] Appellate Body, *US—FSC*, para 90.

[23] ibid.

[24] Appellate Body, *US—FSC*, para 91. In the implementation phase (*US—FSC (Article 21.5 EC)*, para 91) the Appellate Body repeated the same concept: 'in identifying the normative benchmark, there may be situations where the measure at issue might be described as an "exception" to a "general" rule of taxation. In such situations, it may be possible to apply a "but for" test to examine the fiscal treatment of income absent the contested measure'.

[25] Appellate Body, *US—FSC*, para 91.

formalism of the 'but for' test which had been simply hinted at by the EC before the Panel (and partly acknowledged also by the US) were now directly addressed by the Appellate Body which, interestingly, did so *ex officio* as none of the parties had advanced any criticism to the Panel's interpretation.[26]

The crucial warning was that the advantage analysis should not rely only on a *mechanical* process of exclusion which could work only if there is a *clear alternative* in the system which would *formally* have applied in the absence of the contested measure. This was the case of the *FSC* exemption where it was not difficult to establish that the 'foreign-source income of an *FSC* would be taxed "but for" the contested measure'.[27] In other cases, however, the application of a formalistic and mechanical 'but for' test may be unreliable. Its adoption could even create an incentive on Member States to design their tax systems in a way to render it difficult to identify an alternative measure and thus easily circumvent the test.

Despite a tenuous hint at the 'derogation test' (which emerges from the solitary reference to a 'general rule' at paragraph 91), the Appellate Body did *not* proceed further by suggesting an alternative test for those cases where the 'but for' approach does not provide a useful tool. The original proceedings thus finished with new doubts, those on the alternative test(s) that should replace, or at least complement, the 'but for' test.

Preliminary conclusions: the 'but for' test is insufficient

The original proceedings of the *US—FSC* dispute show that the biggest difficulty of the 'otherwise due' requirement is the determination of the appropriate 'normative benchmark' against which to test the tax measure at issue. Neither the Panel nor the Appellate Body provided a comprehensive explanation of how the 'otherwise due' requirement operates. They stated generally that the basis of comparison is constituted by the 'rule of taxation that each Member, by its own choice, establishes for itself' but failed to show *how* to determine what is the actual 'normative benchmark' against which to test the measure.

The 'but for' test has not passed the test. It did not prove to be fully dependable as it seemed to work only in the more straightforward cases being ineffective in more complex ones. What would be required is a *more sophisticated conceptual framework* able to tackle the inconveniences of a too formal test. It is only by going beneath the surface that one is able to explore the mechanism of the tax system and to determine whether the measure at issue confers an advantage and is a tax subsidy.

It is interesting to look at the broader picture and consider the recognition a 'but for' analysis enjoys in other areas. This issue usually comes out in the areas of antidumping, safeguards and subsidy law, when a 'causality' question is posed—along this path it is indeed correct to look at the 'otherwise due' language

[26] ibid.
[27] ibid.

itself as a 'causality' problem. Now, what is the general rating of the 'but for' criterion?[28]

The Appellate Body has never accepted a 'but for' argument to prove a cause and effect nexus, expressly disclosing its reservations in the currently commented *US—FSC*.[29] Only in the recent *US—Cotton (Article 21.5)* report has its application been endorsed by a Panel. This has been explained with various arguments: the room for manoeuvre left by the provision at issue (Article 6.3 (c) of the SCM), the Panel's overall explanation of the causal nexus, and, again, the crucial fact that the existence of a 'link' was not really in doubt, which confirms our analysis of its use in *US—FSC*. The 'but for' approach is an easy test for easy cases. It is however less satisfactory, even insufficient, in more complex settings.

Returning to the *US—FSC* dispute, both the Panel and the Appellate Body made a good attempt of elaboration in the implementation phase where they indicated new standards of assessment.

More sophistication: derogation test and comparative test

Panel (Article 21.5 DSU): a derogation test in disguise?

The implementation Panel took note of the *caveat* of the Appellate Body and accepted that the interpretation of the 'otherwise due' requirement cannot rest on a 'purely mechanical' or 'formalistic' exercise.[30] Nevertheless, it did not formulate in a clear fashion the test that was to be applied. The argumentative apparatus deployed is rather sibylline[31] with the result that the ultimate suggestion is the usual but inconclusive finding that 'the key point [which in fact is merely the 'starting' point] is that the tax rules applied by the Member in question are the *basis* for the comparison'.[32]

Leaving aside the declarations, the examination of the Panel's analysis of the implementing *Extra Territorial Income* (*ETI*) legislation is more revealing. The clear impression is that the Panel is implicitly resorting to a *derogation test*, focused as it is on the affirmation of the *exceptional* character of the legislation.[33] The Panel continues to underline the 'several stringently selective qualitative conditions and

[28] See WorldTradeLaw.net Dispute Settlement Commentary (DSC) on Appellate Body, *US—Cotton (Article 21.5)*, 9 September 2008, 18–19 (available at <http://www.worldtradelaw.net>).

[29] See also Appellate Body, *Canada Aircraft*, n 102.

[30] Panel, *US—FSC (Article 21.5 EC)*, paras 8.14 and 8.15.

[31] With statements like '[t]he key is to apply critical judgment to the facts of the matter' (para 8.17); 'while the enquiry cannot be inherently presumptive or speculative, neither can it be so exacting or confining that it is necessary to attain the level of establishing a mathematical deductive relationship between the contested measure and the default situation' (para 8.18), 'sound basis for exercising reasonable judgment' (para 8.19).

[32] Panel, *US—FSC (Article 21.5 EC)*, para 8.18 (emphasis in the original text, the comment between brackets is made by this author).

[33] See Panel, *US—FSC (Article 21.5 EC)*, paras 8.21 and 8.30.

quantitative requirements' that must be satisfied for the income to be excluded from taxation.[34]

As Professor Hudec observed in one of his last works, the most illuminating passage in this regard is to be found in paragraph 8.29. To give the reader an appreciation of this passage, it is quoted below, together with Hudec's ingenious bracketed suggestions on the underlying references to the concepts of 'general' and 'specific' (and his final perplexities).

> . . . Indeed, discerning what might be described as 'the prevailing domestic standard' for a particular tax regime may be a particularly exacting exercise. In more common usage, it might be rather difficult to discern what is the exception, as it were, and what is the [general] rule . . . [W]e are not, in this dispute, presented with a situation of such complexity. The dispute does not involve a debatable call as to whether the glass is half-full or half-empty. As outlined above, we have looked at the essential shape and the rationale that is exhibited. In examining that, we have weighed such considerations as the degree of conditionality [general-specific?], the range of limitations [general-specific?] and the manner in which the measure at issue related to the overall regime [general-specific?]. Taken together, they enable us to assess the nature of the relationship of the measure at issue and the overall regime [general-specific?]. That is precisely [?] how one is in a position to arrive at the judgment required by the terms of the SCM Agreement.[35]

The first preliminary observation is that this analysis shows the intriguing overlap between advantage and specificity analysis which is indeed a recurring theme (for an explanation of the interplay between and distinction of these two concepts see the next chapter on EC law).

Most importantly for the current analysis, as Hudec underlines, it shows the theoretical framework of the participants in the *FSC* case, whereby national tax laws seems to be perceived as being organized on the basis of *general principles* or *rules*.[36] In this framework, a measure amounts to a subsidy because it constitutes an exception to or a deviation from a general rule operating to the advantage of the undertakings concerned.

Although this framework is not the only possible reading of the 'otherwise due' requirement, it can easily be applied to the counterfactual analysis it requires. This derogation test consists in assessing whether the measure at issue deviates from the regime or rule that *would otherwise have applied because of its general character*. This would give real substance to the 'otherwise due' requirement, providing the interpreter with a useful tool to avoid the inconveniences of the more simple version of the 'but for' test (such as the excessive formalism and risk of

[34] ibid, para 8.21.

[35] RE Hudec, 'Industrial Subsidies: Tax Treatment of 'Foreign Sales Corporations'' in EU Petersmann and MA Pollack (eds), *Transatlantic Economic Disputes—The EU, the US, and the WTO* (Oxford: Oxford University Press, 2003) 175, 196.

[36] ibid, 186. The general principles are at different times referred to by the Panel or the Appellate Body as 'prevailing standards' or 'general rules'. By contrast, the term 'normative benchmark' does not seem to be necessarily limited to general rules.

circumvention, or indeed the lack of consideration of the general or exceptional nature of the measure in question).

Admittedly, the derogation test is not free from difficulties. The search for general rules and exceptions may be a particularly complex exercise, which explains the reluctance to expressly adhere to it (cf in this regard the Appellate Body's remarks in the implementation report below). Its force of persuasion and its utility have however been recognized by the implementation Panel which has implicitly based all its reasoning on it.

Appellate Body (Article 21.5 DSU): the 'new' comparative test

The ambiguous application of the derogation test by the implementation Panel was not the end of the story. The Appellate Body suggested—this time expressly—a different route by formulating the following test:

> . . . we believe that panels should seek to compare the fiscal treatment of legitimately comparable income to determine whether the contested measure involves the foregoing of revenue which is 'otherwise due', in relation to the income in question. [37]

This 'comparative' test is based on the general principle of equality and the related prohibition of non-discrimination: similar situations must be treated in a similar way. The reference in the general introductory findings in the original proceedings to 'some kind of comparison' between revenues due under the contested measure and those that would be due in some other situation,[38] is specified by requiring a comparison between the fiscal treatment of comparable incomes. Interestingly, in assessing an energy tax, the Court of Justice has taken a similar approach, noting that:

> [t]he only question to be determined is whether, under a particular statutory scheme, a State measure is such as to favour [certain undertakings] . . . in comparison with other undertakings which are in a legal and factual situation that is comparable in the light of the objective pursued by the measure in question.[39]

The comparative test is an attempt to combine two aims: the *overcoming of the inadequacy of the 'but for' test* and the *reluctance to fully accept a derogation test* based, as it is, on the identification of general rules and exceptions.

On the one hand, the Appellate Body intends to design a flexible test which certainly gives more importance to the *substance* of the tax system rather than to its *form*, and arguably gets over the insufficiencies of the 'but for' test (and especially the risks of a too formalistic and mechanical interpretation).[40] By requiring the comparative analysis of comparable situations, the new test aims to assess the measure in question closely and to consider its position within the tax system.

[37] Appellate Body, *US—FSC (Article 21.5 EC)*, para 91.
[38] Appellate Body, *US—FSC*, para 90.
[39] Case C-143/99, para 41.
[40] Appellate Body, *US—FSC*, para 91.

At the same time, however, the Appellate Body does not seem willing to fully endorse the derogation test. The expressed reason for this reluctance lies in the inevitable complexities of the quest for general rules and exceptions.[41] The Geneva-based body noted:

[w]e do not . . . consider that Article 1.1(a)(1)(ii) always *requires* panels to identify, with respect to any particular income, the 'general' rule of taxation prevailing in a Member. Given the variety and complexity of domestic tax systems, it will usually be very difficult to isolate a 'general' rule of taxation and 'exceptions' to that 'general' rule. [42]

Despite proposing the comparative test as an alternative, the Appellate Body does not provide much guidance with respect to the *criteria* to follow in the complex and flexible assessment of comparable situations.[43] No guideline is given regarding the *factors* (that is the factual and legal common denominators) that would allow two *situations* to be considered as *comparable*, or those to be taken into account when it has to be determined whether there is an *equal* or *discriminatory treatment.*

The vagueness of the comparative test (but this may well be predicated for the reasoning of all reports in the case) might well have been intentional.[44] The motive for not developing clear tests depended on the will to avoid, in the sensitive area of taxation, the creation of findings that could be viewed as precedents applicable to the countless tax systems that were not subject to scrutiny, and thus to allow more flexibility in the future. This reservation of flexibility, however, coincides with a lack of direction which inevitably perpetuates the uncertainty of the advantage analysis in this field.

Comparative and derogation test between norm and exception

What should now be asked is whether the comparative test is really an alternative to the derogation test, or whether we are in fact confronted with the same substance in a different shape. (The reader may experience a slight sense of déjà-vu here since this issue has already been briefly addressed (and its solution anticipated) in chapter 7.)

While stopping short of expressly accepting the derogation test, the Appellate Body has moved inexorably in that direction. The comparative test requires a

[41] Appellate Body, *US—FSC (Article 21.5 EC)* para 91.

[42] ibid.

[43] cf Appellate Body, *US—FSC (Article 21.5 EC)*, para 91, n 66, where it was recognized that this assessment requires a certain degree of flexibility. The Appellate Body gives just two obvious examples by saying that it might not be appropriate to compare taxation for sales income with taxation of employment income (para 90), or taxation in the hands of a domestic corporation with taxation of income in the hands of a foreign corporation (para 92).

[44] RE Hudec, 'Industrial Subsidies: Tax Treatment of "Foreign Sales Corporations"' in EU Petersmann and MA Pollack (eds), *Transatlantic Economic Disputes—The EU, the US, and the WTO* (Oxford: Oxford University Press, 2003) 175, 200 and 201, cf also 197.

comparison between comparable situations. The goal is clearly to determine whether comparable situations are treated similarly or not. The derogation test enquires as to whether the measure at issue is in line with the appropriate general rule or deviates from it.

There is a clear *link* between these two tests since a *general rule* is such insofar as it applies to *all situations* that, *in the light of a given, inherent objective*, should be considered *comparable*.[45] Although the two tests seem to share the same mechanics, they emphasize different steps of the analysis. The comparative test is clearer in defining the appropriate benchmark, that is the norm that is applicable to comparable situations. The assessment of the (equal or otherwise) treatment of comparable situations is more directly expressed by the derogation test which highlights that the logical process to establish an advantage is whether a deviation from the appropriate norm has occurred.

In sum, the difference in emphasis in the two tests corresponds to a different contribution to the clarification of the working of the advantage analysis. Eventually, the objective and the substance are the same, ie the search for whether the measure at issue, being an exception to what can be viewed as the relevant general rule, confers an undue advantage. It is useful to refer once more to the penetrating observations of Professor Hudec who noted that:

> [the] unstated assumption [would be] that a tax law governing a 'legitimately comparable' kind of income gives some indication of how the exempt income itself would have been treated, especially if that tax law happened to be a general rule or 'prevailing standard'. In other words, looking at the treatment of comparable income could have been a back-door way of looking at how the tax-exempt income itself would have been treated under the general principles of the defendant's tax law.[46]

The inevitable conclusion is that:

> [i]n effect, this would be a back-door version of the 'but for' test, one that could not be blocked by tax laws that try to sever all formal links between the subsidy and the applicable general principles of the defendant's tax systems'.[47]

In conclusion, it seems that in the end we are always confronted with the task of *identifying the general rule* (and the 'comparative' discourse helps us in this regard) and *determining* whether the measure at issue is *in line or deviates from it* (which is the main focus of the 'derogation' approach). Although the Appellate Body tried to distance its comparative test from the identification of general rules and exceptions, quite ironically, the specific contribution of its formulation is *exactly* to indicate how to define a general norm (and consequently to anchor any

[45] The reconstruction of general rules is analysed in detail in relation to the treatment of tax measures under EC State aid law in chapter 10.

[46] RE Hudec, 'Industrial Subsidies: Tax Treatment of "Foreign Sales Corporations"' in EU Petersmann and MA Pollack (eds), *Transatlantic Economic Disputes—The EU, the US, and the WTO* (Oxford: Oxford University Press, 2003) 175, 198.

[47] ibid.

test to the latter). Once the benchmark is identified, the process is to determine whether the Member State is *discriminating* between comparable situations (comparative test variation), or is *deviating* from the appropriate general rule (derogation test variation). Although the substance is the same, the derogation test is more useful in indicating the underlying logical process of the advantage analysis.

The heart of the concept of advantage is the idea that, once a country has adopted a certain rule or regime in its tax (or, indeed, any other) legislation, it should not be allowed to amend it and to introduce exceptions to favour certain undertakings when such need arises.[48] Ultimately, the distinction and interplay between what is norm and what is exception corresponds to the 'common sense' idea of subsidy and captures the sense of advantage which any subsidy should confer. On the premiss that 'general rules . . . have a general scope, reflecting a coherent policy', their derogation may be felt as a particularly sharp 'departure from existing tax policy' and thus involve a 'more tangible sense of gain to a taxpayer'.[49]

C. Some implications of the case-study

We now consider the implications of the findings of the *FSC* case study, focusing in particular on two issues, Member States' sovereignty in tax matters (and its constraints), and the role played by the objectives of the measure in the derogation test.

The share of sovereignty in tax matters: foreign economic processes and local taxation

The subject of this paragraph is the analysis of two cases that should not be considered as involving the 'foregoing of revenue otherwise due', and hence as conferring an advantage, because they are based on a similar rationale concerning the *share of sovereignty* in tax matters. Using the derogation test jargon, they both seem to represent *general rules or principles.*

The taxation of foreign economic processes

The first case deals with an issue that directly emerges from the *FSC* dispute, ie the status of the taxation of foreign economic processes under WTO subsidy rules.

Territorial and worldwide taxation: economic and legal considerations. A tax system may operate on the basis of two different principles. It adopts a principle of *territoriality* if it taxes all income earned (by residents and non-residents) in its

[48] cf RE Hudec, 'Industrial Subsidies: Tax Treatment of "Foreign Sales Corporations"' in EU Petersmann and MA Pollack (eds), *Transatlantic Economic Disputes—The EU, the US, and the WTO* (Oxford: Oxford University Press, 2003) 175, 191.

[49] ibid, 175, 186, and 196.

territory. Accordingly, income earned outside the country's territory is not taxed, and no more than a 'token' tax is imposed on the proceeds of such foreign earnings when they are remitted to the home country. Many European countries adopt a principle of territoriality in their tax law systems. In the context of multinational groups, the beneficial effects of the limited scope of application of territorial tax systems may be maximized if investment is made in low-tax jurisdictions and if transfer pricing is used to shift as much income as possible to those countries.

Conversely, a tax system operates under the *worldwide* principle if it taxes all worldwide income earned by residents. The US adopts such a system by taxing all income earned by US corporations irrespective of whether that income has been earned in the US jurisdiction or abroad. Moreover, it also taxes all income that, although not produced by residents, is 'effectively connected with the conduct of a trade or business within the United States'.[50]

From an *economic* perspective, the broader scope of application of worldwide systems, with the connected disincentive to exploit the opportunities of low-tax jurisdictions, seems to involve that, in international activities, US groups face a handicap if compared with EC groups. It was allegedly to tackle this disadvantage that the US introduced the *DISC* legislation first and the *FSC/ETI* legislation afterwards by exempting from taxation a portion of foreign trade income related to exports.

The *DISC* and *US—FSC* disputes, however, shed light on the *legal* position of these practices. Exemptions of portions of foreign trade income are not consistent with the GATT/WTO subsidy rules *inasmuch as* they derogate from the otherwise prevailing rule of taxation. As far as the definition of subsidy is concerned, it is immaterial that the derogation concerns export-related income, foreign income unconnected to exports, or domestic income. The crucial factor is that there is an exemption from the general tax system adopted by the Member State. The Appellate Body made it clear that if the general policy decision is to tax all foreign source income (worldwide principle), Members are not permitted to carve out an exemption from the system. Once they have made their 'sovereign choice' with respect to the general features of their tax system (it is repeatedly said that Members are sovereign to shape their tax systems as they wish), they are subject to the obligations under WTO law, and in particular the SCM Agreement.

By contrast, it may well be argued that the decision to exclude from taxation all foreign source income should not be regarded as a subsidy. The issue was not examined by the Dispute Settlement Body in the *FSC* case and, indeed, the Panel underlined that its findings should not have been taken as a suggestion that other systems of taxation, and in particular the territoriality principle, were consistent with

[50] See the comprehensive analysis of GC Hufbauer and A Assa, *US—Taxation of Foreign Income* (Washington DC: Peterson Institute for International Economics, 2007).

WTO subsidy rules.[51] This issue has however been subject to analysis in the *DISC* litigation, and in particular in the counter-complaints filed by the US against Belgium, France and The Netherlands. The Panels eventually condemned these laws on the premise that they exempted processes originating in the country. These conclusions were however harshly criticized and consequently reversed by the '1981 Understanding' which accepted the lawfulness of tax exemptions concerning 'economic processes located outside the territorial limits of the exporting country' (and introduced, at the same time, the requirement of the compliance with arm's length pricing to avoid possible abuses).

The common interpretation of this understanding, which reflected the wide consensus of GATT Members on the issue,[52] is that it expressly authorized the effect of territorial tax systems and that, quite probably, it also precluded more limited tax exemptions such as those provided by *DISC* or *FSC* measures. Both the Panel and the Appellate Body eventually concluded that, although in principle the 1981 Understanding could provide guidance as a 'decision' under Article XVI(1) of the WTO Agreement, this was not possible in the instant case because of the fundamental differences between Article XVI:4 GATT (which was interpreted by the Understanding) on the one hand and the discipline on export subsidies of the SCM Agreement on the other.[53]

Although, strictly speaking, this may be true, the significance of this decision for the current analysis depends on the fact that it reflected the *wide consensus* of GATT Members on what principles of international taxation may be legitimate (and, probably, also those that are not legitimate). In the author's view, it accordingly offers an important indication of the characterization of the principle of territoriality under subsidy rules.

We can now attempt to explain the difference in *legal* treatment between two practices that apparently lead to the same *economic* effects.[54]

What can be suggested is that the exclusion from taxation of all income earned abroad, which inevitably derives from the principle of territoriality, should not constitute the 'foregoing of revenue otherwise due' because, unlike the *FSC* and *ETI* mechanisms which were based on pronouncedly targeted exemptions to an extensive principle of worldwide taxation, it represents both a clear and, most importantly, *definite* choice with respect to the general scope of application of the tax system, one that also seems to correspond to both a *neutral* and *convenient* share

[51] Paragraph 7.123. Both the Panel (para 7.122) and the Appellate Body (para 179) generally noted that it is not the choice of a given system of taxation as such—be it worldwide or territorial—which is under scrutiny but the compliance of its rules with WTO obligations.

[52] RE Hudec, *Enforcing International Trade Law—The Evolution of the Modern GATT Legal System* (Salem, New Hampshire: Butttherworth Legal Publishers 1993) 92.

[53] Panel, para 7.79–7.85; Appellate Body, paras 104–19.

[54] RE Hudec, 'Industrial Subsidies: Tax Treatment of "Foreign Sales Corporations"' in EU Petersmann and MA Pollack (eds), *Transatlantic Economic Disputes—The EU, the US, and the WTO* (Oxford: Oxford University Press, 2003) 175, 188–92.

of competence in international taxation. The force of this argument is probably not only legal but also political (and, maybe, even economic).

Border tax adjustments: a confirmation. This point becomes particularly clear if a parallel is made with the treatment of so-called border tax adjustments (BTAs).

Border tax adjustment rules identify which taxes may be rebated on exports and imposed on imports.[55] In this regard, an important distinction is that between taxes on undertakings (ie direct taxes) and taxes on products (ie indirect taxes and import charges).[56] Whereas it has always been clear that the exemption of direct taxes in relation to exports amounts to a subsidy (good examples in this regard are offered by the *DISC* and *FSC/ETI* litigation),[57] the situation is different with respect to the exemption or remission of taxes on products for export where a subsidy occurs only when there is over-compensation. Note 1 to Article 1.1(a)(ii) of the SCM accordingly qualifies the form of financial contribution involving the foregoing of government revenue otherwise due by underlining that the exemption of an exported product from duties or taxes borne by the same product when destined for domestic consumption, or the remission of such duties or taxes in amounts not in excess of those which have accrued, shall not be deemed to be a subsidy.[58]

The traditional consensus on the permissibility of this rule of border adjustment for indirect taxes and other import charges in the event of exportation lies in the recognition of the principle of *destination* whereby it is deemed appropriate that a product should be subject to taxation only in the country of importation.[59] Despite some criticism on the *economic* rationality of having a different treatment between indirect and direct taxes,[60] there has been no serious attempt to modify

[55] GC Hufbauer and J Shelton Erb, *Subsidies in International Trade* (Cambridge, Massachusetts: MIT Press, 1984) 10–11; 51 et seq. For a clear explanation of border tax adjustments see JH Jackson, *The World Trading System—Law and Policy of International Economic Relations* (2nd edn, Cambridge Massachussetts: MIT Press, 1997) 218–21.

[56] For a definition of direct and indirect taxes cf n 58 of the SCM.

[57] cf items (e) and (f) of the Illustrative List on Export Subsidies.

[58] The reference to 'duties or taxes borne by the like product' should be read as referring to final stage indirect taxes (such as value-added or sales taxes). The principle is reaffirmed in the Illustrative List on Export Subsidies and, in particular, in item (g), and also in items (h) and (i).

[59] GC Hufbauer and J Shelton Erb, *Subsidies in International Trade* (Cambridge, Massachusetts: MIT Press, 1984) 10–11 note that they BTA rules 'permit the producer to realize approximately the "world" price for its exports and to acquire traded inputs at their "world" prices for use in export production.' JH Jackson, *The World Trading System—Law and Policy of International Economic Relations* (2nd edn, Cambridge Massachussetts: MIT Press, 1997) 220 explains, that the belief underlying BTA rules is that the different tax burden of indirect taxes would be shifted forward to the purchaser, thus making taxation at destination appropriate. This would not apply to direct taxation which would be shifted backward to the producer.

[60] GC Hufbauer and J Shelton Erb, *Subsidies in International Trade* (Cambridge, Massachusetts: MIT Press, 1984) 54–6, JH Jackson, *The World Trading System—Law and Policy of International Economic Relations* (2nd edn, Cambridge Massachussetts: MIT Press, 1997) 219–21. The criticism is that the traditional assumption concerning the tax burden of direct/indirect taxation is not always correct with the result that a different regulation of indirect taxation (for which adjustment is possible)

the law and, in particular, to consider as permissible also exemptions of direct taxation in relation to exports.[61]

It has been suggested that the general tax exclusion of foreign-source trade is not a subsidy because it seems to depend on a *legal and political* acceptable sovereign choice in international tax matters that involves a *permanent* and *convenient* neutral share of competence. It is now argued that, despite the differences, the functioning of territorial systems (for direct taxes) can usefully be compared with border tax adjustments (for indirect taxes).

While subjecting to taxation the income earned in the territory, the principle of territoriality exempts (in principle without any exception) all foreign-source income. This seems to parallel the logic of competence allocation in tax matters that underlies the rule of border tax adjustment. The outcome is that, in the case of an international activity, only one country, the one *where the taxable activity takes place*, is competent to tax. It is not argued here that this result is necessarily the most efficient from an economic perspective, but that it may, at the very least, represent, as border adjustments rules for indirect taxes, a satisfactory and pragmatic outcome and maybe have same economic grounding too.[62]

The fact remains that, from a legal perspective, the neutrality implied in the strict adherence to a territoriality approach, which defines the international competence in direct taxation in a clear and permanent way, is more likely to be consistent with WTO subsidy rules in comparison with the endorsement of a more extensive worldwide principle which is then adjusted with more or less comprehensive exemptions that progressively redefine the boundaries of the said competence (to the advantage of some undertakings or sectors).

If the above is correct the ultimate finding would be that subsidy rules *do* introduce a significant *constraint* on the often repeated sovereignty of Members in tax matters by creating an incentive to adopt a territorial approach and, conversely, a deterrent towards a world-wide principle of taxation.

and direct taxation (for which it is not) would put those countries that depend more on the latter at a disadvantage. In this regard see DK Tarullo, 'The MTN Subsidies Code: Agreement without Consensus', in SJ Rubin and GC Hufbauer (eds), *Emerging Standards of International Trade and Investment—Multinational Codes and Corporate Conduct* (Totowa: Rowman and Allanheld Publishers, 1984) 63, 73.

[61] Before the WTO GC Hufbauer and J Shelton Erb, *Subsidies in International Trade* (Cambridge, Massachusetts: MIT Press, 1984) 62–3 suggested that the DISC legislation was a 'first step' towards the principle of destination of border adjustments for direct taxes whereby countries could rebate all direct taxes and other social charges incurred in the production of goods for export, and impose those same direct taxes on imports.

The oddity of this suggestion is that it is difficult to fully juxtapose a system devised for products to undertakings. An example may help to understand the point. If a principle of worldwide taxation is adopted, what about direct taxes on foreign income deriving from foreign sales which cannot however be classed as exports (because, eg, the relevant goods are produced abroad)?

[62] As regards BTA, JH Jackson, *The World Trading System—Law and Policy of International Economic Relations* (2nd edn, Cambridge Massachussetts: MIT Press, 1997) 221 underlines that 'perhaps the present rule is as good a rough approximation of equity as can be found, and it is at least administrable'.

Local taxation

An additional confirmation of the previous reading of the legal status of taxation of foreign income is offered by the treatment of local taxation.

The starting point of the analysis is Article 2 SCM which defines the requirement of specificity, ie that a subsidy must be 'specific to an enterprise or industry or group of enterprises or industries within the jurisdiction of the granting authority'.

Article 2.2 provides that 'a subsidy which is limited to certain enterprises located within a designated geographical region within the jurisdiction of the granting authority shall be specific'. The same provision, however, hastens to add that 'it is understood that the setting or change of generally applicable tax rates by all levels of government entitled to do so shall not be deemed to be a specific subsidy for the purposes of this Agreement'.

Although this provision is set in the context of the specificity analysis, it is argued that it has *more* significance with respect to the advantage analysis because it represents an example of a measure that *does not confer an advantage in the first place*. This is again an example of the intriguing interplay between specificity and advantage analysis, which has recurred several times.

A *local* tax measure adopted by a competent *local* authority which extends to all undertakings in the relevant *local* jurisdiction does not confer any advantage at all because it derives from one of the main general features of the (legal and political) *constitutional system* of the Member State at issue. In other words, the measure does not constitute an exception but rather a general tax measure which is the expression of a *general constitutional rule*.

The analogy between international and local taxation under subsidy rules

If we now juxtapose the treatment of international and local taxation under subsidy rules the analogy is clear and interesting.

The exclusion from taxation of all foreign economic processes and the competence of local authorities to impose and collect taxes seem to represent two sides of the same coin. They are both examples of a share of—international and internal—tax sovereignty that is held to be (for practical, political and legal reasons) *proper* under subsidy rules. This substantially depends on the fact that these arrangements can be considered *expression of a general norm*.

Derogation test and objectives: the core of the 'scope/justification' interplay

The aim of this paragraph is to provide a brief analysis of a crucial issue which is discussed at length in the context of EC law (see chapter 10, section I.C) but is of great relevance for the WTO as well. We thus borrow considerably from the jargon and theoretical framework of the EC legal system.

The core of the advantage analysis underlying the 'otherwise due' phrase is to determine whether the measure at issue constitutes a deviation from the appropriate general tax rule. This is the essence of the 'derogation test'.

In tax law, we have many situations which are treated differently. The crucial issue is that, in order to determine whether this differential treatment does in fact constitute a derogation, and hence an advantage, it *is* necessary to analyse the *objectives* of the tax measure and/or of the tax system. This may seem to directly contradict what has been repeated many times so far: when defining subsidies objectives do not matter!

It is therefore necessary to immediately address this point and dispel any uncertainty. Like any public measure, taxes may pursue various objectives. In the context of the advantage analysis, it is fundamental, however, to *distinguish* between objectives. As the EC experience shows, this is a difficult but necessary exercise. In particular, the presence of an objective that is in line with the *logic, nature or general scheme of the tax or the tax system* excludes any advantage element from the differential treatment.[63] This is not the case for those objectives that are *externally* assigned to the tax, ie are not directly linked to the purpose of the tax and/or the tax system, but rather *pursue different policy objectives*.[64] This distinction between 'internal' and 'external' objectives is the fundamental divide to determine whether a tax measure which provides for a differential treatment is ultimately a subsidy or not. The previous analysis recalls Hart's 'shifting and varying criterion used in determining when, for any given purpose, cases are alike or different'.[65] This is the vexating exercise where, in the light of the relevant objectives, general norms and exceptions to them are defined, equal or differential treatment is established.

Returning to taxation, an interesting example of measures that do not imply the 'foregoing of revenue otherwise due', because any differential treatment is in fact justified by the logic of taxation, is that of technical rules. Normally, these rules do not confer any advantage because they define the 'parameters' of the general tax system. In the last analysis, the issue is whether the measure is in line or not with the *inherent* logic of the system. Most of these measures are accordingly justified by the need to shape the system in accordance with generally acknowledged principles, such as that whereby a tax should accord to the 'ability to pay' of the taxpayer.

In *US—FSC*, the EC, clearly drawing from the internal State aid law experience, was arguing that determination of general tax rates, depreciation rules and rules on loss carry-overs, are clear applications of this principle.[66] Admittedly, the same conclusion should be reached with respect to rules to prevent tax avoidance or

[63] For example, in an environmental tax, the main objective is that the 'polluter should pay'. A tax measure that provides a different treatment according to the polluting impact of the activity is therefore in line with this objective, ie the logic of the environmental tax.

[64] Following the example of the previous note, it is common to introduce in environmental taxes, special exemptions for 'heavy polluters'. The goal is to avoid an excessive financial burden which would derive from a strict application of the 'polluter pays' principle. This financial objective is 'external' to the logic of the 'eco-tax'.

[65] See the cover of Part III for a full quotation and reference.

[66] Panel, *US—FSC*, para 4.591.

double taxation, provided that these measures merely address these goals and do not provide any advantage to certain categories of undertakings.

The example of the rules aimed at preventing double taxation is particularly interesting in the WTO context. Footnote 59 to the Illustrative List on Export Subsidies provides that 'paragraph (e) is not intended to limit a Member from taking measures to avoid the double taxation of foreign-source income earned by its enterprises or the enterprises of another Member'. Although this provision merely excludes the conduct at issue from being considered as an export subsidy, it may be argued that, if the measure at issue does not confer an advantage, it should be considered as *not* being a *subsidy* in the first place.

The author believes it is useful to repeat the point of the importance of this exercise of identification, and distinction, of the objectives of the tax measure and of the tax system when carrying out the advantage analysis. This eventually impacts the proper definition of the relation between what is scope and what is justification under subsidy rules.

This brief section has provided a preview of an important debate which is well alive in the EC context. Arguably, it is only a matter of time before these issues about objectives and their distinction, and the underlying interplay between scope and justification, will be debated before the Dispute Settlement Body in a (tax) subsidy context.

The role of 'objectives' in subsidy rules and 'aims' in Article III of the GATT

The previous analysis, and in particular the role played by the objectives of the measure, should have reminded the attentive reader of an intriguingly similar debate in another area of GATT/WTO law. We are referring to the role of the 'aims' of the internal tax or regulation in the analysis of the rule of national treatment under Article III of the GATT.

Article III prohibits both internal tax and regulatory measures that may be applied 'so as to afford protection' to domestic products. This general principle, which informs the various obligations of that provision, essentially forbids discrimination between imported and domestic products.

As has been just seen, however, tax (but this could equally apply to regulation) may be complex and a differential treatment may result from their application. Crucially, we have also seen that such difference may be explained or justified by the objectives the measure aims to achieve.

The key argument that has been put forward in the context of Article III is that we should not limit the analysis to the differential *effects* of the measure since this may be misleading. We should also duly take into considerations the *aims* (or, using a different language, the objectives) pursued by the measure to fully understand whether the tax or regulation at hand is really protectionist (or is, rather, legitimate). The suggested approach is therefore a comprehensive one whereby both 'intent' and 'effects' should be considered in this crucial determination.

This doctrine finds its origins in the GATT, but came to prominence during the WTO era.[67] Despite the express denial by the Appellate Body, the indications coming from its jurisprudence (and often the same decisions that rejects the approach) are contradictory but the distinct impression is that paying some heed to the objectives may indeed be warranted.[68]

Technically, the place where this 'aims-and-effect' analysis should be executed may vary, the most appropriate being the determination of whether the measure defeats the general principle of the first paragraph, whereby no tax of regulation should be applied to imported or domestic products 'so as to afford protection' to domestic production. The alternative to this holistic approach is not the oblivion of the often legitimate tax and regulatory objectives of Members but rather their consideration at the subsequent stage of the general exceptions under Article XX of the GATT.

But, although in practical terms the same result may eventually be reached (ie the measure is GATT/WTO compatible), there are substantial differences between the 'aims-and-effect' and the 'exception' approach.

This not only concerns the different allocation of the burden of proof, and the different substantive requirements under respectively Article III and XX of the GATT. Horn and Weiler have made a more general point, which is indeed applicable in many areas of the law.[69] From a 'symbolic' point of view it makes a difference to conclude that the measure does not amount to discrimination in the first place, or to rather conclude that there is indeed a breach of the prohibition of non-discrimination but this is in fact justified by one (or more) of the

[67] For an excellent overview see MJ Trebilcock and R Howse, *The Regulation of International Trade* (3rd edn, London: Routledge, 2005) chapter 3, and Mavroidis, *Trade in Goods* (Oxford: Oxford University Press, 2008) 216 et seq. See also the classic paper of RE Hudec, 'GATT/WTO Constraints on National Regulation: Requiem for an "Aims and Effects" Test' (1998) The International Lawyer 619. The literature on the topic is extremely rich. See, eg, R Howse and D Regan, 'The Product/ Process Distinction—An Illusory Basis for Disciplining "Unilateralism" in Trade Policy' (2000) European Journal of International Law, 249; G Verhoessel, *National Treatment and WTO Dispute Settlement: Adjudicating the Boundaries of Regulatory Autonomy* (Oxford: Hart Publishing, 2002); H Horn and JHH Weiler, 'EC—Asbestos', in H Horn and PC Mavroidis, *The WTO Case Law of 2001* (Cambridge: Cambridge University Press, 2003) 14; DH Regan, 'Further Thoughts on the Role of Regulatory Purpose under Article III of the GATT' (2003) Journal of World Trade 737; F Roessler, 'Beyond the Ostensible—A Tribute to Professor Robert Hudec's Insights on the Determination of the Likeness of Products under the National Treatment Provisions of the GATT' (2003) Journal of World Trade 771; A Porges and JP Trachtman, 'Robert Hudec and Domestic Regulation – The Resurrection of Aims and Effects' (2003) Journal of World Trade 783; H Horn and PC Mavroidis, 'Still Hazy After All These Years: The Interpretation of National Treatment in the GATT/WTO Case-Law on Tax Discimination' (2004) European Journal of International Law, 39; MJ Trebilcock and SK Giri, 'The National Treatment Principle in International Law', in K Choi and J Hartigan (eds), *Handbook of International Trade Volume II: Economics and Legal Analyses of Trade Policy Institutions* (Oxford: Blackwell, 2005).

[68] See, eg, Appellate Body, *Japan–Taxes II*, and *Chile—Taxes* referring to the 'design, architecture and revealing structure of the measure'. See also Appellate Body in *EC—Asbestos* where it considered the 'carcinogity' of the products at issue as an important factor under Article III:4 analsysis (and in particular the assessment of 'likeness').

[69] H Horn and JHH Weiler, 'EC—Asbestos', in H Horn and PC Mavroidis, *The WTO Case Law of 2001* (Cambridge: Cambridge University Press, 2003) 14, 30–1.

general exceptions. This observation is more political than legal, but politics matters, and symbolism counts for a lot in politics.

In the author's view, the need to consider both the aims underlying the (tax or regulation) measure at issue and its effects is inevitable. Its protectionist, or otherwise, nature can only be truly appreciated in this way. The important point—which is borrowed from our previous analysis and can constitute a contribution of subsidy law analysis to general trade law—is that we should *distinguish between aims or objectives.* Certain aims are strictly linked to the nature of the measure and should certainly belong to this analysis (under Article III of the GATT). Other objectives, by constrast, do not inherently and inevitably belong to its rationale, and—provided they do not have a protectionist nature or impact—should be considered only subsequently, at the stage of the possible justifications of the breach (under Article XX).

In conclusion, the sophisticated analysis of the objectives in the subsidy context has arguably provided a useful input to the 'aims-and-effect' debate. But this is not all. In return, it has received an important confirmation. What the 'aims-and-effect' debate ultimately raises is a delicate interplay between scope and justification, a relationship which is therefore not only recurring in subsidy analysis but is (inevitably) common to other fields of the law.

II. Regulatory measures

Chapter 4 has shown that, under certain conditions, some regulatory measures may be covered by the SCM Agreement if they constitute a form of financial contribution or of income/price support. Thus, for instance, the non-applicability of collective labour agreements and minimum wage levels might be covered by subparagraph (ii) of Article 1.1.(a)(1) insofar as it might involve a loss of government revenue in the form of social contributions or other taxes. The imposition of minimum prices might, by contrast, be covered by subparagraph (iv), as it might be the result of an order or entrustment to a private party to transfer funds, or (more probably) by Article 1.1(a)(2), being an income or price support.

In the context of the advantage analysis, it is sufficient to say that, in these cases, since the governmental conduct is by definition non-economic, the assessment should be carried out by using the derogation test. The measure will be held to confer an advantage if it derogates from the appropriate general rule. The analysis hence closely follows that carried out with taxation measures.

III. Public goods

The conceptual debate on public goods and their current redefinition has been analysed at length. It has been seen that public goods are rare. In this section, the assumption is that we are indeed confronted with a 'pure' public good. In fact, we are abstracting from the precise economic definition of public good and are more generally referring to those situations where, for various reasons, the market completely fails to provide the relevant good or service, and public intervention is hence justified. In this scenario of total lack of private initiative, we would be *beyond* the market, and the public intervention would thus be defined as non-economic.

The most important example of public goods which may be covered by the SCM Agreement is that of some infrastructures, and, probably, also of the services supplied through them.

It has been seen that the third subparagraph of Article 1.1(a)(1) of the SCM provides that there is a financial contribution when 'a government provides goods or services *other than general infrastructure*, or purchase goods' (emphasis added). As happened with subparagraph (ii), this provision offers interesting indications with respect to the advantage analysis. In the analysis of governmental 'economic activity', in chapter 8, two possible readings of the term 'general' have been given.[70] The prevailing line of interpretation is that the exclusion of 'general infrastructure' is in fact superfluous since it would just repeat what is already said under Article 2 and its specificity test. 'General' would thus underline that infrastructures, by not applying to the exclusive advantage of certain undertakings, are not specific in their application.

We have advanced an alternative reading of the phrase. The term 'general' would refer to the fact that the provision of the relevant infrastructure (and service) falls within the *general infrastructure policy* of the government. The conduct is general inasmuch as it is not derogatory from this policy.

In the context of the advantage analysis, what has to be properly defined is the benchmark, the 'general infrastructure policy'. In this regard, the identification of the plan of the government with respect to infrastructures and their relevant services plays a crucial role. A few questions should be addressed at once.

Should the infrastructural plan be viewed in a *static* or *dynamic* way? There is indeed a risk in referring only to the *existing* plans, that of creating an obstacle to the country's infrastructure development. It can thus be advanced that this criterion should be viewed in a *prospective* way. In other words, the government at hand is certainly entitled to update and improve its general infrastructure policy without its generality being defeated.

But, how far can this flexible approach to the definition of general infrastructural policy go? If the government cannot clearly consider that any infrastructure policy or intervention it carries out is a general plan, there is equally a risk that a too intrusive external scrutiny of the government's decisions might lead to the imposition of a specific view of what a general infractructure policy should be about. The right balance needs to be found.

[70] Section II.B.

With this in mind, the author suggests an operative framework to identify whether the creation of an infrastructure can be considered as part of a general infrastructure policy or plan.

The premise is certainty that the 'general' or 'derogatory' character of an infrastructure plan or intervention can be assessed only with a case-by-case and contextual analysis. That said, the use of few criteria which, taken together, can confirm (or otherwise) the 'neutrality' of the action, may be useful. For example: Is the intervention part of an *organic* and *rational plan* of infrastructure development? Considering all circumstances, is there any reasonable *need* to provide an infrastructure of that type in that particular area? What would be the *impact* of the infrastructure on the region/community/economic environment at hand? What, and, more radically, whose, is the *demand* for such an infrastructure? What *procedure* (open, transparent, participative, etc) has been followed in coming to the infrastructure decision? Ultimately, what are the (express or inferred) *objectives* and *motives* that the government is pursuing? Are they characterized by a general and neutral intent, or more simply, do they rather aim to provide a specific favour to a given industry?[71]

IV. 'Derogation' and 'discrimination': a parallel with Article III of the GATT

A nice conclusion to the chapter is represented by a broad parallel between two provisions which are clearly linked between themselves, subsidy rules on the one hand and the principle of national treatment of Article III of the GATT on the other. The allure of this parallel depends on various factors.

We have already seen how the two provisions are connected from the perspective of the analysis of the measure's objective, and the ensuing scope-justification interplay.

More than that, however, the intriguing factor is that, at least in principle, both provisions could apply to the same measure.[72] The possibility of a cumulative application depends on the strict connection between the two key-concepts underlying those provisions.

On the one hand, Article III of the GATT is an express application of the general prohibition of *discrimination*, in the instant case between imported and

[71] Two comments. First, as we have repeatedly noted, the analysis of the advantage is conceptually separate from that of the specific impact of the measure. That said, there is a certain degree of overlap between the two, with similar questions being asked (particularly when *de facto* specificity is concerned; see chapter 13). Secondly, and intriguingly, the proposed test would consider both the 'intent' (objective) and the 'effect' of the infrastructure provision—another parallel with 'general trade law'.

[72] In this context, the *crucial* issue of the excluding effect of Article III:8(b) (which is still vague but seems to be substantially limited) is intentionally left aside. See chapter 6, section III.C for an analysis.

domestic goods. This prohibition covers both tax and regulatory policies. On the other hand, we have seen in this and in the previous chapters that the essence of the notion of subsidy is a *derogation* from the norm which would favour domestic producers/products (almost invariably to the detriment of foreign producers/products).

The analogy between the two situations, and the mischief of the provisions (no 'discrimination', no 'derogation') is clear. The similarity becomes even more apparent if we consider that the analysis of the advantage of subsidies often relies on a comparison between similar situations and on the detected *discrimination* between the two.

The resemblance, and potential overlap, are therefore clear. That said, are there any meaningful differences between the two notions? What distinguishes a *discriminatory* tax or regulation (prohibited under Article III of the GATT) on the one hand from a tax or regulatory *subsidy* (caught by Article 1.1 of the SCM) on the other?

Without claiming to provide a complete analysis of the possible differences between the two provisions, the text below merely outlines what, in the author's view, are the most significant ones. The most obvious differences are described first.

First, Article III applies only to a specific trade scenario, notably the importation of foreign products. Subsidies may take places in the most diverse scenarios, as is reflected by the multiplicity of their categories and, most importantly, 'impact standards' that ultimately regulate them.[73]

Secondly, while Article III applies to products,[74] the focus of subsidy laws is on producers and their activity (which obviously is about making products). Clearly, to be troublesome under subsidy discipline, any benefit to the producer should translate to its products. But this is a further step to be proved, and a further difference with National Treatment (NT).

Thirdly, as has been underlined in chapter 2,[75] the consolidated law is that Article III of the GATT, like any other 'trade' rule, already protects 'competitive expectations' and 'opportunities', and does not focus on 'actual trade effects'. Again in chapter 2, it has been argued that this is not the case for subsidy discipline. Since their deepest concern is the upset of the competitive process, their focus and operation should duly reflect this. In other words, WTO subsidy rules should concentrate mainly on the 'competitive process itself'.[76]

[73] See chapter 14, section II. B.

[74] Note however the ambiguous wording 'directly or indirectly' of Article III:2 of the GATT which might hint at the possibility of covering also taxes that indirectly hit products. But, in the author's view, an interpretation which covered 'direct taxation' too would be over the top. For a commentary see PC Mavroidis, *Trade in Goods* (Oxford: Oxford University Press, 2008) 212–15. See also the ambiguous expression (regulation) 'affecting' in Article III:4 that may open the application of this provision to PPMs. See chapter 6, section III.C for reference to the relevant debate.

[75] Section II.C.

[76] An assessment of the current 'impact standards' in the light of this interpretation is carried out in chapter 14.

10

Non-economic activity and the advantage analysis in the EC

The subject of this chapter is the advantage analysis of public non-economic activity in the EC. It is the natural companion of the previous chapter which focused on similar issues in the WTO context.

The pattern of exposition thus closely resembles that of chapter 9. The core of the analysis is taxation with more limited comments on regulation and public goods.

I. Tax measures

This section examines test and benchmarks used in EC law to determine whether a tax measure confers an advantage. The main difference as compared to WTO law is that the fact that the assessment rests on a 'derogation test', ie on a derogation from the general rule or norm, is virtually undisputed in EC law. The emphasis of the analysis thus inevitably shifts towards the *operation* of the test in this area. And to its problems.

A. The derogation test in taxation

The essence of the advantage analysis lies in the idea, another true paradigm, that a State aid involves a 'derogation from the appropriate norm'. When the government activity is economic the appropriate norm is the market and the test is whether the conduct is in line or not with *market rules*. If the government acts *qua* public authority, for example by imposing taxes, the test is whether the government derogates from the *general rule* otherwise applicable in the relevant field.

Both the Commission and the Community Courts have endorsed this approach. Drawing inspiration from the OECD's definition of 'tax expenditure' as 'a departure from the generally accepted or benchmark tax structure, which produces a favourable tax treatment of particular types of activities or groups of taxpayers', the Commission clarified the relevant test on various occasions which consistently emphasize the ideas of normality and derogation therefrom. In the 1998 Notice on Direct Taxation we find that 'the measure must confer on recipients an advantage which relieves them of charges that are normally borne from their budgets'.[1] Even more explicitly, the 2004 Report on Direct Taxation reads:

to determine whether a tax scheme derogating from the normal system may constitute State aid, it must be established whether the resulting tax burden is lower than that which would have resulted from the application of the relevant Member State's normal taxation method.[2]

The Court has consistently referred to the idea of derogation since its very early decisions. Two classic examples, which are endlessly repeated in the case-law, can be cited. The first is the seminal 1961 *Steenkolenmijnen* decision which includes the oldest case-law definition of aid, and which unmistakably links the notion of aid to the existence of a derogation from the normal course.[3] In 1974 the Court laid down the more elaborate definition of the derogation test, the standard in EC State aid law:

the partial reduction of social charges pertaining to family allowances devolving upon employers in the textile sector is a measure intended partially to exempt undertakings of a particular industrial sector from the financial charges arising from the normal application of the general social security system, without there being any justification for this exemption on the basis of the nature or general scheme of the system'.[4]

This formulation clearly indicates the three steps of the test to determine whether there is a derogation: the identification of the general rule (the 'normal application of the general social security system'), of the differential treatment (the 'exemption' from the latter) and of the possible ingrained justification ('on the basis of the nature or general scheme of the system').

The broad acceptance of the derogation test with respect to governmental taxation does not mean that there is no variety of views surrounding it.[5] For example, both practice and case-law consistently consider it as part of or in any event together with the specificity test, confusing, in the author's view, two steps of the analysis—advantage and specificity—which conceptually should be kept separate. Despite these nuances, the citizenship of the test in the form of derogation from the appropriate general tax rule is unanimously acknowledged in EC law. Before concentrating on its operation which, as in the field of economic activities, presents its own complexities, it is however useful to set forth a conceptual and methodological

[1] Commission Notice on the application of the State aid rules to measures relating to direct business taxation, OJ C384, 10.12.1998, 3, para 9.

[2] Commission, Report on the implementation of the Commission notice on the application of the State aid rules to measures relating to direct business taxation, 9.2.2004, C(2004)434, Box 1, p 6.

[3] A full quotation can be found in chapter 5, section I.A.

[4] Case 173/73 *Italy v Commission*, para 15.

[5] Sometimes, far from being regarded as the core of the advantage analysis, as it is submitted here, it is seen as an additional requirement to the notion of State aid, that is independent from the advantage element. See K Bacon, 'State Aids and General Measures' (1997) Yearbook of European Law 269, 297.

premise concerning its proper location in the context of the advantage analysis, and its relationship with the said specificity test.

B. A conceptual gloss: advantage analysis, derogation test and specificity

The derogation test—and in particular the justification of the differential treatment on the basis of the inherent logic of the system—is often considered in the context of the specificity analysis. More generally, the advantage analysis itself is often not clearly distinguished from the specificity test.

The examples are copious in administrative practice, case-law and literature. In the 1998 Notice on Direct Taxation, the Commission noted that the 'selective nature of a measure may be justified by the "nature or general scheme of the system".'[6] More recently, the Court found that 'a measure which, although conferring an advantage on its recipient, is justified by the nature or general scheme of the system of which it is part does not fulfil that [?!] condition of selectivity.'[7] Along these lines, in the literature, it was observed that, where the State is 'acting in the exercise of public powers, such as in the areas of taxation, social security, etc', the test which should be used to establish the existence of a State aid is whether the measure is 'selective' or 'specific'.[8]

As has already been noted in chapter 8, when discussing infrastructures, this confusion may derive from the ambiguity of the word 'general' which is used in the context of both advantage and specificity analysis. A measure may be considered general because it *objectively* represents the norm in the relevant field—and thus be opposed to the concept of 'exceptional'. From the perspective of its *subjective* application, a measure is general since it does apply to every person across the board—otherwise, it would be denoted as 'specific' or 'selective'. Whereas the first meaning of general is the one relevant to the analysis of the advantage, the second pertains more directly to the specificity test.

It is important to keep the two levels of analysis separate as they address fundamentally different issues. On the one hand, the derogation test, based as it is on the assessment of general rules and exceptions, aims to determine whether the measure at issue departs from the relevant benchmark and thus confers an advantage. Most importantly, contrary to orthodoxy, the analysis of whether any differential impact of the measure is justified by the 'nature' or 'scheme' of the 'general system' is an integral part of this test. On the other hand, the specificity test focuses on the different issue of whether that measure—which grants an advantage—applies selectively, that is whether it is specific to certain undertakings.

[6] Commission Notice on the application of the State aid rules to measures relating to direct business taxation, OJ C384, 10.12.1998, 3, para 12.

[7] Case C-143/99 *Adria-Wien*, para 41. The punctuations mark have been made by the author.

[8] M Hansen, A Van Ysendyck, and S Zühlke, 'The Coming of Age of EC State Aid Law: A Review of the Principal Developments in 2002 and 2003' (2004) European Competition Law Review 202, 203, n 6.

In practice, in most, but not all, of the cases the fact that the measure confers an advantage and is specific are two sides of the same coin since it is clear that a measure satisfies both requirements at the same time.[9] A possible practical overlap does not however justify an ongoing conceptual confusion or a conflation. This is particularly so if, even in practice, there may be measures that confer an advantage but which are not specific in their application, and measures that, conversely, are specific but which do not confer an advantage. Two examples will illustrate this possibility.

Example 1. A measure that introduces differential tax rates, and may consequently affect certain undertakings more than others, may well be justified in terms of the logic of the tax system, for example by the need to tackle tax avoidance. Despite being selective, this measure would not confer any advantage.

Example 2. A Member State may decide to reduce the tax burden related to certain production costs, such as research and development, environment, training, employment. The Commission recognizes that these measures may well not be selective 'inasmuch as they apply without distinction to all firms and to the production of all goods'.[10] This does not mean, however, that they are not apt to confer an advantage on the recipient undertakings.[11] Accordingly, there may be a non-specific advantage.

C. The operation of the derogation test and the critical role of objectives

The derogation test in tax law follows the usual three-step pattern. The first step is the identification of the benchmark, that is the general tax rule applicable in the case.[12] In the light of the general rule, it should then be determined whether (ii) there is a differential treatment in favour of the situation at issue and, crucially, (iii) whether this differential treatment is in fact justified by the 'nature or general scheme of the system' thus excluding the possibility of a derogation from, or, using a different language, a discrimination in light of the general rule.

A few preliminary remarks can be made. First, it should be emphasized that, far from being strictly separate and consequential, the three stages are often

[9] It often occurs that the analysis of the two requirements often rests on the answer to similar questions: compare, eg, the definition of the norm in non-economic context (the example of 'normal infrastructure plan discussed in chapter 9, section III is illuminating in this respect) and the assessment of specificity analysed in chapter 13, section III.B.

[10] Commission Notice on the application of the State aid rules to measures relating to direct business taxation, OJ C384, 10.12.1998, 3, para 13.

[11] W Schön, 'Taxation and State Aid Law in the European Union' (1999) Common Market Law Review 910, 927. Using a language that will become apparent in the following paragraphs, to target factors of production cannot be considered as pertaining to the 'ability to pay' of the taxpayer as it reflects considerations external to the proper functioning of the tax system, that is the pursuit of the government's policy objectives.

[12] cf Commission Notice on the application of the State aid rules to measures relating to direct business taxation, OJ C384, 10.12.1998, 3, para 16.

overlapping in the analysis with the result that the three issues may influence each other. Again, this is testament to the 'shifting and varying criterion' underlying this assessment.[13]

Secondly, objectives play a crucial role in this complex process, particularly at the level of the definition of the general rule and of the enquiry of the 'justification' (as it is known in the EC jargon). This role is critical. As the etymological origin[14] of the word 'critical' suggests, what is required is to separate, to distinguish. In particular, the distinction between objectives is of fundamental importance for the construction of State aid rules, and is linked to one of the *leitmotifs* of this book which is the difficult quest for a legal separation between scope and justification.

What is a general (tax) rule?

As in the WTO, the premise, based on the recognition of the sovereign prerogative to decide the fundamental aspects of the domestic tax system, is that the appropriate benchmark must necessarily be found in the general tax system of the Member State.[15]

Various attempts have been made to define what constitutes a general (tax) rule. As the WTO debate shows, this is not a matter of form or label but of substance. Clearly, however, it is not enough to say that it is necessary to go beneath the surface and assess the substance of the tax system if no principle to use in this assessment is suggested.

Some definitions view as the key factor the fact that the measure *is open to all economic agents* operating within a Member State.[16] As previously seen, however, the subjective breadth of application has more to do with the concept of specificity or selectivity rather than with the conceptually different, and inner, issue of whether the measure represents the norm in the relevant field. In practice, the broadness of the application of the measure may indicate that the measure is the general norm but this circumstance is by no means conclusive. It is an answer to a different question.

Another definition seems more useful. In the *Maribel* case Advocate General La Pergola suggested that 'a measure is general when it is aimed at achieving equality between businesses'.[17] The idea of *equal treatment* is a valuable point of reference. It leads us back to the previous analysis of the formulations of the test of the advantage analysis based on a comparison between 'comparable or like situations' which both the Appellate Body (*US—FSC*) and the Court of Justice (*Adria-Wien*) adopted.

[13] cf HLA Hart, *The Concept of Law* (2nd edn, Oxford: Clarendon Press, 1994) 160.

[14] The Greek verb *krinein.*

[15] cf W Schön, 'Taxation and State Aid Law in the European Union' (1999) Common Market Law Review 910, 923–4.

[16] This is the definition in the 1998 Notice on Direct Taxation, para 13. For a similar definition see K Bacon, 'State Aids and General Measures' (1997) Yearbook of European Law 269, 298.

[17] See Case C-75/97, para 8 of the Opinion.

Taking stock of the analysis of those findings, the suggestion then was that *a general rule is one that, in the light of its inherent objective, applies to comparable situations.*[18]

Having found an intellectually satisfying definition, two questions need to be answered. The first focuses on this 'objective' which would operate as a polestar for the definition of the general rule, the second on the broadness of the scope of that rule.

First, according to the definition just offered, a rule would be general because it applies to situations that are comparable in the light of the inherent objective of that rule. In other words, the objective seems to be the *unifying principle* underlying the general rule, the core concept that leads to the regulation of comparable situations in a similar way. Leaving aside for the moment the meaning of the key attribute of 'inherency' (which we analyse in the next paragraph), let us look at some examples that show what this reference to objectives means in practical terms.

In tax law, the principal, obvious goal of any tax is to raise revenue. It is generally accepted that each tax should do so according to the *ability to pay* of the taxpayer.[19] Since this ability can be measured with respect to each tax by different indicators, such as income, wealth or consumption, we can have general tax rules which respectively use income, wealth, consumption etc, as the criteria defining the ability to pay. To take a second example—the main purpose of the tax may however not be to collect revenue but rather to create a specific *incentive* or a *disincentive* to perform a certain conduct.[20] Energy and environmental taxes, for instance, have a clear objective other than raising revenue which is to disincentivize activities that have a more harmful impact on the environment or, conversely, to incentivize activities that have a less harmful impact.[21]

In conclusion, the different objectives of the tax should be reflected in the criteria used to determine what is the general tax rule that pursue that objective, and whether the measure at issue is in line with the general objective of that tax.

Secondly, if a rule is general because it applies to those situations that, in the light of the *inherent objective* of that rule, should be subject to it, it should further be asked whether the principle of equal treatment which informs this definition should mean that the general rule, to be used, should *consistently* apply to *all* situations that are *comparable* in the light of that objectives.

This is a huge question, with enormous practical implications. It has featured significantly in two high-profile cases.

[18] See chapter 9, section I.B.

[19] cf W Schön, 'Taxation and State Aid Law in the European Union' (1999) Common Market Law Review 910, 925–7). See also Advocate General Stix-Häckl in Joined Cases C-128-129/03 *AEM*, para 18 of the Opinion, and Joined Cases C-266/04 to C-270/04 *Distribution Casino France*, paras 52–3 of the Opinion.

[20] To be fair, this behavioural objective is indeed behind *any* tax policy, but here it would represent the measure's principal objective.

[21] B Renner-Loquenz, 'State Aid in Energy Taxation Measures: First Experiences from Applying the Environmental Aid Guidelines 2001' (2003) European State Aid Law Quarterly 21, 24.

The first is *British Aggregates* which went all the way from the Commission (2002) to the CFI (2006) to eventually reach the ECJ (2008).[22] In a nutshell, the measure at issue was an environmental levy on aggregates introduced in the UK in 2001. The main objective of the tax was to reduce and rationalize the extraction of minerals commonly used as aggregates. To incentivize the replacement of 'virgin materials', an exemption was granted to recycled products or other materials. The Commission did not raise any State aid objection to the planned tax and its exemptions. An action for annulment against the Commission decision was brought by the *British Aggregates Association* before the CFI. The CFI concluded that the various exemptions provided by the measure did not constitute State aid. In so doing, it made many interesting findings. One passage is particularly relevant for the present analysis and is worth being quoted *in extenso*. After saying that in the absence of coordination, it is for Member States to act in the field of environmental law, the Court noted:

> Member States are free, in balancing the various interests involved, to set their priorities as regards the protection of the environment and, as a result, to determine which goods or services they are to decide to subject to an environmental levy. It follows that, in principle, the mere fact that an environmental levy constitutes a specific measure, which extends to certain designated goods or services, and cannot be seen as part of an overall system of taxation which applies to all similar activities which have a comparable impact on the environment, does not mean that similar activities, which are not subject to the levy, benefit from a selective advantage.[23]

This is an important principle in the reasoning of the CFI. Here the Court is indicating how to determine what is the general tax rule, and more particularly the power Member States have to define it.

What the Court is saying is not only that Member States may 'set their priorities' with respect to environmental protection' and they can 'determine which goods or services' subject to an environmental tax. Most importantly, the CFI is concluding that Member States are free to design the tax so as to cover only 'certain designated goods or services' and do not have to introduce 'an overall system of taxation which applies to all similar activities which have a comparable impact on the environment'. This is the key point.

The CFI is clearly rejecting the idea that, to be general, and to comply with the principle of equality, a (tax) rule should apply to *all* comparable situations. In the case of an environmental tax, such as the one at issue in the case, to '*all similar* activities which have a *comparable* impact on the environment'. In other words, although the 'inherent objective' of the tax is to tackle a certain damage to the environment, the same tax should *not necessarily* apply to all situations that similarly produce a comparable negative impact. Although the deference towards

[22] As well as a stop at the UK High Court in *R (British Aggregates Association) v HM Treasury* [2002] Common Market Law Reports 51.

[23] Case T-210/02 *British Aggregates*, para 115.

Member States and their discretion in designing their policies is firmly recognized, the principle of equality is clearly defeated.[24]

On appeal, both Advocate General Mengozzi and the Court of Justice heavily criticized the CFI's reasoning. The crux of the criticism is that the Court is abandoning an objective approach to the notion of State and granting an undue discretion to Member States and the Commission to define what constitutes a State aid. In other words, the CFI would have assessed positively the tax at issue on the sole basis of its environmental objective and irrespective of whether the same tax was properly structured around that objective.[25] For our purposes, the finding that Member States are free to set their priorities and balance all various interests concerned and consequently introduce a tax measure that does not apply to all similar activities that are comparable is not correct.

If this conclusion is sound, can we simply argue *a contrario*? When introducing say an environmental tax, should Member States make it consistently applicable to *all* similar activities which have a comparable impact on the environment? How far shall we go? Do Members still enjoy some discretion in defining the scope of their policies without their generality being denied? If so, do they have to follow certain criteria? Which ones? From another perspective, can we distinguish a blind egalitarian approach to a more balanced one which, although allowing reasonable distinctions, still respects the principle of equality?

These are difficult questions. Some inspiration can however be drawn from another recent ECJ case which focused on the legality of an EC act. Directive 2003/87/EC (the 'Directive') introduced a greenhouse gas emission allowance trading scheme, which was quite innovative, being probably the first of its type in the world. The Directive adopted a 'step-by-step' approach and excluded two sectors from its application.[26] The issue was whether this exclusion amounted to a breach of the general principle of equal treatment or could be justified by the objectives of the Directive.

Both Advocate General Maduro and the Court provided a thorough analysis of the scope of the measure, in light of its objective (environmental protection) and the principle of equal treatment. In particular, it was crucially noted that, the complexity and novelty of the allowance trading scheme fully justified a 'step-by-step' approach and, in this regard, certain sectors could be excluded provided however

[24] In doing so, the CFI also makes reference to Article 6 of the EC which requires the integration of environmental protection in EC policies. According to the Court, this would also refer to State aid law.

[25] The Advocate General clearly stated that 'Neither the competence enjoyed by the Member States in matters relating to taxation or the environment, nor the principle laid down by Article 6 of the EC of the integration of environmental protection requirements into the definition and implementation of Community policies, justifies the wholesale removal of public measures that distort competition' from EC State aid control. See Case C-487/06P, para 102 of the Opinion.

[26] Notably, the chemical and the non-ferrous metal sectors.

that these decisions were based on 'objective criteria' based on technical and scientific information available at the time of adoption of the measure.[27]

It is the author's view that these findings are of considerable use also when determining how broad a national general tax rule should be in the context of the derogation test, and, more particularly, how Member States can draw boundaries around it without breaching equal treatment.[28]

What is a derogation (or discrimination)?

The divergence between the objectives of the measure and the general rule

One of the most delicate steps in the derogation test is the determination of whether the exemption or, to put it differently, the differential treatment flowing from the measure under scrutiny is in line with the objectives of the identified general rule. What is required is in fact a parallel between different objectives, those of the measure at hand and those of the appropriate general rule. The establishment of an advantage ultimately depends on the determination of a *divergence*, rather than a *convergence*, between them.

It must be pointed out immediately that the existence of a differential nature or impact of the measure at issue is not per se conclusive evidence that the measure at issue is a derogation from the relevant general rule. The exemption may in fact be justified by the 'inherent' objective of the general rule.

This important point was laid down by the Court in the definition of the derogation test in the seminal *Italy v Commission* decision quoted above.[29] What is necessary to assess is whether the measure that introduces a differential treatment may be justified 'by the nature or general scheme of the system' or, to put it another way, 'by the logic of the system'. If this is the case, there would be a convergence of objectives between the tax measure and the general tax rule, and hence no derogation or discrimination and ultimately no advantage.

[27] Case C-127/07 *Arcelor*, para 63. In particular Advocate General Maduro noted: 'It is, then, in the very nature of legislative experimentation that tension with the principle of equal treatment should arise. The very idea of "learning by doing" requires that the new policy be applied to only a limited number of its potential subjects to begin with. As a result, the scope of the policy is artificially circumscribed so that its consequences can be tested before its rules are extended, if appropriate, to all operators who might, in the light of its objectives, be subject to it. That said, recognition of the legitimacy of legislative experimentation cannot invalidate any criticism that might be levelled against it from the point of view of the principle of equal treatment. The discrimination which experimental legislation inevitably entails is compatible with the principle of equal treatment only if certain conditions are satisfied' (para 46 of the Opinion). These conditions are: the transitory nature of the experimental measures and the respect of objective criteria (the impact on the greenhouse effect certainly being an objective benchmark in this regard).

[28] For a suggestion of an analytical test to define the generality, or otherwise, of tax measures, see P Nicolaides, 'Fiscal Aid in the EC: A Critical Review of Current Practice' (2001) World Competition 319; id, 'Fiscal State Aid in the EU: The Limits of Tax Autonomy' (2004) World Competition 365.

[29] Case 173/73 *Italy v Commission*, para 15.

The scrutiny of the objectives of the tax measure and of the tax system seems to run counter to the consistent case-law of the Court whereby the notion of aid is 'objective'[30] since Article 87 'does not distinguish between the measures of State intervention concerned by reference to their causes or aims but defines them in relation to their effects'.[31]

Quite interestingly, it is the same *Italy v Commission* case that planted the seeds of controversy by introducing the 'logic of the system' justification. On the one hand, at paragraph 13, the Court says that a State aid is defined in relation to its effects and not to its causes or aims. On the other, at paragraph 15, the Court seems to acknowledge that those aims may indeed become relevant to determine whether the differentiation previously detected may in fact be justified on the basis of the nature or general scheme of the system.

The following paragraphs attempt to show that there is no contradiction between these findings which can in fact be reconciled with each other, at least at a theoretical level. The practical application to a given tax measure is quite another thing.

The distinction between objectives

The tension between the seemingly contradicting *dicta* of *Italy v Commission* can be eased off if consideration is given to the distinction laid down by the Commission in its 1998 Notice on Direct Taxation with respect to the justification on the basis of the logic of the system (which may well apply to any type of tax and, if necessary, also to any other form of non-economic conduct). What is suggested is that the 'objectives which are *inherent* in the tax system itself' should be differentiated from the '*external* objectives assigned to a particular tax scheme (in particular, social or regional objectives)'.[32]

The practical implication of this *distinction* between *inherent* and *external* objectives, which finds confirmation in the case-law,[33] is not spelled out expressly. Since simple logic seems to require that this distinction must have consequences, the only plausible explanation for it is that only measures that pursue objectives inherent in the tax system should be justified on the basis of its logic whereas objectives externally assigned to the system should *not* be considered when it is necessary to determine whether the measure constitutes a State aid.

The Commission offers some direction on the objectives that are inherent in the tax system. The measure would be justified when 'exceptions to the system or differentiations within that system . . . *derive directly from the basic or guiding principles of the tax system*' or where the 'economic rationale' of the measures 'makes

[30] See, eg, Case T-67/94 *Ladbroke v Commission*, para 52.

[31] Case 173/73 *Italy v Commission*, para 13.

[32] Commission Notice on the application of the State aid rules to measures relating to direct business taxation, OJ C384, 10.12.1998, 3, para 26 (emphasis added).

[33] See, eg, Joined Cases T-211/04 and T-215/04 *Gibraltar*, para 144; Case C-88/03 *Portugal v Commission*, para 81.

them *necessary to the functioning or effectiveness of the tax system*'.[34] Bacon underlines that certain rules would be in line with the logic of the tax system since they define its 'parameters'.[35] Schön suggests that only those objectives that relate to the 'structural component' of the tax and are accordingly necessary to implement its fundamental structure are inherent in the tax system, and may thus be used as justification.[36]

'Navigating between the poles': the risk of conflating scope and justification

The system of State aid control in the EC seems to revolve around *two poles*. Each one has its own substantive, procedural, institutional and constitutional characteristics.

The first pole is represented by Article 87(1) of the EC. This provision is based on an essentially technical and objective analysis, aimed at capturing those deviations from the general norm liable to confer an economic advantage on certain undertakings and thereby distort competition across the border. The 'human' factor is there, as the analysis of the complexities and criticisms of the market paradigm has clearly shown. But, the imprinting seems to be substantially denoted by an inevitable *objectivity*.[37]

The second pole is constituted by various norms, notably Article 87(2) and (3) and Article 86(2) of the EC. These provisions feature a more political, discretionary and hence subjective nature. Although, as the current State Aid Action Plan seem to require, this pole too is increasingly subject to more discipline and objectivity, the focus is on the pursuit of socio-economic (efficiency- or equity-related) objectives, which by definition rest on fundamental policy choices. Despite any injection of transparency, predictability and efficiency, the stamp of these rules seems to ineludibly be *subjective*.

The different substantive operation of two poles is echoed by the procedural, institutional and constitutional arrangements.[38] Generally speaking, when we enter the State aid land, apart from the crucial role of national courts in enforcing the standstill and notification obligations under Article 88(3) of the EC, and, traditionally, in ensuring the recovery of incompatible aid, the role played by Member States is rather limited. Centre stage belongs to the Commission which enjoys a monopoly to assess whether the justifications are satisfied and the measure is 'compatible with the common market'. The evaluation of the Commission,

[34] Commission Notice on the application of the State aid rules to measures relating to direct business taxation, OJ C384, 10.12.1998, 3, paras 16 and 23 (emphasis added).

[35] K Bacon, 'State Aids and General Measures' (1997) Yearbook of European Law 269, 301.

[36] W Schön, 'Taxation and State Aid Law in the European Union' (1999) Common Market Law Review 910, 926.

[37] See Case C-487/06P *British Aggregates*, paras 111–14.

[38] To fully appreciate this point an analysis of the landmark decisions in the case-law may be sufficient. See, eg, Case 730/79 *Philip Morris*; Case C-354/90 *Salmon*; Case C-39/94 *SFEI v La Poste*.

which requires a complex economic and social assessment, is normally considered as rather flexible. The current modernization does not touch the fundamentals of this arrangement.[39]

The interpreter has to navigate between these two poles. It is of great practical importance to him to understand where he should direct his ship for a safe harbour. The maps at his disposal are not always fully clear however. Although there seems to be agreement that the separate issues of scope and justification should not be conflated at the stage of the advantage analysis,[40] the distinction between inherent and external objectives is not fully sorted. The *British Aggregates* case provided a good and recent example of these difficulties. Some years ago, Bacon reported the two most common errors encountered in the application of the justification on the basis of the logic of the system by English Courts: first, 'to regard the general system as *the aid measure itself*, and to State that because that measure is objectively justified, or based on solid policy reasons, the measure is not aid' and, secondly, 'to import into the concept of aid the possibility of an "objective justification" analogous to that employed in the field of free movement'.[41]

These examples highlight the risk of an incorrect interpretation with the result that the advantage is generally charged with public interest considerations that are in fact extraneous to its analysis. As seen, this risk is particularly high in the context of non-economic activity of governments where the public policy considerations are by nature pervasive.

An assessment of the case-law

The argument that any differential impact is inherent in the logic of the system is very attractive to governments and is often raised. However, both the Court and the Commission have so far been quite reluctant in accepting it. In its 2004 Report

[39] The aims are to introduce a bit more of coherency and efficiency in the system, by adopting a 'more refined economic approach', by consolidating secondary legislation and by significantly introducing extensive block exemption mechanisms. See chapter 2, section III.

[40] cf, eg, M Ross, 'Decentralization, Effectiveness, and Modernization: Contradiction in Terms?' (2004) in A Biondi, P Eeckhout, and J Flynn (eds), *The Law of State Aid in the European Union* (Oxford: Oxford University Press, 2004) 85; K Bacon, 'State Aids in the English Courts: Definition and Other Problems' in A Biondi, P Eeckhout, and J Flynn (eds), *The Law of State Aid in the European Union* (Oxford: Oxford University Press, 2004) 337; A Biondi and L Rubini, 'Aims, Effects and Justifications: EC State Aid Law and Its Impact on National Social Policies', in M Dougan and E Spaventa (eds), *Social Welfare and EU Law* (Oxford: Hart Publishing, 2005) 79.

Attempts to further complicate an area which is already in great need of legal certainty should not be warranted.Some years ago, K Bacon ('State Aids and General Measures' (1997) Yearbook of European Law 269, 305–11) suggested the idea of introducing a 'third' category whereby a derogation from the general system should be justified in consideration of the 'special characteristics' of the undertakings concerned with the result there would be no aid in the first place. Despite its intellectual flair, the idea of a special 'justifiable derogation' risks muddying the waters further with the final result that scope and justification are again unduly merged at the level of the advantage analysis.

[41] K Bacon, 'State Aids in the English Courts: Definition and Other Problems' in A Biondi, P Eeckhout, and J Flynn (eds), *The Law of State Aid in the European Union* (Oxford: Oxford University Press, 2004) 337, 350–1.

on Direct Taxation, the Commission expressly indicated that it adopts a rather restrictive approach to this justification, even suggesting that it might apply it only 'in exceptional circumstances'.[42]

In the text that follows, a review of the most recent case-law is provided, with the aim of giving a snapshot of the treatment of the 'justification on the basis of the logic of the system'. Some of the most interesting cases are analysed separately below. The decisions are here grouped in three categories where both the correctness of the outcome and the soundness of the reasoning are taken into account.

(a) Correct reasoning and correct outcome

In some cases the reasoning is clear, and sound, and this results into a correct outcome of the case. The defence is accepted because it is clearly founded on objectives that are inherent in the system.

This is the case for tax avoidance in *Gil Insurance*[43] which is analysed at length below. Similarly, although there is no express reference to the 'logic of the system' language, essentially the same reasoning seems to underlie the positive assessment of the tax arrangements of reserves of nuclear stations in the recent *Stadtwerke* case.[44] Another good example, which can be nicely juxtaposed with the *British Aggregates* (CFI) case and where the Court thoroughly assesses the appropriateness of the measure with its environmental objective, is *Dutch ETS*.[45]

Tax measures adopted in line with the autonomous powers granted to regional governments by national constitutions have been considered as justified by the logic of the system.[46] Some recent cases have discussed the conditions under which the conferral of such autonomy would correspond to the 'constitutional' logic of federal or decentralized tax systems.[47] These will be analysed briefly below.

In other cases, although the objective may in principle qualify as inherent in the logic of the tax system, the defence is rejected because the Court subjects the measure at issue to a close scrutiny with respect to its necessity and/or proportionality

[42] Commission, Report on the implementation of the Commission notice on the application of the State aid rules to measures relating to direct business taxation, 9.2.2004, C(2004)434. See, eg, para 76 and ibid, Box No 7, p 10.

[43] Case C-308/01.

[44] Case T-92/02. Crucially, the Court was satisfied about the objective of the reserves and its proportionality. The fact that they were not 'earmarked' did not constitute an argument for considering them as granting an undue advantage. For two comments on this important case, one before and one after the decision, see DG Reich and M Helios, 'Do Reserves for the Disposal of Nuclear Waste and Shutdown of Nuclear Power Plans in Germany constitute State Aid?' (2002) European State Aid Law Quarterly 207; DG Reich, 'No Level Playing Field for Nuclear Power Reserves? Comment on the Judgment in Case T-92/02 of 26 January 2006' (2006) European State Aid Law Quarterly 445.

[45] T-233/04 *Netherlands v Commission*, paras 87–99.

[46] See, eg, Case 248/84 *Germany v Commission*, para 17. More recently, Cases T-127/99; T-129/99 and T-148/99 *Territorio Histórico de Álava*, paras 142 and 146; Cases T-92/00 and T-103/00 *Territorio Histórico de Álava*, para 57; Cases T-269/99, T-271/99 and T-272/99 *Territorio Histórico de Guipúzcoa*, para 56; Cases T-346/99, T-347/99 and T-348/99 *Territorio Histórico de Álava*, paras 52 and 62.

[47] See Case C-88/03 *Portugal v Commission*, para 66 et seq. See also Joined Cases C-428/06 to C-434/06 *Unión General de Trabajadores de la Rioja*; T-211/04 and T-215/04 *Gibraltar v Commission*.

to reach that aim (*MINAS*)[48] or with the general consistency of the measure with its objective (*British Aggregates*, ECJ).[49] Finally, in many cases the claim is not accepted because the measure clearly pursues an external objective (eg *Heiser*,[50] *Cassa di Risparmio di Firenze*,[51] *Air Liquide*[52], *British Aggregates*, ECJ).[53]

(b) Unclear reasoning but correct outcome

In other cases, although the final decision made by the Court seems correct, the reasoning leading to it raises some doubts.

The *Maribel* decision is a good example.[54] The practice at issue was an increased reduction of social contributions for certain industrial sectors which were particularly exposed to international competition. The defending Belgian government argued that the reduction was a 'choice of economic policy, consisting in a decision to promote the creation of jobs in industrial sectors employing mostly manual workers earning low wages owing to their low qualifications' and this particularly occurred in those sectors that were 'most affected by redundancies and restructuring'.

Before rejecting this claim, the Court spent considerable energy in considering the alternative explanation even noting that the said reduction 'does not at first sight appear to derogate from the nature and scheme of the general system of social protection'.[55] The remainder of the reasoning does not, however, give any intellectually satisfying explanation for that finding.[56]

The famous *Adria-Wien*[57] decision, which involved an exemption from an energy tax in favour of undertakings of the manufacturing sector, is in the author's view comparable to *Maribel*. Although the conclusion of the Court is sound, the reasoning does not always support it.

[48] Case C-159/01, *Netherlands v Commission*, paras 42–7.

[49] C-487/06P *British Aggregates v Commission*, paras 86–92.

[50] Case C-172/03, paras 43–9; see also the Opinion of Advocate General Tizzano, paras 48 and 49. See O D'Ormesson and A Bouin, 'Review of the ECJ Judgment in Case C-172/03 Wolfgang Heiser v Finanzamt Innsbruck, 3 March 2005' (2005) European State Aid Law Quarterly 335 for a note.

[51] Case C-222/04, para 137; see also the Opinion of Advocate General Jacobs, paras 104 and 105. An interesting case note which also broadens the picture showing the interesting connections with the law on free movement is A Biondi, 'Review of Judgment in Case C-222/04—Ministero dell'Economia e delle Finanze v. Cassa di Risparmio di Firenze SpA et al.' (2006) European State Aid Law Quarterly 371.

[52] Case C-393/04. Although no defence in this regard is raised by the defending authorities, the point is analysed and dismissed by Advocate General Tizzano, paras 42 and 43 of the Opinion.

[53] C-487/06P *British Aggregates v Commission*, para 88.

[54] Case C-75/97.

[55] ibid, para 36.

[56] What the Court should have clearly explained—and did not—is the alleged nexus between (i) the said reduction of social contributions, which finance the social security system, and (ii) the convergence of the objectives of the measure and of the social security system. In short, what is missing in the reasoning of the Court is the explanation of the link between social security protection and job creation. Had a nexus been found, the Court should have subjected the measure to a close scrutiny in terms of necessity/proportionality to reach the proposed aim.

[57] Case C-143/99, see in particular paras 49–52.

Even here the tax exemption was aimed at preserving the competitiveness of that sector. There was another more plausible justification though: environmental protection. While the Court accepts that this objective is in line with the logic of the energy tax, it underlines that the distinction between undertakings supplying services and undertakings supplying goods is not tenable since 'energy consumption by each of those sectors is equally damaging to the environment'. So far so good.

The Court however also addresses another argument, noting that there was no evidence that the manufacturing sector would have been disproportionally affected from the tax from the financial standpoint. This is an economic argument that sits uneasily with the logic of an energy-tax. It is clearly external to its logic. Rather than positively addressing it, the Court should have more simply dismissed it as irrelevant.

Two more recent cases (*Italy v Commission* and *Unicredito*) raise again the issue of what objectives may be included in the logic of the tax at issue or more generally of the overall tax system. What was at issue was a tax exemption in favour of Italian banks. The clear aim was again to improve the competitiveness of certain undertakings, this time at a certain stage in the development of the sector.[58] The Court thus had no difficulty in dismissing the allegation. Having found the real aim of this measure, it is interesting that in the same paragraph the Court added that the tax reduction is not justified by the nature of the tax in question because 'it is not an adaptation of the general scheme to the particular characteristics of banking undertakings'.

This argument, which also finds support in the Commission's quarters,[59] whereby differential measures for certain sectors,[60] would be in line with the logic of the system, cannot be accepted. In most of these cases, arguments about the 'particularities' of certain undertakings or sectors, which would put them at a disadvantage if the normal rule were applied, are simply misplaced and cannot be justified in terms of the logic of the tax at issue or, more generally, of the general tax system.[61] Normally, the separate provisions governing justifications are the proper place for considering specific disadvantages and redistributive rationales.

[58] See Case C-148/04 *Unicredito*, para 51; Case C-66/02 *Italy v Commission*, para 101.

[59] See, eg, the Commission Notice on the application of the State aid rules to measures relating to direct business taxation, OJ C384, 10.12.1998, 3, paras 26 and 27; Commission, Report on the implementation of the Commission notice on the application of the State aid rules to measures relating to direct business taxation, 9.2.2004, C(2004)434, paras 32–42.

In a similar vein see also K Bacon, 'State Aids and General Measures' (1997) Yearbook of European Law 269; C Quigley, 'The Notion of a State Aid in the EEC' (1988) European Law Review 242; id, 'General Taxation and State Aid' in A Biondi, P Eeckhout, and J Flynn (eds), *The Law of State Aid in the European Union* (Oxford: Oxford University Press, 2004) 207.

[60] Such as agriculture and fisheries, insurance, banking, oil, gas and SMEs.

[61] W Schön, 'Taxation and State Aid Law in the European Union' (1999) Common Market Law Review 910, 926 and 929.

(c) Incorrect reasoning and incorrect outcome

There are not many cases where the Community Courts got it completely wrong. But a few can be found.[62] An incorrect reasoning leads to an incorrect decision. External objectives are accepted as part of the logic of the tax system with the result that the measure does not constitute an aid.

D. Some applications

We can now examine three areas which have increasingly seen a reference to the logic of the system exception, ie technical rules, local taxation and environmental taxes.

Technical rules

Some rules directly reflect the ability to pay of the taxpayer. Accordingly, even though they may have a differential impact, they derive from the logic of the tax system and they do not create any advantage.

Reference is made to technical rules, those that 'define the parameters of the system', for example by determining what a 'corporation' is for corporation tax purposes.[63] According to the Commission, other examples are the setting of the rates of taxation, depreciation of assets, loss carry-overs, and the prevention of double taxation or tax avoidance.[64] We could add provisions that ensure tax neutrality[65] and the efficiency of tax collection.[66] These rules are necessary to implement the fundamental structure of the relevant tax thus belonging to its 'structural component'. With an illuminating metaphor, they have been compared to the 'fine print' of the general decision of a Member State to levy a given tax.[67]

This is the theory. In practice it may be controversial whether a provision containing a technical rule simply measures the 'ability to pay' of the taxpayer or rather provides him with a tax incentive. For example, rather than taking into account the ordinary life of an asset, in accordance with good commercial practice, a depreciation rule may go beyond the objective determination of the financial situation of

[62] Cases C-128-129/03 *AEM*. For a commentary see M Maier and P Werner, 'Review of Judgment AEM Spa' (2005) European State Aid Law Quarterly 657. See, also, T-210/02 *British Aggregates*.

[63] See K Bacon, 'State Aids and General Measures' (1997) Yearbook of European Law 269, 301–2.

[64] cf Commission Notice on the application of the State aid rules to measures relating to direct business taxation, OJ C384, 10.12.1998, 3, para 13. cf also Commission, Report on the implementation of the Commission notice on the application of the State aid rules to measures relating to direct business taxation, 9.2.2004, C(2004)434, para 16.

[65] For an interesting example see the Commission, Report on the implementation of the Commission notice on the application of the State aid rules to measures relating to direct business taxation, 9.2.2004, C(2004)434, para 37.

[66] Some special measures for SMEs are sometimes justified in terms of lower collection costs for the treasury.

[67] W Schön, 'Taxation and State Aid Law in the European Union' (1999) Common Market Law Review 910, 926.

the taxpayer, thus creating an incentive to invest in certain assets.[68] In this regard, accelerated depreciation rates, which allow the undertakings concerned to postpone a proportion of their tax liability and thus confer on them an advantage, may be used to create an incentive for investment in research and development, for adopting equipments serving environmental goals or serving social purposes.[69]

These are, however, policy objectives that are external to the rationale of depreciation and, if they exist, the relevant measures should be considered to be State aid which may be declared compatible with the common market if, for example, the conditions of exemption for research and development or environmental aid are fulfilled.

An interesting example of these difficulties concerns the setting of tax rates. Leaving aside the debate about its rationale,[70] the progressiveness of the tax scale is generally considered as pertaining to the logic of the tax system. Nonetheless, the introduction of different tax rates (for reasons unrelated to tax progression) may sometimes raise some controversy. A typical example is that of eco-taxes which may provide different rates according to the more/less polluting effect.

In this regard it is useful to examine a recent case where the Court found that the adoption of a differential tax rate was justified by the need to prevent tax avoidance.

Gil Insurance

In *Gil Insurance*[71] the Court was called to examine an English tax whose categorization had already been subject to the scrutiny of the English Court of Appeal in the *Lunn Poly* case.[72] The *Finance Act 1994* had introduced the *Insurance Premium Tax* (IPT) on insurance contracts which was charged at a rate of 2.5 per cent (later increased to 4 per cent). That uniform rate was subsequently replaced by the *Finance Act 1997* by two different rates: a standard rate of 4 per cent and a higher rate of 17.5 per cent, the latter applying to insurance contracts connected with the provision of certain services (notably domestic appliances, motor cars and travel).

The initial decision to introduce IPT and, subsequently, a higher rate for connected insurance contracts—which equalled that of Value Added Tax (VAT)—was intended to counteract 'value shifting'. With this practice a low profit margin was set for the principal product (in *Gil Insurance* domestic appliances, in *Lunn Poly* holiday packages) which attracted VAT at a rate of 17.5 per cent. By contrast, a

[68] See Case T-86/96 *Hapag Loyd*, para 61.

[69] K Bacon, 'State Aids and General Measures' (1997) Yearbook of European Law 269, 300.

[70] See Commission Notice on the application of the State aid rules to measures relating to direct business taxation, OJ C384, 10.12.1998, 3, para 24.

[71] Case C-308/01 *Gil Insurance*.

[72] In *R v Customs and Excise Commissioners, ex parte Lunn Poly Ltd and another* [1999] European Law Reports 653, the Court of Appeal concluded that the differential rates of tax on travel insurance constituted State aid under Article 87(1) of the EC. For a note see K Bacon, 'Differential Taxes, State Aids and the Lunn Poly Case' (1999) European Competition Law Review 384.

high margin was set for the connected insurance contract which was exempt from VAT,[73] and only subject to the much lower IPT rate (as said, 2.5 or 4 per cent). The end result of this price manipulation was a loss of VAT receipts for the treasury.

One of the issues before the Court in *Gil Insurance* was whether the differential rate amounted to State aid.[74] With a standard application of the derogation test, the Court accepted the justification put forward—the need to tackle tax avoidance—and concluded, at paragraph 78 of the decision, that:

> . . . even on assumption that the introduction of the higher rate of IPT involves an advantage for operators offering contracts subject to the standard rate, the application of the higher rate of IPT to a specific part of the insurance contracts previously subject to the standard rate must be regarded as justified by the nature and the general scheme of the national system of taxation of insurance. The IPT scheme cannot therefore be regarded as constituting an aid measure within the meaning of Article 87(1) of the EC.[75]

An addendum should be made to this passage. In its analysis (notably at paragraph 74), the Court had considered that, from the perspective of value shifting and the relevant price manipulation, the 'higher rate of IPT and VAT form part of an inseparable whole'. It is with this qualification in mind that the reference to the justification on the basis of the 'national system of taxation of insurance' should be understood.

The issue of negative aid

Another important issue that comes out from *Gil Insurance* is whether there is room within the scope of Article 87(1) of the EC for the concept of so-called 'negative aid'. In other words, the question is whether the imposition of a *burden*, in the instant case in the form of a tax, on certain undertakings can amount to an aid to other undertakings that are not subject to it.[76]

The views differ sharply. Some, as the UK government in the case in question,[77] argue that the general definition of State aid only includes the idea of *positive* benefit.[78] Accordingly, the introduction of a *tax disincentive* can never be held to

[73] Article 13(B)(a) of the Sixth VAT Directives provides that insurance transactions are not subject to VAT. The Court reports that, as a result of this exemption, there was also a trend towards replacing service contracts for the repair and maintenance of domestic appliances (which were subject to VAT) with insurance contracts (which, as noted, were not).

[74] The other questions, which focused on whether the Sixth VAT Directive precluded the introduction of a tax such as IPT, were answered in the negative.

[75] Along these lines, see the Commission 1998 Notice on Direct Taxation, para 13. cf also K Bacon, 'Differential Taxes, State Aids and the Lunn Poly Case' (1999) European Competition Law Review 384, 388.

[76] See W Schön, 'Special Charges—A Gap in European Competition Law?' (2006) European State Aid Law Quarterly 495.

[77] Reported at para 57 of the decision.

[78] W Schön, 'Taxation and State Aid Law in the European Union' (1999) Common Market Law Review 910, 930. An additional argument that is used in support of the traditional view is that when a higher tax is imposed it would be difficult to detect a transfer of State resources. cf K Bacon,

confer an advantage on non-taxable persons.[79] Considering the broad coverage of the notion of State aid in the EC others by contrast believe that there are no reasons for excluding these forms from the notion of State aid.[80] These measures undoubtedly confer an advantage on those that are not subject to the tax.

In the decision the Court did not address the point expressly (which, as seen, was raised by the UK government). At paragraph 78, quoted above, the Court considered, by way of assumption, that the introduction of the higher rate could involve an *advantage* for operators offering contracts subject to the standard rate. However, most of the other findings, which significantly echo the Opinion of the Advocate General that expressly addressed the issue and concluded in the negative,[81] seem to lend considerable support to the traditional view.[82]

Generally speaking, and considering the broad language of Article 87(1) of the EC (it may be recalled that Article 87(1) of the EC covers 'any aid in any form whatsoever'), the first impression is that it should not be excluded that the imposition of a burden or a disadvantage could be considered as a State aid. To put it differently: in many cases it seems indeed that advantage and disadvantage are really two sides of the same coin and the same measure can be construed as either providing the former or imposing the latter.

If however the theoretical framework of the derogation test is applied to the concept of negative aid, it seems that we cannot escape the following incongruous result. Consider the case of a country that introduces two different tax rates for polluting cars (higher rate) and non-polluting cars (lower rate). Admittedly, the former could be viewed as a *disincentive* to use polluting vehicles, the latter as an *incentive* to use more environmentally friendly cars. If the regulation of the two cases is perfectly the same, it is difficult to determine what is the general rule and

'Differential Taxes, State Aids and the Lunn Poly Case' (1999) European Competition Law Review 384, 386–8.

[79] W Schön, 'Taxation and State Aid Law in the European Union' (1999) Common Market Law Review 910, 930.

[80] K Bacon, 'State Aids and General Measures' (1997) Yearbook of European Law 269, 318; id, K Bacon, 'Differential Taxes, State Aids and the Lunn Poly Case' (1999) European Competition Law Review 384, 386–8.

[81] See para 51 et seq of the Opinion. Advocate General Geelhoed found the specific distortions caused by the imposition of a burden can never be regarded as the grant of aid in favour of the market participants coming under the general measure under Article 87 of the EC but should be tackled under Articles 96 and 97 of the EC. The Advocate General expressed his view also extrajudicially. See LA Geelhoed, 'The Demarcation of State Aid and Regulatory Charges' (2005) European State Aid Law Quarterly 401.

[82] When considering whether the differential rate was justified by the nature of the tax, the Court underlined that the higher rate should be considered as a deterrent (to the conclusion of connected insurance contracts) and that accordingly it was not intended to confer an advantage to those operators who offer contracts subject to the standard rate (para 75 of the judgment). The standard rate did not constitute a derogation from the general system of insurance tax as it was introduced to compensate for the fact that insurance is not subject to VAT (para 76 of the judgment). These arguments were the same as those put forward by the Advocate General who opined that the higher rate (like any imposition of a burden) could not give rise to aid.

what is the exception. Two possibilities can thus be envisaged. On the one hand, the higher rate could be regarded as the prevailing rule and the lower rate as the exception. This is the classic example of State aid and there is no need to deploy the concept of 'negative aid'. On the other hand, the imposition of the burden, ie the higher rate, could be viewed as the derogation from the lower rate which would then constitute the *general rate*.[83] Here comes the paradox. It could be observed that it is rather odd to consider that the benefited undertakings are such because they are subject to the *general rule*, and this would ultimately depend on the fact that an exceptional unfavourable treatment has been reserved to other undertakings.

Local taxation

A very topical example of tax rules that may be considered consistent with the logic of the tax system concerns those introduced by local authorities whose fiscal autonomy is recognized in their own jurisdictions.[84]

Along these lines, it would be necessary to distinguish between tax measures concerning a certain region that are instituted by central governments, which even if extending to the whole of the relevant local area would constitute a selective aid, and tax measures adopted by local authorities which extend to all undertakings within the relevant territory and would not amount to aid.

It could be asked why State aid rules should distinguish between these two situations. Arguably, within the context of the Member State at issue, which is principally responsible for the compliance with State aid rules, even *local* taxes adopted by *local* authorities can be viewed as a differential treatment within its (ie of the Member State) jurisdiction. It could further be observed that, from the point of view of its distortive impact, there is probably no difference if the same tax measure is adopted at a central or local level. Aid measures with local scope produce similar effects irrespective of whether they originate and/or are funded at central or local level.

These remarks lead us to consider the commonly already mentioned (chapter 9, section I.C) accepted rationale for justifying the differentiation inherent in local taxation, which is *constitutional* since it relates to the internal share of competence within the jurisdiction of the Member State in question, and involves both legal and political considerations. So far, it seems that the Court has generally accepted this principle (see the cases cited above).

[83] It should be recalled that the existence of a derogation does not necessarily mean that this is always favourable to the relevant undertakings. Once it has been established that the measure at issue deviates from the general scheme, it is still necessary to determine that this exception is advantageous.

[84] See V Di Bucci, 'Direct Taxation—State Aid in form of Fiscal Measures' in MS Rydelski (ed), *The EC State Aid Regime: Distortive Effects of State Aid on Competition and Trade* (London: Cameron May, 2006) 73, 79–81.

The *Portugal v Commission* case directly addresses this issue and particularly the conditions that need to be present for local taxation not to constitute a State aid.[85] Substantially following the Opinion of Advocate General Geelhoed, the Court held that true fiscal autonomy would exist only if it cumulatively occurs at three levels: institutional, procedural and economic.[86]

Environmental taxes

The increasing attention to the protection of the environment has a considerable impact in shaping governmental policies. Its importance is expressly sanctioned in Articles 2 and 6 EC. According to Article 174(2) of the EC, EC environmental law is inspired and moulded by principles that also play an important role in the context of EC State aid regulation.

Among these principles, the 'polluter pays' principle is particularly significant. It requires that all environmental costs should be absorbed (internalized) in production costs.[87] As Advocate General Jacobs clearly explained, in the context of the definition of State aid under Article 87(1) of the EC, this principle is:

> used as an analytical tool to allocate responsibility according to economic criteria for the costs entailed by the pollution in question. A given measure will constitute State aid where it relieves those liable under the polluter-pays principle from their primary responsibility to bear the costs.[88]

Other principles that could arguably play a role in the definition of State aid are the principles of precaution, prevention, and that damage should be rectified at source.

Member States increasingly make use of tax systems to pursue environmental objectives, for example by encouraging or discouraging certain activities depending on their impact on the environment. In some cases, directly or indirectly, these

[85] Case C-88/03 *Portugal v Commission*. For a commentary see P Nicolaides, 'The Boundaries of Tax Autonomy—Comments on the Opinion of AG Geelhoed on Case C-88/03 *Portoguese Republic v Commission*' (2006) European State Aid Law Quarterly 119; V Di Bucci, 'Direct Taxation'—State Aid in form of Fiscal Measures', in MS Rydelski (ed), *The EC State Aid Regime: Distortive Effects of State Aid on Competition and Trade* (London: Cameron May, 2006) 73.

[86] See Case C-88/03 *Portugal v Commission*, para 66 et seq. See also Joined Cases C-428/06 to C-434/06 *Unión General de Trabajadores de la Rioja*; T-211/04 and T-215/04 *Gibraltar v Commission*. A brief parallel with the WTO. There is no case-law on the point. It has however been argued that economic autonomy would not be necessary under Article 2.2 of the SCM. See E McGovern, *International Trade Regulation* (loose-leaf updated biannually, Exeter: Globefield Press, 1995).

[87] The premise is that, inasmuch as they are not internalized in production costs, environmental costs represent a negative externality, that is a loss to society. The 'polluter pays' principle aims to tackle this market failure by requiring that the producer of the damage should also bear its costs. The important role played by the 'polluter pays' principle in EC State aid law is explored by Advocate General Jacobs in his Opinion in Case C-126/01 *GEMO*, paras 66–77.

[88] ibid, para 69.

taxes differentiate between various situations and undertakings and fall within the scrutiny of the tax and State aid provisions of the EC Treaty.[89]

As regards tax rules, reference should be made to Article 90 of the EC that prohibits discrimination with respect to internal taxation between imported and 'similar' domestic products as well as the imposition on imports of 'any taxation of such a nature as to afford indirect protection to other products'. The striking similarity with Article III:2 of the GATT is not accidental since the latter constituted its model. We have seen that the debate of the role of objectives at the level of the prohibition of Article III of the GATT is a very lively one and the orthodoxy is against any reference to the objectives of the measure. A substantially similar approach can be seen in the EC. In *Outokumpu*[90] what was at issue was whether differential tax rates between domestic and imported electricity, which were overall disadvantageous toward the latter, could be justified by an environmental objective. Adopting a strict approach, the Court said that this kind of justification could not be advanced at the level of Article 90 of the EC.

In State aid law the issue is whether the measure at issue provides for a derogation from the general scheme of the tax. As under Article 90 of the EC, the important question is whether any differential treatment can find a justification in the environmental logic of the tax. The fundamental issue becomes whether the environmental objective of the tax is sufficient to define its general nature. The starting point of the analysis has already been expressed previously. Energy and environmental taxes differ from the majority of other taxes because they have a clear objective other than raising revenue.[91] This is an incentive/disincentive effect with respect to the environmental impact of a given activity or goods/service. At least in principle, this lack of ambiguity with respect to the objectives pursued should make the reference to the 'logic of the system' justification easier and at the same time reduce the possibilities of abusing it.[92]

Helpful guidance can be offered by the principles outlined above. We can for example attempt to apply the main one, the *polluter pays principle*. The justification should be acknowledged for those tax measures that, in line with that principle, aim at internalizing environmental costs and accordingly induce a certain environmentally friendly conduct on the targeted undertakings. A tax shaped in this way also seems to be consistent with the principles of precaution, prevention and of rectification of environmental damage at source. By contrast, other

[89] See, generally, G Van Calster, 'Greening the EC's State Aid and Tax Regimes' (2000) European Competition Law Review 294; G Facenna, 'State Aid and Environmental Protection', in A Biondi, P Eeckhout, and J Flynn (eds), *The Law of State Aid in the European Union* (Oxford: Oxford University Press, 2004) 245; A Kliemann, 'Aid for Environmental Protection' in MS Rydelski (ed), *The EC State Aid Regime: Distortive Effects of State Aid on Competition and Trade* (London: Cameron May, 2006) 315.

[90] Case C-231/96.

[91] B Renner-Loquenz, 'State Aid in Energy Taxation Measures: First Experiences from Applying the Environmental Aid Guidelines 2001' (2003) European State Aid Law Quarterly 21.

[92] The *British Aggregates* decision before the CFI stands as good reminder of how the 'logic of the system' justification can be grossly mishandled also in these cases.

differential taxes do not seem to be in line with the environmental objectives of the tax but rather to run against them. Tax concessions inserted within the environmental tax and based on economic or financial considerations seem to be external to the inherent logic of the tax. It is for example common to provide relief for energy-intensive industries. This is motivated by the fact that the normal application of the environmental tax to the relevant undertakings would be too burdensome financially. This measure clearly constitutes a derogation from the general logic of the environmental tax since it is at odds with the *polluter pays* principle and its disincentive effect. It therefore confers an advantage and possibly an aid and, if any, may be eligible for exemption under Article 87(3) of the EC.

It is in this light that the decisions of the Court in *Adria-Wien*, *MINAS*, *British Aggregates* (ECJ) and *Dutch ET* should be read. A differential treatment justified by the environmental objective of the tax should in principle be regarded as pertaining to the logic of the tax. What is always necessary however is to subject the measure to close scrutiny to ascertain the necessity and proportionality towards the stated objective as well as its overall consistency with the latter.[93]

II. Regulatory measures

This section begins by recalling the main finding of the previous Part, and particularly of chapter 5. Under the current law, many regulatory measures are not covered by Article 87(1) of the EC. Since it has been argued however that the net should be cast wider, a brief exposition of the working of the advantage analysis of regulatory measures is justified.

This examination closely follows that carried out with fiscal measures. In the current context of market logic expansion underlined above, it is not always clear whether the conduct should be classed as economic or not, and which test should thus apply. That said, if the activity is considered non-economic, the derogation test applies. In other words, what should be determined is whether the measure favourably derogates from the general regime otherwise applicable by 'lowering' the degree of regulation.

Two cases, concerning employment deregulation and the regulation of debt, are examined in detail.[94]

[93] As the *British Aggregates* cases have shown, the reference to the principle of integration of environmental protection in all EC policies (Article 6 of the EC) in the State aid field can raise concerns, particularly as far as the application of Article 87(1) of the EC is concerned. The proper place for this consideration in State aid policy may be the justification level under Article 87(3) of the EC. See the observations of the ECJ in this regard: Case C-487/06P, paras 91–2.

[94] An intriguing example of advantage analysis in the context of corporate law is C-237/04 *Enirisorse II* where two exceptions to the normal rules in case of shareholders' withdrawal from the company justified each other in the context of a 'micro-system'. An analysis of the facts, and of the separate issue of 'State resources', can be found in chapter 5, section III.A.

A. Employment deregulation

If the departure from the normal application of the regulation of the employment relationship involves a decrease of the level of contractual or legal protection for employees, this form of 'deregulation' confers an advantage for the relevant employers in terms of lower labour costs.

In the *Sloman Neptun* case the partial non-application of German law to foreign crews of vessels flying the German flag but enrolled with an international register meant that the ordinary collective agreement, with its pay and social security level, did not apply to the relevant employment relationships. The Court found that this measure did not constitute State aid. In chapter 5 the findings of the Court were extensively analysed.

What is clear, however, is that the measure at issue did deviate from the normal rule of German employment law and conferred an advantage to the relevant shipowners in terms of lower pay and social contributions burden. This was the stated intention of the legislation and this was also recognized by the Court.[95] At the level of the advantage analysis, the interesting question is whether this differential treatment could be justified by the logic of the measure. In this regard, Advocate General Darmon put forward an intriguing but difficult private international law justification. After carrying out an extensive comparison of the laws of other Member States (see paras 86–96 of the Opinion), he concluded that the measure at issue did not derogate from the system because it 'set the limits' to the application of German Law, enabling in particular individuals faced with an 'extraneous factor' (the seafarers were non-resident) to choose the law applicable to their contractual relationships.'

In *Kirsammer Hack* the exclusion of small businesses from a legal regime requiring payment of compensation in the event of unfair dismissals was not considered State aid.[96] It seems clear that the non-application of the normal rules on liability for unfair dismissal relieved the employers concerned of one cost normally borne by SMEs. What is interesting to consider is the justification for this derogation that the Court seems to have hinted at when it referred to the aim 'to avoid imposing on those businesses financial constraints that might hinder their development'. Advocate General Darmon relied heavily on this aspect, and in particular on the

[95] See para 21. It it interesting to mention a State aid case concerning the *Danish International Shipping Register* (*DIS*) that has recently come before the ECJ (Case C-319/07P *3F*). Although the litigation fully concentrates on procedural issues (ie the standing of the complainant, a trade union), it emerges (see paras 8–11 of the Opinion of Advocate General Sharpston) that the Commission concluded that the *DIS*, which permitted registered shipowners of vessels to employ seafarers from outside the EU on the basis of their own national wage conditions, constituted a State aid under Article 87(1) of the EC. In particular, these employees were completely exempted to pay income tax, a fiscal benefit transmitted to the shipowners. The Commission considered this aid 'compatible with the common market' under Article 87(3) of the EC already in the preliminary phase of investigation and accordingly it did not open a formal investigation.'

[96] As we have seen, this finding is based on arguments remarkably similar to those underlying the *Sloman Neptun* decision.

other characteristics of employment relationships within SMEs, such as their personal character and the 'material impossibility of being able to offer the worker another post within the same structure', to expressly justify this measure on the basis of the logic of the tax system.[97]

Arguably, both the Court and the Advocate General got it wrong. The argument of Darmon is beside the point. What was at issue in the case was not a provision concerning reinstatement into the workplace but rather providing compensation in the event of unlawful dismissal. Although more in line with the rationale of the measure, the Court's argument tries to prove too much. The special problems of SMEs, which would justify an exclusion of compensation should not be considered at the level of the definition of aid and, in particular, of the advantage analysis, but a later stage.[98]

Similar remarks could be made with other cases of employment de-regulation such as *Viscido* where the Court found that the departure from the ordinary rule concerning the open duration of employment contracts, which enabled the Italian Post Office to recruit personnel on a fixed-term basis, did not constitute a State aid. It does not take a lot to appreciate that the measure clearly deviated from the ordinary rule and guaranteed to the Post Office a higher degree of flexibility.

It can be argued that most, if not all, the cases of 'employment deregulation' examined above do confer an advantage to the undertakings concerned since they undoubtedly derogate from the applicable general rule. Importantly, the examination of the arguments based on the logic of the system shows how this justification is difficult to apply. For the same reasons indicated with respect to tax measures, the exclusion of these measures from Article 87(1) of the EC seems to disrupt the proper application of State aid rules falling into the 'trap of conflation' (of justification into scope).

B. The regulation of debt

The expression 'regulation of debt' is used in this context to mean all those forms of regulation that affect the liability of an undertaking for its debts.

Before briefly examining some examples, two general remarks can be made at the outset. First, in general, the approach adopted by the Court with respect to these measures seems to show less deference towards Member States' prerogatives as compared to that concerning the cases of 'employment de-regulation' analysed above. Secondly, this is a grey area of the law from the point of view of the advantage analysis where we see an interesting conceptual interplay between what is

[97] cf paras 64–7.

[98] It is well-known that due to the particular problems they face, and the important role they play in the economy, SMEs enjoy special treatment when the compatibility with the common market of aid measures benefiting them is under scrutiny under Article 87(3)(c) of the EC.

non-economic and what is economic, and hence between what seems to be subject to a normative derogation test and what is subject to a market test.

Three main examples of forms of regulation of debt can be found from the case-law. First, we have special bankruptcy and insolvency rules that exempt certain undertakings from the ordinary regime. Secondly, there may be rules that provide an explicit guarantee or coverage of losses by the State, either unconditional or depending on certain circumstances, such as the acquisition by the State of a holding in a company which entails, in certain cases, unlimited liability. Thirdly, there is the conduct of the government as public creditor when its debtor is in default in the payment of taxes or social contributions.

Starting from the first case, it seems clear, from the advantage analysis perspective, that rules that exempt certain undertakings from the ordinary bankruptcy and insolvency regime should normally be held to constitute a derogation. The two main authorities in this field are *Ecotrade* and *Piaggio* where the Court held that, on condition that it entailed an additional burden for public authorities,[99] the application to large undertakings in difficulties of a system derogating from the rules of ordinary law relating to insolvency, and providing in particular the absolute prohibition of individual actions for enforcement and the suspension of interest on all debts owed by the undertakings in question, and the correlated reduction in creditors' profits, could be regarded as a State aid.[100]

The second category of forms of regulation of debt is more complex because of its ambiguity. This depends mainly on two reasons, partly intertwined, the determination of the appropriate benchmark—normative or market—and the fact that in many cases what is at issue are general rules which are applicable also to private agents.

With respect to those rules that provide an explicit guarantee or coverage of losses by the State, reference should be made to the German system of guarantees to publicly owned banks which ensured an open-ended guarantee against their liabilities and thereby afforded them cheaper funding.[101] After a lengthy negotiation with the Commission, which regarded these measures as a guarantee, the German government agreed to phase out the system. Interestingly, it seems that

[99] See, however, chapter 5, section III.A above, for the serious ambiguity on the point of the conclusion and operative part of the relevant decisions.

[100] For a commentary on the so-called 'Prodi law', and its subsequent amendments to make it EC law compliant, see GM Roberti, 'Public Guarantees and Community Control of State Aids', in CD Ehlermann and M Everson (eds), *European Competition Law Annual 1999: Selected Issues in the Field of State Aids* (Oxford: Hart Publishing, 2001) 278; G Conte, 'Aiuti di Stato e procedure concorsuali nazionali nella recente giurisprudenza comunitaria: il caso della "Legge Prodi"' (1999) Il Diritto dell'Unione Europea 539; MT Cirenei, 'La riforma dell'amministrazione straordinaria alla luce della disciplina comunitaria degli aiuti: fine di un contenzioso?' (1999) Diritto del Commercio Internazionale 199. A Santa Maria (ed), *Competition and State Aid—An Analysis of the EC Practice* (Alphen aan den Rijn: Kluwer Law International, 2007) chapter 4.

[101] A very good discussion on the complex legal problems raised by these German guarantees can be found in CD Ehlermann and M Everson (eds), *European Competition Law Annual 1999: Selected Issues in the Field of State Aids* (Oxford: Hart Publishing, 2001) 177 et seq.

the benchmark applicable to both the 'maintenance' obligation (which obliges the supporting entity to guarantee the stable economic basis of the bank) and 'guarantee' obligation (which obliges the supporting entity to guarantee the claims of creditors of the bank) is a market one.[102] In any event, with language which echoes a possible justification on the basis of the logic of the German (public) corporate law system, Schneider has argued that 'financing and liability rules are a structural element of the law of public corporations' with the result that the said obligations should not be regarded as aid.[103]

As regards the second case, when the acquisition by the State of a holding in a company entails, in certain cases, unlimited liability, it is necessary to mention the *IOR* and *EFIM* decisions of the Commission. The provision at issue was Article 2362 of the Italian Civil Code which provides that, in case of insolvency of a limited company, the benefit of limited liability is lost for those debts incurred when there was only one shareholder, that shareholder thus being liable for all the company's debts during his sole control. According to the Commission, when that shareholder is a public authority this unlimited liability is in effect a guarantee.[104]

This case is paradigmatic to show the ambiguity explained above. On the one hand, this is a general provision of company law applicable to any company and to any shareholder. On the other hand, the Commission thought that a public investor could not shelter itself behind this provision and its apparent inevitability. What should be considered is whether, in the circumstances of the case, a private investor would have reached the insolvency stage or rather, in the knowledge of its possible unlimited liability, would have taken alternative steps, such as going into liquidation. The fact remains that the presence of this rule, when applied to a public shareholder, might have distorted the functioning of the capital market by increasing the rating of the borrower. Despite the sweeping statements in the 1993 *EFIM* Notice,[105] and also in the 1993 Communication on Public Undertakings,[106]

[102] See C Koenig, 'State Guarantees for the German Landesbanken and the EC State Aid Regime' in CD Ehlermann and M Everson (eds), *European Competition Law Annual 1999: Selected Issues in the Field of State Aids* (Oxford: Hart Publishing, 2001), 239, 242, 244–5.

[103] UH Schneider, '"Anstaltslast" and "Gewährträgerhaftung" as Implied Elements of Public Corporations rather than State Aid' in CD Ehlermann and M Everson (eds), *European Competition Law Annual 1999: Selected Issues in the Field of State Aids* (Oxford: Hart Publishing, 2001) 357, 371.

[104] A discussion on the problems raised by Article 2362 of the Italian Civil code is present in various papers of the second part of CD Ehlermann and M Everson (eds), *European Competition Law Annual 1999: Selected Issues in the Field of State Aids* (Oxford: Hart Publishing, 2001). See, in particular, the contribution of GM Roberti, 'Public Guarantees and Community Control of State Aids', ibid, 278.

[105] Commission Notice on *EFIM*, OJ C349/2.

[106] Commission Communication, Application of Articles 92 and 93 of the EEC Treaty and of Article 5 of Commission Directive 80/723/EEC to public undertakings in the manufacturing sector, OJ C307, 13.11.1993, 3, paras 24 and 38.2.

and in the very recent 2008 Notice on Guarantees,[107] reading the two Commission original decisions the impression is however that the real problem is not with the general provision of the civil code, but rather, and more appropriately, with the overall conduct taken by the public shareholder under the cover of that provision.

Finally, we can approach the third example of regulation of debt which focuses on the conduct of the government as public creditor when its debtor is in default in the payment of taxes or social contributions. It seems that these cases too escape from the 'non-market' area since they are consistently assessed on the basis of market criteria. The test is not that of an *investor* but rather that of a *creditor* that, as explained previously (chapter 8, section I.B), mainly aims to recover his credit. This distinction, which has been laid down first by Advocate General La Pergola in the *Tubacex* case,[108] has been reformulated more recently by Advocate General Maduro in the *Grupo de Empresas Alvarez* case.[109]

The conduct of a diligent creditor has been analysed in different cases, where the various courses of conduct of the public authority—and its possible alternatives—have been subject to close scrutiny.[110] The fact that the debt is public since it concerns tax and social contributions arrears does not seem to be relevant. The principle seems undisputed. Once the public law relationship has arisen, the public authority is on a par with that of a private creditor in similar circumstances. It should therefore be tested accordingly. As in the previous example on Article 2362 of the Italian Civil Code, normally, the focus is on the exercise of the conduct by the public authority. Thus, the Commission observed in *Magefesa* that what was at issue in the case was not the Spanish legislation but 'rather the systematic non-payment of certain debts'.[111] This provides another good example of the expansion of the market logic to an area of public activity.

III. Public goods

This paragraph merely sums up the previous findings on the problem of definition of public goods in the context of the advantage analysis, and refers the reader to the relevant analysis.[112] The first important finding is that public goods are quite rare.

[107] Commission Notice on the application of Articles 87 and 88 of the EC Treaty to State aid in the form of guarantees, OJ C 155 of 20.06.2008, 10, para. 1.2.

[108] C-342/96.

[109] C-276/00.

[110] See, eg, C-342/96 *Tubacex*; C-480/98 *Magefesa*; C-256/97 DMT; C-276/02 *Grupo de Empresas Alvarez*; T-36/99 *Lenzing*. In the literature see I Atanasiu, 'EC State Aid Policy with Respect to Soft Budgetary Constraints: Tax and Social Security Contribution Payment Arrears' (2005) European State Aid Law Quarterly 597; P Nicolaides and M Kekelekis, 'When do Firms in Trouble Escape from State Aid Rules?' (2005) European State Aid Law Quarterly 17; A Criscuolo, 'The State in a liberal market economy: a private investor and creditor or a public authority' (1999) European Law Review 531.

[111] C-480/98, para 14.

[112] See chapter 7, section III.B and chapter 8, section II.B.

Consequently, the relevant conduct of the public authority should normally be regarded as economic and should therefore be tested against economic criteria. It is only in those cases where the provision of the goods or service at issue constitutes a true public good that the conduct would qualify as non-economic and the derogation test would apply. In this regard, the analysis made previously in the context of WTO law, particularly with respect to the existence of a general infrastructure plan and to the criteria to define it, is fully transposable here.[113]

[113] See chapter 9, section III.

11

Concluding remarks: objectives and the advantage analysis

This chapter provides a brief summary of the findings of Part III on the advantage analysis and, to further explore one of the main recurring themes of the book (namely the role played by the objectives of the public measure), a topical case-study, focusing on the status of the financing of public services under EC State aid law, will be used. A final section assesses the issue's possible implications in the WTO framework.

I. Concluding remarks: subsidies between market and objectives

Three main conclusions come from the analysis carried out in the previous four chapters. The first focuses on the relationship between subsidy definition and the market. The remaining two lead to a complex exercise centred on the objectives search and their distinction.

The first conclusion, set against the processes of liberalization and privatization of recent decades, but also with the haunting shadows of the current severe financial and economic crisis, is the apparently inescapable expansion of market logic in the determination of whether there is an advantage.

Secondly, the determination of the core of the advantage analysis, which is the idea of a derogation or discrimination, leads to an intricate quest for norm and exception, which ultimately turns on the identification of the objective that underpins the conduct at issue.

The third theme leads on from the second. If it is necessary, particularly in the case of non-economic activity, to consider the objectives of the measure, it is however equally crucial to distinguish between those objectives that are 'inherent' in the measure (which should be considered in the advantage analysis) and those that are 'extraneous' to it (which should not), if one does not wish to take the risk that scope and justification may become unduly conflated.

A. The expansion of market logic: ineluctable process?

The analysis carried out in chapters 7 and 8 has shown two things.

First, it may be difficult to determine whether the conduct at issue is 'economic' or 'non-economic'. There is an inevitable grey area, mainly constituted by 'public goods', where it is not clear whether the conduct is inherently public or could, at least in principle, be carried out by the private sector. This lack of clarity leads to the ambiguity of the test, economic or normative, that should be used in the advantage analysis.

Secondly, especially as a consequence of the processes of liberalization and privatization of recent years, we have witnessed an 'expansion of market logic'. Many areas which were traditionally considered to be public reserves have been increasingly open to the private, to the market and its logic. Again, the example of infrastructure and public goods is paradigmatic in this respect. But certain forms of so-called regulatory conduct may also be used as examples in point.

The question that the current predicament of the world economy may pose is whether the resurgence of State intervention will be accompanied, within the context of subsidy law, and particularly of the advantage analysis, by a confinement, if not a retrenchment, of the expansion of market logic.

The answer depends partly on the criteria that are used to distinguish between the 'economic' and the 'non-economic'. If, as has been suggested in the foregoing analysis, these should draw on the economic distinction between 'public' and 'private' goods, and—most importantly—this distinction should be kept at a rather abstract level, it will be unlikely that the framework and standards of assessment of the advantage will change. By contrast, the need for heavier public intervention may indeed exercise a pressure to limit the scope of application of subsidy laws, which may involve the definition of subsidy but this is not fully calculable at the moment.

B. Derogating? Norm and exception, and the objectives search

The core idea of a subsidy or State aid is that it perpetrates a discrimination, or, using a different language, it introduces a derogation from the normal course of events.

The heart of the advantage analysis is constituted by a 'derogation test', a device which should enable a determination as to whether or not there is a differential treatment. This conceptual and practical exercise inevitably requires the identification of norm and exception. While this can be testing with respect to economic activity and market benchmarks (chapter 8 addressed the difficulties, and criticisms, of the market and its rules), it becomes even more testing when what is under examination is the non-economic conduct of governments, for example, taxation.

In other words, economic conduct is tested against the market and its rules, that is, an 'external' baseline. Non-economic conduct is in principle tested against an 'internal' baseline, constituted by the relevant general norm that the government itself has defined. That said, even though the baseline is 'internal' this does not mean that governments are fully free, or in any event enjoy a greater degree of freedom as compared to the position vis-à-vis their commercial activity.

To escape the classification as subsidy the domestic policy should pass what is essentially a control of 'rationality' and 'consistency'. The normative framework is defined by the government but is then subsequently tested under subsidy laws. This exercise involves a quest for norms and exceptions. And, crucially, this search necessarily turns on the analysis of the objective of the measure. This has been thoroughly analysed in chapter 9 for the WTO and chapter 10 for the EC, particularly in the field of taxation.

C. The attraction of the objectives: scope or justification?

The more focus has been given to the advantage analysis, the more one of the main themes of the book has emerged in all its complexity.

It has been seen that the core determination of whether the conduct under examination, particularly if non-economic, confers an advantage ultimately depends on the identification of the objective underlying the measure and its assessment. The role of objectives to determine whether a differential treatment is a general rule or an exception is fundamental.

In this regard, what has become clear is that there is an irresistible force of attraction between scope and justification. In other words, it is often difficult to keep the assessment of public policy (and other) objectives outside the definition, particularly the analysis of the advantage. For various reasons (legal, political, symbolical: see chapter 1, section IV.B), the definition discourse inexorably 'attracts' an objective discourse.

It is therefore of great importance (and some difficulty) to attempt to distinguish between objectives. The analysis of EC State aid law, and particularly of its wealth of practice and case-law in the area of taxation, has provided a valuable insight into issues which will soon arise in the WTO context as well. To avoid the eventual conflation between scope and justification, which bears important conceptual and practical consequences, a fundamental distinction has to be made between those objectives that are 'inherent' in the measure at issue (and should therefore naturally reside in the advantage analysis, and its quests for general rules and exceptions) and those objectives that are in fact 'external' to the measure (and should hence be kept outside the definition).

Ultimately, this is the core dilemma of the definition of subsidy—under both EC State aid and WTO subsidy rules.

II. Exploring the scope-justification interplay: case-study on the financing of public services

The examination of one of the most important themes of this Part III—the role of public policy objectives in the advantage analysis—may result in an interesting *coda*, ie a brief case-study on the impact of State aid and subsidy rules on the financing of public services. A good reason for putting it at the end of the analysis is that it may concern both market and non-market conduct of public entities.

A. Public services: their mission, their problem, their relationship with State aid/subsidy rules

The provision to all citizens of certain services that present an element of *general* or *public interest* is one of the main duties of the Welfare State.

This is expressly and emphatically recognized in EC law, for example in Article 16 of the EC, which is placed among the 'Principles' of the EC Treaty and recognizes that 'services of general economic interest' belong to the 'shared values of the Union' and fulfil an important role in 'promoting social and territorial cohesion'.[1]

The *protection of public services* is also becoming a topical issue at the international level, as is demonstrated by the heated debate surrounding the impact of international law, particularly the GATS, on their regulation at the domestic level. Concerns are being voiced from various quarters about the interference of international trade law, and in particular its push towards liberalization, with the safeguard of domestic prerogatives in regulating public services, the need to maintain certain standards, and more generally, the protection of the various human rights that are strictly linked to public services.

The supply of public services is affected by an *inherent economic* problem. Their performance, particularly if certain standards of quality and accessibility have to be maintained, which are summed up in the concept of 'universal service', may not be viable from a financial perspective because of the difficulty of covering the relevant costs. Private actors may find it unprofitable to invest in these services, or even to provide them at all under certain, required conditions. The intervention of the government to financially support the provision of these services may thus be needed, and it often (although not always) takes the shape of direct subsidization to the suppliers.

The interesting legal question, which has given rise to a lively debate in the EC is whether the financing of public services, which is clearly motivated by a public policy objective, should be regarded as a State aid, which could be justified by the specific provision of the EC Treaty dealing with the performance of services of general economic interest (ie Article 86(2) of the EC), or whether, more radically, if certain conditions—mainly of *transparency*, *proportionality* and *efficiency*—are fulfilled, it should not be held to be a State aid in the first place. This is the issue that will be dealt with in the first part, focusing on the decision of the Court of Justice in *Altmark*, and, in particular, on its impact on the advantage analysis and on the scope-justification distinction.

[1] This special status is also confirmed in the ill-fated Lisbon Treaty, whose process of ratification is still in doubt.

Although in the WTO, the law of subsidies with respect to services is not as developed as that concerning goods, it is natural—not only from an academic perspective but also from a more practical one—to enquire whether a similar issue could be envisaged in the context of GATS too. In particular, we will analyse whether, as the law now stands, and in the context of the current Doha Round negotiations under Article XV GATS, some inspiration can be drawn from the EC discussion and settlement.

B. The financing of public services under EC State aid rules: the *Altmark* decision

The stakes and the clash

As we have anticipated, a lively debate was sparked off in the EC few years ago on whether support given by the State to enable undertakings entrusted with 'services of general economic interest' (SGEIs or, more simply, public services) to discharge their public service obligations (PSOs) should be considered as State aid. The crux of the matter is the risk that, far from merely compensating the costs of PSOs, the recipient undertaking may redirect the resources intended to finance the SGEIs to support other activities open to competition. This is the competition's concern. At the political and legal levels, the worries are represented by the risk of excluding a whole set of potentially troublesome measures of support from the scrutiny of the Commission and from substantially conflating the separate issues of scope and justification thus rendering useless the bifurcated system of rules provided for by the EC Treaty (Article 87(1) versus Article 86(2)).

These questions have produced a jurisprudential clash between the Community Courts and also between Advocates General, a true clash of Titans, as well as a wide discussion at the political level.

For their significance to the current analysis, we will concentrate mainly on the two cases of *Ferring* and *Altmark*, and in particular on the *findings* that are more relevant to the issue of the role of public policy objectives in the advantage analysis.[2]

The Ferring *and* Altmark *decisions*

Two main approaches ('compensation approach' and 'State aid approach') have traditionally been adopted when analysing the classification of financial compensation of SGEIs under State aid law.

[2] We therefore do not focus on the case-law that has followed the *Altmark* decision where the main principles discussed here have not been changed. It is however important to mention the decision of the CFI in Case T-289/03 *BUPA* which many commentators have read as a rather relaxed application of the *Altmark* decision. The impact of the *BUPA* decision should not be overestimated however. For a commentary, see A Biondi, 'BUPA v Commission' (2008) European State Aid Law Quarterly 401.

The compensation approach considers that financial assistance that merely compensates a PSO does not constitute a State aid. The underlying concept is that the financial compensation is a mere *contropartie* for the public service rendered insofar as it matches the extra costs incurred by the operation of the SGEI.[3] Under the State aid approach the financial compensation of a PSO is always considered as a State aid in the first place which can then be justified under Article 86(2) of the EC.[4]

The Court of Justice was called to decide on the issue in *Ferring*.[5] This case dealt with tax concessions granted to wholesale distributors of medicines. These tax exemptions were granted because of the specific public service obligations the distributors had to bear.[6] The Court found that this exemption could be regarded as compensation for the services thus not constituting State aid. Advocate General Tizzano noted:

> the fact that such measures *do not confer any real advantage* on an undertaking entrusted with a service of general interest and therefore are not likely to alter the conditions of competition appears a decisive argument to me. . . . In other words, *the imposition of the obligation* and *the provision of compensation* cannot be considered as separate matters as they are *two sides of the same public measure* which is intended, as a whole, to guarantee that public interests of primary importance are satisfied.[7]

Thus, these measures did not confer 'any advantage' and could not distort competition since the compensation simply intended to offset the additional costs of the PSO.

The *Ferring* decision was subject to criticism. The official critique came from the Advocate General in *Altmark*. In his two Opinions, Advocate General Léger strongly attacked *Ferring*, arguing that it was liable to undermine the structure and logic of the Treaty provisions in respect of State aid, and reaffirmed the State aid approach.[8] He put forward various arguments in support of his position.

First, State aid must not be defined on the basis of its aims but of its effects. It is an objective concept which focuses on a notion of 'gross' (in contrast to 'net') aid as well as of 'apparent advantage' (in contrast to 'real' advantage). What matters under Article 87(1) of the EC is whether the measure at issue is capable of conferring a selective advantage that distorts competition and affects intra-Community trade. The compensation approach confuses two distinct legal issues,

[3] See Case 240/83 *ADBHU*. This approach has been followed by the Commission's subsequent practice.

[4] This has been followed by the CFI in Case T-106/95 *FFSA* and Case T-46/97 *SIC*.

[5] Case C-53/00 *Ferring*.

[6] Stocking at all times a quantity of medicines sufficient to satisfy the needs of regular customers and to deliver within a 24-hour period any medicines required to any location in their distribution area.

[7] Paragraphs 60 and 61 of the Opinion (emphasis added).

[8] First Opinion delivered by Advocate General Léger on 19 March 2002 in Case C-280/00 *Altmark*. cf also the second Opinion, delivered on 14 January 2003 as a consequence of the *Ferring* decision and the Opinion of Advocate General Jacobs in Case C-126/01 *GEMO*.

the classification of the measure as State aid and its possible justification. Secondly, Article 86(2) would be deprived of any meaningful role in the field of State aid. If compensation would not constitute aid, over-compensation, as was expressly recognized by the Court under *Ferring*, could not be justified under Article 86(2) because it would not be proportionate. Finally, as a result of the compensation approach, the surveillance role of the Commission in controlling measures financing public services would be diminished.

Advocate General Jacobs expressed his view in this debate in *GEMO*.[9] In his Opinion, on the issue of whether the public financing of animal carcass disposal undertakings constituted aid, he presented what has been dubbed as the '*quid pro quo* approach', or the 'differentiated compensation approach'.

The Court should distinguish between two types of situations. Where there is a direct and manifest link between the State financing and clearly defined PSOs (such as a public tender procedure), the sums paid by the State would not constitute State aid under Article 87(1) of the EC. In his view, the financing would represent a mere *contropartie* of the PSO, almost as if the government were *paying* for the public service. Where by contrast there is no such direct and manifest link or the PSOs are not clearly defined, the sums paid by the public authorities would constitute aid.[10]

The Court eventually passed its decision in *Altmark* in July 2003.[11] The question referred to the Court was whether subsidies granted by Germany to an undertaking in order to operate a regular bus service in a specific region had to be considered aid or merely a compensation for the services offered.

The Court held that such compensation did not confer an advantage for the undertaking concerned and therefore could not be considered State aid. In particular, no advantage could be established where a State financial measure must be regarded as compensation for the services provided by the recipient undertakings in order to discharge public service obligations.

However, so that such compensation does not provide any advantage, it should satisfy four conditions. First, the recipient company must have actual public service obligations to discharge and those obligations must be clearly defined. Secondly, the parameters on the basis of which the compensation is calculated must be established in advance in an objective and transparent manner. Thirdly, the compensation cannot exceed what is necessary to cover all or part of the costs incurred in the discharge of the public service obligations, taking into account the relevant revenue and a reasonable profit. Fourthly, and finally, when the company is not chosen through a public procurement procedure, the level of compensation

[9] Case C-126/01.

[10] Along the same lines see Advocate General Stix-Hackl in Joined Cases C-34/01 to C-38/01 *Enirisorse I*.

[11] cf n 8 above.

must be determined in relation to an analysis of the costs that a typical company in the sector would incur (taking into account its revenues and a reasonable profit for the discharging of the obligations).

The academic world has generally welcomed *Altmark*.[12] This decision can be regarded as a desirable 'fine-tuning' of *Ferring* on the basis of some of the arguments that emerged in the debate that followed the latter decision.

It seems indeed that the Court, in adhering to the compensation approach, has been particularly receptive of the Opinion of Advocate General Jacobs in *GEMO* and its differentiated compensation approach based on the dividing criterion of the direct and manifest link between financing and clearly defined public service obligations. More fundamentally, however, the four conditions of *Altmark* represent a rather successful transplant, after the necessary adjustments, of the main requirements of Article 86(2).[13] That is evident with respect to the entrustment of particular tasks of public service obligation, but is also true with regard to the concepts of necessity and proportionality and the underlying idea that distortions are to be kept to the minimum possible. We assess below how, after *Altmark*, the proportionality test under Article 86(2) EC should be assessed.

The *Altmark* conditions clarify *Ferring* by ensuring (i) the adoption of a transparent process (ii) to compensate only those costs that are necessary to execute the SGEI. In this regard, apart from the requirement that compensation be linked to an explicit PSO and does not exceed the latter's cost (paragraphs 89 and 92), two new important conditions have been introduced. First, at paragraphs 90 and 91, that the parameters on which the compensation is calculated must be established 'beforehand in an objective and transparent manner'. Significantly, the determination of the compensation *ex ante* should prevent operators from passing all of their commercial risk to the State and avoid *ex post* rescue of inefficient undertakings. Secondly, that in any event compensation is not supposed to cover any cost claimed to be 'extra' or 'additional' but only those costs that satisfy objective, market-based benchmarks and are determined after certain procedures (see paragraph 93).

[12] See, eg, A Biondi and L Rubini, 'Aims, Effects and Justifications: EC State Aid Law and Its Impact on National Social Policies', in M Dougan and E Spaventa (eds), *Social Welfare and EU Law* (Oxford: Hart Publishing, 2005) 79; E Szyszczak, 'Financing Services of General Economic Interest' (2004) Modern Law Review 982; A Biondi, 'Justifying State Aid: The Financing of Services of General Economic Interest' in T Tridimas and P Nebbia (eds), *European Union Law for the Twenty-First Century, Volume II* (Oxford: Hart Publishing, 2004); P Nicolaides, 'Compensation for Public Service Obligations: the Floodgates of State Aid' (2003) European Competition Law Review 561; JM Thouvenin and MP Lorieux, 'L'arrét de la CJCE du 24 Juillet 2003 Almark' (2003) Revue du Marché commun et de l'Union européenne, 633.

[13] This tendency is not new. See, for instance, Case C-387/92 *Banco Exterior de España*, para 21 where the Court refers to the possibility that an aid is 'capable of falling outside the scope of application of Article [87] by virtue of Article [86(2)] of the Treaty'. See also Case T-106/95 *FFSA*, para 16.

It has indeed been argued that the main finding of *Ferring*, whereby mere compensation of the 'additional costs actually incurred' by undertakings entrusted with SGEIs is not State aid, far from restoring the level playing field would end up strengthening anti-competitive advantages. In particular, the *Ferring* decision did not clearly require the 'necessity' of the compensation. In a word, it did not provide or require any benchmark against which the necessity or efficiency of the financing could be tested.

The proposed solution to the problem was to auction the obligation to provide the relevant services. By creating a market to obtain the services in question, the public authorities would succeed in not favouring any firm and in keeping the subsidy to the minimum necessary.[14] The idea that an open and fair tendering procedure would exclude the existence of any advantage and hence of a State aid is not new.[15]

The Court has taken account of these arguments. The most significant advancement in *Altmark* is that only the compensation of those costs that are *necessary* to discharge the public service do not constitute State aid. To determine the right amount of financing, the Court clearly indicated its preference for public tender procedures. Possibly considering the argument that it would be disproportionate to *require* them,[16] however, it stopped short of imposing them and put forward an alternative benchmark.

The interplay between scope and justification: separation or conflation?

One of the main critiques of Advocate General Léger towards *Ferring* was that it did not distinguish between the characterization of a measure as State aid on the one hand and its justification on the other. To put it another way, the compensation approach would conflate the *separate issues of scope and justification*.

[14] An indication of the repeatedly discussed expansion of market logic, which inevitably creates a competitive pressure on public undertakings, monopolies, and providers of public services, can increasingly be found in various areas of the case-law. Two examples come immediately to mind. On the one hand, the Article 86 case-law which puts pressures on monopolies that are not manifestly able to provide a service (see, eg, Case C-41/90 *Höfner*) or the case-law which puts the necessity of the breadth of the monopoly itself into question (see, eg, Case C-320/91 *Corbeau*). Another example comes from the internal market, and notably from the 'healthcare services' cases (see, eg, Cases C-157/99 *Smits and Peerbooms*, C-368/98 *Vanbraekel*, C-385/99 *Müller-Fauré*). For a similar reading of these internal market cases, which underlines the competitive pressure caused by the Court's decisions, see A Biondi, 'Justifying State Aid: The Financing of Services of General Economic Interest' in T Tridimas and P Nebbia (eds), *European Union Law for the Twenty-First Century*, Volume II (Oxford: Hart Publishing, 2004).

[15] See, eg, Advocate General Jacobs in Case C-126/01 *GEMO*, paras 119 and 129 of the Opinion. cf also CH Bovis, 'Financing Services of General Interest in the EU: How do Public Procurement and State Aids Interact to Demarcate between Market Forces and Protection' (2005) European Law Journal 79.

[16] See Advocate General Stix-Hackl in Joined Cases C-34/01 to C-38/01 *Enririsorse I*, para 157; see also the second Opinion of Advocate General Léger in Case C-280/00 *Altmark*, para 97.

It is argued that this is not the case. Provided that the compensation satisfies the conditions laid down in *Almark*, these cases very much resemble purchases where the compensation is a mere *contropartie* of the PSOs. It is as if the government is *paying* for the public service.

Advocate General Tizzano in *Ferring* already hinted at this logic when he noted that the PSO and the compensation

> cannot be considered as separate matters as they are two sides of the same public measure.[17]

It was Advocate General Jacobs, however, that drew an express parallel between 'public service compensation' and a 'purchase transaction'. He observed that a comparison should be drawn to the situation where a State buys something and pays the price. It seems immaterial that the service is not provided to the State but to the collectivity. According to Jacobs:

> the same global analysis must prevail where the link between State funding and the clearly defined general interest obligations imposed is so direct and manifest that financing and obligation must be regarded as a single measure.[18]

Consequently, there will be aid only if, and only as far as, the *price* paid exceeds the *market price*.

Following the thread of this reasoning, we might consider a compensation, which fulfils the conditions of transparency, proportionality and efficiency of *Altmark*, a (*quasi*)*market transaction*. As such, being comparable to an operation which is consistent with commercial considerations, it should not be regarded as constituting a State aid.

Most crucially, contrary to Advocate General Léger's argument, there would be no intrusion of public policy objectives in the advantage analysis which would rest solely on an *economic* assessment aimed at getting the service done at the lower, ie most efficient, cost/price. *Altmark* cannot be said to conflate scope and justification but is rather in line with the often repeated finding whereby under State aid rules the measure at issue is mainly defined on the basis of its 'effects' and not its 'causes or aims'. The compensation of public services should thus be distinguished from the other measures that are aimed at compensating 'market failures' and 'disadvantages'. Whereas the former seems to largely depend on a purely technical assessment, where there is no significant role for the consideration of the *public* nature or aim of the measure, those cases involve socio-economic assessments which should be properly addressed (i) under the separate provisions that in the system allow for justifications, and (ii) by the Commission that bears legal and political responsibility for its decisions.

Quite similarly, cases involving the compensation of the costs borne by undertakings entrusted with PSOs should be distinguished from those other cases

[17] See para 61 of the Opinion.

[18] Case C-126/01 GEMO, para 122 of the Opinion.

where normal regulations of business introduced to meet various, even social or public, objectives (such as consumer, safety, health or environmental protection) impose costs on undertakings. Indeed it seems that, should governments decide to compensate undertakings for these costs, the financial assistance would undoubtedly constitute a State aid, irrespective of its proportionality with the costs. The distinguishing element seems to lie in the consideration that, whereas these costs are *normally* borne by the undertakings operating in the relevant market, costs for discharging PSOs, which are specifically entrusted by Member States on certain undertakings, do not present the same characteristics of normality, but—as seen—present a more marked quid pro quo nature.

The interesting question that remains open after *Altmark* does not really focus on Article 87(1) EC but rather on Article 86(2) EC. With respect to the financing of public services, what is the role that this important provision can play? To be true, it is accepted that if one of the *Altmark* conditions is not satisfied, and the measure thus qualifies as State aid, it could nonetheless still be justified under Article 86(2).[19] But the intriguing question is whether this availability is open also for those cases where the third condition (lack of over-compensation) has not been satisfied. Can a measure which over-compensates the costs of a PSO still be justified under Article 86 (2) EC?

The answer seems to be a 'qualified' yes. In a nutshell, by underlining in various documents that Article 86(2) could be satisfied by merely compensating the 'costs incurred' or the 'net costs'[20] – without any reference to any external, objective, market benchmark – the Commission would appear to point out that the proportionality test under Article 86(2) EC does not coincide with that under Article 87(1) EC and is in fact 'softer'.[21]

If it is then possible that what could amount to 'over-compensation' under *Altmark* could be justified under the proportionality test of Article 86(2) EC, the next question is: how far can the flexibility of the latter's test of proportionality can go? This is the key question that awaits answer.

[19] See, eg, Case T-354/05, *TF1*, Judgment of 11 March 2009, nyr.

[20] 'See, for example, Commission Decision of 28 November 2005 on the application of Article 86(2) of the EC Treaty to State aid in the form of public service compensation granted to certain undertakings entrusted with the operation of services of general economic interest, OJ L312, 29.11.2005, 67, Article 5; Commission Community Framework for State Aid in the form of public service compensation, OJ C297, 29.11.2005, 4, para 14; Commission Staff Working Paper on the Application of State aid rules to public service compensation for services of general economic interest, SEC(2007) 1516 final, 20.11.2007, particularly 19–20 (and the example in the Box at 20); Revised Draft Communication from the Commission on the application of State aid rules to public service broadcasting, 8.4.2009.'

[21] See along this line, commenting the 2005 Commission Decision and Framework, A Biondi and L Rubini, 'Aims, Effects and Justifications: EC State Aid Law and Its Impact on National Social Policies', in M Dougan and E Spaventa (eds), Social Welfare and EU Law (Oxford: Hart Publishing, 2005) 79, 100–1.

C. The financing of public services under WTO subsidy rules: the GATS

Public services in an international context: between increasing concerns, diversity and official recognition

It has been noted already that the issue of public services has come into prominence in the agenda of the world trading system in recent years.

Many concerns have been raised about the possible negative impact that further liberalization, which would allegedly be requested by WTO rules, and notably the GATS, would have on the access to these services. The ultimate worries are undue interference with domestically made societal choices and standard lowering.[22]

However, two important remarks are necessary at this point.

First, the more we leave a rather integrated and culturally coherent community such as the EC to its own devices, the more the actual definition of what would constitute a public service, and even the perception of its essentiality, tend to blur. Whereas in some societies, especially in the developed world, public services are generally considered as fundamental, in some cases, even inherent in the rights arising from the concept of citizenship itself, in other countries, mainly in the developing part of the world, there is often no concept or recognition of what, in other jurisdictions, are called public services.

Secondly, this degree of diversity inevitably requires the use of basic concepts when defining public services and their contents. From a lawyer's perspective, the progressively diffused perception of the crucial nature of these services and of the access thereto, which is evidently linked to the developing human rights discourse, is embodied in many documents from international organizations which increasingly recognize the importance of public services, their tight link with human rights, and the specific developmental implications of their delivery, protection and liberalization.[23]

It is with these remarks in mind that the current debate on the safeguard of public services and the liberalization of trade can be properly understood. We can now concentrate on the GATS and its current impact on public services, focusing, in particular, on the main issue of this section, that is the interplay between subsidy rules and financing of public services.

[22] An essential reference in this area is M Krajewski, *National Regulation and Trade Liberalization in Services: The Legal Impact of the General Agreement on Trade in Services (GATS) on National Regulatory Autonomy* (The Hague: Kluwer Law International, 2003).

[23] See, eg, WTO and WHO, *WTO Agreements and Public Health* - A Joint Study of the WHO and WTO Secretariats (2002); UN HR Commissioner, *Liberalisation of Trade in Services and Human Rights*, United Nations Economic and Social Council, Commission on Human Rights, Sub-commission on the Promotion and Protection of Human Rights, Report of the High Commissioner, E/CN.4/Sub.2/2002/9, (2002); UNCTAD, *Trade in Services and Development Implications*, Trade and Development Board, Commission on Trade in Goods, Services, and Commodities, TD/B/COM.1/71, (2005).

The current State of the law (and the prospects for the future)

It should be said immediately that the GATS may apply to public services.

In particular, the interpretation of Article 1.3(b) ('"services" includes any service in any sector except services supplied in the exercise of governmental authority') and (c) ('"a service supplied in the exercise of governmental authority" means any service which is supplied neither on a commercial basis nor in competition with one or more service suppliers') seem to indicate that many services, particularly in those Member States where there has been or there is currently a liberalization process, are covered by the GATS.[24] The construction of the provision above, and in particular of the exception as it result from the combined reading of letters (b) and (c), according to the canons of the Vienna Convention on the Law of Treaties (VCLT), would lead to conclude that *only* those services that are not provided for profit (ie not 'on a commercial basis') or are supplied from a (public) monopolist (ie not 'in competition with one or more service suppliers') would be *excluded* from the scope of application of the GATS. It has been said that the concept of service in the GATS is 'near universal'.[25]

Whether or not a certain service is subject to the GATS substantially depends on the degree of internal liberalization of the Member State at issue, that is on a general 'political choice' of the latter.[26] Krajewski clearly expressed the interplay between a domestic and international liberalization decision when he underlined that '*internal* liberalisation can therefore generate and reinforce *external* liberalisation.'[27]

Before moving on to analyse the impact of the GATS subsidy provision on the financing of public services, it is important to briefly underline the peculiar regulatory approach of the GATS. This will constitute the background to our analysis.

The GATS features two different categories of obligations. On the one hand, we have the 'general obligations and disciplines' which in principle apply to all Members and to any service subject to the Agreement (these obligations include

[24] M Krajewski, 'Public Services and Trade Liberalization: Mapping the Legal Framework' (2003a) Journal of International Economic Law 341, 347–59; id, 'Environmental Services of General Interest in the WTO' (2004) Journal for European Environmental and Planning Law 101,106–7.

[25] A Lang, 'The GATS and Regulatory Autonomy: A Case Study of Social Regulation of the Water Industry' (2004) Journal of International Economic Law 801, 816.

[26] Although in principle this choice is autonomous, in reality it may be influenced by various factors, such as the prevailing ideological, political and cultural trends, political pressures and—which should not be forgotten for a 'regime in the making' like the GATS, but more generally the WTO—negotiating dynamics. As a result, it may well be that the ultimate decision of whether to liberalize a service or not would partly fall outside the control of the country at issue. See, eg, L Rubini, 'L'impatto del GATS sulla regolazione nazionale dei servizi di interesse generale' (2007) Diritto del Commercio Internazionale 373.

[27] M Krajewski, 'Environmental Services of General Interest in the WTO' (2004) Journal for European Environmental and Planning Law 101, 107 (emphasis added).

the provision on subsidies, Article XV).[28] On the other hand, there are other obligations, and in particular those on Market Access (Article XVI) and National Treatment (Article XVII), which concern 'specific commitments' inasmuch as they apply only if, and within the limits which, the Member at issue has *committed* itself in its *schedule*. In absence thereof, that is if there are not specific commitments, the service under scrutiny shall not be subject to those specific obligations.

This way of operation, which shows an inherent flexibility, is often expressed as a 'bottom-up' or 'opting in' approach.

All this makes all the more important the drafting of the specific commitments by Members.[29] The 'bottom-up' approach highlights one important fact: that, although the content of the schedule's commitments will result from the bargaining exercise of the negotiating process (and the inherent pressures to liberalize), the ultimate responsibility for the commitments towards liberalization of that particular service lies with the Member that has accepted them.

Having determined that the GATS may apply to certain public services, and explained its particular working, the analysis may now focus on whether an issue similar to that debated in the context of the EC (does the compensation of public services constitute a State aid?) can be envisaged with respect to the GATS provision on subsidies. In this regard, Article XV, which is among the 'general obligations and disciplines', reads:

> Members recognize that, in certain circumstances, subsidies may have distortive effects on trade in services. Members shall enter into negotiations with a view to developing the necessary multilateral disciplines to avoid such trade-distortive effects [footnote on work programme omitted]. The negotiations shall also address the appropriateness of countervailing procedures. Such negotiations shall recognize the role of subsidies in relation to the development programmes of developing countries and take into account the needs of Members, particularly developing country Members, for flexibility in this area. For the purpose of such negotiations, Members shall exchange information concerning all subsidies related to trade in services that they provide to their domestic service suppliers.
>
> Any Member which considers that it is adversely affected by a subsidy of another Member may request consultations with that Member on such matters. Such requests shall be accorded sympathetic consideration.

Even a brief reading of this provision shows that the GATS does not feature any substantial discipline on subsidies. In the absence of any discipline, the issue of the *definition* of subsidy would become largely redundant. In this context, to ask whether there is - or could be - a 'compensation approach' similar to that adopted by

[28] Reference can be made eg to Article II (MFN principle), Article III (Transparency), Article VI (Domestic Regulation), Article VII (Recognition), Article VIII (Monopolies and Exclusive Service Suppliers), Article XIII (Government Procurement), Article XIV (General Exceptions) and, finally, as said, Article XV (Subsidies).

[29] The *US—Gambling* dispute is a good memento of this.

the Court of Justice in *Altmark* with respect to the financing of public services seems to be merely speculative, if not pretentious.[30]

Two remark can be made however, one concerning the current situation and one more focussed on future prospects.

First, albeit rather 'soft', some sort of discipline *is* provided in the second paragraph which refers to the possibility of holding consultations in the event that one Member is 'adversely affected' by a subsidy of another Member. The necessary logical and practical premise of this exercise is the definition of the concept of subsidy and it is in this regard that, as has happened in the EC, the issue of how to consider the compensation of public services obligations may arise.

Further, the text of Article XV might arguably provide some support to the *distinction* we have made above between advantage analysis—merely resting on an economic assessment—and the assessment of public policy objectives, and thus open the way to an argument similar to the EC compensation approach. Reference is made to the separate mention of the 'distortive effects on trade' on the one hand and to the 'development programmes' of developing countries and, more generally, to the 'needs for flexibility' on the other.

Secondly, the issue may gain relevance in the near future. Article XV refers to *negotiations* about the development of a more substantial regulation of subsidies in the service sectors, which are currently underway. Admittedly, they do not seem to have produced many results so far.[31] The *2006 WTO Trade Report* indicated that 'several delegations [had] recently suggested that an acceptable approach [to subsidy discipline] might [have been] to use the SCM Agreement definition of subsidies, appropriately modified, as a working basis upon which to carry forward the negotiations.[32]

Finding an *appropriate* definition of subsidy is of paramount importance for a future discipline on services subsidies. And, in this context, issues on the legal status of the financing of public services will certainly be tabled. Similarly, an appropriate discipline of justifiable subsidies, maybe building up on the

[30] In the context of the specific commitments, a provision that already 'bites' with respect to the issue of the financing of public services, is Article XVII on national treatment.

Suppose that a Member that has specifically committed the public service at issue to commitments, without any express 'condition or limitation', decided to grant a subsidy exclusively to domestic suppliers in order to discharge that public service. Does this amount to a breach of national treatment? If this is so, how should that Member accord a treatment 'no less favourable that that it accords to its own like services and service suppliers'? Admittedly, it could fulfil its national treatment obligation in only two ways. These are either by extending the subsidy to the foreign service supplier(s), or by ceasing to subsidize its domestic supplier(s). This example further demonstrates the importance of schedule commitments drafting.

[31] See, eg, M Wall and D Vis-Dunbar, *The Standstill in Subsidies—Update*, paper produced for the International Institute for Sustainable Development, (2005) 11–14. The latest report (26 May 2008) of the Chairman of the services negotiations is not very promising in this respect, merely reproducing a renewed commitment to conclude the relevant negotiations. See Annex to Report 'Elements Required for the Completion of the Services Negotiations', TN/S/33, Article 6.

[32] WTO, *Annual Trade Report* (2006) 195.

skeleton indications of Article XIV, will be important as well.[33] And, with the inevitable entry of public policy objectives, so will be the issue of the interplay (in terms of separation or distinction) between scope and justification, as is partly indicated by the general guidelines that Article XV drew to the attention of negotiators.

[33] M Benitah, 'Subsidies, Services and Sustainable Development' (2005) Issue Paper No 1 for International Centre for Trade and Sustainable Development (ICTSD) 21, reported that many WTO Members were of the view that 'there is a need to exempt from general subsidy disciplines those subsidies that are necessary to achieve certain public policy objectives'. Three categories were indicated, namely economic development, environmental, and social development (the first being available only to developing countries).

PART IV

BENEFICIARIES

Enter by the narrow gate, since the road that leads to destruction is wide and spacious, and many take it; but it is a narrow gate and a hard road that leads to life, and only a few find it.[1]

[1] Gospel according to St Matthew, Chapter 7, 13–14.

Overview

We have seen in Part III that it is an inherent, and crucial, feature of the definition of both State aids and subsidies that they should confer an advantage.

Whereas in Part V we see how this advantage may negatively alter the competitive process, the two chapters of this Part follow the previous one by focusing on the beneficiaries of the advantage. We deal with two issues in particular.

The first is the *identification* of the beneficiaries, ie of the persons who should be regarded as benefiting from the financial assistance granted through the subsidy. The subjective impact of the measure may be particularly wide and complex as the same measure may affect the economic and financial position of various persons. What matters for State aid and subsidy rules is to establish that an advantage is granted, directly or indirectly, to an undertaking.

The second issue concentrates on the interpretation of the *specificity* or *selectivity test* which is present in both systems. Both EC State aid law and WTO subsidy law are interested only in measures that solely benefit 'certain' undertakings or sectors.

12

The identification of the beneficiaries

This chapter examines the issue of the identification of the beneficiaries, ie the persons that benefit from the advantage granted through the subsidy or State aid. After a few introductory remarks, two case-studies are used to show the complexities of this question. The first focuses on so-called 'input' or 'upstream' subsidies, the second on the identification issues in the context of the sale of companies or assets.

I. Introduction

As with the advantage analysis, the *Canada—Aircraft* dispute provides a useful, somewhat intuitive, starting point. The Appellate Body noted that:

> a 'benefit' does not exist in the abstract, but must be received and enjoyed by a beneficiary or a recipient. Logically, a 'benefit' can be said to arise only if *a person, natural or legal, or a group of persons*, has in fact received something. The term 'benefit', therefore, implies that there must be a recipient.[1]

Thus, it is a 'person, natural or legal, or a group of persons' that will be the 'beneficiary' or 'recipient' of the subsidy or State aid. To produce a distortion, the advantage needs to affect the business activity of the recipient undertaking, ie the production of goods or services for consideration.

The identification of the beneficiaries plays an important role at various levels.

First, it plays a crucial role in determining whether the measure falls within the scope of application of State aid or subsidy rules since the beneficiary must be an enterprise or an undertaking. To put it simply, it must be engaged in an economic activity, ie in the provision of goods or services for consideration, and, quite often, in competition with other undertakings. If the measure benefited only, say, employees or consumers, persons who are clearly not involved in any economic activity, there could be no State aid or subsidy.

Secondly, as we have seen in Part III, the identification of the beneficiaries of the measure is one of the main factors to consider in the analysis of the advantage. The identification of a given undertaking or industry as recipient of financial assistance is certainly of relevance when it comes to determining whether market conditions

[1] Appellate Body Report, *Canada—Aircraft*, para 154 (emphasis added).

are satisfied. Similarly, the process to establish whether a certain measure is a derogation from the general rule depends considerably on the definition of the interested parties and on their position.

The proper determination of the beneficiaries is also key to the definition of the markets affected by the measure and of the effects produced by it which is central in the assessment of any distortion of competition (see Part V).

Finally, the question of who stands to benefit from the intervention also has significant implications from the procedural standpoint, and in particular the application of the remedies.[2] State aid or subsidy granted unlawfully could be withdrawn or recovered. In such cases, it is evident that the definition of who is going to be the target of such withdrawal or recovery is important. The issue of the recovery of (past) paid aid is crucial in the EC, but it is also relevant in the WTO, at least with respect to the category of prohibited subsidies whose withdrawal may include their retrospective repayment. Further, in the specific context of WTO law, countervailing duties may be imposed unilaterally on those products that are held to be subsidized. From this perspective, too, the importance of the identification of who benefits from the subsidy is clear.

As a matter of fact, an advantage may affect the economic position of various individuals. It would therefore be erroneous to concentrate only on the first or more direct recipients of the financial assistance since the advantage may also (or exclusively) be conferred in an indirect way to other persons. A distinction is accordingly usually made between *direct* or *indirect* subsidies.

That said, undertakings can be—more or less directly—benefited in various ways. For example, through the reduction of their production costs (benefits to employees, assistance to research, input subsidies), the increase of their sales revenue (consumer subsidies and benefits to final producers), the provision of capital (aid to investors), the sale of a company or business at particularly favourable contractual conditions, especially as regards price (sale of companies/privatizations).

II. Two case-studies

There are two notable cases where the *buyer* is the indirect beneficiary of the measure of financial assistance and which are worth of further examination. These cases are excellent illustrations of the kind of intricacies the identification of beneficiaries may lead to.

The first is the case of so called 'upstream' or 'input' subsidies. The second is the case arising from the sale of companies or businesses that previously received a subsidy. In both cases, many interesting issues come out from the existence (or not)

[2] See chapter 2, section III.

of a 'pass-through' of the benefit previously granted (as the case may be to the input producers or to the company/assets under sale).[3]

A. 'Input' or 'upstream' subsidies

A particularly interesting case of indirect subsidies is that of so-called 'upstream' or 'input' subsidies.

These cases derive from the interdependence of the various levels of production which substantially flows from one of the most popular axioms of economics, ie the division and specialization of work. In these cases the direct benefit is conferred on the producer of the input (ie upstream in the productive process) and the question is whether this benefit is, totally or partly, passed through downstream to the producer of the final product, typically in the form of a lesser price. As the Panel in *US—Softwood Lumber IV* put it, the 'core of the pass-through issue is the notion of subsidization of a product, ie, in respect of is manufacture, production, or export. Where the subsidies at issue are received by someone other than the producer of the investigated product, the question arises whether there is subsidization in respect of that product.'[4]

The issue is, of course, to determine *when* the benefit granted to the input manufacturer passes through to the downstream producer, which is not always straightforward. Although it has often been underlined how particularly complex this determination is,[5] we can start with some simple remarks. Most of these comments originate from considerations of the seminal work of Beseler and Williams.[6]

It seems fair to begin with the finding that the subsidization of inputs does not *per se* constitute subsidization of the final product. As we will see, one important principle is that no (irrebuttable) presumption can be introduced in this respect. Admittedly, any particular share of the burden of proof can affect the substantive rights to be proven. Accordingly, presumptions (in one direction or another) cannot be lightly introduced as they may (even significantly) shift the burden of proof.

Even assuming that a legal system introduced a presumption that the benefit has passed through, it is of crucial importance to allow the rebuttal of this presumption and to do so on reasonable terms (for example, by permitting the proof

[3] See M Matsushita, TJ Schoenbaum, and PC Mavroidis, *The World Trade Organization—Law, Practice, and Policy* (2nd edn, Oxford: Oxford University Press, 2006) 350, n 56.

[4] Para 7.85.

[5] JF Beseler and AN Williams, *Anti-Dumping and Anti-Subsidy Law—The European Communities* (London: Sweet and Maxwell, 1986), 126, who underlined that GATT experts have considered the issue since 1982 (NB: the authors were writing in 1986) without being able to arrive at definitive conclusions. The issue was also subject to extensive debate during the Uruguay Round of negotiations and has continued to be in the spotlight thanks to the so-called 'privatization' cases discussed below.

[6] JF Beseler and AN Williams, *Anti-Dumping and Anti-Subsidy Law—The European Communities* (London: Sweet and Maxwell, 1986) 125–7.

of significant circumstances). In other words, the share of the burden of proof must be balanced in the sense that it should genuinely lead to the determination of whether the benefit has passed through.

There are some tentative examples of the principles above. It being reasonable to assume that the seller will attempt to maximize its profit, there should be no remaining benefit if the two producers are unrelated and thus really operate at arm's length with each other. It could be counter-argued, however, that, courtesy of the subsidy, the seller may sell at a lower price, and hence pass a benefit on to the buyer. More convincingly, it seems that no pass through should be established when the input is eventually sold at a market price and under normal market conditions.[7] Generally speaking, it might therefore be tentatively concluded that, in the presence of certain circumstances, such as arm's length transactions at normal commercial conditions, it is easier—although by no means conclusive—to presume that no benefit has passed through.[8] This point will be analysed together with the jurisprudence on privatizations of previously subsidized undertakings.

In any case it is important to underline that the specificity test, which requires that the benefit must favour only certain undertakings or industries (and which will be analysed in full in the next chapter), must always be satisfied (and, as has been rightly underlined, this should be done twice: first at the level of the input subsidy and secondly for the pass-through of the benefit).[9]

The case of input subsidies, which was debated during the Uruguay Round negotiations, was the subject of important disputes in the GATT and in the WTO.

The US—Pork *dispute*

In the GATT *US—Pork* dispute subsidies had been granted to Canadian swine producers. The US had consequently imposed countervailing duties on imported pork processed from swine. The whole question in the case was whether the benefit of the subsidies to swine had translated into, or, in any event, could be considered as, a benefit to pork, the product processed through swine, particularly in the form of reduced swine prices. From another perspective, the issue was whether there was

[7] Beseler and Williams underline, however, the difficulties of those cases when there is no benchmark, eg because the only domestic sales of the product are those which are subsidized. In these cases, it is noted, it would be important to consider the price of imports. For similar issues, see chapter 8, section II.

[8] The case would however be different, with a conclusion that there is passing through, when there is a clear evidence thereof, like when there is a governmental requirement to pass the benefit on.

[9] A similar specificity problem occurs for the governmental provision of favourably priced natural resources, such as basic energy products (petroleum, petrochemical products, and natural gas). The issue of whether specificity should be required for upstream and natural resource subsidies has been subject to a certain debate, especially in the US. See GC Hufbauer and J Shelton Erb, *Subsidies in International Trade* (Cambridge, Massachusetts: MIT Press, 1984) 95 et seq.

a direct subsidy to pork producers, or, rather, a direct subsidy to swine producers with a possible indirect subsidy to pork producers.

Before exposing the main allegation of the US, and the findings of the Panel, a brief outline of the main provisions of US law applicable in that case is given.

US law had a specific provision for upstream subsidies (Section 771A of the Tariff Act 1930). This provision required a thorough analysis of whether the upstream subsidy had in fact passed through to the downstream producer. What, in particular, had to be established was that the upstream subsidy conferred a 'competitive benefit' on the downstream product and that this had a 'significant effect' on the cost of manufacturing or producing the merchandise.[10]

A new legislative provision (Section 771B) was introduced in 1988 to avoid the strictures of these requirements in some cases. Section 771B provided that, in the case of an agricultural product processed from a raw agricultural product, a subsidy to the latter should be deemed to have been granted to the former, provided that two conditions were fulfilled: first, there should have been a substantial dependence of the demand for the input product on that of the output product, and, secondly, only a limited value should have been added in the production of the input into the output. In other words, according to Section 771B, the two separate economic processes were fictitiously merged and the subsidy to the input producer was legally regarded as if *directly* granted to the output producer.

On the basis of this amendment, the US were arguing that in the instant case they were dealing with just one single production process. Being confronted with what in their view was a direct subsidy, it was not necessary to prove the strict requirements (of 'competitive benefit' and 'significant effect') provided for upstream subsidies.

The Panel disagreed. In particular, it found first that, under Article VI:3 of the GATT, a countervailing duty could be imposed on pork only if it is determined that a subsidy has been bestowed on the production of pork.[11] In the case in issue, however, although it was not disputed that a subsidy had been granted to live swine, what was under discussion was precisely whether, in the light of Article VI:3 of the GATT, this subsidy could be considered as granted to pork.

The Panel focused on the conditions set by Section 771B to determine whether they were, on their own, sufficient to conclude that, under Article VI:3 of the GATT, a subsidy granted to swine producers should have been deemed as granted to pork producers. Starting from the obvious consideration that, in the instant case, there were two separate industries operating at arm's length, and two different products, the Panel fully recognized the importance of the price effect in upstream

[10] For a commentary see M Benitah, *The Law of Subsidies under the GATT/WTO System* (The Hague: Kluwer Law International, 2001) 269–72.

[11] The relevant part of Article VI:3 reads: 'No countervailing duty shall be levied on any product . . . in excess of an amount equal to the estimated . . . subsidy determined to have been granted, directly or indirectly, in the . . . production . . . of *such product*' (emphasis added).

subsidies cases.[12] In particular, it explained that the determination that a downstream industry had been subsidized by an upstream subsidy necessarily required an examination of the 'impact of the price' of the subsidies on the input product.[13] Consequently, in the case in issue, the existence of an indirect subsidy could be established if:

> subsidies granted to swine producers had led to a decrease in the level of prices for Canadian swine paid by Canadian pork producers below the level they have to pay for swine from other commercially available sources of supply and that this decrease was equivalent to the full amount of the subsidy.[14]

The Panel made it clear that the two factors provided by Section 771B (the substantial dependence of the demand and the limited value added in the production) were not enough to establish that the subsidies to swine had led to a decrease in the price of pork. It was underlined that it was necessary to consider various factors to determine whether there was a pass-through of the benefit, such as, in the instant case, the degree to which swine were internationally traded, and the per unit cost of producing additional output of swine that the subsidies might have caused.[15]

The consequence of the Panel's finding of the inconsistency of US domestic law with Article VI:3 of the GATT, and in particular its distinction between direct and indirect subsidies, was that the admittedly more stringent requirements of the American provision on upstream subsidies could not be by-passed.[16] Before imposing countervailing duties on imported pork on the ground that it was subsidized the US should have proved the existence of a 'competitive benefit' on the downstream product and a 'significant effect' on its cost of production.

There are two lessons to be taken from this case, which can also be applied generally to other cases where there is a similar question of 'pass-through'. There is first a clear reaffirmation of the important GATT(WTO)-based distinction between *direct* and *indirect* subsidies. Generally speaking, the existence of a subsidy to producer A cannot very easily, or even automatically, be presumed to have passed through to producer B. This passage has to be established. Further, there is recognition that the operation of the passing through mechanism may be particularly complex and, accordingly, a thorough analysis of all the factors of the impact of

[12] At the same time, however, the Panel quite intriguingly noted that 'subsidies need not in all cases, particularly in cases involving only one industry, have a price effect to be countervailable' (see para 4.9 of the Panel report).

[13] ibid.

[14] Para 4.10.

[15] For a clear explanation of the relevance of these factors see para 4.10 of the Panel report.

[16] Writing in 2001, M Benitah, *The Law of Subsidies under the GATT/WTO System* (The Hague: Kluwer Law International, 2001) 210–11, noted that Section 771B still existed in US countervailing duty legislation. It is therefore interesting to know how this provision could now be construed in order to ensure GATT/WTO consistency.

the input or upstream subsidy on the downstream level of production may be required.

The US—Softwood Lumber III *and* IV *disputes*

The previous findings have been confirmed in the WTO era, particularly in the *US—Softwood Lumber III* and *US—Softwood Lumber IV* disputes.

The factual background of these cases, which concerned the review of the US preliminary and final countervailing duty determinations on softwood lumber from Canada, is particularly instructive of how complex the production chain of an industry may be. Although the subsidy had originally been conferred on standing timber harvesters, logs were processed, quite often at various stages, to produce softwood lumber and other products.[17] There could accordingly be many subjects (eg harvesters/loggers; sawmills; re-manufacturers) who subsequently acquired the products as inputs for further processing. If these subjects were independent from each other, ie not vertically integrated, issues of the passing through of the relevant benefit could, at least hypothetically, arise out from various separate arm's length transactions.

Focusing now on the *US—Softwood Lumber III* dispute, the important question which was under scrutiny was whether it is possible to use presumptions in the benefit analysis, or, more specifically, whether, in certain cases, it is possible to *avoid* a pass-through analysis altogether.

The issue was whether the US Department of Commerce (DOC) was required to examine whether, in certain transactions covered by the investigation, some or all of the alleged benefit to the holders of harvesting rights was passed through to the producers of the subject merchandise exported to the US, in this case, softwood lumber.[18] What emerged from the record was that in some cases the US DOC had not carried out an analysis of the passing through of the benefit either (i) because it considered that there was no evidence of arm's length transactions between lumber producers and loggers as, in the large majority of cases, they were allegedly not independent from each other, or (ii) because, even in cases of arm's length transactions, all undertakings were producers of the same merchandise and the calculation of the countervailing duty was conducted on an aggregate (vs a company-specific) basis.[19]

[17] For an exhaustive explanation of the various stages of this industry see Appellate Body, *US—Softwood Lumber IV*, para 124.

[18] *US—Softwood Lumber III*, para 7.69.

[19] ibid, paras 7.64–7.67. The possibility of imposing countervailing duties on an aggregate basis can be found in Article 19.3 of the SCM.

With respect to the first argument, having found that there was evidence of arm's length transactions, the Panel crucially reaffirmed that assumptions or presumptions cannot be used to establish that a benefit has passed through:

> we are of the view that an authority may not assume that a subsidy provided to producers of the 'upstream' input product automatically benefits unrelated producers of downstream products, especially if there is evidence on the record of arm's-length transactions between the two. Rather, we consider that in such circumstances the investigating authority should examine whether and to what extent the subsidies bestowed on the upstream producers benefited the downstream producers.[20]

We have already seen that, in principle, it is not possible to presume that an upstream subsidy has necessarily transposed into a benefit at the downstream level. The transmission mechanism of the benefit may in fact be so complex that presumptions of this kind do not easily fit. As said, what seems to be necessary in the case at issue is a more thorough, one might even say empirical, analysis of whether the upstream benefit may have passed through downstream. As hinted at by the Panel, this is particularly so when there are some significant factors, such as the existence of an arm's length transaction, which, under certain circumstances such as the presence of normal market conditions, may in fact lead towards the opposite conclusion (ie that no pass-through has occurred). In this regard, the Panel interestingly cited the *US—Lead and Bismuth II* dispute where the Appellate Body concluded in the different context involving subsidies provided to entities subsequently privatized (which will be analysed in the next section), that an entity other than the original recipient of the subsidy should not be deemed to have received a benefit when an arm's-length price was paid to acquire the entity that had received the subsidies. [21]

The Appellate Body in *US—Softwood Lumber IV* vigorously reaffirmed the *need* to determine the existence of the pass-through of the benefit, when the subsidy has been granted on an input and the countervailing duty is to be imposed on a processed product, and on the connected impossibility of using presumptions when there is an arm's length relationship between upstream and downstream producers.[22]

As regards the calculation of the subsidy on an aggregate basis (ie on a country-wide as opposed to a company specific basis), the *US—Softwood Lumber III* Panel also confirmed that, in the presence of arm's length transactions, it is necessary to

[20] ibid, para 7.71. Similar findings were made by the Appellate Body, *US—Softwood Lumber IV*. See, eg, paras 141, 143 and 146.

[21] Panel, *US—Softwood Lumber III*, para 7.71.

[22] See paras 129–47 in particular. Returning to the GATT *US—Pork* case, these findings of the Appellate Body seems to substantially confirm the correctness of the requirements of a 'competitive benefit' on the downstream product and the 'significant effect' on its cost of production provided for by the US provision on upstream subsidies, since they seem to be in line with the often repeated need to carry out a comprehensive analysis of the effects of the input subsidy before reaching a conclusion that an advantage has passed on.

carry out a pass-through analysis.[23] In this regard, it is interesting to refer to what the Appellate Body said about the relationship between determination of the existence of subsidization on the one hand and imposition of countervailing duties on the other. In *US—Softwood Lumber IV* the Appellate Body admitted that Article 19.3 of the SCM, with the support of Article 19.4, authorizes Members to perform an investigation on an *aggregate basis*.[24] However, any definition of the rate of subsidization for countervailing duty purposes, be it on a country-wide (ie aggregate) basis or on a company-specific basis, can logically take place *only after* the investigating authority has, *inter alia*, established the existence of a subsidy. Referring to the case in issue, the Appellate Body thus underlined that:

> before being entitled to impose countervailing duties on a processed product, for the purpose of offsetting an input subsidy, a Member must first determine, in accordance with Article 1.1 [SCM], that a financial contribution exists, and that the benefit conferred directly on the input producer has been passed through, at least in part, to the producer of the processed product. [25]

The Appellate Body also made it clear that it is in the nature of the imposition of a country-wide (aggregate) rate under Article 19 of the SCM that the rate of subsidization does not necessarily match the precise amount thereof benefiting a specific shipment or, even, that a particular shipment of the subject merchandise is not subsidized at all.[26] The SCM Agreement itself, however, gives a remedy, providing for specific expedited review of the countervailing duty, if any, to be imposed on the exporter not investigated individually.[27]

Input 'State aids' and conclusions

Looking next at EC law, where 'input' subsidy issues do not seem to have arisen with such frequency, it can simply be noted that conclusions similar to those analysed in the GATT/WTO context may also be drawn here. A comprehensive approach, substantially similar to that adopted in the WTO, would be used for determining the impact of input or upstream subsidies.[28]

[23] See para 7.77 in particular.

[24] With respect to the aggregate-based calculation of countervailing duties, Article 19.3 of the SCM *inter alia* provides that 'countervailing duty shall be levied, in the appropriate amounts in each case, on a *non-discriminatory basis* on imports of such product from *all sources* found to be subsidized and causing injury . . .' (emphasis added). Article 19.4 of the SCM reads: 'No countervailing duty shall be levied on any import product in excess of the amount of the subsidy found to exist, calculated in terms of subsidization *per unit* of the subsidized and exported product' (emphasis added).

[25] Appellate Body, *US—Softwood Lumber IV*, para 154.

[26] ibid, para 153.

[27] Article 19.3 of the SCM provides that '[a]ny exporter whose exports are subject to a definitive countervailing duty but who was not actually investigated . . . shall be entitled to an expedited review in order that the investigating authorities promptly establish an individual countervailing duty rate for the exporter'.

[28] cf, in general, GM Roberti, *Gli aiuti di Stato nel diritto comunitario* (Padova, CEDAM, 1997).

In sum, it can safely be concluded that in both legal systems the establishment of a 'pass-through' of the advantage should be based on a thorough analysis of various economic factors involved and that, in this context, the use of assumptions/presumptions should only be made with particular care.

B. Sale of companies or assets

Interesting issues concerning the identification of beneficiaries have also arisen in the context of the sale of undertakings which previously received subsidies. This question has mainly come out in the context of privatizations or reorganizations of companies in difficulties.

Like in the case of input subsidies, one of the issues here is whether, following the sale of the company, of its assets or of an entire business, any advantage has passed through to the *buyer*. As we will see, however, this category raises another fundamental question on the residence of the advantage with the company (or productive unit) which depends on both the complexity of the factual scenario and the need to clearly focus and contextualize the advantage analysis.

The pass-through of the benefit: the position of the buyer between the use of presumptions and the market

We begin our analysis by considering whether, following the sale of the company or the business, the benefit 'passes through' to the *buyer*.

As we are essentially dealing with a 'pass-through' problem, many issues are very similar to those dealt with in the 'input' subsidy context.

Before proceeding to the analysis of these issues, it may be useful to clarify an important distinction between various sale transactions.

On the one hand, in *share deal* cases, what is sold is the firm or the company.[29] The identification of the beneficiary is particularly complex in these cases as they involve the presence of three subjects, namely the company, the owners/sellers and the owners/buyers. On the other hand, we could distinguish between *asset deal* and *business deal* cases. Whereas the former concern the sale of all or part of the assets of a firm, the latter regard the sale of a productive operation as ongoing concern and, as such, they may normally include the transfer of the liabilities of the unit. In these cases the identification of who stands to benefit from the transaction is generally easier as only two subjects (the company/seller and the buyer) are involved. It is therefore natural that in the subsequent analysis we will concentrate particularly on share deal cases because of their greater complexity.[30]

[29] We use the two terms synonymously without referring to any particular legal form of enterprise.

[30] It should be noted that the term 'sale' here generally refer to any sale transaction without distinguishing between share, asset or business deals.

Having set forth these distinctions, we may now analyse the issue concerning the possibility of using presumptions. We can think of two kinds of presumptions which go in opposite directions. First: following the sale, may we presume that the benefit has *simply* passed through? Or, secondly, and to the contrary, should it be presumed that the sale *at certain conditions* (and, notably, an arm's length transaction for a fair market value and in compliance with normal market conditions) *always* extinguishes any benefit? Although we mainly analyse WTO law, we also attempt to draw parallels with EC law.

Presumption of pass-through of the advantage: against automatism

With regard to the first presumption, which is similar to the blunt, and irrebuttable, assumption that an input subsidy should always pass through downstream, both the Panel and the Appellate Body rejected this possibility in the *US—Lead and Bismuth II* dispute. In that case, concerning leaded bars imported into the US and subject to countervailing duties, the issue was whether the subsidies originally bestowed on an undertaking (*BSC*) could still be regarded as being granted to its successors (*UES* and *BSplc/BSES*). Two specific transactions were under examination: the sale of a productive unit to *UES* and the privatisation of *BSC*.

The key premise of the US' argument was that the productive operations of all those companies were essentially the same, and thus there was no need to distinguish between them. This substantially derived from the assumption that, under WTO law, the beneficiary of the subsidy is not a person manufacturing a product but rather the *production operations* themselves.[31] On the basis of this argument, the US put forward an irrebuttable presumption that the benefit of a non-recurring (ie provided on an irregular basis) and untied (ie provided on a company basis and not directed at specific products) subsidy continues to flow, even after changes in ownership.

Both the Panel and the Appellate Body began with the premise. 'Logically' a benefit can only refer to a *person* that has received something, and not simply to its productive operations.[32] They then confirmed that it cannot always be presumed that, in the case of change of ownership of the company or of its assets, the benefit of a subsidy previously granted has passed through to the new owner.[33] In other words, while presumptions that an advantage continues to flow may be used, these can never be irrebuttable. A change in ownership, and in particular the special circumstances surrounding it, such as the compliance with commercial

[31] This allegation was based on note 36 to Article 10 of the SCM and on Article VI:3 of the GATT.

[32] Panel, *US—Lead and Bismuth II*, para 6.78; Appellate Body, ibid, para 58. The principle was laid down by the Appellate Body in *Canada—Aircraft*, para 154.

[33] Panel, *US—Lead and Bismuth II*, para 6.71; see also the Appellate Body, ibid, para 62.

considerations, may require an examination of whether a benefit continues to accrue to the buyer.[34]

The findings of the Panel and the Appellate Body are sound for two reasons.

First, as a matter of general proposition, and as various provisions of the GATT and the SCM Agreement seem to confirm, it is always necessary to prove the existence of a benefit for a subsidy to be deemed to exist and to counteract against it.[35] This is particularly so when we are not talking of a direct but rather of an indirect mechanism of transmission of the advantage which occurs when we have a change in ownership.

Secondly, as we have seen in the context of analysing the impact of input subsidies, the determination of any pass-through effect quite often requires a sophisticated analysis. Irrespective of the rules on the share of the burden of proof, which in any event should respect a balance between the parties, this assessment should properly take into account *all* factors concerned, and in particular the effects of the financial contribution at issue and of subsequent events, such as a change in ownership and the circumstances surrounding it. The presumption that an advantage—quite simply and always—continues to flow, or in any event has passed through, to the new owner does not seem to sit easily in this context.

There is no reason why a similar conclusion should not be reached in EC law as well. As we have shown with respect to input subsidies, there cannot be any irrebuttable presumption that, following a change in ownership, the previously conferred benefit continues to exist. This continuance has to be established and often requires a thorough analysis.

Presumption of exhaustion of the advantage: the market and the government intervention

The more interesting debate, however, is that concerning the second presumption whereby an arm's length sale for a fair market value and in compliance with normal market conditions should be held to *extinguish* the benefit.

What we see here is an intriguingly evolving reasoning of WTO jurisprudence.

[34] See Panel, *US—Lead and Bismuth II*, para 6.70: Appellate Body Report, ibid, para 62. It is however worth noting that the Appellate Body distinguished the scope of this analysis depending on whether what is in issue is an original investigation (Article 11 of the SCM) or only an administrative review (Article 21 of the SCM). See Appellate Body, ibid, para 63.

[35] In the first place, eg, the definition of benefit in Article 1.1(b) of the SCM reads that 'a benefit *is* thereby conferred' (emphasis added). This is also confirmed by the various provisions on the definition and purpose of countervailing duties which clearly imply that such a measure is only there to counteract an existing subsidy (see, eg, the last sentence of Article VI:3 of the GATT which is reprised by word in note 36 of Article 10 of the SCM). This reading is also definitely supported by the uncontroversial language of Article 21.1 which says that '[a] countervailing duty shall remain in force *only as long as and to the extent* necessary to counteract subsidization which is causing injury', emphasis added. This is substantially upheld by the Appellate Body, *US—Lead and Bismuth II*, paras 60–2.

In the *US—Lead and Bismuth II* the issue was whether the fact that a 'fair market value' had been paid for the 'productive assets, goodwill, and all other factors' used by the successor companies in producing imports into the US excluded the existence of a benefit for the new owners.

The focus of the Panel and the Appellate Body was different from that of the US, being more concentrated on the *change in ownership* (of the company and/or the production units) and its *conditions*, and in particular on their compliance with a market benchmark, rather than on the *continuance of the productive operations*.

Having found that the pass-through of the benefit cannot simply be presumed but has to be established, both the Panel and the Appellate Body relied on the often repeated finding that the term benefit implies a comparison with the marketplace. On this basis, they concluded that the payment of a 'fair market value', in the context of an 'arm's length' transaction and in full compliance with 'commercial considerations',[36] excludes that the buyer has 'benefited' from the transaction.[37]

The same principles seem to apply in the EC where the sale of a company at market price is held to extinguish (on the part of the buyer) any advantage accrued from a previous aid. The Court held that:

> where an undertaking that has benefited from unlawful State aid is bought at the market price, that is to say at the highest price which a private investor acting under normal competitive conditions was ready to pay for that company in the situation it was in, in particular after having enjoyed State aid, the aid element was assessed at the market price and included in the purchase price. In such circumstances, the buyer cannot be regarded as having benefited from an advantage in relation to other economic operators.[38]

In *US—Lead and Bismuth II* the Appellate Body seemed however to express some caution, restricting its finding on the inexistence of a pass-through of the benefit to 'the facts of the case'. [39]

This caution can be explained if the more recent *US—Countervailing Measures on Certain EC Products* dispute is considered, where one of the motives underlying this qualification emerged and can be summarized with the following questions. Is the price of an enterprise which is undergoing a privatization and which is determined by the market *always* a reliable indicator in a 'pass-through' assessment? Does the fact that one of the main actors in a privatization process is the *government* have any impact on this answer?

[36] As has occurred in the instant case with the sale of assets to *UES* and the privatization of *BSC*.

[37] Panel, *US—Lead and Bismuth II*, para 6.81; Appellate Body, ibid, para 68.

[38] Case C-277/00 *SMI*, para 80; Case C-390/98, *HJ Banks*, para 77. cf also Case C-305/89 *Italy v Commission*, paras 39 and 40.

[39] Appellate Body Report, *US—Lead and Bismuth II*, para 74. This restriction was recognized by the Appellate Body itself in *US—Countervailing Measures on Certain EC Products*, para 93.

We have already examined these findings previously[40] but, considering their relevance also in this context, it is worth repeating them.

The Panel found that:

privatizations at arm's length and for fair market value *must* lead to the conclusion that the privatized producer paid for what he got and thus did not get any benefit or advantage from the prior financial contribution bestowed upon the state-owned producer.[41]

The Appellate Body highlighted the special role played by governments in the functioning of market economies and, in particular, their ability to direct events and processes, in the instant case privatizations, towards certain, desired directions. The Appellate Body accordingly qualified the finding that privatisations at arm's length and for fair market value would *always* exclude that a benefit is passed through. In particular it pointed out that:

the Panel's absolute rule of 'no benefit' may be defensible in the context of transactions between two private parties taking place in reasonably competitive markets; however, it overlooks the ability of governments to obtain certain results from markets by shaping the circumstances and conditions in which markets operate. Privatisations involve complex and long-term investments in which the seller—namely the government—is not necessarily always a passive price taker and, consequently, the 'fair market price' of a state-owned enterprise is not necessarily always unrelated to government action. In privatisations, governments have the ability, by designing economic and other policies, to influence the circumstances and the conditions of the sale so as to obtain a certain market valuation of the enterprise.[42]

This ability to direct privatizations so as to 'influence the circumstances and the conditions of the sale' inevitably affects the reliability of some indicators such as the 'market valuation' (ie the price) of the enterprise. The Appellate Body thus concluded that:

the Panel erred in concluding that '[p]rivatisations at arm's length and for fair market value *must* lead to the conclusion that the privatised producer paid for what he got and thus did not get any benefit or advantage from the prior financial contribution bestowed upon the state-owned producer.' (emphasis added) Privatisation at arm's length and for fair market value *may* result in extinguishing the benefit. Indeed, we find that there is a rebuttable presumption that a benefit ceases to exist after such a privatisation. Nevertheless, it does not *necessarily* do so. There is no inflexible rule *requiring* that investigating authorities, in future cases, *automatically* determine that a 'benefit' derived from pre-privatisation financial contributions expires following privatisation at arm's length and for fair market value. It depends on the facts of each case. [43]

The main implication of this qualification is, again, an important warning against the possibility of using presumptions, and in particular those that automatically, and without any possibility of rebuttal, tend to produce a solution to the case.

[40] See chapter 8, section II.A.

[41] Panel, *US—Countervailing Measures on Certain EC Products*, para 7.82 (emphasis added).

[42] Appellate Body, *US—Countervailing Measures on Certain EC Products*, para 124.

[43] ibid para 127.

Although it may be assumed that privatizations at arm's length and for fair market value should extinguish the advantage, this is not necessarily the case. It is not a hard and fast rule. Once again, as the case of input subsidies shows, everything depends on a thorough empirical analysis of the facts of the case.[44]

Another implication of the Appellate Body's warning, which we have already examined in the context of the advantage analysis in chapter 8, is the difficulty of defining market criteria, especially when the government intervenes in the market. This qualification does not detract from the fact that, absent any significant interference from the government, the price produced by the market is normally a reliable indicator to determine whether any advantage has passed through to the buyer. It is accordingly argued that the importance of commercial criteria should generally be confirmed.

Turning again to the EC, there is nohing to indicate that the economic and legal remarks of the Appellate Body are not of more general application and could not be used in the EC context too. The fact that the government is not like any other agent in the market, but may instead play a predominant role therein, should be duly recognized when determining the reliability of market indicators.[45]

An interesting issue of the reliability of prices set by the market has arisen in the EC, which could also have an impact on WTO analysis. When the price is determined taking into account the possibility that the buyer might be called to repay the aid, it is likely the value of the aid may not be fully incorporated in that price. The intriguing issue is whether, under these circumstances, such contemplation

[44] cf G Grossman and PC Mavrodis, 'Here Today? Gone Tomorrow?' in H Horn and PC Mavroidis (eds), *The WTO Case Law of 2001* (Cambridge: Cambridge University Press, 2003) 170; id, 'Recurring Misunderstandings of Non Recurring Subsidies' in H Horn and PC Mavroidis (eds), *The WTO Case Law of 2002* (Cambridge: Cambridge University Press, 2005) 78; R Diamond, 'Privatization and the Definition of Subsidy: A Critical Study of Appellate Body Texturalism' (2008) Journal of International Economic Law 649. These authors heavily criticize the analysis of DSM because it would miss the real point at issue. In these post-privatization cases, what should be determined is whether a 'benefit' continues to exist. The price paid for the firm and the financial wealth of its owners is irrelevant in this respect. What counts is whether the competitive position of the firm continues to be advantaged even after the transaction. Legally, this analysis would be done through interpreting the term 'benefit' contextually, in the light of the objectives of the SCM Agreement, as 'competitive benefit'.

This analysis is intriguing, and highly inspiring. The implications of Diamond's analysis of the concept of 'competitive benefit' for the definition of subsidy, and the differences from our approach, have already partly been analysed in chapter 1, section III.

With more specific regard to the issue of the benefit in 'privatization cases', whilst the gist of the argument of these authors is understood, in the analysis presented in this book it is argued that a similar result is reached but in a different way. Rather than interpreting contextually the 'benefit' as 'competitive benefit', we more radically conclude that *a proper* notion of subsidy should already include, as a separate element, a 'distortion of competition' standard (see chapter 14 for an analysis). Reasoning in the framework of the SCM, this means that competitive effects should have been assessed in the 'injury' element. Diamond, ibid, 674, underlines the difficulties of this reading in the context of 'bifurcated' CV duty proceedings and, more generally, in the 'structure of the SCM Agreement's definition of subsidy'. Whereas there is probably not much that can be done with the former, the author believes that the 'structure' of WTO subsidy definition should be clarified to incorporate the suggestions above. This may have an impact on the conduct of CV duty proceedings.

[45] cf the analysis of the *La Poste* saga in chapter 8.

may imply that part of the benefit should really be considered as passing through to the buyer making him liable.[46]

The distinctions between the company and its owners and between share, business and asset deals

We have assessed the position of the buyer as possible indirect beneficiary of the sale, and the role that market considerations may play in determining whether a benefit passes through to him. We now seek to widen the discussion by considering the distinctions between share, asset or business deals on the one hand and, in the context of share deals, between the firm and its owners on the other. Although we examine WTO law and EC law separately, parallels will be drawn between the two.

WTO law

The first step of our analysis comes from an intriguing argument strongly put forward by the US in both the *US—Lead and Bismuth II* and *US—Countervailing Measures of Certain EC Products* disputes.

The US argued that the benefit resides in the legal person of the firm, or in the *production operation*, and continues to accrue to it even if its ownership changes, and can be terminated only with the amortization over time of the subsidy[47] or its reimbursement.

We have seen that, within the context of the determination of whether the benefit had passed through to the buyer, in *US—Lead and Bismuth II* the focus of the Panel and the Appellate Body was different from the one put forward by the US and concerned more the *change in ownership* of the company and/or the production units and its *conditions*, and in particular their compliance with the market, rather than the continuance of the productive operations.

In *US—Countervailing Measures of Certain EC Products*, the Panel, which was asked whether, in the context of the sale of a firm, a distinction should have been made between the 'benefit to the owners of the company' and the 'benefit to the company itself',[48] rejected this distinction put forward by the US.

On the premise that 'when someone purchases a company for fair market value, the purchase price includes the value of the benefit conferred to that company', and, taking into account the relationship between a company and its owners, especially following a privatization where the latter seek to maximize their return through the investment in the company, the Panel crucially noted that, for the purposes of the SCM Agreement, there should be no distinction between the advantage conferred to the company or to its owners as, when reference is made to the recipient of the benefit, this should mean *both of them together*.[49] To support

[46] See Advocate General Tizzano in Case C-277/00 *SMI*, para 79.

[47] Which centres on the average useful life of the subsidized assets.

[48] Panel, *US—Countervailing Measures on Certain EC Products*, para 7.40.

[49] ibid, paras 7.51–7.54.

its reasoning, the Panel also quoted the findings of the Panel in *US—Lead and Bismuth II*, whereby 'it would be misleading in the extreme to suggest that the price paid by the owners of the privatized company is not ultimately paid by the privatized company itself'.[50]

On appeal, the US reiterated their argument. In their view, irrespective of the commercial conditions of the transaction, the benefit always resides with the *legal entity* of the firm.[51] In particular, the conclusion that the privatization (note: even following market considerations) should always extinguish the benefit is founded on a 'basic economic misconception' since the privatization does not move the supply curve to where it has been and thus does not affect the continued existence of the subsidy.[52] In other words, the company that has received the subsidy, being the legal entity that continues to operate on the market, will continue to benefit from it irrespective of its ownership, and its occurrences, and the relevant market will continue to be distorted by the subsidy.

The Appellate Body confirmed that the benefit should be determined with reference to the market. It also explained that a benefit may be provided *indirectly* to a firm via its owners.[53] It thus rejected the strict distinction between company and owners put forward by the US whereby the only relevant consideration for a pass-through analysis would be the continued existence of the same legal person and the position of the owners would be completely irrelevant. The Appellate Body, however, also qualified the broad finding of the Panel, whereby a firm and its owners are, for all purposes of the SCM Agreement, virtually the same, underlining that there *may* well be cases where—from the perspective of the pass-through of the benefit—the distinction between the firm and its owners is indeed relevant.[54]

While the author substantially agrees with the findings of the Appellate Body, it may be useful to emphasize one particular aspect.

The Appellate Body distinguished between *utility value* and *market value* of the equipment that the undertaking has acquired with the subsidy. In the determination of whether a benefit continues to exist, it is the latter that should constitute the focal point.[55] We have seen that the payment of a market price would mean that the buyer of the company cannot be considered as a beneficiary.[56] From this perspective, no advantage would have passed through.

[50] Panel, *US—Lead and Bismuth II*, para 6.82.

[51] Appellate Body, *US—Countervailing Measures on Certain EC Products*, para 88.

[52] ibid, para 99.

[53] ibid, para 113.

[54] ibid, paras 116–19. In particular, the Appellate Body seemed to hint that in other cases (where, eg, a benefit is conferred through a recurring financial contribution, or where the seller retains a controlling interest in the firm) it may be necessary to distinguish between the company and its owners (ibid, para 117). The finding of the Panel should thus have been limited to the 'very narrow' set of circumstances at issue in that dispute.

[55] See Appellate Body, *US—Countervailing Measures on Certain EC Products*, para 102.

[56] Insofar as that price also includes the value of the subsidy it is *as if* the buyer had purchased the shares, which incorporate that value, on the market.

If we adhere to this premise, the focus of the identification of the beneficiaries should therefore shift from the buyers either to the firm as *legal entity* or to its *sellers*.

With respect to the allegation that the firm as a legal entity, and in particular its productive operations, would continue to benefit from the subsidy and, by continuing to operate in the market, this would continue to be distorted, this argument can also be found in the EC.[57] And it is indeed rather persuasive. The changes in ownership do not affect the lines of production of the undertaking which continue to benefit from the granted subsidy. As the US put it, the supply curve is not moved back by privatization and the market will continue to be distorted by the subsidized operations of the firm.

The main issue, which has been underlined by the various critics of the 'privatization' decisions,[58] is whether the firm, as productive operation, continues to enjoy the competitive benefit that the subsidy allegedly granted it. Focusing too much on the financial conditions of the sale transaction may thus be misleading, particularly if it does not take into consideration their impact on what really matters for subsidy law, ie the continuing existence of a 'competitive benefit'.

Accordingly, if it is true that the company should be held to benefit from the transaction if it sells itself the productive operations at market conditions (as we would have a mere exchange of assets for consideration), the analysis is more demanding in the case of privatization through sale of shares. It may well be true, as the Panel suggests, that it is not possible to distinguish between the position of the company and that of its new owners. The *US—Lead and Bismuth II* Panel may be right in observing that 'it would be misleading in the extreme to suggest that the [market] price paid by the owners of the privatized company is not ultimately paid by the privatized company itself',[59] and, accordingly, the latter would be relieved of any advantage.[60]

[57] See, eg, Case C-277/00 *SMI*, para 81; see also in the same case Advocate General Tizzano, paras 82–6 of the Opinion.

[58] See n 47 above.

[59] Paragraph 6.82.

[60] Following this reasoning (the buyer and the company have not benefited), the focus of the analysis of the beneficiaries should shift to those who *sold* their shares. They would be the ultimate beneficiaries of the sale transaction and of the increased value of the company, which would include the value of the subsidy.

In the EC context, where the rule is traditionally that unlawful aid should be repaid, it has been argued that this position may create some difficulties (see Advocate General Tizzano in Case C-277/00 *SMI*, paras 84 and 85). We could mention the case of a public company floated on the stock exchange. If the shares are sold on the market, and the relevant price is by definition the market price, we could envisage that any sale transaction may involve an aid element for the seller. The difficulty of recovering the aid from several hundreds (if not thousands) of sellers can easily be imagined. It is also underlined that the shareholders/sellers may not be involved in any economic activity with the result that they could not distort competition in any way.

As the Appellate Body has expressly acknowledged, however, it may well be that, in certain cases, it is crucial to distinguish between the firm and its owners. The author would like this factor to be emphasized.

In the author's view, this should lead to a fuller, contextual analysis of these cases. The determination of whether a benefit exists, or continues to exist, cannot be resolved by considering only whether the price paid is the market one. A long line of cases has shown how this may be misleading.[61] The complexity of post-privatization situations requires that, even in the framework of the advantage analysis, the focus should be firmly set on the broader goal of subsidy discipline, ie the control of competition distortions.[62]

EC law

After analysing the position as it stands in the WTO, attention is turned to the situation in EC law.

With respect to *asset deal* cases, where the sale concerns the assets of the firm benefiting from the aid, if the transaction has taken place under commercial conditions, the liability clearly belongs to the seller, ie the company.[63] By contrast, in the case of *business deals*, where the transfer regards an ongoing concern, which usually encompass both assets and liabilities, the buyer might be held liable.[64] This would occur not because the buyer is the beneficiary of the aid but because it is the party that has taken over the liabilities of the business.[65]

As regards *share deal* cases, the buyer's liability is excluded when the share price reflects the market price.[66] With respect to the identification of the actual beneficiary, Advocate General Tizzano in the *SMI* case observed that the Court seems to oscillate between two positions, requiring the repayment of the aid either by the company itself or by the sellers of the shares, ie the owners (when the share price reflects the value of the aid granted).[67]

The former position, which echoes that advanced by the US government in the *Lead and Bismuth II* and *US—Countervailing Measures of Certain EC Products* disputes, is well represented by the following findings in the *SMI* decision:

> the undertaking to which unlawful State aid was granted retains its legal personality and continues to carry out, for its own account, the activities subsidised by the State aid.

[61] See chapter 8.

[62] It is worth underlining that, strictly speaking, the advantage analysis should only capture the potential to distort competition. In our 'conceptual framework' (see chapter 1, section III), the assessment of whether this potential translates in an actual anti-competitive effect should be left to the relevant 'impact standards'. See chapter 14.

[63] Opinion of Advocate General Tizzano, Case C-277/00 SMI, para 98.

[64] See Advocate General Geelhoed in Joined Cases C-328/99 and C-399/00 *Italy and SIM v Commission*, para 82 of the Opinion.

[65] This distinction was correctly made by Advocate General Van Gerven in Case C-305/89 *Alfa Romeo*, at para 23 of the Opinion.

[66] See n 41 above.

[67] Case C-277/00, para 82 of the Opinion.

Therefore, it is normally this undertaking that retains the competitive advantage connected with that aid and it is therefore this undertaking that must be required to repay an amount equal to that aid.[68]

We cannot but repeat in this context the remarks made in the analysis of WTO law. The consideration of the 'financial' dimension of what are often complex transactions should not eclipse the underlying core of the issue, and the real concern which, paraphrasing the words of Advocate General Tizzano, is about whether the undertaking at hand 'retains a competitive advantage'.

The case of circumvention of the repayment

We now reconsider the position of the beneficiary, and in particular of the buyer, in those cases where it is alleged that the sale transaction is designed to circumvent the obligation of repayment of the subsidy.

It has been seen that, when the sale transaction takes place under normal market conditions, the buyer is generally safe since he is not considered as benefiting from the aid. Thus he cannot be required to repay anything.

There are however cases where it has been advanced that the buyer is not relieved from the obligation to repay the subsidy. This issue has come out especially in the EC, where, particularly in the case of the reorganization of groups in difficulties or even on occasion of bankruptcy procedures, all the assets—including the benefit deriving from the subsidy—were transferred to a new company, thus leaving the liabilities—including the duty to repay the subsidy—to the original beneficiaries. In these circumstances, the common allegation is that there is an attempt to circumvent the duty to repay an unlawful or incompatible aid.

EC law

The analysis may begin with few general remarks on the importance of the obligation of repayment of unlawful State aid in the EC system. This will prove important when a parallel is drawn with WTO law.

In the EC system the obligation to repay any aid that is 'unlawful' or is in any event considered 'incompatible' with the common market is one of the true

[68] ibid, para 81 of the decision. The Court followed the persuasive reasoning of Advocate General Tizzano in paras 83–5 of the Opinion. See also Case C-303/88, *ENI Lanerossi*, para 57.

As regards the other position of the Court, whereby the repayment of the aid is required by the sellers of the shares, we can refer to the *Banks* decision where it was made it clear that 'where a company which has benefited from aid has been sold at the market price, the purchase price reflects the consequences of the previous aid, and it is the seller of that company that keeps the benefit of the aid. In that case, the previous situation is to be restored primarily through repayment of the aid by the seller'. See Case C-290/98 *Banks*, para 78. See also Joined Cases C-74/00P and C-75/00P *Falck*, para 180; Case C-350/93 *ENI Lanerossi II*, para 22. This is also the conclusion arguably reached by the Court in the recent Joined Cases C-328/99 and C-399/00 *Seleco*, para 85, although the reasoning is rather ambiguous fluctuating between an obligation of the company and of the owners/sellers.

procedural cornerstones of the system of State aid control since it significantly guarantees that the enforcement of State aid rules is effective.[69]

Against this background, where we have the preventive centralized control of the Commission and where the repayment of unlawful or incompatible aid is the rule, the fears that the obligation of repayment could be circumvented through artificial company reorganizations can be seen very clearly. From this perspective, the question becomes whether legal formality should prevail, thus impeding the recovery of the aid from the transferee, or whether the economic substance of the situation should be looked at, thus allowing the said recovery.

If the buyer has to be held responsible this has to occur only in limited and well defined circumstances. This is particularly so if the buyer has paid the market price so that he should in principle be safe from any liability.[70] Moreover, from the perspective of the creditors (including the Member State seeking the recovery of the aid) of the undertaking in bankruptcy,[71] the sale of shares or assets at the market price is not liable to prejudice their position inasmuch as it does not remove resources from the bankrupt undertaking's assets.[72]

That said, it is sometimes alleged that the buyer should be held liable in cases of 'fraud' or 'circumvention of the law'.[73] These concepts are inherently elusive and difficult to define, in particular as far as the proof of their subjective element, the intention to circumvent the law, is concerned. It could be advanced that the presence of certain objective circumstances concomitant with the transfer transaction, such as the opening by the Commission of a procedure of control under Article 88 of the EC, might show the presence of a fraudulent intention. Equally, however, other factors, such as the fact that the transaction has taken place under market conditions or that, in the context of insolvency proceedings, the operation was carried out by administrators or under judicial supervision,[74] may lead to the conclusion that no fraud has been perpetrated. In short, the reality is that the burden

[69] See chapter 2, section 3.A.

[70] cf Case C-277/00 *SMI*, paras 80, 86 and 92. It has however been argued that the 'market' price would not be an appropriate indicator as it would be particularly low because of the situation of difficulty of the seller and would thus allow part of the advantage of the subsidy to pass through to the buyer. This is particularly clear in the case of bankruptcy proceedings. See Advocate General Geelhoed in Joined Cases C-328/99 and C-399/00 *Italy and SIM v Commission*, para 82 of the Opinion.

[71] It may be recalled that it is commonly accepted that the re-establishment of the previous situation and the elimination of the distortion of competition resulting from the unlawfully paid aid may, in principle, be achieved with the simple registration of the liability relating to the repayment of the aid in question in the schedule of liabilities. See Case C-277/00 *SMI*, para 85. See also Case 52/84 *Commission v Belgium*, para 14; Case C-142/87 *Tubemeuse*, paras 60–2.

[72] Case C-277/00, *SMI*, para 92.

[73] L Levi, 'L'identification du bénéficiaire de l'aide', in M Dony and C Smits (eds), *Aides d'Etat*, (Brussels: Editions de l'Université de Bruxelles, 2005), 195, 221; M Rehbinder, 'Recent Developments in Commission State Aid Policy and Practice', in in A Biondi, P Eeckhout, and J Flynn (eds), *The Law of State Aid in the European Union* (Oxford: Oxford University Press, 2004) 117, 129.

[74] See Case C-277/00 *SMI*, paras 92 and 93.

of proof of a circumvention of the duty to repay is not easy to discharge, as it is shown by the case-law on the abuse of right doctrine.[75]

This difficulty does not detract from the fact that (even) Member States often devise mechanisms to circumvent the obligation to recover. The Court has thus found that legislation permitting the transfer, without any consideration, of the personnel and the most profitable assets of an airline, free of all the company's debts, to a new company, and making it impossible to recover the former company's debts from the new firm, constitutes an obstacle to the repayment of the aid and to the effective implementation of the Commission's order of recovery.[76]

WTO law

It can now be asked whether this issue could be relevant in the WTO. This question provides us with the opportunity to consider the general features of the WTO system of subsidy control once again.

It should be recalled that, in the context of WTO law, the importance of the identification of the beneficiary of the subsidy has a double relevance at the remedial level inasmuch as it could be the basis of a withdrawal of the subsidy or of the imposition of a countervailing duty. Clearly, the issue of the circumvention could arise in either context. For the sake of the comparison with EC law, our analysis concentrates only on the possible withdrawal of the subsidy.

Indeed, there is no reason in principle why fraudulent company reorganizations to elude the effectiveness of the remedy could be relevant in the WTO also and the buyer may be held liable of the repayment of the subsidy.[77]

The main obstacle in the WTO legal system is not that of principle but depends on three reasons.

First, it follows from the different emphasis with respect to the retroactivity of remedies.[78] It is indeed known that, according to the *Australia—Leather (Article 21.5)* Panel, the withdrawal of subsidies should include their retrospective repayment, at least with respect to the category of prohibited subsidies (the State of the law with respect to actionable subsidies is still uncertain).[79] This doctrine has not had much success, however. Generally in the WTO remedies continue to be prospective (ie are effective only as far as future conduct is concerned) and only rarely has a retroactive effect been recognized.[80] Clearly, this temporal

[75] A difficult concept that is rarely applied. Despite affirming the doctrine in principle, the Court has thus always been quite reluctant to follow this line of argument. We can, eg, refer to the interesting case law on the establishment of secondary seats of companies. See, eg, Case C-217/97 *Centros*, paras 21–30.

[76] See Case C-415/03 *Commission v Greece*, paras 32–34. For other more recent cases where the claim has been rejected by the Court see Case T-324/00 *CDA; Case T-318/00 Freistaat Thüringen.*

[77] This would be particularly true when it is established that a benefit has in fact passed through in favour of the buyer because, eg, market conditions have not been followed.

[78] For an analysis, and a critique, see chapter 2, section III.

[79] See Panel, *Australia—Automotive Leather Article 21.5*, para 6.22.

[80] Quite interestingly, in some GATT countervailing and anti-dumping duties cases.

limitation would have a significant impact on the possibility of drawing a comparison with EC law where the retroactivity of the repayment is the rule. It cannot be easily disputed, however, that 'purely prospective remedies hardly constitute a deterrent effect against potential violators',[81] as is witnessed by the experience in the EC and by the case-law of the Court of Justice that, despite recent uncertainties, has continuously stressed the importance of the repayment of unlawful and incompatible aid.

Secondly, the weakness of the remedies is accompanied by the known relative flexibility in the compliance with the DSB's decisions. Although full compliance with the rulings and recommendations of the DSB, which usually requires the withdrawal of the measures found to be inconsistent with WTO law, is the first objective of the dispute settlement system, the regime provides for other paths, in the form of compensation or suspension of concessions, that, at least in theory, should only be temporary solutions.[82] A similar flexibility cannot be found in the EC system where compliance with the decisions of the Court of Justice, including non-repayment of unlawfully granted State aid, can be enforced with substantial financial penalties.[83]

Thirdly, these weaknesses are coupled with another general factor that may further weaken the scope of the obligation to recover unlawful subsidies, that is the general laxity of the WTO system of subsidy control.[84] The procedural and institutional frameworks of EC and WTO law are obviously different with the latter still lagging behind the complexity of the former. As a result, WTO law seems to be less rigorous as compared with the EC, and this element too may constitute an obstacle to effectively tackling possible situations of circumvention of the law.

[81] PC Mavroidis, 'Remedies in the WTO Legal Systesm: Between a Rock and a Hard Place' (2000) European Journal of International Law 763, 790.

[82] Article 3.7 of the DSU.

[83] See Article 228(2) of the EC. A good example is that of Greece's persistent non-recovery of aid granted to Olympic Airways and declared incompatible by the Commission in 2002. In his Opinion of 5 February 2009 in Case C-399/07, Advocate General Mengozzi has recommended that the Court of Justice imposes on Greece both a daily penalty (of 15,768 Euros) and a lump sum of 2 million Euros.

[84] See chapter 2, section III above.

13

The idea and analysis of specificity

We now focus on the concept of 'specificity' or 'selectivity'. This idea, which is common to both EC State aid and WTO subsidy laws, raises important conceptual and practical questions, addressed in the two main sections of the chapter.

I. Introduction

Both EC law and WTO law require that a State aid and a subsidy be specific inasmuch as it should confer an advantage only on certain economic subjects. Article 87 of the EC provides that State aid should distort competition by favouring *certain* undertakings or the production of *certain* goods. In the chapeau to an elaborate provision, Article 2 of the SCM defines the concept by referring to a subsidy specific to *certain* enterprises, ie to an enterprise or industry or group of enterprises or industries.

Two remarks can be made at the outset. First, the immediate impression is that this requirement is clearly intended to operate as a tool to *limit* the measures that are regulated by State aid or subsidy rules. Secondly, its underlying *rationale* is not fully clear. Rather, it is not clear whether there is *any* or indeed *more than one* rationale.

We commence our analysis by attempting to answer these questions: does the specificity idea has a rationale underlying it? If so, what is it or what are they? The identification of the justification(s) of the concept of specificity is crucial to approach the second part of the analysis—which focuses on some of its most interesting applications—with confidence. Only by following this process, will we be in a position to assess whether the operation of the specificity test is in line with its alleged justification(s) and, eventually, whether our first impression that it is a *sieve* is in fact validated.

II. The justification of the idea of specificity

The idea of specificity has generally found two broad types of rationales, economic and non-economic.[1] We analyse each in turn.

[1] There is a wide literature on the issue, particularly American, since it is there that the test flourished. See, eg, JJ Barceló III, 'Subsidies and Countervailing Duties—Analysis and a Proposal'

A. Economic rationales

The common proposition that economists make to justify the use of a specificity test is that specific measures would be, or at least would have the potential of being, more distortive than general ones.[2]

This is sometimes linked to the idea of comparative advantage.[3] It is said in particular that specific subsidies would especially interfere with the allocation of resources domestically—and hence internationally—thus shifting artificially comparative advantages between countries.[4] Subsidies may alter the comparative advantage for two reasons: first because they are liable to reduce the costs of the recipient, secondly because they attract resources towards the recipient market. Presumably, the impact on competition and competitors would be particularly noticeable when competitive advantages are not well defined (which occurs when the economies of the two countries and of the two industries are close) and when there is consequently a lot of intra-industry trade in the good or service at issue.

Along these lines, with a dangerous reasoning *a contrario*, Benitah concludes that:

> [t]his type of 'distortion' would not have taken place had the subsidy been generally available to all industries. In such a case, these industries would have been on equal terms for obtaining scarce productive resources and the mechanism described above could not have taken place.[5]

(1977) Law and Policy in International Business 799; JH Bello and AF Holmer, 'Subsidies and Natural Resources: Congress Rejects a Lateral Attack on the Specificity Test' (1984/1985) George Washington Journal of International Law and Economics 297; LA Cameron and GC Berg, 'The US Countervailing Duty Law and the Principle of General Availability' (1985) Journal of World Trade Law 497; MJ Sussman, 'Countervailing Duties and the Specificity Test: An Alternative Approach to the Definition of "Bounty or Grant"' (1986) Law and Policy in International Business 475; JL Panzarella, 'Is the Specificity Test Generally Applicable?' (1986) Law and Policy in International Business 417; PM Alexander, 'The Specificity Test Under US Countervailing Duty Law' (1989) Michigan Journal of International Law 807; JA Ragosta and HM Shanker, 'Specificity of Subsidy Benefits in US Department of Commerce Countervailing Duty Determinations' (1994) Law and Policy in International Business 639.

[2] See, eg, HW Friederiszick, LH Röller, and V Verouden, *European State Aid Control: An Economic Framework*, in Bucirossi (ed), *Handbook of Antitrust Economics* (Cambridge MA: MIT Press, 2008) 625, 628 and 654–5; OFT, *European State Aid Control*, OFT821: London (2005) 35; OFT, *Public Subsidies—A Report by the Office of Fair Trading*, OFT750: London (2004) 22 and 29; Frontier Economics, *The Effects of Public Subsidies on Competition*, a report prepared for the Office of Fair Trading, enclosed as Annexe C to OFT (2004) 15 and 16.

[3] For a general introduction on the theory of comparative advantage cf MJ Trebilcock and R Howse, *The Regulation of International Trade* (3rd edn, London: Routledge, 2005) chapter 1; for a more detailed analysis see PR Krugman and M Obsfeld, *International Economics—Theory and Policy* (5th edn, London: Addison Wesley, 1999).

[4] This is, eg, the argument put forward by W Schwartz and EW Harper Jr, 'The Regulation of Subsidies Affecting International Trade" (1972) 70 Michigan Law Review 831, 840, which seem to imply that subsidies be specific. For a reformulation of this argument (from a critical perspective) see M Benitah, *The Law of Subsidies under the GATT/WTO System* (The Hague: Kluwer Law International, 2001) 258.

[5] M Benitah, *The Law of Subsidies under the GATT/WTO System* (The Hague: Kluwer Law International, 2001) 258.

The fact that more specific interventions would be *more* distortive than generic ones is often criticized.

In this regard, the author cannot resist citing an anecdote. It is reported that, at a Committee's meeting of 25 October 1990 during the Uruguay Round Negotiations, the representative of the United States—the cradle of the specificity test—observed that:

> it had no economic justification. . . . Obviously, the specificity concept was still embedded in US law and regulations. However, the United States had concluded that the concept, which it had created and promoted, did not have the degree of attractiveness once attributed to it. The United States had the intellectual honesty to so admit, and it would seek to convince others in the proper negotiating forum of that change of view.[6]

This comment (and the related intellectual honesty) is noted. Leaving the diplomatic arena to turn to economics again, it is commonly conceded that general measures of interventions are less likely to involve rent-seeking (ie the hunt to get the government to intervene so as to make one's business more profitable).[7] There is on the contrary some disagreement on whether they are more likely to be targeted at—and hence effective at solving—failures and imperfections of the market.[8]

That said, it is however increasingly argued that general measures too may alter the comparative advantage of countries (which are increasingly linked to, for example, social investments in health, education, law and order, basic research, and physical infrastructure) thus distorting competition and trade.[9] According to the OECD, this may occur in particular when the relevant product or service markets are broader than the national boundaries.[10] Even if the measure at issue applies to all firms within the country (and hence is considered as general), it may still be capable of affecting the position of those foreign firms that compete with (that is to say, operate in the same relevant product or service market of) national firms of the benefited industries.

A notable recognition that general measures too might distort competition can be traced back to the very roots of the European Community, the *Spaak Report*,

[6] Minutes of the Meeting Held on 15 October 1990, GATT DOC. No. SCM/M/48 (21 December 1990) 15–16.

[7] MJ Trebilcock and R Howse, *The Regulation of International Trade* (3rd edn, London: Routledge, 2005), 289; OFT, *European State Aid Control*, OFT821: London (2005) 35; T Besley and P Seabright, 'The Effects and Policy Implications of State Aids to Industry: An Economic Analysis' (1999) Economic Policy 15, 20.

[8] For the positive, see T Besley and P Seabright, 'The Effects and Policy Implications of State Aids to Industry: An Economic Analysis' (1999) Economic Policy 15, 20; for the negative see, eg, OFT, *European State Aid Control*, OFT821: London (2005) 35–6.

[9] See MJ Trebilcock and R Howse, *The Regulation of International Trade* (3rd edn, London: Routledge, 2005), 289. See also Sykes, AO, 'The Economics of WTO Rules on Subsidies and Countervailing Measures', Chicago John M. Olin Law and Economics Working Paper No. 186 (2nd Series), May 2003, 4–5.

[10] OECD, *Competition Policy in Subsidies and State Aid*, Competition Policy Roundtable, DAFFE/CLP (2001) 24, OECD, Paris, 29–30.

which laid down the basis for Articles 96 and 97 of the EC (on the approximation of laws to tackle distortions of competition).[11]

One traditional argument in defence of general measures is that they would normally be neutral as any distorting effect would be compensated by other macro-economic factors. It is thus observed that, in the context of a floating exchange-rate world, the effects of general measures would be quite minimal because they would be adjusted by exchange rate mechanisms.[12] Trebilcock and Howse noted, however, that in an international environment where exchange rates are increasingly determined by international capital flows rather than good flows the said adjustment becomes more difficult.[13] It should further be noted that, at least in the context of the EC, this argument can by no means be predicated with respect to those countries that share a common monetary policy whose central element is the adoption of a single currency, the Euro.

Also the argument that the distortive effect of general interventions would be decreased, or even eliminated, because any advantage arising from them would normally be financed, at least partly, by the same beneficiaries of the measures is not far-reaching as there is not necessarily any such symmetry between the financing of the measure and its anti-competitive impact.

Assuming that general measures too may be distortive, the paradoxical nature of the specificity criterion is often highlighted.

Lowenfeld pragmatically observed that, from the perspective of competitors, it is indeed irrelevant whether they are the only ones to be injured or whether other sectors of the economy are distorted as well.[14] Along this path, on the assumption 'the wider the more distortive', it is even argued that it cannot possibly be understood why individual or sectoral subsidies would be caught by the regulation whereas measures of wider scope would be permitted. This is the suggestive argument put forward in the EC by Advocate General Capotorti in *Buy Irish* where he noted that:

> quite apart from the wording of Article [87 EC], it is perfectly justifiable to speak of a general principle of the prohibition of public aids to domestic products.[15]

An alternative, more meaningful concept of specificity would focus on whether that treatment is enjoyed by all competing undertakings in other countries

[11] *Rapport des Chefs de Délégation aux Ministères des Affaires Etrangères*, Secretariat of the Intergovernmental Conference, Brussels, 21 April 1956 (*Spaak Report*).

[12] JH Jackson, *The World Trading System—Law and Policy of International Economic Relations* (2nd edn, Cambridge Massachussetts: MIT Press, 1997) 297; JF Beseler and AN Williams, *Anti-Dumping and Anti-Subsidy Law—The European Communities* (London: Sweet and Maxwell, 1986) 138. For the EC, see also the *Spaak Report*.

[13] MJ Trebilcock and R Howse, *The Regulation of International Trade* (3rd edn, London: Routledge, 2005) 289.

[14] AF Lowenfeld, *International Economic Law* (2nd edn, Oxford: Oxford University Press, 2008) 237–8.

[15] Case 249/81, p 4031.

as well.[16] Although theoretically sound, this is very difficult to administer. It is not therefore subject to analysis in the specificity debate and is certainly not the kind of concept that EC or WTO rules embrace.

What the foregoing shows is that the economics underlying the concept of specificity is not unambiguous. Although the impact of specific subsidies is quite probably more apparent than those of general measures, the specificity test can at most be grounded on what has been termed by Benitah a simple idea of distortion.[17]

The insufficiency of economics to fully justify the idea of specificity cannot however lead to the conclusion that the latter 'stands as a surrogate for an efficiency analysis'.[18] This is not correct for two reasons.

First, as posited in chapter 2, a comprehensive efficiency or welfare analysis should be carried out in a difference context, when the various (negative and positive) effects of the measure at issue are assessed and balanced with each other. In this light, as has been argued with respect to the use of market criteria in the advantage analysis, the fact that the specificity test would be based on a 'simple' idea of distortion is not per se a minus.[19] Neither the advantage nor the specificity elements have the duty to tell us whether there *is* a distortion or a correction of a distortion.

Further, although conceding that the economics underlying the concept of specificity is not fully clear, some agreement can be found for the idea that the specificity criterion may reasonably capture those measures that are *more easily liable* to distort efficient market outcomes.

In the absence of a clear theoretical rationale for judging the welfare implications of a greater or lesser degree of specificity in a subsidy intervention, Low has accordingly acknowledged that specificity should be considered as a 'valid rule of thumb' for focusing on those subsidies that are likely to be more distorting.[20]

[16] AO Sykes, 'The Economics of WTO Rules on Subsidies and Countervailing Measures', Chicago John M Olin Law and Economics Working Paper No. 186 (2nd Series) May 2003; V Di Bucci, 'Comments on the Paper "Selectivity, Economic Advantage, Distortion of Competition and Effect on Trade"' in J Derenne and M Merola (eds), *Economic Analysis of State Aid Rules—Contributions and Limits* (Berlin: Lexxion, 2007) 156; JHJ Bourgeois, 'State Aids, Taxation Measures and Specificity. Some Thoughts', in M Dony and A De Walsche, *Mélanges en hommage à Michel Waelbroeck,* Vol 2 (Bruxelles: Bruylant, 1999) 765.

[17] M Benitah, *The Law of Subsidies under the GATT/WTO System* (The Hague: Kluwer Law International, 2001) 256 et seq.

[18] DK Tarullo, 'Beyond Normalcy in the Regulation of International Trade' (1986/1987) Harvard Law Review 546, 560. cf, along this same line of argument, C Ahlborn and C Berg, 'Can State Aid Control Learn from Antitrust? The Need for Greater Role for Competition Analysis under the State Aid rules' in A Biondi, P Eeckhout, and J Flynn (eds), *The Law of State Aid in the European Union* (Oxford: Oxford University Press, 2004) 41, 54–5, with the allegation that, under EC law, there is not necessarily any direct link between the distortion underlying the specificity criterion and the effects of the subsidy.

[19] See chapter 8, section 3.A.

[20] P Low, 'The Treatment of Subsidies in the WTO Framework' in CD Ehlermann and M Everson, *European Competition Law Annual 1999: Selected Issues in the Field of State Aids* (Oxford: Hart Publishing, 2001) 103, 114, and 120.

For example, certain forms of intervention that are especially likely to distort competition, such as support to failing firms or industries, are usually discriminatory inasmuch as they are given only to firms known to be failing.[21]

In short, this paragraph can be concluded by noting that, although it would be too radical to conclude that the specificity requirement does not have any economic justification (as the US attempted to do at the end of the Uruguay Round Negotiations), economics *alone* does not explain its rationale. As Professor Jackson elegantly put it, 'economic arguments can only go part of the way toward explaining its rationale'.[22]

B. Non-economic rationales

Having concluded that economics alone is insufficient to justify the requirement of specificity, in this paragraph we enquire whether the analysis of non-economic considerations can contribute to define its justification. In particular, we focus on arguments of a political and practical nature.

Indeed it is often argued that the true rationale of specificity should be found in political or practical reasons.[23]

On the one hand, there are reasons of *pragmatic* order. Beviglia Zampetti argues that the requirement that only measures concerning certain undertakings should be subject to the scrutiny of State aid and subsidy rules would avoid a 'painstaking' review of too many governmental measures that may distort competition and trade.[24] (This argument bears a significant resemblance to one put forward by Advocate General Jacobs in the context of the debate on the necessity of a transfer of State resources.)[25] With another nice formulation Hufbauer and Shelton-Erb noted that:

> [t]he special favor concept now appears to serve as Ockham's razor to eliminate a wide range of government programs from the sphere on international law.[26]

[21] OECD, *Competition Policy in Subsidies and State Aid*, Competition Policy Roundtable, DAFFE/CLP (2001) 24, OECD, Paris, 19.

[22] JH Jackson, *The World Trading System—Law and Policy of International Economic Relations* (2nd edn, Cambridge Massachussetts: MIT Press, 1997) 297.

[23] See, eg, JH Bello and AF Holmer, 'Subsidies and Natural Resources: Congress Rejects a Lateral Attack on the Specificity Test' (1984/1985) George Washington Journal of International Law and Economics 297, 308; JH Jackson, *The World Trading System—Law and Policy of International Economic Relations* (2nd edn, Cambridge Massachussetts: MIT Press, 1997) 297; JJ Barceló III, 'Subsidies and Countervailing Duties—Analysis and a Proposal' (1977) Law and Policy in International Business 799, 836; A Beviglia Zampetti, 'The Uruguay Round Agreement on Subsidies—A Forward-Looking Assessment' (1996) Journal of World Trade 5, 21.

[24] A Beviglia Zampetti, 'The Uruguay Round Agreement on Subsidies—A Forward-Looking Assessment' (1996) Journal of World Trade 5, 21.

[25] See, Case C-52/97 *Viscido*, para 18 of the Opinion.

[26] GC Hufbauer and J Shelton Erb, *Subsidies in International Trade* (Cambridge, Massachusetts: MIT Press, 1984) 92.

From this perspective, the specificity rationale would eventually lie in a *lex parsimoniae*, in a law of succinctness. To put it into current parlance, it would lie in a law of administrative/judicial economy. Using rather dramatic language, Sykes defined it as 'little more than *deux ex machina*'.[27]

It is also importantly observed (and here pragmatic and political considerations clearly merge) that subjecting general measures to the scrutiny of subsidy rules could lead to the imposition of countervailing duties on virtually every product entering international trade and could thus jeopardize the functioning of the international trading order itself.[28]

On the other hand, the selection operated by the specificity requirement would find a justification in considerations of more *political* order. General measures would require more deference and self-restraint. We have seen that, contrary to more specific measures, they are probably less distortive of competition and trade and are more easily justifiable in terms of legitimate public objectives. This could in turn reflect more simply the exercise of sovereign prerogatives. This argument is often formulated in terms of an 'everybody-does-so' rationale which would justify the need to eliminate from the scrutiny of State aid and subsidy rules certain measures. This argument is well explained by a passage of Jackson:

> [i]f we recognize the need to eliminate from the subset of subsidies called 'actionable' the general activities that all governments undertake (such as societal infrastructure like police, fire protection, roads, schools, etc), the specificity test can offer a very useful method for doing so. Thus, it can be argued that part of the rationale for the specificity test is that it is useful as a tool of administration (albeit sometimes blunt) to get rid of a number of cases which really ought not be brought into a countervailing duty or other international rule process.[29]

Interestingly, it is recognized that the specificity test can be *blunt*. This echoes our previous finding that, if we wanted to refer to economic analysis, specificity may be viewed as a reasonable approximation, a *rule of thumb*.

As will be explained below, this lack of precision can be reconciled with the *political economy* rationale of the specificity test.

C. A truly political economy justification

We have seen that economics can only partly justify the specificity test, inasmuch as it constitutes, at most, a 'valid rule of thumb' to identify the most blantant distortions.

[27] AO Sykes, 'The Economics of WTO Rules on Subsidies and Countervailing Measures', Chicago John M Olin Law and Economics Working Paper No. 186 (2nd Series), May 2003, 4.

[28] JH Jackson, *The World Trading System—Law and Policy of International Economic Relations* (2nd edn, Cambridge Massachussetts: MIT Press, 1997) 293. See also JJ Barceló III, 'Subsidies and Countervailing Duties—Analysis and a Proposal' (1977) Law and Policy in International Business 799, 836 and GC Hufbauer and J Shelton Erb, *Subsidies in International Trade* (Cambridge, Massachusetts: MIT Press, 1984) 92.

[29] JH Jackson, *The World Trading System—Law and Policy of International Economic Relations* (2nd edn, Cambridge Massachussetts: MIT Press, 1997) 297.

We have also seen that this economic idea of simple or potential distortion should be coupled by important considerations of political and practical convenience.

Combining both lines of argument, it can be concluded that the requirement of specificity finds its grounding in the realm of *political economy*, ie in the place where the findings of economic theory (which are based on efficiency considerations) serve (only) as a basis for political choices. In other words, this term significantly draws attention to *political motivation* giving shape to economic policies and choices.[30]

There is a clear consequence deriving from this political economy rationale which can be summed up in one question: is *specificity* sufficiently *specific?*

This question particularly refers (i) to the *flexibility/uncertainty*, and (ii) to the *expansiveness* that can characterize the specificity analysis once it steps into the realm of political economy.

On the one hand, as a direct consequence of the discretional nature of the requirement, which depends on its political/pragmatic rationale, it can be noted that specificity is a *flexible* tool. As an inevitable corollary, the prediction of the results of the assessment is often *uncertain*. On the other hand, as we will see below, the application of this requirement seems to show a trend towards *expansiveness*. In this regard, a contradiction should be underlined.

The chapeau of Article 2.1 of the SCM explains that the phrase 'certain enterprises' should refer to '*an* enterprise or industry or group of enterprises or industries' (emphasis added). For its part, we have seen that Article 87(1) of the EC regulates those measures that favour 'certain undertakings or the production of certain goods'. It has accordingly been observed that the language used by the two legal systems clearly indicates a limited scope of application (see, again, the article in the singular in Article 2.1 of the SCM).

In other words, it seems that 'certain' should be construed as 'few' (or, in the SCM's language, even as 'one' only). This conclusion seems to be confirmed if the traditional theory of comparative advantage is endorsed, which refers to the competitive position of well-defined industries. However, in many cases, the application of the test in the two systems seems often to indicate a *wide reach* which can in turn put into question the *selectiveness* of the specificity requirement.

III. The application of the specificity test

A. The specificity analysis and its test

Whereas the GATT 1947 did not make any mention of a specificity analysis, the Treaty of Rome adopted a few years later already incorporated the short legal formulation of the specificity criterion of Article 87(1) of the EC (whereby the

[30] Black's *Oxford Dictionary of Economics* (2nd edn, Oxford: Oxford University Press, 2002) 358.

measure at issue should favour certain undertakings or the production of certain sectors). This has never been amended and has been developed in the practice of the Commission and in the case-law of the Community Courts.

Over the years the GATT/WTO faced an interesting evolution. Although not providing an express specificity requirement, various provisions of the Tokyo Round Subsidies Code (see, eg, Article 11.3) were already hinting at this test which was commonly used in the application of CV duties in many jurisdictions, including the US and the EC. It was not until the advent of the WTO, however, that the law expressly provided (in Article 2 of the SCM) an elaborate specificity test with three different progressive stages drawing inspiration from US countervailing duty law.

Despite a different historical development, the specificity analysis in both systems seems to be constituted of *three* different *tests* (or, from another perspective, three *stages* of the same specificity test). Although this is apparent in the sophisticated formulation of Article 2 of the SCM, Roberti noted that this is essentially true also with respect to EC law.[31] It is therefore justified to analyse the law of both systems simultaneously.

The first, and most straightforward, step of the test is to determine whether the measure is *expressly* addressed to certain undertakings or sectors of the economy, which is usually defined as *de jure* specificity. This concept is enshrined in Article 2.1(a) of the SCM which provides that the measure is *de jure* specific when 'the granting authority, or the legislation pursuant to which the granting authority operates, *explicitly* limits access to a subsidy to certain enterprises'.[32]

If this is not the case, it is then necessary to focus on the operation and impact of the measure to determine whether it is specific or not. The second step is thus to assess whether the financial assistance is granted on the basis of objective criteria or on a discretional basis.

The fact that the measure is not explictly targeted at certain undertakings and operates according to objective criteria, however, may not be sufficient to exclude the specificity of the measure if the latter is in fact (*de facto*) capable of conferring an advantage to certain undertakings or sectors. This is the third, and most difficult, step of the test.

The following exposition includes a selection of the most interesting issues arising from the application of the specificity analysis, in particular with respect to the second and third stages of the test. In the examination we attempt to examine particularly whether the specificity analysis carried out in the EC on the basis of the short sentence in Article 87(1) of the EC can be compared with the analysis of the, at least apparently, more sophisticated WTO language. The difference in age of the two provisions may well make a difference, at least insofar as the amount of

[31] GM Roberti, *Gli aiuti di Stato nel diritto comunitario* (Padova, CEDAM, 1997) 200–1.
[32] Emphasis added.

administrative, judicial and scholarly interpretation is concerned. In particular, the case-law on Article 2 of the SCM is still extremely limited.

B. The specificity test between limitation, flexibility, certainty and expansiveness

It has been seen that, in both EC and WTO law, the specificity requirement appears to be a tool to limit the number of measures subject to the scrutiny of State aid/ subsidy rules.

We have also seen, however, that three *inherent characteristics* of the rationales underlying specificity often put into question this general objective of *limitation*. On the one hand, the political/discretional nature of the assessment often implies its *flexibility* and leads to *uncertainty* of results. On the other hand, one of the tendencies of the specificity analysis in both legal systems is its *expansiveness*.[33] As we will see, these *inherent characteristics* can be appreciated in various cases.

The definition of 'certain' (how many is 'certain'?)

We have seen above that the expression 'certain' undertakings or enterprises in the Article 87(1) of the EC and in Article 2.1 of the SCM immediately seems to point to a limited scope of the concept of specificity. According to this reading, the impression is that under those provisions a measure is specific if it benefits only *few* (if not only *one*) undertakings or sectors.

However, even a superficial examination of the case-law leads us to understand that this is not the case and that a measure is held to be specific even though it advantages *several* undertakings and sectors.[34] A brief review of the decisions of the Court of Justice may be useful in this regard.

According to the Court, aid for all exports,[35] for a whole sector of the economy or for a region, is specific.[36] More recently, it was also made it clear that neither the high number of benefiting undertakings nor the diversity and importance of the industrial sectors to which those undertakings belong warranted the conclusion that a scheme constituted a general measure of economic policy rather than a

[33] In the EC, C Ahlborn and C Berg, 'Can State Aid Control Learn from Antitrust? The Need for Greater Role for Competition Analysis under the State Aid rules' in A Biondi, P Eeckhout, and J Flynn (eds), *The Law of State Aid in the European Union* (Oxford: Oxford University Press,2004) 41, 51–4, refer to 'an ever-expanding universe'. In WTO law, M Matsushita, TJ Schoenbaum, and PC Mavroidis, *The World Trade Organization—Law, Practice, and Policy* (1st edn, Oxford: Oxford University Press, 2003) 271, note that the multiple tests of Article 2 of the SCM 'demonstrate the will of the negotiators to include *a priori* as many subsidies as possible under the term "specific"'. This is particularly evidenced by the third step of *de facto* specificity.

[34] See n 31.

[35] See Joined Cases 6 and 11/69 *Commission v France*, paras 20 and 21, Case 57/86, *Greece v Commission*, para 8.

[36] See Case 248/84 *Germany v Commission*, para 18.

State aid.[37] Similarly, the Court of First Instance held that a Spanish scheme to assist in the purchase of commercial vehicles by natural persons, SMEs, regional public bodies and bodies providing local public services was specific because large undertakings were excluded.[38] It has even been assumed that financial assistance to the whole manufacturing sector can constitute State aid.[39]

This short review of EC law can be concluded with a very useful definition of Advocate General Roemer which nicely sums up the approach to specificity in the EC. Using a negative formulation, he suggested that the specificity test would apply to any measure which does *not* apply generally to all the undertakings in a Member State.[40]

It is clear from these statements that a measure may have a broad scope of application and may nonetheless be considered as specific. Hypothetically, a strict application of the negative formulation of Advocate General Roemer would lead to consider as specific a measure that applies to all undertakings of the economy *but* one.

A comparable comprehensiveness can be found in the WTO as well. Thus a subsidy to all undertakings in a region is specific (see Article 2.2 of the SCM). Quite similarly, for export subsidies (and the comparable category of local-content subsidies) specificity is presumed.

This brief examination of the law in the two systems seems to confirm that the definition of specificity is wide and can capture many measures that, at an initial reading, seemed to fall outside the scope of the regulation.

The examples of export and regional aid

It may now be useful to examine two examples of measures that are considered specific in both systems. What is interesting is an assessment of the rationale of this conclusion, which, so it seems, can very much be explained in terms of *political economy*.

The first example is that of *export aid*. Export subsidies are considered in both systems as specific. Article 2.3 of the SCM expressly provides that prohibited subsidies (a category which controversially includes both export subsidies and local-content subsidies) are deemed to be specific.[41] Quite similarly, in the EC, the case-law of the Court has soon held that export subsidies were specific.[42]

[37] Case C-75/97 *Maribel*, paras 32–4; cf also Case C-143/9 *Adria-Wien Pipeline*, para 48.

[38] Case T-55/99 *CETM*, para 47. cf also Case C-351/98 *Spain v Commission*, para 40; Case C-409/00 *Spain v Commisssion*, paras 48–50.

[39] Case C-143/9 *Adria-Wien Pipeline*, para 55. It is interesting to make reference to the practice of the Commission, and in particular to the Irish Corporation Tax case where Brussels changed its view on whether support for the whole manufacturing sector was specific.

[40] Cases 6 and 11/69 *Commission v France*, at 552.

[41] This equivalence has been criticized. See chapter 14, section II.B.

[42] Cases 6 and 11/69 *Comission v France*, paras 20 and 21; Case 57/86, *Greece v Commission*, para 8.

This conclusion is sometimes criticized. Quigley and Collins have thus wondered why aid generally granted to all exporting undertakings and sectors is regarded as specific, and, conversely, aid to all domestic undertakings is not specific.[43]

We have seen in chapter 2 that export subsidies are treated more harshly because they are considered more distorting and more dangerous. Trebilcock and Howse have suggested that their intent is more clearly protectionist and, in contrast with domestic subsidies, they are more difficult to explain in terms of legitimate objectives.[44] Further, they are particularly apt to create diplomatic tensions, subsidy races and trade wars.

This may all be true but it does not fully explain why they should be considered as specific. Once again, the serious candidate for their justification has to be found in a *political* decision. Export subsidies (*et similia*) are so dangerous (and difficult to justify) that specificity is somewhat *assumed* (in the WTO, it is indeed *deemed*).

Quite similarly, the issue of whether measures targeted at certain *regions* should be considered as specific has always been rather controversial. The issue was for example subject to great debate in the Uruguay Round negotiations.[45]

It is important to define regional specificity. The following remarks are made with respect to WTO but are similarly valid for the EC.

Article 2.2 of the SCM talks of subsidy limited to certain enterprises within the region.[46] This language raises the doubt that, to be regionally specific, a measure should not be targeted to all enterprises within the region but only *certain* of them. This doubt is dispelled with a systemic analysis, by considering the rules on non-actionable subsidies where it is clear that regional measures, which are assumed to be specific within the meaning of Article 2 of the SCM, can be justified only if they are not specific within the region. It should be further noted that in both the WTO and the EC, regional measures are justifiable only if they are not specific within the region. The underlying general idea is that the more specific the measure is, the less difficult it is to justify it in terms of positive externalities produced (which, as seen above, is controversial in economic terms).

It is clear that regional subsidies are not as such targeted to specific enterprises operating in a certain sector or industry.[47]

Why then are regional subsidies specific? The tentative answer is that, quite probably, the rationale is based, as Benitah has suggested, on a simple idea

[43] C Quigley and AM Collins, *EC State Aid Law and Policy* (Oxford: Hart Publishing, 2003) 190.

[44] MJ Trebilcock and R Howse, *The Regulation of International Trade* (3rd edn, London: Routledge, 2005) 276–7.

[45] See, eg, MTN.GNG/NG/W/3, para 1.1(b) and MTN.GNG/NG10/W/4, pp 10, 11 and 12.

[46] Article 8.1(a) of the SCM.

[47] Moreover, this category of aid is a good example of those measures that are not necessarily addressed at domestic undertakings. Systems of regional aid are often designed to provide incentives for domestic and foreign undertakings alike in order to relocate in the disadvantaged regions.

of distortion.[48] A regional subsidy would artificially interfere with the allocation of resources shifting them between regions.

What has to be asked is whether the underlying idea is also that of comparative advantage and specialization of countries/regions. However, Trebilcock and Howse also noted that because of an 'unfortunate semantic legacy' from Ricardo's analysis we normally talk of comparative advantage of countries/regions. In fact we should be talking of firms.[49] It seems therefore that this argument could be relevant only if there is a correspondence between region and industry.

Finally, reference should be made to another distinction which is clearly founded on a political choice, indeed (following our analysis in chapters 9 and 10) on a principle of constitutional order. We are alluding to the distinction between local measures with local impact on the one side (which should not be specific) and central measures with local impact on the other side (which should be specific).[50]

Specificity, objective requirements and discretionality

According to Article 2.1(b) of the SCM, there is no specificity if the granting authority or the legislation establishes objective criteria or conditions on the eligibility for, and the amount of, the subsidy. These criteria and conditions must be 'objective', which means 'neutral, which do not favour certain enterprises over others, and which are economic in nature and horizontal in application, such as the number of employees or size of enterprise'. Moreover, they must be 'clearly spelled out in law, regulation, or other official document, so as to be capable of verification', their eligibility must be automatic and they must be strictly adhered to.

A similar conclusion is generally reached in the EC. When aid is granted in accordance with objective, neutral and automatic criteria there is no specificity. Conversely, both legal systems converge in considering that the discretional grant of financial support satisfies the requirement of specificity.[51]

An interesting application of the objective criteria set forth above concerns the support for *Small and Medium Sized Enterprises* (SMEs).

The controversy around the specificity of these measures is proved by the fact that, while in the WTO they are not specific, they are deemed to be so in the EC.

[48] M Benitah, *The Law of Subsidies under the GATT/WTO System* (The Hague: Kluwer Law International, 2001) 260.

[49] MJ Trebilcock and R Howse, *The Regulation of International Trade* (3rd edn, London: Routledge, 2005) 3–4.

[50] cf K Bacon, 'State Aids and General Measures' (1997) Yearbook of European Law 269, 293; M Benitah, *The Law of Subsidies under the GATT/WTO System* (The Hague: Kluwer Law International, 2001) 260; FG Wishlade, *Regional State Aid and Competition Policy in the European Union* (London: Kluwer, 2002) chapter 1.

[51] The case-law on the point is vast. A classic authority in this regard is Case C-256/97 *DMT*, para 27; see also, eg, Cases T-346–348/99 *Territorio Histórico de Álava*, para 51; Cases T-269/99, T-271–272/99 *Territorio Histórico de Guipúzcoa*, para 55.

Applying the criteria under Article 2.1(b) of the SCM, and considering in particular the reference to the number of employees and the size of the enterprise, Adamantopoulos and Pereyra-Friedrichsen correctly conclude that financial assistance to SMEs would not be specific whereas it would be so, although it could be authorized if it meets certain conditions, in the EC.[52]

Interestingly, the Court of Justice was confronted with the argument that a measure favouring *inter alia* SMEs was not specific because it satisfied the criteria of objectivity of the SCM Agreement.

Underlining the irrelevance of WTO-law-based definitions, the Court roundly rejected the argument: 'the fact that the contested aid would not be considered to be a "specific subsidy" under the Agreement on Subsidies cannot reduce the scope of the definition of aid under Article [87(1)EC].'[53] The fact that the measure provides for objective criteria of eligibility does not preclude its classification as specific. The conclusion will be that we are not confronted with an individual aid but rather with an aid scheme or a general aid.[54] It therefore seems that, at least in this regard, EC law is stricter than WTO law.

The EC position does however have its detractors. Schön, for example, criticized the conclusion that measures targeted at SMEs should be specific since it is not based on the activity of the undertakings but rather on their size.[55] Clearly, this issue is independent from the fact that, due to their special role in the economy and their particular problems, aid to SMEs may receive special treatment when justifications are concerned.

Admittedly, the *explanation* of the classification of these measures as specific remains open. Indeed no recognizable economic foundation can be found. Similarly, there does not seem to be any noticeable *pragmatic* or *political* justification, apart from the will to subject these measures to the scrutiny of EC State aid law. This is a good example of the *discretional* element of the specificity assessment—and its *expansiveness*—coming through prominently.

De facto *specificity*

The most interesting step of the test is that of *de facto* specificity which is established when, notwithstanding the appearance of being generally available, the measure at issue is in fact limited to certain enterprises. Thus the *de facto* test does

[52] K Adamantopoulos and MJ Pereyra-Friedrichsen, *EU Anti-Subsidy Law and Practice* (1st edn, Pembridge: Palladian Law, 2001) 109. It is also interesting to speculate that, quite probably, under the SCM aid to large and very large undertakings is more likely to qualify as *de facto* specific than aid to SMEs. Everything however seems to depend on the structure of the market.

[53] See C-351/98 *Spain v Commission*, para 44 and Case C-409/00 *Spain v Commission*, para 56.

[54] Case C-409/00 *Spain v Commission*, para 49.

[55] W Schön, 'Taxation and State Aid Law in the European Union' (1999) Common Market Law Review 910, 929.

not focus on the legislation *per se* but on the actual disbursements made on the basis of that legislation. Article 2.1 (c) of the SCM provides that:

> if, notwithstanding any appearance of non-specificity resulting from the application of the principles laid down in subparagraphs (a) and (b), there are reasons to believe that the subsidy may in fact be specific, other factors may be considered. Such factors are: the use of a subsidy programme by a limited number of certain enterprises, the predominant use by certain enterprises, the granting of disproportionately large amounts of subsidy to certain enterprises, and the manner in which discretion has been exercised by the granting authority in the decision to grant a subsidy. In applying this subparagraph, account shall be taken of the extent of diversification of economic activities within the jurisdiction of the granting authority, as well as of the length of time during which the subsidy programme has been in operation.

A footnote to this indent reads that particular consideration will be given to 'information on the frequency with which applications for a subsidy are refused or approved and the reasons for such decisions'.

This test, which esssentially also applies in EC law,[56] is often considered as a good example of the expansive potential of the concept of specificity. This may well be true, considering in particular the degree of flexibility required by this factual assessment.

Difficulty of distinguishing between specific and generic measures

One of the most significant difficulties of the specificity analysis, and in particular of *de facto* specificity, is that it is sometimes quite difficult to determine whether the measure should be regarded as a *general measure* (which is not a State aid or a subsidy) or as a *specific measure* (which may be a State aid or a subsidy). To put it another way: how general is general? Or, conversely, how specific is specific?

This difficulty depends on the fact that virtually all measures have a differential impact and affect the position of some subjects more than others.

In both EC and WTO law, however, the existence of a differential impact, which is an inherent feature of almost all measures, does not suffice to lead to the conclusion that the measure under scrutiny is specific. Thus the Commission has repeatedly made it clear that the fact that some firms or sectors benefit more than others from some measures does not necessarily mean that they involve State aid. One of the classic examples concerns measures targeted at labour or capital factor. Measures to reduce labour taxation for all firms have a relatively greater effect for labour-intensive industries, while the reduction of taxation on capital tends to favour capital-intensive industries. In neither cases do such measure constitute State aid.[57]

[56] C Ahlborn and C Berg, 'Can State Aid Control Learn from Antitrust? The Need for Greater Role for Competition Analysis under the State Aid rules' in A Biondi, P Eeckhout, and J Flynn (eds), *The Law of State Aid in the European Union* (Oxford: Oxford University Press, 2004) 41, 51–4; GM Roberti, *Gli aiuti di Stato nel diritto comunitario* (Padova, CEDAM, 1997) 201.

[57] See 1998 Notice on Direct Taxation, para 14; OECD, *Competition Policy in Subsidies and State Aid*, Competition Policy Roundtable, DAFFE/CLP (2001) 24, OECD, Paris, 157.

How to distinguish then?

We have seen that the existence of a *differential impact* is not sufficient to conclude that the relevant measure is specific.

The big interpretative issue is thus how to distinguish between those general measures whose differential impact is accepted as an inherent feature, and those measures that, because of their difference in treatment, are sufficiently specific to satisfy the test.[58]

The proposition is that various elements have to be taken into account in the analysis. We can now proceed to indicate those elements that should be considered in order to determine whether a measure is *de facto* specific or is rather general. It seems that the relevant analysis requires two cumulative steps.

The first step, which operates at an objective level, is the *degree of the impact* of the measure. In other words, the *more concentrated* the *effect* of the measure is, the *easier* it will be to find it as *specific*.[59]

Clearly, the difficulty of this step is *where* to draw the line. When does a differential impact, which, as we have shown, is present in virtually any measure, become so significant that the measure should be considered as specific? Conversely, when is that impact not indicative and should not defeat the general availability of the measure? Whilst it is clear that it is not possible to provide arithmetically well-defined ceilings, the foregone conclusion is that it is mainly a case-by-case assessment. In this regard, valuable guidance may be offered by the consolidation of the relevant practice and case-law.

The second step, which operates at a subjective level, is the assessment of the *intent* or objective of the measure. Although we are considering the factual impact of the measure, it is generally recognized that the consideration of this subjective element may play an important role.[60]

The consideration of the intent of the measure may however be subject to two counter-arguments.

On the one hand, it may be correctly underlined that, insofar as we are talking of a *de facto*, ie the factual, objective impact of the measure, the reference to its intent or its objective could seem to be extraneous and, in any event, more appropriate when the *de jure* analysis is carried out which is focused on the explicit purpose of the measure.

[58] There are various controversial examples in the case-law. In some cases, the Court found that an apparently general scheme in fact produced a partial effect: see, eg, Cases 6 and 11/69 *Commission v France*; Case 203/82 *Commission v Italy*. In WTO law, it is interesting to refer to the Panel, *US—Softwood Lumber IV* and to the interesting definition of industry therein.

[59] See C Ahlborn and C Berg, 'Can State Aid Control Learn from Antitrust? The Need for Greater Role for Competition Analysis under the State Aid rules' in A Biondi, P Eeckhout, and J Flynn (eds), *The Law of State Aid in the European Union* (Oxford: Oxford University Press, 2004) 41, 51.

[60] See, eg, MJ Trebilcock and R Howse, *The Regulation of International Trade* (3rd edn, London: Routledge, 2005) 266–8; GM Roberti, *Gli aiuti di Stato nel diritto comunitario* (Padova, CEDAM, 1997) 200.

Although what matters in the context of a *de facto* assessment is whether, irrespective of its intent, a given measure does produce a differential impact such as to favour only certain undertakings or industries, it cannot be denied that the examination of the *more* or *less clearly stated objective* of the measure may be a useful additional element to consider when a complex assessment such as that of *de facto* specificity has to be carried out. In this regard, it is interesting to refer to the assessment made by the Appellate Body in *Japan—Taxes II* in order to determine whether a differential in internal taxation (under Article III:2 of the GATT) was such 'so as to afford protection'. The Appellate Body noted that:

> although it is true that the aim of a measure may not be easily ascertained, nevertheless its protective application can most often be discerned from the design, the architecture, and the revealing structure of the measure.

Apart from being useful in determining whether there is a derogation from the norm, and hence an advantage, in the first place, these criteria can certainly be looked at when the intent of a measure is to be analysed to establish specificity.[61]

On the other hand, what should be avoided—the *leit motif* of the book—is the risk of conflating scope and justification.

This is indeed a recurring issue, and a recurrent risk, at virtually all levels of the analysis of State aid and subsidy rules. We have already seen in the context of the advantage analysis the almost *natural attraction* to consider immediately the objective of the measure and justify it.

In sum, the examination of the criteria considered in the *de facto* analysis has once again shown us that specificity is a *flexible* instrument. *Political* and *discretional* considerations seem to be paramount with the result that the test may well be regarded as *blunt* and at the same time *uncertain* in its outcomes.

One final, interesting issue may be raised. We have seen that the *de facto* analysis is characterized by an almost inherent unstableness. What should the interpreter (ie a reviewing administrative or judicial body) do if, after carrying out the previous analysis and assessing the above mentioned factors, it still has doubts with respect to the generality or specificity of the measure?

Considering that the burden of proving that an aid or a subsidy is specific is always borne by the complainant or the proceeding national or supranational authority, it seems fair to conclude that, in case of doubt, the measure should be regarded as general. Specificity is one of the constituent elements of the definition of State aid and, generally speaking, also of subsidy (see however Article 1.2 of the SCM). This conclusion is in line with the consideration that the classification of a government measure of financial support as State aid or as subsidy may produce

[61] As we have said, although the two levels of analysis are conceptually different, there is certainly some degree of overlap. See chapter 10, section I.B.

significant consequences in terms of constraint of governmental prerogatives and/or reaction against private undertakings.

In the EC, it has been suggested that a different conclusion should be reached from a procedural point of view.

Relying on the duty of cooperation of Member States under Article 10 of the EC, Roberti has argued that, in case of doubt as to whether the measure is a State aid, the Member State should notify the measure to the Commission and wait for its implementation.[62] It is interesting to ask whether the same conclusion could be reached in the WTO and its different procedural and institutional framework. Transparency considerations may favour a positive answer. An obstacle to such a conclusion may however derive from the risk that the notification might signal to the other Members the existence of a possible subsidy and trigger unilateral defensive actions against the beneficiary industry. Good policy and *real politik* may lead to opposite directions.

IV. Conclusions

The specificity criterion has a mixed rationale. It is partly based on an economic grounding, partly on pragmatic and political considerations. To sum it up, it has been suggested that this is a political economy rationale.

The ambiguity of the rationale results in the flexibility of operation of the specificity test with the end result that the latter is not sufficiently 'specific'.

In both systems the filter is not really selective and the net is in some cases cast very wide. With regard to WTO law, and in particular to the test of *de facto* specificity, it has been wittily suggested that 'these multiple tests demonstrate the will of the negotiations to include *a priori* as many subsidies as possible under the term "specific"'.[63] This intention is readily captured by Member States in their domestic application of CV duties.[64]

[62] GM Roberti, *Gli aiuti di Stato nel diritto comunitario* (Padova, CEDAM, 1997) 201. It is interesting to ask whether this conclusion is in contrast with the recent reaffirmation by the Court in Case C-71/04 *Xunta de Galicia* that the concepts of aid under Article 87(1) of the EC and Article 88(3) of the EC are identical. For a commentary, and a positive assessment, on the point see CD Ehlermann and A Vallery, 'Giving Meaning to the Condition of Effect on Trade: The Court's Judgment in Xunta de Galicia, a Missed Opportunity?' (2005) European State Aid Law Quarterly, 709, 710.

The more extensive conclusion, however, seems to be in line with the more recent case-law on parafiscal charges financing State aid. If they are held to constitute an 'integral part' of the aid, they should be notified together with aid itself. See, eg, Joined Cases C-261/01 and C-262/02 *Van Calster and Others*, para 51. This case-law is analysed in chapter 5. The same consideration could apply for the status of tax measures, and in particular the connection between tax liability and exception, in cases such as Case C-526/04 *Boiron*.

[63] M Matsushita, TJ Schoenbaum, and PC Mavroidis, *The World Trade Organization—Law, Practice, and Policy* (1st edn, Oxford: Oxford University Press, 2003) 271.

[64] Thus, eg, the EC institutions tend to adopt a very broad interpretation of the notion of specificity: see I Van Bael, and JF Bellis, *Anti-dumping and other Trade Protection Laws of the EC*, (Brussels: Kluwer Law International, 2004) 541.

Although in some cases the interpretations in WTO and EC law may be different, a similar impression derives from the analysis of the idea of specificity in EC law. This has been summed up neatly by Advocate General Roemer and his *negative* formulation that the requirement of specificity applies to any measure that does not apply generally to all undertakings in a Member State.[65]

[65] Case 6 and 11/69 *Commission v France*, p 552.

PART V

DISTORTION OF COMPETITION

It is the ability to produce at lower cost that constitutes the competitive advantage subsidy recipients enjoy.[1]

I believe you're doing me wrong and now I know
I believe you're doing me wrong and now I know
'Cause the harder I work the faster my money goes[2]

[1] R Diamond, 'Privatization and the Definition of Subsidy: A Critical Study of Appellate Body Texturalism' (2008) JIEL 649, 654.

[2] From the blues song *Shake, rattle and roll* written by CE Calhoun in 1954 and recorded by Elvis Presley in 1955. The lyrics quoted refer to Mr Presley's version.

Overview

Part V focuses on the negative impact that subsidies may have on the international economy, and particularly on the *standards* used to express it.

As Part III underlined, this impact depends on the advantage that the governmental conduct at issue, be it economic or not, may confer. However, whereas the existence of an economic advantage simply signals the *potential* of a negative impact on the marketplace, the 'impact standards' are specifically aimed at capturing these negative effects.

In chapter 2 we have identified two possible types of negative externalities subsidies may produce, in terms of *reduced* (of particularly *expected*) *market access* and *distortion of the competitive process*. The former embraces a trade perspective, the latter a competition one. Together with broader political economy arguments (mainly protectionist reactions and subsidy emulations), these two specific externalities provides support to the need to implement an international system of subsidy control.

It is now inevitable that the 'impact standards' of subsidies closely follow these two negative effects. It is however felt that, while the trade effect (impairment of market access) still examines subsidies at a rather general and superficial level, it is the interference with the competitive process that is really able to identify the specific, and deeper, impact of subsidies. This has led to the conclusion that not only EC State aid but also WTO subsidy laws should be properly construed as 'competition regulation'. In this case, both the emphasis and operation of the analysis is different from the trade one, being concentrated on the actual effects of the measure on the working of competition in the relevant market.

In short, the submission is that the definition of sibsidy (and its regulation) should *mainly* focus on the *competitive* advantage the latter may grant. What chapter 14 proposes to do is to assess WTO and EC law, and in particular the relevant subsidy impact standards, through this lens.

14

The distortion of competition

This chapter analyses the 'impact standards' in WTO subsidy and EC State aid rules. 'Impact standards' are those elements of the definition of subsidy (or State aid) that identify the negative effects produced by the measure.

Building on the findings on the objectives of subsidy control outlined in chapter 2, ie the protection of market access and of competition, the first section analyses the impact subsidies may have on the competitive process. This is arguably the deepest and most specific concern of subsidy rules, and should hence be properly reflected in the 'impact standards' of the relevant definitions of subsidy.

This broad analysis leads to the core of the chapter where the current standards in the EC and WTO are examined and critically evaluated. Among the various findings, we advocate a trend from a 'trade' to a 'competition' perspective'. The chapter is closed with few words of conclusion.

I. Subsidies from market access to distortion of competition

Subsidies can be looked at from a *trade* perspective, notably in terms of their impact on market access of (competing and foreign) non-subsidized products. At a deeper level of analysis, subsidies may interfere with the conduct of economic operators, distorting the competitive relationship between (subsidy) beneficiaries and their rivals.[1] Consequently, subsidization is a natural subject of *competition* discourse.[2]

What the present section attempts to do is to shift from 'trade' to 'competition' discourse, and assess under what conditions subsidies may negatively impact the competitive process.

A. How can subsidies distort competition?

The answer to this question comes from a basic economics lesson, and is succintly conveyed in the quote put at the beginning of this Part: 'It is the ability

[1] See chapter 2, section II.B.

[2] The broader 'welfare perspective', which takes into account of the positive effects that subsidies often pursue, is not considered here since we now focus only on the problems subsidies may pose to the working of competition.

to produce at lower cost that constitutes the competitive advantage subsidy recipients enjoy'.[3]

The impact of subsidies on competition

Subsidies may distort competition. Chapter 2 argued that this is the reading that gives full shape to the negative externalities caused by subsidies. At the same time, this reading provides a workable yardstick with which to determine whether they should be objectionable.

In the context of countervailing duty actions, this distortion of competition has been held to create an 'entitlement' for the harmed competing industry.[4] Diamond lucidly explains this impact:

> [f]or a payment to have this effect, it must lead the [subsidized] firm either to increase the quantity of goods offered or to decrease the price it charges in [foreign] market[s]. Because the recipient firm will produce until marginal revenue equals marginal cost, a payment will only have such a detrimental impact if it either decreases the marginal cost of the foreign producer or increases its marginal revenue. Unless this occurs, the government payment may increase the profits of the foreign firm, but no need for a countervailing duty will exist.[5]

The economic proposition is clear and of general application, even beyond the countervailing duty scenario. Since an efficient firm will produce only until marginal revenue *equals* marginal costs, we cannot talk of any distortion, unless the

[3] R Diamond, 'Privatization and the Definition of Subsidy: A Critical Study of Appellate Body Texturalism' (2008) JIEL 649, 654.

4 The 'entitlement' language has first been used by CJ Goetz, L Granet, and WF Schwartz, 'The Meaning of "Subsidy" and "Injury" in the Countervailing Duty Law' (1986) International Review of Law and Economics 17, 18–19. It is useful to quote the relevant passage *in extenso*: 'We assume that American firms are entitled to that domestic market outcome which would have resulted from a "fair", competitive process, by which is meant one which has not been "manipulated" by foreign government subsidization. The idea then is to restore competition in the American market to its "but for" state by neutralizing the effect of the subsidy'.

The 'entitlement rationale' of countervailing duties has been developed by R Diamond, 'Economic Foundations of Countervailing Duty Law' (1989) Virginia Law Journal of International Law, 767, id, 'A Search for Economic and Financial Principles in the Administration of United States Countervailing Duty Law' (1989) Law and Policy in International Business, 507, and criticized by AO Sykes, 'Second-Best Countervailing Duty Policy: A Critique of the Entitlement Approach' (1989) Law and Policy in International Business 669.

More recently, it has been reinstated in the context of the 'privatization cases' by G Grossman and PC Mavrodis, 'Here Today? Gone Tomorrow?' in H Horn and PC Mavroidis (eds), *The WTO Case Law of 2001* (Cambridge: Cambridge University Press, 2003) 170; id, 'Recurring Misunderstandings of Non Recurring Subsidies' in H Horn and PC Mavroidis (eds), *The WTO Case Law of 2002* (Cambridge: Cambridge University Press, 2005) 78, and by its main developer: R Diamond, 'Privatization and the Definition of Subsidy: A Critical Study of Appellate Body Texturalism' (2008) Journal of International Economic Law 649. cf also MJ Trebilcock and R Howse, *The Regulation of International Trade* (3rd edn, London: Routledge, 2005) 287–8.

[5] R Diamond, 'Economic Foundations of Countervailing Duty Law' (1989) Virginia Law Journal of International Law, 767, 784–5.

subsidy favourably interferes with one of these two variables.[6] The measure should either *reduce* the marginal cost of the recipient ('cost-saving subsidy'), or *increase* its marginal revenue ('revenue-increasing subsidy'). It is *only* this impact on the determinants of an efficient firm's conduct that can cause a change of the recipient's behaviour and eventually adversely affect the position of competitors—in short, distort competition.

Any improvement in the financial position of the recipient that simply enhances it with respect to the situation before but does not produce the said impact cannot interfere with the behaviour of the recipient and hence with competition.[7] It will just increase the latter's wealth but this does not necessarily mean that it will change its pattern of conduct, ie its production decisions.[8] In other words, an increase in wealth or financial strength cannot be equated, *sic et simpliciter*, to distortion of the competitive process.[9]

The clear standard forged by Beviglia-Zampetti brings us to another level of understanding:

> What would be important to prove is that the subsidy has indeed provided the recipient firm or firms with an artificial competitive advantage, affecting its cost and revenue structures, and that this action has distorted the normal competitive process, resulting in injury to the domestic industry.[10]

This passage highlights the two 'causal' steps that should be satisfied to prove that the subsidy actually distorts competition. First, we should have a measure that affects the economic position of the recipient, and in particular its production decisions, which usually happens when marginal costs are lowered. Secondly, this effect should cause a harm to competing producers.[11]

[6] The concepts of marginal cost and marginal revenue refer respectively to an additional increase in cost and revenue for an increase of an activity.

[7] C Ahlborn and C Berg, 'Can State Aid Control Learn from Antitrust? The Need for Greater Role for Competition Analysis under the State Aid rules' in A Biondi, P Eeckhout, and J Flynn (eds), *The Law of State Aid in the European Union* (Oxford: Oxford University Press, 2004) 41, 49–50.

[8] This argument is clearly outlined by G Grossman and PC Mavroidis, 'Here Today? Gone Tomorrow?' in H Horn and PC Mavroidis (eds), *The WTO Case Law of 2001* (Cambridge: Cambridge University Press, 2003) 170, 186–7; and R Diamond, 'Privatization and the Definition of Subsidy: A Critical Study of Appellate Body Texturalism' (2008) Journal of International Economic Law 649, 655 and 666–9.

[9] This analysis is shared also by economists writing with respect to the EC State aid context. See D Neven and V Verouden, 'Towards a More Refined Economic Approach in State Aid Control' in W Mederer, N Pesaresi, and M Van Hoof (eds), *EU Competition Law—Volume IV: State Aid* (Leuven: Claeys and Casteels, 2008) Book 1, Part I, chapter 4.

[10] A Beviglia Zampetti, 'The Uruguay Round Agreement on Subsidies—A Forward-Looking Assessment' (1996) Journal of World Trade 5, 24. For a similar analysis in the EC context, see P Papandropoulos, R Nitsche, B van de Walle de Ghelcke, D Waelbroeck, J Derenne, F Louis, M Merola, P Ibañez Colomo, J De Beys, and J Bousin, 'Selectivity, Economic Advantage, Distortion of Competition and Effect on Trade' in J Derenne and M Merola (eds), *Economic Analysis of State Aid Rules—Contributions and Limits* (Berlin: Lexxion, 2007) 119, 147–9.

[11] The importance of 'causality' and of these two steps in the context of the determination of a damage to competing industry has been recently clarified by R Diamond, 'Privatization and the

Mainly through their 'impact standards' subsidy definitions should aim to control interventions that produce this effect. What eventually has to be ensured is that, through public subsidization, *more, or at least equally, efficient* undertakings are not *damaged* to the benefit of often *less*, and sometimes equally, *efficient* ones.[12]

Three remarks should be made.

First, the distortive character of subsidies should be assessed against 'a pragmatic notion of "normal competition" or the "normal competitive process"'[13] or, to put it another way, 'workable competition'.[14] Although these benchmarks duly recognize that conditions of perfect competition are improbable, they can be distanced from the blurry concept of 'fair competition' which is often used to justify subsidy control, and in particular unilateral remedies. The notion of 'fair' competition is the evocative, more voiced than explained, mantra of lobbying industries seeking protection. The problems come when it is necessary to give some substance to this idea and make it operational.[15] In this respect, the concepts of 'normal' or 'workable' competition combine realism with a solid anchorage to theory. Most importantly, they give full meaning to a discipline that should counteract the negative effects of subsidies *on* (normal) competition, and not protect less efficient operators *from* (normal) competition.[16]

Secondly, following the important distinction between scope and justification, which has accompanied us throughout the book, it can be argued that, in terms of 'welfare standards', what should matter at the level of the 'impact standards' is only the consideration of the 'effects on rivals' caused by the subsidy. If the 'mischief' of subsidy laws is the distortion of competition, it is this factor, and this factor only, that should trigger their application. That said, if subsidy regulation should also consider other positive (or indeed negative) effects and balance them with the distortion of competition, this should be done in a different 'justification' context, when the overall impact and significance of the intervention is considered, possibly applying a more or less broad 'total welfare' approach. From both a conceptual and practical perspective, this distinction seems possible.[17]

Definition of Subsidy: A Critical Study of Appellate Body Texturalism' (2008) Journal of International Economic Law 649, 666–9.

[12] The idea of the inevitability of this damage could not be conveyed better than in the rhymes of the song quoted at the beginning. 'I believe you're doing me wrong and now I know 'cause the harder I work the faster my money goes.'

[13] A Beviglia Zampetti, 'The Uruguay Round Agreement on Subsidies—A Forward-Looking Assessment' (1996) Journal of World Trade 5, 24.

[14] R Whish, *Competition Law* (6th edn, Oxford: Oxford University Press, 2008) chapter 1.

[15] A comprehensive critical overview of the 'fairness rationales' of countervailing duty laws is made by MJ Trebilcock and R Howse, *The Regulation of International Trade* (3rd edn, London: Routledge, 2005) 283–5. See also RA Cass and RD Boltuck, 'Antidumping and Countervaling-Duty Law: The Mirage of Equitable International Competition' in JN Bhagwati and RE Hudec, *Fair Trade and Harmonization—Prerequisites for Free Trade?, Vol 2: Legal Analysis* (Cambridge MA: MIT Press, 1996).

[16] Thus substantially, and incorrectly, operating as a generous safeguard relief.

[17] Despite differences in emphasis, this is substantially confirmed by a review of the (mostly economic) literature. For some references see n 22 below.

Thirdly, subsidies should matter only if they produce distortions or externalities 'across the border'.[18] In other words, public intervention which does not produce an impact beyond the domestic dimension does not raise concerns from an international perspective.[19] If this 'across the border' effect is inherent in export subsidies, the proof of an externality across the border may be more demanding for domestic subsidies. One factor that should be taken into account is that, in an increasingly liberalized and globalized economy, it is easier for a public subsidy—and indeed any public or private economic action—to produce a distortion across the border. This is simply the result of the widening and integration of markets. Further, the distorting effect of subsidies is magnified as other governmental distortions are eliminated. Lastly, it should not be overlooked that policy objectives such as the need to avoid 'unfair' competition between rich and poor countries or the creation or strengthening of an integrated market, like the EC internal market, may make it easier to find international spill-overs.[20]

Assessment of the impact

There is a growing economic literature on the topic, which started in the US[21] and is steadily developing in Europe too.[22]

[18] T Besley and P Seabright, 'The Effects and Policy Implications of State Aids to Industry: An Economic Analysis' (1999) Economic Policy 15, 21; HW Friederiszick, LH Röller, and V Verouden, *European State Aid Control: An Economic Framework*, in Bucirossi (ed) *Handbook of Antitrust Economics* (Cambridge MA: MIT Press, 2008) 625, 638–41, 22; JH Jackson, *The World Trading System—Law and Policy of International Economic Relations* (2nd edn, Cambridge Massachussetts: MIT Press, 1997) 299; J Pelkmans, *European Integration—Methods and Economic Analysis* (2nd edn, London: FT-Prentice Hall, 2001) 241.

[19] There are rare cases of domestic control of public subsidies where the distortions under scrutiny are limited to the boundaries of the national jurisdiction. Denmark is a good example. See OECD, *Competition Policy in Subsidies and State Aid*, Competition Policy Roundtable, DAFFE/CLP (2001) 24, OECD, Paris, 21–2, and 93–124; P Crocioni, 'Can State Aid Policy Become more Economic-Friendly?' (2006) World Competition, 89. More generally, there is an increasing awareness on the national role in the design and control of any public subsidies. The UK represents a good example of this. Significant research has been commissioned at governmental level and various reports issued. See, eg, J Garcia and D Neven, 'Identification of Sensitive Sectors in which State Aid may have Significant Distorting Effects', Report for the HM Treasury, UK, 2004; OFT, *Public Subsidies—A Report by the Office of Fair Trading*, OFT750: London (2004) including the annexed report of Frontier Economics, *The Effects of Public Subsidies on Competition*; OFT, *European State Aid Control*, OFT821: London (2005).

At least part of the rationale for this interest has been conveyed by John Vickers, a former director the OFT, when he noted that 'scrutiny should begin at home'. See J Vickers, 'State Aid and Distortion of Competition', Paper for the State Aid Conference organized by the UK Presidency on 14 July 2005, available at <http://www.oft.gov.uk>.

[20] See A Evans, *European Community Law of State Aid* (Oxford: Clarendon Press, 1997) 80 and 105–6; HW Friederiszick, LH Röller, and V Verouden, *European State Aid Control: An Economic Framework*, in Bucirossi (ed) *Handbook of Antitrust Economics* (Cambridge MA: MIT Press, 2008) 625, 641.

[21] In addition to those cited in the present section, several references can be found in chapter 2, section II.B.

[22] Three works are, in the author's view, particularly useful. The first is the collection of papers of a conference held at the College of Europe in Bruges in September 2006. See J Derenne and M Merola (eds), *Economic Analysis of State Aid Rules—Contributions and Limits* (Berlin: Lexxion, 2007).

The assessment of the impact of subsidies may be particularly complex. Two main dimensions need to be considered: the *characteristics of the subsidy* itself and of the *affected markets*.

The subsidy characteristics refer to the type and amount of the measure of financial support and in particular to its impact on the cost/revenue structure of the recipient. In this regard, reference is generally made to *marginal costs* but 'measuring marginal costs is a notoriously difficult exercise, exacting in its data demands and inherently error-prone'.[23] Consequently, the proxy of variable costs is often used, but in many cases this does not yield accurate results either. Like marginal costs, variable costs, such as labour and raw materials, directly affect pricing and output (as well as entry and exit) decisions of firms since these depend on the level of production. It is not only variable costs that should be taken into account however. Although to a lesser degree, a reduction of fixed costs, which do not depend on output, may also distort competition because it may enable the firm to continue in the market.[24]

The assessment of market characteristics is not easy either. First, a crucial prerequisite of the market analysis is the *definition* of the *relevant* product and geographical *market*. Although inspiration can be drawn from other areas of the law, such as antitrust, the economic scenario is different in the case of subsidies and adjustments should be made. Once the market has been defined, a necessary, but not sufficient, prerequisite for the subsidy to be liable to produce a distortion to competition is that the market is neither monopolistic nor perfectly competitive, which is often the case since most of the markets tend to show oligopolistic tendencies.

The second is a paper co-authored by the former chief-economist of DG Competition that has become something of a classic: HW Friederiszick, LH Röller, and V Verouden, *European State Aid Control: An Economic Framework*, in Bucirossi (ed), Handbook of Antitrust Economics (Cambridge MA: MIT Press, 2008) 625. Finally, the third is a chapter co-authored by the current chief-economist of DG Competition. See D Neven and V Verouden, 'Towards a More Refined Economic Approach in State Aid Control' in W Mederer, N Pesaresi, and M Van Hoof (eds), EU Competition Law—Volume IV: State Aid (Leuven: Claeys and Casteels, 2008) Book 1, Part I, chapter 4.

There are also numerous studies commissioned by authorities dealing with subsidy issues. See, eg, R Nitsche and P Heidhues, *Study on Methods to Analyse the Impact of State Aid on Competition*, Report prepared for the European Commission, Directorate General for Economics and Financial Affairs (Final Report ECFIN/R/2004/004): Bruxelles (2005); J Garcia and D Neven, 'Identification of Sensitive Sectors in which State Aid may have Significant Distorting Effects', Report for the HM Treasury, UK, 2004; J Fingleton, F Ruance, V Ryan, 'Market Definition and State Aid Control' in European Commission (Directorate General for Economic and Financial Affairs) *'State Aid and the Single Market', European Economy—Report and Studies* (1999); T Besley and P Seabright, 'The Effects and Policy Implications of State Aids to Industry: An Economic Analysis' (1999) Economic Policy 15 (which draws on a study for the Commission's DG Social Cohesion).

[23] MJ Trebilcock and R Howse, *The Regulation of International Trade* (3rd edn, London: Routledge, 2005) 287.

[24] Fixed costs (eg factory, machinery) do not affect pricing and output decisions but they have an influence on entry decision, and, in the long run, may act on exit decisions (unless they are 'sunk'). To complicate things further, it is often difficult to distinguish between variable and fixed costs, and to identify whether a subsidy will affect fixed or variable costs.

Various factors may then determine the impact of the subsidy on competition, including the size of the recipient, market shares and concentration ratios, barriers to entry, the degree of product differentiation, how far it complements neighbouring markets, the segmentation of national markets, the tradability of the goods or services and impact on location choices, the process leading to the grant.

Two important economic circumstances stand out. First, a significant factor to consider is whether the beneficiary enjoys *market power*, or may obtain it as a consequence of the subsidy.[25] Secondly, a correct approach to the idea of distortion of competition, and its underlying concept of causality, requires that a subsidy can be determined to have caused the said harm only if that production decision would not have occurred *but* for the subsidy. This requires a *counterfactual* analysis[26] which may be particularly exacting but is in principle necessary if one wants to avoid attributing to the measure at issue an event which would have taken place anyway and is in fact attributable to another factor.

Two case-studies on subsidies and locational competition

In their paper on the economics of EC State aid, Friederiszick, Röller and Verouden set forth four types of distortions of competition that State aid may cause.[27] The first three can easily fit the previous analysis: (i) reducing effective competition by supporting inefficient production; ii) reducing effective competition by distorting dynamic incentives; iii) reducing effective competition by increasing market power.

The fourth reveals a new perspective: distorting production and location decisions among countries. Whereas the first three 'theories of harm' relate to the impact on competition between firms, the last one more specifically refers to the impact of aid on competition between governments. This type of distortion refers to the cases where countries grant subsidies to firms to influence their location decisions. Governments enter into competition between themselves to attract mobile investment.[28]

[25] See, eg, C Osti, 'Di alcuni problemi degli aiuti di Stato' (2006) Mercato Concorrenza Regole 429; D Neven and V Verouden, 'Towards a More Refined Economic Approach in State Aid Control' in W Mederer, N Pesaresi, and M Van Hoof (eds), EU Competition Law—Volume IV: State Aid (Leuven: Claeys and Casteels, 2008) Book 1, Part I, Chapter 4.

[26] A 'comparison between two worlds: one in which the government payment has been made and one in which is has not': R Diamond, 'Economic Foundations of Countervailing Duty Law' (1989) Virginia Law Journal of International Law, 767, 783. For an interesting insight on the complex questions that a 'no subsidy world' may lead to see H Horn and PC Mavroidis, *United States—Preliminary Determination with Respect to Certain Softwood Lumber from Canada: What is a subsidy?* in H Horn and PC Mavroidis, *The WTO Case Law of 2002* (Cambridge: Cambridge University Press, 2005) 220.

[27] HW Friederiszick, LH Röller, and V Verouden, *European State Aid Control: An Economic Framework*, in Bucirossi (ed) *Handbook of Antitrust Economics* (Cambridge MA: MIT Press, 2008) 625, 652–654.

[28] It does not take much to recall that in modern times capital is a mobile resource.

Our understanding of the concept of 'distortion of competition' can be sharpened further with the analysis of two case-studies both relating to situations of 'locational competition'.

The key question for our analysis is whether the incentives that governments may offer to attract investment may constitute subsidies. More specifically, the query is: what is the relation between the concept of 'distortion' of competition outlined above, which focuses on the impact of the intervention on the cost/revenue structure of the recipient and the consequent damage to its competititors, and this 'theory of harm' caused by 'locational incentives'.

Case-study 1: Compensation of regional location costs

The characteristic feature of this case-study is that the measure is intended to specifically compensate a disadvantage faced by a region. Consequently, at least in principle, the amount of the subsidy is merely limited to making up for the relevant location costs.

From a subsidy perspective, the key question is whether financial compensation that *merely* compensates the *costs* for locating in a disadvantaged or, in any event, less attractive area, can distort competition. In other words, in subsidy language, assuming that there is an advantage, and this advantage is specific, does the measure also produce a distortion? This measure will certainly affect the behaviour of the recipient by convincing it to move to that area, or more simply not to abandon it. But, from a competition perspective, *does* this measure produce an impact on the costs of the recipient *so as to alter* its *relationship* with *competitors*? Does it affect the *production*, ie output, *decisions* of the recipient? If the answer to these questions is no, can we then meaningfully talk of any distortion of the competitive process?

Some argue that, insofar as the subsidy merely compensates for the cost of relocating, there would be no distortion.[29] Benitah suggests that this is an example of a sophisticated approach to the concept of distortion, and that no distortion should be found.[30] In particular, if the subsidy covers only fixed (and not variable) costs, there would be no problem since it would not be related to production.[31] Evans takes a more sceptical stance, underlining that 'in most cases it is doubtful whether the disadvantages of an area can be quantified with sufficient accuracy to fix aid at a level which exactly competes for them' and that '[i]n practice, regional aid is

[29] A Beviglia Zampetti, 'The Uruguay Round Agreement on Subsidies—A Forward-Looking Assessment' (1996) Journal of World Trade 5, n 85; M Benitah, *The Law of Subsidies under the GATT/WTO System* (The Hague: Kluwer Law International, 2001) 254; JH Jackson, *The World Trading System—Law and Policy of International Economic Relations* (2nd edn, Cambridge Massachussetts: MIT Press, 1997) 298–9.

[30] M Benitah, *The Law of Subsidies under the GATT/WTO System* (The Hague: Kluwer Law International, 2001) 254.

[31] CJ Goetz, L Granet, and WF Schwartz, 'The Meaning of "Subsidy" and "Injury" in the Countervailing Duty Law' (1986) International Review of Law and Economics 17, 23.

usually set by Member States at so high a level that it provides firms with a positive financial inducement to locate and invest in certain areas'.[32]

These two arguments—the difficulty of quantification (of the disadvantage > cost > subsidy) and the need for amounts higher than mere cost offset to produce an incentive—seem to be crucial. The author would also refer to another, already highlighted, difficulty, that of determining and distinguishing costs. All these uncertainties seem to lead towards a more negative attitude towards the alleged non-distorting effect of this type of subsidy. In short, although a neutral impact may be argued in principle, this conclusion seems to be more difficult to accept in practice.

In the presence of so many uncertainties, there is another fundamental and more general doubt. If accepted, this reasoning—there is no distortion because we merely have a compensation of a cost/disadvantage—could be extended to many other forms of public interventions. This would ultimately lead to the adoption of the 'complex economic' concept of subsidy where the question of whether the measure really confers a benefit depends on a baseline constituted of the whole economic background of the recipient and all its costs/benefits.[33] This way of defining a subsidy—and more crucially its distortion—is conceptually sound but extremely complex. It is not only untenable from an economic perspective, and very difficult to administer, but it would seriously defeat our attempt to disentangle the various externalities of subsidies, and in particular isolate and assess the negative impact of competition. Ultimately, it would risk fully conflating scope and justification which, for the several reasons outlined in this book, is not desirable.

Case-study 2: Mobile investment and location decisions

The analysis now focuses on a case which is partly similar to the previous one, the main difference being that there is no reference to any disadvantage to compensate. Consequently, the incentive is not linked to any costs to offset.

The economic efficiency of this practice is hotly debated. It certainly involves a sophisticated analysis of the possible distortions that it may cause.

On the one side, it has been argued that these incentives would not create any problem in the presence of certain conditions, particularly if they apply in a non-discriminatory manner[34] and there are no barriers to the movement of firms. In the presence of these conditions, there would be no distortion to competition.[35] Locational competition may also tackle institutional rigidities, through desirable

[32] A Evans, *European Community Law of State Aid* (Oxford: Clarendon Press, 1997) 83.

[33] The difficulty of this benchmark has been explained by AO Sykes, 'The Economics of WTO Rules on Subsidies and Countervailing Measures', Chicago John M Olin Law and Economics Working Paper No. 186 (2nd Series), May 2003, 2–3. See chapter 7, section I.A for an analysis.

[34] In other words, they do not discriminate according to nationality or ownership.

[35] OECD, *Competition Policy in Subsidies and State Aid*, Competition Policy Roundtable, DAFFE/CLP (2001) 24, OECD, Paris, 38–41, 170. cf also GC Hufbauer and J Shelton Erb, *Subsidies in International Trade* (Cambridge, Massachusetts: MIT Press, 1984) 105.

'institutional competition' between Member States.[36] Others distinguish 'greenfield', that is 'new', investment from relocation of existing resources.[37] Whereas aid to induce the latter would create negative cross-border externalities, the question would be more open with respect to the former.

The position of the EC is traditionally negative and is concerned that competition between governments might endanger the integrity of the internal market, as well as regional cohesion, and this naturally to the detriment of poorer regions.[38] What is feared is what is perceived as a form of 'unfair' competition between 'haves' and 'have-nots'. Besley and Seabright seem to support the use of aid to attract regional investment and underline the interdependency between efficiency and equity in this regard.[39] Friederiszick, Röller and Verouden however note that this conclusion works only in the presence of certain circumstances, 'when countries are not resource constrained. If this assumption is not fulfilled, 'poor countries will easily be outbid by rich countries.'[40] More generally, they highlight the risks of these incentives in terms of 'inefficient production structure throughout Europe', 'negative spill-overs for other Member States when the good or service is traded' with the possible consequence of 'subsidy races'.[41]

Pausing for a moment, it seems that general political economy considerations seem to connect to, if not supplant, the kind of competition analysis carried out in the previous paragraph, which was strictly based on the micro-economic impact on a recipient's costs. We will return to this at the end to check whether this provisional finding—these are indeed two different notions of 'competition' and hence of 'distortions of competition'—can be confirmed.

With respect to tax competition, which is probably the commonest example of locational competition, Schön highlights that we should talk of *unfair* tax competition in some cases.[42] He notes two elements of the problem, first when the tax does not reflect the true balance between fiscal contribution and public services, and secondly when a foreign investor is influenced to invest capital abroad without having to dispense with public services of high quality at home. What becomes

[36] F Groeteke and K Heine, '"Institutional Rigidities" and European State Aid Control' (2004) European Competition Law Review 322.

[37] J Pelkmans, *European Integration—Methods and Economic Analysis* (2nd edn, London: FT-Prentice Hall, 2001) 242.

[38] OECD, *Competition Policy in Subsidies and State Aid*, Competition Policy Roundtable, DAFFE/CLP (2001) 24, OECD, Paris, 174, where the Commission raises its opposition; A Evans, *European Community Law of State Aid* (Oxford: Clarendon Press, 1997) 82 and 85, who refers to Advocate General Darmon in Case 248/84 *Germany v Commission*, 4031, and to Case 730/79 *Philip Morris*.

[39] T Besley and P Seabright, 'The Effects and Policy Implications of State Aids to Industry: An Economic Analysis' (1999) Economic Policy 15, 36.

[40] HW Friederiszick, LH Röller, and V Verouden, *European State Aid Control: An Economic Framework*, in Bucirossi (ed) *Handbook of Antitrust Economics* (Cambridge MA: MIT Press, 2008) 625, 636.

[41] ibid, 654.

[42] W Schön, 'Taxation and State Aid Law in the European Union' (1999) Common Market Law Review 910.

crucial in these cases is to determine whether the 'harmful tax practice' can *also* amount to a subsidy. Again, if there is a preferential, which means derogatory and selective, regime for foreign companies, there are good grounds for concluding so.[43]

It is very difficult to provide an answer as to whether locational competition can cause distortions of competition, and particularly *what type* of distortions. However, some conclusions will be advanced.

First, a certain degree of competition between countries and regions is an inevitable consequence—indeed a required target—of the idea of trade liberalization itself. Factor mobility, particularly in terms of capital and establishment, should depend on the conditions various jurisdictions offer. Further, the idea that a certain amount of competition between regions may represent a factor of change and be efficiency-enhancing for all has certainly some force.

Secondly, it seems equally uncontroversial to state that there are less reasons to object to the attractiveness which one jurisdiction derives from its *general* tax, labour, environmental regulatory framework.

Thirdly, specific measures, in the sense of both exceptional and non-generally available, makes things woollier as the potential for distortions, and political friction, are higher.

Fourthly, and crucially, what emerges from the various positions is that the debate focuses on the *conditions* (non-discrimination; certain equality in resource endowments among the regions; non-cumulation of benefits) which should be present for locational competition to produce its benefits and not be distortive.

It is clear that the concept of competition that is evoked in the context of locational decisions is 'broader' than that used in our analysis so far. It is more concerned with a macro-economic viewpoint of the correct equilibrium in international economic relations between different countries, rather than to the micro-economic analysis of the specific impact a well-defined tool of intervention may have on the conduct of specific economic operators, and more particularly on their costs and revenues.

That said, we can anticipate our analysis of the 'impact standards' in WTO and EC subsidy laws and assess whether the kind of distortions to competition that locational competition may raise are covered by them.

In general, assuming that locational decisions depend on cost (-revenue) and the incentive has an impact on costs (-revenue), there are no reasons why the subsidy could not be caught by our 'narrower' concept of distortion of competition (the analysis carried out in the context of case-study 1 is instructive from this perspective).

In practice, it very much depends on the rules. The rather precise impact standards of WTO law does not seem to be designed to include the concept of broad

[43] The OECD clearly considers that a tax incentive which discriminate in favour of foreign companies 'distorts the allocation of resources': OECD, *Harmful Tax Competition: An Emerging Global Issues*, Paris (1998).

distortion outlined above. This might be caught only indirectly, as a consequence of the harm produced to competing firms. The outcome may be different in the EC where the briefer but potentially broader wording of the 'distortion of competition' and 'effect on trade' elements may be read to include the distortions caused by locational incentives. It has indeed been seen that EC State aid control itself has largely been explained in terms of a safeguard to 'unfair' competition between governments.

II. Critical interpretation of the standards: from trade to competition

Before proceeding to the actual examination of the impact standards in EC and WTO law, and to their critique, it is important to briefly summarize the core finding of the previous section. Subsidies are premised on the existence of an economic advantage. But it is only the conferral of a *competitive advantage* that may actually cause a significant concern. This impact on—or distortion of—competition depends on whether subsidies may influence the conduct of their beneficiary and, consequently, of its competitors.

In this central section of the chapter, the standards used in EC and WTO law to assess the impact of subsidies are analysed. In particular, reference is made to the 'distortion of competition' and the 'effect on trade' tests in Article 87(1) of the EC, and to the various categories and criteria used in the SCM Agreement.

Our goal is to evaluate whether these impact standards are more in line with the 'competition' approach advanced above, or whether instead they embrace a 'trade' rationale, and, if so, whether a new reading towards the former should be justified.

A. EC law: 'distortion of competition' and 'effect on trade', revisiting two requirements

The definition of State aid under Article 87(1) of the EC provides for two different elements. The measure should 'distort competition' and should produce an 'effect on trade' within the EC. As the following paragraphs show, these two phrases are usually looked at together, and they are very easy to establish. Whenever the other requirements of the definition are fulfilled, ie there is an aid granted by the State using State resources, which favours certain undertakings, a distortion of competition affecting intra-EC trade will almost invariably follow.[44]

[44] See V Di Bucci, 'Comments on the Paper "Selectivity, Economic Advantage, Distortion of Competition and Effect on Trade"', in J Derenne and M Merola (eds), *Economic Analysis of State Aid Rules—Contributions and Limits* (Berlin: Lexxion, 2007) 156, 159.

The following analysis criticizes this automatic approach and aims to restore the meaning and role played by these two requirements.

Two points are in particular posited with respect to both elements. First, they should be emancipated from each other and interpreted separately. Although there are clear links and overlap in their analysis, each of them performs a specific function within the definition of EC State aid. Secondly, far from being almost automatic, their interpretation should be more sophisticated.

We begin with the 'distortion of competition' requirement.

Distortion of competition

The traditional interpretation and its critique

In the EC, for a long time the paradigm of the assessment of the distortion of competition (and the effect on trade) has been set by the *Philip Morris* case,[45] and in particular by a rather loose interpretation thereof.

In this decision the Court requires the strengthening of 'the position of [the recipient] undertaking compared with other undertakings competing in intra-Community trade' to prove a distortion of competition and an effect on trade (which, as is common practice, are not clearly distinguished between themselves).[46] Now, particularly if interpreted loosely, under the *Philip Morris* standard, any form of financial assistance would 'strengthen' the 'financial position' of its beneficiary, and its position relative to its competitors not receiving that money. It is however clear that this does necessarily mean that a distortion of competition in the sense explained above, ie an impact on cost/revenue structure which damages more efficient competitors, has occurred.

Further, according to the traditional line of case-law, while the Commission is required to provide a statement of reasons of its determination of distortion of competition and effect on trade,[47] in principle no type of market analysis is necessary. A good illustration of the low threshold of the traditional approach can be found in the *Wam* decision.[48] Although the Commission's decision was eventually annulled for inadequate explanation of the alleged distortion of competition, according to the CFI, the Commission was not required to define the relevant market, and in particular to determine the market situation, the market shares of beneficiaries, the position of competitors, or the trade flows between

[45] Case 730/79.

[46] It is interesting to note that even stricter positions were present in the EC. In 1981, in its Annual Report on Competition Policy, the Commission essentially rejected the autonomy of the requirement of distortion of competition holding that any aid is liable to distort competition and hence it is not necessary to prove the effects (see point 176). A similar position was taken by Advocate General Capotorti in the *Philip Morris* case where he said that, whenever there is a subsidy, a distortion of competition is presumed.

[47] Cases 296 and 318/82 *Leeuwarder.* This follows from Article 253.

[48] Joined Cases T-304 and 316/04 *Wam* [2006] ECR II-64, para 64.

Member States. More importantly, there was no need to assess the impact of the aid on the prices of the recipient, to compare them with those of competitors or to examine the sales situation of the recipient in a given market. Further, the Commission was not required to prove actual effects on competition.[49] It should be finally added that, in line with this very restrictive approach, another consistent statement in the case-law is the rejection of any *de minimis* threshold.

It is therefore generally noted that the standard of proof is relatively low and that no detailed evidence is required.[50] A true reminiscence of a 'trade' approach (see chapter 2, section II.C above).

This is still the prevailing interpretation of the 'distortion of competition' standard. Certainly, a contextualization of many decisions, and the consideration that, in presence of certain conditions (such as fierce competition, overcapacity or market liberalization), *that* measure is likely to produce an impact on competition, can partly diminish the concerns deriving from the formal rejection of a more sophisticated analysis. In other words, in these cases, despite a laconic argumentation, the Commission and the Courts often reach correct decisions. In other cases, however, there is a significant risk of over-inclusion, ie of measures *not* distorting competition that are actually caught in the definition and prohibited.

Quite interestingly, a few recent decisions seem to hint at a more rounded approach with some focus on competition dynamics.[51] They are too few to represent a trend, but they are certainly significant, not only for their conclusions, but often also for parts of their reasoning. In particular, they offer some support to the thinking that the *Philip Morris*' test of 'strengthening the position' of the recipient can be interpreted in a way which gives more weight to competition rather than financial effects.[52]

In this respect, it is the recent Opinion of Advocate General Sharpston, delivered in the appeal of CFI's *Wam* decision, that offers the clearest statements so far.[53]

The Advocate General begins her analysis by asking whether a 'finding that a company enjoys a "strengthened financial position" suffice to show that aid given

[49] How this long 'list of releases' can be meaningfully reconciled with the Commission's duty to State reasons under Article 253 of the EC is not fully clear. Indeed, it seems inevitable that factors such as those discounted by the CFI should be taken into account to determine whether the measure distorts competition.

[50] K Bacon, *European Community Law of State Aid* (Oxford: Oxford University Press, 2009), para 2.137.

[51] See, eg, Case T-34/02 *Le Levant*, paras 123–4; Joined Cases T-304 and 316/04 *Wam*, para 72. It is also worth mentioning the decision of the ECJ in C-341-342/06P *Chronopost* (July 2008) which used revealing language in one paragraph (130) by linking the 'distortion of competition' to whether the measure 'altered the structure of the market concerned and affected the situation of the competing undertakings already present on that market'.

[52] Joined Cases T-304 and 316/04 *Wam*, para 72.

[53] Case C-494/06P. With a decision of 30 April 2009, the Court of Justice dismissed the appeal and confirmed the annullment of the Commission's decision for inadequate reasoning. For our purposes, it seems that the reasoning of the Court still bears ambiguities of the traditional view of the distortion of competition requirement and has not fully received the signal sent by its Advocate General.

to that company fulfils the conditions set out in Article 87(1) of the EC'. This language, particularly the emphasized words which borrow from the *Philip Morris* test, is sufficient to appreciate that what was at issue was a possible *reconstruction* of the same test in a competition-oriented fashion. And this is exactly what Sharpston did by linking the phrase 'strengthens the position' with the concept of 'competitive advantage'.[54]

After observing that, in its decision, the Commission simply found that the loan at issue constituted an 'advantage' to *Wam*, she noted that 'an improvement to the recipient's financial situation is something which is inherent in all grants of State aid' (the tautology present in the loose reading of the *Philip Morris* test), 'including those grants which do not fulfil the other criteria required by Article 87(1) of the EC' (that is to say, in particular, the 'distortion of competition' requirement).[55] Referring to operating aid,[56] Advocate General Sharpton concluded that what was required was a 'specific' or 'plausible' connection between the grant of the aid and alleviation of the burden of costs that the recepient company would have normally had to bear.[57]

It may well be that these statements remain isolated and the strong flow of the traditional, automatic, and formalistic approach is difficult to divert.

However, there are also other indications of a discomfort felt at the too simplistic 'impact standard' *à la Philip Morris*. Probably following the mounting criticism levelled at the insufficient economic analysis in merger control,[58] one of the first acts of the newly-installed Directorate General for Competition Neelie Kroes was to adopt the already mentioned State Aid Action Plan (SAAP) in June 2005 which, among other things, advocates a 'more-refined economic approach' in State aid cases.[59]

This approach is still at a very early stage and needs to develop. Much discussion, and also critique, is in particular surrounding the 'refined economic approach'.[60]

[54] ibid, para 49 of the Opinion.

[55] ibid, para 47 of the Opinion.

[56] Paraphrasing Case C-256/98 *Germany v Commission*, para 30, this refers to aid granted 'to release an undertaking from the costs which it would normally have had to bear in its day-to-day management or normal activities'. According to the Court, this type of aid distorts competition.

[57] Case C-494/06P, paras 49–50.

[58] Which followed three memorable cases lost before the CFI in 2002 in the span of few months.

[59] 'State Aid Action Plan—Less and better targeted aid: a roadmap for state aid reform 2005–2009', 7 June 2005, paras. 19–23. A more effect and economic-based approach has also been advocated by National Competition Authorities, like the Office of Fair Trading (OFT) in the UK. See, eg, the paper delivered by the former Director of the OFT just at the time of the launch of the SAAP: J Vickers, 'State Aid and Distortion of Competition', Paper for the State Aid Conference organized by the UK Presidency on 14 July 2005, available at <http://www.oft.gov.uk>. The OFT also carried out two studies on the economics of State aid. OFT, *European State Aid Control*, OFT821: London (2005); OFT, *Public Subsidies—A Report by the Office of Fair Trading*, OFT750: London (2004).

[60] A robust critique can be found in JL Buendia-Sierra and B Smulders, 'The Limited Role of the "Refined Economic Approach" in Achieving the Objectives of State Aid Control: Time for Some Realism', in 'EC State aid law-Le Droit des Aides d'Etat dans la CE, Liber Amicorum Francisco Santaolalla Gadea (Kluwer Law International, 2008) 18; JL Buendia-Sierra, 'Not like this: Some

It has been noted that most of the efforts of the Commission in the first years of application of the SAAP have concentrated more on the justifications' side rather than on injecting more economic reasoning in the definition of State aid, including the requirement of 'distortion of competition'.[61] By relying on the complexity of subsidies' effects, the attention of some economists too seems to have been captured more by the input that economic analysis may give at the level of the justifications, without fully neglecting however the requirements of the definition, including the distortion of competition.[62]

No revolution should be expected, nor in any event is it needed. The discussion and the critiques prompted by the SAAP are good opportunities for refinement. For their part, the findings of the case-law may be an indication that the tide is changing. They may often depend on the special features of the cases.[63] They may simply be considered as a call for the Commission to be clearer in its statement of reasons. But, at the same time, they may mean that more economic analysis is needed.[64]

In this regard, the findings of Advocate General Sharpston in *Wam* are particularly interesting. They have indicated the first two important steps towards a sounder approach to the 'distortion of competition', in line with the analysis of section I above.

The first, obvious step should be the rejection of any temptation of automatism. If there is a selective aid granted by the State and through State resources, the 'distortion of competition' should *not* be presumed.

Secondly, the fallacy which equates 'financial advantage' with 'competitive advantage' should be refuted. It is only the latter that matters under a proper reading

Skeptical Remarks on the "Refined Economic Approach" in State aid', in Proceedings of 4th Experts' Forum on New Developments in European State Aid Law, 18 and 19 May 2006, European State Aid Law Institute (Berlin: Lexxion, 2006) 59.

[61] JL Buendia-Sierra and B Smulders, 'The Limited Role of the "Refined Economic Approach" in Achieving the Objectives of State Aid Control: Time for Some Realism', in 'EC State aid law-Le Droit des Aides d'Etat dans la CE, Liber Amicorum Francisco Santaolalla Gadea (Kluwer Law International, 2008) 18, 29–31.

[62] See, eg, D Neven and V Verouden, 'Towards a More Refined Economic Approach in State Aid Control' in W Mederer, N Pesaresi, and M Van Hoof (eds), *EU Competition Law—Volume IV: State Aid* (Leuven: Claeys and Casteels, 2008) Book 1, Part I, chapter 4; HW Friederiszick, LH Röller, and V Verouden, *European State Aid Control: An Economic Framework*, in Bucirossi (ed), *Handbook of Antitrust Economics* (Cambridge MA: MIT Press, 2008) 625.

[63] V Di Bucci, 'Comments on the Paper "Selectivity, Economic Advantage, Distortion of Competition and Effect on Trade"' in J Derenne and M Merola (eds), *Economic Analysis of State Aid Rules—Contributions and Limits* (Berlin: Lexxion, 2007) 156, 159.

[64] See JL Buendia-Sierra, and B Smulders, 'The Limited Role of the "Refined Economic Approach" in Achieving the Objectives of State Aid Control: Time for Some Realism', in 'EC State aid law-Le Droit des Aides d'Etat dans la CE, Liber Amicorum Francisco Santaolalla Gadea (Kluwer Law International, 2008) 18, 3132, who also refer to other cases where the CFI seems to have indicated its support for more enconomic analysis.

of the 'distortion of competition' element. And this should be proved by reference to the impact of the aid on the costs of the recipient.[65]

These are the first two necessary conditions. Almost inevitably then, the use of market and economic analysis, like in antitrust law, will follow. What is needed are *just* those insertions that are instrumental to determining the impact of the State aid on competition. This would also solve the apparent conundrum surrounding the question of what the Commission's decision should include in order to satisfy the duty to State reason (and provide more transparency and legal certainty to everybody).

Crucially, a more competition- (and economic-) oriented approach does *not* exclude the use of 'presumptive rules' (often with the possibility of rebuttal).[66] These could cover the cases where, apart from direct proof of reduction of costs, the characteristics of the subsidy (eg magnitude; conditions attached to it) or the market itself (eg overcapacity; strong competition; liberalization of markets) indicate that a State aid will in all probability create a distortion of the competitive process.

One of the most notable examples of presumptions is that of *de minimis* thresholds. Although firmly established in the legislation, this idea still finds difficulties in being accepted in the case-law.[67]

Further, in consideration of the link between 'distortion of competition' and 'effect on trade', *de minimis* rules usually refer to both. While we leave for the moment more specific considerations on the 'trade' aspect of *de minimis*, in this paragraph, we provide a few remarks which mainly concern its relation with possible distortions of competition.

The purpose of *de minimis* rules is to put less significant and dangerous forms of State aid outside the scope of the rules. Currently, they operate on the basis of the amount granted to undertakings. If they are below a certain sum, they are automatically permitted.

[65] This may indeed be enough to capture the anti-competitive potential of the State aid without there being a specific requirement to separately prove the specific impact of the aid on competitors, impact which may in any case emerge from the factual circumstances at hand. 'When subsidies affect the recipient firms' behaviour, rivals' profits are likely to be affected': P Papandropoulos, R Nitsche, B van de Walle de Ghelcke, D Waelbroeck, J Derenne, F Louis, M Merola, P Ibañez Colomo, J De Beys, and J Bousin, 'Selectivity, Economic Advantage, Distortion of Competition and Effect on Trade' in J Derenne and M Merola (eds), *Economic Analysis of State Aid Rules—Contributions and Limits* (Berlin: Lexxion, 2007) 119, 146.

It should be noted finally that Article 87(1) of the EC covers also cases where the measure 'threatens to distort competition'. A proper reading of the concept of 'threat' should mean that the measure *can* produce an impact on the behaviour of the recipient (although it has not done that already), not that it is *less likely* to produce an impact. In other words, the standard and the factors to consider within it (eg costs) are the same. What changes is simply the fact that the impact and damage have not materialized yet.

[66] See the analysis of HW Friederiszick, LH Röller, and V Verouden, *European State Aid Control: An Economic Framework*, in Bucirossi (ed) *Handbook of Antitrust Economics* (Cambridge MA: MIT Press, 2008) 625, 656–60.

[67] This point is discussed in the next paragraph.

This technique, and in particular the mere reference to the amount of the aid, has been criticized. It is noted that the amount of the subsidy is meaningless in identifying the potential of distortion. Again, we should relate the subsidy to its recipient and its economic situation. The same amount may mean different things to different recipients. What would make more sense would be to link any presumptive permission to market power and use it as a controlling criterion.[68]

Effect on trade

The analysis now turns to the other element of the definition of EC State aid, the 'effect on trade between Member States', which is traditionally analysed together with the 'distortion of competition'.

Three points are posited here with respect to the 'effect on trade', the first two are in common with the previous analysis of the distortion element, the third one is peculiar to this requirement.

First, this element has a specific role to perform within the definition of State aid and should therefore be examined separately from the 'distortion of competition'. Secondly, the 'effect on trade' should require an analysis more sophisticated than the very basic one currently carried out. Thirdly, this element has a dual function, having both a jurisdictional and a substantive value.

Effect on trade: a jurisdictional and substantive requirement between free movement and State aid

O'Keeffe and Bavasso detected the 'common ancestry of competition and free movement' in the fact that both rules are 'subject, albeit in different forms, to an assessment of the effect on trade between Member States'.[69] Whereas this element, expressly worded in competition (both antitrust and State aid) rules, has traditionally been interpreted as a jurisdictional test, the effect on trade obviously represents the substance of free movement rules.

The proposition here, however, is that the effect on trade should be interpreted *both* as a *substantive* and as a *jurisdictional* test not only with respect to free movement, as has been convincingly explained by O'Keeffe and Bavasso, but also in the area of State aid.

It has been said that the requirement of an 'effect on trade between Member States' under Article 87(1) of the EC is rather easy to prove. More interestingly,

[68] C Osti, 'Di alcuni problemi degli aiuti di Stato' (2006) Mercato Concorrenza Regole 429. For another critique of the traditional way of dealing with *de minimis* aid see Merola, M, 'Comments on the Paper "The Most Appropriate Economic Tools for a Better Targeted State Aid Policy"' in J Derenne and M Merola (eds), *Economic Analysis of State Aid Rules—Contributions and Limits* (Berlin: Lexxion, 2007) 68, 70.

[69] D O'Keeffe and A Bavasso, 'Four Freedoms, One Market and National Competence: In Search of a Dividing Line' in M Andenas and D Fairgrieve (eds), *Judicial Review in International Perspective: Liber Amicorum in Honour of Lord Slynn of Hadley* (London: Aspen, 2000) 541, 544.

it has often happened that this element has been treated together, almost merged, with the distortion of competition test. The simplified competition analysis has inevitably meant a simplified effect on trade test. The fundamental step in this direction has been made by the Court in the *Philip Morris* case where it was crucially held that, once the position of an undertaking active in Community trade is 'strengthened', an effect on trade should almost invariably be assumed.[70]

There is indeed an inevitability in considering the distortion on competition and effect on trade together. This conclusion derives from the *substantive* nature of the effect on trade. It has been seen that an appropriate definition of State aid should be concerned with the actual effects created by the latter. In this regard, the execution of market analysis is required. More specifically, since we are dealing with a supranational regulation of subsidies, the concern should be the detection of distortions across the border.

It is argued that, in the context of Article 87(1) of the EC, this is the substantive role played by the effect on trade element. This has been implicitly recognized by Ehlermann and Vallery who have crucially linked the establishment of an effect on trade to 'market analysis' whereby the 'relevant geographic and product markets must first be defined'.[71] Fundamentally, this requires a serious analysis which should not rely on 'negative' and 'vague' statements such as that an effect on trade is 'not inconceivable'.[72]

To repeat the point, at a substantive level, the element of the effect on trade is strictly linked to that of the distortion on competition. To trigger the application of State aid law, what should be proved is that the measure creates a negative externality, a distortion, across the border. The 'effect on trade' is looking at this externality from the perspective of trade patterns. In a word, 'distortion of competition' and 'effect on trade' seem to represent two sides of the same coin.

This is the first step to giving full meaning to the effect on trade element. Although not fully separate from the distortion of competition from a substantive point of view, the *effet utile* of the effect on trade element would also be safeguarded in another way, ie by redefining its *jurisdictional* function. This should be done by considering it as an 'appropriate filter'.[73] Even at the very preliminary stages of the investigation, it may be apparent immediately that the measure under scrutiny cannot have an impact going beyond the domestic borders and should therefore be disposed of immediately. Quite intriguingly, a similar argument has been put

[70] Case 730/79.

[71] CD Ehlermann and A Vallery, 'Giving Meaning to the Condition of Effect on Trade: The Court's Judgment in Xunta de Galicia, a Missed Opportunity?' (2005) European State Aid Law Quarterly, 709, 711.

[72] Case C-172/03 *Heiser*, para 35. For a similar language ('conceivaible') see Case C-71/04 *Xunta de Galicia*, para 47.

[73] CD Ehlermann and A Vallery, 'Giving Meaning to the Condition of Effect on Trade: The Court's Judgment in Xunta de Galicia, a Missed Opportunity?' (2005) European State Aid Law Quarterly, 709, 712.

forward in the WTO context by Jackson who suggested introducing a 'distortion across the border' test as a 'pre-requisite'.[74] Its functionality, very similar to the 'filter' image put forward in EC law, would be to dispose of the clearly non-troublesome subsidies at the preliminary stages of countervailing duty investigations.

This redefinition of the effect on trade element leads us to reconsider the role of a *de minimis* test in State aid law. The link with the 'distortion of competition' element is crucial in this respect with the result that the substance of the analysis on the principle made in that context should be transposed here.

That said, it is extremely interesting to assess the legal status of the *de minimis* principle under EC State aid law. On the one hand, the case-law consistently repeats its dislike for this filter. There is no threshold below which it may be concluded that aid does not distort competition or affect intra-EC trade.[75] On the other hand, the practice of the Commission has now gained legislative recognition.[76] Crucially, how can these two different strands of legal development be reconciled? More specifically, how is the Court reacting to the legislative status of *de minimis*? Does its consolidated case-law, which interprets primary provisions of the EC Treaty, prevail over secondary legislation? Even the recent case-law seems to show a steady resistance to acceptance of the principle of *de minimis*, often resorting to an ambiguous approach. Thus, the legal instruments are either found to be inapplicable on the facts of the case[77] or the traditional case-law position is simply reiterated while ambiguously referring to the *de minimis* legal principle.[78]

When discussing the *de minimis* principle, a parallel with the law on free movement is again useful. The traditional approach in the internal market is 'no *de minimis*'. The *Keck* judgment has however kicked off a process of debate and rethinking about the rationale and working of internal market rules and their limits.[79] A landmark in this process is represented by the market access test proposed

[74] JH Jackson, *The World Trading System—Law and Policy of International Economic Relations* (2nd edn, Cambridge Massachussetts: MIT Press, 1997) 298–9.

[75] See Case C-71/04 *Xunta de Galicia*, para 41.

[76] See Council Regulation (EC) No 994/98 of 7 May 1998 on the application of Articles 92 and 93 of the Treaty establishing the European Community to certain categories of horizontal aid ('Enabling regulation'), OJ L142, 14.5.1998, 1; and Commission Regulation (EC) No 1998/2006 of 15 December 2006 on the application of Articles 87 and 88 of the Treaty to de minimis aid, OJ L 379 of 28.12.2006.

[77] See, eg, C-256/98 *Germany v Commission*, paras 39–40. See also Case C-382/99 *Netherlands v Commission*, paras 37–9 where the Court analyses the compliance with the Commission Notice on *de minimis* applicable at the time. Compare with Case T-453/99 *Kuwait Petroleum*, paras 71 and 72 in which, on essentially the same facts, the CFI does not address the *de minimis* point at all. See also Case C-172/03 *Heiser*, paras 32–4.

[78] See, eg, Case C-280/00 *Altmark*, paras 80 and 81; Joined Cases C-34/01 to C-38/01 *Enirisorse I*, para 28; Case C-71/04 *Xunta de Galicia*, para 41.

[79] Cases C-267-268/91 *Keck*. See, eg, S Weatherill, 'After *Keck*: Some Thoughts on How to Clarify the Clarification' (1996) Common Market Law Review 885.

by Advocate General Jacobs in his Opinion in *Leclerc-Siplec* which also features a *de minimis* assessment.[80] This approach has found some indirect support in the case-law[81] and more solid approval in the literature.[82] It is conceptually sound. It may certainly involve some practical difficulties but no more than those encountered in the antitrust field.[83]

Considering this, at least partial, recognition in the 'internal market' field, the question that can be posed in the context of our analysis is clear. Why is the Court still so reluctant to accept it in State aid law, particularly given that in this area there is a consolidated legislative choice in this direction?

B. WTO law: a bundle of standards, but what rationales?

A simple juxtaposition of EC and WTO 'impact standards' shows a stark difference. While the former is recognizable by two brief and apparently simple sentences, the latter is the land of fragmentation. Three elements contribute to this complexity. The bilevel nature of available tracks, the taxonomy of subsidies, and eventually, which matters in the present analysis, the multiplicity of 'impact standards'.

We can immediately achieve some simplicity, at least at the level of the exposition of these standards. The following analysis concentrates on the two categories of subsidies, 'prohibited' and 'actionable' ones, and on the relevant 'impact standards'. Since one of them, ie the 'injury' test, is common to both unilateral and multilateral tracks, we deal with it together with the other standards of the 'actionable' category.

Prohibited subsidies

The SCM Agreement prohibits two types of subsidies. First, export subsidies, ie those that are 'contingent' on export performance. Secondly, 'local-content' (or 'import-substitution') subsidies, ie those that are 'contigent' on the use of domestic over imported goods.

The rationale, or in any case the intention, underlying the adoption of this strict *per se* rule is clear. These forms of subsidies are considered particularly negative. It has been noted already that export subsidies have always been considered as

[80] See chapter II, section II.C.

[81] See eg, Case C-67/97 *Bluhme* in the field of free movement of goods.

[82] See P Craig and G De Búrca, *EU Law—Text, Cases and Materials* (4th edn, Oxford: Oxford University Press, 2007) and see, eg, S Weatherill, 'After *Keck*: Some Thoughts on How to Clarify the Clarification' (1996) Common Market Law Review 885; C Barnard, *Fitting the Remaining Pieces into the Goods and Persons Jigsaw?* (2001) European Law Review 35.

[83] D O'Keeffe and A Bavasso, 'Four Freedoms, One Market and National Competence: In Search of a Dividing Line' in M Andenas and D Fairgrieve (eds), *Judicial Review in International Perspective: Liber Amicorum in Honour of Lord Slynn of Hadley* (London: Aspen, 2000) 541, 552.

troublesome for international economic relations, and difficult to justify in terms of legitimate domestic policy objectives.[84] This has been consistently reflected in their discipline that, along the years, has been increasingly rigorous with the end result that the WTO simply prohibits them.

According to Article 3.2 of the SCM, 'a Member shall neither grant nor maintain' them. The 'impact standard', which is an irrebuttable presumption, is clear and immediate. The occurrence of negative externalities, and serious ones, is simply presumed for these two types of subsidies. Consequently, the SCM Agreement does not require the establishment of any distortion, in whatever sense.

First, we should immediately underline that, in general terms, the adoption of a 'competition approach' does not necessarily exclude the use of presumptions, even non-rebuttable ones. Both empirical evidence and administrative efficiency may point towards considering certain measures prohibited because they almost invariably distort competition. The cost may be that innocent instances of conduct be caught. But this 'over-inclusion' may be reasonably calculated and taken into account in the final decision to go ahead with the presumptive rule. As already noted, but worth repeating, as with any *per se* rule, presumptions are easily administrable. This is an important point. The efficiency of a legal system goes hand in hand with its sustained ability to produce sound decisions and acceptable outcomes. It should finally be accepted that the 'distortion of competition' as we analysed it (ie in terms of impact on production decisions of undertakings) is not the only possible rationale underpinning subsidy control, and consequently the 'impact standards' it adopts. We have already highlighted how subsidies may raise other concerns ranging from political rows and global inefficiency to market access frustration.[85] An 'impact standard' may thus indeed be inspired by one, or indeeed many, legitimate justifications.

Secondly, the broadness and strictness of the prohibition themselves have been subject to criticism.[86]

Although it is generally accepted that the prohibition of export subsidies makes sense, because they would be liable to both upset 'market access expectations' and

[84] See chapter 2, section III.A.

[85] See chapter 2, section II.

[86] It is interesting to note that, in the context of the current Doha negotiations, the US proposed to sensibly enlarge the category of prohibited subsidies including virtually all cases that were previously presumed to cause adverse effects in the actionable category and introducing the 'most extreme forms of government economic intervention' (like debt and equity financing not in line with commercial considerations). See Proposal from the US, TN/RL/GEN/146, 5 June 2007. This did not really come as a surprise since it corresponds to their negotiating stance during the Uruguay Round Negotiations as well. See PJ McDonough, 'Subsidies and Countervailing Measures' in TP Stewart (ed), *The GATT Uruguay Round—A Negotiating History (1986-1992)*, Volume I (Deventer: Kluwer, 1993) 809. What is interesting to ask is whether this stance will be affected by the current economic climate where public assistance in one of those forms is likely to be required, and with significant magnitude and frequency.

be a 'source of economic distortion',[87] it is also noted that, in some cases, like oligopolies or 'experience goods', export subsidies may be justified.[88]

In practical terms, this could require a flexible and differentiated approach, going beyond the provisions of 'special and differential' treatment provided for developing countries and economies in transition. As Green and Trebilcock have clearly suggested, this need for flexibility could impact both the actual design of the requirements (which could be 'rules' or 'standards') and also remedies.[89] In other words, this could mean that certain subsidies that are now automatically prohibited would be objectionable only if certain negative effects, maybe reaching a certain threshold of significance (eg above a *de minimis* or 'serious' effect level), are established. Certain cases, or circumstances, may further warrant the use of presumptions, possibly rebuttable ones. Others may finally require that a case-by-case analysis is always carried out. Further, if the basic negative rationales against this type of subsidies is adhered to, a progressive realignment to a stricter discipline should be envisaged. This may be subject to temporal deadlines, or to the occurrence of certain events. In short, the guiding principle of a prospective discipline is as clear —and sound—as ever, that different situations may require a different treatment.

Thirdly, the current assimilation between export and local content subsidies has been criticized.[90] 'Local content' subsidies were not prohibited in the 1979 Tokyo Round Subsidies Code regime. They were just part of domestic subsidies. That said, the first doubt concerns the possibility that the effects of 'local content' subsidies can really be equated to those of 'export subsidies'. If not, the justification of a similarly harsh treatment would beg a question. More intriguingly, it is observed that this prohibition would conflict with the positive assessment of 'local content' or similar practices made by other WTO law provisions. 'Import substitution' subsidies would at least partly overlap with the 'effect of normal, WTO-permitted tariffs'. In a similar vein, relying on Article III:8(b), which allows the 'payment of subsidies exclusively to domestic producers', Sykes is 'led to wonder . . . why the domestic producer subsidy is widely tolerated while the subsidy to domestic purchasers conditioned on the purchase of domestic goods is prohibited.'[91]

[87] AO Sykes, 'The Economics of WTO Rules on Subsidies and Countervailing Measures', Chicago John M Olin Law and Economics Working Paper No. 186 (2nd Series) May 2003, 18–19.

[88] See A Green and M Trebilcock, 'The Enduring Problem of WTO Export Subsidies Rules' (2007) and KW Bagwell and PC Mavroidis, 'Too Much, Too Little . . . Too Late?' in KW Bagwell, GA Bermann, and PC Mavroidis (eds), *Law and Economics of Contigent Protection in International Trade* (Cambridge: Cambridge University Press, forthcoming 2009).

[89] ibid.

[90] See, eg, AO Sykes, 'The Economics of WTO Rules on Subsidies and Countervailing Measures', Chicago John M Olin Law and Economics Working Paper No. 186 (2nd Series) May 2003, 19; GN Horlick, 'Subsidies Discipline Under WTO and US Rules' in CD Ehlermann and M Everson (eds), *European Competition Law Annual 1999: Selected Issues in the Field of State Aids* (Oxford: Hart Publishing, 2001) 593, 594.

[91] Sykes, ibid.

In conclusion, the 'impact standards' regulating export and local content subsidies cannot be explained simply in terms of a 'distortion of competition' approach as we have explained it. Their hard-and-fast treatment seems to be motivated by broader efficiency and political economy considerations which are largely still tenable. The rule may however need some fine-tuning and provide for a more flexible approach for certain circustances where, far from being inexorably presumed, negative externalities are to be established, if they are present at all.

Actionable

The category of 'actionable' subsidies is the most comprehensive, including all subsidies that cannot be classified export or local-content since they do not fulfil the relevant and particularly stringent requirements. In short, it includes all domestic subsidies. These interventions represent, to a large extent, the most debated class of subsidies because they are often introduced to address legitimate policy objectives. Since, following the expiry of the idea of 'non-actionability', no express recognition of this important public policy dimension is now present in the SCM Agreement, governments should be particularly cautious that, by designing and granting them, they do not cause 'adverse effects' to the interests of other governments.

This is the general approach to the distortions that domestic subsidies may cause as expressed by the SCM Agreement. Following the regulation of the 1979 Tokyo Round Subsidies Code, the current WTO regulation identifies three different 'impact standards' under the general expression of 'adverse effects'. These are: (i) 'injury to the domestic industry of another Member' (the same test used to impose countervailing duties), (ii) 'nullification or impairment of benefits' of other Members and in particular the benefits of tariff commitments, and (iii) 'serious prejudice to the interests of another member'.

Before analysing the various standards in more detail, some general comments can be made.

First, even a quick read through the various provisions shows that geographical location seems to be a key consideration in the differentiation of standards. This is certainly correct, but warrants more consideration when we analyse each of the tests in turn and then attempt to draw final conclusions on 'actionable subsidies' and their 'adverse effects'.[92]

Secondly, it should be recalled that the main goal of this chapter's analysis is the identification of the 'mischief' that this variety of standards address (trade? competition?). More particularly, the thesis to be tested is whether any, some or indeed all of them can be justified or construed in line with our main finding that the deepest concern of subsidies is that they distort competition by directly interfering with the behaviour of economic operators. Considering the variety, and the different,

[92] And the author considers whether it is desirable that the multitude of 'impact standards' be simplifed.

even historical, origins of the various tests, it would not come as a surprise if we were to find that different objectives underpin the numerous 'impact standards'. In principle, complexity is acceptable in a complex system. This is the main lesson to be learned from the analysis of the category of 'prohibited subsidies'. Assuming that different rationales justify the various 'impact standards', our effort will however be aimed at assessing whether they are still properly tuned to the objectives underlying the system of subsidy control.

Thirdly, the main principle leading our analysis is that, at a deeper level, causality is the key. It is a causality analysis that allows us to distinguish whether the harm is produced by subsidized imports or, more simply, by competing imports.[93] The choice of a more or less sophisticated causality analysis is also important to determine whether the rules are mainly about protecting 'market access' or 'competitive effects'.

Fourthly, we should recall the observations on the use of presumptions and (*de minimis* or otherwise) thresholds made in the context of the analysis of prohibited subsidies. *Mutatis mutandis* they can be applied here too. A complex reality like domestic subsidies, which produce a network of different, even conflicting, effects, demands a regulatory framework that duly takes this complexity into account. And this is particularly true now since an important leeway for 'policy space', in the form of 'non-actionability', is gone.

Presumptions and thresholds of various types do help in guaranteeing this much needed flexibility. Although we are not endorsing its content unreservedly, the kind of *normative order* initially provided by Article 6 read in its entirety is a sort of model to the flexible approach we are hinting at.[94]

Fifthly, we already expect that a question will be posed after the painstaking analysis of the several 'impact standards' for domestic subsidies. It is the same question that Hufbauer and Shelton-Erb posed in 1984 while commenting on the then in force Tokyo Round Subsidies Code and its tests.[95] Why so many standards? Would it not be better if we could simplify? Although a fuller answer to these questions must be left till the end, a few points can be ancipated. Even in a complex area, simplification is welcome. This is no contradiction. The complexity of domestic subsidies, their objectives and effects has been underlined, and, on this basis, the need for a 'complex' discipline has been argued. But complex means comprehensive and compound, not complicated and Gordian. Some simplification of the

[93] See R Diamond, 'Privatization and the Definition of Subsidy: A Critical Study of Appellate Body Texturalism' (2008) Journal of International Economic Law 649, 667–75. Causality concerns usually raise eyebrows for the 'injury' test particularly in the context of countervailing duty determinations. Apart from Diamond, ibid; see, eg, AO Sykes, 'International Trade: Trade Remedies' in AT Guzman and AO Sykes (eds), *Research Handbook in International Economic Law* (Cheltenham: Edward Elgar, 2007) 62.

[94] See, in the context of Doha Round negotiations, the comments of Canada in this regard. See Communication from Canada, TN/RL/GEN/14, 15 September 2004.

[95] GC Hufbauer and J Shelton Erb, *Subsidies in International Trade* (Cambridge, Massachusetts: MIT Press, 1984) 43–4.

'impact standards' of domestic subsidies can probably be achieved, particularly if it is found that those, currently distinct, standards pursue the same target. Further, simplicity should be coupled by coherency. Any attempt to simplify (domestic) subsidy 'impact standards' would need to take the schizophrenic nature of the WTO system of subsidy control, with two distinct remedial routes, into proper consideration.

Injury

The concept of 'injury' to the domestic industry is used in the same sense as in the context of countervailing duty and anti-dumping duty procedures.[96] Article 15 of the SCM specifies this concept in great detail.

Before commenting, it may be useful to quote the text of the relevant provision, Article 15 of the SCM and, in particular, paragraphs 1, 2, 4 and 5:

A determination of injury . . . shall be based on positive evidence and involve an objective examination of both (a) the volume of the subsidised imports and the effect of the subsidised imports on prices in the domestic market for like products and (b) the consequent impact of these imports on the domestic producers of such products.

With regard to the volume of subsidised imports, the investigating authorities shall consider whether there has been a significant increase in subsidised imports, either in absolute terms or relative to production or consumption in the importing Member. With regard to the effect of the subsidised imports on prices, the investigating authorities shall consider whether there has been a significant price undercutting by the subsidised imports as compared with the price of a like product of the importing Member, or whether the effect of such imports is otherwise to depress prices to a significant degree or to prevent price increases, which otherwise would have occurred, to a significant degree. No one or several of these factors can necessarily give decisive guidance.

The examination of the impact of the subsidized imports on the domestic industry shall include an evaluation of all relevant economic factors and indices having a bearing on the State of the industry, including actual and potential decline in output, sales, market share, profits, productivity, return on investments, or utilisation of capacity; factors affecting domestic prices; actual and potential negative effects on cash flow, inventories, employment; wages, growth, ability to raise capital or investments and, in the case of agriculture, whether there has been an increased burden on government support programmes. This list is not exhaustive, nor can one or several of these factors necessarily give decisive guidance.

It must be demonstrated that the subsidised imports are, through the effects [as set forth in paragraphs 15.2 and 15.4] [97] of subsidies, causing injury within the meaning of this Agreement. The demonstration of a causal relationship between the subsidised imports and

[96] The Agreement on Safeguards (SG) also provides a concept of 'injury' which relies on a 'causality' standard. The Appellate Body in *US—Wheat Gluten* has told us that the causation standard under the SG should amount to 'a genuine and substantial relationship of cause and effect' (para 69). This is useful. But, as the following exposition shows, the problem of the injury analysis in the subsidy context is that disorientation on the identity of the cause of the injury (imports? subsidy?) is still particularly acute.

[97] The text in brackets appears in a footnote in the original text.

the injury to the domestic industry shall be based on an examination of all relevant evidence before the authorities. The authorities shall also examine any known factors other than the subsidised imports which at the same time are injuring the domestic industry, and injuries caused by these other factors must not be attributed to the subsidised imports. Factors which may be relevant in this respect include, inter alia, the volumes and prices of non-subsidised imports of the product in question, contraction in demand or changes in the patterns of consumption, trade restrictive practices of and competition between the foreign and domestic producers, developments in technology and the export performance and productivity of the domestic industry.

Despite its high sophistication, the language of this provision is fundamentally indeterminate. In particular, the most serious problem is the interpretation of the causation standard.

It has been noted: 'there is no precise definition in the Uruguay Round Agreement of "cause", beyond a list of factors that may be examined, leaving the appropriate standard to the discretion of the investigating authorities'.[98] Such indeterminacy depends on the fact that 'each provision is drafted in such a way as to refer to another and this interrelation and interdependency forms an almost closed loop'.[99] In short, the language 'seems deliberately designed to perpetuate the debate over the proper standard'.[100] Indeed, all relevant provisions attribute a language of causality alternatively to 'subsidised imports' or to 'subsidisation'.[101] The most difficult issue is raised by the hermeneutic equivalence between 'through the effects of the subsidy' in paragraph 5 and 'subsidized imports' and their 'effects' in paragraphs 2 and 4.[102]

Two constructions of the causation standard thus seem possible.

On the one hand, and this seems to be the prevailing interpretation, a determination of injury to the domestic industry is made even though the adverse effects do not depend on subsidization but more simply, and ironically, on imports' competition. In the GATT era, support for this reading has been found in the *US—Atlantic salmon* report[103] which had to apply the virtually identical provision of the Tokyo Round Subsidies Code. The Panel noted that the expression 'through the effects of subsidies' referred to the effects set forth in the paragraphs on volume increase, price effects and impact on industry which are centred on' subsidized imports'. It thus concluded that that expression does not require proof that

[98] MJ Trebilcock and R Howse, *The Regulation of International Trade* (3rd edn, London: Routledge, 2005) 380.

[99] M Benitah, *The Law of Subsidies under the GATT/WTO System* (The Hague: Kluwer Law International, 2001) 281.

[100] AO Sykes, 'International Trade: Trade Remedies' in AT Guzman and AO Sykes, (eds), *Research Handbook in International Economic Law* (Cheltenham: Edward Elgar (2007) 62, 92.

[101] See also Article VI:3 of the GATT reading that '[n]o contracting party shall levy any . . . countervailing duty on the importation of any product . . . unless it determines that the effect of. . . . subsidisation . . . is such as to cause or threaten material injury to an established domestic industry'.

[102] Link created by footnote 47 of Article 15.5 of the SCM.

[103] GT Panel, *US—Atlantic Salmon*, para 328 et seq.

subsidization is the cause of the injury, but merely that the subsidized imports are the cause. This reading has been confirmed recently by the Appellate Body in *Japan—DRAMS*. The Appellate Body held that the 'architecture of Articles 15.2, 15.4, and 15.5' clearly shows that, for 'determining whether the "subsidized imports are, through the effects of subsidies, causing injury" to the domestic industry', what is required is only the examination of the 'effects of the subsidized imports' on prices (Article 15.2) and consequently on domestic producers (Article 15.4).[104]

Situations can easily be imagined, however, where subsidized imports prove popular with purchasers, and therefore injure the domestic industry, for reasons other than price (depending on mobilization), for example quality, design, consumer preferences, innovation. The Appellate Body rejected this remark, observing that this would require two additional enquiries, notably (i) how the exporting company use the relevant subsidies and (ii) a counterfactual analysis of whether a similar injury would have occurred in the absence of the subsidies, both of them going beyond the standard of Article 15.[105]

Quite interestingly, the Appellate Body also rejected the argument that there is a need to ensure a consistent interpretation of the 'injury' standard (in the context of Part V of the SCM on countervailing duty actions) with the other standards of 'adverse effects' or 'serious prejudice (in Part III) that expressly concentrate on the 'effect of the subsidy'. Different parts of the agreement differ in 'text, context, rationale and object' and it should not be warranted that the relevant standards should be interpreted similarly.[106]

Leaving aside the double role of the 'injury' test which is also one of the 'adverse effects' in Part III (the fundamental question is: shall we resort to a different interpretation of 'injury' depending on the, unilateral or multilateral, context of the action?), the indirect confirmation that the 'impact standards' of the 'adverse effects' might be interpreted differently is promising.

On the other hand, a different construction of the 'injury' standard, directly focusing on the 'effect' of 'subsidies' and on their 'use' by recipients could be put forward.

It is clear that 'injury to the domestic industry cannot be equated to distortion of competition. Injury to competitors is not the same as injury to competition.'[107]

[104] Appellate Body, *Japan—DRAMS*, para 264.

[105] ibid, paras 265–6.

[106] ibid, para 272. It is worth quoting the Appellate Body: 'In view of the difference between the text, context, rationale, and object of the provisions in Part III and Part V of the *SCM Agreement*, we see no basis for importing the specific obligations of Part III into the provisions of Part V of the *SCM Agreement*. Although both Articles 6.3 and 15.5 refer to effects of the subsidies, the meaning of this phrase must be interpreted in the light of the substantive obligations within which the phrase is located. Articles 6.3 and 15.5 deal with different subject matters and therefore it is not appropriate to accord an identical meaning to the common phrase in these Articles.'

[107] M Benitah, *The Law of Subsidies under the GATT/WTO System* (The Hague: Kluwer Law International, 2001) 23.

It has accordingly been suggested that, perhaps through a progressive judicial interpretation, the injury test (as well as the other two types of 'adverse effects' provided for in Article 5 of the SCM) should be construed so as to guarantee what is seen as the underlying aim of the GATT/WTO system, the safeguarding of 'normal competition'.[108]

Despite the difficulties in defining the purpose of the WTO system, and of subsidy rules in particular, this 'competition-oriented' interpretation seems to be in line with the wording and purpose of Article 15 of the SCM.[109]

The first sentence of Article 15:5 of the SCM expressly sets out the object of the determination and, in doing so, it defines the relationship between 'subsidized imports' and 'subsidization'. According to that clear passage, 'it must be demonstrated that the subsidized imports are, *through the effects of subsidies*, causing injury within the meaning of this Agreement'.[110] It is indeed reasonable to require such causal link, as the object of the SCM Agreement is to regulate subsidies and responses to them.[111]

Therefore, if the injury depends on factors other than subsidization no determination of injury should be made. Article 15.5 of the SCM accordingly requires the examination of 'any known factors other than the subsidised imports which at the same time are injuring the domestic industry' and makes it clear that 'the injuries caused by these other factors must not be attributed to the subsidised imports'. Among these factors, 'competition between the foreign and domestic producers' is also included. The Appellate Body recognized this[112] but suggested a schizophrenic approach where different sentences in the same provision are interpreted differently. Contextualization requires that all sentences in Article 15:5 (and more generally 15) should be read harmoniously.

A 'competition-oriented' interpretation would also contribute to safeguarding the system's coherence. Indeed, Article VI GATT and the SCM Agreement concern *subsidies* and responses to *subsidized* imports. The need to provide, under certain exceptional circumstances, import relief to the domestic industry should be addressed by the appropriate safeguard mechanisms, and not by subsidy rules.

[108] A Beviglia Zampetti, 'The Uruguay Round Agreement on Subsidies—A Forward-Looking Assessment' (1996) Journal of World Trade 5.

[109] This argument was put forward by Korea in *Japan—DRAMS*. The Appellate Body however opined that its interpretation was in harmony with the object and purpose of the SCM Agreement (see para 276 of the Report).

[110] Article 15.5, first sentence SCM (emphasis added). cf also Art 19.1 of the SCM.

[111] With respect to the latter, if there is no subsidy then there cannot possibly be any countervailing duty. cf Panel, *US—Lead and Bismuth II*, para 6.48 et seq. Article 21.1 of the SCM is clear on this point, expressly stating that 'a countervailing duty shall remain in force only as long as and to the extent necessary to counteract *subsidisation which is causing injury*' (emphasis added). cf also Article VI:3 of the GATT and footnote 36 to Article 10 of the SCM which read that countervailing duties are levied for the purpose of offsetting any subsidy.

[112] Appellate Body, *Japan—DRAMS*, para 267.

Nullification or impairment of benefits

One of the forms of 'adverse effects' in Article 5 of the SCM is the 'nullification or impairment' (NI) of benefits to other Members under the GATT, and in particular the benefits of concessions bound under Article II.

The term NI has the same meaning as in the relevant provisions of GATT 1994, notably Article XXIII:1. However, as Article 5(b) specifies, it refers 'in particular' to those cases of 'breach' of the 'GATT bargain' described in chapter 2.[113] In other words, it refers to those cases of 'non-violation nullification or impairment' (NVNI) where a Member that has given a tariff concession acts in a way that denies the 'competitive opportunity' that other Members could reasonably expect.

The NVNI was a controversial GATT remedy already being described as 'legal fantasy' or a 'diplomat's legal concept of legal order'.[114] Against these judgments, it is no surprise that its carry-over from the GATT to the WTO has raised considerable debate, with various views (still mainly negative) being expressed.[115] It seems however that, so far, WTO claimaints relying on it have not been very successful with no such complaint being upheld.

This test has been inherited from the GATT and adjusted by the WTO. In general, the main change is that, while before the remedy was 'compensation', what is now provided is 'reasonable adjustment'. However, the NVNI remedy has a specific status in the subsidy context since it is expressly inserted into the SCM agreement as one of the forms of 'adverse effects'. As a result of this insertion, it has been 'transformed'.[116] If the NI derives from a subsidy, this concept is now expressly defined in the SCM Agreement (Article 1). Further, since the NI standard is included in Part III on actionable subsidies, it is clear that the relevant subsidy should satisfy all conditions for being admitted to the category, ie should also be specific (Article 2).

What is interesting to see, however, is to what extent this transformation has taken place. The comments just made (we need a specific subsidy under Articles 1

[113] At least on its face, the wording of the Tokyo Round Subsidies Code was more comprehensive, using the term 'include' (see n 24 of the Code). In actual fact, however, most of the cases of NVNI have concerned the negating of tariff concessions through the grant of subsidies.

[114] The two expressions are respectively attributable to P Pescatore, 'The GATT Dispute Settlement Mechanism: Its Present Situation and Its Prospect' (1993) Journal of World Trade 5; and RE Hudec, *Enforcing International Trade Law—The Evolution of the Modern GATT Legal System* (Salem, New Hampshire: Butterworth Legal Publishers, 1993) 7.

[115] A broad analysis of non-violation complaints is that of T Cottier and K Nadakavuakeren Schefer, 'Non-Violation Complaints in WTO/GATT Dispute Settlement: Past Present and Future in T Cottier, *The Challenges of WTO Law: Collected Essay* (London: Cameron May, 2007) 75. For a defence of non-violation complaints see C Larouer, 'WTO Non-Violation Complaints: A Misunderstood Remedy in the WTO Dispute Settlement System' (2006) Netherlands International Law Review 97. See also KW Bagwell and PC Mavroidis, 'Too Much, Too Little . . . Too Late?' in KW Bagwell, GA Bermann, and PC Mavroidis (eds), *Law and Economics of Contigent Protection in International Trade* (Cambridge: Cambridge University Press, forthcoming 2009).

[116] R Howse, 'Do the World Organization disciplines on domestic subsidies make sense? The case for legalizing some subsidies' in KW Bagwell, GA Bermann, and PC Mavroidis (eds), *Law and Economics of Contigent Protection in International Trade* (Cambridge: Cambridge University Press, forthcoming 2009).

and 2) are relatively uncontroversial. What is important to know in the context of our analysis is whether the inclusion in the 'adverse effects' has repercussions on the interpretation of the actual 'impact standard' required.

We do not have any jurisprudence on the application of this standard in the SCM Agreement's context. We therefore need to return to the GATT era and to the admittedly scarce case-law we have on the subject. This will enable us to assess whether the interpretation of that standard is still valid in the new context.

It seems that in the GATT three elements are needed to successfully prove a NVNI claim: (a) benefit which usually refers to assurance of better market access; (b) nullification or impairment, which depends on a showing of adverse effect and frustration of reasonable expectation; (c) as a result of a measure (causality).[117]

Crucially, as with other GATT trade rules, like Article III or XI, the case-law on NVNI focused on the impact on the 'conditions of competition for trade, not on volumes of trade'. In the *EEC—Oilseeds I* report, which concerned a claim that a domestic subsidy was emptying a tariff concession, the Panel noted:

> These arguments of the parties raise the question of the nature of the benefit accruing under Article II: does that benefit consist of the protection of expectations on competitive conditions or on trade flows? The Panel noted that the CONTRACTING PARTIES have consistently interpreted the basic provisions of the General Agreement on restrictive trade measures as provisions establishing conditions of competition. Thus they decided that an import quota constitutes an import restriction within the meaning of Article XI:1 whether or not it actually impeded imports and that an internal tax on imported products does not meet the national treatment requirement of Article III whether or not the tax is actually applied to imports. A previous panel pointed out that Articles III and XI are 'to protect expectations of the contracting parties as to the competitive relationship between their products and those of other contracting parties. Both articles are not only to protect current trade but also create the predictability needed to plan future trade'. In the past Article XXIII:1(b) cases, the CONTRACTING PARTIES have adopted the same approach: their findings of nullification or impairment were based on a finding that the products for which a tariff concession had been granted were subjected to an adverse change in competitive conditions. In none of these cases did they consider the trade impact of the change in competitive conditions to be determining. In one case they specifically rejected the relevance of statistics on trade flows for a finding on nullification and impairment. It is of course true that, in the tariff negotiations in the framework of GATT, contracting parties seek tariff concessions in the hope of expanding their exports, but the commitments they exchange in such negotiations are commitments on conditions of competition for trade, not on volumes of trade.[118]

This language, and the relevant standard, are very clear. The question now is whether, in the Article 5 of the SCM context, which generally requires the NI should be caused through the 'use [of the] subsidy', the relevant 'impact standard'

[117] See M Matsushita, TJ Schoenbaum, and PC Mavroidis, *The World Trade Organization—Law, Practice, and Policy* (Oxford: Oxford University Press, 2006) 121–2.

[118] Paragraph 150.

should still be read in this way, as relating to the mere propensity to cause adverse effects, without any need to prove a specific and actual impact on trade flows; in short, in the same way that traditional trade rules are construed.[119]

Just after the entry into force of the SCM Agreement, Beviglia Zampetti argued that, like all other subsidy 'impact standards', this provision could be interpreted in a 'competition oriented' way. The author has some reservations, however. It seems contentious that the proof that the 'legitimate market access expectations' of another Member have been frustrated should require an actual analysis of the impact of the measure on the competitive position of the recipient and hence of the competitors.

The author believes that the NVNI has *not* been transformed in this respect by the insertion in the SCM Agreement. It is still the best example of a remedy trying to tackle the first type of negative effects subsidies may cause, ie impairment of market access. As such, it still operates in the typical blunt fashion of other trade provisions, protecting expectations of competition and not enquiring as to actual effects. Even in the new 'adverse effects' context of Article 5 of the SCM, and even assuming that a 'competition oriented' approach should inform the impact standards of WTO subsidy rules, it is difficult to conclude that the NVNI remedy is more about protecting 'actual competitive process' than 'market access'.

Serious prejudice

Like the NVNI, 'serious prejudice' claims have not been very common, although there have been more claims recently.[120] It seems indeed that, among the three forms of 'adverse effects', this is the one that is most often pursued.[121]

The original basis of the 'serious prejudice' language and tests can be found in Article XVI:1 of the GATT. It was then developed in the 1979 Tokyo Round Subsidies Code under Article 8(4) and now in Article 6.3 of the SCM that clearly shows its origins in the latter.

The 'serious prejudice' standard is without doubt the most elaborate of the 'impact standards' of the SCM Agreement. The 'injury' test is elaborate too, but in another sense. There, the interpreter has to find which (one) rationale is underlying a single standard. Here, he is faced with various standards, with the possibility that each of them has a different justification.

The current discipline of Article 6 is not only elaborate but also incomplete. The first paragraph, which laid down few cases of presumption of 'serious prejudice',

[119] See chapter 2, section II.C.

[120] It is however the case that the multilateral route of actionability is not much followed. The 'injury' test, courtesy of its double-cap (playing a pivotal role in multilateral and unilateral actions alike), is more used but almost exclusively in the countervailing duty context.

[121] For its part, the NVNI complaint route is not very attractive. Not a single claim on this basis has succeeded in the WTO. But, more fundamentally, its inherent problem is that it brought the 'original' uncertainties, or weaknesses, of its GATT period into the WTO, to which one should add, in the subsidy discipline context, those deriving from its 'transformation' due to its insertion in the 'adverse effects'.

lapsed in 2000.[122] These presumptions could be rebutted demonstrating that the subsidy had not produced any of the 'effects' described in the crucial paragraph 3.[123] This paragraph includes the actual 'impact standards' that may lead to establishing serious prejudice. It is these tests that we are going to analyse in the rest of this section. We should however commence by quoting the relevant provision.

Serious prejudice in the sense of paragraph (c) of Article 5 may arise in any case where one or several of the following apply:

(a) the effect of the subsidy is to displace or impede the imports of a like product of another Member into the market of the subsidizing Member;
(b) the effect of the subsidy is to displace or impede the exports of a like product of another Member from a third country market;
(c) the effect of the subsidy is a significant price undercutting by the subsidized product as compared with the price of a like product of another Member in the same market or significant price suppression, price depression or lost sales in the same market;
(d) the effect of the subsidy is an increase in the world market share of the subsidizing Member in a particular subsidized primary product or commodity[17] as compared to the average share it had during the previous period of three years and this increase follows a consistent trend over a period when subsidies have been granted.

---

17 Unless other multilaterally agreed specific rules apply to the trade in the product or commodity in question.

Two linguistic features strike immediately the reader. First, all items expressly and unequivocally correlate the 'serious prejudice' to situations which are the 'effect of the subsidy'. This, it is argued, may play an important role in the interpretation of the various cases listed in Article 6.3 since it is stressing the importance of *causality* discourse, and in particular the direct link between the subsidy and the negative effect.

Strictly intertwined to that is another argument which emerges from the case-law on 'serious prejudice'. The various situations that may establish it should be proved on the basis of *positive evidence*. This may not only be a procedural remark but, more deeply, it may reinforce the interpretation of the substantive requirements. In other words, it is clear that the kind of evidence that has to be adduced to prove

[122] A serious prejudice was deemed to exist when (i) subsidization exceeded a certain percentage of the product value (normally 5%); (ii) in case of subsidies to cover operating losses to an industry or enterprise (unless, in the latter case, they were a non-recurrent measure and were given merely to provide time for the development of long-term solutions and to avoid acute social problems); and (iii) when debt was directly forgiven, or when grants to cover that debt were given.

In the context of the Doha negotiations Canada has proposed to reinstate this provision. See Communication from Canada, TN/RL/GEN/14, 15 September 2004.

[123] These 'effects' have a double relevance for the determination of serious prejudice. On the one hand, if one of them is established serious prejudice *may* arise (Article 6.3). On the other, if it is proved that none of them is present then *no* serious prejudice may be established (Article 6.2).

a breach of 'expectations' on the one hand and an actual negative impact on trade and competition on the other is different, the latter being more demanding. It is only if this is the type of 'impact standard' to be adhered to that the adjudicator may feel it necessary to underline that positive evidence, and not mere circumstantial evidence or even speculation, is required.

Secondly, the chapeau intriguingly say that 'serious prejudice . . . *may* arise' when one or more of the various situations indicated immediately below occur. How should we construe this? The first, still superficial meaning is that there is no inevitability. Even if one of the situations that are listed is proved this does not necessarily mean that a 'serious prejudice' *is* established (under Article 6.2 the contrary is true, however). What fundamentally enables us to take the step from the demonstration that one situation from (a) to (d) is present and the final determination that there is a 'serious prejudice'? What makes a 'may' an 'is'? There is certainly some judgement and discretion to be exercised here. How should this be done? What are the guidelines? These are important, and legitimate questions. It seems however that the case-law bluntly dismisses them by observing that the listed situations 'in themselves constitute serious prejudice'.[124] The author is still not convinced that 'may' should mean 'is'.

But there is another, more significant question.[125] Does 'may arise' mean that when trying to establish that a subsidy causes a 'serious prejudice' we could, and probably should, start from letters (a) to (d) but, in case of negative results, we should not be limited to them? Can other circumstances (and, if so, which ones?) assist and establish that a serious prejudice is indeed present? This question, which is different from the previous one, is equally important.

After these testing questions, and doubts, we can move on to interpret the individual situations and assess the 'mischief' they are trying to capture. In our framework of analysis, the issue is: is this rule more about 'trade' or 'competition'? We look at the first two paragraphs together, since they concern similar situations and raise analogous issues. Then, we move on to paragraph (c) and analyse it in depth. The final situation, in paragraph (d), will be dealt with only very briefly, because of its limited practical importance, and only to the extent that is necessary to answer our fundamental question about the rationale of 'impact standards'.

The first two situations, governed by paragraphs (a) and (b), are corresponding. They concern the cases where the 'effect of the subsidy' is 'to displace or impede' imports or exports of like products of another Member respectively into the market of the subsidizing country or from a third country market.

[124] Panel, *US—Cotton (Article 21.5)*, para 10.255; Panel, *Korea—Commercial Vessels*, paras 7.581–7.587.

[125] See J Flett, AC Jessep, and K Talaber-Ritz, 'The Relationship between WTO Subsidies Law and EC State Aid Law' in *EC State aid law—Le Droit des Aides d'État dans la CE, Liber Amicorum Francisco Santaolalla Gadea* (Kluwer Law International, 2008) 441, 463–4.

Although strictly speaking it directly applies only to 'export' cases, Article 6.4 offers more general indications on the impact standards under (a) and (b) suggesting that displacement or impediment 'shall include' cases where it is 'demonstrated that there has been a change in relative shares of the market' to the disadvantage of non-subsidized products. What seems to be involved is not just a protection of 'expectations' but actual 'effects'.

The only Panel that dealt with the case, *Indonesia—Automobile Industry*, laid down interesting findings for understanding the rationale of these 'impact standards'.[126] Its analysis of the concepts of displacement and impedance in particular confirm that what matters is the *actual impact* of the measure (which would distinguish these cases from those of NVNI complaints). Significant indicators such as lost sales and market share data are used but, in eventually rejecting the claim, the Panel repeatedly confirms that proof of serious prejudice should be based on 'positive evidence' which does not rely on speculation only, and may require a counterfactual analysis. The ingredients of a 'competition analysis' are certainly there. Although no direct inquiry of the 'effect of the subsidy' on the cost/revenue structure of the recipient is hinted at, the interference with the latter may inevitably be correlated to the demanding standard and evidential examination followed by the Panel.

In conclusion, although one might initially entertain a doubt that these cases are similar in nature to NVNI ones, a closer scrutiny reveals that they are not only about a simple protection of market access in domestic or export markets. Rather, they indicate the direction that a 'newly-transformed' NVNI remedy complaint might follow if it were decided that a mere trade perspective has to be abandoned.

The situation under paragraph (c) refers to those cases where the effect of the subsidy is a 'significant price undercutting' by the subsidized products of a 'like product of another Member in the same market' or 'significant price suppression', 'price depression' or 'lost sales'. This situation is the one that more easily lends itself to being construed in a 'distortion of competition' way.

This is for two reasons. First, the factors that define this situation are 'prices' and their occurences.[127] Prices are directly linked to the kind of cost-analysis we have developed. In the famous *US—Cotton* dispute, the Panel in the original proceedings distinguished 'price-contingent' from 'non-price-contingent' subsidies, or, to put it another way, payments related to production or 'decoupled' payments.[128] Only the former involved a clear nexus between subsidy and price suppression, and should have been considered.[129]

[126] See paras 14.207–14.236.

[127] One case also refers to lost sales and can thus be assimilated to the previous two situations. which according to our reading, may lead to a 'competition oriented' approach.

[128] Panel, *US—Cotton*, paras 7.1289–7.1307.

[129] ibid, paras 7.1307 and 7.1350.

Secondly, the case-law expressly underlines the importance that the situation be 'the effect of the subsidy'. The Appellate Body in *US—Cotton* and *US—Cotton (Article 21.5)* has thus made it clear that this effect implies a 'genuine and substantial relation of cause and effect'.[130] The impact of the subsidy is the focus, causality is the key.[131]

A final comparison, which reveals a stark contrast in the case-law in the interpretation of two different 'impact standards', is useful to corroborate our conclusion. The approach taken by the Appellate Body in the context of Article 6.3(c), fully focused on subsidies' effects, can be juxtaposed with that in the 'injury' context as evidenced by the *Japan—DRAMS* decision where, it may be recalled, it was concluded that it is not necessary to establish that the injury should be the effect of the subsidy.[132]

Finally, it is interesting to note that in the more 'competition-oriented' of the tests a little, but significant, word has been added. The effect of the subsidy should produce a 'significant' impact. Otherwise, logic demands, serious prejudice should not arise.

Just one word on the final situation under paragraph (d) which only concerns primary products and commodities and in particular targets subsidies that produce an 'increase in world market share'. After analysing paragraph (c) it seems clear that this standard does not immediately involve a true competition analysis. It may in fact be more related to the standards under paragraphs (a) and (b) analysed above, with an actual impact to be proved through positive evidence.

III. Conclusions

After this analysis of 'impact standards' in both EC and WTO law three conclusions can be drawn.

First, building on the findings of chapter 2, and their development in section I of this chapter, it has been posited that, since the main concern of subsidies is their negative effect on competition, 'impact standards' in the relevant discipline should ideally be informed to reflect this. This thesis was however made more specific in two ways. On the one hand, subsidies *do* create other concerns (like subsidy wars,

[130] Appellate Body, *US—Cotton*, para 433; *US—Cotton (Article 21.5)*, para 372.

[131] With respect to the methodology, the Appellate Body in *US—Cotton (Article 21.5)* notes that the Panel is free in choosing it. A 'but for test' may be fine provided that it is not construed as one of the extremes 'necessary but not sufficient' or 'the only cause'. 'Other factors' that can impact the relation should also be considered. The Panel in *Korea—Commercial Vessels* used the 'but for' test for both price depression and price suppression claims.

Further, the Appellate Body intriguingly observes that since, unlike 'price depression', 'price suppression' cannot be observed, the relevant analysis is 'counterfactual in nature'. The interesting question is whether this means that counterfactual analysis should not be resorted to in other cases.

[132] See R Diamond, 'Privatization and the Definition of Subsidy: A Critical Study of Appellate Body Texturalism' (2008) Journal of International Economic Law 649, 673.

global inefficiency, and market access frustration). It cannot therefore be excluded that subsidy discipline may take these into account as well, and, from our perspective, this would influence the design and operation of impact standards. On the other hand, it is *not* necessary that an individual analysis be required in any case and that resort to more or less restrictive rules and presumptions should be precluded.[133]

The overview provided in this chapter confirmed that in both systems certain impact standards are already applied (see Article 6.3(c) of the SCM), or should be increasingly being applied (see Article 87(1) of the EC or the 'injury' test in Article 15 of the SCM), in a 'competition-oriented' perspective. At the same time, however, various provisions seem to have considered other concerns raised by subsidies, linked to global, political economy rationales (see the 'prohibited subsidies' category), the frustration of market access expectations (NVNI), or (in ways which still need specification) the actual impact on trade and competition (see the situations under paragraphs (a), (b) and (d) of Article 6.3).

We have also found quite a variety of techniques. Whereas most of the standards involved a case-by-case analysis, there is also a notable exception, that of prohibited subsidies, which resorted to a hard-and-fast prohibition.

Secondly, an easy parallel between EC and WTO law shows how a similar interpretation of the idea of 'distortion' can in fact be motivated by opposite goals, ie trade liberalization or protectionism.

On the one hand, the rather automatic, and combined, construction of the two requirements of 'distortion of competition' and 'effect on intra-EC trade' are fully consistent with the fact that State aid control in Europe was created in the context of the promotion of a common market.[134] In other words, a simplified idea of distortion is easy to prove and, by catching many measures within its net, may fully contribute to an integrationist aim by removing 'obstacles to trade'.

On the other hand, the use of a similarly simple idea of distortion may find a different—and indeed an *opposite*—justification in the context of the GATT/WTO. The extremely simplified concept of distortion which underlies the interpretation of the 'injury' test in the context of countervailing duty actions (only?) is in line with the general and blurred idea of *fair* competition. The relevant conceptual benchmark (What is fair? What is unfair?) is, probably intentionally, difficult to identify. From a practical perspective, this idea would inform a particularly low evidential threshold which would serve the objective of protecting domestic industry injured by unfair foreign imports. The risk is clear. This simple idea of distortion easily becomes a powerful tool in protectionist hands.

For similar reasons—a subsidy discipline properly informed by its deepest concern, the distortion of competition—it has been suggested that both the EC and

[133] This order of issue has been developed also in chapter 2, section III.B.

[134] See the Commission' statements in OECD, *Competition Policy in Subsidies and State Aid*, Competition Policy Roundtable, DAFFE/CLP (2001) 24, OECD, Paris, 173.

the WTO should abandon their simple idea of distortion and adopt a more conceptually and practically sound, sophisticated approach.

The third, and final order of conclusions, concerns the WTO in particular, and its multiplicity of standards. Commenting the Tokyo Round Subsidies Code, Hufbauer and Shelton-Erb had the opportunity to note that '[a]s a result of the give and take of political compromise, far too many trade-impact standards have been devised, and simplification would be most welcome'.[135] What was suggested was a more stringent approach for unilateral action, based on a material injury test, and a looser approach when multilateral control is involved, interestingly relying on clear data, like lost sales and lower prices, and with a flexible use of presumptions (subject to rebuttal). Thus, adverse effects would have been presumed for export subsidies and for those countries obtaining a certain minimum market share.

Although the author does not specifically comment on these plain suggestions, it is clear that there is much merit in them. The conclusion that we have far too many impact standards is still partly correct in the WTO era. There is certainly a good case for rationalization and simplification. This would bring clarity and coherency, two much sought commodities.

[135] GC Hufbauer and J Shelton Erb, *Subsidies in International Trade* (Cambridge, Massachusetts: MIT Press, 1984) 43.

Conclusions

The stated goal of this book is 'to provide an analytical and conceptual framework' of the legal definitions of WTO subsidy and EC State aid.

As noted in chapter 1, the decision to embark on this effort was due mainly to two reasons. First, the conceptual and practical importance of these notions. They tell us whether a given discipline, with all its requirements, exceptions and legal paraphernalia, applies or not. And, since any discipline embraces its own balance of values and interests, this issue also has clear political and symbolic dimensions. Secondly, despite its significance the 'definition' of subsidy is still an 'issue'. The definition of the subject of a legal discipline is the *basic controlling* factor. Everything begins with, and possibly returns to, it. In both the WTO and the EC, this is an area that is surprisingly full of continuing controversies and lack of clarity. This uncertainty—and the willingness to find coherent answers—is the ultimate justification of this book. We cannot avoid recalling the concluding words of Professor Jackson's chapter on subsidies in *The World Trading System*: 'The subject probably merits other efforts of elaboration and definition also'.[1]

This book offers a distinct, conceptual framework for analysing the definition of subsidy in the two legal systems and their various issues. A subsidy language, made of issues and tests, concepts and categories, has been developed. Most importantly, some general elements have emerged as essential characteristics, and useful tools of interpretation, of a more abstract concept of subsidy, transcending, but always connected to, the actual definitions posited in WTO and EC law. The first is a form of public action, the second the conferral of an economic advantage, the third an impact on the competitive process. These constitute the subject of the analysis in the three main parts of the book (respectively Parts II, III and V).

It is hoped that with this packaged conceptual toolbox the 'interpreter and policy-maker' may have a better understanding of the topic. And this is for the readers rather than the author to say. What can be done here is to outline the main conclusions that the use of that conceptual framework has allowed us to reach.

The preliminary remark is that, maybe not so surprisingly, the topic is not exclusively or mainly technical. Certainly both the concepts of WTO subsidy and EC State aid raise intricate and esoteric issues, all of great practical impact.

[1] JH Jackson, *The World Trading System—Law and Policy of International Economic Relations* (2nd edn, Cambridge Massachussetts: MIT Press, 1997) 303.

But, under this buzzing world of technicalities (made up of notions and categories, rules and exceptions, tests and benchmarks), there is a most interesting flow of more general themes. The emerging scenario is not the dry land of experts or the battlefield of lawyers and diplomats. It is the subject of the discourse of the most diverse disciplines, such as political science, economics, sociology, and philosophy, on one of the most intriguing topics in the field of international economic law. As a result, together with technical issues, broader themes, of both conceptual and policy nature, have thus naturally emerged from the analysis.

Let us briefly see what these themes are.

The main theme, with different variations, is the role played by objectives. This is a complex discourse operating at various levels.

In particular, one of the first realizations of whoever has to deal with subsidy or State aid issues, and all the more so with foundational ones like their definition, is that questions which we could easily call existential ought to be posed. In progressive, and escalating order—What is the purpose of this definition? What is the purpose the discipline of which it is part and defines the scope? And, ultimately, what are the more general, overall objectives of the political and legal system which accomodates the subsidy discipline?[2] These critical questions have been addressed in the Part on the 'Introduction and Foundations', and particularly chapter 2.

Only the answer to these questions enables the interpreter to approach more technical issues, like the definition of subsidy, and give it a meaning. An exegesis which does not solidly rest on an objective analysis is purposeless and will eventually be sterile. Its results will be merely descriptive, even tautological, and no added value on which to build further exploration, interpretation or law reform will be yielded.

But it is not only the level of the objectives of the legal system at large and of subsidy control—and its definition—that matter. An important variation to the main theme is also that the objectives of the subsidy itself (ie of the measure specifically contemplated or adopted by a given government) are capable of revealing equal, if no more, intriguing aspects of the analysis.

At the level of the actual examination of the subsidy measure a fascinating interplay emerges, that between scope and justification. Definitions are a matter of 'scope'. They define the ambit of application of certain rules. At the same time, however, subsidies are an important tool of public intervention in the economy, often motivated by public policy goals. This is the 'justification' of subsidy.

[2] Howse recently observed that: '[o]ne of failures of Doha negotiation is about the dissensus on the very purpose or nature of the WTO as a rule-based system'. See R Howse, 'Do the World Organization disciplines on domestic subsidies make sense? The case for legalizing some subsidies' in KW Bagwell, GA Bermann, and PC Mavroidis (eds), *Law and Economics of Contigent Protection in International Trade* (Cambridge: Cambridge University Press, forthcoming 2009). Indeed, it is high time for both the WTO and the EC (see the current constitutional malaise in Europe) to ask questions about purpose and direction.

For two reasons—one technical, one political—legal norms cannot possibly, distinguish in a precise manner scope from justification. On the one hand, the determination of whether we have a subsidy, often depends on the perusal of *certain* objectives. On the other hand, the attraction exerted by scope discourse is too strong for lawyers and politicians to resist. 'If we manage to have them conclude it is not a subsidy . . .' is the motto. For reasons of various orders, legal, political, even symbolic, to secure the notion that the public policy at issue is *not* a subsidy grants it a safe harbour, at least for the time being.

Returning to a few lines above, the reader can see that we have not predicated the statement that, technically, to define a subsidy we have to look at objectives in general terms. The phrase 'certain' objectives was used. This implies that a painstaking distinction has to be made. The difficulties of this technical exercise arise particularly in the area of taxation. What has to be done is to distinguish those objectives that are 'inherent' in the measure, and are thus relevant at the definitional level, from those that are 'external' to it, and should be eventually considered only afterwards, when a subsidy possibly 'breaching' the rule could nonetheless be 'justified'.

At a deeper and more theoretical level, revolving around the concepts of equality and distributive justice, this 'scope-justification' discourse has evidenced an intriguing paradox which is ubiquitous in non-market activities (especially in the area of taxation).[3] One would expect a perfect overlap between the distinction (i) 'breach of equality-definition-scope', and (ii) 'distributive objective-justification' on the other. The fascinating conclusion, which confirms from another perspective the attraction exerted by the scope analysis, is that the distributive objectives of certain measures are already considered at the level of the definition. The first term of the distinction above would thus have to be reformulated as follows: '*substantive* equality-definition-scope'. As noted in chapter 1, the more general question is to determine the degree of (re)distribution that the definition of subsidy is ready to accept. As most tax cases examined by the Commission or the Community Courts show, there is a balance and a limit to be found.

We can now outline the other themes that emerge from the book.

First, the difficulty, if not impossibility, of drawing clear lines around what forms of governmental actions are covered by the definition and what not. This depends on the natural 'pliabibility' of the concept of subsidy—an expression masterly crafted by the late Professor Hudec.[4] More specifically, the question is whether, and if so to what extent, 'regulatory' subsidies, where governments do not

[3] The paradox depends on the relevance of the concepts of equality and distributive justice for subsidy discourse. On the one hand, if found to exist, subsidies breach equality. They introduce a differential treatment with no immediate and inherent justification. At the same time, however, subsidies are a policy instrument often used to pursue policies of redistribution fostering equality.

The jurisprudential link between scope- justification, equality and redistributive justice is analysed in chapter 1, section IV.A.

[4] Re Hudec, 'Difference in National Environmental Standards: The Level-Playing-Field Dimension' (1996) 5 Minnesota Journal of Global Trade 1, 15.

act through the traditional tools of taxation and expenditure, but through the broader power to regulate the economy, should be covered. In no system, the status of regulatory measures is fully clear yet. This issue has been dealt with mainly in Part II of this book.

Secondly, two general phenomena have an important impact on the definition of subsidy (see Part III). These are the redefinition of the roles of the market on the one hand and of the public intervention in the economy on the other. Till very recently, before the financial and economic crises, and now recession, erupted, the trend was very clear. For decades governments have been retreating from various parts of the economy, liberalizing markets and privatizing companies. The most immediate consequence, also in the context of the definition of subsidy, was the seemingly unstoppable expansion of market logic. In the context of subsidy definitions, this meant two things. First, more and more instances of public action occured in a market context and were hence to be tested against market baselines. Secondly, the explanation of how markets worked has to be found in economic analysis. As a consequence, what has been witnessed is an increasing use of economic jargon and tests to assess the economic activities of governments. The impact on these conclusions of the current economic climate, which is bringing another redefinition of the respective roles of market and public sector—truly two characters in search of identity—is still to be seen.

Thirdly, within the broader context of WTO and EC law and their objectives, and more specifically of the relevant disciplines of subsidy control, we have concluded that what we are confronted with are essentially 'laws about competition'. This 'competition' theme goes through the whole book. It is introduced in chapter 2 and then developed from an operational perspective in chapter 14. Certainly subsidies may act as obstacles to international trade, frustrating market access, and the relevant commitments and expectations. At a deeper level, however, they have the potential to directly interfere with the determinants of firms' behaviour and thus affect the competitive process. This is, in the author's view, the main 'mischief' both EC State aid and WTO subsidy rules *should* attempt to address. Consequently, more than traditional 'trade regulation' (aimed at removing obstacles to free movement of economic factors), they should be looked at as 'competition regulation' (aimed at directly controlling the impact of subsidies on the cost/revenue structure of recipients and, via this, on their competitors).

This difference—it has been suggested—is not just a conceptual nicety. Although, as has been noted, a risk of oversimplification is present, we believe that the distinction is tenable and desirable. Since the *focus* and *operation* of trade and competition rules respectively is different, this conclusion may have great practical importance. In particular, the general adoption of a trade approach, focusing more on trade expectations and opportunities rather than on actual effects and competitive process, typically involves a rather blunt mechanism of operation, prohibiting measures that may be permitted within a more 'competition-oriented' scrutiny. The risk is thus one of 'over-inclusions'.

Quite significantly, a trade approach has traditionally prevailed in both the administration of EC State aid and WTO subsidy laws. But, intriguingly, for completing opposite causes. In the EC, the blunter internal market approach, which presumed that any State aid was distorting competition and trade, was instrumental to liberating and protecting the economic forces of an increasingly enlarged internal market while avoiding unfair competition between Member States. In sum, a free trade-and-competition aim. In the GATT/WTO context, on the other hand, where trade remedies, ie countervailing duties, unilaterally administered and imposed on foreign imports, have always had the upper hand, the construction of the relevant 'injury' standards in a relatively loose way meant that it was easier to trigger the discipline and to protect the domestic industry from external competition. The main substantive suggestion of the book is the shift from a 'trade' to a 'competition' perspective.

Fourthly, it is clear that the 'internal perspective' on the discipline, and definition, of subsidy, which is constituted by EC State aid and WTO subsidy rules themselves is inextricably linked to the 'external perspective', controlled by other rules and disciplines that may apply to the measure under examination. The possible applicability of specific rules on trade obstacles, taxation and regulation does play an important role in the determination of the scope of application of subsidy rules. In this regard, we have sketched some of the terms and issues coming out from this most interesting interplay between 'internal' and 'external' views in chapter 6.

Finally, the book has confirmed the utility of a comparative analysis. Indeed, the comparative approach has been one of the driving forces of this research, and its distinct flavour is pervasive in all the arguments presented. Its perspective has dramatically sharpened the awareness of issues, and the possibility of solutions, always in a fully contextual settings. In many ways, St Paul's exortation—'Probe everything and keep the best'[5]—has accompanied and guided this effort.

Similarities and differences have been detected, some expected, others not. Some issues that have come out in one system only are more than likely to emerge in the other as well. No one system is however better than the other. Any statement in this respect would be utterly simplistic. Within their own specific political, economic, social, legal, etc, context, each system has strengths and weakenesses. A process of cross-fertilization between the two is not only possible but desirable, and is conducive to the inevitable critical step of comparative exercises that has often led us to criticize current solutions and suggest new ones.

Further, a comparative exercise can lead us to better understand the inconsistencies between the two systems, in our case particularly with respect to the definitions of EC State aid and WTO subsidy, and approach with more awareness the possible 'conflicts' between two disciplines which do not live in splendid isolation but may well simultaneously assert their rights over what they call subsidy. Although

[5] *First Epistle to the Thessalonians*, 5, 21.

the topic is complex and goes well beyond the subject of this book, in the first chapter we have sketched the terms of the issue—always from a definitional perspective—and attempted to offer few guidelines.

'The major problem identified is the issue of the definition.' It is the author's hope that, if he has not succeeded in providing many answers in the controversial area of subsidies, and in the most controversial topic within it, his effort has at least raised new questions, or in any event put old ones in a newer perspective. If so, it will have provided useful inspiration on which to build new endeavours.

Bibliography

Abbamonte, G, 'Cross-subsidization and Community Competition rules: Efficient Pricing versus Equity?' (1998) European Law Review 414

Abi-Saab, G, 'The WTO Dispute Settlement and General International Law' in R Yerxa and B Wilson (eds), *Key Issues in WTO Dispute Settlement—The First Ten Years* (Cambridge: Cambridge University Press, 2005) 7

Adamantopoulos, K, and Pereyra-Friedrichsen, MJ, *EU Anti-Subsidy Law & Practice* (1st edn, Pembridge: Palladian Law, 2001)

Ahlborn, C, and Berg, C, 'Can State Aid Control Learn from Antitrust? The Need for Greater Role for Competition Analysis under the State Aid rules' in Biondi, A, Eeckhout, P and Flynn, J (eds), *The Law of State Aid in the European Union* (Oxford: Oxford University Press, 2004) 41

Albors-Llorens, A, 'The European Court of Justice: More than a Teleological Court' (1999) Cambridge Yearbook of European Legal Studies 373

Alexander, PM, 'The Specificity Test Under US Countervailing Duty Law' (1989) Michigan Journal of International Law 807

Alexis, A, 'Notion d'Aide d'Etat—Remarques sur l'arrêt Stardust Marine du 16 mai 2002' (2002) European State Aid Law Quarterly 149

Andreassen, BA, and Marks, SP (eds) *Development as a Human Right—Legal, Political, and Economic Dimensions* (Cambridge MA: Harvard School of Public Health, 2006)

Arhold, C, 'The 2007/2008 Case Law of the European Court of Justice and the Court of First Instance on State Aid' (2008) European State Aid Law Quarterly 441

Aristotle, *Ethica Niconchese* (Oxford: Clarendon Press, 1925)

Aristotle, *The Politics* (Oxford: Oxford University Press, 1995)

Arnull, A, *The European Court of Justice* (2nd edn, Oxford: Oxford University Press, 2006)

Atanasiu, I, 'EC State Aid Policy with Respect to Soft Budgetary Constraints: Tax and Social Security Contribution Payment Arrears' (2005) European State Aid Law Quarterly 597

Atanasiu, I, 'Chronopost II: The Application of the Market Economy Investor Principle in Reserved Sectors' (2008) European State Aid Law Quarterly 571

Bacchus, J, 'Appellators: The Quest for the Meaning of And/Or' (2005) World Trade Review 499

Bacon, K, 'State Aids and General Measures' (1997) Yearbook of European Law 269

Bacon, K, 'Differential Taxes, State Aids and the Lunn Poly Case' (1999) European Competition Law Review 384

Bacon, K, 'State Aids in the English Courts: Definition and Other Problems', in Biondi, A, Eeckhout, P and Flynn, J (eds) *The Law of State Aid in the European Union* (Oxford: Oxford University Press, 2004) 337

Bacon, K, *European Community Law of State Aid* (Oxford: Oxford University Press, 2009)

Bagwell, K, and Staiger, RW, *The Economics of the World Trading System* (Cambridge MA: MIT Press, 2002)

Bagwell, K, and Staiger, RW, 'Will International Rules on Subsidies Disrupt the World Trading System?' (2006) The American Economic Review 877

Bagwell, KW, Bermann, GA and Mavroidis, PC (eds), *Law and Economics of Contingent Protection in International Trade* (Cambridge: Cambridge University Press, forthcoming 2009)

Bagwell, KW, and Mavroidis, PC, 'Too Much, Too Little ... Too Late?' in Bagwell, KW, Bermann, GA and Mavroidis, PC (eds), *Law and Economics of Contigent Protection in International Trade* (Cambridge: Cambridge University Press, forthcoming 2009)

Barceló, JJ III, 'Subsidies and Countervailing Duties—Analysis and Proposal' (1977) Law and Policy in International Business 779

Barnard, C, 'Fitting the Remaining Pieces into the Goods and Persons Jigsaw?' (2001) European Law Review 35

Barshefsky, C, Mattice, AL and Martin II, WL, 'Government Equity Participation in State-Owned Enterprises: An Analysis of the Carbon Steel Countervailing Duty Cases' (1983) Law and Policy in International Business 1101–58

Bartosch, A, 'Clarification or Confusion? How to Reconcile the ECJ's Rulings in Altmark and Chronopost' (2003) European State Aid Law Quarterly 375

Bartosch, A, 'Distortions of Competition on the Markets for the Operation of Airport Infrastructures: the Commission's New Guidelines'(2005) European State Aid Law Quarterly 621

Basquero Cruz, J, and Castillo de la Torre, F, 'A Note on PreussenElektra' (2001) European Law Review 489

Begg, D, Fisher, S, and Dornbusch, R, *Economics* (5th edn, London: MacGraw-Hill, 1997)

Bello, JH, and Holmer, AF, 'Subsidies and Natural Resources: Congress Rejects a Lateral Attack on the Specificity Test' (1984/1985) George Washington Journal of International Law and Economics 297

Benitah, M, 'Les divers sens du concept de distortion et leur rôle dans la définition juridique actuelle d'une subvention compensable: Les normes internationales et le cas des États-Unis' (1996) Canadian Yearbook of International Law, 137

Benitah, M, *The Law of Subsidies under the GATT/WTO System* (The Hague: Kluwer Law International, 2001)

Benitah, M, 'Subsidies, Services and Sustainable Development' (2005) Issue Paper No 1 for International Centre for Trade and Sustainable Development (ICTSD)

Benyon, F, and Bourgeois, J, 'The European Community—United States Steel Arrangement' (1984) Common Market Law Review 305

Beseler, JF, and Williams, AN, *Anti-Dumping and Anti-Subsidy Law—The European Communities* (London: Sweet & Maxwell, 1986)

Besley, T, and Seabright, P, 'The Effects and Policy Implications of State Aids to Industry: An Economic Analysis' (1999) Economic Policy 15

Beviglia Zampetti, A, 'The Uruguay Round Agreement on Subsidies—A Forward-Looking Assessment' (1996) Journal of World Trade 5

Bhagwati, J, *In Defence of Globalization* (Oxford: Oxford University Press, 2004)

Bhandari, JS, and Sykes, AO, *Economic Dimensions in International Law* (Cambridge: Cambridge University Press, 1997)

Bigdeli, SZ, 'Incentive Schemes to Promote Renewables and the WTO Law of Subsidies', in Bigdeli, SZ, Cottier, T, Nartova, O (eds) *International Trade Regulation and the Mitigation of Climate Change* (Cambridge: Cambridge University Press, 2009)

Biondi, A, 'BUPA v Commission' (2008) European State Aid Law Quarterly 401

Biondi, A, 'Free trade, a mountain road and the right to protest: European economic freedoms and fundamental individual rights' (2004) European Human Rights Law Review 51

Biondi, A, 'Justifying State Aid: The Financing of Services of General Economic Interest' in Tridimas, T and Nebbia P (eds) *European Union Law for the Twenty-First Century*, Volume II (Oxford: Hart Publishing, 2004)

Biondi, A, Eeckhout, P and Flynn, J (eds) *The Law of State Aid in the European Union* (Oxford: Oxfrod Univeristy Press, 2004)

Biondi, A, and Eeckhot, P, 'State Aid and Obstacles to Trade' in Biondi, A, Eeckhout, P and Flynn, J (eds) *The Law of State Aid in the European Union* (Oxford: Oxford University Press, 2004) 103

Biondi, A, and Rubini, L, 'Aims, Effects and Justifications: EC State Aid Law and Its Impact on National Social Policies', in Dougan, M and Spaventa, E (eds) *Social Welfare and EU Law* (Oxford: Hart Publishing, 2005) 79

Biondi, A, 'Review of Judgment in Case C-222/04—Ministero dell'Economia e delle Finanze v. Cassa di Risparmio di Firenze SpA et al.' (2006) European State Aid Law Quarterly 371

Biondi, A, 'Some Reflections on the Notion of "State Resources" in European Community State Aid Law' (2007) Fordham International Law Journal 1426

Bishop, B, 'From Trade to Tutelage: State Aid and Public Choice in the European Union', Presentation to Conference to ACE, Copenhagen, 2 December 2005

Black, J, *Oxford Dictionary of Economics* (2nd edn, Oxford: Oxford University Press, 2002)

Black, O, *Conceptual Foundations of Antitrust* (Cambridge: Cambridge University Press, 2005)

Bognetti, G, *Introduzione al Diritto Costituzionale Comparato* (Turin: Giappichelli, 1994)

Boltuck, RD, 'Innovations in support of the unitary injury test in US unfair trade cases', in Bhandari, JS and Sykes, AO (eds) *Economic Dimensions in International Law* (Cambridge: Cambridge University Press, 1997), 166

Bourgeois, JHJ, 'The GATT Rules for Industrial Subsidies and Countervailing Duties and the New GATT Round: The Weather and the Seeds', in EU Petersmann and M Hilf (eds) *The New GATT Round of Multilateral Trade Negotiations: Legal and Economic Problems*, Vol. V (Deventer: Kluwer, 1991) 231 et seq

Bourgeois, JHJ (ed) *Subsidies and International Trade—A European Lawyers' Perspective* (Deventer–Boston: Kluwer, 1991)

Bourgeois, JHJ, 'State Aids, Taxation Measures and Specificity. Some Thoughts', in Dony, M and De Walsche, A, *Mélanges en hommage à Michel Waelbroeck,* Vol 2 (Bruxelles: Bruylant, 1999) 765

Bourgeois, JHJ, 'EU Rules on State Aids and WTO Provisions on Subsidies Compared: The Case of State-Owned Banks', in Ehlermann, CD and Everson, M, *European Competition Law Annual 1999: Selected Issues in the Field of State Aids* (Oxford: Hart Publishing, 2001) 209

Bovis, CH, 'Financing Services of General Interest in the EU: How do Public Procurement and State Aids Interact to Demarcate between Market Forces and Protection' (2005) European Law Journal 79

Brander, K, and Spencer, B, 'Export Subsidies and International Market Share Rivalry' (1985) Journal of International Economics 82

Breyer, S, *Active Liberty: Interpreting a Democratic Constitution* (rev edn, Oxford: Oxford University Press, 2008)

Bronckers, M, and Quick, R, 'What is a Countervailable Subsidy under EEC Trade Law?' (1989) 6 Journal of World Trade 5

Bronckers, M, and Van der Vlies, R, 'The European Court's PreussenElektra Judgment: tensions between EU Principles and National Renewable Energy Initiatives' (2001) European Competition Law Review 458

Brown, NL, and Jacobs, FG, *The Court of Justice of the European Communities* (5th edn, London: Sweet & Maxwell, 2000)

Brownlie, I, *Principles of Public International Law* (6th edn, Oxford: Oxford University Press, 2003)

Buendia-Sierra, JL, 'Not like this: Some Skeptical Remarks on the "Refined Economic Approach" in State aid', in Proceedings of 4th Experts' Forum on New Developments in European State Aid Law, 18 and 19 May 2006, European State Aid Law Institute (Berlin: Lexxion, 2006) 59

Buendia-Sierra, JL, and Smulders, B, 'The Limited Role of the "Refined Economic Approach" in Achieving the Objectives of State Aid Control: Time for Some Realism', in 'EC State aid law-Le Droit des Aides d'Etat dans la CE, Liber Amicorum Francisco Santaolalla Gadea (Kluwer Law International, 2008) 18

Calamai P, and De Moor A, *Subsidizing Unsustainable Development—Undermining the Earth with Public Funds* (Geneva: Earth Council, 1997)

Cameron, LA, and Berg, GC, 'The US Countervailing Duty Law and the Principle of General Availability' (1985) Journal of World Trade Law 497

Cass, RA, 'Trade Subsidy Law: Can a Foolish Inconsistency be Good Enough for Government Work?' (1989) Law and Policy in International Business 609

Cass, RA, and Boltuck, RD, 'Antidumping and Countervaling-Duty Law: The Mirage of Equitable International Competition', in Bhagwati, JN and Hudec, RE, *Fair Trade and Harmonization—Prerequisites for Free Trade? Vol 2: Legal Analysis* (Cambridge MA: MIT Press, 1996)

Cass, RA, and Knoll, MS, 'The economics of "injury" in antidumping and countervailing duty cases: A reply to Professor Sykes', in Bhandari, JS and Sykes, AO (eds) *Economic Dimensions in International Law* (Cambridge: Cambridge University Press, 1997) 126

Cass, DZ, *The Constitutionalization of the World Trade Organization: Legitimacy, Democracy, and Community in the International Trading System* (Oxford: Oxford University Press, 2005)

Cho, S, 'The WTOs *Gemeinschaft*' (2004) Alabama Law Review 483

Cirenei, MT, 'La riforma dell'amministrazione straordinaria alla luce della disciplina comunitaria degli aiuti: fine di un contenzioso?' (1999) Diritto del Commercio Internazionale 199

Clarke, PA, Bourgeois, J, and Horlick, GN, 'WTO Dispute Settlement Practice Relating to Subsidies and Countervailing Measures', in Ortino, F and Petersmann, EU (eds) *The WTO Dispute Settlement Syste, 1995-2003* (Kluwer Law International, 2004) 353

Coccia, M, 'Comment' in Bourgeois, JHJ (ed) *Subsidies and International Trade—A European Lawyers' Perspective* (Deventer-Boston: Kluwer, 1991) 139

Conte, G, 'Aiuti di Stato e procedure concorsuali nazionali nella recente giurisprudenza comunitaria: il caso della "Legge Prodi"' (1999) Il Diritto dell'Unione Europea 539

Cottier, T, 'Limits to International Trade: The Constitutional Challenge' (2000) American Society of International Law Proceedings 220

Cottier, T, 'From Progressive Liberalization to Progressive Regulation in WTO Law' (2006) Journal of International Economic Law 1

Cottier, T, *The Challenges of WTO Law: Collected Essays* (London: Cameron May, 2007)

Cottier, T, and Nadakavuakeren Schefer, K, 'Non-Violation Complaints in WTO/GATT Dispute Settlement: Past Present and Future in Cottier, *The Challenges of WTO Law: Collected Essay* (London: Cameron May, 2007) 75

Craig, P, and De Búrca, G, *EU Law—Text, Cases and Materials* (4th edn, Oxford: Oxford University Press, 2007)

Crawford, J, *The International Law Commission's Articles on State Responsibility—Introduction, Text and Commentaries* (Cambridge: Cambridge University Press, 2002)

Criscuolo, A, 'The State in a liberal market economy: a private investor and creditor or a public authority' (1999) European Law Review 531

Crocioni, P, 'Can State Aid Policy Become more Economic-Friendly?' (2006) World Competition, 89

D'Ormesson, O, and Bouin, A, 'Review of the ECJ Judgment in Case C-172/03 Wolfgang Heiser v Finanzamt Innsbruck, 3 March 2005' (2005) European State Aid Law Quarterly 335

Davey, W, 'The Dispute Settlement Mechanism', Illinois Public Law and Legal Theory Research Paper Series, Research Paper No 03-08, 25 June 2003.

Davies, P, 'Market Integration and Social Policy in the Court of Justice' (1995) Industrial Law Journal 49

De Búrca, G, and Scott, J, *The EU and the WTO—Legal and Constitutional Issues* (Oxford: Hart Publishing, 2001)

De Búrca, G, (ed) *EU and the Welfare State—In Search of Solidarity* (Oxford: Oxford University Press, 2006)

Derenne, J, and Merola, M (eds), *Economic Analysis of State Aid Rules—Contributions and Limits* (Berlin: Lexxion, 2004)

Diamond, R, 'A Search for Economic and Financial Principles in the Administration of United States Countervailing Duty Law' (1989) Law and Policy in International Business, 507

Diamond, R, 'Economic Foundations of Countervailing Duty Law' (1989) Virginia Law Journal of International Law, 767

Diamond, R, 'Privatization and the Definition of Subsidy: A Critical Study of Appellate Body Texturalism' (2008) Journal of International Economic Law 649

Di Bucci, V, 'Direct Taxation'—State Aid in form of Fiscal Measures', in Rydelski, MS (ed) *The EC State Aid Regime: Distortive Effects of State Aid on Competition and Trade* (London: Cameron May, 2006) 73

Di Bucci, V, 'Comments on the Paper "Selectivity, Economic Advantage, Distortion of Competition and Effect on Trade"' in Derenne, J and Merola, M (eds) *Economic Analysis of State Aid Rules—Contributions and Limits* (Berlin: Lexxion, 2007) 156

Didier, P, *WTO Trade Instruments in EU Law—Commercial Policy Instruments: Dumping, Subsidies, Safeguards, Public Procurement* (London: Cameron May, 1999)

Dominick, MF, 'Countervailing State Aids to Steel: A Case for International Consensus' (1984) Common Market Law Review 355

Dougan, M, and Spaventa, E (eds) *Social Welfare and EU Law* (Oxford: Hart Publishing: 2005)

Douglas-Scott, S, *Constitutional Law of the European Union* (Harlow: Pearson Longman, 2002)

Duchêne, F, *Jean Monnet: The First Statesman of Interdependence* (New York: Norton, 1994)

Dworkin, R, 'Is Wealth a Value?' in *A Matter of Principle* (Cambridge MA: Harvard University Press, 1985) 237

Dworkin, R, 'Why Efficiency?' in *A Matter of Principle* (Cambridge MA: Harvard University Press, 1985) 267

Eeckhout, P, 'Constitutional Concepts for Free Trade in Services', in De Búrca, G and Scott, J (eds) *The EU and the WTO—Legal and Constitutional Issues* (Oxford: Hart Publishing, 2001) 211

Eeckhout, P, *External Relations of the European Union—Legal and Constitutional Foundations* (Oxford: Oxford University Press, 2004)

Eeckhout, P, 'Remedies and Compliance' in Bethlemen, D, McRae, D, Neufeld, R and Van Damme, I (eds) *The Oxford Handbook of International Trade Law* (Oxford: Oxford University Press, 2009) 438

Ehlermann, CD, 'The Contribution of EC Competition Policy to the Single Market' (1992) Common Market Law Review 257

Ehlermann, CD, and Everson, M (eds) *European Competition Law Annual 1999: Selected Issues in the Field of State Aids* (Oxford: Hart Publishing, 2001)

Ehlermann, CD, 'Six Years on the Bench of the "World Trade Court"—Some Personal Experiences as Member of the Appellate Body of the World Trade Organization' in (2002) 36:4 Journal of World Trade 605

Ehlermann, CD, and Vallery, A, 'Giving Meaning to the Condition of Effect on Trade: The Court's Judgment in Xunta de Galicia, a Missed Opportunity?' (2005) European State Aid Law Quarterly, 709

Ehlermann, CD, and Goyette, M, 'The Interface between EU State Aid Control and WTO Disciplines on Subsidies' (2006) European State Aid Law Quarterly 695

Eksridge, WN Jr, 'Dynamic Interpretation of Economic Regulatory Legislation (Countervailing Duty Law)' (1989) Law and Policy in International Business 663

Evans, A, *European Community Law of State Aid* (Oxford: Clarendon Press, 1997)

Facenna, G, 'State Aid and Environmental Protection', in Biondi, A, Eeckhout, P and Flynn, J (eds) *The Law of State Aid in the European Union* (Oxford: Oxford University Press, 2004) 245

Fingleton, J, Ruane and F, Ryan, V, 'Market Definition and State Aid Control' in European Commission (Directorate General for Economic and Financial Affairs) *'State Aid and the Single Market', European Economy—Report and Studies* (1999) 65

Flett, J, Jessep, AC, and Talaber-Ritz, K, 'The Relationship between WTO Subsidies Law and EC State Aid Law' in 'EC State aid law-Le Droit des Aides d'Etat dans la CE, Liber Amicorum Francisco Santaolalla Gadea (Kluwer Law International, 2008) 441

Fox, E, 'Competition Law and the Agenda for the WTO: Forging the Links of Competition and Trade' (1995) Pacific Rim Law and Policy Association 1

Fox, E, 'Toward World Antitrust and Market Access' (1997) American Journal of International Law 1

Friederiszick, HW, Röller, LH and Verouden, V, *European State Aid Control: An Economic Framework*, in Bucirossi (ed), *Handbook of Antitrust Economics* (Cambridge MA: MIT Press, 2008) 625

Frontier Economics, *The Effects of Public Subsidies on Competition*, a report prepared for the Office of Fair Trading, enclosed as Annexe C to OFT (2004)

Galbraith, JK, *The Affluent Society* (5th edn, London: Penguin, 1998)

Gambaro, E, Nucara, A, and Prete, L, 'Pearle: so much unsaid!' (2005) European State Aid Law Quarterly 3

Garcia, J, and Neven, D, 'Identification of Sensitive Sectors in which State Aid may have Significant Distorting Effects', Report for the HM Treasury, UK, 2004

Garner, BA, (ed) *Black's Law Dictionary* (7th edn, St Paul, Minnesota: West Group, 1999)

Geelhoed, LA, 'The Demarcation of State Aid and Regulatory Charges' in (2005) *European State Aid Law Quarterly* 40

Gerber, DJ, 'Competition Law and the WTO: Rethinking the Relationship' (2007) Journal of International Economic Law 707

Goetz, CJ, Granet, L, and Schwartz, WF, 'The Meaning of "Subsidy" and "Injury" in the Countervailing Duty Law' (1986) International Review of Law and Economics 17

Goh, G, and Ziegler, A, 'Retrospective Remedies in the WTO after *Automotive Leather*' (2003) Journal of International Economic Law 545

Goossens, A, and Emmerrechts, S, 'Case Note on Case C-379/98 *PreussenElektra AG* v *Schleswag* AG' (2001) Common Market Law Review 991

Grane, P, 'Remedies under WTO Law' (2001) JIEL 755

Gray, JM, 'Taxation: Foreign Sales Corporations Replace Domestic International Sales Corporations' (1985) Harvard International Law Review 293

Green, A, and Trebilcock, M, 'Enforcing WTO Obligations: Whan Can We Learn From Export Subsidies?' (2007) Journal of International Economic Law 653

Green, A, and Trebilcock, M, 'The Enduring Problem of WTO Export Subsidies Rules' (2007) in Bermann CA, Mavroidis PC and Bagwell, KM (eds) *Law and Economics of Contigent Protection in International Trade* (Cambridge: Cambridge University Press, forthcoming 2009)

Groeteke, F, and Heine, K, '"Institutional Rigidities" and European State Aid Control' (2004) European Competition Law Review 322–31

Grossman, G, and Mavrodis, PC, 'Here Today? Gone Tomorrow?' in Horn, H and Mavroidis, PC (eds) *The WTO Case Law of 2001* (Cambridge: Cambridge University Press, 2003) 170

Grossman, G, and Mavrodis, PC, 'Recurring Misunderstandings of Non Recurring Subsidies' in Horn, H and Mavroidis, PC (eds) *The WTO Case Law of 2002* (Cambridge: Cambridge University Press, 2005) 78

Habermes, J, 'Does the Constitutionalization of International Law Still Have a Chance?' in Habermes, J, *The Divided West* (Cambridge: Polity Press, 2000)

Hallstein, W, 'The European Economic Community' (1963) Political Science Quarterly 161

Hancher, L, and Buendia-Sierra, JL, *Cross Subsidization and EC Law* (1998) Common Market Law Review 901

Hancher, L, 'Case note on Case C-482/99 *French Republic* v *Commission* ('Stardust Marine')' (2003) Common Market Law Review 739
Hancher, L, 'A Pearle of Wisdom' (2004) European State Aid Law Quarterly 363
Hansen, M, Van Ysendyck, A and Zühlke, S, 'The Coming of Age of EC State Aid Law: A Review of the Principal Developments in 2002 and 2003' (2004) European Competition Law Review 202
Hardin, G, 'The Tragedy of the Commons' (1968) Science 1243
Hart, HLA, 'Definition and Theory in Jurisprudence' (1954) Law Quarterly Review 70
Hart, HLA, *The Concept of Law* (2nd edn, Oxford: Clarendon Press, 1994)
Hencsey, M, Reymond, O, Riedl, A, Santamato, S and Westerhof, JG, 'State aid rules and public funding of broadband' (2005) Competition Policy Newsletter 8
Hoekman, BM, and Mavroidis, PC, 'Policy Externalities and High-Tech Rivalry: Competition and Multilateral Cooperation Beyond the WTO' (1996) Leiden Journal of International Law 273
Hoekman, BM, and Kostecki, MM, *The Political Economy of the World Trading System* (Oxford: Oxford University Press, 2001)
Horlick, GN, 'Subsidies Discipline Under WTO and US Rules' in Ehlermann, CD and Everson, M (eds) *European Competition Law Annual 1999: Selected Issues in the Filed of State Aids* (Oxford: Hart Publishing, 2001) 593
Horn, H, and Weiler, JHH, 'EC—Asbestos' in Horn, H, and Mavroidis, PC (eds) *The WTO Case Law of 2001* (Cambridge: Cambridge University Press, 2003) 14
Horn, H, and Mavroidis, PC, 'Still Hazy After All These Years: The Interpretation of National Treatment in the GATT/WTO Case-Law on Tax Discrimination' (2004) European Journal of International Law 39
Horn, H, and Mavroidis, PC, 'United States—Preliminary Determination with Respect to Certain Softwood Lumber from Canada: What is a subsidy?' in Horn, H, and Mavroidis, PC, *The WTO Case Law of 2002* (Cambridge: Cambridge University Press, 2005) 220
Howse, R, and Regan, D, 'The Product/Process Distinction—An Illusory Basis for Disciplining "Unilateralism" in Trade Policy' (2000) European Journal of International Law 249
Howse, R, and Nicolaides, K, 'Enhancing WTO Legitimacy: Constitutionalization or Global Subsidiarity?' (2003) Governance 73
Howse, R, 'Post-Hearing Submission to the International Trade Commission: World Trade Law and Renewable Energy: The Case of Non-Tariff Measures', 5 May 2005, Renewable Energy and International Law Project
Howse, R, 'Do the World Organization disciplines on domestic subsidies make sense? The case for legalizing some subsidies' in Bagwell, KW, Bermann, GA and Mavroidis, PC (eds), *Law and Economics of Contigent Protection in International Trade* (Cambridge: Cambridge University Press, forthcoming 2009)
Hudec, RE, 'GATT or GABB? The Future Design of the General Agreement on Tariffs and Trade' (1971) Yale Law Journal 1299
Hudec, RE, *Enforcing International Trade Law—The Evolution of the Modern GATT Legal System* (Salem, New Hampshire: Buttherworth Legal Publishers 1993)
Hudec, RE, 'Differences in National Environmental Standards: The Level-Playing-Field Dimension' (1996) 5 Minnesota Journal of Global Trade 1

Hudec, RE, 'GATT/WTO Constraints on National Regulation: Requiem for an "Aims and Effects" Test' (1998) The International Lawyer 619

Hudec, RE, 'Industrial Subsidies: Tax Treatment of 'Foreign Sales Corporations" in Petersmann, EU and Pollack, MA (eds) *Transatlantic Economic Disputes—The EU, the US, and the WTO* (Oxford: Oxford University Press, 2003) 175

Hufbauer, GC, and Shelton Erb, J, *Subsidies in International Trade* (Cambridge, Massachusetts: MIT Press, 1984)

Hufbauer, GC, and Assa, A, *US—Taxation of Foreign Income* (Washington DC: Peterson Institute for International Economics, 2007)

Hufbauer, GC, Moll, T, and Rubini, L, 'Investment Subsidies for Cross-Border M&A: Trends and Policy Implications', Occasional Paper Series No 2, United States Council for International Business Foundation, New York, 2008

Hufbauer, GC, and Brunel, C, 'The US Congress and the Chinese Renminbi' in M Goldstein and NR Lardy, *Debating China's Exchange Rate Policy* (Washington: Peterson Institute for International Economics, 2008)

Hufbauer, GC, Charnovitz, S, and Kim, J, *Global Warming and the World Trading System* (Washington DC: Peterson Institute for International Economics, 2009)

Hylton, KN, *Antitrust Law—Economic Theory and Common Law Evolution* (Cambridge: Cambridge University Press, 2003)

Instructions for American Servicemen in Britain 1942: Reproduced from the Original Typescript, War Department, Washington, DC (2nd edn, Oxford: The Bodleian Library, 2004)

Irwin, DA, Mavroidis, PC and Sykes, AO, *The Genesis of the GATT* (Cambridge: Cambridge University Press, 2008)

Jackson, JH, *World Trade and the Law of GATT* (Indianapolis: Bobbs Merrill, 1969)

Jackson, JH, 'The Jurisprudence of International Trade: The DISC Case in GATT' (1978) American Journal of International Law 747

Jackson, JH, 'Perspectives on Countervailing Duties' (1989) Law and Policy in International Business 739

Jackson, JH, *The World Trading System—Law and Policy of International Economic Relations* (2nd edn, Cambridge Massachussetts: MIT Press, 1997)

Jackson, JH, *The World Trade Organization: Constitution and Jurisprudence* (London: Royal Institute of International Affairs, 1998)

Jackson, JH, *Sovereignty, WTO and Changing Fundamentals of International Law*, Cambridge: Cambridge University Press, 2006)

Jacobs, FG, 'Varieties of Approach to Treaty Interpretation: With Special Reference to the Draft Convention on the Law of Treaties before the Vienna Diplomatic Conference' (1969) International and Comparative Law Quarterly 318

Jacobs, FG, 'The Uses of Comparative Law in the Law of the European Communities, Legal History and Comparative Law' in Plender, R (ed) *Legal History and Comparative Law: Essays in Honour of A. Kiralfy* (London: Frank Cass, 1990)

Jacobs, FG, 'Is the Court of Justice of the European Communities a Constitutional Court?' in Curtin, D and O'Keeffe, D (eds) *Constitutional Adjudication in European Community and National Law* (Dublin: Butterworths, 1992) 25

Jacobs, FG, *The Sovereignty of Law—The European Way*, The Hamlyn Lectures 2006 (Cambridge: Cambridge University Press, 2007)

Jaeger, T, 'The CELF-Judgment: A Precarious Conception of the Standstill Obligation' (2008) European State Aid Law Quarterly 279

Janow, ME, and Staiger, RW, 'Canada—Measures Affecting the Importation of Dairy Products and the Exportation of Milk' in Horn, H and Mavroidis, P *The WTO Case Law of 2001* (Cambridge: Cambridge University Press, 2003) 236

Janow, ME, and Staiger, RW, 'United States—Measures Treating Export Restraints as Subsidies' in Horn, H and Mavroidis, P *The WTO Case Law of 2001* (Cambridge: Cambridge University Press, 2003) 200

Joerges, C, and Petersmann, EU, *Constitutionalism, Multilevel Trade Governance and Social Regulation* (Oxford: Hart Publishing, 2006)

Kaplow, L, 'Rules Versus Standards: An Economic Analysis' (1992) Duke Law Journal 557

Karyfis, G, 'Le principe de l'opérateur économique privé, critère de qualification des mesure étatiques, en tant qu'aides d'Etat, au sens de l'article 87, par. 1 du Traité CE' (2003) Revue Trimestrielle de Droit Européen 389

Kirch, P, d'Ormesson, O, Rodriguez Curiel, JW, 'Transfer of State Resources' in Derenne, J, and Merola, M (eds) *Economic Analysis of State Aid Rules—Contributions and Limits* (Berlin: Lexxion, 2007) 105

Klabbers, J, and Vregdenhil, A, 'Dispute Settlement in GATT: DISC and its Successor' (1986/1987) Legal Issues of European Integration 115

Kliemann, A, 'Aid for Environmental Protection' in Rydelski, MS (ed) *The EC State Aid Regime: Distortive Effects of State Aid on Competition and Trade* (London: Cameron May, 2006) 315

Koenig, C, and Bartosch, A, 'EC State Aid Law reviewing Equity Capital Injections and Loan Grants by the Public Sector: A Comparative Analysis' (2000) European Competition Law Review, 377

Koenig, C, 'State Guarantees for the German Landesbanken and the EC State Aid Regime', in Ehlermann, CD, and Everson, M (eds) *European Competition Law Annual 1999: Selected Issues in the Filed of State Aids* (Oxford: Hart Publishing, 2001), 239

Koenig, C, and Haratsch, A, 'The Logic of Infrastructure Funding under EC State Aid Control' (2004) European State Aid Law Quarterly 393

Koenig, C, and Kiefer, S, 'Public Funding of Infrastructure Projects under EC-State Aid Law' (2005) European State Aid Law Quarterly 415

Krajewski, M, *National Regulation and Trade Liberalization in Services: The Legal Impact of the General Agreement on Trade in Services (GATS) on National Regulatory Autonomy* (The Hague: Kluwer Law International, 2003)

Krajewski, M, 'Public Services and Trade Liberalization: Mapping the Legal Framework' (2003) Journal of International Economic Law 341

Krajewski, M, 'Environmental Services of General Interest in the WTO' (2004) Journal for European Environmental and Planning Law 101

Krugman, PR, *The Return of Depression Economics and the Crisis of 2008* (2nd edn, London: Penguin, 2008)

Krugman, PR, and Obsfeld, M, *International Economics—Theory and Policy* (5th edn, London: Addison Wesley, 2000)

Kutscher, H, 'Methods of Interpretation as Seen by a Judge of the Court of Justice', in *Reports of the 1976 Judicial and Academic Conference* (Luxembourg: Office for the Official Publications of the EC, 1976)

La Spina, A, and Majone, G, *Lo Stato Regolatore* (Bologna: Il Mulino, 2000)

Lang, A, 'The GATS and Regulatory Autonomy: A Case Study of Social Regulation of the Water Industry' (2004) Journal of International Economic Law 801

Larouer, C, 'WTO Non-Violation Complaints: A Misunderstood Remedy in the WTO Dispute Settlement System' (2006) Netherlands International Law Review 97

Lennard, M, 'Navigating by the Stars: Interpreting the WTO Agreements' (2002) Journal of International Economic Law 17

Lesguillons, H, 'Comment' in Bourgeois, JHJ, (ed) *Subsidies and International Trade—A European Lawyers' Perspective* (Deventer-Boston: Kluwer, 1991) 151

Levi, L, 'L'identification du bénéficiaire de l'aide', in Dony, M and Smits, C (eds) *Aides d'Etat* (Brussels: Editions de l'Université de Bruxelles, 2005) 195

Low, P, 'The Treatment of Subsidies in the WTO Framework' in Ehlermann, CD, and Everson, M, *European Competition Law Annual 1999: Selected Issues in the Field of State Aids* (Oxford: Hart Publishing, 2001) 103

Lowenfeld, AF, *International Economic Law* (2nd edn, Oxford: Oxford University Press, 2008)

Lübbig, T, and Von Merveldt, M, 'Stardust Marine: Introducing Imputability into State Aid Rules—Plain Sailing into Calm Seas or Rowing Back into Shallow Waters?' (2003) European Competition Law Review 629

Luengo Hernández de Madrid, G, *Regulation of Subsidies and State Aids in WTO and EC Law—Conflicts in International Trade Law* (Alphen aan den Rijn: Kluwer Law International, 2006)

Luengo Hernández de Madrid, G, 'Conflicts Between the Disciplines of EC State Aids and WTO Subsidies: Of Books, Ships and Aircraft' (2008) European Foreign Affairs Review 1

Maier, M, and Werner, P, 'Review of Judgment AEM Spa' (2005) European State Aid Law Quarterly 657

Majone, G, 'The Rise of the Regulatory State in Europe' (1994) West European Politics 77

Malinconico, C, 'Aiuti di Stato' in Chiti, MP, Greco, G, (eds) *Trattato di diritto amministrativo europeo* (Milan: Giuffré, 1999) 55

Matsushita, M, Schoenbaum, TJ, and Mavroidis, PC, *The World Trade Organization—Law, Practice, and Policy* (1st edn, Oxford: Oxford University Press, 2003)

Matsushita, M, Schoenbaum, TJ, and Mavroidis, PC, *The World Trade Organization—Law, Practice, and Policy* (2nd edn, Oxford: Oxford University Press, 2006)

Mattoo, A, and Subramanian, A, 'Currency Undervaluation and Sovereign Wealth Funds: A New Role for the World Trade Organization', World Bank Policy Research Working Paper 4668 (July 2008)

Mavroidis, PC, 'Remedies in the WTO Legal Systesm: Between a Rock and a Hard Place' (2000) European Journal of International Law 763

Mavroidis, PC, 'Come Together? Producer Welfare, Consumer Welfare, and WTO Rules' in Petersmann, EU and Harrison, J (eds) *Reforming the World Trading System—Legitimacy, Efficiency and Democratic Governance* (Oxford: Oxford University Press, 2003) 277

Mavroidis, PC, *Trade in Goods* (Oxford: Oxford University Press, 2007)

McCormick, N, *Who's Afraid of a European Constitution?* (Exeter: Imprint Academic, 2005)

McDonough, PJ, 'Subsidies and Countervailing Measures' in Stewart, TP (ed) *The GATT Uruguay Round—A Negotiating History (1986-1992)*, Volume I (Deventer: Kluwer, 1993) 809

McGovern, E, *International Trade Regulation* (loose-leaf updated biannually, Exeter: Globefield Press, 1995)

Meicklejohn, R, 'The Economics of State Aid' in European Commission (Directorate General for Economic and Financial Affairs) *'State Aid and the Single Market'* (1999) European Economy—Report and Studies 25

Merola, M, 'Comments on the Paper "The Most Appropriate Economic Tools for a Better Targeted State Aid Policy"', in Derenne, J and Merola, M (eds), *Economic Analysis of State Aid Rules—Contributions and Limits* (Berlin: Lexxion, 2007) 68

Morgan De Rivery, E, Le Berre-Dodet, N, and Thibault-Liger, S, 'Une application sectorielle: l'exemple de la Poste' in Dony, M and Smits, C (eds) *Aides d'Etat*, (Brussels: Editions de l'Université de Bruxelles, 2005) 157

Mortelmans, K, 'Towards Convergence in the Application of the Rules on Free Movement and on Competition?' (2001) Common Market Law Review 613

Motta, M, *Competition Policy: Theory and Practice* (Cambridge: Cambridge University Press, 2004)

Moura Filho, HP, 'Pioneering Multilateralism: The Sugar Agreements 1864-1914', paper presented at the XVI International Economic History Congress, Helsinki, Session 109, 2006

Neven, D, and Verouden, V, 'Towards a More Refined Economic Approach in State Aid Control' in Mederer, W, Pesaresi, N and Van Hoof, M (eds), *EU Competition Law—Volume IV: State Aid* (Leuven: Claeys & Casteels, 2008) Book 1, Part I, chapter 4

Nicolaides, P, 'Fiscal Aid in the EC: A Critical Review of Current Practice' (2001) World Competition 319

Nicolaides, P, 'Compensation for Public Service Obligations: the Floodgates of State Aid' (2003) European Competition Law Review 561

Nicolaides, P, 'Fiscal State Aid in the EU: The Limits of Tax Autonomy' (2004) World Competition 365

Nicolaides, P, and Kekelekis, M, 'When do Firms in Trouble Escape from State Aid Rules?' (2005) European State Aid Law Quarterly 17

Nicolaides, P, 'The Boundaries of Tax Autonomy—Comments on the Opinion of AG Geelhoed on Case C-88/03 *Portoguese Republic* v *Commission*' (2006) European State Aid Law Quarterly 119

Nicolaides, P, 'Where Is the Advantage? The Case of Public Funding of Infrastructure and Broadband Networks' (2007) European State Aid Law Quarterly 615

Nitsche, R, and Heidhues, P, *Study on Methods to Analyse the Impact of State Aid on Competition*, Report prepared for the European Commission, Directorate General for Economics and Financial Affairs (Final Report ECFIN/R/2004/004): Bruxelles (2005)

O'Brien, A, 'Countervailing Low Wage Subsidies: A Counter to the Leveling of Labor Conditions' (1994) 4 Transnational Law and Contemporary Problems 825

O'Keeffe, D, and Bavasso, A, 'Four Freedoms, One Market and National Competence: In Search of a Dividing Line' in Andenas, M and Fairgrieve, D (eds) *Judicial Review in International Perspective: Liber Amicorum in Honour of Lord Slynn of Hadley* (London: Aspen, 2000) 541

O'Keeffe, D, and Branton, J, 'State Aid and Urban Regeneration: A UK Perspective' (2007) European State Aid Law Quarterly 484

OECD, *Harmful Tax Competition: An Emerging Global Issues*, Paris (1998)

OECD, *Consistencies and Inconsistencies between Trade and Competition Policies*, Joint Group on Trade and Competition, COM/TD/DAFFE/CLP(98)25/FINAL, 1999, OECD, Paris

OECD, *Competition Policy in Subsidies and State Aid*, Competition Policy Roundtable, DAFFE/CLP (2001) 24, OECD, Paris

OFT, *Public Subsidies—A Report by the Office of Fair Trading*, OFT750: London (2004)

OFT, *European State Aid Control*, OFT821: London (2005)

Ortino, F, *Basic Legal Instruments for the Liberalisation of Trade—A Comparative Analysis of EC and WTO Law* (Oxford: Hart Publishing, 2004)

Osti, C, 'Di alcuni problemi degli aiuti di Stato' (2006) Mercato Concorrenza Regole 429

Oxfam, *Rigged Rules and Double Standards: Trade, Globalization, and the Fight Against Poverty*, 2002

Panzarella, JL, 'Is the Specificity Test Generally Applicable?' (1986) Law and Policy in International Business 417

Papadias, L, Riedl, A, and Westerhof, JG, 'Public Funding for Broadband Networks: Recent Developments' (2006) Competition Policy Newsletter 13

Papandropoulos, P, Nitsche, R, van de Walle de Ghelcke, B, Waelbroeck, D, Derenne, J, Louis, F, Merola, M, Ibañez Colomo, P, De Beys, J, and Bousin, J, 'Selectivity, Economic Advantage, Distortion of Competition and Effect on Trade' in Derenne, J, and Merola, M (eds) *Economic Analysis of State Aid Rules—Contributions and Limits* (Berlin: Lexxion, 2007) 119

Parish, M, 'On the Private Investor Principle' (2003) European Law Review 70

Pauwelyn, J, *Conflict of Norms in Public International Law—How WTO Law Relates to Other Rules of International Law* (Cambridge: Cambridge University Press, 2003)

Pauwelyn, J, Book review on Cass, DZ, *The Constitutionalization of the World Trade Organization: Legitimacy, Democracy, and Community in the International Trading System* (Oxford: Oxford University Press, 2005) (2006) American Journal of International Law 986.

Pauwelyn, J, 'The Transformation of World Trade' (2005/2006), Michigan Law Review 1

Pauwelyn, J, 'Fragmentation in International Law' in *Max Planck Encyclopedia of Public International Law*, 2008

Pauwelyn, J, 'New Trade Politics After the Doha Round', *Center for Trade and Economic Integration, Working Paper 1/2008*

Pauwelyn, J, Testimony before the US 'Subcommittee on Trade of the House Committee on Ways and Means', 24 March 2009

Pelkmans, J, *European Integration—Methods and Economic Analysis* (2nd edn, London: FT-Prentice Hall, 2001)

Pescatore, P, *The Law of Integration: Emergence of a New Phenomenon* (Leiden: Sijhoof, 1974).

Pescatore, P, 'The Doctrine of 'Direct Effect': An Infant Disease of Community Law' (1983) European Law Review 155

Pescatore, P, 'The GATT Dispute Settlement Mechanism: Its Present Situation and Its Prospect' (1993) Journal of World Trade 5

Pigman, GA, 'Hegemony and Trade Liberalization Policy: Britain and the Brussels Sugar Convention of 1902' (1997) Review of International Studies 185

Plender, R, 'Definition of Aid' in Biondi, A, Eeckhout, P, and Flynn, J, (eds) *The Law of State Aid in the European Union* (Oxford: Oxford University Press, 2004) 3

Porges, A, and Trachtman, JP, 'Robert Hudec and Domestic Regulation—The Resurrection of Aims and Effects' (2003) Journal of World Trade 783

Quigley, C, 'The Notion of a State Aid in the EEC' (1988) European Law Review 242

Quigley, C, and Collins, AM, *EC State Aid Law and Policy* (Oxford: Hart Publishing, 2003)

Quigley, C, 'General Taxation and State Aid', in Biondi, A, Eeckhout, P, and Flynn, J, (eds) *The Law of State Aid in the European Union* (Oxford: Oxford University Press, 2004) 207

Qureshi, AH, and Grynberg, R, 'United States Tax Subsidies Under Domestic International Sales Corporation, Foreign Sales Corporation and Extraterritorial Income Exclusion Act Legislation within the Framework of the World Trade Organization'(2002) Journal of World Trade 979

Ragosta, JA, and Shanker, HM, 'Specificity of Subsidy Benefits in US Department of Commerce Countervailing Duty Determinations' (1994) Law and Policy in International Business 639

Rapport des Chefs de Délégation aux Ministères des Affaires Etrangères, Secretariat of the Intergovernmental Conference, Brussels, 21 April 1956 (*Spaak Report*)

Rasmussen, H, *On Law and Policy in the European Court of Justice* (Lancaster: Martinus Nijhoff, 1986)

Regan, DH, 'Further Thoughts on the Role of Regulatory Purpose under Article III of the GATT' (2003) Journal of World Trade 737

Regan, DH, 'What Are Trade Agreements For?—Two Conflicting Stories Told by Economists, with a Lesson for Lawyers' (2006) Journal of International Economic Law 951

Rehbinder, M, 'Recent Developments in Commission State Aid Policy and Practice' in Biondi, A, Eeckhout, P and Flynn, J (eds) *The Law of State Aid in the European Union* (Oxford: Oxford University Press, 2004) 117

Reich, A, 'Privately Subsidized Recycling Schemes and their Potential Harm to the Environment of Developing Countries: Does International Trade Law Have a Solution?', Bar Ilan University Public Law Working Paper No 2-5, 4 March 2004

Reich, DG, and Helios, M, 'Do Reserves for the Disposal of Nuclear Waste and Shutdown of Nuclear Power Plans in Germany constitute State Aid?' (2002) European State Aid Law Quarterly 207

Reich, DG, 'No Level Playing Field for Nuclear Power Reserves? Comment on the Judgment in Case T-92/02 of 26 January 2006' (2006) European State Aid Law Quarterly 445

Renner-Loquenz, B, 'State Aid in Energy Taxation Measures: First Experiences from Applying the Environmental Aid Guidelines 2001' (2003) European State Aid Law Quarterly 21

Roberti, GM, *Gli aiuti di Stato nel diritto comunitario* (Padova, CEDAM, 1997)

Roberti, GM, 'Public Guarantees and Community Control of State Aids' in Ehlermann, CD, and Everson, M, (eds) *European Competition Law Annual 1999: Selected Issues in the Field of State Aids* (Oxford: Hart Publishing, 1999) 278

Rodrik, D, 'Industrial Policy for the Twenty-First Century', November 2004, CEPR Discussion Paper No. 4767

Rodrik, D, 'How to Save Globalization from its Cheerleaders', JF Kennedy School of Government, Harvard University, Faculty Research Working Papers Series, September 2007, RWP07-038

Roessler, F, 'Beyond the Ostensible—A Tribute to Professor Robert Hudec's Insights on the Determination of the Likeness of Products under the National Treatment Provisions of the GATT' (2003) Journal of World Trade 771

Ross, M, 'State Aids: Maturing into a Constitutional Problem' (1995) Yearbook of European Law 79

Ross, M, 'State Aids and National Courts: Definitions and Other Problems—a Case of Premature Emancipation?' (2000) Common Market Law Review 401

Ross, M, 'Decentralization, Effectiveness, and Modernization: Contradiction in Terms?' (2004) in Biondi, A, Eeckhout, P, and Flynn, J, (eds) *The Law of State Aid in the European Union* (Oxford: Oxford University Press, 2004) 85

Rubini, L, 'Brevi note a margine del caso *PreussenElektra*, ovvero come "prendere seriamente" le norme sugli aiuti di Stato e la tutela dell'ambiente nel diritto comunitario' (2001) Diritto Comunitario e degli Scambi Internazionali 473

Rubini, L, 'Comments on the US—Cotton dispute' in Ortino, F, and Ripinsky, S, (eds) *WTO Law and Process* (London: British Institute of International and Comparative Law, 2006) 133

Rubini, L, 'L'impatto del GATS sulla regolazione nazionale dei servizi di interesse generale' (2007) Diritto del Commercio Internazionale 373

Ruggie, JG, 'International Regimes, Transactions, and Change: Embedded Liberalism and the Post-War Economic Regimes' (1982) International Organization 195

Rydelski, MS, (ed) *The EC State Aid Regime: Distortive Effects of State Aid on Competition and Trade* (London: Cameron May, 2006)

Sacco, R, 'Legal Formants, A Dynamic Approach to Comparative Law' (1991) American Journal of Comparative Law 343

Sacco, R, *Introduzione al Diritto Comparato* (Turin: UTET, 1992)

Santa Maria, A (ed), *Competition and State Aid—An Analysis of the EC Practice* (Alphen aan den Rijn: Kluwer Law International, 2007)

Santamato, S, and Westerhof, JG, 'Is Funding of Infrastructure State Aid?' (2003) Europaische Zeitschrift für Wirtschaftsrecht 645

Scalia, A, *A Matter of Interpretation: Federal Courts and the Law* (Princeton: Princeton University Press, 1998)

Schneider, UH, '"Anstaltslast" and "Gewährträgerhaftung" as Implied Elements of Public Corporations rather than State Aid' in Ehlermann, CD, and Everson, M, (eds) *European Competition Law Annual 1999: Selected Issues in the Field of State Aids* (Oxford: Hart Publishing, 2001) 357

Schön, W, 'Taxation and State Aid Law in the European Union' (1999) Common Market Law Review 910

Schön, W, 'Special Charges—A Gap in European Competition Law?' (2006) European State Aid Law Quarterly 495

Schwartz, WF, and Harper, EW, Jr, 'The Regulation of Subsidies Affecting International Trade' (1972) Michigan Law Review 831

Schwartz, WF, 'Countervailing Duty Law for the 1990s—A New Look at the Law and Economics of Subsidies' (1989) Law and Policy in International Business 503

Sen, A, *On Ethics and Economics* (Oxford: Blackwell, 1987)

Sengupta, A, 'The Human Right to Development' (2004) Oxford Development Studies 179

Shaw, MN, *International Law* (5th edn, Cambridge: Cambridge University Press, 2003)

Shleifer, A, *Inefficient Markets: An Introduction to Behavioural Finance* (Oxford: Oxford University Press, 2000)

Shorter Oxford English Dictionary on Historical Principles (5th edn, Oxford: Oxford University Press, 2002)

Sinclair, I, *The Vienna Convention on the Law of Treaties* (2nd edn, Manchester: Manchester University Press, 1984)

Slocock, B, 'EC and WTO Subsidy Control Systems—some Reflections' (2007) European State Aid Law Quarterly 249

Slot, PJ, 'Case note on Case C-199/06, *Centre d'exportation du livre Francais (CELF) v Société internationale de diffusion et d'édition (SIDE)*' (2009) Common Market Law Review 623

Slotboom, M, 'State Aid in Community Law: A Broad or Narrow Definition?' (1995) European Law Review 289

Slotboom, M, 'Subsidies in WTO Law and in EC Law: Broad and Narrow Definitions' (2002) Journal of World Trade 517

Smith, A, *An Inquiry into the Nature and Causes of the Wealth of Nations* (Oxford: Clarendon Press, 1976, originally published 1776)

Smits, C, 'La notion d'avantage et le critère de "l'opérateur en économie en marché"', in Dony, M, and Smits, C, (eds) *Aides d'Etat* (Brussels: Editions de l'Université de Bruxelles, 2005) 53

Snape, R, 'International Regulation of Subsidies' (1991) 14:2 World Economy 139

Soltész, U, 'The New Commission Guidelines on State Aid for Airports: a Step too Far' (2006) European State Aid Law Quarterly 719

Staiger, RW, and Sykes, AO, 'Currency Manipulation and World Trade', December 2008, NBER Working Paper No. W14600

Stiglitz, JE, *Economics of the Public Sector* (3rd edn, New York: Norton, 2000)

Stiglitz, JE, *Globalization and its Discontents* (London: Penguin, 2002)

Sussman, MJ, 'Countervailing Duties and the Specificity Test: An Alternative Approach to the Definition of "Bounty or Grant"' (1986) Law and Policy in International Business 475

Sykes, AO, 'Countervailing Duty Law: An Economic Perspective' (1989) Columbia Law Review 199

Sykes, AO, 'Second-Best Countervailing Duty Policy: A Critique of the Entitlement Approach' (1989) Law and Policy in International Business 669

Sykes, AO, 'The economics of "injury" in antidumping and countervailing duty cases', in Bhandari, JS, and Sykes, AO, (eds) *Economic Dimensions in International Law* (Cambridge: Cambridge University Press, 1997) 83

Sykes, AO, 'The Economics of WTO Rules on Subsidies and Countervailing Measures', Chicago John M Olin Law and Economics Working Paper No. 186 (2nd Series) May 2003

Sykes, AO, 'International Trade: Trade Remedies' in Guzman, AT, and Sykes, AO, (eds) *Research Handbook in International Economic Law* (Cheltenham: Edward Elgar (2007) 62

Szyszczak, E, 'Financing Services of General Economic Interest' (2004) Modern Law Review 982

Tarullo, DK, 'The MTN Subsidies Code: Agreement without Consensus', in Rubin, SJ, and Hufbauer, GC, (eds) *Emerging Standards of International Trade and Investment—Multinational Codes and Corporate Conduct* (Totowa: Rowman and Allanheld Publishers, 1984) 63

Tarullo, DK, 'Beyond Normalcy in the Regulation of International Trade' (1986/1987) Harvard Law Review 546

Tarullo, DK, 'Norms and Institutions in Global Competition Policy' (2000) American Journal of International Law 478

The Economist, 'The Return of Economic Nationalism', 7–13 February 2009

Thouvenin, JM, and Lorieux, MP, 'L'arrét de la CJCE du 24 Juillet 2003 Almark' (2003) Revue du Marché commun et de l'Union européenne, 633

Thucydides, *The Peloponnessian War* (Oxford: Oxford University Press, 2009)

Tönnies, F, in Harris, J, (ed) *Community and Civil Society* (Cambridge: Cambridge University Press, 2001)

Trachtman, JP, 'The Constitutions of the WTO' (2006) European Journal of International Law 6233

Trebilcock, MJ, 'Is the Game Worth the Candle? Comments on *A Search for Economic and Financial Principles in the Administration of US Countervailing Duty Law*' (1989) Law and Policy in International Business 723

Trebilcock, MJ, and Giri, SK, 'The National Treatment Principle in International Law', in Choi, K and Hartigan, J (eds) *Handbook of International Trade Volume II: Economics and Legal Analyses of Trade Policy Institutions* (Oxford: Blackwell, 2005)

Trebilcock, MJ, and Howse, R, *The Regulation of International Trade* (3rd edn, London: Routledge, 2005)

Tridimas, T, 'The Court of Justice and Judicial Activism' (1997) European Law Review 199

Twining, W, *Globalization and Legal Theory* (London: Butterworths, 2000)

UN HR Commissioner, *Liberalisation of Trade in Services and Human Rights*, United Nations Economic and Social Council, Commission on Human Rights, Sub-commission on the Promotion and Protection of Human Rights, Report of the High Commissioner, E/CN.4/Sub.2/2002/9, (2002)

UN International Law Commission, *Fragmentation of International Law: Difficulties Arising from the Diversification and Expansion of International Law*, Report of the Study Group of the International Law Commission finalized by M Koskenniemi, A/CN.4/L.682, 13 April 2006 ('Analytical Study')

UN International Law Commission, *Fragmentation of International Law: Difficulties Arising from the Diversification and Expansion of International Law*, Report of the Study Group of the International Law Commission, A/CN.4/L.702, 18 July 2006 ('Conclusions')

UN International Law Commission, *Draft Articles on the Law of Treaties, with Commentaries, Yearbook of International Law Commission*, 1966, Vol II

UN International Law Commission, *Draft Articles on the State Responsibility for Internationally Wrongful Acts, with Commentaries, Yearbook of International Law Commission*, 2001, Vol II, Part II

UNCTAD, *Trade in Services and Development Implications*, Trade and Development Board, Commission on Trade in Goods, Services, and Commodities, TD/B/COM.1/71, (2005)

Van Bael, I, and Bellis, JF, *Anti-dumping and other Trade Protection Laws of the EC* (Brussels: Kluwer Law International, 2004)

Van Calster, G, 'Greening the EC's State Aid and Tax Regimes' (2000) European Competition Law Review 294

Van Damme, I, 'Jurisdiction, Applicable Law, and Interpretation' in Bethlemen, D, McRae, D, Neufeld, R, and Van Damme, I, (eds) *The Oxford Handbook of International Trade Law* (Oxford: Oxford University Press, 2009) 298

Van den Bossche, P, *The Law and Policy of the World Trade Organization—Text, Cases and Materials* (2nd edn, Cambridge: Cambridge University Press, 2008)

Verhoessel, G, *National Treatment and WTO Dispute Settlement: Adjudicating the Boundaries of Regulatory Autonomy* (Oxford: Hart Publishing, 2002)

Vesterndorf, B, 'A Further Comment on the New State Aid Concept as this Concept Continues to be Reshaped—Pearle—A Further Piece of the State Aid Puzzle?' (2005) European State Aid Law Quarterly 393

Vickers, J, 'State Aid and Distortion of Competition', Paper for the State Aid Conference organized by the UK Presidency on 14 July 2005

Viner, J, *Dumping: A problem in International Trade* (New York: Kelley, 1966)

Wall, M, and Vis-Dunbar, D, *The Standstill in Subsidies—Update*, paper produced for the International Institute for Sustainable Development (2005)

Weatherill, S, 'After *Keck*: Some Thoughts on How to Clarify the Clarification' (1996) Common Market Law Review 885

Weiler, JHH, 'The Transformation of Europe' (1990–1991) Yale Law Journal 2403

Weiler, JHH, *The Constitution of Europe* (Cambridge: Cambridge University Press, 1999)

Weiler, JHH, (ed) *The EU, the WTO and the NAFTA—Towards a Common Law of International Trade* (Oxford: Oxford University Press, 2000)

Weiler, JHH, 'The Rule of Lawyers and the Ethos of Diplomats: Reflections on the Internal and External Legitimacy of WTO Dispute Settlement', Harvard Jean Monnet Working Paper, 9/00

Weiler, JHH, and Wind, M, *European Constitutionalism Beyond the State* (Cambridge: Cambridge University Press, 2003)

Weiler, JHH, 'Editorial: Marking the Anniversary of the Universal Declaration; The Irish No and the Lisbon Treaty' (2008) European Journal of International Law 647

Weizmann, L, 'The Making of an Export Subsidy: DISCs and FSCs in Compliance with the GATT' (1987) World Competition 57

Whish, R, *Competition Law* (6th edn, Oxford: Oxford University Press, 2008)

Wishlade, FG, *Regional State Aid and Competition Policy in the European Union* (London: Kluwer, 2002)

WorldTradeLaw.net Dispute Settlement Commentary (DSC) on Appellate Body, *US—Cotton (21.5)*, 9 September 2008

WTO, *World Trade Report* (2006)

WTO and WHO, *WTO Agreements and Public Health—A Joint Study of the WHO and WTO Secretariat* (2002)

Zweigert, K, and Kötz, H, *An Introduction to Comparative Law* (Oxford: Oxford University Press, 1999)

Index

Lightning Source UK Ltd.
Milton Keynes UK
UKOW031447150113

204912UK00001B/22/P

9 780199 533398